AN INVISIBLE CHILD

LENORE OSSEN, MSW

Review Rating: 5 Star s - Congratulations on your 5-star review!
Reviewed By Christian Sia for Readers' Favorite

In the introduction to An Invisible Child: A True Story of Hope for Victims of Abuse, Lenore Ossen writes: "This is a true story. This is my story. This is about a child who grew up in a lonely, isolated world with a mother who was out of reality." The narrative follows the journey a child suffers at the hands of a controlling mother who won't allow her to connect with anyone else. Shut up in a world that limits her to her mother, Lenore is deprived of the basic right to grow up in a supportive environment, the right to make friends, and the right to education. But when she becomes a teenager, she revolts against her mother, and gets out in the world. But what does she know about this world? She is shocked because what she'd secretly dreamed about is far different from the reality that awaits her. Follow her journey as she moves from one crisis to the next, seeking love in places it doesn't exist, and how she gradually heals through an understanding of where she came from.

Lenore Ossen's memoir is engrossing, a story that explores the psychological and behavioral consequences of child abuse. It is poignant, filled with insightful passages and emotionally rich moments. An Invisible Child: A True Story of Hope for Victims of Abuse is a story of abuse simply told, a story with powerful lessons and tools to enable readers to heal. It is interesting how writing her story became a healing journey for the author. While this story castigates abuse, it explores powerful themes like the strength of family, hope, and healing. Listening to Lenore Ossen's reassuring voice offers hope to readers that they can rise above their emotional and psychological abuse, and that they can connect to their purpose and come home to themselves. It is both inspiring and thought provoking.

LITERARY TITAN

Congratulations!

We are proud to present you with our Literary Titan Book Award.

Your book deserves extraordinary praise and we are proud to acknowledge your writing talent.

The Silver Award is bestowed on books that expertly deliver complex characters, intricate worlds, and thought provoking themes. The ease with which the story is told is a reflection of the author's talent in exercising fluent, powerful, and appropriate language.

Thomas Anderson

Editor In Chief

Literary Titan

Jan 30 Posted by Literary Titan

"An Invisible Child is a story based on the heart wrenching experiences of Lenore Ossen. It tells the tale of her lonely and traumatic childhood, growing up with a mother suffering from mental illness; isolated and trapped away from the real world. Deprived of social interaction, friendships and even family relationships she tells the story of how she endured life living within the restrictive and peculiar rules set by her mother, living in a constant state of fear… Although this is a shocking and heart-breaking story, it is also a story of hope. As she grows older, she slowly gains confidence. She pushes herself far beyond her comfort zone, and literally steps out of the apartment. Lenore attempts everyday tasks and teaches herself age-appropriate skills for living in society. At times she makes mistakes, however she learns from these as any intelligent person does. She gains the courage and confidence to overcome her life of abuse, showing others that no matter what road you have traveled there is hope for your future."

AN INVISIBLE CHILD

Contents

Part One
Growing Up Invisible

**Part Two
Becoming Visible**

**Part Three
My Life In Review**

Cover Photo of Lenore Ossen as child

Names Have been changed to protect anonymity

Cover Design by Bonnie Toews ©

Enjoy Yourself (It's Later Than You Think) by Carl Sigman and Herb Magidson

Time and Time Again by Fred Spielman and Earl Brent

A Wonderful Guy

This book is dedicated to all the children who are abused, abandoned, and forsaken, in the hopes that they too will be able to rise above their despair and overcome.

I want to acknowledge the people who have encouraged and supported me during the time I was writing this book: Susan G., Joyce S., Rick S., Irene K., Robert H., Bob K., Julius R., Dr. Anna B., Dr. Charles K., Dr. Ronald S., Prof. Gustavo E., Bonnie T., Ann E., and my uncle Will for his contribution in making this book possible.

Special thanks to my husband and editor, Jonathan Hillel, for his patience, understanding, and insightful suggestions.

This is a true story.

People who tell me that they can recall
nothing of the early years of their childhood
have greatly surprised me. For my part, I have
retained vivid memories of the time when I was
a very small child.

—Anatole France, Le livre do mon ami

Introduction

This is a true story. This is my story. This is about a child who grew up in a lonely, isolated world with a mother who was out of reality. She made her own rules and I lived by them. I was there for her to control and abuse emotionally and physically. She didn't allow me to be touched, not even by my own father. She did not allow me to talk to anyone but her. I did not attend school. I had no friends. Because there was no one to turn to except my psychotic mother, I lived in an inner world of fear, chaos, and fantasy.

As I came into my teens, something within me rebelled. I wanted to free myself of my mother and her horrible abuse. I went through a continuous hell trying to dig myself out of the black hole I was living in. I was fighting my way out of isolation into a world I knew nothing about. I was groping with the simplest things that children are accustomed to—like going out by themselves and coming back by themselves.

As I ventured out of my mother's asylum, I found each new experience devastating and frightening. I was walking the streets, looking for the love I never had as a child. I was turning to men, but what they were offering me was not what I was searching for.

I kept talking to people who crossed my path. I was turning to any source that I felt could help me and show me how I could find my life. And it went on like this, as I drifted from one crisis into another. From the life I had lived, my feelings and thoughts were jumbled, and I couldn't get a grip on either. I never knew what I would encounter in my hapless state of existence. But I had to find a way to move through this nightmare and learn how to live in the world.

I went through periods of deep despair. I was experiencing continuous anxiety that was wrapped around feelings of gripping fear. I was constantly reliving trauma I had experienced in my early years. As a young adult, I was struggling to find my true identity, while searching for some sense of sanity. I had to find me.

With each new encounter, I was learning to think… to feel… to function… I was having new experiences all the time, some of them good—many of them, horrible. But, like a baby, I was learning how to stand on my feet. I was finding out that I could do things and think for myself. As I floundered and made mistakes, I was becoming aware of the world around me—how people live, act, and interact with each other. But I felt so different and unlike anyone else. Sometimes I wanted to give up and quit, but I kept going.

This book is about how I survived the obstacles I endured in my life. It is about having inner strength and courage to persist and not give up when things look bleakest.

As someone who likes to express her thoughts and feelings on paper, I started to write the story of my life for myself. My goal was to free myself of the demons that held me in psychological paralysis from childhood. I found comfort in releasing my emotions in writing, but I also found it exceedingly difficult to describe what it felt like to be me, growing up in isolation with a psychotic mother. I had to turn myself inside out to turn feelings into words, as I tried to capture the reality and truth of my life.

With the help of information contained in an awesome file my uncle kept on me as I was growing up, I learned things about myself that I was able to use in my writing. In the process, I gained a greater understanding of myself. And because this is a compelling story, I felt a need to put it out into the universe.

I do hope this book will be helpful to those of you who feel lost in a world that can be cold, cruel, and indifferent. One can suffer, the human spirit can be crushed, and one can plummet into an abyss, but one can also rise above despair and make a life that is fulfilling, with pleasures and joys from just being alive. I know because I have.

I have done the best I could to recollect my myriad memories from so many years ago. I have presented everything the way I remembered it. Each chapter speaks for itself. This story is not written as a novel nor is it intended to be.

One Day

At last, my life is making some sense. I feel useful. I have a purpose. I feel that I am finally fulfilling my destiny. I'm working with women who have been abused, and I feel a close kinship with them.

It is July, and it is hot, even with the air-conditioning. But it's always hot and humid in New York in the summertime. As the rain trickles down on windows that are worn and weather-beaten from a multitude of storms, I cannot help but feel it is appropriate to the setting I am working in.

I am sitting behind my desk, and a new client comes in. She sits down in a chair opposite mine. It feels strange; not so long ago, I was sitting in her place.

My client, Nancy, is a young woman in her twenties, with long, dark hair and hazel eyes. Her sad expression is familiar. It's like seeing my reflection in a mirror.

As she talks, tears fill her eyes: "I feel like I can't go on another day. Sometimes I feel like I want to die—it hurts so bad . . ."

As Nancy speaks, a picture of myself as a child flashes before me: *I am sitting in the kitchen with my mother. I'm afraid to move. I dare not make a sound. I'm cowering in my chair, wondering if*

I'll be able to make it through another day. Suddenly, I am feeling uneasy. I take a few deep breaths and shift my focus back to what Nancy is saying. I am distracted by the jarring sounds in the street below.

Nancy is now looking out the window. Her eyes are scanning the busy throng of the hectic West 90's, and she seems dazed as she speaks: "The other day, I overhear my boyfriend Danny talking on the phone. He's saying, 'Sure, honey, I'd love to! When do you want to come over? I'll see what I can do . . .' "

Nancy begins to cry. "I ask him, 'What's going on?' and he tells me, 'I have a few female friends, and I brought one over the other day when you were out working.' Suddenly, my heart is thumping, and I feel like I'm going into a spin. I come right out and ask him, 'Did you sleep with her?' He says, 'Yeah. So what! What's the big deal! I didn't mean it that way—it just happened . . .' "

Nancy's eyes are now blazing with anger. "I feel like I'm going crazy. I yell, 'How dare you! You're living in my apartment, and you're sleeping with other women while I'm out working?' "

Nancy starts to cry some more, and then she continues. "He comes towards me and smacks me across my face, and then he slaps me some more. I manage to run into another room and lock the door. That's when I call the police. He runs out of the house and I yell after him, 'Don't you ever come back here anymore!' "

"That must have been just awful for you," I empathized. "Did you make a complaint when the police came?"

"No, I didn't. He's beaten me many times before. I've been in the hospital a few times. He thinks nothing of punching me and beating me up. He has fits of anger, and he's broken a few of my ribs. When he gets like that, he can't control himself."

A wave of anger sweeps over me. Thoughts keep rushing into my head. *This is appalling! How can she allow herself to be beaten like that? This guy is a real bastard!* I try not to voice my opinion as Nancy continues to tell her story. I am sad as I look at her. I can see that she's hurting, and I wish I could say something to ease her pain, but I know she has to feel her feelings.

Nancy soon starts to cry again as she clutches her hands to her face. "He's done this so many times. He pushes me around and hurts me. I don't know why I take it. It's terrible; I can't put it into words." Her eyes roam over the dark, speckled linoleum as she holds a tissue tightly in her hand. "You don't know what it's like to feel so worthless and unloved . . ."

I think to myself: *If she only knew* . . .

Nancy sits there for several minutes, staring at a blank wall, and then she says, "He hollers at me. He uses his hands on me. And now, he's cheating on me . . ."

As she speaks, I am hopeful that she will be strong enough to keep away from the batterer. I want to tell her how I really feel— but I have to remain objective. I learned in my training, and in my own therapy, that the client must be allowed to have her own thoughts and feelings and make her own decisions. Nancy is having trouble with all of this. I am intent upon helping her get in touch with her true feelings. The goal here is for Nancy to become self-empowered and gain better control of her life.

But there is a deeper problem. She seems to need this abuse, so then the question is, why does Nancy have a need for abuse? I surmise it is a part of some kind of pattern from her childhood. I hope Nancy will be able to talk about this at some point.

Meanwhile, I am very concerned about her. I know that battered women have a tendency to return to their batterer when the tension lifts and things return to the status quo. I am wondering if Nancy is safe and if she will be returning to her batterer. There is always danger lurking when a woman is involved with someone who has a violent temper. My mind flashes: *What is the next step to take if her life is in immediate danger?*

I find the sordid stories that Nancy has been telling me about her boyfriend very distressing. I'm wondering what this guy Danny is all about, and I have questions. When I perceive the time is right, I ask, "Why is Danny in your home when you're out working?"

"He can't find employment now. Acting jobs are hard to find, so he has time on his hands." Nancy quickly changes the subject. "I'm afraid if he comes back, I'll end up in the hospital again."

"Nancy, there is something called an order of protection. It's a legal document that protects women in situations like yours. Have you thought about that? It can help to keep him away from you."

Nancy reflects for a moment. "I know what that's all about—I don't want that right now. I'm not going back to him! I don't want him back. I don't ever want to see him again!" She began to sob. "I don't know what I'm going to do. I can't eat . . . I can't sleep . . . I don't care about anything anymore . . ."

"Are you suicidal?"

Nancy is fast to reply, "No, I'm not. I've gone through this before . . ."

But Nancy doesn't look well, and I need to pursue this further. "Do you want to see a psychiatrist? A psychiatrist could prescribe medication for your depression."

"No, I just want to see you," she softly says.

I am surprised to hear that. It does not sit well with me, and I am feeling some anxiety now. She might be better off with a psychiatrist because she might need to be medicated. I feel an urgency to consult with my supervisor about Nancy's case. Meanwhile, I make another appointment to see her.

I am aware that women are abused every minute of the day and that they are sometimes even murdered by their batterers. Working with a client is a big responsibility, and it is something that I take very seriously. I am now in a situation where someone's life is at stake. When you have someone's life in your hands, there is no room for error. I want very much to help Nancy, but I don't know if I can. I will speak to my supervisor about it, and then we will see how to proceed.

That night I am worried about Nancy. *Will she be all right?* I can't get any sleep. I keep thinking about the things she's told me, and I recall memories from my childhood. I recall how violent my mother would become with me. I have a vision of her coming towards me and turning into a monster before my eyes. She's chasing me all over the place and when she finally catches me, she grabs me and pummels me. I'm shaking with fear. I feel the pain as if it were only yesterday.

As I feel the pain of my early years, I recall how horrible it is to be beaten, especially by a significant person in one's life. I was a child and couldn't run away from my mother. But why is Nancy, a grown adult, allowing her boyfriend to abuse her? The thought keeps running through my mind, and it rotates round and round, like a phonograph record.

The following day, I talk to my supervisor about Nancy's case. She says, "Let's wait and see if she comes back."

But what if she doesn't? I'm on edge. While I'm there, I ask my supervisor about Nancy's safety: "If her life were in immediate danger, what would I have to do?"

She says, "There are all kinds of measures we can take. One option is a women's shelter. But we're not there yet. Let's take one step at a time."

I begin to think that I am getting ahead of myself. Maybe my supervisor is right. I attempt to stay in the moment.

A week later, I'm sitting at my desk, waiting for Nancy. It's getting late and there is still no sign of her. I'm feeling very nervous. I go outside and look for her in the waiting room several times. Finally, Nancy appears. I am relieved. As she begins to speak, I'm thinking about how very pale and thin she looks. I ask, "Are you taking anything for your depression?"

She quickly replies, "No, but I'll be all right. I try not to take drugs. They don't agree with me." Nancy pauses and then says, "I don't know how I ever got involved with a man who makes me feel so bad. He makes me feel like I belong in the gutter."

I am trying to be careful and not say the wrong thing as I empathize with her and what she is going through. Her pain is talking, and I'm listening. At times, I feel helpless. How can I help Nancy in her despair?

As our session draws to a close, Nancy says, "I don't think you could possibly understand what it feels like to be hollered at for the least thing . . . to feel you don't count . . . that you're nothing . . ."

What Nancy doesn't know is that I'm very familiar with those feelings. I know them all too well. I have experienced all of them—and more.

These sessions trigger many emotions in me. I keep hearing, *Hollered at for the least thing . . . you don't count . . . you're nothing . . . you're worthless . . ."*

I am disturbed by those words. Memories are triggered in me about how invisible I was growing up. And then I remind myself of my uncle's file.

One day, I was visiting my uncle Will, and I was eager to find an article on a mental health topic. I knew he had a proclivity for collecting information on various subjects and stashing it all away in his file cabinets, so I asked him if he had this particular article. "I might have it—look in the file cabinets."

As I was rummaging through the drawers, I came upon a folder with my name on it. I was stunned. The folder was brimming with papers. *My goodness, what could this be?* I ran into the living room with the folder in my hand, my heart beating fast, and excitedly said, "What is this?"

My uncle casually replied, without emotion, "I've collected information about you when you were growing up. We were planning to write a book about you, but we never got around to it."

Write a book about me? I was flabbergasted! My uncle Will and his wife, Jessie, never said a thing about it to me. And now, suddenly, I had a huge manila folder in my hands. I said, "I want to take this home and read it."

Will was reluctant, and then Jessie interjected, "Billy, I don't think we should give the file to Lenore . . ."

Goodness, gracious, what is she saying? Here is a big, thick folder with my name on it, and they don't want to give it to me? They were now bickering as I stood by and watched, with my heart pounding. I was soon pleading, "Please, Will, let me have it. I'll give it right back to you, I promise."

He finally agreed on one condition: that I return it to him "as soon as possible." Jessie looked distraught as I put the folder into my tote bag. I couldn't wait to get home and read it.

As I left their apartment, I had a terrible feeling. *My goodness, they were going to write a book about my life!* The thought of it made my skin crawl. Good Lord, this file was thick enough for several books! How could my uncle be so detached? If I were a total stranger, I could understand this better—but not his very own niece!

When I arrived home, I hesitated. Would I be opening Pandora's box? I opened the file just the same and came upon the statement that my father signed to have my mother put away in Bellevue Hospital. Oh, my God, my mother was going to commit suicide and take me with her! How devastating it was to see those words in print. And there were more disturbing things about my childhood that rattled me. I soon became overwhelmed and quickly put the file away in a drawer.

Will and Jessie never mentioned the file to me again.

For some time, I had no desire to open "Pandora's box" again, but I am now overtaken by my curiosity to find out what's in that file. My hand is a little shaky as I open the drawer that contains the horrors of my childhood. Soon the file is before me. I see all kinds of correspondence, notes, and cards. My uncle was communicating mostly with my grandmother and my father to find out whatever he could about the way I was living with my mother. I was astounded. Was I some kind of a lab experiment or research project? How could he sit back like that and collect all this information without taking some kind of action to help and protect me?

While I found this all very disturbing, at the same time, I am learning things about myself I had never known. From these papers come a flood of memories and an awakening of old feelings from so many years ago.

I have written the story of my life based upon childhood recollections and the material accumulated in my uncle's file, which he collected until I was nineteen. This is the story of a child trapped in isolation with a psychotic mother and of my lifelong struggle to overcome her abuse. This is a true story of personal growth that has a clear message to impart: we can triumph over adversity if we persevere. There is hope, there is healing, and ultimately, there are people who care.

PART ONE

GROWING UP INVISIBLE

1

The Onset

My name is Lenore Ossen. I was born in the Bronx on a cold, icy day in January. Soon after, my mother, Hedda, began to act strange. When I was 4, my father, George, visited Hedda's brother, Will, to discuss her deteriorating mental condition.

"I am very concerned. My mother keeps telling me that Hedda and Lenore haven't been out of the house all winter. What's going on?"

"Yeah, Hedda's acting really strange. She's doing all sorts of strange things. She's even talking strange. But she'll get over it."

"Is my sister still putting books in the refrigerator?"

"That's just a part of it," George responded. "She doesn't want anyone in the house—not even her own parents! She keeps saying: No visitors!"

"There's no doubt this needs attention. If my memory serves me right, Hedda became reclusive when Lenore was approximately two years old. Now Lenore is four, so this has been going on for just about two years. Her germ phobia appears to be getting worse."

"It's really getting worse! She keeps the house like a sweatbox. The windows are shut tight—she's afraid that a drop of air will come through. When I come in at night, I feel like I'm in a Turkish bath."

"She doesn't want to open the windows because she's afraid Lenore will catch cold. Go over to the window and open it a crack. Tell her, 'It's not healthy for you, or Lenore, to live in such a hot apartment.' Don't be afraid to tell her."

"I can't tell her anything! She gets all upset and yells, 'You drive a cab, that's your business. I have a baby and she's my business. Don't tell me what to do!' "

"George, you're in a tight bind. My mother comes back with all kinds of stories, too. She complains, 'You can faint up there from the heat.' I went over and brought a hygrometer to show her the unhealthy humidity in the apartment. Hedda raged, 'I don't want that thing!' She practically threw me out. No doubt, my sister is very difficult to deal with. Hedda allows my mother in about every two weeks. She stays for about fifteen minutes and Hedda says, 'The baby gets too excited when you come. When everybody stays away, the baby is best off!' Hedda then asks her to leave."

George agreed, "The thing she wants most is to be left alone with Lenore."

"I went to your apartment recently, and she was reluctant to let me in. But she did. I told her to consult a psychiatrist or even a medical doctor about her condition. She became enraged. 'There's nothing wrong with me! Just leave me alone! Don't tell me what to do!' You can't mention the word psychiatrist to her. She equates that with insanity and becomes very upset. She'll tell you, 'I'm not crazy.' "

"It's like a mad captain running a ship! To tell you the truth, Will, I don't know what to do. I woke up in the middle of the night, I had to go to the bathroom, and there was Lenore, in her crib, wide-awake, staring at me. She was bundled up in so many blankets she couldn't sleep. And there was Hedda sitting up in her chair, watching to see that the blankets remained in place. One slipped off and she quickly put it back on again."

"I know what you're up against. My sister has a closed mind, you can't tell her anything. Right after Lenore's birth, I gave her some U. S. Government publications on childcare. And now she says: 'If you didn't give me those damn books, I wouldn't have all these troubles!' She admits to having a 'germ craze' and she blames it all on me. It's obvious that Hedda doesn't want to listen to reason!"

"Listen to reason? She walks around the house saying, 'My baby is a very bad baby. She's always cross and cranky. When she grows up and gets better, I'll get better, too.' Maybe that's so, but right now, she's kind of weird. She doesn't trust the baby out of her sight—not even with me, and I'm the father!"

"That must be really rough on you, George. Have you noticed if she's washing her hands any less these days?"

"I was home on Saturday morning, and I saw her washing her hands and Lenore's. She was also washing toys, tables, and chairs that Lenore used. I don't know how many times she did it. I didn't count. But she did it over and over. I don't know what to make of it."

"I go up there and try to reason with her. My mother tries too, but to no avail. My mother tells me she walks around the house saying, 'My child is different from other children. Nobody else can understand my child, not even the doctors.' Now, if the doctors can't understand her child, who can? If I tell her that all children have similarities, that she should talk to other women with babies and see how they manage, she says, 'No two babies are alike.' "

"She says Lenore is very bad. I came in the other night and Hedda was sitting there and crying, 'She's so bad, I wish I were dead!' She says that from time to time. I don't know what to do, Will, I just don't know…"

"This is serious, George. My mother goes up there and she hears Hedda saying: 'I love my baby. She's all I have in this world.'"

"She may say she loves the baby, but she doesn't permit Lenore to have any love or affection. She does not touch Lenore. She doesn't kiss her, and she doesn't allow anyone else to kiss her or touch her. I am the father, and even I am not allowed to go near her! And Lenore must not touch me! She becomes very upset if anyone, including her own mother, even goes near the baby. How do you account for that, Will?"

"You have to realize that your wife has a germ phobia. But it may be more than that. From what you're telling me and from what I've observed, it looks like she's fearful and worried that something will happen to Lenore. Keeping the windows tightly closed, bundling Lenore up when she goes out, making sure she's securely covered with blankets at night—these are but a few indications of her fears about Lenore becoming ill. Can you see that George?"

"I guess you're right, but I don't know how much longer I can put up with it. I have no life with her. She's always telling me to wash my hands and I do it to please her. She sends me out shopping. Sometimes she sends me over to her mother to pick up food or something else. When I'm not working on the weekends, I usually leave the house early in the morning for breakfast, I come back for a short while, then I leave again after lunch to go to the movies and I come home late in the evening. It's gotten to be a routine. I'm lucky that I have my taxi. At least I don't have to worry about a job and money. My job is my life. It's all I really got."

"Do you know why she constantly sends you out of the house? She wants to keep you away from Lenore. She has all kinds of tricks to do this. I know what you're up against. My mother is very upset about this, too. She's very worried about Hedda and Lenore. She feels a pressure to help out as best she can. She does the major part of the shopping, she prepares meat and vegetable dishes for you and Hedda, and she tells me she cooks special foods for the baby twice a week."

"And I go over there to pick up the food and bring it home. She gets upset when her mother comes over. I say Hedda's acting very strange. She's got to get over it!"

"How do you think that will occur? Hedda needs psychiatric help to get over this obsession with germs."

"If we leave her alone, she might improve on her own."

"George, I don't think you're aware of the seriousness of her condition. My mother went to visit Hedda last week. She was standing outside the door with pots of food for Hedda and Lenore, but Hedda would not open the door! She was hollering and banging on the door, 'What's going on in there? If you don't open this door, I'm going to have it broken down!' But Hedda just ignored her. She would not open the door to her own mother! My mother comes to me and tells me what's going on. She had several incidents like that one. The last time that happened she threatened, 'I'm going to call the police. Something has to be done!' But she was afraid to act. She told me, 'If we do something drastic, my daughter may lose her mind completely.' "

"I've been saying it all along: her behavior is really weird!"

"It's worse than weird. Something has to get done. Do you realize that they rarely go out? And when they have gone out, she wouldn't permit Lenore to walk. Lenore was all bundled up and wedged into a stroller designed for a child half her size. I got news for you—her behavior is bizarre. Lenore is now four years old, and Hedda is but a shadow of her former self. She's eating little, and from what my mother tells me, she has not experienced a sound night's sleep since Lenore was born. How long do you think she can go on like that, George?"

"I don't know what the answer is."

"Lenore has not been examined by a physician for over two years. Hedda argues that she must be taking good care of the baby because the child has not suffered from any childhood ailments in the four years of her life. She says, 'I must be doing something right!' I find that incredible. My sister is impossible. I wind up having a fight with her every time I go up there. You don't know what this is all doing to me, or for that matter, how it's affecting my mother. She's heartbroken. I saw my mother the other day and she was on the verge of tears. She said, 'Lenore is four years old and she's never played with other children. She's not even been in contact with other children.' Except for two visits to my mother, she's never visited another home. Do you know why that is? She's afraid that Lenore will come down with a contagious disease if she plays with other children. My mother also tells me that Lenore is still drinking from a bottle. What's that all about?"

George paused to reflect and said, "Lenore is drinking from a bottle because Hedda doesn't want to use drinking glasses. She sterilizes the bottles and even the drinking water is boiled. Lenore drinks from a bottle like a baby…"

"It's amazing, a child of four years, drinking from a bottle…"

"It does sound incredible, Will, and I don't understand it."

"Don't try to understand it, you're not the only one who doesn't understand it. Tell me, how long is it now that Hedda and Lenore have not gone out of the house?"

"I believe it started in November, and now, it's the end of April. I think it's something like five months."

"Does she talk about going out at all?"

"She says she's waiting for the weather to get warmer…"

"Do you really believe that?"

"Look, Will, I don't know what to do. What do you want me to do?"

"For almost two years, I have tried to convince the family—that includes you and my parents—that Hedda is becoming worse rather than better, and that her problems require professional treatment. Taking no action will only aggravate the situation more and make any solution increasingly difficult. The last time I went to Hedda's house, she yelled at me: 'What do you know about babies? You haven't any of your own. Get out of here and leave me alone!' But I didn't stop there—although I did stop going over to visit Hedda. I contacted her physician and I asked him to casually pay a 'friendly' visit to Hedda at semi-weekly intervals. Dr. Wyckoff paid three calls to Hedda and she reacted unfavorably."

George frowned as he said: "I remember that time. She told me to call the doctor and tell him not to come again."

"Do you know why she ordered you to cut off those doctor visits? It was because she was afraid that he might be coming from homes with contagious diseases."

"I heard her say something about pneumonia."

Will agreed rather somberly: "That is correct. Soon after, I consulted six psychiatrists. I have the letters here if you want to see them. Each of the psychiatrists I contacted agrees that Hedda needs immediate treatment. One physician believes that psychosis is already developing, and in all probability, she will either go completely out of her mind and develop dementia praecox—an incurable form of insanity—or she will commit suicide and kill Lenore at the same time. They recommend hospitalization."

"I don't know what the answer is," George grimly responded. "All I know is that this has been going on for some time. If the doctors say she needs hospitalization, then maybe she does…"

Will and George soon agreed that this was the way to deal with the problem, and they discussed the steps needed for immediate action. Will soon provided George with the necessary papers, and George signed the following statement:

"….*My wife and the baby have not been getting along very well lately. On one or two occasions, she threatened to take her own life and that of the baby's. I do not believe that either she or the baby are safe… The family doctor has advised us to send her to Bellevue for observation.*"

2

Because I Was Bad

I saw her put books in the refrigerator, books that I wanted to look at. She said the books needed to be "aired out." How could she do that when I wanted those picture books so badly? At some point, she would reach into the refrigerator to see if they were "ready" to give to me. There were times when they were "not ready." I recall reaching in to grab a book. She would take my hands and hit them so very, very hard, and I would stand there and cry. My heavens, what had I done?

I only wanted to look at a book.

She was sitting on a chair near the gas stove and was looking at me in an odd way. Her eyes were glassy, and she was sobbing. She was saying things I did not understand: "God give me the strength to live another day. Help me not to take my life and my baby's."

Just looking at her face as she said that was enough to make me tremble. Her cheeks were wet with tears. I had a dreadful feeling that something terrible might happen at any moment.

I lived in fear for days on end. And soon, that dreadful feeling became real.

Early one morning, I suddenly heard a loud banging on the door. Someone was shouting, "**Open up**!"

The next thing I knew my mommy was being dragged out of the apartment in her nightgown, her hair hanging loose like strings, and her feet bare. She was sobbing uncontrollably as she began to scream "My baby, my baby…" She was trying to reach out and grab me when suddenly I felt someone pulling me away from her. I turned around and saw my grandma Elly. I didn't even know she was there. I was in turmoil and crying convulsively as I saw two men carrying my mommy out. I was now shaking with fear.

Grandma went over to the window and I followed her. As we stood there, looking out at what appeared to be a truck in front of the building, we heard screams in the street below. Grandma was closing the curtain with one hand and holding me with the other, shielding me from the ugly scene that was taking place. She did not want me to see the policemen pushing my mother into the ambulance and closing the doors. I cried and cried, but she didn't say anything. The sad, somber expression on her face told me how distressed she was.

I continued to cry. I had a terrible feeling: *Whatever it is, I made this happen! I made Mommy sick! I did something to her, and I'll never see her again. They had taken Mommy away because I was bad!*

I guess I was no angel, but what had I done? When I was about three, I was making a mess all over the floor and soiling myself. Mommy looked like she was about to have a fit. When Grandma came over, Mommy told her, "She did it again today! I had her trained. She was trained so well. I don't know what to do with her. She says 'Caca, caca,' and then she makes."

When it happened, Mommy would look at me with a strange look, and then she would hit me.

Another time, I was sitting in my little chair, watching Mommy and Daddy talk. In no way did I want that. I wanted him to talk to me and only me. I wanted his attention more than anything else. So, I made sounds that kept them from talking. Mommy said it nice and loud: "I can't get a word in edgewise with her around!"

She seemed angrier all the time, but who cared? I didn't—not when Daddy was around.

One night, when I was in bed, I overheard Mommy talking to Daddy. "I want to have another child. I can't manage her. She's such a bad child. Maybe a brother or sister would help . . ."

I got scared when I heard that. I didn't know why, but I didn't want a brother or sister. I calmed down—when Daddy didn't say anything.

My daddy was a quiet man. He said very little. He drove a taxi and lived in our home. I thought he was the best looking man in the entire world. He was not too tall and not too short. He was not too fat and not too thin. He was just right. And he had these big brown eyes and straight, dark-brown hair. Sometimes he looked so sad as he peeked out at me through his glasses. But I loved the way he looked at me. He did not have to say much; he was kind, and I could feel it. But he seemed so unreachable. If only he would leave Mommy and take me to live with him somewhere away from her. That's all I wanted. But she was so pretty, with that red color on her lips and her hair so short with every curl in place.

When he did glance my way, I recall a special feeling I had for him. I would smile at him, and there was something that felt very good about that. If only he could have sent just a little smile my way! But no, he seemed like he had bigger, more important things on his mind.

And now, Mommy was gone.

The next thing I knew, Grandma was taking me to her home. I did not know if I would ever see Mommy again. I would just sit there and stare off into space. I disliked Mommy at times, but I didn't want anything to happen to her. And there I was, feeling I had made something happen to her—what it was, I didn't know.

Grandma did not say much. She would sit in her chair and look at me with those big green eyes, and frown. I hated to see Grandma unhappy.

I saw little of Grandpa Moe. But I do recall him sitting with a newspaper, and all I could see was his white hair and big, black, bushy eyebrows rising above his paper. I felt sadder than usual when I looked into his dark-brown eyes. Sometimes a chill would go through me, and I never knew just why. And then I would hear Grandpa say, "There's nothing wrong with Hedda. The baby is a bad baby. If Hedda was left alone, everything would be all right."

I heard it all the time: "It's all the baby's fault."

Sometimes Grandpa would come over to me and say, "You're a bad girl!"

I did not like that great, big smile that came on his face when he said those words, for I did not think it was funny at all. How could those few words cause his teeth to show and his eyes to light up? What was he so happy about—because I was "bad"?

Grandma had a few visitors. I recall trying to listen to what they were talking about, but everything was said so low and hushed up. At one time I overheard Grandma telling her friends, "The child is four years old, and she's so difficult. She doesn't want to go out of the house. Her mother had so much trouble with her—she's a bad child. My poor daughter . . ."

Her voice dropped low, and I could not hear anything else. Grandma, too, was saying bad things about me. I wanted to go and hide. Again, I felt that I had done something terrible. Maybe my mother would never come home.

I became very frightened when there was a thunderstorm. I heard a sound of thunder and I would start to shake and tremble. Grandma saw this, and she came over to me. "Gawd is angry. (She could not say God.) When you're bad—and you do bad things—Gawd shows his anger. Gawd punishes bad little girls!"

My eyes widened in awe. Then Grandma pointed to a mole on her face. "Do you see this? This is what happens when little girls are bad, when they tell lies—or when they do bad things."

The mole was big and ugly. It scared me. Did she get that mole because she had done something bad? I wondered if God was angry with me; I wondered if I would be punished. Maybe it was true: bad things happen when people are bad. Was I being punished for all the harm I had done to my mother?

I sat in Grandma's kitchen on a rocking chair and held on to my mother's slippers. It gave me some comfort, and I felt, in some strange way, that it brought me closer to her. Then I held the slippers to my cheeks and pressed my lips against them as I rocked back and forth. And I cried and cried some more. How I wanted to be with my mother! But my mother was nowhere to be found.

My father took me out for a brief stroll in the neighborhood. He also took me over to my uncle's house. Both times, I cried so much, I had to be brought right back to Grandma's.

One day my uncle Will and his wife, Jessie, came to visit Grandma. I heard Jessie say, "She's such a sad child, she came to our home and she didn't smile once. She has that blank look on her face—and her eyes are so big and sad!"

Nothing seemed to bring a smile to my face. My only relief came from listening to songs on the radio. There was one song I especially liked: "Don't Sit under the Apple Tree (with Anyone Else but Me.)"

I listened to that song over and over. I don't know why, but that song gave me hope.

And I sat in my chair with tears in my eyes. *Where is Mommy? Will she ever be coming home? Will I ever see her again?*

3

Bellevue and Beyond

I was four years old when my mother was committed to the psychiatric ward of Bellevue Hospital for observation. Her brother, Will, was concerned about her, so he paid a visit to the lady psychiatrist assigned to her case. And he was taken aback. She told him, "I'm trying to find out why this woman hates her child so much!"

Will became very angry and responded, "If anything, her plight is the result of the very opposite—she loves her child too much!"

Words flew thick and fast. Afterward, Will noted, "She practically threw me out of her office when I bluntly told her she didn't know what the hell she was talking about! What nonsense!"

Hedda's stay at Bellevue was very brief. After four days, the family had her removed to a private sanitarium. Her discharge record at Bellevue indicated "undiagnosed psychosis."

Hedda was now in a peaceful, country-like environment, and George was visiting her regularly. After one of his visits, Hedda sent a letter to him:

"I felt very lonesome when you went away and I am counting the minutes and days when we will be together again—not for a few hours, but for good . . . I'm telling you I feel fine and I'm not

kidding—I see everything in a different way now and my mind is normal again and I want you to find me a changed person in every sense of the word for the best . . . Give me a good chance to show you how improved I am, and I'm sure you'll be happy with me again. Bellevue gave me the works and how! You'll never realize how very sick I was there, but I want to forget that terrible experience. The things that happened to us cannot and will not happen again. I feel happy and well and expect to remain so . . . I want to live and enjoy myself. I suffered enough at home and since I've been away, I think I deserve some pleasure out of life and I expect to get it, hook or crook, and I'm not fooling . . ."

At about the same time, her father, a man who said very little, became enraged: "There's nothing wrong with her! There's no mental illness in this family! It's all the baby's fault! The baby is very difficult to manage. I want Hedda out of there! I have a cousin who's a lawyer, and I will take legal action if anyone tries to prevent her from coming out."

It is not clear what transpired, but shortly after that, Hedda was released. She came into Grandma's apartment with her brother, Will, and how surprised I was to see her! It was a miracle! My mother was alive and well. I couldn't take my eyes off her. How very different she looked! She wore bright-red lipstick, her hair was short, curly, and combed, and she had even put on a little weight. I thought she was the most beautiful lady in the whole world, but she had an odd look on her face. I wondered if she was angry with me. Suddenly she slapped my uncle across his face. I heard her say loudly, **"You just try to put me away again and I'll never talk to you as long as I live!"**

I became very upset. What did he do to make her so angry? She may have looked different, but something told me Mommy had not changed. I had wanted her back more than anything else in the world, but there she was, hollering and screaming in her same old manner. In that moment, I knew: Mommy had come home!

Soon we were back in our apartment on Belmont Avenue. Hedda looked like a new person. She was combing her hair. She put on a simple dress and even wore shoes. I felt a sense of comfort in that. It seemed as if the worst had passed and things were getting better.

Unfortunately, it was all wishful thinking. My mother was as angry as ever. For the least thing, she would explode and hit me. I watched her eyes bulge and her jaw clench tightly. I would sit cowering in a corner; I couldn't move, and I was afraid to cry. I wanted to be as far away from her as possible when she was like that.

Soon, she was standing at the sink, scrubbing her hands like crazy. Her hands became so red, they would bleed. And soon I saw her once again airing out books in the refrigerator. I had a sick feeling when I saw her doing that, I didn't like to look at books that were wet and soggy. There was nothing I could do but cringe inside and long for her to stop. And I saw book after book, like *The Bobbsey Twins*, finding their way into our refrigerator.

I was so glad to see Grandma. Schlepping up the stairs with her shopping bags, Grandma gave a little knock on the door and called out "Hedda." And soon she was in our home. She stood in the hallway for a few moments, trying to catch her breath, and then slowly, she took off her coat and sat down. She tried to put on a happy face as she asked Hedda, "How is everything here?" She paused for a moment and then said, "I just saw Willie. He keeps asking about you. He wants to see you."

"I never want to see him as long as I live!" snapped Hedda. "Look at what your precious son did. That bastard! He sent me to the loony bin. He had the police come up here and pull me out, like some kind of nut. And right in front of the building I live in! He had some nerve! He can never come up here again."

Pacing up and down, Hedda continued: "He and his wife— those bastards—they're responsible for my troubles. I was planning to take her out that week when they put me away in the nuthouse . . ."

Hedda began to cry. "I took her out one freezing day, and I met the super's wife. She said, 'Your little one looks so cold—she's such a dainty thing, she's so delicate . . .' After that, I couldn't take her out. She knew how delicate my baby is, so I kept her in the house. I was waiting for the weather to get warm. They should be ashamed of themselves—putting me away like that!"

Hedda came up for a breath of air and went on: "My brother and his wife—I know they wanted me out of the way. You wanted to get your hands on her too. Then you all could raise her—you're not fooling me!"

Grandma sat there with a blank look on her face. She listened to Hedda ramble on. Then suddenly, her face was flushed with anger. "You don't know what you're talking about. I spoke to the super's wife. She told me that the neighbors had been talking about you for months—that if we hadn't sent for the ambulance, they would probably have done it themselves. If you don't believe me, go over and ask her!"

Hedda shot back: "You're just like your son! You're a troublemaker! You come up here and you make trouble! I've had enough for one day. Leave me alone!"

Grandma's eyes were blazing as she reached for her coat and her bundles. "Every time I come up here, I go away sick!"

And she left. That was a scene that would repeat itself over and over.

Grandpa paid us brief visits. As soon as he came in, he sat down and lit a cigar. He looked deep in thought. With his cigar dangling from his mouth, he would take a few puffs and look at his fingers as if he were studying them. Then, with a frown, in a low, sad voice, he would say, "It's no good." He said it so often, I just about knew what he was going to say before he said it. I felt the gloom from those words; things appeared darker than usual.

The three of us sat together as a cold, dead silence permeated the air. It was so quiet in the house, you could hear a pin drop. Then suddenly Grandpa would chuckle heartily as he pointed his index finger at me: "You're a bad girl!" Every time he saw me, he said that, and each time, I cringed. I hated to hear it, for he was only confirming what I already was feeling inside. Did he have to remind me how bad I felt about myself?

I knew my mother didn't like me talking to anyone, so I remained silent. I wondered if she was going to say anything to Grandpa; he was one person she didn't talk about in a bad way. But she just sat there, looking on. And the time passed. Then Grandpa would stare at the floor for a few minutes and boldly say, "After rain comes sunshine." That's when my mother snapped: "What sunshine? That's real crap! Don't tell me about sunshine! I don't want to hear that crap!"

A hush fell over the room. Grandpa would gaze at his hands and mutter, "It's no good." He became silent for a little while, and then, looking rather sad, he would go for his hat, coat, and cane and depart.

Despite what Grandpa said about me, I felt bad for him in the moment. He said so little, and when he tried to say something nice and comforting, there was Hedda, slapping him down. He walked away looking more wounded than when he came in.

There were times when Grandma came up, and Hedda couldn't wait to lash out about "the crazy house." She began a long rant about the things that had happened to her there. She angrily boasted about being "the perfect patient" and how she had developed a remarkable strategy for getting out. She called it "fooling the doctors."

"They wanted to catch me washing my hands. But I fooled them! They even had me mopping floors! And I did not cry. One of the patients came up to me and said, 'Honey, if you cry, you'll never get out of here!' They wouldn't catch me crying. Not after I heard that!"

In a defiant tone, she went on. "I was watched by a bunch of crazy psychiatrists, and they gave me all kinds of stupid pills. I never took them—I spit them out and threw them away when they weren't looking."

She laughed as she said, "There was one psychiatrist who walked around with a limp and a shaking hand. He was a real nut if ever I saw one. He was more confused than the patients. He came up to me and asked, 'Why are you here?' and I said, 'Because I wash my hands.' He said 'Well, don't wash your hands!' And that was it. I never saw him again.

"There was only one thing that kept me going while I was there—coming home to my baby!"

I listened to my mother speak. She was usually angry, and she would go on and on. I just sat there. I didn't know what I was thinking or feeling; I was only a child. The only thing I knew was that I felt bad—really bad—and I didn't know why.

Grandma listened too. She just sat there; she didn't say anything. Soon Mommy finished, and Grandma was gone. I was grateful for that; I wouldn't have to hear Mommy continue her rant—not until the next time.

Soon Mommy was acting very strange. I don't know what came over her, but suddenly, she had a weird look on her face that scared me. And then I heard a strange noise. Mommy was growling and gritting her teeth! Her fingers curled over like animal claws, and her eyes were bulging. As her back began to hunch over, she looked incredibly ugly.

What's happened to Mommy? She no longer looks like my mommy. Oh no! She's turned into a monster!

I was scared out of my wits. As she reached out to grab me, I ran away from her, but she came after me and chased me all over the house. I heard her scream, **"You little bitch—wait till I get you!"** My heart was beating faster with each step. As I raced into the kitchen, she cornered me and shook me. She began to make more noises, like an animal, as she slapped me around and punched me. I was shaking with fear. *What's going to happen to me?*

Then, suddenly, it was over. Just like that! She snapped out of whatever had taken hold of her. The monster was gone, and my mother was back. But the turmoil within me didn't stop. I was trembling, and my heart was beating like a drum. I had some redness on my skin where she socked me, and it hurt—but it was nowhere as bad as the pain I felt inside. I don't recall what happened after that; I was in a state of shock, and I don't know how long I was like that.

How did this happen? What brought this about? What did I do to make her so upset? I couldn't get it out of my mind.

These episodes continued to occur again and again. I lived in dread of her next attack.

Hedda was pacing up and down. She was having a monologue with herself as she complained: "Why did I come back to Belmont Avenue? This place is a dungeon! The dark rooms, the long hall, it's like a cellar—it's so damn cold in here!"

Hedda reached for a cigarette (something she had learned to do in Bellevue). She lit it and went on. "The neighbors are talking about me. And I know what they're thinking. They saw me dragged out of here. They see me in the street, and they stare at me. They think I'm crazy!"

Hedda confronted George and adamantly said, "You have to find a new apartment—or I'm not going out of this house!"

"I'll see what I can do."

By this time, my father had lost a lot of weight. He looked very pale and drawn. And there was a sadness about him that could be felt as he just about made it out of the house to his taxi route.

George couldn't find an apartment for us, but he found a temporary solution for the summer months: a resort hotel in Spring Valley. We did not know that a new pattern of spending our summers at this resort had begun. It was an opportunity to step out of the darkness of despair and into the light of hope.

4

A Breath of Fresh Air

The time came for us to go to Spring Valley. I recall my mother opening the door to the back seat of my father's cab, as we edged our way inside. After just a short distance, I was throwing up, and needless to say, that didn't make my father happy, but he didn't say a word. He cleaned it up, and we went on with our trip, as if nothing had happened.

It seemed like we were traveling forever when finally, we arrived at the hotel. I felt a discomfort in the pit of my stomach as I slowly moved out of the cab. I looked around. I saw trees, flowers, and greens, and I smelled the clean fresh air. It seemed as if there was nothing to be afraid of. Then I saw people, and my heart began to beat fast. *What will things be like here? Will I be safe?*

I couldn't stop feeling that something bad was about to happen. I turned to my mother for a feeling of safety and comfort. Somehow, I needed to be with her—and only her. We walked around on the premises, and wherever she went, I was right there, hanging on to her skirt. It seemed that as much as I needed to cling to her, she wanted me with her as well.

Soon, my mother and I were sitting at a table in the dining room. I was amongst a large crowd of people in a strange, new environment. This gave me the most eerie feeling and I began to block out most everything around me.

A man soon came over to our table. He was carrying a tray in his hand. On this tray were various platters of food that he put down before us. My mother immediately told me it was okay to eat some things, but not others. The food was so tasty, so very delicious and different from anything I had at home. I wondered why she said I wasn't to have certain foods.

Soon my mother called back the waiter to return something that was "too cold" or "not right" for me. She simply said: "These foods do not agree with my daughter." But how did she know that? I had never tasted any of it, but it seemed that she knew what was best for me. The same thing happened each time I went into the dining room and I didn't tell her how awful I felt because I sensed it wouldn't make any difference.

In the mid-afternoon, my mother and I went into the dining room to have tea and cookies. Harry, the waiter, brought out trays with all kinds of deserts, and Tom, the bus boy, took away the empty plates. I enjoyed watching them as they whirled by our table. I began to smile at them, and they smiled back at me. I appreciated the attention they were giving me. I was fast becoming a little flirt at the tender old age of four and a half!

When there were not that many people around, the boys frequently found a few minutes to stop by our table and talk. And I loved it. Harry said funny things as he leaped up in the air, with a dishtowel over his shoulder. "I'll jump over any one of those tables if you want to see it!" *How will he ever be able to do that?* It sounded kind of silly to me. I just laughed and laughed, and he laughed too. But Tom was not like that; he didn't make any jokes. He was tall, good-looking, and serious. I liked the way he looked at me. He smiled at me with his eyes. I eagerly looked forward to seeing Tom and Harry every day.

I soon found something that gave me a great feeling; I loved to go on the swings. My mother would swing me back and forth and it was wonderful to go high up into the air! I could never get enough. In that moment, all my cares were whisked away on a cool summer breeze. I loved that feeling!

I continued to cling to my mother. I couldn't stand the thought of being away from her. I would never stray far enough from her to make a friend. How nice it would have been to have someone to play with, but something about it just didn't feel right to me. In fact, it scared me. I only wanted to be with Hedda.

As my mother and I strolled along the grounds together, we came upon all kinds of farm animals. I delighted in seeing cows, pigs, chickens, and geese. I had not seen real live animals before, and I was eager to touch the chickens and geese, but I soon found they were just as timid as I; as soon as I came close, they would all run away.

And then I came upon the cat. Immediately, I loved the way it looked: the soft, silky fur, the colorful markings, and the expressive, soulful eyes. This creature—the cat—seemed to speak to me with its eyes; there was a certain inner something that I could feel, but I did not know what it was; I just knew it gave me a good feeling.

There were quite a few cats and kittens on the grounds, and I would stand there and look at them in wonderment. How beautiful they were! Sometimes I reached out to pet one, and it felt thrilling. When I got a bit bolder, I began to play with them. I had a little string that I would dangle before the kittens, and if I were not fast enough to pull away, I would get scratched. Hedda, standing a few feet away, saw blood trickling out of an open wound and she would give out a yell: **"I told you not to fool around with cats. Now look at what you've done!"** She looked frantic as she came running over and slapped me. My world collapsed around me. I thought I did something awful, and that something terrible was about to happen to me—just what, I didn't know. My zest for playing around with cats quickly waned, and I soon stopped altogether. But I never stopped admiring the cat and its beauty.

As we walked around, I was particularly attracted to the green hills that surrounded me. They looked so beautiful and inviting, I suddenly felt an overwhelming urge to run up one. Disregarding the unhappy expression on Hedda's face, I raced ahead enthusiastically toward the grassy slope. Running up and down the hill was an exciting experience for me, until I lost my balance and fell. Blood was oozing down my knees, as Hedda, standing nearby, came towards me, screaming: **"You did it again!"**

I saw that look of hatred on her face. I was cringing, as she lashed out with a hard smack. How frightened I was of my mother's rage! Then, as I looked down at my knees and elbows, I felt panic. When would this bleeding stop? I was in a state of turmoil as Hedda dragged me back to the hotel room. As she began to apply iodine, I didn't know what hurt more: the iodine, or the look of disgust on her face.

Things could get pretty rough at times and I didn't know what to do. Most of the time, I remained sad and frightened. But when Hedda started to take pictures of me with her Brownie camera, I somehow found it in me to smile. So, there I was, smiling up a storm as if I didn't have a care in the world. Something about that camera felt so good. When I saw the camera's eye, it brought me to life and made me sparkle. It was as if the camera was paying attention to me and asking me to pose for it. With a snap of a button, I appeared to be one of the happiest, most well-adjusted children you would ever want to see.

But there were times I couldn't get that sad, blank look off my face and my mother continued to take pictures anyway. I didn't like to see how distraught I looked on these pictures.

When I saw pictures of me smiling and looking pretty, I couldn't believe my eyes. Is this really me? For the most part, I adored the pictures where I looked like a happy child. And the pictures started to accumulate in a photograph album.

Friday night was a special night for me. My father came up from the city on weekends and stayed until Sunday evening. I thought about seeing him all week, but I was rarely with him on these visits. He was mixing with people in the hotel, and he appeared so happy; his eyes were beaming, and he had a great big smile on his face. I could see that he genuinely enjoyed people, and yet, he looked so gloomy around my mother and me. Hedda and George continued to live the same in the country as they did at home; they were under the same roof, but they acted as though they were total strangers. Hedda kept herself distant, while my father remained his usual silent self. And, as usual, I felt sad and alone.

One night, when my father was outside, getting ready to return to the city, my mother said she would be right back. That kind of startled me, for she usually didn't leave me out of her sight. But suddenly I was all by myself.

It seemed like an eternity that Hedda was gone. *Did she leave me this time for good?* I began to panic. I reached up for the knob of the door, but I couldn't get at it for I was so small. I kept straining to reach the knob. I started to cry. Soon my cries turned into screams. Suddenly the door opened from the outside, and a lady appeared. "Where is your mother, little girl?"

The next thing I knew my mother was walking very slowly down the hallway. She was coming towards me and I ran to her. I started to cry. "Mommy, Mommy…"

My mother turned to the lady and said: "I hope she didn't bother you, I just had to go out for a few minutes…"

But it felt like forever! Then again, what appeared like an eternity to a scared little child might have only been moments in time. How relieved I was to see my mother.

The lady was soon gone, and I was with my mother once again. But my feelings of fear and abandonment still lingered. I would have liked to have my mother comfort me by putting her arms around me, but it was just a fantasy; Hedda would never do anything like that. I felt as alone as ever. I was still thankful for one thing: my mother had returned. She did not abandon me after all.

Towards the end of the summer, I had a pleasant surprise. Grandma and Grandpa came out to visit. What stands out in my mind is that special moment when Grandma, smiling happily, reached out to me, and tried to sneak in a kiss—but she got caught in the act! Hedda hollered: **"What are you doing? That's a lot of nonsense—all that kissing—she doesn't need that crap."**

I felt my heart sink. Grandma did not say anything; she stopped immediately and stared off into space, while Grandpa stood there, as though he didn't see or hear a thing. Hedda's Rules were reinforced: nobody was allowed to show me any love or affection— and I was not allowed to show love and affection to anyone. I swallowed my feelings of sadness and hurt. *Why does Hedda have to be so mean?*

My first summer in Spring Valley drew to a close. It was a special time for me, even though the scars of my mother's hospitalization were still fresh. I would remember the warmth of the summer days, and the pretty country scenery. I would miss the smell of the fresh air in the morning, and the beautiful flowers on a bed of green. I would miss my friends, the animals. And I would miss Tom and Harry.

What a shame it had to come to an end.

5

A Letter to Annie

Hedda had a high school friend, Annie, who later moved to California. Over the years, Hedda maintained contact with Annie through letter writing. In this long, detailed letter, Hedda pours her heart out to Annie. It reads as follows:

Dear Annie,

I have not written to you in some time because there was not much to say. As the expression goes, no news is good news. But my life has become such a mess, I have no one to tell my troubles to, so I thought I would get them off my chest and write to you.

Things have gotten very bad since I had the baby. I never should have had her—it was all my mother's idea. She would say, "It's good to have a child for your old age. What will happen to you when you get old? Who will take care of you? What if you're all alone in the world?" I hear stupid things like that, and what happens? I get talked into having a baby.

Do you know it took ten years for me to have that baby? When it happened, I swear to you, my mother was happier than me.

Babies. They scream, they have to pee or make number two and then you have to change diapers. Who needs that?

Things were so peaceful before she came. When my mother got sick and needed someone to take care of her, I gave up my job and became her nursemaid. And it was like that for years. I stayed in the house with my mother and lived a quiet life. I didn't need to go back to work. My mother said let's go out and do the shopping now, and we did the shopping. In the morning she'd say let's have juice now, and we had juice. There was not much to do.

Then I got pregnant. My first pregnancy ended with a miscarriage. That was a warning, but I paid no attention. Then I had her. I have to tell you the story now.

Before she was born, I told my husband that I was in pain. He called the doctor and the doctor said it would be just a few hours before I'd give birth. My dear husband said he had to go to work. Could you believe it? He left me with labor pains to go to work on a cold icy day in January. When the pains got bad, my mother went out and got a taxi to take us to the hospital. I never forgave my husband for that. He should be ashamed of himself!

And then she was born. The nurses commented on a baby that would cry so much. They made a joke of it. They said she could become an opera singer. Her lungs are good and strong. That's for sure. She screams enough for ten.

They also spoke about her one dimple. They asked if she slept on a button. I knew right away that my baby is different.

The fun, or should I say horror, really started when I came home from the hospital. She didn't stop screaming. We had several doctors, and they all said she was a colicky baby. She had one formula after another and nothing was right. Meanwhile, she laid there and screamed. It's like a bullet in the head.

My father was the only one who had a way with her. He could walk the floor with her and carry her around on his back as if she were some kind of toy. She liked that. Plenty of attention. She stopped that carrying on at least for the time he was there. The rest of us were just a bunch of slaves for her to make mincemeat of. We didn't know what the hell to do with her.

There was always fighting in the house. My mother and I didn't see eye to eye and we couldn't stop that crying. My husband went to bed. He had a fine excuse. He said he had to get his sleep so he could get up early in the morning to be on his taxi route. Like Hell, he did!

When she was one and a half, my husband tells me that we have to leave my parents, or he will pack his bags and leave. He said he couldn't take it anymore. Look at who's talking! Where the hell did he get off to tell me something like that? He wasn't even around.

We left my parents' home and moved a few blocks away to Belmont Avenue. Things got only worse. I found myself alone with this screaming kid. I was doomed.

Such a bad baby! I could sit here and tell you stories about her, but I don't want to waste the paper. I will say she is different. She is cranky and unmanageable. She'd be better off in strange hands. I keep telling my husband we should have another baby. Two is better than one. Maybe she wouldn't be so bad if she had someone to play with. He doesn't want to know of it. Talking to him is like talking to the walls.

My mother comes up and tells me what to do. I tell her to skip a while and let me live. My brother and his wife think they're so smart. They have no children of their own, and they have all the answers. I tell them to mind their own business. My brother has six degrees, and he thinks he knows it all. He only knows what's in the books. He has no common sense.

As much as I hate to say it, she is still my baby. As bad as she is, I have to take care of her. I don't have much else in my life.

You should see what I look like now. When I was a young girl, I was so attractive, I'm sure you remember. I was slim. I had short curly hair and bangs. I was nice and quiet, but my home was like a battlefield. I never told you about it, but there were terrible fights in my home.

My mother would tell me to go outside and play with the other children. But I didn't want that. I wanted to stay with her and that's how I grew up. I didn't have any friends. I think you're the only friend I had in high school.

I had to make good grades. I studied so much, I got headaches. I had to graduate from high school and for what? To end up like this?

My husband is no good. There's a lot about him you don't know, and I'm going to tell you now.

I met George when he was working as a waiter in the mountains. I was there for the summer with my parents. He wasn't a bad looking fellow. He had dark hair and brown eyes, nothing very special, just average. He looked poor. I think I felt sorry for him. He said he came over from Lithuania during the First World War. I didn't want to get involved with boys. I told him I was going to high school and I had another year to graduate. I didn't take him seriously.

Can you imagine what happened? He came back for me. Exactly one year later, he came to my door. He said he fell in love with me when he first saw me. His exact words were, "You're such a beautiful girl, and you're so intelligent, I couldn't get you off my mind."

You know, I went to a relative's wedding and my mother told me there was a lawyer asking about me. He wanted to know who that beautiful girl was and he wanted to meet me. But it was too late. I was already with George.

What a damn fool I was. I was 19, he was 20, and we got married. I had just gotten over a terrible experience. I saw a man in the hallway, exposed. I screamed and he ran up the stairs to the roof. A few weeks later I heard that a little girl was taken to the roof and was attacked and killed by a man. They caught the rapist. I think it was that same man. I was scared out of my wits, I was afraid to go out of the house. I met George that year. Sometimes I think I was sorry for him, he dressed so shabbily and I don't know, something about him was just plain pathetic. Or maybe I married him because I was afraid to go out by myself. I can't figure that one out.

He didn't have much education. He was working as a shipping clerk when we married. One day he said he wanted to drive a cab. He started to work long hours. I swear he developed a love affair with that cab and he bought one after another.

I never felt like that about my work. I didn't like secretarial work. I was scrawling those lines for my bosses and half the time I couldn't read it back. It was no great shake to give up that job when my mother had back surgery. I stayed home and took care of her. I didn't bother to go back to work.

When George and I got married, we went to live with my parents. That was a big mistake. George was stingy and wanted to save a few dollars. I often told him that he should have married my mother, he got along so well with her. My brother also lived there, and George got along with him even though I didn't. My mother and father had their usual terrible fights but we managed.

The best thing about my husband was his mother. The rest of the family could go jump in the lake. I have no use for them. When George's mother died, he was named executor of her will and his sister Bea accused him of being a thief. Did you ever hear such a thing? A bunch of low lives, if ever there were. George was weak and never fought back, he stood there and took it. I didn't bother with any one of them after that.

I recently had a terrible thing happen to me. My doctor came to visit me, and he kissed me on the lips and fondled my breasts. I told him never to come back. Everything happens to me.

I hope you get an idea of what my life is like. There's much more I can't even talk about now. My heart is heavy. I'll say good-bye.

Hedda

6

Back Home Again

We stayed in Spring Valley for a couple of months, then we returned to the city. I was about four and a half at the time we moved into our new home. And Hedda was very angry. She lit a cigarette and raged: "It's bad enough I got pulled out of the house like some kind of nut. Now I meet people who look at me like I'm crazy. Your father is so damn stupid. He found an apartment just a few blocks away. I didn't have to move for that. I could have stayed on Belmont Avenue."

She paused to catch her breath, and then she went on: "My brother—he's no damn good! I'll never forgive him for signing those papers. That bastard put me away and ruined my life!" As I listened to her rant, I got the feeling that my uncle was a very bad man.

Hedda went around for some time like that. She held Uncle Will responsible for putting her away in a mental institution. But those several weeks that she was away may have saved her life— and mine. And now, despite her anger and hostility, it felt like we were making a new start in a new apartment. At least, it seemed that way.

We had two bedrooms, a living room, and a kitchen. I liked it as only a child can like something new. I frequently stood near the entrance to the living room and admired it; it was so nice and large. I especially liked the long, white, sheer nylon curtains that were hanging on the bedroom doors when we moved in. I kept staring at them. Something about those curtains fascinated me.

We didn't have much furniture, and what we had was rather shabby. A large bureau, an easy chair, a rocker, and a floor lamp were all we had in the living room. I recall my father pleading, "Let me get a sofa."

Hedda had one adamant response: "I don't want a sofa in this house! Don't bring any sofa in here, or you'll go out with it!" At times, she would turn to me, face all flushed, veins in her neck protruding, and say, "What do I need a sofa for? Sofas breed bugs! Who's going to stand and clean it?" Other times she would say, "I don't want your father coming home from work, flopping down on that sofa, and falling asleep . . ."

I cried in my heart when she said that, for I wanted my father home with me. And I would think about the sofa. I didn't know what a sofa was, but it sounded like something nice to have. I secretly longed for something that would make our home look better.

I saw the easy chair stacked high with newspapers. I often looked at that chair, and I felt sad. I had a secret wish to have someone—anyone—come into our home and have a nice easy chair to sit down on. Hedda made it quite clear, however, that she did not want anyone in the house—including my father.

How very dark it was in the apartment, and how very dreary it looked. The overhead lighting was only 40 watts, and our old floor lamp was no better. Hedda said, "What do we need more light for? This is good enough!" But it didn't feel good to me.

The off-white kitchen curtains turned tattletale gray in no time, and the shades on the windows changed from beige to dirty yellow. I overheard Grandma talking about something called "drapes and blinds," and I wondered what they looked like. I thought anything would be better than what we had.

Hedda did not like the new apartment any more than the one we had just moved from. She walked around, complaining bitterly:

"It's so damn cold in this dump. You don't get a bit of steam! Look what your father found. It's like that cellar on Belmont Avenue."

Then, at some time during the day, we would hear someone banging on the pipe to get steam heat. Hedda would go next. As she banged on the pipe, I would hear her say, "He should only go to hell! All those goddamn supers should drop dead!" By now her face was reddened with anger. I sat there, gaping at her. How I wished she would stop.

Usually, when the apartment was very cold, the kitchen was the best place to be in; Hedda made sure that several pots of water were on the stove so there would be plenty of heat in the room. There were times when it became very hot. When Grandma came, she often complained: "You could faint in here, it's so hot! For God's sake, open a window!"

Usually, Hedda had a deaf ear. Sometimes, however, she would holler: "If you don't like it, don't come up!"

Grandma might then take a sheet of paper from her shopping bag and use it as a fan. She then would roll her eyes around or say something that made Hedda more upset. Words flew back and forth. I was too scared to open my mouth. Eventually, Grandma would get up and leave. I felt better because I didn't have to watch the two of them fight.

I looked around me and saw dust and dirt growing all over the place. I didn't like what I saw. But it didn't seem to bother my mother; she was too busy washing her hands and airing out books in the refrigerator to kill germs. I anxiously waited to look at those nice picture books of the Bobbsey twins, but I tried not to make a wild grab for them when they came out of the refrigerator. I dreaded seeing my mother's face turning red and then that smack once again!

While Hedda kept busy worrying about germs, little visitors had come to call. They were marching their way right into our refrigerator. For the most part, Hedda did not seem to mind. But there were times she would squash one with her wet hands. I had a horrible feeling about that. I could never understand how she could do that.

Grandma came up one day and noticed the roaches crawling around the apartment. She turned to me and said, "Roaches are dirty; they creep all over and they bring disease . . ." I felt a chill go through me: *Would I become ill from these roaches?*

Grandma had more to say, but Hedda abruptly cut in: "What are you bothering her with that nonsense? **She doesn't need that!** She knows enough already. Leave her alone!" It was rare for Grandma to speak to me at all. How very much I wanted to hear what she was going to say.

It was amazing: Hedda was "airing out" things to make them "clean" while these "dirty" bugs were creeping all over the house. And the dirt continued to grow.

I watched her "clean up" after Grandma and Grandpa left our home. She walked around with a washcloth in her hand, washing off the chairs they sat on and anything they touched. I just watched, I never asked what she was doing or why she was doing it.

Grandma came up one day and told me about how we need to wash our bodies to keep ourselves clean. She said, "That's the difference between humans and animals. If we don't wash ourselves, we begin to stink." She showed concern about the germs and dirt that live on one's body, but according to Hedda, showers and baths were not necessary. "A little dirt never killed anyone."

Hedda did not show any shame about the way we were living. She acted as if dirt was a part of our household and belonged where it was. She rarely picked up a broom or washed a floor. Once in a while, my father would take time to get down on his hands and knees and scrub the kitchen floor. Sometimes he would wash the windows, which you could hardly see out of. Then suddenly he stopped—and the dirt began to grow all over again.

I was an extremely nervous child, and it began to show in different ways. Drinking glasses would slip through my fingers and fall on the floor. That made my mother crazier than ever. I was panicky as I looked at the pieces of glass scattered all over the floor. I knew what was coming. Just before she was about to clean it up, she would give me a hard slap on my fingers, as if I were doing it for spite. This made me even more nervous. It seemed that the more upset I became, the more glasses I dropped.

I was paying the penalty of being a child and making mistakes. I had become nothing more than a receptacle of bad feelings about myself: *I'm clumsy; I'm stupid; I'm unlike other children who obviously never broke a glass.*

Hedda did not like to do anything. She could sit on a chair for hours without budging. She did as little cooking as possible. What she did make was very simple. We ate a lot of dairy and some hamburger patties. As she made the food, she put it on the table. We got into the habit of eating our meals separately at different times during the day.

I would hear a key in the lock every night. My father came in, took off his short brown leather jacket, washed his hands, and sat down at the kitchen table. My eyes were fixed upon him as I sat there, watching him eat. He had the same meal every night: sour cream and potatoes. I wondered if he ever ate anything else.

Sometimes he nodded to me, but nothing was really said. I would have liked to say something, but somehow, it didn't feel right. I still very much wanted to see him and be in the same room with him. He was a very special person in my eyes. He was my father.

When he finished his meal, he retired to the bedroom and went to sleep. It was pretty much the same every day he came home from work.

I was a little over six years old, and I was still sleeping in a crib. When Hedda noticed my feet curling up, she decided it was time to send George out to buy a bed with rails around it so that I would not fall on the floor. Hedda said, "She needs a youth bed."

George said, "I'll go out and get one."

But he did not buy the bed Hedda wanted. He bought a regular single-sized bed and put it into the small bedroom. That made Hedda very upset. "I sent him out for a youth bed and look what he comes home with!"

For some time after that, whenever my mother was annoyed at George, she would say, "How stupid your father is! You send him out for one thing, and he comes back with something else!"

My father soon wound up in the small room, and I started to sleep with my mother in the double bed in the large bedroom.

It was about the same time that my father, as quiet as ever, came into the living room with a pen and paper. He would sit down next to me and draw lines. When he put them all together, he had a figure of a woman in a long, pretty dress. I wished I could look like that lovely lady. I marveled at the way he could draw. I soon found myself making lines also. It was the beginning of something that I would learn to appreciate and cherish.

Just as I was beginning to make little drawings, my father introduced me to something else that fascinated me; it was a water paint set. He showed me how to wet the brushes, dip them into colors, and make pretty designs. I was painting! And my father was joining me. That was really nice. My mother passed by, and I became tense. *Would she stop us? Would she take this away from me?* But she didn't say anything. I was relieved and thankful at the same time.

Soon, on Sunday mornings, a new routine came about: my father brought newspapers into the house. Again, Hedda was silent. The newspapers, however, did not go into the refrigerator. They somehow managed to escape the fate of the magazines and books.

My father would now sit down with me at the kitchen table and open the newspaper to the comic strips. He looked so relaxed and comfortable as he smoked his pipe and read to me *Dick Tracy*, *Gasoline Alley*, and other strips. He made them come to life. He also made me laugh—something I was not used to. And how astonished I was when he taught me how to use tracing paper and a spoon to make pictures of my favorite characters! We were making little creations of our own.

But as nice as he was, I saw another side to my father—and that was the taskmaster. He bought me coloring books and crayons and showed me how to color "in the lines." He smiled at me when I did well, but when I didn't color the way he wanted me to, I saw how unhappy he was. He would frown and tell me, "Stay in the lines!"

I hated to see that disappointed look on my father's face. I wanted so very much to please him, for his love meant so much to me. I wanted his love as only a little child could want her father's love. But I was failing my father. *Why can't he accept me and love me for myself?* How truly sad it is when a parent can't accept and love a child just the way she is rather than for how well she can perform.

I continued to make mistakes, and I tried harder, but I wasn't doing well. I felt the same ache each time: *Why can't I learn? Why can't I do it right?* My striving for perfection had begun.

As I look back, I find it rather amazing that Hedda let me out of her sight long enough to participate in those Sunday morning activities with my father. But then again, she was not far away. She would pace up and down in the apartment, and I could feel her presence even though she was in another room.

Although my father was interacting with me more, he was still a stranger to me. He never gave me a hug or a kiss, and he remained at a distance. I guess he knew better; he knew the rules—Hedda's Rules.

Regardless of the many mixed feelings I had for my father, I felt fortunate to have shared those precious moments with him. When would I ever have those moments with my father again?

The Sunday morning juncture with my father lasted for about a year until school began, then everything changed once again.

7

School Daze

My mother kept me home as long as she could, but when I was seven years old, it was mandatory for me to be in school. I became terribly frightened. *School? What is school? Why do I have to go to school?* The word "school" made me cringe.

One morning my mother took me for a walk in the neighborhood. We soon were in a wide open space that turned out to be a schoolyard. Children were gathering as lines were forming. Suddenly, my mother was putting me on one of these lines. I desperately grabbed her hand, but she pushed me away, saying: "I have to go now, I'll be back later." An overwhelming fear crept over me that threw me into a panic. I was now pulling on her skirt for dear life, sobbing uncontrollably, begging her not to go. As tears came streaming down my face, she turned her back to me and walked away.

The line of children was now slowly moving into this great big building that stood before me—and I was on that line! *Where am I going? Why am I here? And where did my mother go?* I was so frightened, I felt as though my heart were about to leap out of my chest.

I continued to follow the girls and boys up several flights of stairs into a room where there were many desks and chairs. Everyone was soon seated, and I sat down, too. There was a lady in front of the room who announced: "I am your teacher, and this is your classroom. Welcome…"

What? This is a classroom? I was so frozen in fear I could barely move in my seat. What do they want with me? I sat there, yearning to see my mother. *Will she be coming back for me? Or will she leave me here?* It seemed that Hedda wasn't coming back. As a feeling of abandonment crept over me, I found myself in a frenzy, alone and lost. I don't recall how long it was before Hedda appeared. I was relieved; I could breathe more easily.

In the days that followed, the same scene pretty much repeated itself. My mother was dropping me off at school in the morning, leaving me there, bringing me back and forth at lunchtime, and picking me up at the end of a school day. I nervously managed to get through one day, then another and still another, with a feeling of anxiety hovering over me.

Although we lived only two blocks from the school, I still didn't know how to cross a street without my mother. I would wait for her at the school to take me home. Again, I had the most terrible feeling: *What if she doesn't come? What will happen to me then…?*

One day she wasn't there on time. I waited a few minutes for her and then I felt a dreadful panic come over me. I started to run halfway down the block, heading in the direction of my home. Suddenly, I didn't recognize my surroundings. My heart was thumping wildly when I saw my mother coming toward me. *What a relief!* I ran to her. She had come for me after all, and I was able to calm down.

I wasn't in school that long. I went for perhaps a week or two, when I became ill with what the doctor called "an upper respiratory infection" or "the grippe." Sometimes he called it the flu or bronchitis. Whatever it was, I dreaded it. My body ached all over, I had temperature and soon I was choking on a cough that took my breath away. When I started to cough, it didn't seem I would ever stop. *How will I get over these violent infections?*

But eventually, I did get better. I would return to school and it happened all over again. It seemed that if someone just looked at me and sneezed, I came down with some bug. Then I would be home weeks at a time. It was a disaster. Germs seemed to be everywhere and I couldn't hide from them. I would move away from anyone who coughed and sneezed, but I found it rather amazing; I still got sick!

I recall how my heart would pound at the thought of telling my mother. She would nervously snap, "What? You're sick again?!" Then she went crazy. She hollered at me and gave me a hard slap on my hand. She made me feel that I had done something awful. I began to panic whenever I felt myself coming down with a sniffle or scratchy throat.

The little time I spent with my father on Sunday mornings had come to an end. I so very much looked forward to those moments with him, but once I began school, everything changed. My father came into contact with people in his cab and handled money. That meant germs. Hedda, with her fear of germs, went around the house talking to herself: "I have enough trouble. I don't need her getting sick on me again."

I soon noticed a strange look on Hedda's face when I came near my father. She made me feel there was something bad about that. Hedda would be standing there watching as my father and I walked in the same space. If I accidentally brushed up against him in the hall, I became nervous. *I mustn't come close. My clothes must not touch his; Hedda's Rules.* I was learning to avoid my own father. I was frightened to even look at him. And it bothered me. I hated to pass him in the hallway and not even say hello. But I had a gripping fear: *I must not get sick again.*

But I got sick anyway. Avoidance. Avoidance. Avoidance. How awful it felt. I was avoiding my life.

I soon had a fear about everything making me ill. I even worried about the books in school that were not "aired out" in the refrigerator to "kill germs." I had to handle them. *Will the books make me ill?*

In the classroom I sat quietly and prayed that the teacher would not call on me. Because I found it so difficult to say words properly,

I was very self-conscious about the way I sounded. I was ashamed to talk to my classmates, let alone say anything in front of the class. Would they poke fun at me? I didn't have the guts to find out.

I no longer was a small child, but I spoke like one. Teachers inquired about my speech. They asked my mother questions like, "Where does she get that accent from? Do you speak to her in a foreign language? Do you talk baby talk?" A few of the less sensitive kids in my class made comments directly to me: "You talk funny. What country do you come from?" I wanted to run away and hide.

The sad truth is that my mother hardly spoke to me at all. As long as I didn't bother her and she could have her "peace and quiet," she would sit on her chair for hours without saying a word. When she did speak, she was usually hollering about something. I heard her ranting, and it made me scared. I could tell, just by looking at her face, that she didn't want to hear from me. It didn't feel safe to talk to her. So how was I going to learn to speak?

I recall when I tried to say the word "milk," it came out "mook." I listened, as I spoke each word, but as much as I tried, I just couldn't make the correct sounds. It felt awful. As I grew older, the problem persisted. I yearned to speak like everyone else, and I agonized about it. One of my teachers said, "You'll have to go to a speech class for that impediment." But I wasn't in school long enough to attend.

I listened to the radio: singers, dramas, mysteries, comedy shows, all kinds of programs. I began to imitate the sounds of words I heard. And slowly, I was learning to talk. But I still heard, "What kind of accent is that?"

One day in class, my teacher, Mrs. Goldberg, a lady who was big, heavy, and boisterous, asked the students to bring their assignments up to her and she would check them over. When she called my name, I went up to her desk with my composition book in my hand, and my heart pounding in my chest. "No, that's not right!" she lashed out in a loud, nasty tone, as she glanced at my work. She then took her pen and made a long, black line down the page. I stood there, gaping at her as I held back my tears. I was crushed. I sulked about that long ugly black line for some time after that.

I didn't seem to fit into the school setting. I felt so different from everyone else. As if that wasn't painful enough, I continued to have a terrible dread that the girls and boys would ridicule me because I was different. I certainly did not dress like the other girls. I had three black-and-white checkered jumpers. Each one had a different insignia sewn on by my mother. If you didn't look for the insignia, you would think I had only one jumper. I hated wearing them. I thought they were really ugly. I admired the soft, frilly clothes that my classmates were wearing.

I felt rather awkward in brown oxford boy's shoes and dark lisle stockings. My stockings were constantly falling because my garters were loose, and my shoes looked like something an old lady would wear. I was aware that no one dressed like me.

When I looked in the mirror, I saw a pretty face, and that pleased me. But I was also chubby, and the mirror reflected that as well. Those few extra pounds made me more self-conscious. I wondered if the kids at school were making fun of me because I was overweight. Had they also noticed that frightened look in my eyes and that shy, insecure manner to match?

Other kids went to school. They were liked and accepted by their classmates and were able to make friends. But I was hardly in school, and I didn't have any friends. I only had my mother.

It became a nightmare. I hated to become ill then get better, only to go back and start the cycle all over again. I would have to face the same kids, the same teachers, the same everything that made me anxious and tense. Each time I entered the classroom, after being absent for some time, I was overwhelmed with feelings of shame. Kids were laughing, talking to one another, and there I was, all alone, sticking out like a sore thumb. I wanted to cry. And it continued like this—until one classmate showed an interest in me.

As I was standing on line one day, a soft voice said to me, "Why are you out of school so much?"

I turned around and saw Barbara. I couldn't believe it. Was this real? Barbara was one of the brightest kids in the class—and she was talking to me!

Dark haired, wide-eyed, with a long, thin face, Barbara had a natural curiosity about people and life. I would hear her asking intelligent questions in class, and I thought she was very smart. And now, she was reaching out to me in her kind, gentle manner.

I was stunned; I didn't know what to say, but we were soon speaking to each other, and I became less self-conscious. Suddenly, Barbara reached for her handkerchief. That made me uneasy. I asked her if she had a cold. Stone-faced, she replied: "That's what everyone thinks. I have allergies, and I'm going for treatments."

I didn't know what she meant by "allergies," but I accepted what she said without asking any questions. Whenever I saw her, she usually had a handkerchief in her hand, or she was blowing her nose. That, of course, made me very uncomfortable. I moved away as best I could, hoping she wouldn't notice it.

During the short time I was in school, Barbara and I had become quite fond of each other. She soon said, "Can I visit you in your home?"

I was ecstatic. She had accepted me despite my frailties. It was a great feeling. I felt like I finally had a friend. I told my mother about Barbara and constantly asked her if Barbara could come over. She casually kept putting me off. "We'll see about it." But I was glowing inside. I was hopeful that I was going to have Barbara in my home.

When my mother was with me at school one day, I joyfully pointed out Barbara. "That's my friend—the girl who wants to visit me."

My mother glanced at Barbara and said, "Is that the girl blowing her nose?"

Suddenly I felt terrible. I knew then and there that she would never allow this girl into our home. I brooded about it, but I knew there was nothing I could do.

Barbara continued to ask me if she could visit with me. Soon, I became ill, and once again, I was out of school. I thought a lot about Barbara during that time, and I missed her. I wanted to see her and have her in my home. I was angry with my mother for not allowing this to happen.

When I went back to school, things were not the same between Barbara and me. Barbara was aloof, and I couldn't make a connection with her. In my heart I cried as I mourned the friendship I would never have.

I wondered what it was like to have a friend. The girls and boys in school appeared so happy. They were talking and laughing, and their faces were beaming, and I was so sad. I thought, *How wonderful it must be to have a friend to talk to, someone to laugh with* . . . I sat in the house and daydreamed about having a friend.

I found a way to lessen my sadness. I turned to the one companion I had—my radio. And I turned to my schoolwork so I could be like the kids who went to school.

Hedda was now scurrying over to school, just a couple of blocks away, to pick up my lessons. I just couldn't get over the amazing transformation in her. She looked great! She combed her hair, colored her lips with an attractive bright-red lipstick, and powdered her face. She put aside the ragged, water-stained jumper she wore every day of the week and left the house in a dark-blue spangled dress and black wraparound coat. I found it shocking that she could come out of herself long enough to become an altogether different person when she went to see a teacher in school. I couldn't believe that this was my mother.

Each time she returned with a new challenge, and I was eager for it. Studying hard at home gave me a sense of satisfaction. It was a reminder that I was not left out of life—that I could be like everyone else who went to school. Regardless of how sick I was, I managed to sit up at the kitchen table, dressed in my black-and-white checkered jumper, with my schoolbooks spread out in front of me.

Hedda was now helping me with my lessons. For a great part of each day, she and I sat in the kitchen, working on assignments until we both were exhausted. I did very well with spelling and grammar, but I struggled with all the other subjects, especially arithmetic. I dreaded it. I found it difficult to learn anything that had to do with numbers and the strange-looking signs that were attached to them. I just wasn't taking it in. I was constantly annoying Hedda to go over it with me one more time. I was trying to understand and get it right. I kept plugging away until we both were irritable and cranky.

There were times when I couldn't wait to finish and put the books away. I would fidget in my chair and say, "How much more is there?"

When I completed my lessons, I was relieved. I had a feeling of accomplishment. I felt I now deserved to drift off into another world—a world of popular music and soap operas. I ran over to the radio and put it on. My mother sat there with me. Her moods were more under control, and she usually appeared calmer when the radio was on. It seemed to work wonders for both of us.

This was becoming a way of life for me. I had no desire to return to school. School was scary; it felt safer to work hard at home. But when I was well enough, I did go back. And it was amazing: I was on the same academic level as my classmates, and even a bit ahead! I felt really good in those moments.

During one of my brief encounters in school, I had a fantastic experience. The class was covering the topic of settlers moving out west, and the teacher said that each of us would have to give a presentation on some aspect of this, in front of the class. *Oh no!* I had enough problems speaking as is—and now, this! Intimidated as I was, I knew I had to go through with it.

I selected a poem, "Not So Very Long Ago." It had eight stanzas about settlers traveling across the country in covered wagons and all they had to endure along the way. I worked at memorizing the poem every spare moment I had, but I still worried if I would be able to speak well enough to present it in class.

Soon the day came for me to recite my poem. When my name was called, I left my seat with some trepidation and staggered forward to the front of the classroom. I forgot about how I sounded, and there I was, nervously reciting the stanzas by heart. Suddenly, I forgot the words and I panicked—but the words came right back to me. I recall a spark of relief when I reached the last sentence.

The class went wild! I got a big round of applause, and I couldn't believe it was for me. It didn't feel real—but it was real. I had just presented eight stanzas, four lines in each, on sheer memory, and I had performed this overwhelming feat in front of an audience of my classmates. I got the feel of what it's like to do something well and have the recognition of others. I could feel proud of myself. I could even feel smart. This was something very new to me. For once, I liked being in school, and I wanted to have more experiences like this.

I was only in school for a brief time when I became ill again. I was disappointed because I was becoming more comfortable within the school setting and I was connecting with my classmates.

After one of my mother's trips to school, she told me that a few of my classmates were asking for me. My heart was jumping with joy. I couldn't believe it. *My classmates are asking for me! My goodness, they care; they haven't forgotten me.* How I wanted to see anyone from my class. I anxiously asked, "Who are these girls?"

Hedda barked back: "How should I know?"

"If someone wants to see me, could you let them come over? Please, please . . ."

She nodded and said, "I'll see what I can do."

But no one came. I was very disappointed. I just couldn't get it through my head that Hedda didn't want anyone in our home.

However, sometime later, Hedda came back from school and told me that a classmate, Jodi, offered to bring my lessons over. What a surprise! I remember Jodi as a shy, thin, little girl who wore glasses and rode around on a bicycle. I wondered why she volunteered.

Soon, Jodi was standing in the hallway of our apartment with my lessons in her hand. She came inside and handed them over to my mother. Jodi was now staring at me, and I was staring back at her. I thought, *What a sad look on her face!* We continued to stare at each other as my mother looked on. Jodi didn't talk to me, and I couldn't find the words to say anything to her except "Thank you." She came a few times, and each time it was the same; she handed over the assignments, stayed a few minutes, and left. She soon stopped coming over.

It still felt good to have someone in our home. I suppose that's the reason I so very much looked forward to seeing Grandma. Since I was so isolated from the outside world and usually didn't see anyone, it was a treat for me when I heard Grandma's knock at the door. I anticipated her visits with glee. She stopped by with bags of food for us on her way to Grandpa's necktie store. She immediately handed the bags over to Hedda, and soon, they were counting change, trying to straighten out how much Hedda owed Grandma. I just sat there, not paying attention to what was going on around me. It all seemed so trivial. I was just too excited when Grandma was in our home.

But I perceived an underlying tension that threatened to erupt at any moment. Grandma was deeply distressed about the way we were living. She saw me studying in the dark, dismal kitchen, or rocking in my rocking chair to music on the radio. She lamented: "The whole world's in school, and that's where she belongs!" As she looked at Hedda, daggers were jutting out of her eyes and her voice rose in anger. "There's nothing wrong with her. She should go to school like everybody else. She belongs in school with children her own age. No one lives like this. She's been in the house for weeks now. She doesn't get a breath of fresh air. For crying out loud, when are you going to take her out and let her go back to school?"

I was squirming as Grandma spoke. Her words hit me like a thunderbolt. Why was Grandma pushing so hard for me to go to school? Couldn't she see that school was making me sick? Why would I want to go to a place that's making me sick? Besides, I usually felt like an outcast in school—I was so unlike the other children. Grandma kept saying that I "belonged in school" with those children. But did I really "belong"?

I sat in my chair, afraid to move, afraid to say anything, while Grandma was having a war of words with Hedda. And it was all about me. I was only a few feet away, but they didn't see me. Were they even aware of my presence in the room? I didn't think so; I felt invisible.

The argument escalated. Hedda's face was reddening like a beet, and the veins in her neck were protruding. "Don't you mix in my business. I don't tell you what to do, don't you tell me what to do!"

Words were flying back and forth, and they were now yelling at each other like two crazy people. It was frightening to see my mother and Grandma so much out of control. I sat there and felt sick to my stomach.

"You keep her locked up in the house. She sits and rocks in that rocking chair like an eighty-year-old woman!" Grandma's words cut like a knife. She was attacking the one thing that gave me a little pleasure: rocking myself to the music on the radio. It was the one thing that brightened my sad, dreary world. Why was she knocking something that meant so much to me?

My mother was furious by now and yelled back: "Skip a few days! I don't need this aggravation. You come up here and you make trouble. Stay away!" And then she showed Grandma the door. Grandma reached for her coat and shopping bags, mumbling something under her breath, and left in a huff.

I sat there and cringed.

This was a recurrent scene—a scene that was as frequent as the infections I came down with. Afterwards, I would sit and think about it. It troubled me that Grandma could criticize my mother like that. Hedda knew what she was doing; Hedda knew what was best for me. She was protecting me from school and those wretched germs. I was safe at home with her. Why couldn't Grandma see that? She was beating up on my mother, and I didn't like that. It was pretty clear that Grandma didn't understand. Sometimes I didn't like Grandma.

But what Grandma said lingered with me. Maybe she wasn't altogether wrong. She was saying things that made me think: *Maybe the whole world is in school, and here I am, sitting in the house with my mother, rocking myself in my rocking chair. Will I be living like this for the rest of my life?*

There were times when I was too sick to care about anything. I would sit on the edge of the bed, with my head bent over, choking on a cough, and gasping for breath. But this was nothing new. Most of my infections were like that.

During one of these coughing episodes, my mother walked into the room, and with absolutely no feeling in her voice, proclaimed, "Teddy Roosevelt was always sick, and he grew up to be a Rough Rider!" Now, what in the world was a "Rough Rider"? And why would I want to hear something like that when I was struggling to catch my breath?

I was about eight years old and back in school after a bronchial-asthmatic attack. I was sitting in front of the classroom, and I complained to the teacher: "I can't see the words on the blackboard!" She immediately sent me to the school nurse, who then asked to see my mother. When my mother arrived, the nurse told her, "Your daughter has trouble seeing the blackboard. I recommend that you take her for an eye checkup as soon as possible."

Hedda appeared annoyed but nevertheless took me to a neighborhood optometrist. He gave me an eye examination and said, "Your daughter has a nearsighted condition known as myopia. As she grows older, it will worsen. She should avoid small print as much as possible. I'm giving her a prescription for glasses right now."

I didn't like to wear glasses. I only used them when I had to. I put them away in a drawer, and I went on reading and writing in a dark kitchen under a 40-watt ceiling bulb.

About this time, my mother received a letter in the mail stating that a school official would be coming over to see her. Within a few days, the doorbell rang, and a short, stocky, grey-haired lady was standing outside our door. In a firm voice she introduced herself: "I'm Miss Paul. I'm a truant officer. I've come to talk to you about your daughter's attendance in school."

My mother invited Miss Paul in, and they spoke in our hallway. Miss Paul asserted: "Your daughter is home more than in school. We've been much too lenient with you. From now on, your daughter must be in school, or there must be a doctor's note that indicates why she's out. Keeping her home like this is not acceptable to school standards."

What did all this mean? I felt myself starting to shake. Something about the whole thing seemed very scary. My mother stood there and listened. Her face looked flushed and she seemed confused. Then she told Miss Paul what she wanted to hear: "I will have notes for you in the future when she's out sick."

When the truant officer left, I said to myself: *Thank God, she's gone!* But her words were not gone from my mind.

My mother started to call a neighborhood physician to come to our home each time I became ill. Dr. Weisner, a tall, hefty, good-looking, brown-haired man, was amiable and matter-of-fact in his approach. He came in, slammed his satchel down on the kitchen table and asked: "What's the problem, Mother?"

"My daughter is sick all winter. She's more out of school than in. She loves school, but she just can't make it. I need a note for school that says she's sick."

After a quick examination, Dr. Weisner took out his pad and jotted down a prescription. "This is an antibiotic. Have her take this every four hours. I'm also giving her something for that cough."

He then scribbled a few words on his pad: *"Lenore Ossen is ill with the flu and unable to attend school."*

I was tickled to have that note; it would allow me to be home without having the truant officer breathing down our necks.

Dr. Weisner became a steady visitor in our home. In the times he came, and there were many, Dr. Weisner refrained from questioning or challenging my mother. Once or twice he casually remarked, "The more she's shielded from bacteria and viruses, the less likely she is to build up immunity. She goes back to school, comes into contact with a cough or sneeze, and then she's sick all over again. She's susceptible; her resistance needs to be built up, but that can't happen in the house. She has to go out there!"

My mother's response was simply "So what am I to do? Send her out sick when she's coughing like that?" Dr. Weisner declined to respond.

I became used to seeing Dr. Weisner as soon as I began to sneeze or feel a sore throat. I would hear his loud voice and watch his smug smile as he said, "Take a laxative to clean yourself out on the first day of a cold. Drink a lot of fluids. Don't go to sleep late. Stay out of drafts . . ."

I knew what he was going to say before he said it and I was annoyed because he repeated the same things over and over every single time he came. I tried to tell him, "Doctor, I do that . . ." But it was pointless to tell him anything; he didn't hear me because he was speaking over me. I continued to take the medication he prescribed. I was practically living on penicillin or tetracycline. I was also taking Cheracol cough syrup regularly for my persistent coughs.

There were times, however, when I continued to cough into the night. Exhausting days turned into sleepless nights. When Grandma came over, she would tell me, "Get it up! Cough it up!" I was already spitting up green phlegm, and I became irritated when she said that. But in some strange way, it did feel good to hear her concern.

On one occasion, Dr. Weisner came to our home, and I had a temperature of 102. My mother complained: "My daughter is so sick, and I can't get the books away from her. She's learning to write the alphabet, and she can't make each letter just right, so she's writing on the walls. Look at the walls! I don't know what to do with her!"

Dr. Weisner hollered: "Nonsense! I would put all those books in a briefcase, lock them in the closet, and I would break her neck if she attempted to touch them!" He roared like a lion and his face became red. **"Put those books away right now!"** My mother sheepishly took the books off the table and packed them in my briefcase. The books went away, and I meekly went to bed.

How could they do this to me? When I was working on my lessons, I could feel smart; I could feel that I was doing something worthwhile. And now, they're taking my books away! I felt so lost, I didn't know what to do. I was very annoyed with Dr. Weisner for some time after that, and I didn't want to see him anymore. But we needed him to write out those notes.

"Take her to Florida!" Dr. Weisner barked this many times. I thought it was a wonderful idea. New York's cold winters certainly weren't for me. But how was I going to get to Florida when I can't even get out of the house?

My mother, fed up by this time, walked around the house, wailing: **"The goddamn school and the goddamn books! The school should only burn down! And the teachers . . . they should all go to hell!"** As she went into one of her tirades, I sat there in anguish.

When I felt better, I was able to work on my lessons. Once again, I didn't feel I was doing very well, and I agonized about it. *Why can't I make my work perfect? Why do I have to make so many errors?* The more I tried, the harder it became and the more mistakes I made.

In my frenzy, I found a way to give myself permission to stop obsessing. I put a few words together, and I kept saying to myself. *Period, comma, period.* It was magical thinking, but it actually worked! I convinced myself to take a break and let it go. I devised other little thoughts to guide me when I was feeling overwhelmed. I came back to my lessons calmer and refreshed. I was then able to resume where I left off.

Through all this turmoil, I welcomed the doctor's notes; they were a godsend. No longer was there pressure for me to return to school. I now felt I had the right to be "homebound."

Sometime later, we received another letter from the Board of Education that specified the time and date when we would be receiving another visit from a school official. Again, I was anxious and frightened. Soon, I heard the doorbell ring. This time I heard a man talking to my mother: "My name is Mr. Flarney, I'm a truant officer, and I want to speak with you. It'll only take a few minutes."

Mr. Flarney was a tall, thin man who looked rather old. puffing on a big cigar as he followed my mother into the kitchen. I was sitting at the table, my schoolbooks spread out in front of me and I was choking on a cough as he passed by. *Why is he here? And what does he want with us?*

Each time I saw a truant officer in our home, my heart skipped a beat. I felt fear. *Is this man, Mr. Flarney, going to make trouble for us?* It seemed as if something terrible was about to happen.

Mr. Flarney was now asking my mother, in a demanding tone, "When do you plan to send her back to school? We need another note that will say just how long she will be out. It's simply procedure. It's for our records."

My mother's face flushed, and she looked upset as she pleaded, "But I just gave a note to the school."

"We need a specific period of time. We need to know approximately how long she's going to be out. She's never in school, and it's my job to check for attendance."

My mother assured Mr. Flarney, "I'll get another note from the doctor."

My schoolwork was a great source of comfort for me at times like these. I went into my books and studied harder.

Soon, my mother obtained doctor's notes that indicated a specific time period, but the notes weren't working very well, for it was difficult to determine just when I would be able to return to school. But it was what they wanted, and my mother complied.

Hedda continued to go to school for my lessons and resented it no end. She hated to be confronted by teachers who would ask, "When is she coming back?"

At home, she sat in the kitchen with a cigarette dangling from her lips. She griped: "I'm not the only one around here who can pick up your schoolwork. Everything gets dumped on me, and I'm sick of it. Let your father take time off from his cab and go to school. Let him talk to the teachers. I don't need this!"

Of course, she was just blowing off steam. My father was at his taxi stand come rain or shine and was not very articulate or convincing. But my mother was. She made sure she looked and dressed well when she came to school with doctor's notes and did a good job at impressing the teachers and the principal with the same story she had told the doctor: "She wants very much to be in school. She works so hard at home to get her lessons done, you can't get the books away from her. She really loves school!"

My mother would then reach into her bag, and like a magician pulling a rabbit out of a hat, she pulled out a great, big composition book. "Look at all the work she does when she's home. When my daughter is well enough to go back to school, she knows her work better than the kids in her class! But she can't go back when she's sick and coughing. My daughter's well all summer, and when she goes back to school, she gets sick all over again. Ignorant mothers send their kids to school sick, coughing, blowing their noses, and my daughter is home all winter because of them."

She made it clear that keeping me home from school was the right thing to do. She spoke of her plight with sincerity and passion, and they ate it up. She usually closed her argument with a statement I heard her say all the time: "Every mother knows her child best."

My uncle points out in his file, "The school officials, teachers and principal alike, are sympathetic to her plight. One teacher commented on Hedda's 'zeal and devotion' to her daughter. Another said: 'If every mother were like you, our children would grow up to be wonderful men and women!' When she finished, they accepted what she had to say without question or dispute. They were like putty in her hands."

Because my mother was such a "nice" lady and I was doing my work at home so well, how could they refuse to give her new assignments or not promote me? In appreciation, my mother endeared herself to the teachers by showering them with gifts such as scarves, gloves, slips, and aprons.

My mother was in school one day collecting my lessons when she was confronted by the school principal—a tall, slim, regal lady with white hair and a soft-spoken manner. She had usually shown concern about my school problem. This time she said, "I have some bad news for you. The doctor notes are no longer sufficient. Your daughter is only attending three weeks out of the school year. She is spoiling the school attendance record, and she will be dropped from the school register. I recommend very strongly that she receive her education at home from private teachers."

My mother was taken aback by this and asked, "Can my daughter be allowed to attend school on a part-time basis?"

The principal replied, "It has to be complete attendance or none at all. I suggest you take her out of school at this time." The legality of the principal's decision was never questioned; my mother accepted it then and there. When she told me about it, I felt a sense of relief; *I don't have to go to school!*

When my father came home from work, Hedda immediately told him, "She's spoiling the school's attendance record and they want her out. I told you all along, she belongs in a private school. The classes are smaller, and the coughs are less. Dr. Weisner says, 'Take her to Florida!' The way she gets sick all winter, she belongs in Florida. But you're so stingy—why should you care about your daughter? Now, she needs a private tutor, and I need money for that."

My father responded, "I don't have money for that. Who says she needs a private tutor?"

My mother started to yell, and as usual, my father handled her outburst in silence. He picked himself up, put on his jacket, and went for the door.

"He's a real scrooge! Your father spends his money on one thing: those damn cabs!"

Later that night, while I was lying in bed, I overheard my father arguing with Hedda: "What do you think I am? A mint? I don't manufacture greenbacks!" I was trembling in the dark as I tried to hear their voices in the background, but I only heard bits and pieces. My father never raised his voice to her, so I knew he was really upset. Somehow that made me even more anxious. I felt something terrible was about to happen, but what it was, I didn't know. I lay in the dark, troubled, and scared.

The next morning, my mother was at the kitchen sink, scrubbing her hands as usual. I heard her muttering something under her breath, "Too wise you are, too wise you be, I see you are too wise for me! Your father thinks he's so smart—but you just wait and see!" I wondered what she was talking about, but I felt it was better not to ask.

A few hours later, Dr. Weisner appeared in our home. He was pleasant enough when Hedda asked for another note. This was the big one—the note that said, *"Lenore Ossen is suffering with chronic respiratory infections. Private home instruction is recommended in this case."*

My mother and I now possessed a piece of paper that indicated I had the right to stay out of school for the remainder of the school year. A new procedure was now in effect for the rest of my elementary school life: I would come to school at the beginning of each new term, and when I became ill, the doctor would write a note that would keep me home for the rest of the school year.

The next thing I knew, the doorbell rang, and a private tutor came into our home. I was not aware just how starved I was for human contact until I met Miss Costello. She was a pretty young woman with short brown hair and big, brown, sparkling eyes. I recall her warm, radiant smile and that touch of concern in her voice as she softly said, "I'll be coming to your home twice a week, and together, we'll go through everything you need to know."

I needed to hear that. Miss Costello made me feel that I could calm down with my schoolwork and relax. She was easy to talk to, and we worked well together. Sometimes, she shared a thing or two about herself. My unhappy world became a little easier to bear when she was around. As the days passed, I would look at the clock and wait for the time when I would see her again.

Now that I wasn't going to school, I worried that maybe I wasn't learning what the kids in school were learning. Although Miss Costello had an outline of the school requirements, I still had some concern that I was falling behind on what I needed to know.

The more anxious I became, the greater was my need to do more. My anxiety was quite apparent to Miss Costello, and she took care of that. At the end of each tutorial session, she would firmly say, "Now, I want you to pack your books into your briefcase and put them away. I'll wait here until you do." As Miss Costello stood hovering over me, with a kind, loving smile on her face, I took my books, one by one, and slipped them into my briefcase. She was giving me permission to stop working and worrying. I was a little less anxious by the time she went home.

Unfortunately, this dear lady did not stay long. She was with me for a short time and then she left to be married. I hated to see her go. In my heart, I was grateful to her for stepping in at that crucial time.

Other private tutors followed, and I was thankful to have them coming to my home and helping me with my studies. They interrupted my isolated existence and gave me some contact with the outside world.

In the days and months that followed, I was becoming more confused and ambivalent about school. Schoolwork was becoming more taxing, and my concentration was poor. Concepts did not penetrate easily. I was never quite sure of what I was doing or if I was doing it right. At times I didn't think I had the capacity to learn, and that thought was quite appalling. Sometimes I felt just plain stupid.

At the age of ten, my main goal was to muddle through my studies as best I could. It was crucial for me to move on to the next grade and not be held back. Actual failure would have shown me that all the bad things I felt about myself were justified, and I could not allow that to happen. So, I had to work—and work really hard.

I remember writing notes in a black-and-white composition book that said, "**I am smart. I am a smart girl**." I felt so bad about myself I had to say I was smart just to keep going. Perhaps if I said it often enough, I might even believe it.

8

The Mad Hedda: A Monarch of Many Moods

Things had to be done her way. Hedda had to be in control. She created her own little universe and became the sole ruler in it, with no understanding of what she was doing, or of the consequences of her actions.

"I want to be alone." She would say that all the time. And we were alone. Visitors were not wanted or permitted in our home. Only those who served a purpose were allowed in—such as the doctor, the grocery boy, and homebound tutors. Grandma was tolerated because she did food shopping for us. Since we didn't have a phone, if school officials wanted to see Hedda, they would have to write to her ahead of time to say they were coming. Relatives and neighbors—well, they just were not welcome and, inevitably, stayed away.

Hedda seldom left the house except when she needed a few items for immediate delivery from the corner grocery store, or when she went to the butcher a block away.

Occasionally, the downstairs bell would ring. It was a joyful moment for me. I became excited when I thought of seeing another human being walk through the door. But Hedda just let it ring and ring. Whoever it was soon became tired of pressing the button and left. I wondered who it could have been. Perhaps someone cared enough to come over and see me? I sat there and quietly grieved about the visitor I never saw.

When I asked Hedda about it, she was very casual. "If anyone wants to come up, they can; I'm no ogre—I don't chase people out of my house!" But it confused and bothered me. If it was true that people were welcome in our home, why didn't Hedda answer the bell?

Hedda wasn't very happy about it, but a few people had to come into our home out of sheer necessity. Hedda had something nasty to say about each one. "That truant officer is vicious and trying to make trouble." "The super is a no good liar." "That tutor is a real phony." Didn't she have anything nice to say about anyone?

According to Hedda, everyone was bad and out to do you in. "It's bad to talk to people—you don't know who they are and what they can do. People can't be trusted. You'll find that out and you'll think of your mother." My world began to shake even more. Something about this didn't feel right and it troubled me, but I dared not question what she said. I listened to her faithfully. She was my mother. Why would she tell me something that was not so?

Grandma came in with shopping bags of food on her way to Grandpa's necktie store. I was under Hedda's watchful eye more than ever when Grandma was in our home. I could feel the tension in the air. If Hedda walked out of the room, I had the feeling that she was listening, and that her eyes were upon me, no matter where she was in the apartment. If I were alone with Grandma for a few minutes, she would anxiously ask me later, "What did she say to you?" I couldn't understand what was so important about that.

And heaven forbid if I tried to speak to Grandma. It was as if Hedda were biting her lip if I opened my mouth to speak. She would cut me off, and later lash out: "Children should be seen and not heard! You haven't learned that!" It felt terrible to be scolded like that just for speaking to my grandma. It seemed that being able to speak out was a part of being alive—but not for me. I was there, but it felt as though I wasn't there; I was invisible.

Grandma's visits usually ended in heated words with Hedda. They had terrible fights. I sat there, distraught, and helpless, as I watched them in one of their shouting matches. Grandma usually flew out of our home in a huff.

Hedda had kind words for Grandpa. "My father is the only good one from the whole damn bunch! He doesn't mix in and minds his own business!" Grandpa came to see us about once a month and said almost nothing for the short time he was in our home. He appeared to be bogged down in thought, and sometimes he expressed his unhappiness. "That woman—it's impossible to live with her!" I knew he was talking about Grandma. I felt sad as I looked at him. I wanted to say something to him, but what, I didn't know; then again, it was against Hedda's Rules for my voice to be heard.

A cold war continued to exist between Hedda and my father. It was rare that I saw them speak to each other. When they were in the same room, they didn't even look at each other. You could feel the tension in the air. My father still came home from work at 6 o'clock in the evening. He looked sad and dejected as he took off his jacket, went over to the sink and washed his hands. He then sat down at the kitchen table and gulped down the usual dish of potatoes and sour cream. As we sat there together, my father and I did not speak. I felt an ache inside. The pain seemed to say: *I wish he would talk to me. If only he would say something—anything.* But he didn't. I didn't have the courage to say anything either. Father and daughter: two strangers in the same house.

Soon he was ready to leave. "I'm going to the garage," he casually said, as he approached the door. I wondered: *Why the great rush? And why is he always "going to the garage"?*

I recall a day when he was busy going through a drawer of shirts and Hedda, a few feet away, came upon him with a snicker and an odd tone of voice: "Too wise you are, too wise you be, I see you are too wise for me." I thought this was a strange comment, coming out of the blue. She continued to blurt out more nonsensical rhymes. "What's good for the goose is good for the gander." Both times George didn't appear interested and displayed a deaf ear. And then she was smirking as she said, "You know, George, you're losing your hair." Again, he did not respond. As I watched her standing there, chiding him, I was taken aback. Something about the whole scene seemed bizarre to me. I wished I knew what was going on.

Later on, I heard Hedda rant: "You're lucky you have me. I know you love your grandmother. Well, I got news for you. She doesn't want any part of you. You'll see how much she loves you if something happens to me. She loves you as long as I'm around and she doesn't have to take care of you. She comes and goes and throws a few kisses. I'm left with all the misery. What did I ever do to have it so bad!"

Those words cut like a knife and tore me up inside. *Is it true what she said about Grandma? Am I so bad that Grandma has no use for me?* I wanted to believe that my grandma cared for me, but my mother was putting doubt in my mind. I didn't know what to believe. I wondered: *Why is my mother telling me all these awful things about Grandma?* It made me feel more alone than ever.

The feeling became stronger that something terrible might happen to me if Hedda was not around to keep me safe. The thought of it made me shudder. Many times I heard her say, "Just you remember, I'm the only one in this world who will ever care for you!" She usually sounded very hateful when she said it, so this disturbed me even more.

"…And your father—he's so damn selfish, he doesn't care for anyone but himself. Just you remember that!"

It seemed like there was no one I could turn to and trust—just her.

It was madness, sheer madness. I watched her put books into the refrigerator to air out germs. I saw her hands bleeding from washing them under scalding hot water. She appeared to be in agony, tortured from something deep within that made her do crazy things. I wondered what was troubling Hedda. Why was she so disturbed?

She walked around the house in a water-stained black jumper and a faded old blue corduroy robe. Her hair was stringy and hanging loose. She was smoking one cigarette after another, and her eyes were wet with tears. Usually, she didn't care to do anything but sit on her chair in the dark, dismal kitchen with the most morbid expression on her face and a strange, faraway look in her eyes. As I watched her staring off into space I wondered: *What is she thinking? What is she feeling?* She seemed so forlorn, so lost in a world of her own. As I sat there and looked at her, I felt helpless and I thought to myself: *Isn't there some way I can make things better for my mother?*

Hedda usually didn't want to talk, but once she got started, she couldn't stop. I was amazed at how long she could stay on one topic. It was as though she was talking to herself. She didn't seem to care whether she was being heard or not. I just sat there and cringed.

There were times when, out of the blue, she broke down and cried. "I don't know what I did to deserve this. I don't know what I was born for. I wish I were dead." It felt awful to hear my mother talk like that. I sat there, aching inside, as I stared at her. *What did I do to cause her such pain?* I must have been very bad to make my mother so miserable.

I was rocking in my chair in the living room when I heard Hedda retching in the kitchen. I hurried in to see what was going on. She soon came over to me and pointed to her chest: "You're killing me. You're giving me heart trouble. It's all because of you I'm having this pain. You will be punished as sure as there's a God above."

I stood there, with eyes wide open, as if God had spoken. I was overcome with fear. As she ranted on, I had the most terrible feeling her illness was my fault, and that God was going to punish me. I slinked off to my rocking chair and withdrew into myself. My mind went blank and I couldn't speak. I don't know how long I sat there like that…

"What I wanted all my life was a sister, not you, you little Moloch Hamovess!" I cringed every time she said that. It sounded like something awful. If I worked up some courage, I would ask her, "What does Moloch Hamovess mean?" But she wouldn't tell me. (When I grew older, I learned it was the Hebrew name for the Angel of Death.) I never got used to the terrible things Hedda would say about me. *Maybe I was bad. Maybe I was no good. Maybe I was killing my mother.*

I don't know when it started but I had the feeling that something awful was about to happen to me and I went around with a terrible dread. It seemed like there was a large cloud hanging overhead heralding in some awful disaster. I was listening to the radio when I heard talk about something called "an imminent doom." It sounded like something that might apply to me. Many times, when I was ill with severe bronchial asthma, coughing so profusely that I couldn't catch my breath, I became very anxious. *Is this the imminent doom?* But as things improved and changed for the better, my fears abated, and I could let go of my panic—at least until the next time.

And I watched my mother as her moods continued to fluctuate.

I must have been about 8 or 9, and it was still happening as much as ever. Out of the blue, I would see her body hunching over, her eyes filled with rage, and her face on fire. My mother was becoming something else before my eyes. The monster was back! It was coming towards me and I made a mad dash into another room, but I couldn't hide from it. When it got its hands on me, I was unable to escape from its clutches. It began pounding my arms with its fists as it rasped: "I'll fight you to the finish!" By now I was terrified. I didn't know what was going to happen to me. The monster continued to pummel and slap me around until it suddenly let me go. Tears were running down my face. I was aching all over as I staggered over to my rocking chair.

It took me some time to recuperate from each of her attacks upon me. Amazingly, Hedda would be calm and serene, as if nothing had happened.

How was I to deal with my mother's brutal behavior? I was lost and confused. I tried my darndest not to provoke that terrible creature in her, but no matter what I did, the monster appeared. As many times as it happened, it always seemed like the first time.

I fantasized about running away—anywhere—to be free of my mother. But where could I go? I tried to sneak in a few moments, when Hedda was out of the room, to write a note to Grandma: *I can't live with my mother. She is so mean to me. Please take me away from her.*

But whom was I kidding? I couldn't leave Hedda. It was just a fantasy. I was stuck—and I knew it. I continued to have a longing to tell someone, but who was there to tell? Even if there were someone to talk to, I don't think I would have been able to reveal what was going on between my mother and me; I was much too immersed in Hedda's Rules to say anything to anyone.

I kept thinking it was all a mistake. Maybe I was given to the wrong mother at birth. This awful woman could not be my mother! I held a prayer in my heart that one day someone would ring the doorbell and tell me that Hedda was not my mother, and I would be taken away from her. But that was just wishful thinking.

As I became bigger and stronger, Hedda stopped stalking me around the house. The days of her turning into a monster and scaring me half to death were over. But she was still striking me with a punch on my arms and other parts of my body. As in the past, my skin became discolored and swollen, but my long sleeve blouses hid it nicely. I began to hit back. And she would scream at me: **"You're a little bitch!"** I would echo back, **"No, you're the bitch!"** Soon we were having fistfights. This went on for some time.

Ironically, in my uncle's file, it was noted that doctors and teachers knew my mother as a "doting, caring, concerned mother"—a mother terribly concerned about her child not being in school. Similarly, it was very disturbing to hear Grandma whisper to me, when Hedda walked out of the room, "I hope you realize your mother is sacrificing her life for you!" I felt sick to my stomach. How could Grandma say something like that?

I saw my father come in one day with some groceries and a small bag, which he handed to Hedda. He said, "This is for Lenore." She opened the bag and exclaimed, "Oh, it's a whistle!" Then she quickly put it away. Later, I asked her about it and she casually said: "I don't know what happened to it." The look on her face betrayed her words.

I became very upset. The whistle held great meaning for me, and I could not keep quiet. "My father bought that whistle for me, what did you do with it? You threw it out! I know you threw it out. How can you be so mean?"

Well, I cried and cried—but the whistle was gone. Even worse than that was the thought that my mother would take something meant for me, throw it out, then stand there and lie to me about it. (I found out, later on, that other things were sent to me through the years, which I never received.)

It was a dreadful existence. I didn't know what to think, or how to feel. There were times when I was in so much emotional pain, I found myself yelling and screaming and banging my head against the wall. Hedda would rage, "What the hell are you doing? Stop that carrying on!" But I couldn't stop. Nothing seemed to matter when I felt like that. I had bottled-up feelings to express, and this was the only way I knew to get them out. Despite my outbursts, she did not come after me.

"I AM A GOOD GIRL TODAY." I kept printing that in big black letters in my composition book. I guess I felt a need to say it—it helped me get through the day and not feel so bad about myself.

So, there I was, home sick and unable to go to school. I was straddled down with loads of homework, so I turned to Hedda for help. I now saw a completely different Hedda. She could be raging or depressed, and yet snap out of her mood and work with me on my lessons for hours on end. In those moments I looked up to Hedda as a very smart lady who understood all the things I knew nothing about. I marveled at that, as I struggled to learn.

Afterwards, we went into the living room. There, in a corner, stood this great big radio with a dark circle in the middle of it. When Hedda turned it on, the circle became a green light. She would take a long hard look at it and then exclaim: "That damn green eye—I hate it!" I wondered why that made her so upset. What was so bad about it? I didn't see anything wrong with it. In fact, I thought it was rather pretty.

Soon, I would be listening to the radio and rocking myself in my rocking chair. I would soothe myself as I rocked back and forth to the rhythm of the music. A few feet away sat my mother in her chair. She would listen to the music with me. Some songs made her cry; some songs made me cry, too.

Once in a while I wondered: *Do other people live like this?* I had no friends, and I did not visit the homes of other people, so I had no way to know. But I dared not think about it. I had to live my life the way it was—it was the only life I knew.

As I busied myself with my schoolwork, I continued to read and write for hours at a time with very little light in the kitchen. My eyesight, already quite poor, had worsened. I could only see things up close, and even then, I would strain to see clearly.

One day my father came into the kitchen and spoke to Hedda. He meekly said, "I want to put a lamp on the table. It's so dark, she can hardly see what she's doing."

How wonderful it was to hear him say he wanted to get me a lamp. I felt he cared about me. Finally, there would be light! My heart was beating fast at just the thought of it. How I wanted that lamp!

But in seconds, everything changed. Hedda was blazing with anger. Her face was all red and her eyes got big and glassy. The veins in her neck were showing. I thought she looked so ugly. And then she started to yell at my father: **"No! She doesn't need that! What does she need a lamp for? She can see well enough! Don't bring any lamp in here! If you do, you'll go out with it!"**

I flinched as she spoke. My father just stood there, dumbfounded. Soon he left the room without saying a word. I wished he had said something—anything. I found myself numbing out to escape my pain.

The lamp became a dead issue in our home. Hedda had spoken! She wildly screamed: **"No! She doesn't need that!"** and **"No!"** it was. I guess I should have known better; it was too good to be true. I was sad and disappointed for some time. I gave up all hope of ever having that wonderful light for my eyes, and I was fuming with anger. Once again, my mother ruined something I wanted so badly. But she was like that with most everything. **"No! She doesn't need that!"** How I dreaded to hear her scream those hideous words! They seemed to permeate just about everything in my existence. According to my mother, I didn't need anything... anything... anything...

I silently sat in my rocker and nursed painful feelings I couldn't express. How I hated Hedda!

I had an overwhelming curiosity to explore things in the apartment. Hedda was on guard and didn't want me near the measly furniture we had. Sometimes I became really bold; I would sneak into the bedroom and attempt to open a drawer. But Hedda would catch me and, with a weird look on her face, she would screech: **"What do you think you're doing?"**

She would slap me hard for that, and my curiosity waned quickly enough. However, deep in my heart, the more she said **"No!"** the more I wanted to explore the things around me.

The refrigerator was something else that was off limits to me. It was but a few feet away from where I studied in the kitchen. I often had an urge to eat something when I was doing my schoolwork. If I attempted to go near the refrigerator door when Hedda was out of the room, she would come running in and scream: **"Get away from there!"**

My goodness, is everything forbidden to me? I had become afraid to touch anything and everything. I was doing something "wrong" or "bad" if I just moved! It seemed that my mother had eyes in back of her head, for she was there, on the spot, to constantly tell me **"No!"** I learned that I should not explore my surroundings— that it is best to sit in a corner, squelch my curiosity, not ask any questions, and stay out of trouble.

I soon found that I was unable to do some of the easiest things, like tying the strings of a woolen hat. I must have been about 8 years old, and, after being cooped up in the house for quite some time, my mother and I were going out. I remember standing in the hallway of our building, struggling to make a bow. My mother was showing me how "simple" it was; how one string fits over the other—but that's as far as I got. I could not complete it, as much as I tried. Exasperated, I finally gave up and said, "Please tie it for me."

When a neighbor walked by, and saw my mother tying a bow for a "big girl" like me, my face turned red. Hedda seemed ashamed, too. She quickly pulled on the strings and tied the bow for me. Then she muttered, "Why can't you tie it yourself? There's nothing hard about it!"

As much as I would have liked to do things for myself, I found myself under Hedda's thumb and I resented it. I was still 8 years old when Hedda was dressing and undressing me, as I stood on the bed. One night, Hedda was getting me ready to go to bed. I asked her to let me undress myself, but she said no. We began to quarrel; then it escalated—and I spit at her.

I thought she would strike me, but in that moment I just didn't care. Soon she started to rage: **"You're just like your father's sister, Bea. She used to spit at her mother, and her mother was so good to her. You're a disgrace. You're no damn good!"**

Suddenly, the pain that was bottled up within me came flowing out like a pipe that had burst. **"I don't care. I want to be like her! You're mean! I hate you! I hate you!"**

It took guts, but I felt relieved. Hedda shouted back: **"You're like Bea, all right! She wanted to kill her mother, and you'd like to see me dead, too. I know that. And after all I do for you! You should be ashamed of yourself! They say you need children. Like a hole in the head!"** I could feel the venom in each word she spoke.

Soon I would hear her bemoan her fate. "Children! They're not worth having, I swear! You work so hard to have them and what do you get from them? Only heartaches and misery. She opens up such a big mouth to me. I had to become a mother for that! I waited ten years. My mother was nagging me to have a child. 'It's good to have a child in your old age.' For what? I'd be better off dead!"

Those words were cutting. I couldn't speak. I was aching inside, but I buried my feelings. What else could I do?

As I lived each day, my dependence on Hedda grew more intense. In one breath I had a desperate need to be free of her, and in the next, I knew she was all I had. I felt dependent on her for my life. I turned my thoughts away from the turmoil I had inside, only to be confronted by the call of Mother Nature. It was time to go to the bathroom—and Hedda had to be there, too!

Not only was Hedda the caretaker of my mind, but she was still inspecting my bowel movements at age 8. It happened more and more that I would not go to the bathroom. As much as she pressured me, I resisted. So Hedda began to load me down with laxatives. I hated to take them, but I did. And I still continued to hold in my bowels. This was one thing Hedda had no control over. For quite some time it went on like that.

I still wasn't taking any showers or baths. To keep me clean, Hedda simply used a wet washcloth with some soap on it to wash various parts of my body, especially when it was time to see the doctor. As for Hedda, I didn't see her taking showers or baths. She was constantly at the sink scrubbing her hands, which were red as ever. Water was splashing all over her black gabardine jumper, and a patch of fabric had worn away and become stiff. The jumper now looked like a rag, but she continued to wear it. And she continued to wash her hands.

When my hair became oily, hanging like strings, Hedda led me to the bathroom. I saw her open a shampoo bottle and my heart began to pound as I stood in front of the sink. *Oh no, she's going to do it again!* And soon I heard her say: "Bend down and stand still!" Before I had a chance to close my eyes, water and suds came streaming down my face, with a sting to my eyes that made me cringe. I cried, "My eyes are burning—please stop." She went right on until she finished. I wondered: *Do other children go through this to get clean hair?*

Dental hygiene was never mentioned in our home. There had to be a real emergency for Hedda to take me to the dentist. I was growing up on chocolate pudding, Hershey bars and Fig Newtons. Decay and plaque were rapidly forming in my teeth, but how could that be avoided? And I was brushing my teeth as if I knew what I was doing.

One day I had a toothbrush in my hand, and I was about to brush my teeth when my father sneaked up behind me and followed me into the bathroom. He had a grin on his face as he whispered, "I want to show you how to brush your teeth."

I was excited about that. Just as my father was beginning to show me how to brush my teeth, Hedda came storming in: "Don't tell her how to brush her teeth! She knows enough already! Leave her alone. **She doesn't need to know that!**"

With that half-smile on his face—reserved only for moments when he was under attack—he ran out of the room, mumbling something under his breath. Minutes later, he was out the door. I felt a pain go through me. *What did he want to say?*

"She doesn't need to know that." Apparently, Hedda didn't want me to know anything. How delighted I was whenever my father or grandmother reached out to me with something they wanted me to know. Then Hedda would appear on the scene, ready to explode into a tirade. I didn't know what to make of it. Whichever way I looked at it, I felt trapped. So, I would sit there, holding in my pain as she continued to rant and rage. Her voice was like a loud radio I couldn't shut off.

One day an incident occurred in the hallway of our apartment as my father was getting ready to leave for work. It was a rare moment when I shared a smile with him, and it made me feel good. We spoke a few words that encouraged me to go further. I playfully kneeled down before him to take a bow. I don't recall where I had seen it—most probably in a magazine—but there I was, coming out of my shell and taking a risk.

My father, looking disappointed, said: "No, you're not doing it right. That's not the way to curtsy. You're clumsy!" He then bent over, very slowly, and with magnificent grace, he showed me what a curtsy should look like. It seemed so easy to do, but I didn't feel there was any way I could do it like that. I wound up feeling stupid. *Why can't I do anything right?* I stood there in shame, my face flushed, not knowing what to say or do. I thought I would sink through the floor.

There was now sadness written all over my father's face as he put on his jacket and walked towards the door. When his hand was just about on the knob, Hedda pounced. "Look what you've done! You got her all upset! Why are you upsetting her with all that nonsense? Leave her alone! Mind your own business! She can live without knowing how to curtsy. **She doesn't need to know that!**"

My heart dropped. I tried to say something, but I couldn't speak. I was numb as I watched my father walk out the door.

There was Hedda, her face reddened with anger and contempt. The words, **"She doesn't need to know that!"** were still ringing in my ears. It was a constant reminder that I was invisible … that I was not to be seen or heard … that I didn't need to know anything. Nor was I supposed to have any needs or wants for that would make me too human. She made me feel that I was her possession and I existed solely for her. She was denying my very existence and she didn't want anyone else to acknowledge me either. And there was nothing I could do about it but brood and feel the pain of my reality.

I went over to a chair and sat down. It felt terrible to be me. I wanted to make the pain stop, but I didn't know how to do that. I soon went over to the radio, turned it on, sat down in my rocking chair, and started to rock. Rocking away my cares: it meant salvation for me.

So, this is the way we lived our lives, day in, day out, year after year, destined to live in a world of doom, darkness, and despair—Hedda in the role of the monarch, with me by her side.

9

My Fantasy World

How fortunate for me that my mother liked to listen to the radio. It seemed to help her relax and calm down and she allowed me to listen with her. It was one of the few things she permitted me to do. The radio was a source of comfort for me, and an outlet for my feelings. It turned out to be the one friend I could turn to when I needed a friend.

One of the first songs I ever learned was a song she taught me when I was five: "Show Me The Way To Go Home." I had a funny feeling each time I heard that song. Something about the words did not seem right. (It was about a drunk who couldn't find his way.) But my mother was singing it to me—so it had to be okay.

I found I could lose myself in the world of music. I did not need to be afraid to sing along with any song I heard. Not a care in the world, as I sat in my rocking chair, swaying to and fro with the gentle sounds that came from my radio.

The lyrics of some songs touched me deeply. They were saying things I could not openly express. Lyrics about sadness, hurt, being unloved and seeking love: my feelings were alive and scattered throughout each song. And so were the tears that trickled down my cheeks. It was therapy—musical therapy. I rocked back and forth in my rocking chair and sang. It was a cleansing process that kept my spirits alive. It was my connection to the outside world.

I couldn't get some songs out of my mind. The song, "If I Loved You" from *Carousel,* went round and round in my head as it tugged away at my heart. I felt the melancholy sting of "My Happiness" with a spark of hope that accompanied it. While I was experiencing and working out my saddest feelings in song, I also found an element of hope and joy. A happy, perky melody like "Everything's Coming Up Roses," or "Who Cares," was enough to make my heart race with exhilaration. How could anything out there in the world be that scary or bad after experiencing such happiness in a song? It felt great! Everything in the world was good and new. Fear was but an illusion; my sadness had disappeared. It was from these melodies that contained the sparkle and glow of being alive, and from the precious joy that is inherent in life itself, that my spirits were lifted enough to sustain me in a cold, hostile world.

While I indulged myself in musical mirth, I stepped out of my role as a sad, suffering child. I could withstand Hedda's cruelty to me. I no longer was the victim of one bronchial-asthmatic attack after another. I didn't see the bleak, poverty-stricken environment I lived in. I could see myself as a happy, healthy, young adult with a love of music and an ability to sing. In my mind's eye, I was not a child, but someone much older. It felt good. I was free to feel whatever I needed to feel. And there was satisfaction in this new role I had secretly created for myself. My make-believe world became more real to me than the world I was living in, which began to look more like a fantasy.

I could sit at the kitchen table and do my schoolwork for only so long. Eventually, I was rushing through my lessons, so eager was I to finish. I then put on my radio and was transported to my wonderful world of fantasy. When I felt up to it—that is, when I wasn't choking on a cough or feeling very ill—I would participate by singing along.

At some point I developed intense crushes on male singers. It may have started with Frank Sinatra. I was very young when I first heard him sing on the radio. There was something about the way he could express feelings in a song that made me want to listen more.

I loved to hear his voice. I saw pictures of him, and I adored his dreamy look; he was so cute.

When I was about eight or nine, I discovered Bing Crosby. He was singing from the heart, and I was moved by the gentle, intimate quality of his voice. As I listened to him sing, I found his voice so warm and soothing, I was able to calm down and find a sense of tranquility. I loved the poignant feeling he gave to songs like "The Day After Forever" and "I'll Be Seeing You." Tears filled my eyes.

His songs brought me to a wonderful place where I felt alone with Bing, and it seemed as though he was singing just to me. I felt special and cared for in those moments. I felt especially close to Bing when he sang the tender "Close As Pages In A Book":

We'll be close as pages in a book
My love and I
So close, we can share a single look
Share every sigh

So close that before I hear your laugh
My laugh breaks through
And when a tear starts to appear
My eyes grow misty too

Our dreams won't come tumbling to the ground
We'll hold them fast
Darling, as the strongest book is bound
We're bound to last

Your life is my life
And while life beats away in my heart
We'll be close as pages in a book
Never to part

I started to sing along with Bing. I soon knew his songs by heart. We were now singing to each other. I lived for those moments. Bing made me feel as if nothing else mattered but those moments. He was singing about something enchanting and filling the void in me. I didn't think about my mother during those times, or how unhappy I was; I had a sense of freedom—if only in my mind.

There was now something to look forward to, something that was uplifting and beautiful. I could feel a spark of hope in my heart. I felt good. I felt alive. I felt at one with the universe. Bing's soft, warm voice created an atmosphere that strengthened Little Lenore with the feeling there was something out there to live for. Bing was conveying, in his songs, a feeling of love—and I was taking it in.

But what did I know about love and what the words in the songs really meant? All I knew is that without actually understanding the lyrics, a wonderful sensation came over me. When I heard Bing, I wasn't that sad little girl anymore; I felt a glow inside. It was magic, and I was thriving on it.

For quite some time, Bing was my world. Later on, I became fascinated with other male singers whose songs could also touch my heart and keep my spirits alive. I felt sad and disappointed when I learned about their romances, wishing it were me.

I admired female singers as I sang along with them and tried to imitate their singing styles. Doris Day was high on my list. I loved her sunny smile and the warmth in her voice. Her singing created moments of peace and calm for me. There was a refreshing sincerity about her that I gravitated to, a sort of wholesomeness I found very special.

And how I adored Toni Arden; she was my favorite. She was often referred to as "the little lady with the great big voice." She started out as an opera singer and decided she liked pop music better. I found it thrilling to hear her sing Italian melodies as well as the pop songs of the day. The feeling she put into the lyrics of a song touched me deeply and often brought tears to my eyes. She had a uniquely sensitive way of pouring her heart and soul into a song. It is very difficult to describe in words the magic that Toni Arden creates with her voice and feeling for music. One has to experience it—and then the beauty of it resonates and becomes clear.

I was writing down lyrics of songs that were most meaningful to me. It was an endless endeavor, and I found a sense of fulfillment in this. Soon, I was singing songs from memory, and enjoying every moment of it.

I must have been about nine years old when I began to fantasize about becoming a singer. This was an exciting thought that put life into me. I loved to sing. Perhaps I could even become famous and be renowned the world over. My idols were talented and loved by millions. If I were to acquire such fame, wouldn't it mean that I, too, could be loved and adored by millions of people?

I was afraid to tell Hedda or Grandma about this, for my dream might be discouraged and destroyed. I couldn't deal with that, so I kept it to myself. It became my own little secret.

I was switching the dial back and forth when I began to hear all kinds of stories about people's lives. "Can a poor girl from a small mining town in the west find happiness…?" I must say it was reassuring to hear the multitude of miseries that others were overcoming in their lives. Before long, I tuned in to just about every soap opera there was. In addition, the Lux Radio Theater had a repertoire of movie dramas that I found intriguing. I didn't have to go out to a movie; I heard the latest Hollywood movies on my radio.

I still had trouble with my speech. I was unable to enunciate my words and speak clearly. When I was listening to my radio programs, I often tried to pronounce the words I heard, but I wasn't doing very well. I knew I sounded funny, and it continued to bother me. I became more self-conscious, and my shame intensified. But I kept listening to my friends on the radio, and I was getting a better feel for the English language. Slowly, very slowly, my speech was improving, as I kept on struggling to do better.

I had created my own little world. It was a special place where I could feel safe and serene with my radio friends. They would talk to me, and I would listen. They would sing to me, and if I were up to it, I would join in. And when I was ill, my fantasy world helped me to remain hopeful.

I don't recall exactly how old I was—possibly about eight or nine—when my mother went downstairs to the candy store on the corner and came back with a movie magazine. I was drawn to the faces on the cover. I reached out for it, but Hedda slapped my hand. "**No!** Don't touch that!" In an angry voice she said, "**You'll get it** later!" Then I saw her go over to the refrigerator and put it in. I should have known better; I had forgotten Hedda's Rules: books had to be "aired out" before I could touch them. They had to be "clean." I guess this rule included magazines as well. This upset me, but the only thing I could do was wait. It felt like forever. I was very anxious to have it in my little hands. I cried, "When are you going to give me that magazine? You're ruining it! You're making it wet!" Hedda turned a deaf ear to me once again.

In a few hours, the magazine was "ready." My mother was in a nasty, grumpy mood as she pulled the magazine out of the refrigerator. Soon, I had the magazine in my hand. As I turned the pages, I saw so many pictures of pretty people. I was elated. I didn't know where to look first.

Soon, Hedda began to buy just about every movie magazine in the store. They were in our home as soon as they came out. I eagerly went through each one from beginning to end. It wasn't long before I knew the names and faces of just about every movie actor and actress in Hollywood.

It was a great moment for me when Hedda would open the refrigerator door and, like a magician pulling a rabbit out of a hat, a small stack of movie magazines would suddenly appear on the kitchen table. "Well, now you have them! Leave me alone and don't bother me!" I cringed when she spoke, but I finally got my magazines. But maybe she was right. Maybe there were germs on the magazines. Maybe airing them out in the refrigerator was the way to get rid of something awful that could make me sick. What did I know? I wondered if other people aired out magazines to kill germs. I didn't know what to believe. I only knew what my mother told me.

And it went on like that.

I now had something else to look forward to, besides my radio friends. I was in sheer ecstasy when I had the romantic, illusory world of Hollywood at my fingertips. I loved seeing the sparkling, winning smile of Esther Williams, decked out in one of her fabulous bathing suits. Doris Day radiated a glowing charm with her sunny smile. I marveled at the glamour and the striking beauty of Elizabeth Taylor and Ava Gardner, with their dark black hair and alabaster skin. They looked so good on the outside; I wondered what they were like on the inside.

And I kept staring at the pictures of the Hollywood starlets. *My goodness, these are gorgeous creatures! How does one get to look like that?* I cut out pictures and kept them in special scrapbooks of my favorite stars and admired them every so often.

Hedda opened up to me one day and revealed that she had been quite an avid movie fan in her youth. She showed me pictures of herself in her late teens and early twenties. She wore short skirts and loose blouses in the Flapper/Vamp style. She had short dark hair with bangs, and her lips were shaped like a heart. I thought she looked every bit as pretty as any starlet in the magazines. She reminded me of Clara Bow, an actress of her day (known as the "It" girl), and when I told her that, she closed her eyes in a swoon and sighed: "She was beautiful, so very beautiful…"

So Hedda and I had something in common: we both admired the beautiful and scintillating female stars of the silver screen. But the male movie stars were no stepchildren to Hedda. She admired them just as much, if not more. Her eyes lit up and she glowed. "You know who's really fantastic? Joel McCrea. And John Payne— he's so handsome!" She spoke some more about her Hollywood heroes, and I noticed that her dark world brightened, as she lost herself in movieland fantasy.

I must have been about nine or ten when I was reading all about these movie stars. I wanted to know how they lived, what they thought, what they liked to do in their spare time, what made them happy, and what made them sad. I wanted to know about their worries, their fears, and concerns. It became a pastime that enthralled me for hours on end. I was especially curious about how they attained success and fame so young. What does one have to do to achieve worldwide stardom?

I was very impressed with those who had suffered great obstacles and overcome them, prospering in the face of great adversity. I think that was one reason I admired Doris Day so much. When she broke her leg and was told her dancing career was over, she turned to singing. I thrived on such success stories, probably because I needed to identify with a heroine.

The more I read about the Hollywood stars, the more incredible their lives appeared to me. Here I was, living with dirt in every nook and cranny, and our furniture looked as though it was found in the street. My mother and I wore the same old, shabby clothing day in, day out. And what was I doing? I was reading about the lives of movie stars: their luxurious homes, the parties they attended, the expensive clothing they wore, their work that had so much meaning for them—and their romances. I didn't know people could live like that. Perhaps ordinary people could also live well—even if it wasn't in the lavish and luxurious lifestyle of Hollywood.

Despite my fascination with Hollywood stars, I never aspired to become one of them. It seemed rather far-fetched to me. I was just too involved with popular music and radio personalities to give a second thought to anything like an acting career. I held on to my dream of becoming a popular singer, and that was good enough for me.

And soon things would change once again. Regardless of how involved I was with my fantasy world, I still had to contend with the disturbing behavior of my mother. When Hedda was in one of her moods, I knew it was time to break away from my fantasy world and go on alert. When I came back to reality, I was still a very frightened little girl, but I was managing to survive and gain some courage to go on. Sadness and hurt continued to gnaw away inside of me—but my fantasy world made it just a little easier to bear.

10

Another Side of Hedda

There was another side of Hedda. How surprised I was to see a different face—one that could smile! I lived for moments like these. I certainly did not expect Hedda to praise me as I sang along with the radio. Nevertheless, she turned to me and said, "Very nice," sending a slight smile my way. How I welcomed that smile! It carried the hope that she might be able to like me—maybe even love me? You would never think that this was the same woman who, a few hours earlier, commiserated about her "wretched life," her "rotten daughter," and that she would be "much better off dead." Despite the horrible things she would say, I still wanted to have her love; I wanted her to be a mother who could love me.

But her mood would soon change again. I went through a monologue with myself: *That frown on her face—I think she's mad at me again. What did I do now? She was just smiling at me. What can I do to get her to be like that again? I think she liked me before. What can I do to get her to talk to me now? Maybe I'll put on the radio and sing—she likes that. But that look on her face—maybe the radio will annoy her. What am I going to do?*

I often wonder where I got the emotional stamina from—the strength that enabled me to come out of myself and pull my mother out of her troubled world—if only for a short time.

I came upon a picture of a Dalmatian dog in a magazine. The dog was white with big black spots, and it was used as a "fire dog." I had an idea. Why not make up a little story that might amuse her? I said, "Hedda, you and I are two Dalmatians, and we're going out to fires together."

She giggled. I said, "Why don't you be Gamber-Gamber Wackee, and I'll be… Hearty?" Now, she was actually laughing!

We began to talk about our lives as Dalmatians. We soon invented our own little language and we had interludes where we communicated with each other in a unique, crazy way. It was fun. My mother was enjoying herself, and I would enjoy myself, too. It broke up the tension that existed between us. I was bringing Hedda out of her moods with nonsensical stories. But there were times when my attempts were non-productive and short-lived. She soon would slink off into her own world again, looking miserable and depressed.

In her changing moods, Hedda could fluctuate from a state of supremacy—where she could do no wrong—to becoming as helpless as a kitten. When she was in this child-like state, I was able to change my personality to conform to her needs. I no longer was a child reliant on my mother for survival. I stepped out of my fearful, docile self and became the adult she needed me to be. I was now the adult advising the monarch, who temporarily was unable to rule.

In this state, Hedda would confide in me, sharing stories about her early years. "There was so much fighting in my home, I was afraid I would come home from school one day and find my mother or father dead. I hated the way my mother treated my father. She was so mean to him…"

I listened with sadness as she went on: "My brother was the favorite. My mother had no use for me. He got piano lessons and everything he wanted, I got nothing…" I knew I could safely tell her, "But that's not true, you also had piano lessons, and you can play the piano very well." She calmly listened with a tear in her eye.

It was weird how I could voice my opinion about anything during those rare times, and she appeared interested in whatever I had to say. I no longer was an enemy or a threat to her existence; I was her friend.

And I was using my newfound "power" constructively. I spoke my heart out about putting books in the refrigerator, and I begged her not to do it. Hedda appeared to be listening, and I hoped something would come of it. (Later, she seemed to be "airing out" fewer books. I wondered if I had anything to do with it.)

But this did not last long. I found it amazing how Hedda could spring back in moments, take the reins and be in full control once again! No one was going to tell her what to do. Not Hedda. She knew what she was doing; it was only the world around her that was "wrong." And I soon was back to being the fearful, passive little girl once again.

However, when she could give me a smile—that is, when she was still in an approachable mood—I thought it might be safe to go over to her and put my arm around her. But she didn't want that. She pushed me away. "I never had all that when I was growing up. If you ask me, it's a lot of crap!" Her response left me speechless and distraught. Maybe I should have known better. Hedda's Rules: no touching—that meant I was not to be touched and she was not to be touched either. How awful it felt to know I wasn't allowed to touch my own mother. I felt like something less than human.

How terribly upsetting it was when Hedda was friendly with me one moment and then completely oblivious of me in the next, as if I didn't exist. Worst of all, my nerves became frazzled when she would explode into an outburst of rage, then withdraw into herself and become mute. I never knew which Hedda would appear next.

One day Hedda sat down and started to weep. "I once had a doll. I was playing with the little girl from next door, and my doll fell off the bed and broke into pieces. I cherished that doll." She was now sobbing bitterly. "It was a small cheap doll—the kind they sell in Woolworth. No other doll could take the place of the one that broke."

Whenever she spoke about that doll, there was grief in her voice and tears rolling down her cheeks. I was touched by her grief.

I sat there and listened to her; I was feeling helpless. I didn't know what to say to comfort her. After all, I was only a child.

Hedda was constantly buying dolls for me. Eventually, she bought just about every doll on the market: Sonja Henie, Anne Shirley, Carmen, and Sparkle Plenty—to name a few—each one in a colorful outfit, one more beautiful than the other. When she asked my father for extra cash, he would say: "What is it for? Another doll?" And he would grunt a little, but he would give her the money. She then made the purchase through the mail.

When I opened the boxes to admire the dolls, I caught a glimpse of Hedda looking over my shoulder, sort of smiling. Was she buying those dolls for me? Or was she buying them for herself? They were so pretty, so very delicate… I would have liked to hold them and caress them, but somehow, I just couldn't touch them. And neither could she. Could it be that, in some sort of fantasy, I became a replacement for her doll? Could it be that she was afraid to touch me—and didn't want anyone else to touch me—lest I break like her doll?

But a human being is not a doll. A doll doesn't need a light to read by. A doll doesn't need to know how to brush its teeth or wash its body. A doll doesn't get sick. It doesn't have to walk or talk. A doll just has to be there, sitting nice and quiet in a corner, not saying anything. If a doll has any needs, or tries to assert itself, then it's a bad doll. Bad Doll! I guess I needed to be a nice, quiet, motionless doll for Hedda—but I turned out to be a living, walking, talking little person—with thoughts and feelings. Apparently, I couldn't please my mother; I was not a doll.

11

A Man Named George

It was summertime. I was nine years old and back in Spring Valley. I excitedly waited for the weekends, for then I would see my father again. Words could not express the inner glow I felt as I watched my father walk down the path to meet us. He said hello, went to wash up, and began mingling with the crowd in the hotel. He loved being around people. He began to crack jokes, as he became an all-around "good guy." I felt a funny feeling come over me when someone approached him and said: "Darn it! I've just run out of cigarettes." No sooner were those words spoken then my father drove into town and picked up a carton. It seemed that he liked pleasing others. *But what about me? I'm his daughter.*

How disappointed I was as I watched him with a big smile on his face, beaming from ear to ear, chatting with various people on the premises. He seemed too busy having a good time to even notice me.

I recall the time I was standing outside the hotel when a man came over to me and said, "What does your father do for a living?" I found his question strange. I usually did not speak to anyone, but somehow I felt compelled to respond. I nervously said, "My father drives a taxi."

The man walked away, but afterwards, something told me I should not have said that. I saw my father in the distance and I ran over to him, hoping to hear him say that I didn't do anything wrong. Instead, he nervously replied, "You didn't say I was a cab driver, did you?"

I became flustered by his tone of voice and the expression on his face. I never saw him like that. I could see he was upset, and that, in turn, made me upset too. I didn't feel safe telling him the truth, so I made up a story to appease him. I had to get away. I walked as fast as I could, and soon, I was back in the hotel with Hedda.

I wondered why my father had acted so strangely. I didn't know he was ashamed of driving a cab. Then again, what did I really know about my father?

One day a woman in Spring Valley, who heard me address him as "George," approached my father and said, "How do you allow that? Don't you mind your daughter calling you by your first name? I would be insulted if my child called me by my first name!"

My father broke out in a grin, and laughingly replied: "That doesn't bother me. She can call me George. You've heard the old saying: 'You can call me anything, just don't call me late for dinner!'"

I was a few feet away, and I overheard them talking. My father made a joke of it, but it was true: he didn't care what I called him. In fact, he even encouraged me to call him George. I didn't know why it bothered me, but suddenly, I started to feel bad.

Who was this man named George? What was he really like? He remained a stranger to me, but I adored him from afar. I would fantasize about getting to know him. Maybe someday, in my teens, when I would be old enough to break away and leave my mother, we could meet and talk. We could even laugh and show affection for each other. Wouldn't that be wonderful? When I thought about this, it took away my pain, and gave me some hope.

I was sitting alone, outside the hotel, waiting for my mother to come out and join me. It was seldom that I was without her, but this was one of those rare occasions. I was busily doing some embroidery work with a small needle, when suddenly the needle slipped through my fingers. My eyes turned to the ground, but it was nowhere to be found.

I was terrified of losing needles because Hedda had once said that a needle could be deadly; it has no head and can travel through your body, reach the heart, and cause instant death. And I had lost the needle! I was filled with anxiety and fear.

I began to scurry around the grass, hunting for the needle as one would look for a diamond. The grass was higher in some spots than in others, so it was not easy for the naked eye to see something so small. It seemed as if the earth had swallowed it up.

Soon I had a terrible thought: What will happen if my mother comes out and sees me scurrying around in the grass, no less, looking for a needle. *My God, where can it be? I just have to find it.*

In my state of panic, who should walk by but my father! He no sooner looked my way when I pleadingly cried out: "George, I lost my needle, please help me find it before Hedda comes out."

He stared at me for a moment, and then joined me in the hunt. He began to fumble around, searching in the tiny blades of grass. Suddenly, I saw him laughing. He was jumping up and down. "I found it! I found it! The needle in the haystack!"

He was dangling the needle in his hand. He looked so joyous, so triumphant. And I was so happy as I ran over to him and grabbed the needle from him. I then heaved a sigh of relief, and we both laughed.

Suddenly, I had an uncomfortable feeling in my stomach. I was alone with my father, and I became frightened. I wanted to be with him very much; now that we were alone, I didn't know how to act, what to say, or what to do. Neither did he. We were strangers to each other.

I said, "Thank you," as I stuck the needle into the fabric and ran back inside.

How well I remember that day. My father was laughing; he was happy. I was overjoyed when he found that needle. We shared a few delightful moments together. And then, a cloud came over me; I did not feel safe with my father. So, what did I do? I thanked him and ran away!

But he didn't come after me either. I called him George. I guess that is how I saw him—not as a father, but simply as "George"; a man named George.

12

Physical Development

I was over five feet tall, my breasts were developed, and my hips were large for a girl my age. I thought I looked more like a woman than a little girl of ten. It was a strange feeling to be growing so rapidly.

Then I got a big scare. I was sitting on the toilet seat when I noticed vivid red blotches on my underwear. Because I had a fear that something awful was about to happen to me at any moment, I worried: *Is this the impending doom that I heard about? Maybe this is my punishment for being a "bad girl."*

I yelled out to my mother, and she came right in. She appeared shocked and ran out of the room. A few minutes later, I heard her speaking to my father. This was very unusual since they rarely spoke to each other. Now they were whispering in the hallway. *What are they saying?* I could only hear the faint sound of their voices. My heart was pounding as I looked down at the bright-red color on the toilet tissue. The more I looked at it, the more frightened I became.

It seemed as if time stood still, but Hedda finally came back to the bathroom. I was still sitting on the toilet seat, in a state of panic, as I waited to hear what she was going to tell me. And then Hedda very casually said, "You're bleeding . . . you're unwell." *What did she mean by "unwell"?* She mumbled a few words, but I was too upset to hear. As I looked at Hedda, I saw she no longer had that worried expression on her face, so I was able to calm down a little. But I was still scared. Why couldn't I stop bleeding?

Hedda soon showed me something she called a "sanitary napkin." It was a long, white, cloth-like fabric that looked very strange to me. She put it on for me, and it immediately absorbed the blood. With this bleeding came sweats, chills, and stomach discomfort. For the first few hours, I was sick with cramps, and then the pain subsided. But when I was in the midst of it, I didn't think it would ever go away. The bleeding lasted for a few days, and then it stopped. Goodness gracious, I was so glad it was over. After a month, however, it was back!

I don't recall just how I found out, but I soon became aware that this condition was part of "becoming a woman" and that all women experience this on a monthly basis. I thought to myself, *If this is what it's like to be a woman, I don't want any part of it.* But Mother Nature had a different view. I began to look at the calendar every month so I would not be surprised when my period came. This was my startling introduction into the world of menstruation.

As if I wasn't feeling different enough from everyone my age, there was still something else that came to me as a shock—something that made me feel even more self-conscious. It was summer, we were in the country, and my mother and I were just returning from a walk when one of the well-intentioned ladies on the premises approached my mother and asked: "How old is your daughter? Hedda replied: "She's ten. Why?" The woman was quick to respond: "Your daughter is very well developed for her age. I was like that when I was a child. She really needs to wear a bra. I was so much more comfortable when I started to wear one . . ."

And from that day on, each time she saw my mother, she tried to convince her how necessary a bra is for any girl with large breasts. Hedda listened and seemed rather amused. She herself was slim and never wore a bra. However, a couple of months later, my mother took me to a local lingerie store in the neighborhood. I tried on a few bras, and Hedda made a purchase. I soon became accustomed to wearing the bra, and I even thought I might get to like it.

So, there I was, ten years old, wearing a bra and wondering if people noticed me in my bra and what they were thinking.

At about the same time, a slight protuberance on the right side of my back had become more pronounced. Grandma pointed it out and seemed very concerned, but I wasn't. I continued to spend a great part of each day writing and studying at the kitchen table. I wasn't aware that I had a tendency to lean towards the left, elevating my right shoulder, which had become slightly higher than the other. I was too intent upon doing my schoolwork to be bothered by improper posture.

Grandma began to express her fear that my back was becoming crooked. When Hedda was out of the room, she would thrust her shoulders back, her head up, and say, "Stand up straight!" As if Hedda had a radio antenna attached, informing her of my every move, she came dashing into the room, barking at Grandma: "Don't tell her what to do! **She doesn't need to know that**—she knows enough already! There's nothing wrong with her back. Leave her alone!"

I could feel the hatred in her voice. I just sat there, immobilized, as I watched my mother and grandmother exchange words once again. Grandma did not give up easily in this instance, and whenever she could sneak in a gesture of "standing up tall" or whisper some advice on posture to me, she would. I appreciated her concern, but I would forget almost immediately. And I continued to slouch.

During one of my illnesses, Dr. Weisner came to the house. "How is the patient today?" He then rolled back his shoulders, and like a sergeant in the army, he staunchly commanded in a loud tone, "Stand up tall! Don't slouch!"

I recall how I shuddered at the sound of his voice, but I did what he told me to do. Then, as I began to undress for the examination, I saw an odd expression on the good doctor's face. "Your bra—it's yellow!" he lashed out. "It's dirty! You have to wash that bra in lots and lots of suds and scrub it real hard to get out all that dirt!"

My back was curving to a side, but did that really matter? Not when my bra was yellow and dirty! As he was about to leave, he held the doorknob in his hand and called out: "Don't forget to wash that bra!" How could he show more concern for the condition of my bra than the curvature of my spine?

I was sitting in the house most of the time; I did very little walking. And yet I felt pain in my feet when I got up and walked around. I wondered if the Buster Brown boy shoes had anything to do with it. My mother bought them from a store in the neighborhood, and they did not feel right on my feet. The small toe of my right foot was badly inflamed, and there were calluses on the soles of my feet. But what can you expect when you don't go to a shoe store to try on your own shoes?

I would tell myself that things were not as bad as they seemed. I was experiencing the joys of having the breasts of a woman in the body of a child; beginning menstruation while not even knowing where babies come from; and wearing a bra at the ripe old age of ten. Who could ask for anything more?

13

My Mother's Operation

I was ten years old and my mother was very ill. She frequently went over to the sink and threw up. She constantly complained about stomach pains and nausea, but she refused to see a doctor. One day she experienced so much pain my father went downstairs and made an emergency phone call. Dr. Weisner came right over and examined Hedda. He appeared worried as he said: "I don't like the way this looks. There's a bulge in her stomach and it has to be taken care of immediately. I'm putting her in the hospital."

"You're putting her in the hospital? What's wrong with her? Will she be all right?"

By now Hedda was convulsing in pain. I became panicky and started to tremble. I recall the grim expression on the doctor's face as he said: "We'll do all we can for her."

I didn't hear anything after that. I stood there in a daze. The sound of a siren brought me back to the moment. An ambulance was in front of the building, waiting to take Hedda away. I can't remember what happened after that. All I know is that I was trembling.

Before I knew it, Grandma was in our home. She told me she would take care of me while my mother was away. I felt a little safer when I knew I wouldn't have to leave the house. But inside of me was the dreadful fear that something terrible was about to happen to Hedda. Then what would happen to me?

I was too overwhelmed by feelings of fear and despondency to know what was going on around me. Soon my father brought back news about Hedda. "They had to do emergency surgery. The doctor said she had a strangulated hernia. She was able to get through the surgery, but she's still critically ill."

Thank God, Hedda survived.

I nervously asked: "What is a strangulated hernia?"

"The doctor said it was a lump in her side that cut off her blood supply. It's a very dangerous condition, that's why they had to operate right away. That's all I can say for now. We'll have to wait and see."

In the days that followed I remained tense and on edge as I anxiously waited to receive more news. The morbid expression on Grandma's face told me that she too was very worried about her daughter.

"Willie will be coming over this afternoon. When I'm at home he usually comes every day after school and has a cup of tea and some cookies." I was glad that Grandma let me know this, so that I would be prepared. How I dreaded the thought of seeing him. I remembered that big black mustache and ear-to-ear grin when he would bring thermometers into my mother's apartment on Belmont Avenue. He would say, "I'm giving you these thermometers so you'll know when to take Lenore out." But Hedda did not want them. She would nervously pace up and down, saying: "My brother and those goddamn thermometers!" Just as she disposed of one, he gleefully brought over another. Hedda was fast becoming a nervous wreck and screamed: "Don't come up here anymore! You're not welcome in this house!" I was only four years old, as I stood at Hedda's side in the hallway. I hated to see my mother so upset while Uncle Will had that big grin on his face.

Soon Will was at my door and I was face-to-face with him. I felt a chill soar through me. It was quite some time since I had seen him, and yet it seemed like only yesterday. From what I could recall, he looked pretty much the same. He was tall and thin, and he wore glasses; his hair was black and wavy—and he still had that big, black mustache and wide toothy grin. Strange, how memories cling. I looked at magazines and I saw pictures of men with mustaches, and I cringed. When I saw my uncle Will that day, I knew why. I did not like my uncle Will.

I recalled Hedda's warning: "I don't want you to ever have anything to do with my brother. He's rotten. He's no good. He put me away. He can't be trusted. He'll ruin your life like he ruined mine. Remember I told you that!" I then made a faithful promise to my mother: "I will never talk to him or have anything to do with him."

As he entered my mother's apartment, he gave me a great big "Hello, Lenore." I was hoping that the unhappy expression on my face wasn't too obvious. He was gracious and friendly as he tried to connect with me. But I still managed to keep myself at a distance.

I was emotionally starved. I had a hunger to talk and share my thoughts and feelings with anyone who might listen to me. Usually, I had to push my feelings down as I tried to avoid any controversy with Hedda. But here was an opportunity for me to speak my heart and my mind. My uncle Will was coming over daily and showering me with a lot of interest and attention. Because I was feeling so lost and lonely, I was open to it.

Little by little, I began to talk to Will. As I began to converse with him, the promise I made to Hedda began to fade. I felt like a traitor as a gnawing feeling of guilt came over me. I couldn't help but wonder: *Is my uncle really the "bad guy" my mother made him out to be, or is he as nice as he appears?* I guess I had to find that out for myself.

Soon Will came with news about my mother. "The doctor said it was touch and go. She almost died on the operating table. Then she had a bout with pneumonia. Your mother is still quite ill, but she's receiving the medical attention that is required."

I could feel anxiety pulsating throughout my body as he spoke. It didn't sound good. I nervously asked: "Do you think she'll recover?"

Will responded stoically, "It's too soon to know." After that, I heard him talking, but I couldn't absorb what he was saying. The rest of his visit became a blur in my mind.

As Will continued to make brief visits to my home, I listened to him converse with Grandma and I was impressed. I thought he was very knowledgeable. And he continued to pay lots of attention to me. He made me feel so good when I was around him that I began to look forward to his visits. But I was still on guard.

As much as I always wanted to live with Grandma, I began to realize it was no picnic. She would get upset very easily over miniscule things. An example of this is the night Grandpa hobbled in on the way home from his store. Grandma and I were listening to the radio when Grandpa joined us. The hit song from Porgy and Bess, "It Ain't Necessarily So," was now playing when they began to fight: "Does the word necessarily have two c's or one?"

What is going on? What is wrong with them? Have they gone mad? I sat on the edge of my seat, feeling tears well up in my eyes as I watched my grandparents hurling angry words back and forth while their daughter was lying so very ill in the hospital. I couldn't understand how they could fight about something as miniscule as the spelling of a word. It seemed surreal.

And I continued to walk around the house with one concern on my mind: *What's happening with my mother?*

When I saw my uncle again, he said, "I would like to do things for you, Lenore." I liked the sound of that. I was beginning to lose a lot of my bottled-up fear of him. Then he said, "I'd like to show you the outside world. It's about time you came out of the house. There's a whole world out there. I want to take you downstairs now!"

That was one thing I didn't want to hear. I immediately became anxious and upset. I wasn't used to going outdoors, nor did I have any interest in going out of the house. When I did go out, I was with my mother, and I certainly would not leave the house without her. The thought of going outside with someone I didn't really trust was terrifying to me.

So, what am I going to do?

Grandpa was sitting nearby, supposedly reading his newspaper, when he overheard his son talking to me. He came to my rescue. In a burst of anger, Grandpa defiantly declared: "Her mother left strict instructions that the child is to remain in the house!" It was a moment I would not forget. Grandpa was trying to save me from the horrible fate of facing the outside world with my uncle Will.

Will fired back in a tone of exasperation: "It is an outrage to keep this girl locked up in the house. She should be allowed to go out like everybody else. You are only helping to destroy this child."

A panic came over me. *Will I be forced to leave the safety of my home?* It was especially scary to face this with someone I had sworn to stay away from for the rest of my life. I suppose the worst of it all is that no one bothered to ask me what I wanted to do. While my grandfather and uncle were busy arguing about taking me out, they showed absolutely no interest in what was going on inside of me, as I sat there, nervous and tense, barely able to move. How awful that felt. They were squabbling over me as if I were some kind of object without any thoughts or feelings of my own. I felt invisible. Everyone knew what was best for me. Or so they thought. Even Grandma surprised me; she just sat there, sadly nodding her head. After an intense squabble, my uncle, in a fit of rage, ran for his hat and coat and hurried out the door. And I remained in the house. I was relieved, but very distraught.

Later, I thought about that afternoon. It was humiliating. Would anyone ever recognize me as having thoughts and feelings of my own? I kept saying to myself: *There's no me. There's no me…* There was no me.

I was especially annoyed with myself because I couldn't find the words to tell my uncle how frightened I was of going outside and how very sensitive I was about being locked up in the house when I knew people were going out, doing things and enjoying themselves. It felt awful to be me.

And I continued to worry about my mother: *Will she be all right?*

Grandma soon came in with good news: "Your mother is on the road to recovery. She is still very ill, and it's not known how long she will be in the hospital, but she seems to be doing better."

How relieved I was to hear that. "When will she be coming home?"

She replied, "No one seems to know."

I would just have to hope and pray.

I continued to live within my shell. Day in, day out, things were pretty much the same. There was a gloom that could be felt throughout the house. Then, one day my father, who was seldom at home, came over to me and said, "I want to take you out." *Oh no, not that again!* I felt my heart leaping in my chest as he pulled out a nail clipper from a shirt pocket and said, "But first, I want to clip your nails. They're much too long. It will only take a few minutes."

I said, "George, I don't want my nails cut." He proceeded to clip them anyway and I started to cry. "Now look what you've done. They're too short. They look terrible." I paused and pouted. "I'm not going out. I'm not going out. Now leave me alone!" George didn't say a word. He took a look at me, then reached for his jacket and walked towards the door. I was relieved to see him go. It meant I could remain indoors.

I soon had a pleasant surprise. The doorbell rang and standing before me was a lady with snow-white hair, bright, beaming eyes and a broad, happy smile. I had only seen Will's wife, Jessie, a few times in my life and my memory of her was very vague. But there she was, with a warm greeting for me: "I wanted to see how you're doing, dear. I just returned from Florida and I'm stopping by on my way home." She appeared to be very kind and I hoped she would stay, but she said she was in a hurry. "I'll see you again real soon, then I'll spend some time with you." I was joyful as I thought about it.

Soon after Jessie's visit, I received some good news: Hedda was coming home! I was so grateful. I said a prayer of thanks to God for saving her life.

When I first saw her, I noticed how pale and drawn she looked. She had lost considerable weight and it was obvious that she had been through a terrible ordeal. She complained of being very weak and hardly able to stand on her feet. Soon, a home aide was hired, and everything possible was done to make her comfortable. That included cleansing Hedda's wound in which pus formed and applying fresh dressings twice a day. The aide also helped out with cooking and various household chores. Grandma was only too glad to return to her home, but she continued to do most of the food shopping.

About this time, I contracted intestinal influenza. I had not gone out of the house and, as far as I knew, I was not in contact with anyone who was ill. So how did I get this infection? I dwelled upon this in between hours of vomiting, diarrhea, and high fever. The doctor speculated: "Someone must have brought it in from the outside."

Soon, Jessie came to visit again. It was an afternoon that started out very slowly and rather quietly. Jessie and I were seated at the kitchen table and Hedda was nearby, lying in bed. Jessie was speaking to me and I was basking in the tones of her soft, gentle voice. Soon she was telling me, "I have a niece, Elaine. She's about your age, and she goes to public school. She's a very bright girl. One day the weather was bad and it looked like it was going to rain. Elaine put on her raincoat and boots, went for her umbrella, and said: 'If it rains, I won't have to get wet. Now, I'm ready for a storm'!" Jessie was glowing as she spoke. "Don't you think that's a delightful story, dear? Elaine is so smart."

Up to that point I liked Jessie, but suddenly I became disenchanted with her. I was being consumed with a feeling so strong it was tearing me apart. Why was I so upset? I didn't even know this girl, Elaine, but she was so "bright" and could do things I couldn't do. I was afraid to go out of the house, but there she was, fearless and ready for a storm! *Who cares about Elaine? Not me.*

I listened some more to what Jessie had to say, so as not to appear rude, but I was choking up inside. Then she asked if I had been outdoors and I said no. "You know, dear, girls and boys your age go to school and have friends; they go to each other's homes, they enjoy things together…." And on and on she went, but I couldn't take it in. Her talk was making me sick. Soon, her words passed through me and I couldn't hear anything, nor could I feel anything. I finally found the guts to say: "I really don't want to hear what other girls and boys are doing."

The tone of endearment was now gone from Jessie's voice and she had a frown on her face. "Dear, you have a closed mind." Why did those words hurt me so much? I felt as though I was slapped in the face, as I sat in my chair, emotionally crushed, unable to speak or even move. The pain of my existence came crashing down around me. Why did I have to hear how other girls and boys are enjoying their lives? I was not like other girls and boys. Couldn't she see that? It was bad enough I felt so different from everyone else; did I need her to make me feel even worse about myself?

I was on the verge of tears when suddenly Hedda appeared. "You're coming up here and making a lot of trouble. We know all about the girls and boys in school. She can't go to school. She goes out and comes home sick and you know that. So why are you starting up with this school business?"

Heated words were exchanged, and soon Jessie, in a huff, face all flushed, ran for her hat and coat. As she headed towards the door, she yelled back, "My God, you can't say a thing to them! They're crazy!"

I had a hope in my heart that I would have a friend in Jessie, but it was a dream, which fell apart before my eyes. An aching emptiness festered inside of me as I grieved about my loss. Then I became angry; Jessie didn't understand, she didn't care about me. I knew I would not be seeing Jessie any time soon, and that was fine with me.

Soon after that, Grandma came up and said that Jessie may have been suffering from some kind of infection when she came back from Florida. Hedda began to speculate: "It must have been from your sweet Aunt Jessie that you got so sick. She had no business coming up here if she was sick. And you think these people care for you. They only care about themselves!"

I didn't know how to respond to that. Maybe Hedda was right.

When Uncle Will came to our home again, Hedda confronted him on the spot. "I wish you would mind your own business once and for all. The same goes for your wife. Now I know what got my daughter sick—your wife coming up here with the flu. You people are such know-it-alls and yet she doesn't know enough to stay away when she's sick. If you ask me, you both know a lot of nothing."

I left the room. I heard raised voices coming from the kitchen, but I paid no mind to what they were saying. However, Hedda's voice was so loud, I couldn't escape hearing: "Don't you ever come up here again. I never want to see you or your wife again!"

With those words, Will and Jessie were banished from our home.

14

In The Valley of My Dreams

He cracked jokes about it, and he laughed at it. He called it "the valley of my dreams." From the tone of his voice, it sounded as if my father would have wanted to be anywhere in the world—except Spring Valley. Nevertheless, when summertime rolled around, he would take us there without comment or complaint.

I was back in the country again, and there before me were the winding lanes and open roads, the multicolored flowers enhancing the greens of the earth, the gentle breeze swaying over spacious grassland, and the sweet, fresh aroma of country air. It felt good, in the moment, to be back.

I was now ten years old, and things were pretty much the same as ever. I was still wearing the same clothes I wore the previous year and two years before that. My skirts, however, had become too short, and my mother had to piece a strip of white material to the bottoms. It wasn't particularly attractive, but I didn't complain about the way they looked. The rest of my attire was far worse. I wore heavy-textured lisle stockings, even during hot summer days. I thought they were as atrocious as my Buster Brown boy shoes, which I continued to wear, even as calluses were growing on the bottoms of my feet. I was very self-conscious of my appearance, but I tried to put it out of my mind as best I could.

I watched the other children in the hotel. Girls my age were in their pretty summer dresses and playsuits. With lustrous hair, sparkling eyes, and big, wide, happy smiles, there was an air of ease and confidence about them. I compared myself to them, and I felt shame and envy. I was nowhere like them. Then I would hear someone on the premises talking to Hedda: "What a pretty daughter you have! She has one dimple and such a pretty smile." But I didn't see myself that way. For the most part, I saw myself as clumsy, overweight, and not particularly attractive. I was so top-heavy that I needed to wear a bra. And I kept feeling that no one would ever like me—let alone love me. The way I was dressed compounded the way I felt about myself. I agonized that I was not like everyone else—and I so wanted to be.

One day I was walking with my mother along a country road when I saw a sight that startled me. A few feet from the road, there was a small, weather-beaten house with a fence around it, and near that house stood a child. She was small and slight; she must have been about four or five. She had dirt all over her face, and her clothing was soiled. Her hands hung limply at her sides. Her eyes were big and sad, and she had a forlorn expression on her face. There were no shoes on her feet.

But there was one thing that stood out more than anything else: one of her legs was chained to a tree. She looked stiff and motionless as she stood there, staring at us. I said hello, but she did not respond. Was she unable to talk or just too scared? I will never forget that vacant stare. Tears welled up in my eyes as I looked at her. I wondered why anyone would chain a child to a tree. It seemed such a cruel and inhuman thing to do.

The sight of her stayed with me—the child on the chain. Something frightened me and made me sad. Was I identifying with her? How different from that little girl was I? I was on a chain too— although it was not a visible one. It was a heavy, emotional one that tied me to my mother. I was no freer than she to smile, to laugh, and to enjoy a summer day—to be a child. She on her chain, and me on mine—the difference was insignificant.

Not allowed to be a child. Not allowed to romp in the beauty of a summer day. I wondered if that little girl had ever eaten ice cream. I know I had never tasted it in all of my ten years! I wondered what it tasted like as I watched the children and grown-ups make a mad dash to the ice cream cart. I saw my father scoot over there, smiling from ear to ear. He looked like the cat that swallowed the canary as he danced away with a great, big cone in his hand. As he passed by, he would look at me looking at him, and he would happily sing, "You scream, I scream, we all scream for ice cream. Rah! Rah! Rah!"

I was feeling more invisible than ever. Couldn't he see how bad I felt? I was so choked up with emotion, I couldn't say anything. I just stood there and watched him. That cone looked delicious, and my father was guzzling it down with such vim and vigor. Would he offer me any? He dared not! He knew better. And if he did, would I accept it? My mother's voice in my head was telling me, *No! It's not good for you! You don't need ice cream!* She did not say why, and I would not ask. The decision was made for me long before I could make it for myself. And I sulked about it in my state of deprivation.

As stifling as it was, I didn't think about any other way of life except being with my mother. It was all I knew, and I guess I was afraid to even entertain the thought of anything else. I was tied to her emotionally as much as ever. I couldn't even think of going from one place on the premises to another unless she was with me. Younger children traveled around freely, with or without friends, and parents were not watching their every move. Because I was not a little child, I was very ashamed that anyone should know how attached I was to my mother (as if they couldn't tell just by observing).

I resigned myself to watching the passing parade. I saw children at play, running about happily on the lawn. Grown-ups were laughing and talking with each other as they went strolling by. I stayed on the side with my mother; I couldn't move—and I didn't have a chain on my leg.

Even though I sensed my mother didn't want me to mingle with other children, she didn't stop me from talking to them. She was just a few feet away when two girls came by and started to speak to me. I felt awkward and ashamed as I attempted to talk; I could feel how unlike them I was and how unlike me they were. It was as if we came from two separate worlds and spoke a different language, and I suppose, in a way, we did. I didn't understand their way of life, nor did they understand mine.

It was usually the same with every child I met. Misunderstandings would occur. I was very insecure and couldn't hold my own. Frequently, a child made fun of my poor speech. "What kind of accent do you have? You speak funny . . ." And I was taunted because of my inability to speak clearly like other kids. My self-consciousness made it all the more difficult for me to speak at all. The way I dressed and looked was still another source of discomfort that I had to cope with. I wasn't like other kids—and they knew it. And so did I.

On top of that, I was extremely sensitive about every little thing. I hated to be ridiculed and didn't know how to respond. I felt a need to cry, but I just couldn't show that I was hurting. My mother would soon step in and handle the situation for me. My shame and anxiety abated—until a similar incident arose. And it went on like this from one episode to another.

I came away from these encounters feeling more alone and more let down than ever. How very much I longed to have contact with children my own age, but it wasn't happening. I was getting hurt emotionally, and I dreaded it. Children seemed to know how vulnerable I was, and they knew how to make me cringe. It was just too risky for me to try to make any friends. I was so glad that my mother was there to protect me. I felt safe with her around.

The feeling that I couldn't be liked by anyone intensified, and these experiences added more emotional scarring to what was already there. I just couldn't get over how very cruel children could be. Why was that so? It preyed on my mind. How insensitive they are, yet how sensitive they can be to perceive when something is wrong. They can just zero in on it and derive satisfaction out of making a peer feel bad. I would sit and wonder what it was in them that made them feed off someone else's discomfort and pain.

The horrible situations I found myself in only caused me to withdraw more into myself and to cling even more to my mother. I would console myself: *I don't really need them. I'm okay without them.* But I knew I was only kidding myself. And I continued to ache for the social contact I couldn't have.

Then one day I had a pleasant surprise. My mother and I were coming out of the dining room when my mother strolled over to the piano in the lobby. She sat down and started to play. She looked calm, composed, and rather pretty as her hands glided over the keyboard. I recognized the melody as the beautiful "Missouri Waltz." A few people stopped to listen. I was very proud of my mother. I soon asked her to play one of my favorite songs: "Laughing on the Outside, Crying on the Inside." She knew that song too, and she played that as well. I never knew she could play like that.

I soon found something to occupy my lonely moments. As I looked around, I saw blue skies, green grass, flower beds, and a little river in the distance. It was all so peaceful and refreshing. It was also very inspiring. I felt a need to capture the beauty that was surrounding me. I went inside to get my watercolors, and I was soon painting a little brick hut and a tiny bridge over a waterway. And I surprised myself; it actually looked good! One or two people who passed by were staring at it and said, "Did you do that?" I now had a sense of satisfaction, knowing I could create something beautiful like this, and I continued to make some more paintings.

There was something else that gave me a good feeling that year. I found myself attracted to a handsome young waiter at the resort. Alvin was tall, thin and had the most charming smile. He was holding down a summer job to pay expenses for medical school. I was particularly impressed that he was studying to become a doctor; I thought he must be very smart, and I looked up to him all the more. I just wished I were older than my ten years.

One day my mother left me alone on the porch of the main building and said, "I'll be back in a few minutes."

I was sitting on a small couch, and who should sit down next to me but Alvin! He started to speak to me, and I could feel my cheeks flush. A strong desire to kiss him welled up inside of me. I sat there as he smiled and made casual conversation. Before I knew it, my mother returned. Alvin sprung up from his seat and offered it to her. It was a sad moment for me. My mother was back—and Alvin was gone!

Whenever I was near Alvin, the song "It's Magic" popped up in my mind. I began to associate the song with Alvin. What a beautiful song of love it was! I remember going to bed at night with tears in my eyes and that song whirling around in my head. And I thought about Alvin.

I was sitting with my mother in the dining room, and I was staring at Alvin; he was so cute! I couldn't keep my eyes off him. Suddenly, out of the blue, my father appeared with a hurt smile on his face and announced in a loud, clear voice, "I don't know why I even bother to come out here when she has Alvin."

I was startled. I didn't know what to say. Everyone at the table was staring at me—including Alvin. I wanted to hide my face and run out of the room, but I didn't have the courage. So, I sat there, humiliated. My face was a bright red for all to see.

What made my father say something like that? We didn't have any kind of relationship. For the most part, he didn't even look at me. There was an uncomfortable distance between the two of us. Yet there he was, noticing me noticing Alvin!

Yes, I was infatuated with Alvin. I thought the world of him. I wanted to talk to him and take long walks with him; I wanted to hug and kiss him. But I was only a child.

How I hated the summer to end. How I hated to say good-bye to Spring Valley and its beautiful country land. Most of all, I hated to say good-bye to Alvin. Good-byes always made me sad—especially when I knew I would never see Alvin again.

15

He Left

We had just returned from the country, and I was sad that the warm, pleasant days of summer had come to an end. But I was thankful that my mother was feeling better after her operation. She continued to abuse my father with her verbal tongue-lashings, and he would shrug his shoulders and break out into a silly grin. Or he might just ignore her altogether. But it really bothered me: *Why can't he speak up to her?*

He still came home to eat dinner. Then he would leave, telling us he had things to do at the taxi garage. But suddenly he started coming home about three or four in the morning. Hedda began to notice some of his clothes missing. Something strange was going on.

About this time, I made another attempt at going back to school. After a few days, I began to feel chills and my throat was scratchy. I thought I would be bold and attempt to be like everyone else and go to school anyway. I made an announcement to Hedda: "I'm going to ask George to take me to school. We can all go together." Hedda did not seem to object.

I rarely asked my father for anything. I found it very hard to do, but I finally approached him and said, "Could you give me a ride to school? I think I'm coming down with something . . ."

"I can't do it. I have to go to work now." And he flew out the door.

I felt more than disappointed. The school was only two blocks from our home, and he wouldn't take me over there in his cab. I went with my mother that morning, and I felt kind of shaky. The next day I awoke with fever. I had aches and pains all over. My mother called the doctor. "She has it again! She has the grippe!"

I felt a burning anger. After the doctor left, I said to Hedda, "If he cared about me, he would have taken me to school. I hate my father! I never want to talk to him again!"

Shortly after that, Hedda and George had an argument late one night. I overheard her saying, "You couldn't make time to take your daughter to school when she was sick! Well, she has no use for you. She told me she hates you. Your daughter hates you!"

I lay in my bed, afraid to move or make a sound. I started to tremble. Those words stung: "Your daughter hates you!"

Then I heard my father speak in a low voice: "Now I know what I have to do."

I was frightened—terribly frightened. What did he mean by that?

Two weeks later, in the early morning, I heard my mother sobbing. I got out of bed and ran into the kitchen. I saw my mother standing there, clutching a note in her hand. She moaned, "Your father left . . ." Blood came rushing to her cheeks as she spoke; then I could barely hear her voice. I became very upset. What was she talking about? She went on. "I found a note on the table from George." And she handed it to me:

Dear Hedda,

As you know we have been unhappy for a very long time. I don't think that we can ever have a happily married life. I think it is for the best that we face the situation, and separate. I think that you, Lenore and I will be happier this way. I shall send you every week sufficient money for the support of you and Lenore. I am sorry that things have turned out this way, but as I said before, it is for the best for all of us.

Good luck.

George

What? He left? Oh no! I was startled. I felt sick, and then I didn't know what I was feeling. I blocked out everything around me. I don't recall how long I remained in that state of numbness, but when I began to recover from the initial shock, I looked around and saw my one friend, the radio. It seemed to be waiting for me. I went over and switched it on, and it came alive. I turned the dial and I heard songs with sad lyrics—songs that hurt and made me want to cry. As I lingered in fantasy, I was getting a taste of reality: my father had left. Maybe he was gone for good.

Why did I have to hate my father just because he didn't drive me to school? Why did I have to say those nasty things about him? Why did she have to go back and repeat them? I was angry with myself; I felt it was my fault that he had left.

One day Grandma came in looking more downcast than usual as she started to speak with Hedda. "I just came from the grocery store. George has a friend in the neighborhood, Hal. He drives a cab and lives somewhere around here. Hal is spreading stories that George left home because he gave you money and you didn't put any food on the table. He said George didn't have anything to eat when he came home at night. He also said that you kept him away from his child, and he couldn't bear his life anymore—so he left home and went out dancing. Oy, it's no good."

Hedda's eyes began to bulge. "I knew it! I knew it! He's running around with women and having a good time! And who the hell is this 'Hal'? And where is he getting his stories from? George always had a meal when he came home."

Hedda turned to me. "See how nice your father is. He slowly sneaks out a pair of shoes, then a pair of pants, then some shirts. And where does he go? He goes out dancing! I knew something funny was going on. I never should have married him. He should have married Toby, that big, fat slob who worked in the launderette."

Hedda stopped for a breath then waved her hand and said, "Good riddance to bad rubbish!"

I sat there, confused, and lost. It felt awful to hear those horrible stories about my father. Soon afterwards, when Grandma came with our groceries, she was unable to contain herself. "He should be ashamed of himself—running around to dances, leaving his wife and sick child. He should only break his hands and legs. He's rotten to the core . . ." She continued to talk in a loud voice as her face reddened with anger. I sat there, looking at Grandma in a fit of rage. Oh, how I wished she would go home.

Soon Grandpa came up and started to rant. "He's a bum. He left his wife and child to run around with women. He's no good. He'll get what he deserves, just wait and see!" I never saw Grandpa so angry as he waved his finger back and forth, sounding like the voice of authority. All this talk was making me more nervous and on edge. I couldn't wait for him to take his predictions and leave.

Yes, it was a terrible thing my father did, and I was very disturbed by it, but my grandparents coming up and cursing him out didn't change the situation or make things any better. I cringed as they spoke. I began to tune out their voices. I was feeling bad— really bad.

When I turned the radio on, I heard songs that made my sad feelings come alive. Then I began to cry. I didn't realize how much I was missing him even though he was seldom around and not available to me. I suddenly had a strong need to see George, but he was nowhere to be found. It was as if he had vanished into thin air.

I continued to sing along with songs of despair and loss that I heard on the radio. The things I could not express in words I was able to express in song. There was one song in particular that brought tears streaming down my face. It was "Maybe You'll Be There," and it was on the radio all the time. The lyrics would haunt me. It was all about the pain of losing someone and desperately trying to find the person who disappeared. I listened for that song. The words helped me to feel my pain and to tell my father, in my heart, how very much I missed him. The song also gave me hope. I told myself that he couldn't dismiss me from his life forever. Sooner or later, he would return.

In the mail came weekly checks for fifty dollars. No note attached. No return address. Hedda said, "The postmark says Brooklyn. He must be staying with his brother, Marvin, or his glorious sister, Bea. So, let him stay there."

I often wondered what we would do if there was an emergency and we needed to reach him. The thought was very disturbing, so I quickly put it out of my mind. And I stood at the window watching the cars scurrying up and down the block. I saw taxis stop in front of the building. But they were not my father's yellow cab with Father Knickerbocker on the door.

The days were slipping away—and still no George. I began to think that I would never see him again. But then I told myself that it was a silly thought. I listened to my radio and cried some more. *Will I ever see my father again?*

I kept having fantasies about growing up and breaking away from my mother; I would go downtown and look for my father at his taxi stand. Wouldn't he be surprised to see me? Perhaps we could share some happy, tender moments together. Perhaps we could even make up for lost time.

It began to rain and snow. It felt dreary even when the sun was out. *Where's George?* And the same question came up again to haunt me: *When will I see him again?* I put on the radio, and I heard that song again. Life was nothing more than waiting for that doorbell to ring. *Will I ever hear his voice at the door?*

And I was still waiting.

16

He Came To Visit

The night before my eleventh birthday, the doorbell rang. My mother opened the door, and there was my father! I was in utter disbelief; I could feel my heart pounding. Three months had passed, and we hadn't heard from him. I thought I would never see him again.

He looked different. I didn't know what it was; maybe it was his new horn-rimmed glasses that gave him a new appearance. I thought he looked good, but somewhat tired and unhappy, as if he were carrying the weight of the world on his shoulders. From the moment he came in, he was on pins and needles to leave. "I can't stay. I just wanted to stop by because it's her birthday."

I don't think he stayed for more than ten minutes. As he was getting ready to leave, I suddenly picked up the courage to say, "George, I miss you. When will you come again?"

I was surprised to hear him say, "I'll be here next Monday night."

How delighted I was to hear that! Perhaps there was a chance he would come home to stay. I held that hope in my heart.

The following Monday I was eagerly watching the clock. He came at seven o'clock, as promised. He went into the living room and sat down in the easy chair opposite me in my rocking chair. He closed his eyes and seemed to be listening to the soft, relaxing music on the radio. He did not utter a word and I wondered if he was sleeping. I began to feel bad. My father was sitting in the same room with me, and he had absolutely nothing to say to me. Was I invisible? Did he know I was there? At eight o'clock, he picked himself up and left.

He began to see me every Monday night; he would come in, sit down in the easy chair, and close his eyes for an hour. Then he would leave.

Finally, I said: "Don't you sleep at night? You always sleep when you come here to see me."

He replied: "I'm depressed when I come here. The apartment is dark and dreary. Everything in this house is depressing to me."

Then he closed his eyes again. I did not know how to respond. *Am I dark, dreary, and depressing like everything else in the house? Why can't he talk to me? Why can't he say something—anything?* How I longed to hear my father's voice. But it continued this way; he had nothing to say to me, and I couldn't find the voice to say anything to him.

I was very sad after his visits. I might say that I felt more alone than ever. My father was there in the room with me, but he wasn't really with me. I didn't know where he was.

I wondered why he was coming to see me. It was obvious that he wasn't interested in talking to me. I felt very hurt to see him sitting there, sleeping for the hour he was with me, ignoring me as if I weren't there.

(Later, I found out that he did not come of his own volition. In my uncle's file I saw a notation that he urged George to visit me because Grandma was telling him I was crying all the time and I missed him very much. I was very angry when I learned this. He didn't really want to see me. It was someone else's idea.)

On the nights when he came to visit, my mother dressed up and looked positively beautiful. What an amazing transformation in her. She put away her raggedy, worn-out jumper and dirty robe, and looked tall and stately in her royal blue dress. Her hair was combed and fluffed out. Her lipstick was a vibrant, glowing red, which she applied in the shape of a heart. She used a little powder and a touch of rouge. It was obvious that she was trying to make herself attractive for my father.

While I was in the living room with my father, Hedda spent most of her time in the kitchen. At times I would hear her pacing back and forth between rooms, trying to be inconspicuous. For the most part, she was very quiet, but I surmised she was listening in another room. Whenever my father and I would exchange a word or two, Hedda would walk into the room rather casually, supposedly looking for something or other. When she left, my father broke out in a big grin and winked at me with a rather engaging smile. "There goes Hawkeye!" It was a rare moment I shared with my father; I felt he was able to see me, and the world I was living in with Hedda— at least in that moment.

At times I saw him tapping his feet to the music on the radio, and eventually I said: "George, why don't you sing along with me?" He quickly replied, "I can't sing, I don't have enough breath." I wondered what he meant by not having enough breath, but I did not ask.

One evening he actually spoke to me; he told me about his sister Bea's daughter. "Lisa runs over to me, puts her arms around my neck, and she kisses me." I could see that hurt look on his face. Was he asking me to come over to him, put my arms around him and kiss him like Lisa? I suddenly felt my cheeks flush. I didn't know what to say. I didn't know how to tell him that I wanted to hug and kiss him, too, but I was not supposed to hug or kiss anyone—nor was I to be hugged and kissed. He knew that. These were Hedda's Rules. I was much too afraid to tamper with them, and I didn't know how to be different. Then again, neither did he.

"Your cousin Lisa is a very talented girl. She's only thirteen, and she's giving a piano recital at Town Hall…"

I felt an ache that made me want to cry. I was not like Lisa. I couldn't do things like Lisa. She was a success; I was a failure. I was nothing. I couldn't even show affection to my own father!

I didn't want to hear any more stories about Lisa. I was very hurt and envious of her. I felt bad enough about myself and didn't want to feel worse. I hated to feel that stifling pain. But the things he told me about her lingered in my mind and continued to haunt me.

Valentine's Day was fast approaching, and I had an idea. I would sing "My Funny Valentine," a song of love, to my father on a day that signified love. I was afraid he might laugh at me, but it was something I had to do. Nothing would stop me—not even Hedda. She heard me sing all the time, so she would never know I was singing to my father.

Valentine's Day came, and my concern was to find that song on the radio during my father's visit. As I turned the dial from station to station, I finally came upon it. When I heard the announcement that "My Funny Valentine" would be next, my heart began to beat like a drum. It was my opportunity to show my father that I loved him. I quickly sat down in my rocking chair and whispered, "George, I have a song just for you."

His eyes met mine, and he smiled that sad smile. I went ahead and sang the song to him, pouring my heart into each lyric. He just sat there, seemingly unmoved, with a blank look on his face. Soon he closed his eyes. I felt my spirit shatter into pieces. It all seemed so futile. Again, I sadly realized that I was physically in the same room with my father, but he was miles and miles away, and I was all alone with my pain.

Despite his inattentiveness, I still yearned for my father's love. I pleaded with my mother to have some private time with him. "If I could be completely alone with him, then maybe I could talk to him about coming home." She finally agreed. "Next time, I'll leave you alone with your father."

When Monday night rolled around, Hedda slipped into her coat and casually said, "I'll be back shortly."

I wondered if he was surprised at Hedda's sudden departure, but he didn't say anything. He sat in his chair, quiet as usual, and I sat in mine. I was very nervous. What was I going to say and how was I going to say it? All I knew was that I had to make him understand. "George, I have to tell you something. I miss you very much. If you would come home, we could try and make things different…."

My father sat there, totally unmoved. A few minutes later, a slight smile appeared on his face, and then he spoke. "From the day I married your mother she wanted to live with her parents. I wanted to be alone with her. It was crowded, living with her parents and brother. There were many fights, and this went on for years. When you were born, I couldn't tolerate it any longer. I threatened to leave, and I asked Hedda to go with me. Hedda finally consented to leave her parents after eleven years."

My mind drifted a bit. Hedda had told me an altogether different story: "I wanted to move out and live alone with your father, but he wanted to live with my parents. He was so damn stingy. He didn't want to know from bills and paying rent when he could get it for free."

When I returned to the present, I heard George saying: "I loved your mother very much at one time, but I could never be happy with her anymore. There's nothing between us."

What could I say that would make him want to come home? It now seemed so hopeless.

After a pause, he asked: "Would you rather have a dead father in the house, or a live father out of the house?"

I was startled and confused by his question. I didn't know how to respond. I finally forced the words out: "A live father out of the house."

A hush fell over the room. He had a look of anguish on his face. My mind went blank, and I couldn't feel anything.

I soon heard a key in the lock. It seemed like an eternity and yet it was less than an hour. Hedda was back! I felt more despondent than ever.

My father reached for his jacket and said, "It's time to go."

He walked towards the door. I felt my world crumbling, as I gave up hope that my father would ever return home to stay.

A couple of months later, George and his brother, Marvin, went to Miami Beach. He said he needed a short vacation to "get away from it all." There I was, sick all winter, cooped up in the house with debilitating respiratory infections, and my father was off to the beautiful warm climate of Florida! I said to myself: *For all I care, he can stay there! If I never see him again, it will be too soon!*

However, I was glad to see him when he returned. He came in sporting a golden tan that gave him a vibrant look of good health. And again, he was wearing new spectacles that gave him a distinguished appearance. I commented, "You look very handsome with your new eyeglasses."

He smiled and said, "My brother, Marvin, said I look like Harry Truman." I didn't see the resemblance, but I wasn't about to go there. I wondered what we could talk about, and then I blurted out: "I hate to go out in cold weather. I'm always getting sick. I hear it's so nice and warm in Florida."

"Well, kid-o, you need to acclimate yourself to the winter weather."

"Acclimate"? I never heard that word before. And why was he calling me "kid-o"? The old George was simple, unpretentious, and very plain. I said, "Gee, you're so different. I hardly know you."

"I'm attending lectures with my brother. Maybe that has something to do with it."

I was disappointed. There I was, telling him about my inability to handle the cold weather, and he wasn't showing any interest in me or how I was living. Couldn't he see that I was hurting inside? But I overlooked all of this, because I was so glad my father had come to see me.

He came to visit one Monday evening when one of my favorite songs was playing on the radio. It was a hit song from the Broadway musical, "South Pacific." I made the radio louder and sang along with it. How I enjoyed singing "I'm In Love with a Wonderful Guy" and somehow, I wanted to share this with my father.

There he was, sitting in the easy chair, eyes closed—as usual—with his hand holding up his head, as his elbow rested on the arm of the chair. I kept on singing after the song ended: "I'm as corny as Kansas in August, I'm as normal as blueberry pie…."

George opened his eyes and suddenly looked up. With an odd smile on his face and a mocking tone in his voice, he made a comment: "Normal? Did you say you were normal?"

His words stung and so did that pained look on his face. I wanted to cry, but I didn't want him to see how hurt I was. I flashed back to the time when he said: "You're clumsy!" He made me feel

I was incapable of performing a simple feat like taking a bow. Now he was saying I wasn't "normal."

I suddenly felt as if a hole had opened and I was falling into it. I found myself staring at him. I didn't know how to reply. I certainly did not feel "normal," but I hated to hear my own father say it. The truth was painful; I was different. Is that why he was sleeping when he visited me? Because he didn't want to see a daughter who was not like everyone else?

I felt that no one in the world would ever like me or accept me. Long after he left that night, his words were ringing in my ears. I no longer had the same desire to sing my songs when he was around, but what else could I do? Just sit in my chair and watch him sleep? So, I continued to sing along with the radio, as if nothing had happened. My radio, my music—it was my source of comfort; it was my connection to life.

One evening in March, after my twelfth birthday, my father came in and said, "I won't be here next week. I'm going back to Florida."

My goodness, another trip to Florida? I didn't know what to say. I had to work hard at holding back my many mixed feelings of envy, anger, and disappointment, but I had become quite good at that. How I wished I could go to the Sunshine State, but I knew it wasn't about to happen. So, there was no point dwelling on it and yet I couldn't stop myself.

Soon I received a picture postcard from Miami. I didn't want to see it; I didn't want to know how much he was enjoying Florida, when I was plodding through another frigid winter in New York. As I looked at the beautiful beach and palm trees on the postcard, I thought about the doctor telling me, "Go to Florida. Your health will improve there." I suddenly felt sick to my stomach.

It was about two weeks later when my father returned. He was very tan and looked like the picture of health. Although he had put on a little weight, I still thought he looked absolutely fantastic! He came into the kitchen just as the hit song "Enjoy Yourself" was playing on the radio.

As I looked at George, I could sense something was wrong. He looked tense and troubled. And then the lyrics of the song came bouncing by in a light, jubilant manner: "Enjoy yourself, enjoy yourself, it's later than you think…" George quickly responded. "That's right, I better enjoy myself—it's later than I think!" What a strange thing to say! *What did he mean by that?*

The song finished, and he was staring at me. He turned to Hedda and said: "She's wearing glasses? Since when?" As he spoke, his voice dropped. He seemed anxious as he waited for her answer. But she didn't respond. I thought, *"That's how much he's noticed me! I've been wearing glasses for years!"*

He frowned when he saw a coat hanging on the bedroom door. "Why, that's a brand new coat! It looks like it never was worn."

He was right; it was never on my back. My mother said, "I had a tailor come up to make that coat for her." I saw a pained look on his face.

He soon turned to Hedda and said, "I'd like to speak to you alone."

I could feel my heart pounding. I knew now that something was very wrong. As they walked into the kitchen, I felt a need to eavesdrop.

"I can't take this life any longer, and I have no intentions of returning to it. I am suing for a legal separation and ultimately, a divorce. I have pains around my heart, and I have high blood pressure. I will not be able to work as much, and I will have to give you less money."

There was silence. Then Hedda pressed the question: "Did you meet someone in Florida?"

My father was slow to respond. "Yes, I met a woman who I think I can be happy with. At least, I'm going to try."

It suddenly felt like the end of the world to me; I began to tremble. And then I heard my mother say, loud and clear: "I will not give you a divorce!"

They continued to talk, but I didn't hear a thing. My emotions were running wild. *I hate that woman in Florida. I don't want him to marry her. I wish he were dead rather than marry her!*

I ran into the kitchen and started to cry. My mother said, "Look at her! Look at what you've done to her!"

George looked at me and turned to Hedda: "I'm sorry for her. Someday she'll know the truth. She'll see it all when she gets older."

George headed for the door. Without turning back, he put his hand on the knob and said goodnight. And he was gone.

I frantically worried: *Oh no! He's going to make a new life for himself, and he'll forget all about me. He'll never want to see me again!*

Several weeks passed, and there was no word from him. The regular weekly check came in the mail—and stopped. And then we received a letter from George. He said, "I went to a doctor and was diagnosed with a heart condition. The doctor advised me not to work. I need money for living and medical expenses. Can you send me money from our joint account to my sister's address in Brooklyn?"

"**No!** He's not getting any money from me! It's a lot of crap. I know what he wants that money for. He wants to go to Reno for a quickie divorce!" My mother held steadfast to her belief, and she did not send any money.

But what if he isn't lying? Maybe he needs that money for medical expenses. Conflicting thoughts whirled around in my head. But eventually a fit of anger overtook me, and I convinced myself that my mother was right.

There was no further word from him. My mother said, "Maybe I'll send a detective to his sister's place in Brooklyn to find out what's going on." But later she said, "Why bother?"

17

Time and Time Again

"Spring will still follow December. Stars will continue to shine. And through the years I'll remember the love that was never quite mine . . ."

I heard a song that charmed me—and haunted me. It was a tender refrain that would sweep over me like a gentle breeze on a balmy summer day and captivate me with its moody, touching quality. I was moved by the magic of David Rose and his strings. The lyrics of "Time and Time Again" kept spinning around in my head. Whether I sat on a chair in my living room or lay in my bed with my eyes closed, I kept hearing that song. It brought out the sadness in me.

Two months had passed. Not a word from my father. I tried not to think about him as my mother prepared for our trip to the country. Summer had just begun, and it was time to go back to Spring Valley. But this year would be different; the days of the resort hotels were over. My mother said, "We're going to a bungalow." I thought to myself, A bungalow? What is a bungalow? How did she find this place? But I wasn't about to ask. I trusted my mother. She was a smart lady; she knew what she was doing. Or so I thought.

She soon called a taxi service, and in no time, we were there. The bungalow looked like a small house with a big porch. There weren't any other houses around, and it looked kind of deserted to me. It would have been nice to see people passing by. But that didn't really bother me; I was used to being alone with Hedda. But there was something troubling me deeply: What had happened to my father?

It was the first week in July, and my mother lit the Sabbath candles as usual on Friday night. The candle flame began to flutter wildly, almost as if a strong wind was blowing it. I had never seen a candle burn like that before. I moved away from it. The strange flickering frightened me.

I had on the radio and I heard Toni Arden singing the song "Tonight." I could not relax and enjoy the warmth of her voice; I was too busy watching the candle flame flicker in a fit of frenzy.

I was out on the porch the following day when I saw two people heading towards our bungalow. I was very surprised, and shocked, to see my grandmother. Even more alarming, she was accompanied by a man I had never seen before. As she came closer, I saw her eyes were red and swollen. I could barely hear her voice as she asked, "Where's Hedda?"

Hedda heard us talking and came right out. She looked stunned as she said to me, "My mother and George's brother, Marvin. What are they doing here?"

I thought to myself, So this is my father's brother! I heard so many bad things about him. He looked very sad, too.

Grandma beckoned to Hedda to come down. I watched my mother descend the steps of our porch into the beautiful July sunshine. I stayed on the porch and watched them talk, but I could not hear what they were saying.

Suddenly, my mother reached out and leaned her hand on the wall of the bungalow as if she were about to fall. I panicked. Oh, my God, something terrible must have happened! A cloud of dread came over me. Where was Grandpa? He wasn't there. From the way Hedda was sobbing, I thought that something had happened to Grandpa. And why was Uncle Marvin there?

My mother soon said, "We're going to be leaving now. We're going back to the city. Your father is very ill in the hospital, and I have to see him—but you will be staying home."

I began to tremble. If he were sick, why couldn't I see him?

We were heading back to the Bronx in Marvin's taxi, and I was shaking. I looked over at Grandma; an expression of grief covered her face. Tears were in my mother's eyes. Marvin kept his eye on the road and didn't talk. I could feel that something terrible had happened.

That night I went to bed with a dreadful feeling that my father had died. I said to myself, My heart is breaking into a million pieces—I'll never be the same. I lay there, in the dark of night, trembling in my bed as a wave of panic swept over me.

And soon I was struck by some very disturbing thoughts: It was only two months ago that he wanted a divorce to marry that woman in Florida. How I hated him. I wished him dead. Oh, my God, what a terrible thing! If only I hadn't wished that. Did I have some kind of demonic power to cause my father's death?

Emotional pain surged within me with such intensity that I wanted to scream: No. No. I didn't mean it! I didn't mean it!

However, at the time, I did mean it.

But perhaps he was not dead. Somewhere within, there was a hope in my heart that this was some kind of a bad dream, a figment of my imagination. When I had last seen him, he looked so healthy, so robust, how could this possibly be? Maybe my mother didn't want me to see him ill in the hospital.

But that didn't feel right either. I had seen that look of terror upon my mother's face. I was feeling her grief. I felt as though I was in mourning, and yet I couldn't begin the mourning process. I was twisting back and forth in my turmoil. Soon I found it more comforting to hold on to the belief that George was alive rather than think he had died, his life obliterated like a candle snuffed out in the night. Yet I couldn't get out of my mind those candles burning with such intensity that night.

And I kept hearing that song. It was whirling around in my head: "Time and time again you'll hear me call and darling then, you'll know I need you (I need you) . . ."

The following morning, Grandma and Grandpa came over. They both looked troubled and worn. My mother appeared in a black dress, looking pale and fragile. Grandma was also dressed in black. She had come to accompany my mother "to the hospital."

My heart started to pound, and I gathered the courage to timidly ask, "Did something happen to my father?"

I held my breath, afraid to hear the answer. Both my mother and grandmother became rather guarded. My mother said, "Your father is very ill in the hospital."

Grandma, however, said, "Gawd takes people who are very ill—it's for the best, so they don't have to suffer."

I didn't seem to hear those words, or perhaps I didn't want to. If it were true that my father had died, how would I ever be able to deal with it? I chose to believe what I wanted to: my father was alive and sick in a hospital. It had to be true; my mother told me so.

I stayed with Grandpa all afternoon. I nervously paced up and down. And more thoughts came to me. My mother and I are rarely apart. Why did she suddenly leave me with Grandpa? Again, I sensed that my mother had gone to my father's funeral, but I prayed in my heart that I was wrong.

As I moped around the apartment, I had a flashback of my father. He looked so nice and peaceful with a pipe in his hand. And then suddenly he stopped smoking—just like that. I went over to him and asked, "George, why don't you smoke your pipe anymore?"

He somberly responded, "I had chest pains right after mowing the lawn in Spring Valley. So, I went to see the doctor. He told me I strained a ligament around the heart. He said I should stop smoking, and I did just that. No more pipe."

That happened some time ago, but now that scene was vivid in my mind. He must have been ill for some time with a heart condition. Oh, my God, I didn't know. I didn't want to know.

That memory was tearing me apart.

And soon my mother was back. Her eyes were red, and her face was white as a sheet. She appeared weak, as if her legs were not strong enough to support her body. Grandma's face told a story of despair. I did not want to look at Hedda or Grandma; I had to turn away.

That haunting melody kept coming back to me: "And time and time again, my heart will sigh remembering when I gave my love to you."

It seemed as if those lyrics were trying to tell me something. Suddenly tears started to roll down my cheeks.

Within a few days, we returned to Spring Valley. I would frequently turn to Hedda and ask, "How is George?" I always received the same response: "Your father is very sick in the hospital."

She had a sad look on her face, and her tone rarely changed. My eyes met hers, and a feeling of helplessness overwhelmed me. I was left at a loss for words. But distraught as I was, I had asked the question I needed to ask, and she had answered it. It was what I had expected. For the time being: subject closed, no further questions.

As usual, Hedda said little and showed no feeling other than the times when I asked about George. Then some emotion might trickle through. But Hedda remained aloof.

Bungalow life was really lonely. I don't recall seeing many people around. If we needed something in the village, my mother would phone the taxi service. It may have been somewhat extravagant, but she got used to calling for taxis on a regular basis. I could now ride in a car without throwing up, so traveling around Spring Valley, and other nearby towns, became a diversion for both of us. It took us away from our nothingness existence. Except for these taxi excursions, the summer was just a continuation of an isolated existence for me.

Labor Day had come and gone, and it was time to say good-bye to Spring Valley. My mother was packing, and we were getting ready to leave, when I began to feel ill. I was extremely flushed, and I had pains in my legs that were so bad, I could hardly walk.

My mother located a local doctor, who came to our bungalow. It felt strange to be treated by a doctor whom I didn't know. Rather befuddled, he said, "There's nothing so far that tells me what's wrong with her."

I became more frightened as he spoke. Why couldn't I walk?

Finally, he came upon what appeared to be a slight scratchiness in my throat. "It seems like a bacterial infection, and it should clear up nicely with penicillin."

He took out his pad and wrote a prescription. He was right. My symptoms abated nicely on the drug. In a few days, we were ready to leave. I was relieved and so thankful that it wasn't polio.

It had been a long, tough summer, but we managed to muddle through. My mother called the cab service, and we went back to the city. It was back to life the way we knew it. But memories of this summer did not fade easily. It was a summer I would remember time and time again.

18

Eight Months Straight

I was twelve years old, and the fall semester had already begun. I was supposed to return to school, but I couldn't make it. The bacterial infection I had contracted in the country left me tired and weak. It was a blessing in disguise. I had a perfect excuse to remain at home.

A month later, there was a new physician coming to our home. He was replacing our regular doctor, who was away on vacation. As Dr. Gross walked into our living room, I thought, *Such a handsome man. My goodness, he could have been a movie actor!* He stood tall in his long overcoat and dark-gray hat, with satchel in hand. When he removed his hat, his slightly-graying hair added to his stately, dignified appearance. He greeted us with a smile and said, "What can I do for you?"

My mother's eyes were gleaming. I could tell that she had taken an immediate liking to the doctor. Then she spoke. "My daughter became ill in the country, and she's still not well . . ."

He began to examine me, and she went on. "The least thing, my daughter gets sick. She's like this all winter when she goes out to school . . ."

She filled him in on my infections and soon asked him for a note. She handed him a piece of paper and said, "This is the kind of note I need for school."

Dr. Gross took out his pen and pad and began writing: *"Lenore Ossen is subject to frequent upper respiratory infections, and these attacks do not respond too well to treatment. I believe that private home instruction would be beneficial to her health."*

It was as simple as that. A brief note, and I was on my way. I did not have to worry about school until the next note was due, which was in the fall of the following year. The doctor notes had legitimized my right to stay home. I was grateful to have them. I would not have to go out into the cold and bundle up as if I were Alaska-bound. I could avoid the wretched winds of winter. I could forget about the teachers, the children, and everything else about school that made my stomach churn. I could curl up inside my cocoon and escape from the outside world. For me, there was no world outside my windowpane.

But it was not as comfortable as it appeared. Since my mother had her hernia operation, her side became permanently swollen, and she started to experience other physical complaints. One of them was a scratchy throat. She held a mirror to her throat and saw white spots. Was it some kind of an infection? I suggested that she see the doctor. "Maybe he could give you penicillin for whatever it is."

Hedda became very annoyed. "I'm not taking any penicillin! And I'm not seeing any doctor!"

Grandma had now become Dr. Grandma; with a flashlight and a mirror in her hand, she would look into my mother's throat and sadly comment: "Those white patches are still there."

I found it rather nerve-racking. *What is this all about? When will those "white patches" go away?* Hedda now refused to venture out of the house. She soon made an announcement: "I'm not going out till I get rid of these spots!" And I, of course, would not go out without her. In October of that year—just three months before I turned thirteen—we locked ourselves away in the house. But I was used to spending most of my winters indoors anyway, so I really didn't mind.

I felt sorry for Grandma. The total shopping burden fell directly upon her. She was now making daily stops in the neighborhood for both herself and for us. She climbed the stairs to our apartment, huffing and puffing, carrying shopping bags full of food. Then I saw my mother and Grandma figuring out what my mother owed for the groceries and produce. Grandma looked so tired; I often wondered how she managed. I also wondered how we would have survived if it hadn't been for her.

Grandma was now in her early sixties, and she displayed a robust, healthy appearance with just a tinge of powder and rouge. But most of the time, she didn't wear makeup; she liked things natural, and she enjoyed being natural herself. She wore her long, dark hair twisted neatly in a bun on the back of her neck. Sometimes I would just sit and look at her and feel a warm glow.

Grandma continued to live a very unhappy life with Grandpa. As soon as she came through the door, she would plop into a chair and talk about her woes. "He's so stubborn, you can't do a thing with him. He can hardly walk, yet he goes to work. You can't keep him home! You don't know what I have . . ."

And there were times when she would forget about her troubles. Sometimes she might tell a joke and break out in laughter, as if she didn't have a care in the world, but those times were rare. There were moments when she'd curse like a sailor. I did not find that aspect of her particularly attractive, but Grandma was a very important person in my life. I accepted her however she was. I knew her heart was heavy with sorrow. I also knew that she was not well.

Sometimes Grandma spoke about my father. "What Gawd takes is for the best . . ."

I didn't want to hear that, but I didn't know how to tell her. Soon, my mother came into the room and cut her off. "Leave her alone! You keep on stirring up trouble! You don't know when to leave well enough alone." And with a sad, troubled look on her face, Grandma would stop talking.

Soon, Grandma would leave. Her visits were usually short, unpleasant, and filled with tension. But how wonderful it was to hear her knocking on the door, if only for that moment. Life with my mother was an ongoing nightmare. I was living a scary, isolated existence under my mother's relentless control. I turned to my radio to help me get through the day.

And soon I found something that brought a smile to my face. As I browsed through my movie magazines, I came upon pictures that caught my eye. I found some of them exciting and some quite exotic. After a long time of not caring to do any artwork, I suddenly had an urge to reproduce what I saw. I took a plain sheet of paper, a pen or pencil, and sometimes, colored pencils, and I started to draw. Just like that!

I particularly liked to draw dancers. I found it exciting to capture the spirit of a dancer in action. I drew a male dancer in what appeared to be midair. His eyes were popping, and his mouth was wide open, and he appeared to be having a great time. I caught that feeling with my pen, and I loved it! I drew many dance scenes after that. I was constantly on the alert for pictures that appealed to my fancy. If I could catch a happy expression, I was in my glory. It was all so satisfying and serene. I could snap out of the doldrums and feel exhilaration as I made my subject come to life on a sheet of paper. I now had something to look forward to besides my music and my radio programs.

One day two visitors came to our door. It seemed like ages since I had last seen them, but there they were: my uncle Will and his wife, Jessie. Suddenly, my mother was smiling and welcoming them into our home. Why would my mother want to see her brother when one of her favorite pastimes was cursing him for wrecking her life? She spoke harshly of his wife as well. I just couldn't figure out if they were our enemies or friends, but somehow, it didn't matter; a part of me was glad to see them. In fact, I was glad to see anyone!

Will and Jessie were now visiting us regularly. They stayed for a short time, and their visits were nice and pleasant. I was not aware of anything unusual going on, but in my uncle's file, I found several letters that my mother wrote to them. And this is a part of one that Hedda wrote to Will:

"She just went to bed and I thought of a few things. When you have a little time, please write a few answers to the questions you think they may ask. Don't give any unnecessary information.

I also may have a few things I'd like to ask you next time I see you. Don't say you got this letter, as she is suspicious and worried about George. They may ask when and how George got ill? If they ask would you say I was in the country? Don't say we were separated.

If you have anything to say (and I know you will), I'll look in your pocket for a note next time you come up . . ."

What was this all about? I had no idea. And this is a small excerpt from a letter to Jessie:

"You will never know how much I appreciate your going to school for me. I'd very much like to know what you said about George. Will you please write a note and put it in your pocket or Will's pocket when you come up and I'll take it out?"

I was shocked to learn of these maneuvers. Where was I when all this pickpocketing was going on? I had no knowledge of the things that were going on right before my eyes.

Will responded to one of Hedda's letters with this simple statement:

"Positively nothing will be disclosed about Belmont Avenue or George's separation."

Whatever it was, the issue was resolved quickly enough. Soon, there was a note in the file that my uncle wrote to himself:

"Heated controversy with Hedda; she asked me not to come again. Will abide by her wishes."

Hedda's vendetta against her brother was as strong as ever. What did he do now to make her so upset? My uncle was banished from our home once more, and I wondered if I would ever see him again.

It was back to our lonely existence. I was sitting in the kitchen with Hedda and she had that mournful look on her face. I had seen it so many times, but I never got used to it. The sound of silence was making me uneasy. I needed my radio to soothe me and make me feel better. I went into the living room and put on my music. I sat down in my rocking chair and soon, I was rocking my cares away. Hedda came in and perched herself on a nearby chair. She was listening to the music with me. It was pretty much what we were doing for years—in between all of the tumultuous times we endured. Only now, there was no prospect of going out of the house.

The tutor came several hours each week, and I kept muddling through my lessons. I could hardly concentrate, but I did the best I could. I felt fortunate that my homebound teachers did not make great demands upon me. Some of them took time to talk about themselves. It was a welcome relief from the monotony of schoolwork. I was at a point where I wanted to free myself from anything and everything that was related to school.

And I constantly asked about George. Hedda continued to tell me the same story: "Your father is very ill in the hospital."

I went along with it. But if that were true, why didn't she go to see him? I was afraid to mention it. I somehow needed to go along with her story. Maybe I was living in a world of make-believe, but I needed to be reassured that my father was alive. Then things would be okay in my world.

But, in reality, things were not okay in my world. I was George's daughter, but I had not been a real daughter to him. I did not show him love and affection. When he stopped visiting me and said he was ill, I did not believe him. When I heard the word "divorce," I wished him dead. How much more terrible could I be?

I was more than depressed. There were times when I was so despondent, I didn't know if I could make it through another day. I was fortunate to have one friend—a constant companion that stuck with me through thick and thin. This friend continued to tide me over the worst times and keep me in touch with the outside world. Thank God for Mr. Radio. I began to think of it as the best friend I would ever have. The music, the singers, and the soap operas—they were helping me to survive.

Grandma continued to make her short visits. As the months went by, Grandma remained the source of our food supply. And when Hedda walked out of the room, Grandma would whisper to me: "What Gawd takes is for the best—when a person is suffering."

There was a look of despair on her face. I still did not ask any questions, but I felt awful inside. As we looked into each other's eyes, I had a feeling she knew that I knew.

I held on to my fantasy. If Hedda wanted me to know that my father was dead, she would have told me. But I could not come out and say it myself. I felt compelled to do it Hedda's way; it seemed like the only way.

Just before she would leave, Grandma would ask for the flashlight and look into my mother's throat. Each time she would sadly say, "Oy, those spots are still there—they're still white!"

My mother would then take out her hand mirror, look at the spots, and say, "I can't get rid of them!"

I felt sad too. I didn't know if those spots would ever go away.

It went on like that until one day my mother put the mirror down—and Grandma put her flashlight away.

It was a bleak eight months in the house. We did not inhale a breath of fresh air during that time. With the onset of summer, we finally broke out of our cocoon; we had been hibernating long enough. It was time to come alive and do things we were afraid to do—like venture outside.

19
Coming of Age

A few words appear on a plain white piece of paper from my uncle's files:

"Lenore seems to have asserted herself over the summer. For the first time in her life she goes downstairs alone, comes up alone, and runs errands. The adolescent has come of age."

My mother and I had just lived through an eight-month period that seemed like an exile from the world. When summer came, my mother felt well enough to go out—and I went with her. It was my first summer in the city since my mother was taken away to Bellevue.

Summer was a wonderful time of the year for me. It was a time when we went to the country, and I saw life outside my four walls. I could come out of hibernation and experience the beauty and comfort of a warm, sunny day. It was a delight to breathe in the fragrance of fresh air. I had a feeling of freedom as I tossed aside my heavy clothing. I was free of my winter ailments, and I could feel the joy of good health. There was a ray of hope and promise in the caress of a gentle breeze that seemed to say, "Don't be afraid."

But this summer was unlike any other. I felt sadness that not even the glow of summer could erase. I was consumed by emptiness. I felt a sense of loss. I missed George. Where was he? What happened to my father?

And there I was, with Hedda, strolling along the streets of the Bronx. It did feel kind of strange. At thirteen, I was rather confused about the "outside world." I guess I could say I felt somewhat disoriented. But I suppose it was a normal reaction to all those years I spent in the house. What was it like out there?

Then again, it really didn't matter. I didn't care where I was going; my mother was with me, and we were walking. I didn't like or dislike it; I was there and yet not really there. The expression on my mother's face told me that she, too, didn't care one way or another. We were coming out of seclusion and getting away from our gloomy life, trapped in the house.

For the first time, we were strolling through the neighborhood. When we came upon a cluster of stores, we stopped to look in the windows. Sometimes we might even go inside and browse around. At other times, we would sit down on a street bench. My mother seemed to be lost in her thoughts whenever I looked at her. I soon turned away to watch people going by. Some were moving slowly, and others were hurrying about. It seemed like so many people had somewhere to go, something to do. I watched the cars and buses coming down the street, moving at different speeds. There was a boundless energy in the air, and I could feel it.

Country life was so simple and relaxed. But city life seemed like an ongoing stream of brimming excitement; I sensed that as we crossed one street after another. It certainly was different from the summers I knew in Spring Valley.

There we were, going out more and more. Hedda would complain to Grandma: "We are up and down some twenty times a day!" Of course, that was an exaggeration, but we did go out quite a lot. The rest of the time, we lived much the same as before: we sat in the kitchen, listened to the radio, spoke when we needed to, and argued when we didn't need to. And I still clung to Hedda as much as ever.

When I was hungry, I still didn't go to the refrigerator because I didn't want to make Hedda angry. She allowed me to eat only when she put food on the table. It was a life of deprivation, but I was used to it. What else was there?

I suddenly got a feeling that I didn't want my mother to check my bowel movements any longer. Hedda was quite disturbed, but I needed to have that bit of privacy. This was a step towards independence. I was proud of myself for standing up to her.

I now had a strong urge building up inside of me to go downstairs on my own. I was worried about upsetting Hedda, but I would have to tell her. I struggled to say, "I want to get the mail."

In a pressured tone, she cried out, **"Don't do it! I'm going to do it! Don't go down!"**

That voice of control once again! I just couldn't tolerate it any longer. It was so demoralizing: a girl of thirteen not allowed to go downstairs to the mailbox without her mother! She was making me feel that I couldn't open a mailbox!

Freedom! To be as free as a breeze on a summer day! That's what I suddenly wanted. I was tired of being cooped up in the house year after year, not being allowed to stand on my own two feet. I was angered at being told that I couldn't do this, I couldn't do that— I couldn't do anything. I was sick of her control. I craved that precious thing called freedom—and I wanted to experience it on a warm, carefree summer day. It was time to fight back with courage and conviction.

She hollered, **"Where are you going?"**

I didn't respond. I walked over to the door, grabbed the knob, turned it, and stepped out. Then I walked down a flight of stairs, right past the mailbox, and into the lobby. I stood there for a long anxious moment, looking at the door that led to the street. Then I went over, pulled it open, and walked outside.

It was a strange feeling to be out in the street by myself—but there I was. I felt a surge of fear as I stood on the sidewalk and looked around. A part of me wanted to turn back, but something within told me to keep moving. I soon found myself walking even though I had no idea of where I was going. There was no Hedda near me to tell me what to do. So, I kept walking; I had to, lest the spell be broken.

I was feeling shame. I thought it horrendous to be a big girl like me and to never have been on the street by myself. I felt like a thief; I dare not look at anybody lest they discover my secret.

And I kept walking.

My breathing quickened when I found myself at the curb. How I wished that Hedda was with me then. That old feeling of not being safe was steadily creeping up on me. My heart was beating faster with every step I took. I wanted to run home. But I didn't.

So, there I was, with a terrible dread of crossing a street on my own. What did I know about crossing a street by myself? I stood there, gaping at the streetlights that were changing from red to green, as I watched the oncoming traffic. It seemed that the cars would just as well run you down as stand still for you to cross. *How reckless can they be?*

I watched the other pedestrians gather at the curb and cross in a wave. As I watched and waited, a slogan rang in my head: "Cross at the green, not in between." Suddenly I found courage and became part of the throng as I raced along with them. I soon found myself crossing one street, then another, and still another.

Just as I was coping with one fear, another one crept up on me; I was afraid of getting lost. I had no sense of direction, and one street looked just like another. I remember crossing corners and looking back so as to be able to maintain some sense of where I had come from. I tried to memorize street names. I also moved slowly, for if I walked too fast, I might not be able to keep track of where I was, and then I would surely get lost. Then what would I do? Step by step, it was quite an adventure. I was like a baby taking its first steps.

I was also noticing people passing by. Just about every young woman looked so pretty and well groomed. I kept admiring how beautiful they were. Where had they ever learned to apply their makeup so well that they looked as if they just stepped out of a movie magazine? They had an air of confidence about them in the way they dressed and moved. As they went prancing by, I was envious. *Why can't I be as beautiful and confident as these young women?*

So, there I was, wearing a skirt and blouse that were outdated and shabby. I was dressed just like my mother, and I hated it. But I wasn't going to lament about my clothes; I was too busy taking in the sights around me. I couldn't help but stare at the young men who were walking by. *My, they're handsome! If only I had one of them in my life. But why would anyone bother with a girl like me?*

I also saw a strange sight: a young woman with a big, swollen stomach. *My God, how did she get to be like that?* I remembered asking my mother what a pregnant woman looked like. She once called me over to the window and said, "You see that woman over there with the big belly? Well, she's pregnant!" I could barely see what she was talking about as I stood there squinting, trying to catch a quick glimpse. As I walked along the street, I realized, *That woman must be pregnant!*

Through the years, I asked my mother, "What is sex? How are babies made?" She would snicker with the silliest grin on her face then clam up like a shell. It seemed like some kind of dark secret, something I shouldn't know about. Now, already in my teens, I still knew nothing about sex or babies, and there was no one else I could ask.

As I continued my walk, I found people were staring at me as much as I was staring at them. Especially men. I was very well developed for my age. I had the appearance of a girl much older than my thirteen years. However, the men who gave me sexual glances were not the ones I would have selected to be with, but I must admit, it was kind of nice, even flattering, to receive some attention.

I did not go very far, just a few blocks. Then I turned around. I slowly retraced my steps, and before I knew it, I found myself in front of my apartment building. I made it back all by myself. I was safe!

My mother greeted me with a long face. I could tell she was on the warpath by the look in her eyes. Pretty soon she was ranting and raving. I had expected that. "What happened to you? Where were you? You said you were going down to the mailbox and look how long you were gone!"

What was I to say to that? Yes, I was flustered, but I was able to bark back: "I did something I should have done a long time ago; I went out!"

Soon words were flying back and forth. That went on for a while. When things subsided, I went into the kitchen and sat down. I felt emotional pain welling up inside of me, and then I turned on the radio. I was able to distract myself considerably when I heard some of my favorite music.

Later, a sense of accomplishment came over me. I went outside by myself; this was my first step in separating myself from my mother. I began to have a growing desire to try new things and to further remove myself from Hedda's emotional leash.

Hedda was now becoming even more irate and high-strung. It was almost impossible to approach her. She snapped at the sound of my voice. I knew if I wanted to find my freedom, there was only one way I was going to succeed: I would have to fight her every inch of the way.

At times, a spell of uneasiness came over me, blotting out any good feelings I was experiencing from the small progress I was making. It wasn't long before my discomfort turned into agitation. Suddenly, everything seemed upside-down and wrong.

I knew it would be a long time, if ever, until I would be able to function like other people in the world. Meanwhile, the parade of life was passing me by. But I had made a start.

20

Junior High Times

"It's time to try again." The doctor did not want to write another note to keep me out of school. I had to go back. How I dreaded the thought!

I was thirteen and about to go to a brand new school. If I attended elementary school 2 to 3 weeks out of the year, it was a lot. *How am I going to function in junior high school? Can I do the schoolwork adequately? What will the kids be like? Will they accept me?*

It was the same old fears all over again. I felt anything but safe. I wished there was a way out, but there just didn't seem to be any. The years of being locked away in the house were catching up with me. With anxiety blurring my emotional vision, I worried about going back and forth to school. But Hedda solved that problem; she said she would go with me.

Changing classrooms was another source of concern for me. In elementary school, there was one classroom for the whole day. In junior high, there would be several, some of them on different floors. I wasn't sure I would find my way.

Most of all, I perceived I would need to be very much on guard with my fellow students. I could not let them know about my fears and anxieties; it would be just too embarrassing. They would never understand. I was entering junior high school like a babe in the woods: in awe of it and very naïve.

I was in the home classroom when I found myself seated amongst a number of students—all girls—at a long table. They were talking and laughing amongst themselves, while I sat there, feeling lost, lonely, and afraid to open my mouth. I felt like an outsider looking in. I wanted so much to be a part of their group, but they disregarded me as if I weren't there. What did I have to do to be recognized by my fellow students?

A couple of days had passed, and it continued like this; no one spoke to me, and I couldn't muster the courage to say anything to them. My frustration was growing as I sat at the table and watched them engage in conversation. How was I going to break the ice and communicate with them?

I was feeling sick to my stomach. I didn't know what to do. When I couldn't cope with my discomfort any longer, I introduced myself to the girl who did most of the talking; she sat opposite me and appeared to be the spokesperson for the group. I recall, as if it were yesterday, opening my heart to this tall, stringbean-like creature with dark, crossed eyes and short, blond, frizzled hair, who called herself Bonnie. I was eager to have her like me, so I began to tell her things about myself. I told her I had been ill and unable to attend school. I said I received my education from private tutors at home. She seemed friendly enough as she listened to me and replied with pertinent questions. At times, she seemed to be overly interested and even amused.

I thought I had finally made a breakthrough, that I would be a part of the group, that these girls would see me as a nice person, and like me for myself. But that was a mistake. Bonnie apparently discussed what I had told her with her friends. I don't know just what she said, but I soon found myself the center of attention, with six girls popping questions at me from all sides.

A few days passed, and I perceived some kind of change in their behavior. They no longer asked questions about me. If anything, they looked at me as if I were some kind of curiosity, a freak, someone they could make fun of.

They began to ask me about the size of my bra cup. They were using sexual terms I had never heard. They spoke about their boyfriends and what they did with them, and for them. Not knowing anything about sex, or what they were talking about, I didn't know how to respond. I became confused and embarrassed. It all seemed so wrong, so vulgar. I wished I had not opened my mouth and spoken so much. I sensed I was being ridiculed and rejected for being different. Pretty soon, I was feeling helpless. I started out just wanting to belong to the group and be accepted by my classmates.

A few more days passed, and I realized that I could no longer endure their bullying. It had gotten so out of hand that I was unable to concentrate on what I was there for: to learn. My anxiety blocked out all learning, and all I could focus on were the girls and what they were saying about me. I was becoming obsessed with it.

I finally went to the homeroom teacher and said, "The girls at my table are upsetting me. I can't concentrate on my schoolwork."

She asked me what they were saying, and in detail I told her what had occurred. She asked me who these girls were, and I pointed them out. She assured me, "They will be taken care of."

When I returned to my seat, Bonnie asked me what I had said to the teacher. Defiantly, I replied. "I told her the things you've been saying to me, and I let her know how upset I am."

I was proud of myself. I was speaking up. I was saying, "There! You're not going to get away with that crap anymore!"

Bonnie's eyes widened. "You shouldn't have done that."

She paused for a second then said, "We have boyfriends, and they'll be waiting for you after school. You're going to get the beating of your life!"

When I heard that, I started to panic. What had come before sounded like child talk compared with the threats they were now making.

When my mother met me at school that day, I told her what had happened. I broke down and cried. "I don't ever want to go back there again!"

The following day I came down with a viral infection. And that was the end of junior high school for me.

21

Home Instruction

Hedda needed another doctor's note to excuse me from school. She ran downstairs to the candy store to phone Dr. Gross. Within an hour, he was at our door. As soon as he removed his hat and coat, Hedda let him know about the note. He went on to examine me. "She has one of those respiratory infections again."

He reached for his pen and pad and started to write out a prescription when Hedda said, "What about the note, Dr. Gross?"

He looked my mother in the eye and said, "It's a big mistake. She really needs the social contact that school provides, and I feel it's wrong to keep her home."

It looked like Dr. Gross was about to leave. I felt my heart beating fast, and I saw Hedda's face all red. She was really flustered. Then she spoke. "She just went back to school. It's only a couple of weeks and she's already sick! She does very well at home. She knows all her work, and she's never sick when she's not in school. She works well with her tutors . . ."

Dr. Gross replied, "I don't like doing this, I don't feel this is the answer, but I'll give you a note this time."

Begrudgingly, Dr. Gross wrote a few words on a piece of paper. Thank goodness for that. My mother had to work hard but she got her note. I would now be receiving home instruction from the Board of Education. My days of private tutelage were over. I wondered how different it would be from the private instruction I had received in the past.

One day, a strikingly handsome man came to our home. Mr. Schultz became my homebound teacher. He was fairly young, and well over six feet tall. A lock of black wavy hair rested comfortably on the side of his forehead, and his piercing brown eyes sparkled. I had seen pictures of male models, and when he walked into our living room in his suit and white shirt, it seemed as if he'd just stepped out of a Sears catalog.

I'd watch the expression on Hedda's face when Mr. Schultz spoke. There was a gleam in her eyes, and her face would light up. He bore a striking resemblance to the well-known movie actor, Fred MacMurray, whom Hedda adored. When I mentioned that to her, she appeared surprised and said, "I didn't think of that, but he does look a lot like MacMurray."

Mr. Schultz came to our home several days a week. There were times when he would teach, but most of the time he would talk. Mr. Schultz had done extensive traveling around the world, and he had a multitude of stories to share. I didn't need a history or geography book—not with Mr. Schultz around. He loved to talk about the wonderful times he had in various countries. He had a fantastic flare for drama. He made his experiences come alive as he discussed the people, their backgrounds, and traditions of various countries. Soon, he was lost in detail. Time just seemed to evaporate, and he was still talking.

"From all the places I've seen, I would say that Spain and Mexico are probably two of the places I liked best. There's something about the Mexican culture that I keep going back to. There is a certain beauty and delight about the country. I love the food—it's so tasty and exotic. Here I am, a Jew, and I love Jewish cooking, but I got to tell you there's nothing like Spanish food!"

With a grin on his face, he added, "If you want to live longer, do what the Spanish people do and take a siesta! A nap in the afternoon replenishes the soul and gives you more zest to go on with the rest of the day."

I wasn't very interested, but I tried to listen. My mother, seated nearby in the living room, had a wide-eyed look as he spoke about his tales of travel and the bullfights he attended. He'd rise out of his chair to demonstrate the motions of the bullfighter in the ring, gracefully displaying each movement as he swirled his imaginary cape from side to side. A sweet aroma of cologne filled the air as he performed his twirling motions. I sat there and watched his tense facial expression, his rapid hand gestures and changing body movements. I thought, *All this to kill some poor bull?* Something about this whole scene turned me off.

While I didn't share his enthusiasm about bullfighting, I was interested in hearing about his personal life—which he loved to talk about. He'd met his wife on one of his traveling expeditions, and it sounded so romantic. There was a sense of pride in his voice when he spoke about her. "She's a gorgeous redhead. She models, and she loves her work."

Jealousy pulsed through my veins. I asked, "What does she model?"

"Hats."

I couldn't help thinking, *So she models hats! What's so great about that? But he loves her. Why do some people have all the luck?*

As for my schoolwork, well, I muddled through it as best I could. I did dribs and drabs here and there when I had to. Sometimes I received a difficult assignment, but it was rare. Mr. Schultz was carefree and applied little pressure on me to do anything. He was so involved in his travels and personal life, why should he tax himself to discipline someone who really didn't care to learn?

The weather was now cold, and as usual, I resigned myself to staying in the house with my mother. I had no desire to go out. I was a teenager who still had no social contact. Things remained the same as always. Grandma stopped by on her way to Grandpa's store with bundles of food for us, and my mother was constantly hostile to her. Grandpa would hobble up on a Sunday afternoon, and was tolerated because, as Hedda usually reminded me, "He sits there and doesn't butt in!"

Mr. Schultz's visit to my home became the highlight of my day. He was able to communicate his enthusiasm for life, and I think this helped me to deal better with my dismal moods. I know it toned down some of the tension between my mother and me.

But nice as he was, I understood that Mr. Schultz came to my home in the capacity of a teacher. I was especially aware of this when he gave me an assignment. I dreamed about the time when I would turn sixteen, so that I could quit school and not have to account to any teacher. I felt angry that I had to waste more time on something so superfluous. After all, I was already imprisoned in my mother's house. Did I need this too?

When I opened a book, my mind would wander. I found myself drifting off into space. Mr. Schultz may have noticed this, but he never mentioned it. He'd just continue to talk about some occurrence or event, totally engrossed in his own world.

One day I told Mr. Schultz that I intended to quit school as soon as I was eligible. He reflected for a moment and then expressed his concern: "I think you'd be making a big mistake if you drop out. When the time comes and you need to take the Regents, I'll prepare you for the tests. But get your high school diploma. You never know when you might need it."

I thought about what he said, he just might be right. Maybe I should get a diploma. But hearing about the Regent tests frightened me; I didn't think I would be able to pass them. How could I graduate from high school when I didn't think I knew anything, nor did I have any desire to know?

So, I sat on a folding chair at the bridge table in our living room, with Mr. Schultz seated opposite me, and Hedda a few feet away. I continued to anticipate the day when I would finally make a clean break and be finished with school. No more home instruction! No more schoolbooks! And, as nice as he was, no more Mr. Schultz!

Then I would begin my life.

22

And Then I Knew

Time passes. We go about our business, keeping as busy as we can, trying to ward off the pain and discomfort of life. We dodge reality as much as we can. Then one day, it catches up with us. Truth creeps out of its crevice, where it was hiding for so long.

About a year and a half had passed since I was told, "Your father is very ill in the hospital . . ." I'd think about him, and then I tried to put the thought out of my mind. I continued to soothe myself, as I rocked in my rocking chair. My mother was my audience, as I sang along with the songs I heard on the radio. The movie magazines were still coming into the house in droves, and I continued to hate the homework I had to do. I didn't really question anything, and nothing seemed to really interest me. I was growing up in ignorance, and I couldn't care less.

I was about fourteen when one day Grandma paid us her usual visit. Things seemed to be going rather well, until she started talking about money, and my mother's love of spending it. In the past, my mother had spent over eighty dollars on a tailor-made winter coat that I never wore. Riding around in taxis that last summer in Spring Valley had cost a pretty penny. She could be extravagant—when she wanted to be. I didn't know why, but it troubled me to no end. I just hated to see her spend my father's money so frivolously, as if it grew on trees.

Suddenly my mother and grandmother were having a heated discussion about finances. Grandma became very excited and blurted out angrily, "You can't spend money like you used to! You're a widow now!"

Those words "You're a widow now!" went right through me like a bolt of lightning. I could no longer deny the truth I had somehow known all along: *My father is dead.*

My mother raged at Grandma. "You had to open your big mouth! You had to tell her! She didn't have to know! Everything was fine up to now!"

Grandma, waving her arms about (which was customary for her to do when she became upset), retorted, "It's about time she knew! You can't keep her stupid all her life!"

I sat there, stunned, and listened. All I heard were words, and more words. Then I heard nothing. There was too much going on in my heart, and in my head, for me to be concerned about their foolish argument. *It's true. My father is gone. My mother wore black that day. She left me with Grandpa and said she was going to see my father in the hospital, but she went to his funeral. How could she live with such a lie?*

I asked, "Why didn't you tell me?"

My mother replied, "I saw a rabbi at the time. He said, 'Your daughter has enough troubles.' He told me not to say anything to you."

I wanted to believe what she was saying as only a child can believe her mother. The things my mother told me, were they actually real or part of her imagination? There were times when I would sense that something was very wrong and even absurd. Did she really believe what she was saying? Or was it easier for her to manipulate the truth in order to suit her way of thinking? Did a rabbi really advise her not to tell me that my father had died?

She held on to her story: "Your father is very ill in the hospital." Every time I asked about him, she would tell me the same thing. She had deceived me. She invented a story, and in so doing, had prevented me from expressing my grief. I had played into her madness. I was not allowed to mourn the death of my father.

I had also lied to myself. I had become complacent—at least, on the surface. My feelings were locked away. I would not admit to myself that I had figured out the truth. I was not supposed to know. But then again, it was easy for me to keep my head in the sand. It seemed to tie in so neatly with what was expected of me. But did she really think I would never find out? I was amazed that she could keep the story going for so long.

But now I knew. My father was dead.

He was only forty-two years old. His death was a tragedy that could have been averted, and I blamed my mother for it. Whatever else in his life may have caused his demise, I did not know, but I knew one thing: My mother helped kill him. It was not done with a weapon. It was something that did not happen overnight. She was abusive. She was cruel. She had made his life miserable and had driven him out. There was no doubt in my mind that unhappiness and suffering had eaten away at his heart. If anything, he died of a broken heart. Was she just evil? Or was it her madness that made her that way? She certainly was capable of destroying those she came in contact with.

A vision of Grandma came before my eyes. All I had to do was look at the sorrowful expression on her face and see how torn she was. Much of her distress emanated from our home. Grandma suffered, like my father, but there was a major difference between them. Grandma fought back whenever she could. She voiced complaints about the misery she witnessed in our home: "It's impossible to see what goes on here! There's not one in the world who could see this! I must be made of iron." My father remained silent; he never let it be known how he felt about anything.

I, too, was in the process of being destroyed, but I didn't know it at the time.

I suppressed my rage as best I could, but in my heart, I despised my mother. I would have liked nothing better than to walk away from her, and never see her again, never to return. But whom was I kidding? Where would I go?

23

After the Fact

I could see him standing there, in our living room, large as life. He had just come back from Florida, and he looked so healthy. Just two months later, at the age of forty-two, my father was dead. How could that be?

I had many questions to ask. Grandma had been in contact with Uncle Marvin at the time of my father's death. He was close to my father; they went out and did things together. I wondered how much he revealed to Grandma. She was visiting one day when I asked her if she could tell me what happened to George. With a morbid look on her face, she said, "Your father complained of not feeling well. He had chest pains. He laid down to take a nap and that was it. He never got up..." Her voice trailed off into the distance.

Before I could respond, Hedda broke in and angrily began to rant: "Your father went to a doctor, and the doctor said he needed bed rest and no work. Do you know what your father did? He was back driving that cab the next day! That was your father. He never listened to anyone—not even to a doctor!"

It was all so tragic. I wanted to cry, but instead, I sat there, distraught and listened some more as Hedda continued: "I went to

Brooklyn to see his doctor; I had to get a death certificate. You should have seen that doctor's face when I told him your father had gone to work. He said, 'You mean he went to work after I told him what a sick man he was, and that he was not to do anything but get plenty of bed rest?' The doctor slammed his hand on the table and said: 'If I knew he was going to work, I would have wiped my hands off this case. That man should have been in the hospital, and I told him that!' "

I found the courage to ask, "But what was the cause of my father's death?"

"The doctor said your father had the worst type of heart disease: coronary thrombosis. If he had lived, he would have been very ill. The doctor said your father had the heart of a man of eighty in the body of a forty-two year old."

I felt torn up inside. For the first time, I realized how very ill my father was.

"Right after your father died, I went over to the private house in Brooklyn where your father lived. You should have seen how happy that landlady was to get rid of your father's things. She said, 'Take it all with you, I don't want that stuff here!' She was another one of your dear father's friends!"

Grandma sat silently as Hedda spoke non-stop.

The veins in Hedda's neck were protruding as she continued to rant. Her eyes had a mad look. "That landlady had plenty to say! She told me all about your father and his fabulous family. She said his sisters promised to take care of him when he was lying there, sick in that room. They were supposed to bring him food, but they didn't show up. Or they came late—or some other nonsense. What a family!"

Hedda broke down and sobbed: "I paid $600 for a beautiful mahogany casket. I picked out a headstone and had it engraved:

FOREVER IN OUR HEARTS
BELOVED HUSBAND AND DEAR FATHER.

My goodness! When he was alive, she didn't even look at him. Now, he was "beloved" in death? I was aching inside as I listened to her ramble on. I couldn't find the words to say what I was feeling.

"Your father would never have done what he did if it weren't for his brother. Marvin pulled him out of the house. He took him out dancing. He introduced him to women. It was Marvin who went to Florida with him and carried on with women. That Marvin is no damn good!

"Your father and I were not right for each other. We never should have married! You know what it was? Your father didn't know how to live. He was stingy. All he ever cared about was making money. When we lived with my parents, he read a paper when he came home at night. There was one easy chair in the house, and your father and grandfather fought over it. Your father went to bed at eight o'clock every night. He never smiled. Something seemed to be bothering him."

I felt barraged by all these stories. I sat there, not knowing what to think or feel. But that was nothing new. And my mother continued her angry monologue. "Your father wanted a mother. He came to this country from Europe when he was just a kid. His father brought him and his sister, Bea, over. His mother came years later with the rest of the brood. He had no family life. Maybe that's what bothered him. But with your father, you could never be sure!"

I had heard those stories so many times. But that's the way it was when she got all wound up. It was talk, talk, and more talk.

I looked at Grandma off in a corner, eyes downcast with the saddest expression on her face. As I looked at her, I wanted to cry. I turned away and my mind soon drifted off to something George said in one of his last visits. Hedda was telling him, "I don't have your address and I don't have a number where I can call you in case of an emergency."

I was taken aback by his reply: "If there is any emergency, it will be mine." I wondered what made him say something like that, but I could understand now.

Soon I was back in the moment. My mother was still talking, but I was no longer listening.

I brooded a lot in the days that followed. My poor father. I wondered what the last months of his life were like. How did he manage when he was so ill? I had questions, but there were no answers.

One day the bell rang, and I ran to the door. Before me stood a nice looking man, slightly balding, with dark brown eyes and a serious expression on his face. He looked vaguely familiar to me, and then it popped into my mind: *It's Uncle Marvin!* It was a pleasant shock. I never expected to see him at my door. And what a strange feeling it was—seeing my father's brother again. I had seen him only once in my life and that was in Spring Valley when I was a girl of twelve. He had come to deliver the bad news about my father. It seemed like an eternity since I had seen him.

I was delighted to have Marvin in our home. I was eager to speak to him about the man who was my father. I had so many questions, I just hoped Hedda would allow me to talk to him and not take over.

Marvin immediately said: "I miss my brother. I loved him very much. George was such a wonderful guy, so very warm…."

I sadly said, "I never knew him."

Marvin replied, "What a shame!"

I mustered up the courage to ask, "What was my father like?"

"Your father had a great sense of humor. He loved to laugh and have fun. He was kind, warm—a real nice person. We went to places together. He liked to socialize. He said he never knew there were so many things in the world to see. He loved life. When I lost him, I lost a good friend."

Marvin spoke slowly with feeling. I was touched by the words he used to describe his brother and the relationship he had with him.

Looking directly at my mother, he said, "George was angry at my sisters and me. It went back to the time when there was that stupid fight over our mother's will. I would say some twenty years went by before I saw George again. One day, out of the blue, he called me, and we resumed our friendship. He came back to his family."

I was attentive to every word he said, but Hedda had a blank stare as Marvin was talking. Surprisingly, she didn't have anything to say. In Will's file he mentioned that Hedda had "a severe depression" during this time. I guess that accounts for why she was so calm and quiet.

Marvin's eyes were fixed upon me as he continued: "We went to lectures; we went to dances; we went to Florida together. George's eyes lit up when he said, 'My God, I never knew anything like this existed!' That year-and-a-half was the happiest time of his life!

"George was a very noble man. He once said to me: 'I make one hundred fifty dollars a week. I put aside one-third for my car; one-third for myself; and one-third for my wife and child.' That's the kind of man George was."

I soon asked: "What happened to him when he became ill?"

"Your father was living in a private house in Brooklyn. He had a furnished room and he lived there for two years until he died. When he became ill, we took turns at helping him. I must say my sisters worked very hard—the girls were very good. Bea was making trips over there, and Rose was coming in from the Bronx. They were bringing him food and feeding him soup when he was too sick to feed himself. We all tried to do whatever we could to make him comfortable.

"George stayed a couple of days with me. You know, I had my own house. I was married then. It didn't work out… Well, that's still something else. I believe he also stayed a couple of days with Bea. His landlady was a wonderful person. She cooked and brought food up to him. He was not really alone. Her husband and son were there—you know, it was a family."

Marvin caught his breath and heaved a sigh. "George started to feel better. He was going to the country to recuperate. He shaved and was packing when he started to have chest pains. He said he wasn't feeling well, and he laid down on the couch to take a nap. He was supposed to leave that afternoon to go to the mountains." Marvin paused, then raised his voice: "Instead, he went to the cemetery!"

There was silence. I could feel Marvin's hurt, his anger, his caring for George. Each of us seemed to be somewhere else. I had a vision in my mind of that Friday night in Spring Valley, the night

George died. The candles in our bungalow were flickering furiously until they burned out. I thought of his life snuffed out like a candle that flickers and then is no more.

I was lost in sadness as Marvin spoke: "It was a mistake. George should never have been at home, he was much too ill. The doctor who took care of him was not even a cardiologist. George should have been in a hospital where he would have received medical care. If he had, I think he would be alive today."

Those words dug deeply into my heart. I thought of the money he had asked my mother to send for medical expenses. A wave of remorse swept over me. That money may have saved his life.

Marvin kept on talking, but I didn't hear a word. I had thoughts of George, lying there in a furnished room, sick and alone. My mother didn't believe he was ill. I didn't believe him either. Now it was too late.

I don't know how long I sat there, lost in my own little world, when I heard Marvin saying, "George really loved Florida. He said there was no place in the world like it. He called it 'God's Country'."

As Marvin spoke, I thought about the last time I saw my father. He was tan as a berry. He had just come back from Florida and mentioned something about meeting a woman there he wanted to marry. I asked Marvin, "What was she like—this woman my father wanted to marry?"

"I didn't like Peggy, she was not for him. She was getting a divorce when he met her. I told George: 'Stay away from her,' but he didn't listen to me. When he told me he wanted to marry her, I was very much against it, but he had made up his mind. He was crazy about her. There was nothing I could do to change his mind."

Suddenly Marvin stopped short as he looked down at his watch. "I was so busy talking, I lost track of the time. I have to be leaving." He quickly got up from his chair, reached for his coat, and said goodbye. Then he was gone. But he was not gone from my mind. There was something nice about him that appealed to me. There was a caring tone in his voice when he spoke about his brother that told me he loved George very much. I was so glad that he came by. I wondered if I would ever see him again.

Yes, I found out a lot about my father. But much of it was very disturbing and I didn't know how to process the information I received. As a young teenage girl, with no one to talk to, all I could do was ruminate about the tragedy of my father and brood. But a great part of my mission was accomplished. I had a need to find out whatever I could about George because I wanted to know this man, my father. Although I was upset and confused by many of the things Marvin revealed to me, deep down I realized it was better to know the horrible truth than to be shielded from it. It seems the truth has ways of making itself known, even if we don't want to know it.

And I kept saying to myself: *If only I could re-do the past. If only I could have known my father….*

I had a dream about seeking out my father when I grew up. I was going to make up for lost time, for all the love I could never show him. But that dream was not to be; it died with my father. And I mourned that dream, too.

24

My Father's Secret Life

Although some time had passed since I found out about my father's death, I was still enmeshed in sadness. I went around with tears in my eyes. My mother's eyes were reddened too, but it was not unusual for Hedda to cry.

Grandma came in one day and appeared quite distressed. She looked at the two of us and exclaimed: "I don't know what you both are crying about. He doesn't deserve all those tears. At the time he died, I went over to the garage to pick up his personal belongings. A garage man who cleaned out George's cab found a cigar box and gave it to me. There were letters in that box—letters to women!"

My mother and I both looked at her, amazed. *Letters? What letters?*

Hedda was at a loss for words, as Grandma continued: "George wrote letters to women. The letters were coming into the garage and the garage men knew about it. They knew he was running around with women. One of them said, 'He had a wife and child. It's disgraceful! He got what was coming to him!' "

My mother looked bewildered and I just stood there, staring at Grandma. Neither one of us could utter a word. Then Grandma announced, "I'll bring the letters over to you, and you'll see what I'm talking about."

A few weeks passed, but I did not see Grandma bringing any letters into the house. I had a feeling they were there, and I just had to see them. I had to know more about this man who was my father. But I was also afraid to see those letters and I didn't know why. Yet I continued to ask Hedda and each time she said, "I don't have them." But I was persistent, and one day she slowly went into the small bedroom, walked over to the closet, and came out with a cigar box in her hand. She did not say a word, but I detected a tear in her eye as she handed it to me.

I opened the box, and my heart was pounding. I leafed through it and saw numerous letters my father had written to various women over a period of several years. There were also responses from these women.

I came upon a steady stream of correspondence between my father and someone named Gloria. From the dates on the letters, it seemed that they had known each other for some time. The relationship ended with Gloria accusing my father of being dishonest. He replied: "I feel like I've been stabbed in the back with a knife!"

My goodness, this was a most disturbing letter. It sounded like my father and this woman, Gloria, had a very intense relationship. I figured out that I was only six years old at the time this letter was written. It seemed to me that he cared very much for this woman. As I continued to read on, I wondered how he could care so much for these women and have no feeling for his own daughter. I was sad and hurting and didn't know what to do with my pain.

And I went on. One piece of mail had our address on it, and on the return address was a man's name. But inside the envelope was a spicy note written as only a woman would write to a man. George was upset that she had written to him at his home and said so in his return response. He asked her to "send any future mail to the garage."

I wondered: *Who are these women?* As I thought about it, it seemed most likely that he met them in his taxi or a dance hall. I was feeling more disheartened with each letter I read. This man, my father, was not the cold, detached man I had seen in my home. He described deep, intense feelings in each of his letters.

One letter that really stung was the one he wrote to the woman he met in Florida, who he was planning to marry. He spoke about lying quietly in his room, listening to Victor Herbert music, and thinking about the sweetness and warmth of Peggy. As he described the lyrics of the haunting Herbert melody, "Ah, Sweet Mystery of Life," he revealed how much she meant to him. How ludicrous it was. My father was in love. And I was in pain.

At the bottom of the cigar box were a few pictures of my father and one of a young woman, fairly attractive, with short hair and a jubilant smile on her face. Around her face was drawn a large heart. *Oh, my goodness! This must be her!* My heart dropped. I looked at the picture for a few minutes. Then I closed the box and sadly walked away.

The thought of my father's love for that woman filled me with jealousy and rage. I burst into tears and said to myself: *He's no good! He didn't care about us. He was running around, having affairs with women. He was having a good time, while I was sitting in the house with my mother yelling at me.*

I ran for the album that contained our country photos and then I went for a pair of scissors. I took out each and every one of his photos and cut them in half. I felt he deserved that. I felt the love that he gave to those women should have been given to me. I needed to obliterate him completely from my mind, my heart, and the album.

All of a sudden, I felt sick. I looked at the severed pictures in my hand and I asked myself: *What have I done? This is all I have of him!*

I began to sob. I felt as if I had cut my own heart in half. I ran over to the drawer where the Scotch tape was kept, pulled it out, and started taping the pictures back together again, as Hedda yelled: "What are you doing? Have you gone crazy?"

The photos never looked the same, as much as I tried to mend them. I had done a terrible thing, and I knew it. I kept asking myself: *How could I do that?*

I looked at the album many times after that and was especially saddened when I saw a torn photo of my father and me. We were posing for the camera and sharing a loving glance. It was the only photo I had like that—a rare moment captured by the camera—and then gone, never to be again.

I had wanted to know more about my father. Now I knew too much. And I was still very confused. It soon did not matter what Hedda said, what Grandma said, what Marvin said, what the garage men said, or even what the letters said. Whatever he was, good or bad, he was still my father.

25

The Letters They Wrote

In my uncle's file was a note about a conversation he had with my father. It was the last visit my father would make to Will. "I'm suing for a legal separation and then, a divorce," George told him. "I am very ill. I have high blood pressure and pains around the heart. I can't take it any longer. I've been away from Hedda for seventeen months now, I met someone in Florida, and I want to make a new life. I will be giving them less money."

Will was upset to hear this. "You are responsible for Hedda's plight because you let things ride and did nothing about getting psychiatric help for her. You are evading a moral responsibility to both your wife and daughter in walking out permanently, and they'll probably crack up even further. Hedda might ultimately turn on the gas jets. You will never be happy as long as your wife and daughter are unhappy. You will never find happiness by shirking your moral responsibility. Go to a psychiatrist with your wife and daughter and reestablish a family unit in another house in another neighborhood."

George's response was "I don't know how long I'm going to live. I'm entitled to some happiness in life. And I intend to get that happiness!"

When the evening ended, Will added this statement to his notes: *"We parted on cool, but not hostile terms."*

It seems their conversation had some effect upon George. Several days later, Will received a note from him: *"No doubt you will be surprised to hear from me. I had to write to you for I wasn't feeling well, so I saw a doctor, and he took electric cardiogram and it shows I have a heart condition. I told the doctor the first time I had the pain was three years ago. That is what they called a mild heart attack. It's not nerves it's the heart. All problems if exchanged would be solved. For each of us knows how to solve the other fellow's problem."*

Will sent a letter to George, reiterating much of what he had said before:

"You have a moral responsibility toward Hedda and Lenore. They are both physically and emotionally ill and both will continue to deteriorate as time passes unless you help them.

We all experience guilt feelings when we attempt to evade a responsibility and an obligation. Under these circumstances happiness cannot be attained. Your sick wife and daughter will always come between you and your happiness.

To urge Hedda to study shorthand and get a job is to show an amazing lack of understanding of the whole problem. If Hedda could be persuaded to get out and leave Lenore with other people, she would not be emotionally ill and there would never have arisen the need for you to leave her in the first place.

The physical and emotional well being of Hedda and Lenore are tied up with you, and your own health is tied up with the solution of their problem. You all stand or fall together.

4. Your best solution would be:

a.) Make an attempt to rehabilitate Hedda and Lenore through psychiatry, with your participation. Although this may be a slow process, we are certain that she would undertake the treatments if you say so.

b.) Get a new apartment (which really looks like a home) in a new neighborhood. A new start for all.

c.) Keep a calm, patient and hopeful attitude toward the entire situation.

Will soon received a response from George:

"Dear Counselor:

Are you trying to prosecute me on my sick bed? Didn't I write you I have a heart ailment? Did you have to write a form with numbers and letters stating word for word what we have discussed formally? Are you trying to send me to my doom? You tell me I have an obligation to support Hedda and Lenore. Yes I have a moral obligation for my own health and happiness. I will fall, if I come back to my old environment, and I aim to stand for my life."

Less than two months later, George was dead.

Shortly thereafter, my uncle wrote a lengthy letter to a relative in California. This is an excerpt from it:

"Several days after the funeral, Hedda and Lenore went back to Spring Valley where they are now. My mother and father are bitter but heartbroken. Jessie and I are very upset. To us it all is a very great tragedy, which could have been averted. George was a plain, simple fellow who wanted what all men want: a wife, a home, the love and affection of his wife and child. He had none of these.

When he finally left, he was just as unhappy as when he had been home, but he insisted he couldn't take it any longer. If my father and mother had stood behind me and helped get Hedda the psychiatric help she needed so desperately, the story might have had a happy ending. Despite what faults George might have had in this whole tragedy, and he was certainly not free from fault, he died from a heart, which was broken in the stresses and strains and tensions of the last 10 years. Hedda was a very sick woman who could not help herself without outside assistance. But the results were still very bad for George.

My mother is angry because George did not warn Hedda before he left that if she did not change, he would leave. Just before he left, George came up to us and told us that it was futile to try to talk to Hedda because she got very excited and shouted at him. It is not for us to judge George. There is no doubt that he was a weak personality, but it is very doubtful if such last words would have made much difference."

26

Neglect

"Lenore is 14-and-a-half-years old. It is almost unbelievable that she:

1) Has never been on a subway or elevated train.

2) Has never been to Manhattan.

3) Has never visited any other house except her grandmother's (infrequently).

4) Never played with other children in the street or in her own home.

5) Has never gone into a store alone to purchase anything— even the corner candy store.

6) Has never been in a department store."

This is a note my uncle wrote to himself, as he kept track of my life for the purpose of writing a book. I am amazed at the accuracy of this information. But there were so many other things he didn't know about. For example, I had never spoken into a telephone; or handled money. I never went to the refrigerator to feed myself. I never ate any cold foods. If I were to make up a list, it would be endless.

Grandma was telling me, "Stand up tall!"

My mother came running in like a tiger: "Leave her alone! **She doesn't need that!** She knows enough!"

I cringed as she said that.

But Grandma would not stop. "Look at the way she sits there, bending over those books! She's all hunched over!"

"She's okay the way she is," Hedda hollered. **"Don't mix in so much! Mind your own business!"** Grandma would just sit there, very sad, and look away.

But Grandma could not keep quiet for long. I would hear her say, "She's growing up crooked!" And that's exactly what happened. I had a slight bulge on the right side of my back that had been developing over the years. My right shoulder blade had started to protrude, and a curve was quite noticeable by the time I was fourteen. Dr. Gross, our family physician, spoke to Hedda about it. "She has a curvature of the spine, otherwise known as scoliosis. She will have to wear a brace to help correct this condition. If this is left untreated, the curve will progress and worsen."

When the doctor said that, I became very worried. What did he mean by "progress and worsen?" If a brace could correct this condition, I wanted it. I pleaded with Hedda to get it for me. But Hedda responded, "You don't need that!"

A note from my uncle's file reveals the following: *"According to my mother, Hedda seems quite upset that a doctor told her that Lenore would have to wear a brace. Hedda warned the doctor not to mention this again in Lenore's presence."*

And the doctor never mentioned the brace again. I found it incredible that my mother was able to silence our doctor from his persistent urging: "This girl needs a brace to stop her back from becoming crooked." And how I begged her for that brace. I often wondered what my mother said to the doctor that made him clam up about something so vitally important for my health?

As the curve progressed, I kept begging Hedda for the brace. But she displayed the same deaf ear each time. And I continued to read and write at the kitchen table, in a slanted position. I would try to remember to sit up straight, but soon I would become busy with my schoolwork and I would forget.

There were times, however, when I could not help but worry about my back; things occurred that reminded me something was wrong. I had a tendency to tire easily. (The doctor had mentioned this is a symptom of scoliosis.) Grandma would also point out that one hip was slightly higher than the other, and my clothes were pulling to a side. Sometimes I noticed it in the mirror, and I felt bad. I yearned to be straight and I would brood about it; then I tried to put it out of my mind, for I knew nothing would be done.

The curvature of my spine was ignored. And so was my dental care. Like most everything else, seeing a dentist was of no importance to Hedda. It had to be an emergency to get my mother to knock on a dentist's door.

"Leave her alone. Don't tell her how to brush her teeth. She knows enough already. **She doesn't need to know that!**" I recall my father, with an embarrassed grin on his face, running out of the bathroom. He was only trying to show me a little dental hygiene.

One day, when I was fifteen, I was biting down into a hard candy bar, and suddenly I felt something crack. In a state of panic, I ran to the bathroom mirror. I was flabbergasted. I saw part of a front tooth had broken off. My goodness, I looked like a jack o'lantern!

It was time to see a dentist. I had not seen one since I was about eight years old. At that time, I had a toothache, and my mother took me to a dentist in the neighborhood. Dr. Schwartz treated my tooth. Then, in a loud tone, he confronted my mother, "Your daughter has decay in several teeth." He went into detail. "This can present some serious problems. These teeth need immediate attention. If you don't do this now, she's going to have real problems later on."

Hedda did not respond. She just stood there, staring at the dentist. In exasperation, he declared, "Mother, you look like you're in a fog!"

Hedda stared at him for a moment more, then headed for the door. I followed. That was the last time I would have dental care in my childhood.

Now, as a teenage girl, I was going to see a dentist around the corner from where we lived. Dr. Feinman was Dr. Schwartz's son-in-law, who now had a practice of his own. He was a very attractive young man, with a tall, lean frame, dark brown wavy hair, and sparkling smile. He was attired in his white professional jacket when he walked into the waiting room and came over to us. He smiled and said, "What is the problem? How can I help you?"

Hedda stood there gaping at him, and then she smiled. She said, "My daughter has a broken tooth…" Dr. Feinman warmly said, "Let's take a look, and see what we can do."

I nervously sat down on his chair and he examined my mouth. He then took an x-ray and pronounced the verdict: "The tooth will have to come out. It has broken off substantially, and it makes no sense to try and save it. I can cap the tooth, but in the long run, capping only does more harm than good. It can promote decay, since rotting could occur underneath it, and it would still have to come out eventually. The tooth next to it will also have to be removed so I can make a stationary bridge. The one I have in mind is a Cantilever bridge. In summary, I will remove both teeth: the broken tooth and the one next to it."

I was inwardly trembling as Dr. Feinman made his assessment. *Oh no! He wants to remove two of my front teeth, just like that!* I looked at my mother and I was appalled; I could see she was considering it. Suddenly, I felt helpless as reality set in: *My mother is agreeing with the dentist, and he's going to pull my teeth!* Looking up to my mother as if she were God, I felt powerless to object; I just didn't feel safe enough to speak up and express myself. I sat there holding in my pain.

I started thinking: *Maybe it is necessary to have my two front teeth replaced.* I hated the thought of rotting that could occur under capped teeth. Maybe this bridge will prevent me from having further problems later on. These thoughts gave me some relief and helped me fight my fear of the inevitable.

Still, what did I really know about any of this?

When I came back to the moment, I heard my mother talking to the dentist. "How much will all this cost? Money is a problem since my husband died." Looking directly into her eyes, in the most sincere tone, Dr. Feinman replied: "I'm going to do my very best for you. Under the circumstances, I'm offering my services for a flat rate of $125 for the entire job. That includes the extraction, materials, labor, and whatever else is involved. You can't go wrong!"

He put his arm on her shoulder and reassured her, "It will come out just fine. Don't worry about a thing! Leave it all up to me."

My mother looked enchanted, standing there, gazing into his eyes. She smiled and said, "I trust you, and I know you will do a good job for my daughter."

Overcome with anxiety and fear, I was sitting in his chair when he came over to me and softly said, "I'm going to give you an injection now. It will not hurt."

I remember feeling a sharp jab into my gum. And soon, it was over. My tongue hit a wide empty space at the roof of my mouth. It was a strange sensation. My heart sank. Dr. Feinman stood there, smiling triumphantly, dangling my teeth in his hand. Soon everything around me became a blur.

The next thing I knew, he was taking impressions for a permanent bridge and inserting something temporary to cover the empty space in the front. When I left his office, I was in a state of shock.

Within a few weeks Dr. Feinman cemented a stationery bridge in my mouth. He smiled as he held the mirror for me. He proudly exclaimed, "It's a perfect piece of dentistry." I must admit those teeth looked good—but I didn't like them; they were not mine. Dr. Feinman added a warning: "Eat soft foods and don't bite into anything hard."

My mother came over to marvel at his work. He proudly said, "You've heard of a two-sided bridge—well, this is a Cantilever Bridge. It's one-sided, and one of the best bridges there ever was."

I didn't care to hear about the technicalities. It was over, and now I would have to live with the aftermath. As we were about to leave his office, in his soft, sweet manner Dr. Feinman said, "She has a mouth full of decay. If we don't take care of this right away, she will lose more teeth. What do you want to do?"

I soon found myself making regular visits with Hedda to Dr. Feinman's office. As he worked in my mouth, he had a habit of humming a tune while running his finger across my nose, as if he were playing a violin. He usually had a great big smile on his face.

That really annoyed me, but I couldn't find the voice to make him stop. One day, I was sitting in his chair—which I had nicknamed "the electric chair"—and he was making the violin gesture. I didn't like his clowning around when I was in distress. I gently lowered my teeth on the hand he had in my mouth. He laughingly said, "Oh, you bit me!" And I, in turn, laughed with him. But he got the message; and he stopped the violin movement.

I came away with a lot of mixed feelings. For a long time after the dental work was completed, I couldn't help thinking about Dr. Feinman with contempt and rage. I also felt the same contempt towards my mother for the total neglect of my teeth that made such dentistry inevitable. It was a pain that would not go away.

But neglect did not stop there. When I crossed the street, I found those moving vehicles coming up close; my glasses were not as clear as they used to be. I thought back to the years I had spent reading and writing under a 40-watt ceiling bulb. I felt heartsore and angry. Had working in a dark kitchen hurt my eyes?

When I was fifteen, I went with Hedda to an optometrist in the neighborhood. He gave me two prescriptions: one for reading and the other for distance. I wound up wearing the distance glasses most of the time. I only read what I had to, mostly for my school assignments and no more.

My mother refused to accept responsibility for my physical conditions. She showed no signs of remorse about my eyes, my back, or my teeth. She sat in her chair, expressionless, almost as if she were viewing a film of someone else's life. It was as if everything that happened to her, or to me, was someone else's fault—not hers. And this was the woman who led others to believe that she was sacrificing her life for me. It was something to think about.

27

In Love with A Dream

Grandma was visiting one day, and we were listening to a radio program, when we heard the voice of a new singer. The announcer said his name was Eddie Fisher. Apparently, Grandma had heard of him; she smilingly said, "Ah, he is a nice Jewish boy. I hope I see the day when you marry a nice Jewish boy like him."

Well, that was a mouthful! Those words went right to my heart. I considered Grandma to be sharp and alert. I respected her, and the things I heard her say. Now, she was telling me about this wonderful young Jewish singer.

I had fallen in love with radio singers before, as I was growing up. Bing Crosby was one, and there were many others. But after my father's death, I was just plodding along, not very interested in anything. Not until Grandma told me about Eddie Fisher.

I anxiously listened for his songs on the radio. His voice, so strong, yet tender, conveyed a message to me of love and hope. I saw pictures of him in magazines, and I loved the way he smiled. He looked so cute and boyish. When I learned that he was in his twenties and single, I found this very appealing.

I began to collect his pictures and clip articles about him. Like his hit record, "Thinking of You," I found myself thinking about him constantly, as I sat in a corner of my kitchen, or on my rocking chair in the living room. Suddenly, nothing in the world mattered to me like Eddie Fisher.

I liked to believe that inevitably our lives were destined to become intertwined, and that we would meet and fall in love. But the competition was keen. I became terribly upset when I read in a magazine or newspaper that he was dating, and that it might be serious. I was jealous when he had female guests on his radio program. I lived in mortal dread that he would suddenly go off and get married. I hated being only fourteen years old. I wished I could leap over the years and be old enough to marry him. It was something to live for. Being married to Eddie Fisher became my raison d'etre.

I wanted to make myself beautiful, like the women he was going out with. As I walked past my mirror, I wasn't too happy with what I saw. I went into a local drug store and got on a scale; I found out that I was over one hundred thirty pounds. At 5'2", I knew I would have to lose a considerable amount of weight to be attractive to him. I always wanted to have a slim Hollywood figure, and this was as good a time as any to pursue that goal. It was time to go on a diet.

On a radio program I heard about a protein powder to lose weight. My mother ordered it for me, and soon I was taking it fervently. In just a few months, I went down to ninety-eight pounds. I soon found that losing too much weight too soon could be a dangerous thing. I became very ill with pains in my stomach, and I found it difficult to eat just about anything. I went to Dr. Weisner, looking like a shell of my former self. I was under his care for several months. Gradually, I put back some weight and began to feel better.

I continued to listen to the radio, and the music that made me feel good. I loved to sing, especially when I was singing along with Eddie Fisher. But I was deeply distressed. I kept reading the newspapers and saw his name linked with various Hollywood beauties. My mother told me, "Don't believe it. They make up all those stories just to sell their damn papers!"

I prayed she was right. Those romance rumors just had to be something invented by some news-hungry columnists! Nevertheless, I was in deep sorrow as I imagined his involvements. I began to have fears and doubts as to whether I would ever be his one and only. I felt a pang in my heart as I checked the gossip columns daily for the latest word on his love life. It became emotional agony. Why would he pick me over all those gorgeous women he was going out with?

But I would not give up hope. I would not relinquish my dream of Eddie Fisher giving me the love and happiness I was yearning for all my life.

Grandma went back to my uncle and told him about this. He wrote in his file, *"Lenore's mother has 'solved' the Eddie Fisher problem by banning all newspapers and magazines from the house so that Lenore will not read anything about Eddie Fisher, which is likely to excite or disturb her further."*

But I was still able to get a hold of the information I craved. I had begun going out alone, and there were two candy stores on the block where I lived; they both carried a raft of newspapers and magazines. All I had to do was walk over to either one, and I could find out for myself what I needed to know. The storekeepers scowled at me, as I quickly leafed through the gossip magazines and put them back on the shelves.

When I read something about Eddie Fisher that got me down, I would take a brisk walk in the neighborhood. It was therapeutic and it eased my anxiety, but mostly, it was a means of escape. I found myself walking quite a bit. I began to come out of my shell in the warmth of a summer day. I would meander over to the street benches on Southern Boulevard. It was only a few blocks from where we lived. I would go there a lot and sit there for I don't know how long, just observing the passing scene.

I started to wear halter tops, low-cut blouses, and snug pants that accentuated the contour of my body. I was full breasted, with hips that jutted out too much for my own liking, but I didn't allow that to bother me. A bright red lipstick and a smear of rouge created an image of someone older than my fourteen years. I felt a need to look as good as I possibly could.

But I was feeling funny about the way I dressed. I guess I had been looking at too many movie magazines over the years. I certainly didn't want to go around looking like my mother. But I didn't feel comfortable when people stared at me either. I walked down the street self-conscious with shame.

And soon I was attracting attention wherever I went. It felt like the eyes of the world were upon me. I noticed people, young and old, gaping at me. Women were eying me up and down with a curious stare. I wondered what they were thinking. Some kids would look at me, make a remark to their friends, glance my way again and laugh. That really bothered me. Did they think I was some kind of freak?

But the response from men—that was still something else. There were men whistling at me, calling to me from cars and trucks. Men, whom I had never seen before, passed me on the street, smiling, and saying hello. Sometimes they would say more. I didn't know what to make of it. I was bewildered, but at the same time, flattered in an odd sort of way.

I was also scared. Perhaps talking to strangers could get me into trouble. So, in most instances, I pretended not to hear. I simply minded my business and walked ahead.

I was a real attention-getter sitting on a street bench. Many a man sat down next to me. Most of them were older, average looking, and casually dressed. They were not very impressive. They would usually approach me with a question: "Do you know what time it is?" "Are you waiting for somebody?" "Haven't we met before?"

I was feeling quite uncomfortable. I usually begged off with "I'm sorry, I don't talk to strangers," or "I'm sorry, I don't know you." If I spoke to any one of them, it was only because I was curious; I wondered what they were going to say.

There were still other men, whom I ignored altogether; something about them appeared vulgar or repulsive to me. I would politely get up and leave, without saying a word.

Well, the whole scene made me feel bad, really bad. I usually walked away dejected and disappointed. But I could not pull away from the scene. I was meeting men, all types of men, and it became intriguing. My need for love and attention was now so overpowering, I felt compelled to take this path wherever it would lead me. Underlying my sexy exterior, I was nothing more than a frightened little girl who hoped to meet someone, sooner or later, with a warm heart and the ability to care. But the men whom I was attracting were not the kind I wanted in my life.

Meanwhile, Eddie Fisher remained the love of my life. After meeting those wretched men in the street, I wanted to marry Eddie Fisher all the more. He was not like them. He was a young man who could touch my heart with his songs. He sang of love with a sweetness and sincerity in his voice that made me glow and feel alive. I could not get him out of my mind.

I had been bothering my mother for some time to buy a phonograph for me, and one day I was able to talk her into it. I no longer had to wait patiently to hear Eddie Fisher on the radio. I had my magical machine. I could place a disc on the turntable and out would come Fisher's voice! What a thrill it was.

I would now walk over to a neighborhood store with my mother, and she would buy me all the Eddie Fisher records I craved, as well as any other records that suited my fancy. I was amazed that I did not have to beg for what I wanted; she bought whatever I requested without any hesitation or reservation. When I complained that I wasn't happy with the 78-rpm records because they were big, clumsy, and broke so easily, my mother went to a record store where she bought me the same records in the compact, unbreakable 45-rpm speed. I now had a double set of records. My collection was growing.

When my uncle Will found out about all the records that were coming into the house, he made a statement in his file: *"Hedda gets her way in big things by 'buying Lenore off' with phonograph records . . . She feels she is losing Lenore, and it's a means of keeping Lenore in the house with her."*

I was on a drug—a self-induced drug called rapture—as I listened to Fisher sing his songs of love. I remained in this state of ecstatic delight until once again word came that he was seriously involved in a romance. Things changed within seconds, as I plunged into despair. How empty my world was whenever I felt I was losing him.

My uncle once again made some notes in his file: "Lenore may be but one of a million girls or more who want to marry Fisher . . ." And he may have been right. But I couldn't let go of my feelings for Fisher. I may have been upset about his romances, but with him in my life, I had something to live for.

Grandma saw my constant mood swings, but she didn't make any comment. She would come up, stay less than an hour, and then leave. She continued to bring stories back to Will, who continued to write notes for his files: *"My mother visited Hedda and Lenore yesterday. She came up with a newspaper in her hand. Before Lenore could see it, Hedda hid it. When my mother left, Hedda gave her a note, admonishing her for bringing a newspaper lest Lenore read something about Eddie Fisher."*

I still was not aware of all this. But I probably would not have known what was going on, even if it happened before my eyes. My mind was elsewhere. Besides my constant roller coaster emotions about Fisher, I was now going out, and I was trying to find my way in a strange world I knew nothing about.

Soon, however, the summer was over. As the weather was changing, I retreated back to the house. My uncle wrote in his file *"Lenore is kept isolated from everyone, except Hedda. No one is welcome in their home . . ."*

At this time, Grandma reported to my uncle an incident he included in his file: *"Hedda's germ phobia seems to be getting more pronounced again. A plumber came the other day to fix a stuffed kitchen drainpipe. For several days thereafter, Hedda did not put the kitchen utensils back in place. She left them in another room, indirectly giving the germs a chance to dissipate themselves."*

I guess I was too busy with my own anxieties to get caught up in Hedda's. My uncle, however, was keeping abreast of what was going on in our home: *"Hedda is extremely depressed—more so than usual. Lenore's spirits are also very low. They are getting on each other's nerves as much as ever, arguing about the least thing . . ."*

I heard about television somewhere, and I began to want it desperately. If I had a TV, I could see dramas, comedy shows, movies, and most of all, I could see Eddie Fisher. I delighted in that thought alone.

I was pestering my mother to buy a TV. Hedda had a deaf ear, and I was frustrated to tears, but I would not give up. I knew it was not a matter of money; my father had left us a substantial amount in savings, bonds, and a valuable taxi medallion. Hedda did not want a TV set. She remained contented to sit in her chair and do nothing.

Again, I had to fight for what I wanted. "We don't have visitors, with the exception of Grandma and Grandpa, and they're here for short visits. We don't have friends. We don't go to movies and shows. We have no entertainment other than the radio and the phonograph. So why can't we get a TV?"

Well, I must have talked myself blue in the face until Hedda finally agreed to go with me to a small TV store across the street. We looked at a number of sets. A very accommodating young salesman, who called himself Vic, recommended a small black and white Motorola. It showed a clear picture, and it played well. So Hedda purchased it on the spot.

Before long, there was a TV in our home. It was a very exciting moment for me. At first, there was just a flickering, but then there was a steady picture on the screen. As my mother turned the knob, I saw people dancing, laughing, talking to each other, and telling jokes. My goodness, this is a marvelous machine!

I couldn't wait to see Eddie Fisher on my screen. But I was also very nervous. What if I saw him and didn't like what I saw?

And soon the big moment came: Eddie Fisher in my living room on my TV! There he was, smiling, holding a Coca-Cola in his hand as he said, "The pause that refreshes." I thought he was very cute with his glowing grin and an impish charm that radiated through the television screen. But he wasn't all that I had built up in my mind. I don't know what I expected, but I was disappointed. The image I had in my mind was very different from what I saw before me. The more I saw him, the more my fantasy faded.

But I still held on to my feelings for Eddie Fisher. What else was there?

28

Handling Money

When I was in my early teens, and the weather was nice and warm, my mother and I went out walking in the neighborhood. I was not very zealous about anything at the time, but I was getting out of the house, and so was my mother. We walked around, not talking much, but just walking, and soon we came upon a large shopping area. As I looked around, I was overwhelmed. There were many clothing stores, a bunch of restaurants, movie houses, record stores and so much more. I didn't know where to look first.

We went into many of the stores and sometimes we made a purchase. I felt good about one thing: Hedda showed no fear of handling anything — including money. What happened to her fear of germs and contamination? I really can't say. But it seemed to be under control, at least in the stores, and I was happy about that.

Money was something foreign to me. I knew it was there, and that my mother could spend it without a second thought. But I didn't care about it until I, myself, had a need to buy something. As I started to go out by myself, I found I was at a loss. *How do I make sense of this thing called money?* As far as I was concerned, it was just pieces of green paper, with coins of different sizes. I was familiar with the saying "Money is meant to be spent" but how strange it felt to have a dollar bill in my hand. Then again, what could I expect? I wasn't allowed to touch money when I was growing up. Hedda believed that money contained germs, but since I generally did not go out of the house, I didn't need to worry about it. But now it was different. I couldn't sit in the house any longer and avoid it. As a teenage girl I needed to go out and buy things for myself.

Once or twice I approached Hedda and said, "Can you teach me how to use money?" She was very nonchalant in her response and I was even more frustrated. I soon went to Hedda and asked for some spending money and she reluctantly gave me a few dollars.

With much discomfort, I journeyed forth and attempted to make small purchases in local stores. How very embarrassed I was when I tried to make change. I broke out in a cold sweat as the cashier watched me in my struggle. I was flustered. Questions kept running through my head: *What do I do with these coins? How much do I give? How much do I get back?* My face was turning red.

When the cashier, or storekeeper, saw I was having trouble, they usually gave me a look that seemed to say, "Don't you know how to count? Where do you come from?" I was on the spot all right, and I tried to hide my ignorance as best I could. I stood there feeling self-conscious and stupid as I handed over my money and accepted whatever change was given to me. Then I made a mad dash to the door, as if there was a tiger on my tail.

What did they think of me? I was ashamed to go to the same store twice, but it was unavoidable; there were only so many stores in the neighborhood. And I wondered: *Why can't I do the things that even small kids know how to do?*

As for the germs that Hedda had spoken of as I was growing up, oddly enough, I didn't feel infected when I handled money. In fact, the thought of washing my hands after a money transaction rarely entered my mind unless I was going to eat, in which case I washed my hands anyway.

For quite some time, my mother and I were living on the money my father left when he died. There was a considerable amount, and yet I felt poorer than poor. It was hard to tell if that was because we did not have any real income, or because I felt so poor at heart. When I went to buy in a store, I didn't feel that I could afford anything. It was an eerie feeling that came over me. To buy or not to buy, that is the big question. When I saw something I really liked, I had to force myself to buy it. I might feel guilt at first, but later, I was glad I did it.

Money. It was new to me, but I was getting used to it. I began to see it not only as a necessity, but also as a good thing to have.

29
With a Song in My Heart

I was still receiving home instruction from the Board of Education and the school semester was coming to an end. I was anticipating the lovely warm summer months when I could go outdoors and experience life beyond my four walls. But now I wanted something more. Ever since I can remember, I had a secret wish to become a singer. My intense feelings for Eddie Fisher gave me motivation to make my dream real. It was time to pursue a singing career, and I worried what my mother's reaction would be. Would this be upsetting to her and cause her to fly off into a rage?

My heart was racing wildly when I said, "Hedda, I've been meaning to tell you for some time, I want to become a singer." There was silence. She just sat there and stared at me. Then I quickly added: "I'm going to need singing lessons…" I was happily surprised that she didn't snap at me with her usual "no." Instead, she seemed to be calmly taking it in. So, I went a step further. "I'm also going to need a gown. I'll need to have it ready for my debut." I was amazed that Hedda didn't say a word. I had yet to take a single singing lesson, and there I was, talking about my "debut." What was Hedda thinking? I dare not ask. And then I heard her say, "We'll see." Suddenly, my spirits soared. I had a feeling she was going to say yes.

The following day, Hedda and I went out to take a walk in the neighborhood. Around the corner from where we lived was a little shop that catered to women's clothing. A short, black-haired lady usually smiled and waved hello when we passed by. I said, "Let's go inside and look around." Hedda agreed, and soon we saw quite a few gowns hanging on the rack. I told the lady what I wanted it for, and she suggested a light blue chiffon gown. She brought it over to me. It was pretty enough, and I tried it on. It fluffed out a little too much at the waist and it made me look a trifle heavy; I was not happy about that. The lady saw my hesitancy and said, "It's not that expensive, and it does look good on you. The color blue is very becoming to your eyes. It just needs a little shortening."

I started looking at the gown more closely. I wasn't sure that this was the one for me, but before I could say anything, Hedda cut in and told the lady to shorten it. She then reached into her bag, took out some cash and paid for it on the spot! I was pleasantly surprised that my mother would do this for me. I would usually have to plead with her to get anything, but she seemed to be different now.

I went home and thought about the gown; it was beautiful, and I was glad we bought it. It was very different from anything I ever owned. I became excited about it, like a child with her first toy. I was going to have this gorgeous garment for my singing career. I might even wear it on a date with Eddie Fisher! My thoughts were running rampant.

But what about the bra? I would need a strapless bra for the gown. Then I worried about what kind of shoes I would need, and the accessories for the gown. How would I wear my hair? I was getting myself into a dither over something that wasn't happening or about to occur.

Soon something dawned upon me that I hadn't really thought about before. I failed to consider, after spending all those years locked away in the house, how was I going to suddenly branch out and perform in front of a crowd of people when I was so afraid of people in general? This was a real problem, but I couldn't focus on it; my head was in the clouds.

When the time came, I went to the ladies' shop around the corner and picked up my gown. The alteration was a success, and the gown fit as though it were made for me. I took it home and hung it in the closet. Just knowing it was there put my mind at ease. I admired it on the clothing rack and cherished it as if it were some sacred cloth. It was just too delicate and much too beautiful to touch.

My mother and I were taking a stroll in the neighborhood one day when we came upon a music school. I was thinking about singing lessons when I asked: "Could we go upstairs, and see what it's like?" Again, my mother was agreeable.

We climbed up a long, dimly lit stairway that led into a dingy, dilapidated room. The furniture was old and shabby, and coldness permeated the place. In some bizarre way, it reminded me of the place I called home.

Near a beat-up piano stood several racks of music sheets. I saw some of my favorite songs: "Hey There," "Wish You Were Here," and some Bing Crosby hits. My heart was dancing with delight as I held them in my hand; it felt like I had the world at my fingertips. Soon we came upon the posted prices for music lessons. I turned to Hedda and said, "The lessons are not that expensive."

Just then, a short, blond-haired man walked over. He was pale, slender, and somewhat on the frail side. He introduced himself: "I'm the singing teacher. I have sung professionally for years and I'm now rendering musical services to the public."

I could feel enthusiasm well up inside of me; I would finally be working with a professional, someone who would teach me to sing well enough so that I might make a living at it. Eventually, I might even be able to sing with Eddie Fisher!

The teacher suggested that I come for several lessons each week, but my mother explained that she could not afford it. I wound up going once a week for about an hour. My mother bought a slew of song sheets and we brought them with us each time.

"Breathe deeply and sing from the diaphragm!" He would say it over and over as he sat at the piano and provided musical accompaniment for me. He would soon show me how to breathe from the diaphragm, and how to project my voice. He sang in a high pitch as he vigorously pounded the keys of the piano. As his voice came bursting forth, it didn't sound like music to me, it sounded more like a screeching noise.

But I was so very eager to learn. I stood there, trying hard to take in his breathing technique, but the notes were not coming out right. I was straining; I was singing from the throat. I could not achieve the proper breath control. But I continued to persevere.

On these hot summer days, the windows were wide open, and I became overly self-conscious as I heard the sound of my voice soar through the air and fill the room. Beads of perspiration were forming on my forehead as I struggled to hit high notes and I wondered: *What if people in the street below hear me singing and make fun of me? And what if someone were to scream up something nasty or vulgar?* It was not such a far-fetched thought since the music school was just one flight above street level. At any moment, I expected a loud **"Shut up!"** But it never happened. How thankful I was. Every now and then I wondered how I would ever become a singer with such negative thoughts spinning around in my head.

And I continued to struggle with my singing lessons. It still troubled me: *Why can't I do what the teacher is asking of me? Will I ever be able to sing from my diaphragm?*

I was discouraged. I wanted to change teachers, but that was not an option; he was the only singing teacher in the school. I was achieving nothing more than a state of frustration and I finally decided to stop. Somewhere in my heart was the hope that I might be able to find another teacher—someone who could actually help me with my singing.

In the meantime, I had to recuperate from my disappointment. I would continue to sing at home. My mother was still my audience. When she heard me sing, she would continue to smile and say, "very nice." When I was courageous, I might sing a little in front of Grandma. She would sit and listen with my mother, then gently clap her hands when I finished. It was a heartwarming moment for me. They liked my singing; I liked the applause. I had a good feeling about myself.

I soon had an idea to have a piano in our home. When I told Hedda this, she said: "What do I need a piano for?" I gingerly explained to her that she could accompany me when I was practicing. I pleaded my case. She was now the judge and jury. What would her verdict be? How ecstatic I was when she finally said yes.

I ran over to the music school and let them know that I was looking for a piano. I soon received good news: a used piano was selling for a nominal fee—would I be interested? A voice within me screamed: *"I must have that piano!"*

I could hardly wait. I will never forget how overjoyed I was the day the piano was delivered. I stood there, marveling at it. It was a gorgeous piece of furniture and it had a wonderful sound. The tone was loud and clear, and it looked brand new. I wondered why anyone would ever want to sell it for ten dollars. It seemed like a giveaway.

But the piano became an ornament in the house, like everything else. Hedda didn't touch it. She was her detached, lethargic self, sitting in her chair, not interested in anything, unless it was something she was compelled to do. From that point on, I would just stand there and admire this beautiful piano in an otherwise dark and dreary room.

So, what was I going to do about my singing career? Perhaps I didn't need a piano or even a singing teacher. I had the records of my favorite female singers. I could study the styles of Patti Page, Rosemary Clooney, and Doris Day, to name a few, and I could continue to sing along with their records. They became my new singing teachers.

Sometimes it seemed like I was on a hopeless mission. I persevered at practicing with my records until I became exhausted. I didn't feel like I was accomplishing anything, but I continued. The other part of my day I was ruminating about Eddie Fisher and his romantic escapades. I was becoming more and more pessimistic with each passing day. Would any of my hopes ever be realized?

I was feeling sad again when something happened out of the blue that astounded me. My mother and I were sitting and listening to the radio when I heard about a contest to interpret the lyrics of the song, "Nina Never Knew." It was about a girl who didn't know anything about love. I was intrigued by the lyrics and could identify with this girl. So, I sat down and wrote out what I thought she was feeling. Then I put it into an envelope and mailed it off. The prize was a date with the well-known singer, Vic Damone, who had recorded the song.

In a couple of weeks, the name of the winner was announced. As my mother and I sat there listening, we looked at each other in disbelief. I let out a scream. **"Did you hear that? Oh my God! I won the contest!"** What a great feeling! I was bursting with joy. I said, "Now I have to get something to wear for my date." Hedda and I dashed around the corner to the dress shop. We saw a dark red velveteen suit that was simple, inexpensive, but elegant. My mother bought it then and there.

Surprisingly, the date never came off and I wondered what went wrong. But I didn't pursue it since I wasn't a fan of Vic Damone anyway. I entered the contest because I identified with Nina and I had something to say. And I won! I was inspired. I told myself I would not give up, and I would find more ways to move forward and do good things for myself. I could be successful, after all.

30

Starving for Love

I was a young girl of fifteen with an intense desire to find someone who would give me the love and affection I never had. I was starving for love. How very much I wanted to be held, hugged, and kissed. I could no longer live in fantasy. I had to find someone real.

But I didn't know where to turn. I did not have any friends, nor did I know anyone who could introduce me to a nice, attractive young man. After being locked up in the house all those years, I wondered if I would know Mr. Right if I were staring him in the face. I didn't even know how to behave in the presence of others. *What is expected of me? What can I expect from others?* I told myself it really didn't matter; I would just go out into the street and find someone who could love me.

It was summertime, and I was wondering how I could attract the man I was looking for. And just what was I looking for? I really didn't know, and I didn't give much thought to it. I was just hoping that there would be someone out there for me.

I remembered all the attention I got the year before when I went out in those halter-tops and tight pants, much like the movie stars I would see in the magazines. I didn't see anything wrong with the way I dressed. Maybe this year things would be different, and I would meet a man who would accept me not as a sex object but for myself. So, I continued to follow my instincts. I again put on my halter-top, tight pants, a smear of red lipstick and rouge—and I was on my way.

So, there I was once again, on the streets of the Bronx, drawing attention to myself wherever I went. It gave me an uneasy feeling, but it was not unusual for me to feel self-conscious. On the other hand, I was finally out of the house and people were now noticing me. Yes, I was getting plenty of attention, but from the wrong people. One man approached me and asked: "Do you have the correct time?" Another came up to me and said, "I'd like to get to know you over a cup of coffee." Still, another man came over and asked: "Would you like to make easy money?"

I found myself more and more disturbed by the men I was attracting. I abhorred being viewed as a sex object. Sometimes I would sit down on a park bench and think about it: *Why are they treating me like that? I may look sexy, but that doesn't mean I want to have sex—whatever that is. My goal is to find love and I'm going to do whatever I can to get it. I'll get dressed in the sexy garb of the movie stars so I can attract the love I crave into my life. How else am I to find this love?*

I liked my clothes, and I liked my make-up. I did not want to make any changes on behalf of guys who had only one thing on their minds or for that matter, anyone else who was critical of my attire. I wondered: *Why can't they accept me for the way I am?* I had reached a point in my life where I needed to do things my way, right or wrong. If those guys can only see one thing—well, that's too bad. I regarded it as their problem—not mine. But it still bothered me.

I saw girls in the street who were pretty, and others who were plain. And then there were girls who were just as sensuous as I. I wondered if any of them were bothered by men on the street. Were they, too, treated like sex objects? What was it about me that made men come up to me and proposition me? I just couldn't understand it.

I also noticed girls simply dressed in blouses and skirts walking with clean-cut, handsome young men. I admired them. What were they like? What did one have to do to have a fine young man interested in her?

I somehow felt, in my heart, that I could never be like those girls. There was something about them that was different, and I couldn't put my finger on what it was. It was useless to compare myself to any one of them, but I couldn't stop. I continued to be plagued by these thoughts.

And I continued my walks. I would disappear for hours at a time. I was meeting more men—men who gaped at me with a wild gleam in their eyes. I spoke to some who told me stories pertaining to sex that confused and disturbed me. I didn't know what to make of it. I was meeting one character after another. No, I didn't want the money I was offered, nor did I want to get to know any one of them "over a cup of coffee." I wanted love, real genuine love. What did I have to do to get it?

One day I was feeling very low and I thought of Vic, the salesman from the TV shop across the street. He was a young man with dark brown eyes, black kinky hair, and a warm personality. He had asked me to stop by and say hello, so I decided to pay him a visit. He was delighted to see me. We chatted and I sensed something about him that was wholesome and refreshing. We talked about a lot of nothing, but it felt good to have the companionship of a male who treated me with dignity and respect. Was it possible that anyone would like me for just being me? I was grateful that Vic was accepting me as a human being—not as an object. This was something new and spirit lifting for me. We spoke for a while until he became busy, and then I left.

I went back several times and we talked some more. Vic had a way of welcoming me and making me feel like an old friend who just came back into his life. One day I mustered up the courage to ask, "Are you married, Vic?" His quick response was, "Why no, I'm not. Should I be?" It really wasn't that important to me, and yet it was a relief to hear him say that. As he spoke, I noticed a twinkle in his eye that lit up the serious expression on his face. Soon something about Vic began to bother me. Was it his overly friendly manner? I thought he was flirtatious at times, and that made me wonder if he was really being genuine with me. Was this his real self, or was this a face that he presented to the world?

Hedda did not like Vic. But then again, whom did she like? She gave me all kinds of reasons why I shouldn't bother with him, none of which made any sense to me. She told me she saw him one day walking in the street holding the hand of a child. "He's probably a married man posing as a single fellow." I wondered about that. Then again, did it really matter? He was not a love interest; he was an acquaintance who I knew in the neighborhood. Despite her warnings, I managed to maintain friendly contact with Vic whenever I saw him, which was not that often.

I was aware that whenever I said good things about someone, the inevitable occurred: Hedda would verbally tear that person to pieces and I wound up turning away from the person she was badmouthing. She had an extraordinary way of influencing me and making me feel miserable. One day I got up the nerve to tell her: "You just want to get rid of anyone I might have as a friend so that you can keep me in the house with you!"

She did not respond.

I was still very attached to Hedda emotionally. I told her about the experiences I had with men in the street, and although she didn't say much, I could see she was distressed. It was clear to me that she didn't like me going out on my own and breaking away from her. When I left the house, she looked depressed; there were tears in her eyes and she seemed more down in the dumps than usual. Still, I had to do what I felt was right for me.

So many times, Hedda would ask, "Where are you going?" and I would reply, "Out for a walk." Not knowing exactly where I was going, that is all I could honestly say. I had more important things to worry about—like finding a way to bump into the man who would change my life.

I once again walked over to Southern Boulevard. I picked a spot where there were some benches, a few trees and little traffic. It was about 9:30 on a quiet weekday morning. The area was practically deserted, except for a few people passing by. I was sitting on a bench, wearing the same sexy attire and quite a bit of make-up, when a man sat down next to me. He was dark-skinned and attractive, with black, straight hair and dark brown eyes. I felt a little nervous when he started to stare at me. I tried to act casual and avoid eye contact, but I wasn't doing very well. How confusing it was: I wanted so badly to meet someone, and when I had the opportunity staring me in the face, I was too afraid to open myself to it. Maybe that's because I sensed there was something wrong about it.

Suddenly, he broke the silence and started a conversation. He smiled and said, "Hello. My name is Jim." I had the strangest feeling; it was as though he knew I was waiting there for someone— possibly him.

There was a sincere look in his eyes, and his voice was soft and low. "Do you come to the benches often? Do you live in the neighborhood?" I began to talk to him. It seemed there couldn't be anything wrong with that. Yet, as we spoke, I was on edge.

And we continued to talk. Something about Jim appealed to my little girl instincts. It was when he spoke of taking me out for a cup of coffee that I began to panic. *Who is he? I don't really know him!* Even worse, I had never been in a restaurant before, and that in itself made me nervous. My heart was pounding. I wanted to run back home as quickly as my legs could carry me. I said, "I'm sorry, I have to go now. Perhaps we can meet some other time."

"When will you be on the Boulevard again?" he asked. I simply told him "I'm around." He wanted to set a date to meet, but I reassured him, "I come here frequently, I'm sure we'll meet again."

Jim did not pursue the issue. He allowed me to leave in a quiet, dignified manner. It was a relief to be home and feel safe again. I had escaped without having to reveal myself to someone I just met on a park bench. I had no intention of letting him know that I had never been in a restaurant, and that the thought of it made my skin crawl. And I kept thinking: *Who is this man, Jim?*

I continued to think about my brief encounter. I somehow knew I would see Jim again. And I did. It was another lovely summer morning when I sat on the same bench at about the same time that Jim came by. This time, however, Jim did not have patience to linger over words. He sat down next to me and said, "You know,

I'd like to take you to the zoo. My car is parked right there at the curb. What do you say we go now?"

Suddenly, my anxiety zoomed. My mother had always said: "Remember, if you go in a car with a man, you're asking for trouble!" Now Jim was asking me to go into his car. I surmised some kind of danger. I nervously told Jim: "I don't go in cars with strangers."

However, in his soft-spoken, gentle way, he was able to assure me: "Nothing is going to happen." His eyes met mine as he said, "We'll ride over to the zoo and then we'll take a nice stroll through the park. We'll enjoy the passing scene."

I heard my mother's voice telling me: "Don't go!" But my heart had made up my mind. I nervously got into the car. Suddenly I felt trapped. My heart was racing, and I was trembling inside. *Where is he taking me? What does he want with me?* All I knew about him was that his name was Jim, and I wasn't even sure of that.

I had done a crazy thing. I was expecting the worst at any moment. Why was I jeopardizing my life by going into a car with a total stranger? It was mind-boggling. But I was fortunate; I did get to the zoo, unharmed. I felt safe when I saw other people around, and I knew I was not alone with Jim. But when we came to spots that were deserted, my fear started to escalate.

Jim took me further into the zoo, and I tried hard to conceal my fear. At some point he casually slipped his hand into mine. It might have been the most natural thing in the world, if he were my sweetheart or even a friend. I suddenly felt annoyed. *Why am I holding hands with someone I don't even know?*

It was absurd. I didn't want to be holding hands, I didn't want to be in the zoo, and I did not want to be with Jim. So why was I? I couldn't answer that question. I was gazing off into the distance, staring at trees and greens — but I didn't see a thing.

What will Jim's next move be? Is this handholding a prelude to something else? If so, what can I expect? A thought ran wildly through my mind: *I don't know a thing about sex!*

We walked a little more, and then suddenly Jim turned to me and said, "Let's go back. Where do you live? I'll drop you off."

How happy I was to hear that! I quickly replied: "You can drop me off where we met."

We did not speak on the way back. And before I knew it, I was back on the Boulevard. What caused Jim to have a sudden change of heart? I didn't know. But I was glad he was gone, and that I was safe. I knew I didn't want to see him again.

And I hurried home. I told my mother about Jim. "I met a man in the street, and I went out with him — in his car!"

She was not upset. I thought it incredible. She had always warned me how bad men were; that girls go out, get "knocked up" and have babies; and that I was never to go in a car with a stranger. I had defied what she had told me; I went into a car with a stranger. I had stared danger in the face. She had nothing to say about this. But what did I expect? Hedda was enmeshed in her own world, as usual.

I kept thinking about my experience with Jim. It wasn't so bad. Nothing terrible had happened. It was still summer: sunny, warm, and the time of the year for love…

31

Sunday Morning In The Park

I discovered an area of Bronx Park at least ten blocks from where I lived. It was nice and large, with a lot of trees and benches. I felt something special about being there. It had the feel of a romantic setting. I saw many young people holding hands and looking lovey-dovey. As they strolled by on a summer afternoon, I all the more longed to have someone of my own.

I began to take long walks in the early morning. About seven o'clock on a Sunday morning in September, I left the house and began my walk. The streets were deserted and there was a nip in the air, reminding me that fall was on its way. I was wearing a blouse, skirt, and medium heel shoes, with enough makeup to appear older than my fifteen years. I recall feeling chilly. I was sorry I hadn't taken my jacket.

I was halfway towards Bronx Park when I saw a young man walking in the same direction. He was tall and thin with sandy brown hair. A quick glance told me he was either in his late teens or early twenties. He had his hands in the pockets of his jacket and, as he moved along in a huddled posture, he appeared to be either cold or deep in thought. He looked in my direction and, as our eyes met, he said, "Hi. Mind if I join you?"

No, I didn't mind at all. In fact, that sounded just fine. He was attractive and had a boyish quality about him that I liked right away. He introduced himself as "Joey."

I told him my name, and I proceeded to walk with him. Suddenly, I felt Joey's hand in mine. Again, a stranger was holding my hand! I felt tense and uncomfortable, as I did with Jim. Something did not feel right about holding hands with a man I just met, but if it felt bad with Jim, it was much worse now; Joey was gripping my hand. Why was he pressing my hand like that? Was he afraid that if he didn't hold on tightly, I just might slip away? I wanted to turn back, but somehow, I couldn't do that. And then Joey told me, "I'm a bum. I've been out all night. I'm just getting back now. I've been at a party—you know, drinking and all that . . ."

I wondered why he was telling me such things. I thought it rather strange to tell a girl you've just met that you're a bum, when you should be trying to impress her. I closed my ears to what he was saying and asked, "Do you have a job, Joey?"

Rather spontaneously, Joey answered, "I'm a printer. I work in Manhattan—you know, a printing shop in Manhattan . . ."

I was not sure I believed him, whether it was about his job or the party. But it did not seem to matter; I was living in the moment, and for the moment.

We continued to walk in the direction of the park. When the conversation came to a halt and silence filled the air, I had a sick feeling in my stomach. Where were we going? Why was I going into the park at seven o'clock on Sunday morning with someone who had just told me he was a bum and had spent the night drinking? I perceived imminent danger. I struggled with a feeling that said, *Turn back!*

When we arrived at the park, Joey did not take me into the entrance I was familiar with. We walked beyond for almost a street block. We then came upon another opening, one I had not seen before. Joey seemed quite familiar with the area. He escorted me along a path that led into a huge, secluded grassland. It seemed that not a soul had been there in ages. An eerie feeling swept over me, as I gazed around. I felt that I was standing in the middle of nowhere.

What was this all about? Joey had taken me all the way to this desolate spot. *What is he going to do with me? What have I gotten myself into this time?* Love. Finding someone to love me. Those songs that spoke of love never indicated moments like these! I suddenly felt threatened by something I did not understand. A Sunday morning. Not a person around, just Joey and me. We had the park all to ourselves. I wanted to scream, but I knew no one would hear me.

As soon as we came to the end of the path, Joey stopped. He then opened his pants and exposed himself. I was aghast. A gripping fear came over me. Joey stood there, looking at me, and then he said, "Aw, come on, do for me what you do for all the other guys!"

What did he mean by that? A sweat of panic passed through me. *What should I do for him that I do for all the other guys?* Joey, who had appeared so attractive to me, now looked sinister. I suddenly started to tremble. Joey kept demanding: "I need it, I got to have it!"

Then he started to talk vulgar to me. He used words I didn't understand. I stood there, frozen. *What am I going to do?* Joey soon became violent. He started to shake me by the shoulders and rasped, "Some other guy might be beating you up by now! I ain't kidding you. You gotta give it to me—now!"

What in the world is he talking about? What if I don't give him this thing he wants? Is he going to hurt me, or possibly kill me? My heart was pounding, as I saw Joey take off his jacket and lay it down on the grass. I didn't know what sex was about, but something told me I was going to find out. And then the realization: *This must be how girls get pregnant!*

I had to tell him the truth, whether he believed me or not: "I've never had sex before. I don't know what it is. You have to believe me when I say this: I'm a virgin! I am a virgin!"

He looked at me as if I were crazy. Then he uttered, "You're no cherry!"

I said to myself, *What does he mean by "cherry"? What is a cherry?* Again, he adamantly repeated, "Look, I have to have it. I must have it!"

The urgency in his voice told me if I did not comply, something terrible was about to happen to me. I had heard about something called "rape."

Oh no! I'm going to be raped. I'm going to be forced into having sex! I don't know what to do. I'm in his clutches and there's no way to escape. If I resist, I may not get out of the park alive. I have to do whatever he wants.

The next thing I knew, Joey was trying to force himself upon me. I started to cry, and I begged him to stop. I repeated, "I'm a virgin, I've never had sex! I'm a virgin . . ." He paused for a moment, and said, "Okay. Just let me try, and if it hurts, I'll stop."

Moments later, I cried, "It hurts! It hurts! Please stop!"

Joey hesitated, and then said, "If you want to get out of here, you're gonna have to do what I tell you . . ."

He forced me to engage in a sexual act that made me sick to my stomach. But I remained a virgin.

I recall heading back along the grassland path in a kind of daze. Joey turned to me and said, "You're over eighteen, aren't you? I hope you're not a minor!"

He had a frightened look on his face. Why was he looking at me in such a peculiar way? He repeated the question, and I could feel his tension. Why was my age so important? Something did not feel right in telling him my real age (fifteen), so I assured him I was over eighteen. He didn't say another word.

It seemed like such an endless walk. I couldn't wait to get out of the park, and away from Joey. I soon saw the pavement of the street, and it looked so good to me. And then Joey disappeared. I took a deep breath. *Thank God, he's gone!* In a sort of trance, I found my way home.

I still kept no secrets from my mother. Defiantly, I told her about my experience. Suddenly, a cold silence fell over the room. I saw that wild look in her eyes that penetrated every nerve and cell of my body. Her face reddened, and her eyes began to bulge. "You know that woman, Doris, who lives around the corner? Well, she slept with a man and she had a baby. **If you have a little bastard, you know where you're going—you're going right out of here with it! You're not going to bring shame into this house!"**

I don't know what I expected, maybe some compassion or words of comfort from my mother. To look at me in that moment, anyone could tell how distraught I was. But not my mother. She didn't want to know anything about my confusion, my pain, or what I was going through. She had one concern, and that was how disgraced she would be if I were to bring home a baby out of wedlock. Perhaps I should have been used to her noncaring, her indifference, but I never was.

"Look at what I raised! A little tramp! One of these days you're going to get into a lot of trouble. Just remember, you come home with a little bastard, and out you go!"

Her cheeks were now blazing and veins were protruding in her neck as she hollered, **"If you get pregnant, you'll go to a work farm! That's where girls like you end up—on a work farm!"**

A work farm? I had never heard of that before, and I became frightened. What did she mean by that? Then she added, **"You'll yet end up as a prostitute!"**

I didn't like it, but I had it coming to me. Perhaps that's all I was. Perhaps I was nothing more than a little tramp.

I sang love songs when I was a little girl. I heard songs that spoke about the wonder of love. I heard songs that stressed the joy and happiness that comes with love. I heard that a tender, caring love could take the pain away from one's lonely existence. Perhaps there was a special someone out there who could change my life with his love. It seemed like all I had to do was find that love. But it wasn't happening. What was happening certainly did not feel like what I heard in those songs. I was looking for love. I was getting attention, but it was all about sex, and nothing about love. I was on the road to self-destruction.

32

The Facts of Life

"Just remember, you come home with a little bastard, and out you go!" Those words were ringing in my ears. It was just a few words, dripping in venom, but Hedda had made her point.

I was just forced to indulge in sexual activity against my will. I didn't know at the time this was rape. I started to worry: *If there is another Joey incident, I might very well become pregnant. The last thing in the world I want is a baby!*

The very thought of having a baby terrified me. I must have been about nine years old when I said to myself, *I will never have children.* Motherhood seemed like a terrible trap to me. I saw how horrible my mother looked in her old, raggedy jumper, and how angry and bitter she was, as she yelled and screamed and used her fists on me. *Is this what you become when you're a mother? Will I wind up like that? Oh, God, no, I don't want any part of it. Motherhood is not for me!*

But I could not allow my fear of pregnancy to overtake me and diminish my dream of finding the genuine love I heard about on the radio. I would continue my search and not let anything get in my way.

I was back in the park the next week. I was once more meeting fellows looking to satisfy their sexual urges. I guess I disappointed them, for hugging, kissing, and petting were as far as I went. Then I managed to slip away. Because I was so love starved, so deprived of touch and affection when I was a little child, I was eager to be hugged and kissed and held in someone's arms. But very soon I was becoming disillusioned. Who were these men? They didn't want to know me; they just wanted my body. How terrible that made me feel. And how crazy it was. I might have been risking my life, but I didn't want to stop and think about it. My need to find "love" was overpowering my better instincts. I was obsessed, and I badly needed to talk to someone—anyone—but whom?

It was a joyless existence, a sordid life I had chosen for myself. But it still was better than being shut away in the house with my mother. I didn't like the guys I was meeting, but maybe they were not all like that.

The amazing thing here (or should I say the sad thing) is that I still knew very little about sex. Despite my various encounters with men, kids in elementary school probably knew more about sex than I. When I was a little girl, I would ask my mother how babies are made, and she would get a silly grin on her face and clam up. At some point, I became aware that sex, men, and babies were all tied in together, and I had to keep that in mind. Although I was vigilant when I was with a man, there still was a possibility that I could become pregnant. So far, I was very lucky.

I kept walking around in my neighborhood. A feeling of emptiness continued to follow me wherever I went. I was glad to talk to anyone who would listen to me. One day I came upon a young woman feeding a stray cat near the curb. I thought it was a kind gesture on her part, and being a cat lover myself, I felt a need to talk to her. So, I introduced myself and she told me her name was Madelyn.

I immediately noticed that her eyes were large and glassy, and that gave me a peculiar feeling, but it didn't stop me from speaking to her. She wore her sandy brown hair pulled away from her face, and I thought she was attractive in a strange, unsettling way. As I became involved in a conversation about cats, there was something about her that continued to bother me; I didn't know what it was. And we continued to talk.

Madelyn soon told me that she lived with an older woman, Sonia, in the neighborhood. Several times she referred to her as "my landlady." She did not talk about herself; she continuously made references to Sonia as if she were her other self. I thought the conversation was somewhat odd, but I had found someone to talk to, so I decided to disregard it; I was most intent upon making a friend.

The next time I saw Madelyn, her hair was hanging loose and stringy, and the strange look in her eyes appeared more prominent. She asked if I would like to come over and visit her. I jumped at the opportunity. She gave me her address and emphasized, "If I'm not in when you come, mention my name and wait with Sonia." The way she said it sounded strange, but I agreed. Since I didn't have any friends, I figured anyone might be better than no one.

I soon decided to pay a visit to Madelyn. I walked over to the address she gave me and nervously rang the bell. A short, stocky woman came to the door. She told me her name was Sonia. She was clad in a loose house robe and held a glass in her hand. When I asked, "Where's Madelyn?" Sonia told me, "She's expected later. Come in and sit down. You can wait here for her."

Sonia sat down with the glass in her hand and offered me a seat on her couch. She was sipping on her drink, as she started to speak. She had many stories to tell, and strangely enough, it was all about sex, things I never heard before, things I knew nothing about. It felt weird; I had never seen this lady in my life, and yet, there she was, sharing with me her knowledge about something so very personal. I felt somewhat uncomfortable as she spoke, but there was a part of me that was really curious to hear what she had to say. I sensed she knew that from the way I reacted.

"Men make babies. You go to bed with a man and he plants the seed. And the seed gets fertilized . . ."

As Sonia continued, I became frustrated; I didn't know what she was talking about. When I tried to find out, her explanation became even more confusing. I decided not to pursue it, lest I show more of my ignorance. However, one thing was very clear to me:

she did not approve of sexual relations between men and women. She was rambling on, trying to teach me the facts of life from her viewpoint and, as much as I wanted to hear her stories, I found them quite disturbing. "Men make babies. They plant the seed." She kept repeating that in a derogatory tone. Was she telling me to stay away from men?

I never bothered to find out. When I became disturbed to the point where I could not take in another word, I rose from my chair and politely said that I had to be leaving. Enough was enough! Sonia graciously extended an invitation: "Come back another time. Madelyn is usually here."

So much for that! I knew I would never go back there again.

I thought a lot about Madelyn and Sonia—Madelyn gazing at me with a glassy stare, and Sonia sipping on her beverage as she bashed the world of masculinity. The more I thought about the two of them, the more puzzled I became. I had heard somewhere about women who were infatuated with other women. I wondered if Sonia was one of them, and if that was so, was she hoping to entice me into that kind of lifestyle?

This thing called "sex"—it was getting in my way. It seemed that wherever I turned, the issue of sex was there to fascinate, confuse, and upset me. I began to wonder, *Is love and sex one and the same?* As I encountered each new experience with disappointment, I asked myself the same question over and over: *Is this what life is all about—just sex?*

33

The Outside World

At the age of fifteen, I would sit in the kitchen and reflect upon the outside world. I didn't understand it; I wasn't able to become a part of it. I thought it was a pretty tough place.

Throughout my childhood, I heard talk about the outside world. I wondered, *Why do people rave about it? What is all this stuff about it being so wonderful, so fantastic?* According to Grandma, I was missing out on my life. Repeatedly, she would tell my mother, "It's a big world out there! Take her downstairs. Let her see the world!"

I remember my father coming home from work and eating his supper. He didn't talk; he was the silent man. Then, all of a sudden, I heard him say, "Did she go out today?" That was about all he said. It bothered me: *What is so important about going out?*

Every now and then my father asserted, "I want to take her downtown to see the Great White Way!" Hedda, plainly annoyed, would hatefully retort, **"She doesn't need any 'Great White Way.' She has enough right here!"** Didn't he know that she was going to say no?

I wondered, *What is this "Great White Way"? And why was it so important that I see it?* It must have been something very special, for when he spoke about it, there was a sparkle in my father's eyes that I rarely saw.

When I was a little girl and my mother was in the hospital, my Uncle Will was fighting with Grandpa for permission to take me out. But I was much too scared to leave the safety of my home. I would sit in my chair and ruminate about it: *What is it like to be out there? What am I missing? They all talk about how great it is—how can they all be wrong?*

The few times I saw my Uncle Will and Aunt Jessie, they would enthusiastically endorse the magic of the outside world. Jessie would tell me, "There are movies, and shows, and art museums, and restaurants to eat in. There's just so much to do out there!" But I wasn't interested in any of it.

The outside world seemed so mystical and unattainable. It preyed on my mind as I kept telling myself, *I'm safe at home. Why abandon something secure and subject myself to the unknown?*

I was just entering my teens when I had my first real exposure to the outside world. I went downstairs by myself, into the street. I didn't know where to turn first. I saw people scurrying to and fro and there was constant movement all around. *How overwhelming!* It seemed like there were a multitude of things to do and places to see. But there was also something strange; I sensed that strangeness wherever I went, and it troubled me.

I looked at the people around me. It seemed they wore many faces, and I was intrigued, and frightened, by what I saw. Some looked plastic and cold, as if carved in stone. Some were happy and exuberantly alive, while others looked as if they were about to cry. Still others had an air of indifference about them.

I passed neighbors in the hallway and on the street; I sensed them looking at me as if I were a creature from outer space. Some might say "Hello." Otherwise, I received a nonverbal message that seemed to say, "You keep your distance, I will keep mine!" Did they think I was strange because I rarely went out of the house? I often felt like a leper in my own building. I longed for social contact, and I could not understand why people had to be so aloof. What was it about me that made people distance themselves from me?

I gave it a lot of thought. I concluded that I was different, and people just didn't like me. It seemed that life in the real world was difficult and hard—even cruel. You had to be smart, informed and really aware, not only to succeed, but also, to survive.

I would stand in front of my building and watch people pass by. I saw tongues wagging wildly; smiles extending from ear to ear; eyes that would dilate and beam, and then the faces went blank. It was almost as if they wore masks that could be taken on and off. And I watched some more.

I felt diminished every time I walked past the candy store. When the fellows there saw me coming down the street, they would have something vulgar to say or snicker about. They didn't even know me. Did they single me out because I looked different? Did they have x-ray vision where they could see inside of me and know just how different I felt? The more I thought about it, the more agitated I became. It took great effort to walk past them and their mocking expressions without bursting into tears.

Yes, I was very sensitive to my surroundings. Quite a few times I saw people on the street who I thought were making fun of me. Sure enough, as I turned around, they, too, turned around; they were looking at me and laughing! I wondered, *What's so funny?* A few women snickered and made comments to each other as they passed by. *What was that all about?*

Then there were the men who would try to pick me up. Truck drivers hollered out the windows as they drove by. That, too, made me feel awkward and uncomfortable. *If only this would stop!* But it didn't. I couldn't understand what I was doing to bring on this kind of response.

I felt like one great oddity in a very strange society. Wherever I went, I felt empty and lost. I didn't seem to fit in anywhere. How awful that was! Nobody cared about me, or what I was feeling. I was just there, sticking out like a sore thumb, trying to hide from ridicule, and yet desperately longing to be accepted by those who were ridiculing me. As terrible as the whole scene appeared to me, I still longed to be a part of it.

Many a time I had wanted to approach a person in a store or on the street. I would gaze their way and hope for a response, but the look I received seemed to say, "Why are you staring at me? Don't you have anything better to do?" I felt an ache inside. The more I wanted to "belong," the more alone I was.

As I watched people on the street talking, laughing, sharing with one another, I was reminded that I had no one. How I hungered for the friendship I never had. I thought so much about it as I was growing up: *What was it like to have a friend? Would I ever be able to have a friendship with another human being?* As I looked around, I didn't think it would ever happen.

I retreated to the house. I was timid; I was lonely and sad. I was struggling with feelings—all kinds of feelings—over which I didn't seem to have any real control. I needed someone to talk to, possibly a shoulder to cry on, and a helping hand. But there was no one. I felt hollow inside, and there didn't seem to be any way to fill that hole.

And I continued to observe people on the street. They were part of a throng that was foreign to me. I thought about the passing parade. I could have been drowning in buckets of tears and I don't think anyone would have noticed or cared.

So, I stepped out of a dark, sedentary existence into a supposedly better way of life. It was different from anything I surmised. I thought I was missing something being locked away in the house. But at least I felt safe. I did not feel safe in the outside world.

34

Sweet Sixteen

"There are gang wars in the neighborhood. These gangs take young girls off the street and rape them! There was an abduction of a teenage girl just the other day…"

My mother was telling me horrible stories about girls my age, and I was becoming very frightened. Soon, I had no desire to go outside by myself. I didn't even want to go out with her. I was not very happy in the outside world anyhow. The one good thing about going out was the sense of freedom I had breaking away from Hedda. I was asserting my independence, and, for about three years, I was slowly getting the feel of going downstairs by myself. When the weather was warmer, I had an urge to go out, but when it began to change and get colder, I was back in the house. This time, with the sinister stories my mother was telling me, I didn't think I would ever go outside again.

I was now as homebound as I ever was. Once more, I was completely under my mother's thumb. I felt as though an emotional paralysis had taken control of me. I had regressed; I was helpless. I was back in my childhood again.

Just as before, Hedda didn't want people in her home. My uncle Will wrote a letter to relatives in California, saying: *"Before the summer vacation, I visited them about once every two or three weeks for a short while. Since I have come home from Martha's Vineyard, Hedda and Lenore do not answer the doorbell when I ring. They only answer my mother's knock on the door and her call, 'Hedda....' My mother goes up to see Hedda almost every day. She does some shopping for them. But otherwise she too is not very welcome. Hedda often tells her not to come up the next day. 'Skip a day. We have too much to do here'.*"

Dear Grandma. She lived such a pained existence. Will wrote about Grandma in his file: *"My poor mother. Jessie and I often wonder how she is able to take all this. But she lives on—not too well, and very unhappy."*

But Grandma kept coming back with the same concerns. She reminded me about my back as usual: "You're slouching again! Stand up tall! You're a young woman now and you're bending over like an old lady!" I was annoyed hearing this over and over, but it was true. My curvature of the spine had progressed, and I continued to tip to the right side. When Hedda walked out of the room, Grandma once again sneaked in another reminder. She would thrust her shoulders back and staunchly tell me to "straighten up!" If Hedda caught her in the act, she would give her a contemptuous look and say, "That's enough mixing in! Enough telling her what to do! She knows enough already—too much!"

It made me hurt and angry that my mother had no caring about my back. There I was, growing up crooked and my mother couldn't care less. But my grandma seemed worried. Whenever she could, she communicated her concern and I appreciated it so much.

There were times when Grandma would refrain from telling me anything. But when she felt something was very wrong, she would harp on it. When my mother was out of sight, she whispered to me: "Your clothes are not fitting right. When you wear a skirt or anything with a belt, raise the right side to make both sides equal. Otherwise, you look lopsided."

It seemed like a clever trick, camouflaging my curvature. When I looked in the mirror, I felt grateful to Grandma for bringing it to my attention and I thanked her for letting me know. I felt cared about in that moment. But many a time Grandma became frustrated. "No, you're not doing it right! Let me show you…"

When Hedda came into the room and caught Grandma showing me how to wear my skirt, she raged, **"What are you doing? She doesn't need that!"**

It tore me to pieces. Grandma was showing concern about my scoliosis, and Hedda was showing her disdain. Hedda was like a broken record spinning out of control. How I wished I could turn her off. I never got used to the emotional pain she inflicted on Grandma and me. Many a time Grandma would brave my mother's wrath and yell back: **"Don't tell me what to say! If I want to tell her something, I will!"**

I silently applauded Grandma for putting my mother in her place. But most of the time Grandma looked away. I could see that Grandma was hurting, and I wanted to say something comforting, but I would not dare—I knew Hedda would become more enraged and I didn't want that. Sitting in our kitchen, with sad, downcast eyes, Grandma often reflected: "I have a heavy heart." I knew she wasn't talking about her physical condition.

I recall the day when Grandma, more distressed than usual, whispered to me: "My daughter is rotten, she's no damn good! She opens up such a big mouth to me…" I didn't know what to say; I was just glad Hedda didn't hear Grandma say that.

Grandma was used to biting her tongue until she couldn't any longer. When she spoke up, she and my mother continued to have a war of words. They both had their points to make. Who was right? Who was wrong? I was already sixteen and it made me sick to my stomach to hear them fighting as much as when I was a child of ten. I thought their fights were ridiculous and I continued to tune them out. And Grandma continued to run out the door in a state of upheaval.

Why is my mother so mean? That thought constantly crossed my mind. And I often wondered why Hedda was usually hostile to Grandma. I sat there ruminating for a while, squelching my hurt and anger. I soon numbed out.

Through the years, I longed to see people in our home but, with the exception of the homebound tutor who came on a mandatory basis, we had no visitors. Grandma was the one person who braved the storm of Hedda and came into our home. These were precious moments for me. I respected Grandma and thought of her as a very smart lady. When she talked, I listened. She knew how to be blunt, open, and honest, and I liked that aspect of her.

Grandma was now coming up and telling us stories about the people who came into Grandpa's necktie store. She spoke with zest and zeal about happy people on trips, traveling around the country and enjoying their lives. Hedda became irritated and barked: "Who wants to hear that? I have enough troubles. I don't care what others are doing."

That was the end of Grandma's stories for that day. But those stories had an effect upon me. I was extremely envious. It seemed to me that just about everybody in the world had some kind of happiness, some sort of achievement, some kind of meaning in their lives. What did I have? What could I hope for?

Mr. Schultz, my homebound teacher, continued to come twice a week for two hours at a time, to give me "home instruction." I think the only reason Hedda allowed him into the house is because the Board of Education required that I receive an education and, since I wasn't going to school, the only way I could receive it was at home. So, this was a necessity and something over which my mother had no control.

Mr. Schultz, pleasant as ever, continued to talk about things that interested him, with no particular emphasis on schoolwork. However, when he did speak about schoolwork, I sat there and appeared to be listening. I'm pretty sure he knew I was placating him, as I tried to get away with the least studying possible. I thought I was doing a pretty good job at it.

I once was a girl who wanted to study and learn and "be smart." An amazing transformation in me had occurred. At sixteen, there was very little I wanted to do. I had no interest in education or the world around me and no thoughts about the future.

I had become an awful lot like my mother. She had no interests, no passions, and no real concern about anything. I would sit in the house with her and listen to the radio. I sensed that my mother didn't want me to learn about the world or become part of it and function on my own. She certainly didn't want me to be "smart." And I didn't feel smart, especially when she said, "She doesn't need that!" She didn't even want me to know that my father had died. Why did she want to keep me stupid? Did she want me to sit with her in the house for the rest of my life?

We were watching a TV show about a so-called "dumb blond." In that role, Marie Wilson made one stupid mistake after another. My mother laughed and said, "She's doing the kind of things you would do." I didn't find it funny, but she seemed to enjoy ridiculing me for being dumb. It made me cringe inside that my own mother could laugh at me and make me feel worse about myself. Couldn't she see that she was the one encouraging me to be "dumb"?

One day Mr. Schultz was telling us one of his amusing personal stories and the subject of death was mentioned. I felt sad and I guess it showed. My mother stepped in and said, "Please don't speak about that to my daughter. Her father recently died." Mr. Schultz apologized and said he would not mention it again.

Later that day I asked, "Why didn't you tell me when my father died? You said you saw a rabbi. What did the rabbi say?"

Very casually Hedda replied: "I never said that. I never saw a rabbi." I didn't know what to make of this. When I found out about my father's death, I recall her saying, "The rabbi told me not to say anything to you." Now, she was denying it. Her mixed-up stories and cover-ups were causing me to experience more anxiety and distress. I wondered: *If I can't trust my own mother, how will I ever be able to trust anyone?*

I continued to practice my singing. I felt safest when I was singing. It was just about the only thing in my life that gave me some sense of fulfillment, some ray of hope. Grandma was speaking with my uncle about all the hours I put into it. A note in his file said: *"Nobody has the heart to disillusion her. She is therefore becoming more tense, jumpy and easily moved to anger than ever before. Hedda, who is in very bad straits herself, does not realize that this is the fruit of her own doing—Lenore was raised on motion picture magazines when she should have been reading children's books, playing with other children, and going to school."*

Sweet sixteen—not a very sweet time for me.

35

Another Crisis

History has a way of repeating itself and it was repeating itself when I was seventeen. My mother was ill again with symptoms that were very similar to her previous illness. She was throwing up and complaining of stomach pain. This was happening more and more. I was very worried about her and pleaded: "You have to see a doctor." She responded with her usual "No, I'm not seeing any doctor."

Grandma was visiting one day when Hedda was doubling over in pain. Grandma became very upset and said, "I'm going downstairs to call the doctor." Dr. Weisner was at our door in no time. He did a quick examination and announced: "Hedda is critically ill. She has to go to the hospital right away. I'm calling for an ambulance." A wave of panic swept over me as the doctor uttered something about Hedda's condition that I didn't understand. I asked if she would be okay as my heart continued to pound in my chest. I don't recall what he said, and soon, everything around me became a blur. I heard the loud sound of a siren, and I felt an involuntary shaking throughout my body. Hedda was whisked away in an ambulance. I didn't feel any different at seventeen than when I was a child of ten, and she was taken away so very ill. Once again, I was lost in panic and fear.

"You'll have to come to my house this time." I heard Grandma's voice and although I dreaded the thought of leaving my home, I knew there was no other way.

So, there I was at Grandma's, overwrought with anxiety, expecting to hear bad news at any moment. Soon Grandma came in with a grim expression on her face. I held my breath as she spoke: "Hedda had emergency surgery for gallstones and now there are complications. She's in critical condition."

I was relieved to hear that Hedda made it through surgery. But I was still very worried that Hedda would not recover. The thought of it frightened me and made my heart beat faster.

In my distress I blocked out most everything that was going on around me. I didn't realize how very much a part of me Hedda still was, and I was grieving for her. When I looked at Grandma, I saw a look on her face that told me she too was very distraught, but we didn't talk about it.

The next day the doorbell rang and Uncle Will was standing at the door. I remembered the promise I made to my mother and I had every intention of keeping it. I wasn't about to betray her. Or so I thought.

Will had a big smile on his face, and I felt a certain discomfort seeing him again. He tried to make friendly conversation, similar to the last time my mother was in the hospital. Again, I tried to maintain an emotional distance. I remained very tense in his presence and tried my best not to show it.

During this time, I became very run-down. My energy was low, and I was tired all the time. The stress was more than I could handle. Out of the blue, I developed a cough. I couldn't figure out how I got it; I wasn't going outdoors, and as far as I knew, I didn't have contact with anyone who was ill. But there I was, lying awake at night, choking on a cough. I was keeping Grandma awake, and soon she called the doctor. He made an immediate assessment: "She has a bad case of bronchitis. I'm prescribing cough syrup for that, and make sure she gets plenty of rest. She can increase the dose if the cough worsens."

One night my cough was so bad, Grandma got out of bed to make me a cup of hot tea. I heard a thud in the kitchen, and I ran in to see what happened. Grandma was on her knees, trying to get up from the floor. She looked up at me and said, "I don't know how that happened. I must have tripped over something." Fortunately, she was not hurt. As she put it, "It was just a freak accident." But I knew the nights of losing sleep were catching up with her. And I blamed myself: *This wouldn't be happening if it weren't for me.*

I observed Grandma sitting in her chair. She was pale and didn't look well. After she did a few things around the house, she would sit down to catch her breath. She had seen a doctor who told her she had an enlarged heart and advised her to "take it easy." Her reaction was: "What do doctors know?" So, she went about her business doing whatever she felt she had to do, within moderation.

Grandpa was sick, too. His legs were very stiff, and he hobbled around, struggling to move one leg in front of the other. I wondered how he was able to get around as he did. Nevertheless, he defied his hardening of the arteries by staggering out of the house every morning, with cane in hand, to the bus stop a couple of blocks away. He arrived at his necktie store at nine-thirty without fail. Not even inclement weather would keep him away. I marveled at his courage and perseverance. He braved winds, rains, and even snowstorms—but he got to his store.

In a remarkably good mood, Grandpa laughingly reminisced about a day in his boyhood: "I braved the blizzard of '88. When I got to school, I was the only one in the classroom! None of the other kids showed up. I was never afraid of things like that." I thought that was an incredible story. I wondered if he exaggerated a little, or if it was really true. But he looked so happy. Did it really matter? Now, he was elderly and frail. I confronted him one day and asked, "Grandpa, how can you go to work so sick?"

"What am I going to do? Stay home with her? I might as well be dead!"

And the usual fighting continued. When Grandma and Grandpa were in the same room, I witnessed either a war of words or a daunting cold silence. Most of the fights were about Grandpa schlepping to his store. "You should be home like any man your age who is old and sick!" Grandma's eyes would blaze with venom as she spoke. "People must think you have ten children to support and a wife who chases you out to work." She begged him not to go. "You don't even make enough money to cover your expenses."

Grandpa didn't bother to respond and soon Grandma became irate: "You should only go to Hell! You shouldn't have bread to eat!"

I couldn't believe my grandma was saying such mean things. I didn't like Grandma when she cursed like that. It made me very uneasy. Soon Grandpa came up with a retort: "At least I don't sit around with those snakes in the grass!"

And whom was he referring to? Grandma had a couple of female friends she would see every now and then, who he disliked with a passion. If he were moved enough, Grandpa would accuse her of having boyfriends. That would really raise Grandma's eyebrows, and an emotional tug of war would reach its peak.

I found it very disturbing to witness their fights. There were times when Grandma was very much out of control. One such time was when Grandpa was getting ready to leave the house and Grandma reached for his cane and threw it at him. He made a grab for the cane, finally got a hold of it, and headed for the door with Grandma screaming in the background. It was a very sad sight: an old man, almost lame, reaching for the cane that his wife threw at him. I stood there, distraught, and helpless, watching this horrific scene unfold before my eyes.

Living with my grandparents turned out to be nothing short of bedlam, and there I was, right smack in the middle. Endless fights and tensions were the norm. I could only surmise how difficult it must have been for my mother and uncle growing up in that environment. The whole scene made me sick to my stomach. Day after day, they were so busy tearing each other apart, I often wondered if they were aware of my presence. How was I to say anything to them? I was a guest in their home.

I remained indoors during this time, as I continued to worry about my mother. Then Grandma, appearing more relaxed, came over to me and said: "Your mother seems to be improving. She's making a slow recovery, but she's doing much better." When I got that wonderful piece of news, I felt better, too.

Meanwhile, I was on guard not to speak too much to my uncle. I was nice and polite to him. I thought I was doing a good job at hiding my true feelings from him, but Will was quite aware of how I felt. In his file, there was a note he wrote to himself: *"I see her every day. The systematic poisoning of her mind against Jessie and me has been going on for at least 10 years. On the surface, she is friendly, but there is a deep-seated antagonism. We'll both try to reach her, and perhaps may persuade her to visit us."*

A feeling of emptiness kept gnawing away at me. I was lonely and depressed and struggling to avoid my uncle's overture of friendship. Similar to the time of my mother's last operation, my uncle was paying a lot of attention to me. I felt a need to speak to him, but I didn't think it was the thing to do. When he offered me pamphlets on teenagers and their problems I asserted, "I don't want that; I would much prefer a psychology book. Do you have any psychology books I can read?"

That started the ball rolling. The next time I saw him, he handed me two psychology books: Dorsey's "Why We Behave Like Human Beings" and Messinger's "The Human Mind." I was intrigued. I happily declared, "This is much better." My uncle Will had given me an introduction into the world of psychology and how grateful I was for that. *With that black mustache and great big grin, he's not such a bad guy after all!*

Afterwards, I leafed through the books, but I couldn't really get into reading them, so I put them away. But my curiosity was aroused.

My mother remained in the hospital for several weeks and I continued to think about her: *How is she doing? When is she coming home?*

Grandma came to me one day in good spirits. "It looks like the worst is over and your mother will be coming home any day now." When? She couldn't tell me. From where did she get the information? She didn't tell me and I didn't ask. The crisis was over and that's all that really mattered. I could breathe a sigh of relief.

Hedda came home looking emaciated. My first glimpse told me she had been through an awful lot; she looked gaunt and had lost quite some weight. "They didn't know if I would make it. My heart stopped while I was on the operating table, but they brought me back. And here I am to tell the story."

Hedda then reached into her pocketbook and proudly pulled out a small jar of greenish-gray pebbles, which she held in her hand as if they were souvenirs. "My nineteen gallstones!"

My goodness! Nineteen gallstones! I was overwhelmed at the sight of them. Each one looked like a little gem. I said, "It's amazing that those stones could grow in your body. How do such stones develop?"

She responded, "No one knows. The doctor told me I have to be careful what I eat. No fats! I listened to my mother and took that damn mineral oil all these years. I even took it when I was pregnant with you! I'm not taking any more of that crap!

"They only took out half the gall bladder, they couldn't get it all. I was sick as a dog. I had peritonitis, and they had to give me blood transfusions. I don't know how I made it. Maybe it would have been better if I hadn't. Sometimes I wonder if it's all worth it."

36

What Can I Do With My Life?

My uncle Will made this statement in his file at the time I quit school: *"Their world continues to grow smaller and smaller. Hedda has poisoned Lenore's mind against everybody without exception. Now, at 17, the last contact with the outside world has been broken off: The Board of Education teacher for the homebound has ceased to come, at their request."*

I couldn't wait to tell my home instruction teacher "I'm going to quit." Once again, Mr. Schultz's reply was not what I had hoped to hear. "It's a big mistake. I'm willing to help you until you get your diploma. If you leave now, you'll regret it later on."

Regret it later on? I wasn't doing anything more than going through the motions of learning—merely opening and closing a book. I stayed on longer than I expected, but I finally made my decision. It seemed long overdue. I had mixed emotions though, about losing Mr. Schultz. He came in from the outside and distracted me from my lonely existence with my mother. There was a part of me that was sad to see him go.

My mother and I continued to hibernate in the apartment. She sat in her corner, and I stayed in mine. My uncle wrote more about this particular period in our lives:

"The outlook does not look too bright. Lenore and Hedda continue to remain indoors almost continuously. My mother does the shopping for them. Hedda is going to keep Lenore locked up as long as she (Hedda) lives. After that, Lenore won't be fit for anything else . . ."

"Mother and daughter do not get along well. There is endless friction. Daughter rebels, but so far domination by mother is almost complete . . ."

"Hedda looks bad and is very unhappy; she is almost continuously depressed and in a state of anxiety, according to my mother. She is worried about Lenore, but is unable to do anything. She probably realizes that any effort to reorient Lenore would take her away. Hence anxiety and status quo! What an unhappy situation!"

So, there I was, living in the shadow of my mother. I wasn't doing much of anything, and I had no interests. Even my love for Eddie Fisher had faded. My life was meaningless. I desperately needed something, or someone, to believe in. I wondered, *What can I do with my life?*

Summer was approaching, and the weather was getting warmer. Soon, my mother and I were taking walks again in the neighborhood. One day we saw a sign in the window of a ground-floor apartment that said, "Professor Rosa, Singing Instructor." Although I still loved music, I no longer gave much thought to singing as a career. However, this presented an opportunity to put some meaning back into my life.

We knocked on the door, and out came a small, elderly white-haired man. He had a twinkle in his eye, and a confident manner that appealed to me. He told me he could see me once a week for an hour's lesson. My mother agreed to this, and I was at his door the next day.

Professor Rosa was an easygoing gentleman who said, "Things have to come naturally, like breathing from the diaphragm, for proper breath control." He devoted much time and patience to me, but it was the same old story: "You're not singing from the diaphragm!" No matter how much I tried, the sound came out flat, from the throat. After each singing lesson, I came away emotionally drained and disheartened.

My uncle wrote a note about this in his file: *"Lenore still hopes to be a singer, although that hope has probably become somewhat dimmed. Ambitions and hopes aside, there does not seem to be any great talent along these lines . . ."*

But singing gave meaning to my life. I wasn't about to give it up. I had to pursue it further. There was another singing teacher in the neighborhood, Mr. Marcos, who was said to be "good and inexpensive." I went over to see him. He was a plump little man whose cheeks became red when he laughed. I thought he looked like a wonderful ad for a beer commercial; I could see him holding a mug of beer in his hand, making a toast.

Mr. Marcos was also trying to get me to sing from "deep down," (pointing to my diaphragm). He even went so far to say, "Make believe you have to go to the bathroom. Breathe and push down!"

Well, I tried, but it seemed easier to go to the bathroom. I was becoming very discouraged. I soon realized it didn't make sense to keep going to instructors if I wasn't able to do what was asked of me. As I said good-bye to Mr. Marcos, it became obvious to me that a singing career was not for me. I felt sad for some time. I kept asking myself, *What can I do with my life?*

I was reaching for the television dial more and more. It was fast becoming an avenue of escape for me. From a variety of programs I would watch, I found the musical-variety shows most captivating. I became aware of the dancers who came soaring across my screen. As they came floating through air, it seemed as if they didn't have a care in the world. I was fascinated.

Sometimes my mother would join me. She seemed to like the musical shows I was watching. I commented on the expertise of the dancers, but she sat silently in her chair and continued to watch. The smile on her face told me she was enjoying herself.

For a while we were glued to the screen. When it came time to shut off the TV, my mother walked out of the room and I was left alone with my feelings and thoughts. All of a sudden, I got out of my chair, put a record on the phonograph and started to dance.

I felt a need to let loose and feel the music in my soul. No longer was I the little girl in her rocking chair; I was now a young lady who was moved by rhythm, with a need to express it. As I swirled around the living room, I could feel the tempo of a melody, like "The Melba Waltz", from my head to my toes. I soon was dancing to one melody after another until I became exhausted and collapsed into my chair. But I was exhilarated; I had come alive. I was in love with life. To hear those musical strings twirling about, with a gaiety inherent in each melody, was enough to set my heart aglow with a passion for the purity and beauty of life. But when the music ended, my joy disappeared, and I would slink back into reality. I became sad once again.

I went out for a walk one day and I became aware of a store with a sign in the window that said, "Dance Studio." It was only a few short blocks from where I lived. I was surprised that I hadn't noticed it before. I stood there, staring at photos in the window of an attractive young woman with a vibrant smile and sparkling eyes. She was clad in a multitude of different costumes, and she was beautiful. In a corner of one of the photos was her name: Ellen Marino. My mind began to race wildly, and I said to myself, "This is it. I know what I want to do. I'll take dancing lessons. I'll take lessons with Ellen Marino. I'll become a dancer!"

I rushed home and eagerly told my mother that I wanted to take dancing lessons. Hedda showed no emotion, but I didn't think she would. She sat in her chair and let me ramble on. I was relieved that she didn't try to talk me out of it.

The next day I went over to the "Dance Studio." Ellen Marino was in the middle of a class when I came in, so I stood off to a side and watched. She appeared just as radiant in person as in her photos. Her titian hair, tied back in a ponytail, kept bouncing up and down as she glided around the dance floor. She looked as young as a teenager. I admired the elegance and poise in her movements. I wondered how I would approach her.

When the class was over, I found the courage to go over and say, "I'm interested in taking lessons with you."

She gave me a wide-eyed stare and asked me my age. I was embarrassed, but I told her. With a startled look on her face, she said, "You're seventeen? You're rather old to begin ballet, but that's where you'll have to begin. All dance is based upon ballet."

I said, "I want to learn to dance the way that you do."

She began to speak about her many years in the theater and her accomplishments. She was aglow as she spoke. She emphasized that "it's a lot of hard work," but the happiness in her eyes seemed to say it's worth it. I felt her passion for dancing, and I sensed what it must be like to have something you love to do. *Perhaps I can find something that would make me so happy. Maybe it will be dancing. Maybe I could be like Ellen . . .*

She continued to speak about her career, and then suddenly she stopped and looked into my eyes. "Okay, I will work with you." There was one problem: I was limited in what I could pay. When I told her that, she gave me a warm smile and said, "Let's start out with class lessons, they're less expensive, and I think you'll probably do better in a group—for now anyway."

I was nervous, but very excited, on the day of my first dancing class. There I was, in my black turtleneck sweater and leotards, all ready for my lesson. Then, as I looked around, I felt a little self-conscious; the girls in the class were much younger than I, and slimmer; they moved with ease and grace, and were experienced. I didn't know if I would fit in. I couldn't help but feel awkward and out of place. But I wouldn't let that stand in my way. I wanted to dance. I thought if I could dance in my living room, it would be a cinch to do well in a class. But I was mistaken. Ellen tapped the tempo with her stick: "and one and two and three and four . . ." I felt sick; I couldn't follow the rhythm.

I approached Ellen after class and said, "I need to take lessons privately. I'll pay you more for the lessons. I just think I would feel more comfortable if it were one-to-one. I might even do better with the rhythm."

Her eyes were intensely fixed upon me as I spoke, and I think she detected my desperation. "I'm going to make a concession," she said in a sensitive tone. "Because dancers need to practice on a daily basis—and you cannot afford to pay that much for lessons—I'll see you privately for abbreviated sessions a couple of times a week. And you may practice at the bar when there is no class."

That sounded like music to my ears. Ellen was giving me special attention; I would work hard and learn to dance.

I came for my lessons and spent time at the bar, bending, stretching, and trying to coordinate my body with the rhythm of the music. She tapped her stick to each beat, and I heard the same old "one and two and three and four . . ." But her commands didn't register with me. The problem persisted. I was creating my own rhythm; the way I felt it was the way I danced it.

Ellen looked at me with her wide-eyed stare and her mouth wide open. "This is elementary. There's nothing hard about this. It's just following a beat. It's really very simple."

I could not find the words to express my anguish. All I could say was, "I'm trying." It may have been simple to do, but it wasn't that simple for me. I went home discouraged. Why wasn't I able to follow the beat?

It wasn't long before Ellen said to me, "We need to talk."

I was all ready to be admonished for my lack of rhythm when Ellen declared, "You don't have a theatrical appearance, and you need to do something about that if you want to get into show business." She paused and took a long look at me. "First of all, you need to lose some weight. And look at your hair—it's not the right length. It either has to be long or short; yours is neither—it's in between. And your makeup is on wrong. That shade of lipstick isn't right for you. It's a dark red with too much blue in it, and it's not applied properly; you need a lip brush, and it should be applied in the shape of a heart."

I interrupted and said, "My lips are not heart shaped." She looked at me for a moment, and then turned away. "And by the way, you have to do something about your rhythm."

A cloud of despair came over me. I became more nervous and anxious as I sat there, listening to Ellen take me apart, piece by piece. I didn't know how to respond to this verbal onslaught. I wasn't emotionally prepared to handle anything like this. Was my appearance that bad? I was becoming more and more self-conscious about the way I looked, and I felt a deep sense of shame. If there were a hole in the wall, I would have crawled into it. I didn't think I would ever be able to make myself look that attractive.

I had an overwhelming need to get up and leave—or should I say escape? But there I was, stuck. I was curious to hear what else she had to say. So, I sat there, hanging on to every word that came out of her mouth, as if my life depended on it. I was overcome. I couldn't get out of my chair. What a relief it was when she finished her little analysis. My legs couldn't carry me out of there fast enough.

Feelings of hopelessness overwhelmed me on my way home. I moaned the blues to myself: *I can't sing. I can't dance. My hair is not right. My makeup is on wrong. Everything about me is wrong, wrong, wrong! I'll never be able to get anything right.*

I didn't want to ever go back and see Ellen again, but when I calmed down, I had different thoughts. I hated to admit it to myself, but there were many things about me that were crying out for change. Just thinking about making myself over catapulted me into a state of anxiety, but I couldn't go on like this; I was just burying my head in the sand like an ostrich. Maybe Ellen could help me, somehow, with the negative things she told me about my appearance. I could even learn from her, if I were able to keep an open mind and not be sidetracked by emotions.

So, I stashed away my resentment and returned to the Dance Studio. I suddenly felt a need to try harder if that were at all possible. I was practicing with Ellen one day when I attempted to do the split. It came easy to me. I was ecstatic about it, and so was she. Ellen looked utterly amazed. She gleefully said, "It's incredible that a girl your age can do the split! Usually, bones are developed and matured by your age. Your limbs are still very flexible, and you do it so gracefully!"

My head was in the clouds. Was Ellen really speaking like that to me?

I went on to excel at other dance movements, but still couldn't perform in time with the rhythm. One night I gracefully took my lesson, said good night to Ellen, and never went back.

But that was not the end of dancing for me. I thought that possibly another, more patient instructor would have greater tolerance for my deficiencies. I found a couple of dance instructors in the neighborhood, but I still created my own rhythm. I soon had to acknowledge that I wouldn't be able to have a career in dancing. Once again, I was down in the dumps.

On a balmy summer morning I went out for a walk and bumped into Vic, the salesman who sold us our TV. A friendly smile covered his face as he said, "Well, hello there. How have you been? I was thinking of you. I haven't seen you in some time." As we talked, Vic went on, "I'm on a break now, and we're not too far from the Boulevard. What do you say we go on over there? We can sit down and talk." It sounded like a great idea. As a gentle breeze swayed to and fro, we walked a few blocks and found a bench. Vic smiled and said, "So what's been going on with you?"

I reflected for a moment about my experience at the Dance Studio and replied, "I would like to have your opinion about my appearance."

He began to look me over and wound up staring at the hair under my arms. "First of all, attractive young ladies do not display unsightly hair. You have to shave off that hair. Your lipstick is too dark; the color red gives you a harsh look. You should be using a lighter shade, maybe orange or light pink. And your clothes: you need a wardrobe that makes you look smart and sophisticated . . ."

Each word stung. I was overwhelmed. Talking to Vic seemed to be an opportunity to find out how I could improve my appearance—or so I thought. But he was too blunt, and I was too sensitive. Couldn't he see I was hurting and on the verge of tears?

I went home with an urge to cry, but I bottled up my pain. I continued to carry around an ache inside. *Do I look that bad?*

I grew up in isolation. There was no one to teach me how to dress or how to apply makeup. More importantly, there was no one around to show me how to live in the real world. My only teachers were the radio and movie magazines.

Yes, I wanted to make myself look better. I wanted to be the very best I could be; I just didn't know how to do it. I was angry with people like Ellen and Vic for making me feel even worse about myself. It didn't take much to shatter the little self-esteem I had. And I was angry with myself for being the way I was: weak, helpless, and taking to heart every little thing that was said to me. I was emotionally fragile and unprepared to handle the most benign, or even friendly, feedback. I would have to learn how to live in the world and not fall apart so easily.

I had a lot of growing up to do.

37

Visiting Grandma

I saw Grandma as a ray of sunshine that came into my life and stole the gloom from it—at least for the brief time I saw her. I would have liked to talk to Grandma, but Hedda's Rules did not permit it, and my mother was usually right there in the room as an enforcer on the beat. However, the sight of Grandma, and the sound of her voice, was a comfort to me.

I was already eighteen, and Hedda's Rules remained pretty much the same. I waited for Grandma's knock on the door just as much as when I was a child of five. She came into our home from the outside, and that was kind of special to me. She was reminding me that there was life outside our four walls.

Hedda regarded Grandma as "a trouble maker," but she needed her to do our food shopping, so she let Grandma in. Throughout the years, as they continued to have their fights, Hedda would scream at Grandma to "stay away," or "skip a few days." I worried that Grandma would take her seriously and not come back anymore, but thank God, that never happened.

For as long as I knew her, Grandma walked around as if she were carrying the world on her shoulders. I could see the pain in her eyes as she silently sat in the kitchen with my mother and me.

Sometimes it seemed as though Grandma was biting her tongue not to speak.

As Grandma approached her 70's, she looked like a woman much younger than her years. A little on the stout side, she always appeared neat, with her hair braided in a bun on the back of her neck. She usually wore a simple dark dress and a navy sweater over it. She would say, "The simpler, the better."

Why hadn't I thought of visiting Grandma sooner? She lived just a couple of blocks away and I could walk right over. I guess I didn't want to disturb Hedda; I knew she would be very upset and I wanted to avoid the aftermath. I realized, however, that it was something I had to do. I would see Grandma, whether my mother liked it or not.

Then I finally did it. My heart was beating a mile a minute as I stood there, ringing Grandma's doorbell. When she came to the door, she looked at me with wide eyes. "What a surprise!"

Grandma took me into the living room, where I saw a gigantic dining table with several large chairs surrounding it. It took up most of the room. There were pictures all over the walls. Staring me straight in the face was a large black and white charcoal portrait of a young man. Grandma said, "That's your uncle Willie. He was in his twenties at the time."

I couldn't get over how handsome he was, even with his big black mustache. I couldn't take my eyes off this portrait. Will hadn't changed that much, only now he was somewhat older, and his hair was graying a little. I liked the nice, pensive expression on his face. *Is this the same man who ruined my mother's life? He doesn't look so bad to me!*

Grandma looked sad as she talked about the portrait. "It was done by a young artist in California. She liked Willie, but he wasn't interested in her." She had a morose look on her face when she said that. She didn't say anything more about it, and I didn't ask.

As my eyes roamed across the room, I caught a glimpse of a great big wooden object standing in a corner. I asked Grandma about it and she said, "It's a hutch." I wondered: *What in the world is a hutch?* I walked over and opened the door. I was amazed to see shelves filled with antiques that Grandma collected over the years.

Amongst these were several green and pink flowered plates that I found appealing. I was afraid to touch them, lest they slip out of my hands and break. I reminded myself how angry Hedda would become when I broke a glass. I stood there admiring them.

When I entered the bedroom, I saw a huge, framed photo of a young woman. I kept staring at it. Her hair was short, in bangs, and she had on a long dark dress. She was tall and slim, and I thought she looked regal. Grandma told me, "That was your mother when she was sixteen." Her face had deep, penetrating eyes and a soulful sadness. She was beautiful.

Then I saw a large picture of myself. There I was, two years old, chubby, with long, falling stockings and a facial expression as if I were about to cry. I wondered why Grandma had chosen that particular picture to frame. But it didn't matter; Grandma had a picture of me on her wall. It was a very pleasant surprise.

As I looked around, I couldn't help but comment: "Grandma, you have such a nice place. Things are in such good order, and you don't have that much space. I don't know how you do it."

Her reply was, "You get rid of things you don't need. When I don't need something, out it goes! A clutter in the house is like a clutter of the mind—you don't need either." I thought she made a lot of sense. Grandma could be so wise.

I kept looking around in astonishment. I had stayed at Grandma's when my mother was in the hospital. I had seen the pictures on the walls, the tables, chairs, and various ornaments, but I had been oblivious to my surroundings. It was an eerie feeling to have lived somewhere, and yet, have hardly any recollection of it. My anxiety must have blurred my vision when I was there.

But now, things were different. Grandma and I were finally together. We could speak freely to each other without Hedda coming into the room like a lion about to pounce. If God forbid, she caught Grandma whispering to me or trying to give me a kiss, we both were in trouble. **"What's going on behind my back?"**

I was now visiting Grandma on a regular basis. She began feeding me a delicious grain called kasha. When she knew I was coming over, she had a bowl on the table for me. She flavored it with butter, and my mouth watered at just the thought of it. When

Grandpa was home, he would walk by and laugh, "Kashi, kashi…" That's all he said, but he was grinning from ear to ear. And Grandma looked happy, too.

I thought it was wonderful to see Grandma and have quiet moments with her. I could confide in her. I could talk to her about my problems. "Grandma, those boys at the candy store bother me when I go by. They say all kinds of nasty things about me…" And I would talk to her about the things they said. I told her about Jim, the man I met on the parkway. I even told her about that morning in the park with Joey. "Oh Grandma, what am I going to do? It's so hard for me to find love."

Grandma sat still and listened. As I spoke, I saw that sad look on her face. Her downcast eyes and mournful expression told a story of their own. I knew she was hurting, but I needed someone to pour my heart out to, and I was thankful that I had Grandma.

Grandma soon responded: "Oy, what you're making of yourself! You're wrecking your life! Foolish child. What do you need all those no-good bums for? They don't love you! They want what they can get from you. You'll see. You'll get into serious trouble if you keep on like this. Mark my words. I'm an old lady, but you'll say your grandmother knew. I hope I'm wrong."

And in a loud voice she added: **"Men! They want one thing! They all can go to hell!"**

Staring at her, I could feel my heart pound. My mother often said the same thing, but somehow, it felt worse to hear it from Grandma. Was there nothing good about men? For a few moments there was silence. Then Grandma said, "I tell you this because you're the eyes in my head."

I needed to hear that, and the sincere tone in which she said it. I would hold on to that feeling for as long as I could. Those words gave me an inner strength when I felt the lovelessness of my existence.

I soon stopped telling Grandma stories that were upsetting to her. Then, one day when I was sitting with her in her living room, I saw her staring at me peculiarly. "You don't look good in bangs. It gives you a hard, fast look." Grandma got up from her chair and came back with a mirror in her hand. She swept my bangs back with her fingers and handed the mirror to me. "See how much nicer you look now."

I was flabbergasted; I stared at myself in the mirror. How different I looked. I was very pleased. I acknowledged, "It's quite a change, Grandma. I like it very much."

Grandma smiled with a tone of joy in her voice. "Now you look like an attractive young lady. Don't you ever cover up a pretty face with bangs! You should always wear your hair off your forehead."

Although I wasn't that interested in hairstyles, I was very interested in what Grandma had to say. She continued, "And don't ever wear your hair behind your ears." As she spoke, she pulled back a strand of hair and exposed her ears. After one look, I saw why she was so strongly opposed to it. But I didn't think it was bad for everyone—or was it? As I tucked my hair behind my ears, the mirror told me that Grandma was right.

Grandma continued to talk to me about things she felt I should know, and I was always receptive, but what really mattered was the interest she showed in me. I felt a genuine concern that I needed so very badly to survive. And yet, there was no physical closeness between us. We didn't touch, hug or kiss, and still remained at arm's length from each other. Hedda's Rules prevailed, even though she wasn't there to implement them.

While Grandma and I spoke about many things, the subject of my mother was never brought up. I guess on some level it felt safer that way…

As I continued to visit, I observed Grandma sitting in her chair looking tense and worried. One day she said to me: "I want to take you downtown. You're eighteen years old, and you've never been in a subway. A girl of your age should have been in the subway years ago!"

Suddenly I became very nervous. How was I going to express what I was feeling inside? How was I going to say: "I don't want to go"? I had the same anxiety about a year before, when I heard Grandma saying to my mother: "When is she going to travel like the rest of the world? It's about time she learned to use the subway. I'll take her downtown myself!"

At that time, my mother fought vigorously against it. "She doesn't need the subway. I knew all about the subway and where did it get me? She has plenty of time for that. Leave her alone!"

Grandma let it go, but something told me she was going to fight to make it happen this time. A fearful side of me said: *I dare not explore anything new and risky,* while a more courageous side said: *If I'm going to do anything with my life, I'd better get on that subway now!*

When I returned from one of my visits to Grandma, my mother confronted me. Her face was long, and her voice harsh. "You love your grandmother, and you run to her, but you don't know your dear grandmother. I know you think I'm the bad one, but what you don't know is what your dear grandmother says behind your back. She's sweet to your face, but when you're not here, she talks about you. 'Look at what she turned out to be—a little prostitute! She'll yet bring you home a baby!' That's your dear, sweet grandmother!"

I was devastated. Did Grandma really say those things, or did Hedda fabricate the story as a means of keeping me away from Grandma? I never found out. I closed my ears, and my heart, to what my mother said.

38

The Subway and The Telephone

In my late teens, there were myriad things I hadn't done. For example, I had never:

- spoken into a telephone
- been exposed to a bath or shower
- eaten in a restaurant
- tasted cola, ice cream, or any cold drink
- traveled on a subway
- visited Manhattan
- been in a department store
- had a friend

And there were many more.

I wasn't in any hurry to find out what I was missing. I was too immobilized, too traumatized, to care. I accepted things the way they were. I was living one day at a time, with no thought of tomorrow, and no desire for anything in the present. I was sitting in the house with my mother, allowing precious time to slip away, without realizing that once it is gone, it cannot be renewed like a magazine subscription—or relived like a memory.

There was a part of me, however, that wondered about "normal" people, and how they lived. I wondered if I could learn to do things like everyone else. The feeling gnawed away at me, then receded, and came back to haunt me.

Even if I felt strong enough to emotionally pursue something new, I was very slow in attempting it. The unknown was very scary. Usually, something had to propel me into action. Then, when things didn't go right, I would crawl back into my shell. That's exactly what happened when I failed at my singing and dancing lessons. I went back to the safety of my home. But each time I became a little stronger just by having had the experience.

It had become almost impossible for me to speak to my mother without antagonism or exasperation. I was like a pressure cooker boiling over with anger. My mother was still pretty powerful and overbearing, but I could now pull away from her dictates without overwhelming guilt or anxiety. I would do things without her approval, and I didn't have that awful fear that suffocated me when she became enraged. I made my way over to the refrigerator and got food for myself when I was hungry. I even forced myself to go to a neighborhood movie by myself.

True, none of these things occurred without some trepidation, but I had to go through that turmoil to discover there was nothing to be afraid of. As I took baby steps and succeeded, I had a good feeling about myself—a sort of self-satisfaction that made me want to do more.

Manhattan: It was just the name of a song I had heard on the radio, until Grandma declared, "I want her to see Manhattan. It's time for her to go into the subway! It's time for her to see how the whole world lives!"

I suddenly felt it was something I had to do.

Hedda fought the idea. She once again said to Grandma, "All you do is come up here and make trouble. You never know when to leave well enough alone. She doesn't need any subway! If you want the subway, you go!"

But I had already made up my mind, and I would not allow my mother to hold me back. I turned to Grandma and said: "I want to go on the subway. I want to see what Manhattan is like. I will go with you, whenever you are ready." I was proud of myself for making that decision, and speaking up, and even more proud of Grandma for making the demand.

Soon I found myself with Grandma standing on an elevated platform in the Bronx. We were waiting for a train to come. I was very nervous wondering what it would be like. All of a sudden, the platform started to tremble and sway. As the vibrations grew stronger, I heard a strange squealing sound. Soon, the platform was shaking. The train was becoming taller and taller as it rushed into the station. It felt like the train was shaking down the platform. Windows came whizzing by. Suddenly the train squeals came to a halt. The doors burst open, and people came rushing out. I stood there stunned. Grandma grabbed my hand and dragged me into the train.

The train was crowded. Grandma put my hand on the pole and said, "Hold on to this!" Then the doors slammed shut. The train lurched forward, and I felt myself flying backward. I just managed to keep my grip on the pole. We started moving faster and faster. As the train rushed onward, I had a feeling that I was going to lose my balance and fall. Apartment buildings were flying by, and the speed of the train frightened me. I felt at any minute it would crash.

My heart was racing. I was too scared to move. I kept looking at Grandma to see if she was frightened, too, but she appeared unconcerned. Then I looked around me. I saw men and women, young and old. I saw children with their parents. They all seemed perfectly calm and relaxed. They were not frightened, so why should I be? But I couldn't help myself.

Soon I heard Grandma say, "We'll be downtown in no time. You should have been on this train years ago!"

I stood there, looking at her, hardly able to open my mouth. The noise of the train was loud, and I could barely hear her voice. The train kept moving on and making stops. My hands were shaking as I nervously held on to the pole. I asked Grandma, "How many more stops till Manhattan?"

Grandma took a long look at me and uttered something. Suddenly, the train went underground. I looked out the window, and it was dark as night. I became terrified. I couldn't believe it—we were now in a pitch-black tunnel. I started to cry. "Grandma, when are we getting off this train? I want to go home."

Grandma said, "We'll be getting off the next stop." Soon the train started to slow up and come to a halt. Within a split second Grandma pulled my hand, moved me towards the door and said: "This is our stop. We're getting out." The doors opened. People were pushing out and others were shoving in. I felt jostled and confused. It was scary, but I was out of the train. I could take a deep breath. I was safe and unharmed. We were now outside on the platform in this great big cavern. Then I heard Grandma say, "We're going over to the Uptown platform. We're going home." Thank God for that!

Although we never made it into Manhattan that day, I got a taste of what it's like to ride on the subway. To say I didn't like it would be putting it mildly. I didn't think I would ever ride on a train again. However, this experience aroused a restlessness in me.

There were times when I worried about the things I had never done. I felt shame when I just thought about this. For one, I had never used a telephone. It was an enigma to me. *Suppose I had to make a phone call. What would I do? Maybe I should learn how to use a phone, just in case.*

I went to a local store and stood there, staring at this strange-looking gadget. How does it work? What are all those numbers and letters that make up a circle? Suddenly I felt more shame. I was eighteen years old and didn't know how to make a phone call. I would see people of all ages, even little kids, using the telephone. It seemed that the whole world knew how to use this gadget but me. I went home and asked my mother, "How do I use a telephone?"

"What is there to know? There's nothing to it." She explained it to me very casually, but I was very confused. I asked her: "Can you come out and show me how it works?" Then I realized I should have known better; she wasn't about to go out of the house to show me how to use a telephone.

So how do you dial a number? I felt as thick as molasses when I went to a phone booth and found I couldn't understand the letter-number combinations. Staring at the rotary dial, I felt just plain stupid. Maybe I would never learn this contraption. Then suddenly, out of the blue, it happened; I had someone to call.

I was watching musical variety programs on television, and I was fascinated with one show and the dancers on it. Their names were mentioned and I was drawn to one. When the camera came in close and caught his profile, I thought: *How handsome he is!* Bobby moved so gracefully and danced so beautifully; he looked like a debonair storybook Prince Charming, as he blissfully glided over the dance floor with a partner to the then popular "Melody of Love."

Out of curiosity, I checked the Manhattan phone directory to see if Bobby was listed. I was quite surprised to see his name in the book. Suddenly, I had a desire to call him. I now had a goal. *But what if he doesn't want to speak to me? Perhaps he wouldn't want to be bothered.* I hated to think that he might reject me, or even hang up on me. But I decided to take the risk.

I went to a phone booth in a coffee shop. I nervously put a dime in the slot, got a tone, and, as my heartbeat quickened, I slowly placed my finger into the digit slot. I attempted to dial the number as I turned the rotary disc clockwise. Was I right? I hung up and dialed again. I sat in the phone booth for a few minutes in contemplation and confusion. I stared at the phone, trying to make heads or tails of it. I finally left the booth in dismay and defeat. I was about to go home when I had a change of heart. I sheepishly stood in a corner of the store, trying hard not to look conspicuous, as I waited for someone to pass by. I approached an elderly gentleman who appeared nice and kind, and with some reluctance I found the courage to say: "I'm having trouble dialing a number. Can you dial it for me?"

I felt terribly embarrassed as I handed him a dime and a piece of paper with a phone number on it. The stranger smiled, dialed the number, and handed me the phone. I thanked him, as I pressed the phone to my ear. I heard it ringing for a few seconds, and then there was a voice at the other end. I could feel my heart thumping as I spoke into the mouthpiece and said, "I would like to speak to Bobby."

"Speaking," said the voice at the other end. In that moment I realized that a phone is a magnificent invention, for there I was instantaneously connecting with another human being at a distance. What a moment of joy that was for me. I was too excited to speak, but somehow I found the words: "I enjoy watching you dance on television."

Bobby shyly laughed and said, "Oh, thank you, I enjoy my work." He had the most delightful southern accent, and a warm friendly manner. We only spoke for a few minutes, then Bobby said, "I have to go, I have a rehearsal coming up." As I placed the receiver on the cradle, I was so glad I made the call. I knew I would be calling Bobby again.

I soon asked Grandma to help me learn the telephone. I hated to bother her, but she didn't turn me down. Together, we went to a store in the neighborhood, and she went over each aspect with me. I might have lost a few coins along the way, but I finally mastered it. *Hallelujah!* That was a great day for me.

A few weeks later, I worked up the nerve to call Bobby again. I went back to the coffee shop, now determined to call him on my own. I was very nervous when I picked up the receiver, got a dial tone, and dialed his number. Was I right? I hung up and dialed again. I held my breath. I heard a voice at the other end. It was Bobby. I did it! I made the call!

Bobby didn't seem surprised, or annoyed, to hear from me again. He was warm and outgoing. I heard some noise in the background. "Did I interrupt something?" I asked.

He chuckled and said, "I'm just cooking."

"What are you making?"

"I'm scrambling up some eggs," he casually replied.

When I asked if he did much cooking, there was a tone of joy in his voice. "Oh, yes, I love to cook; it's my pastime."

Bobby was talking to me as he would to a friend, and he didn't even know me! I couldn't believe it—the fabulous dancer Bobby taking the time to talk to me! I so very much wanted to see him in person. *Could I even suggest it?* I somehow mustered up the courage to say, "Would it be possible for us to meet?"

My heartbeat quickened as I waited for his reply.

He said cheerfully, "Sure, when would you like to meet?"

Was this real? Bobby proceeded to give me his address on West 86th Street and set a date and time when he would be available. "All you have to do is ring the bell, and I'll come down."

I couldn't be more excited. I wondered what I would wear, and then I remembered that lovely dark red velveteen suit hanging in my closet. I tried it on, and it was still a perfect fit. I now had an occasion to wear it. I was jumping for joy.

The song, "Picnic," kept running through my mind. Bobby had just danced to it on TV, and there was a certain element of romance in it. I was mesmerized as I watched him perform. To think, I was soon going to spend some time with Bobby. It was an exciting thought. Will I be having my own "Picnic" time with him? I could hardly wait.

I was not very happy, though, when I thought about traveling into Manhattan. *Where was 86th Street and Central Park West?* I went to the closest subway station and spoke to the token booth clerk. He readily gave me directions on how to get there.

As I thought about it, I was frozen with fear: fear of riding in the subway, fear of traveling underground, fear of being in a strange new place, fear of the unknown. There was even a certain amount of fear attached to meeting Bobby. *Who was Bobby? What was he like?* I ruminated about it. Maybe it was wrong for me to have made this appointment. Maybe Bobby would treat me like the other men I met. What a horrible thought. I couldn't allow myself to think that way. Soon, my need to meet Bobby became so strong it overcame my fears. I would force myself out of my state of complacency and do whatever was necessary to keep my appointment.

On the subway platform I recalled what it felt like with Grandma, especially shaking in that black tunnel as the train moved at lightning speed. The memory of it made my heart pound. I didn't know how I would be able to confront it on my own. Thoughts and more thoughts were whirling around in my head. My imagination was running wild. What if I make the wrong connection? What if I miss my stop? The tremendous speed at which trains move—there could be an accident! But I had to go. I would not yield to my fears. I had a date to keep.

I could feel my heart in my mouth when the train came, but I met the challenge and went in. A shudder went through me. I was now on a Manhattan-bound train. I was on edge throughout the ride. It was more unsettling than I thought. When it was time for me to switch to another train, I felt my anxiety soar. I turned to strangers on the platform with many questions, and I finally made my connection. When the train pulled into the 86th Street station, I jumped out of my seat and ran for the door. *Thank God, I made it!* I couldn't wait to get out into the open.

Manhattan: Something told me the songs about Manhattan sounded better than the real thing. I had to find that out for myself. When I came off the subway, I felt as if I was in a different world. I looked up and saw big, tall buildings looking down at me. They appeared so much taller than the ones in the Bronx. Were they really that towering, or was I so much in awe of this great big metropolis that my reality became distorted?

The streets were brimming with people. I wondered: *Is it always this crowded?* But even with all that traffic and excitement, I felt as if I were in the middle of nowhere. I stood there lost, confused, and very alone. I could empathize with a foreigner getting off a boat in a strange land; I was a foreigner in my own country. I didn't know where I was, or how to get around, but I knew I had to be somewhere at a certain time.

I pulled out a piece of paper from my purse and approached people on the street, timidly asking for directions. As usual, I felt ashamed, but it was something I had to do. I finally found Bobbie's building, and I made it on time.

Suddenly, I wanted to be anywhere but there. My heart was leaping in my chest as I forced myself to ring Bobby's doorbell. I was waiting in the lobby only a few minutes when a young man came towards me with a dog. He was dressed in an old pair of jeans, plaid shirt, and casual jacket. He was short, his hair was sandy brown, and his skin was ruddy. He smiled and said, "Hi. I'm Bobby."

I was amazed and disappointed; he was nowhere near what he looked like on my television screen. I looked at him as though he were two different people: the captivating dancer on a television show, and the plain, ordinary man I just met in a Manhattan lobby.

I felt more disenchanted, if not somewhat uncomfortable, to see that Bobby had brought along a small poodle on a leash! It seemed that Bobby was taking his dog out to do its thing and had fitted me into his schedule. My spirits dropped pretty low. I wanted to feel more important than being part of a dog walk.

Soon I was walking briskly with Bobby and his dog, not paying any attention to my surroundings, not even knowing where I was going. Just walking. Before I knew it, I found myself heading into a park. The street sign said Central Park West.

From our phone conversations, I perceived Bobby as kind and gentle. He seemed like a really nice guy, so unlike the men I had encountered before. I could feel safe with him. But I did not feel safe in Central Park. It was an immense piece of land, stretching out in all directions. As I looked around, I was overtaken by fear. What would happen if Bobby suddenly said, "Well, good-bye, I have to go," and left me there in the park? I dared not have such a thought.

I couldn't tell Bobby what was going on inside of me. I wanted him to think I was smart, knowledgeable, and that I had been around; I didn't want him to know that I spent my childhood locked up in the house with a mother who kept me away from people. *What would he think?* I worried that he would see me as "different" and "strange." I was embarrassed just thinking about it.

We kept walking. I kept feeling anxiety, as thoughts came racing through my mind: *Where are we going? When are we turning back? What is Bobby thinking about me?*

Bobby was overly quiet and that bothered me. I thought he was very guarded, and I wondered why. When I spoke to him, I felt as if I were talking to myself. Every now and then he responded with a smile or chuckle, not saying much of anything. Hoping to get him to open up and talk about himself I said: "You dance so well. How did you get into dancing?"

He casually replied. "I came to the big city to start my career. I've been dancing all my life, but I think I'm getting too old for that now."

I was taken aback. "You don't look old to me." (I thought he might be in his thirties.)

He quickly countered, "Too old for a dancer on the stage."

I detected a bit of sadness in his voice, which led me to say. "What would you like to do?"

Reflectively, he replied: "I don't like living in New York. I'm planning to go back to my hometown, New Orleans, and open a dancing school in the near future."

And that was the brunt of our conversation. Neither one of us said much more. Bobby remained non-communicative, and soon he said, "Time to be getting back." We left the park and said good-bye. I was in a pretty downcast mood as I found my way back to the subway.

For the rest of the evening I thought about my meeting with Bobby. It was very disappointing. I brooded, as I tried to sort things out in my mind. Bobby was aloof and distant. Although I asked many questions about him, he didn't ask one question about me. He was totally disinterested, and I found that kind of appalling. I hated to be treated as if I were a non-person.

But what did I expect? Bobby was a stranger, a dancer on a musical variety show—and I was his fan. However, Bobby treated me like a lady, and that was very important to me. Bobby was not the Prince Charming I imagined him to be when he appeared on my television screen, and that was okay, too. I guess this was just another romantic fantasy that I built up in my mind.

So, things were changing for me. I had made a start. I learned to use the telephone. I had my first taste of Manhattan. I made my first solo trip on the subway. I even reached out to another human being. It seemed that I had made some progress, but I knew I still had a long way to go.

39
Shopping for Me

At the age of eighteen I had a lot of catching up to do. From a life of deprivation, I felt a hunger for things I never had. Everywhere I turned, I was reminded of the many things I missed out on as I was growing up. A feeling of helplessness came over me when I realized I was left out of life. I wasn't a part of anything—and it hurt.

There were a variety of stores in my neighborhood, each with something different to offer. It was all there for me; all I had to do was step outside my door. As I peeked in store windows and browsed through shops, I was overwhelmed and confused. I didn't know where to look first, there was so much to see. I was especially attracted to clothing stores; I just couldn't stay away from them.

Although I wasn't out in the world that long, I was out long enough to know I had to do something about the way I dressed. I was tired of wearing sexy tops and snug pants. I said to myself, "No more sexy garbs for me." So, I reverted to wearing the least attractive clothes I had. I now had a desire to have clothes that were not suggestive, but more fashionable and in good taste.

Although I still didn't know anything about what was considered "fashionable" or "in good taste," I suddenly was eager to learn. I opened my eyes to the classic lines. I was not aware there

257

were clothes that could look so elegant. I had heard it said somewhere that what you wear is an expression of how you feel about yourself. To look pretty then, is to feel pretty. Or so I thought…

As I browsed the stores, I became terribly flustered. Some clothing seemed too beautiful, much too splendid to wear, and some were just too costly. I would just stand there in a daze, admiring the various styles before me. What was "really me": the fancy, frilly, or the plain and simple? I was utterly confused. When I was overcome with fashion fatigue, I picked myself up and walked out.

Then the question arose: *What can I afford?* I didn't have much money to spend, but I knew how to stretch a dollar and wound up doing just that. The cheaper the item, the more I gravitated toward it. But I didn't buy easily; a lot of anxiety went into every purchase.

While I meandered around shopping for inexpensive clothing, I soon realized I could get great buys. I discovered the stores had something called "sales." *My goodness, I can get beautiful items at half the price or even less! Why hadn't I seen this before?*

Soon I was going into stores with an intent to buy. I found many stores in my neighborhood that I thought had fantastic merchandise at great discounts. Whether it was a small store or a large one, I found myself thumbing through racks of clothing, then heading into a dressing room with a number of items on my arm. One by one, I tried them on and looked at myself in the mirror. Too bad the mirror wasn't always my friend; I was not very happy with what I saw. Most of the clothes I selected didn't look good on me. *Oh my God, I have to do better than that!* And I kept bringing into the dressing room clothes that looked better on the racks than they did on me.

I was glad there was a salesperson on tap, so I could ask for an opinion. Many a sales attendant said, "You're no size 16! You look much smaller. You're not even a 14!" Perhaps they were right, but when I tried smaller sizes, the clothes didn't fit properly. (I later found out I was trying on misses' sizes when I was only a junior.)

And while I was trying on clothes, I worried about my curvature of the spine. How much of it could be noticed? I was especially self-conscious of my scoliosis when I was in the fitting room.

However, there were times when I came upon merchandise that fit just right and looked super on me. I was in my glory. I couldn't believe my eyes. When I looked in the mirror, I asked myself: *Who is that girl? Is that really me?* My spirits soared and I was elated when I knew I could look that good. I felt that the world was mine and nothing could ever go wrong.

It was great merchandise and I wanted to own it right away. But I would get cold feet when it came to an actual purchase. There I was at the cash register, and something seemed wrong, very wrong. Although the merchandise was usually inexpensive, I struggled with a feeling that said I shouldn't be doing this. I was anxious and confused as I finally talked it into myself that it was okay to buy. How I hated the trepidation I experienced over a piece of clothing.

Soon I was back home holding the pretty, new fabric in my hands. I told myself that I would never again wear old shabby garments or that atrocious sexy attire. I felt like a new me as a feeling of joy swept over me. But these good feelings didn't last long enough, and as they wore off, my sad feelings returned to haunt me.

When I opened my closet door, a smile came to my face as I marveled at a variety of brightly colored garments, all so pretty and new, hanging on the rack. However, I rarely experienced the pleasure of wearing any of them. In fact, I was very uncomfortable when I went out with these eye catchers. I usually wound up wearing a very plain blouse and skirt. And I felt bad. *When will I ever wear these pretty, colorful clothes?*

If I didn't make an immediate purchase of something I liked, I would go home, ruminate about it, then hurry back to the store to see if it was still there. Many a time, the item was gone and I chastised myself: *Why didn't I buy it then?* I tried to convince myself that I would know better the next time. And I obsessed some more. I was driving myself crazy.

My shopping career was turning into nothing short of mass confusion. I kept searching and buying, but something didn't feel right. As I continued to shop around, I found more items that were "not me." Many times I made returns, but my mistakes often wound up taking up space in my closet. What was I looking for? I had no idea. Whatever it was, I couldn't find it. And I went out to shop some more.

My mother wasn't interested in hearing about my clothing excursions. I showed her what I bought; she smiled and said, "Very nice." And it ended there. So, I turned to Grandma. When she was visiting one day, I showed her my latest purchases. Grandma was not a lover of clothing, but her reaction startled me: "They're all very nice, but all clothes are rags. You wear them a few times and all you have are shmatas! Rags! That's all they are."

I was taken aback. There I was, sharing my joy with Grandma and she was slapping me down. For the next few days, I brooded as I wondered: *Are all clothes rags?* Even if it was so, I still wanted to buy more.

Soon I was on a blouse-buying spree when I had an unpleasant experience. I was in a small local shop, going through the racks, when I noticed I was the only one there. The shop owner, an elderly man, appeared to be agitated and grumpy as he paced back and forth. I could feel his eyes upon me, but I tried not to let him upset me. I had my eye on a long sleeved orange shirt and several other blouses that appealed to me and went into the dressing room with them. I spent a long time there; I just couldn't make up my mind which ones I wanted, if any. I finally decided not to buy anything. Disappointedly, I put them all back on the rack.

When I returned to the dressing room to pick up my tote bag, the shopkeeper came running in. He had a crazed look in his eyes as he grabbed my bag and began rummaging through it. I stood there, gazing at him in horror, as my heart started to thump. *My goodness, does he think I'm stuffing blouses into my bag?*

In a state of frenzy, he was searching the crevices of my bag for something that was not there. *How can this be happening?* I was so humiliated I wanted to cry. This man was acting crazy. Suddenly, he flung my bag at me and said, "Get out of here and don't come back! I don't need customers like you!"

I was shaking as I grabbed my bag and headed for the door like a bat out of hell. The experience was a traumatic one for me. I went into that store with an intention to buy and came out feeling like I had committed a crime. I was not emotionally prepared to deal with the shopkeeper's abuse. His behavior was so much like my mother's emotional outbursts. As I rushed home, I felt sick to my stomach.

I stayed indoors for the next several days to lick my wounds. Then, demoralized as I was, I found the emotional strength to put this episode behind me and go on.

It was time to buy a winter coat, and I didn't look forward to it. I considered this a real ordeal. I grew up hating coats, and with good reason. When I was a little girl, a tailor came to my home and made a couple of matronly coats for me that were just plain ugly. I rarely had either one on my back. Now that I needed a new coat, I wondered where I could get one that was warm and inexpensive. I heard about a large department store in Manhattan called Klein's that always had a sale going on.

I dreaded the thought of shopping in the city by myself. What did I know about coats? It seemed too overwhelming to select a big item like a coat without having someone there to give me an opinion and some support. Grandma wasn't well, so whom could I ask? On impulse, I turned to my mother. She barked, "Me go into a subway down to 14th Street? You have to be crazy! You won't catch me dead down there in Klein's!"

I guess I should have known better; I knew she detested the subway with a passion. I sadly realized that if I wanted it enough, I would have to do it on my own. I soon summoned the courage to go downtown on the subway to Klein's.

Klein's was one gigantic fairyland of clothes. I didn't know where to look first. I held my breath in astonishment as I marveled at the beauty of the styles, textures, and designs. I gaped at racks and tables that were overflowing with stunning eye-catchers. I was bewildered; I wanted everything in sight. And what sales, it was like a give-away! Surrounding me were shoppers grabbing clothes off the racks, from the tables, and from each other. I was appalled as I looked down at the floor and saw beautiful sweaters and blouses scattered all over. My goodness, these people were like a pack of wild animals!

I started to feel light-headed as I found my way through the crowd. After much wandering around, I finally found the Misses'

Coats section. *My goodness, there are so many coats, where will I look first?* I didn't see any salesperson around, so I began to search on my own. The coats came in a myriad of styles, colors, and sizes, and I was soon trying on one coat after another. Before long, I was becoming tired and frustrated. Either the coats didn't look good on me, or they were too expensive, or they were not warm enough. But I persisted. When visions of coats, coats and more coats began to swirl before my eyes, I knew it was time to leave. I pushed my way through the crowds until I finally found a door and edged my way out into the street. I left Klein's empty-handed, with my head spinning.

Thank God, I'm out of there! It's a madhouse!

I didn't think I would ever be able to buy in a store like that; there was too much going on. In the street I felt triumphant: *I made it out of the famous Klein's Department Store alive!*

But I knew I would return.

40

Will and Jessie

There were times when my uncle Will rang our doorbell and my mother didn't answer. Once, when I was at the window, he waved to me and I turned away; I was afraid to look at him, as if he could destroy me with a glance.

Over the years, my mother held steadfast to the belief that her brother, Will, had put her away in a mental asylum. "I saw his name on the committal papers." And she continued to hold a grudge against him. Over and over, she would tell me: "Your uncle is no damn good. He will ruin your life like he's ruined mine."

Then she demanded: "I want you to promise me that you will never have anything to do with my brother and his wife."

I looked upward as one would look to God, and I faithfully pledged: "I will never have anything to do with my uncle Will and his wife as long as I live."

My oath to my mother lingered in my mind like a mantra. But on occasion I did have contact with Will and Jessie. These were the times when there was a crisis, and they were in our lives again. Once the crisis was resolved, Hedda adamantly dismissed them: "Don't come up here anymore, I don't need this aggravation!" And out the door they went.

I was nineteen and in despair. I was walking around my neighborhood in a fog, with tears in my eyes, oblivious to my surroundings. I didn't realize that I was on the block where Will and Jessie lived. I looked up and how startled I was. There they were, Will and Jessie, only a few feet away! They seemed surprised, but happy, to see me. I didn't know how to react when I saw them. Jessie's eyes gazed into mine and in a low soft voice she asked: "How are you, dear?"

Suddenly the promise I made to Hedda didn't matter. Something inside told me I could talk to Jessie and not be afraid. Somehow I was able to say: "I'm very unhappy. I'm struggling just to get by. I have so many problems. It's all such a mess."

She warmly asked, "Do you think we could be of help to you, dear?"

I was touched by the sincerity in her voice and the kind expression on her face. Suddenly I felt a door opening for me. How I desperately wanted to accept her offer but all I could utter was, "Thank you, I'll think about it."

She continued, "If you would like to come up and see us, dear, you would be more than welcome in our home." I came alive when Jessie said that. I was drowning and she was grabbing my hand, towing me in. Maybe I would not drown after all.

But I was not used to visiting people. The only person whose home I went to was my grandmother's. The thought of visiting anyone made me uncomfortable and from all that I knew about Will and Jessie, I didn't think I would ever be able to visit them. So, what could I say to them? I managed to blurt out: "I may take you up on that, but not right now." Shortly after that, we parted. Inwardly, I doubted that I would ever go to their home.

In the days that followed, I thought about Will and Jessie. The little bit of interest they showed me triggered a desire to see them again. I reminded myself that I was no longer a child and what my mother told me was not law. However, I was not very good at hiding things from Hedda. Although I dreaded her response I said, "I met Will and Jessie in the street. They were very nice to me. They asked me to come over and I want to see them."

She looked at me with daggers in her eyes. "You're going to my brother? If you go up there, you're asking for trouble. Damn it! You'll never learn! My brother will do to you what he did to me!"

I expected that, but I wouldn't allow it to keep me away. I knew what I had to do. On a warm, sunny day, I stood before the brown, four-story apartment building in which Will and Jessie lived. I was hesitant and nervous, but I finally rang the bell. Could it be they weren't home? What wishful thinking. Soon, the buzzer echoed back. I slowly climbed the three flights of stairs to the top floor. My heart was racing wildly when my uncle opened the door. I was overwhelmed with mixed feelings. Suddenly, this felt like a big mistake. I wanted to turn around and run home as fast as I could, but there they were, Will and Jessie, smiling and inviting me in. I felt fear as I entered their apartment.

The first thing I noticed was a wall in their living room covered with books—my goodness, books on shelves from floor to ceiling, wall to wall. It was immense. My uncle was the owner of a library in his living room! As my eyes roamed the shelves, I was amazed to see so many books with so many names I never heard of: Socrates, Plato, Aristotle, and many others that meant nothing to me. It made my head spin.

In an adjoining room, my eyes wandered to walls that were decorated with large portraits of strange-looking men. One of the faces staring at me was extremely tense looking. This man had dark, piercing, angry eyes, and I felt a little uneasy as I stared back at him. (Later, I learned this was Beethoven.) I saw other portraits of men with long hair and bland expressions. I thought some of them looked grotesque. My uncle said, "You're looking at musical geniuses." I stared at them some more.

I noticed two desks in a small corner of an adjacent room. It seemed like a cozy setting for two people who share togetherness. In my mind, those desks symbolized a loving, caring relationship. Suddenly, I felt envy.

As I went from room to room, I marveled at this place that was spotlessly clean. Apparently, roaches hadn't become boarders in their home. *Could there really be a home that was roach-free, or for that matter, dirt-free?*

Soon I understood why their home was so immaculate. In the kitchen I met their housekeeper, Mary. I liked her immediately. She was a short, plump lady who smiled a lot and laughed even more. Her easy-going attitude seemed to say, "I'm happy here; I'm part of the family." As I watched Will and Jessie interact with her, I got the impression that Mary was indeed a valuable person in their household. I enjoyed being in her presence.

We soon went back into the living room. We sat down and talked, and I was beginning to lose some of my uneasiness when Jessie asked: "Have you given some thought to what we spoke about? Can we be of any help to you, dear? A psychotherapist could help you work through your problems. You could get the kind of insights that would enable you to have a better life. If you decide to see a therapist, let us know and we'll see what we can do."

They were offering to send me for therapy and I was deeply moved at just the thought of it. How very much I wanted to say yes on the spot, but I just couldn't; it didn't feel right to me. But I could say, "Thank you, I don't know right now what I want to do. I'll get back to you on that." We didn't discuss it further. A spark of hope was aroused in me that made me feel I was going to get better.

Soon, my thoughts drifted to the nasty things Hedda said about Will and Jessie, but after being with them, I felt differently: *These people are kind; they are not my enemies.*

From that day on, Will and Jessie became an important part of my life. I started to visit them regularly. I found myself opening up to them and speaking about the things that were on my mind: "I don't know what to do with my life. I don't know how to find relief from my problems." I went on to tell them how I wasn't able to handle anything without trepidation.

In the beginning, Will seemed to be listening, although not saying very much. Sometimes he shook his head and looked annoyed. He soon became impatient with me and started to cut me off as I was speaking. I felt the things I had to say were of little or no significance to him. He had his own ideas and opinions about most everything. I felt it wouldn't do me any good to tell him that he was hurting me with his uncaring attitude.

Will soon expressed his frustration to me: "Lenore, you've never learned how to live in the world or how to do things like other people…" He had the most morbid expression on his face as he spoke, and I was feeling the pain and anguish of being me.

On the other hand, Jessie responded with warmth and understanding. She appeared concerned and interested in whatever I had to say. I was soon sharing my most intimate stories with her, as well as my fears and anxieties. It was a relief to tell Jessie about the men I met in the street, and how they wanted to go to bed with me. I told her about the teenage boy who lived in my building and how he was trying to seduce me. I complained about the sex-hungry boys at the corner candy store: "I'm ashamed to pass them on the street. They talk to me as if I were a streetwalker!"

Jessie listened with a heartfelt expression on her face as I revealed one episode after another. It was amazing; she didn't even bat an eyelash. She was so unlike Grandma, who became upset over every little thing I told her. I liked the way Jessie could sit there quietly and not pass any judgment.

"When will I ever find the 'right' someone for me? How will I find the love I need so badly to survive?"

Soothingly, Jessie assured me: "Someday, dear, you will meet someone who will be worthy of you—someone who will love you very much for the good person you are. You must have patience, and above all, you must give yourself time." How I hated the thought of waiting. It made me more tense and restless, but at least she had given me hope.

Before long, Jessie became my refuge, my pillar of strength, and my tie to life. Her spontaneous smile and soft, firm voice told me it was okay to be me. She accepted me the way I was, and I was grateful for that. She was not about to reprimand me and tell me "the right way" to do things. I was relieved that I could feel so much comfort in her presence.

One morning Jessie, Will and I were having breakfast together when we started talking about my scoliosis. Jessie turned to me and angrily said, "Dear, you were born straight as an arrow!" I was surprised to hear this, and I didn't know how to respond. I wondered why Jessie was speaking about it, and why she was so angry. And shortly, the topic was dropped. But the subject of scoliosis remained on Jessie's mind.

Soon, Jessie was speaking to me about something she considered of prime importance: "Your uncle and I want to take you to an orthopedist for your back. We are very concerned about your scoliosis. We're taking you to one of the leading specialists in Manhattan."

I didn't see the necessity of this. My back wasn't bothering me, and this seemed like a waste of time, but since Jessie was strongly suggesting it, I thought it might be a good idea. So, I went with them to see an orthopedist, who did an examination, took a number of tests, and made an assessment. "You're just past the age when corrective surgery can be done. Do you have any pain in your back?"

I said, "No, but I wouldn't want to have surgery in any case."

The doctor took a long, slow look at me and said, "You're a very wise young woman. I have girls coming in here who want surgery for cosmetic purposes, and they go berserk if it can't be done. You have the right attitude. In any event, your scoliosis shouldn't cause you any problem."

Will and Jessie seemed satisfied with his diagnosis. It was good to know that I didn't have to worry about my back. I wanted to get back to the things that were actually bothering me. I felt I had real problems that needed immediate attention and they were cropping up all over.

One of my problems was about being in the outside world. I would speak with Jessie about how different I felt from other people and how very troubled I was about it. "How will I ever fit into a world I don't understand? The girls out there—they're so bright, so pretty, they know how to fit in. I'm nothing!"

"Dear, you are intelligent. You are bright. You are pretty. You have a very good head on your shoulders. The problem is you just don't believe it!"

I began to think about what Jessie said. It was true; I couldn't believe there was anything good about me. Tears were rolling down my face as I bitterly sobbed: "Everything is so bad, I just can't go on. What am I going to do?"

"Yes, dear, you've had a very bad life. But there are people in the world who have suffered like you, and they have survived. You will survive, too. You'll go for therapy. You'll get a job. You'll make friends. Things will change, and you'll feel better. But you must make an effort. You must fight what bothers you. You must pull yourself up by your bootstraps and go on!"

I wanted very much to believe what she said, but my resistance was very strong. Jessie sat down with me one day and told me about herself. "Do you think I've had it easy, dear? I wanted very much to become a medical doctor. I was in my sophomore year in college when my father died. I had to quit school to contribute money to the household, so I took a job as a school secretary and I've been a secretary ever since. I like my work very much. It's what you make of your life that counts."

I needed to hear that. Jessie became more real to me as a person who had to deal with her own problems and turn them around to work for her. I had the feeling that Jessie could handle any challenge that came her way and remain cool and confident in the face of it. I all the more admired her emotional strength. I didn't know if I could ever be that strong, but I was going to learn from her whatever I could.

Jessie became the mother I would have wanted, but never had, yet I felt that she was distancing herself from me. It often seemed as if she was in the same room with me, but not really there. I sensed a sort of aloofness, and it troubled me. I thought it might be my imagination running away with me, but at times I couldn't help but wonder if she really cared, or was she listening to my problems out of a sense of duty? As close as I felt to her, I wondered why, when I was upset or crying, she never put her arms around me or gave me a hug. I didn't know how to ask for it; nor did I know how to show my affection for her. And it continued like this.

I was now seeing Will and Jessie almost every day. I no longer had that desire to go out into the street seeking "love." I now managed to put my search for love on a back burner. Every so often, however, a spark would ignite. It was no wonder that my uncle was concerned about those "bums and tramps," for no one knew when I would once again become involved with one of them—least of all, me.

Through those tumultuous times, my stories remained the same; it was just the names of the characters that changed. My uncle hollered: **"You're above all those goddamn bums and tramps! When are you going to wake up—when it's too late? One day you'll get yourself into plenty of hot water. Then don't come crying to us!"**

I just couldn't understand my uncle. *Why is he so short-tempered with me?* It seemed that he cared about me, yet he was always scolding me for one thing or another, especially when I didn't see things his way. I wanted to voice my feelings to him, but I couldn't find the right words; I was too afraid of saying the wrong thing. And inevitably, I did. Then he gave me a dirty look—a look that hit me as hard as any verbal attack. I tried to cover my hurt and anger as best I could, until I couldn't; then there would be an exchange of harsh words.

Will had great respect for the intellect, but very little patience for feelings. He would walk into the room, hear me speaking to Jessie about my feelings, and fly into a rage: **"Feelings! Feelings! What crap! Have you ever heard of thinking more and feeling less? Have you ever heard of reason?"**

I stared at him in wonder. *Why was he so upset about feelings?* Undoubtedly, his standards were very high. Will had several degrees and a doctorate. He was also a member of Phi Beta Kappa. He could converse on just about any topic. This presented a challenge to me: I didn't have the knowledge or background to communicate with him on his level. I felt small as a mouse in his presence.

I complained to Jessie about the way Will was treating me. "Dear, your uncle loves you very much, but he becomes impatient with you…" I wanted to hear her, but I couldn't take it in. It didn't feel good to have my uncle yelling at me for the least thing. This was so reminiscent of Hedda and her tirades, it made me cringe. As a child of abuse, I didn't want any more.

But the things I spoke about seemed to upset him so much; he couldn't control himself. An example of this was my worship of show people. Both Will and Jessie knew about this, but Will reacted with disdain: "Those show people are a bunch of neurotics! They lead sordid, mixed-up lives. Trash! I have no use for them!"

It was demoralizing to hear him speak like that. Why did he have to knock my idols? Yes, I grew up with Bing Crosby, Frank Sinatra, and Doris Day, to name a few. Who else did I have? I couldn't speak about it, so I wrote a note to him: *"…if you don't like all the things I like, you don't have to lash out so sarcastically. You say plenty of things I don't like, and yet I don't release my feelings to you in such a manner…."* He didn't stop—but it felt good to express my feelings on paper.

When my uncle was in an exceptionally good mood, I said: "Jessie is so calm. We can sit and talk for hours and she never gets upset with me, and you get upset all the time…"

Will retorted, "I say what I think; Jessie bites her tongue."

Was he saying that Jessie was not telling me the truth? The thought of it made me break out in a sweat. I put it out of my mind as quickly as he said it.

One day Will spoke about himself. "When I graduated from law school my goal was to become a lawyer, but during the Depression, jobs were scarce. So, I became a teacher. It was the only living I could make at the time…" He spoke so matter-of-factly. I couldn't help but wonder: *Is he really as content as he appears to be, or just making the best of things he is unable to change?*

He soon volunteered: "My life is based on logic and reason. I've been a student of Greek philosophy all my life. Eventually, you might want to look into a philosophy of life. But right now, there are other things you will need to do."

I was so worried about getting through each day, I wasn't ready to hear this. But I began to think about what he said: *What in the world is a "philosophy of life?" and how can this "philosophy" help me?*

I was becoming more and more aware that my uncle Will was no ordinary person. I had a growing reverence for him because he was so highly intelligent. He amazed me with his knowledge and insights. How was he able to pinpoint and recommend solutions with only minimal facts? And I kept turning to my uncle for answers only he could give. I knew I could depend upon his wisdom to guide me. Most of the time he was very generous with his thoughts and ideas. In a voice of authority he would say, "The answer is…" And he was right so much of the time.

Yet, when it came to my personal problems, I perceived the things he was telling me were not "right" for me. I often came away confused and distressed. I wasn't about to blindly follow my uncle's dictates, especially since I spent my childhood dominated by my mother and her control. It wasn't easy turning off her voice in my head, and her rants were still very much a part of me. I didn't want to be taken over by anyone else.

"Lenore, you are stubborn and you won't listen to reason." I wondered why Will couldn't see me the way I was. Why couldn't he understand that I was not like the boys and girls in his class? Couldn't he see that my background was very different from theirs? He couldn't tolerate my problems; they just didn't make any sense to him. He had an image of how his niece should be: standing tall in the face of everyday problems; thinking, instead of feeling; and in total control of her life. As much as I tried, I couldn't live up to his expectations. This left me feeling sadder and even more distraught.

So often, I wasn't sure of what path to take. And so often, Will chuckled as he made light of my concerns. "Lenore, you remind me of a donkey caught between two bales of hay. It didn't know which one to choose, so it starved!"

"So, it looks like I'm going to starve…"

I didn't make a decision easily, but when I did, I usually stuck with it tenaciously. Will was opposed to so many of my choices and vehemently complained: "When you get a thought or idea in your head, nothing will stop you. You will follow your instincts, regardless of what anyone tells you. You refuse to listen to reason." I agreed with him on that. When I made a good choice, it was great, but when I was wrong—oh brother!

I kept running over to Jessie with my problems, desperate to get her thoughts and insights, but much to my dismay there were times when she just sat there perplexed, sadly staring at me. "You're very confused dear, very confused." I knew I was confused—but what was I going to do about it? I couldn't find the voice to tell her how hurt I was to hear her say that.

On one of my visits, I found my uncle in an unusually cheerful mood. He was smiling from ear to ear. "My students are coming over tomorrow. They're such lovely girls and boys. They're very bright. I'm very fond of them…"

That's when I found out that my uncle was inviting the brightest teenage students from his class to participate in informal gatherings in his home. Apparently, this was nothing new; it was going on for some time, but I wasn't aware of it. I wondered what those get-togethers were like. I would have loved to be a part of it, but I didn't feel I belonged in that group. I felt an ache inside. As I compared myself with his students, my feelings of worthlessness came to the surface. I wasn't like them; I was not one of his "girls and boys."

One day I came to their home very upset. As I spoke to Jessie, I broke down and sobbed. "I'm no good… I'm ugly… I'm nothing… I'll never be loved… I'll never be anything…" I became hysterical. When I couldn't stop, Jessie got up from her chair and came toward me. She yelled, **"Stop it!"** and gave me a smack across my face. I snapped out of it at once. Startled that Jessie would raise a hand to me, I told myself I would never behave that way again in her presence. And I never did. I tried to leave this incident behind me.

I continued to visit them as usual, although at times I felt like I was wearing out my welcome. Both Will and Jessie had jobs that were hectic and demanding. Sometimes, towards the end of the day, I would be waiting for them with my problems. I was especially hopeful of speaking to Jessie. While I waited for her, I might pick up a book and glance at it or talk with Will about superficial things. Then Jessie would appear. Most of the time she would tell me: "I'm so tired, I have to lie down and take a nap." At about 6 o'clock, Mary rang a bell to announce dinner. Then the three of us went into the kitchen and had the nice, simple meal that Mary prepared for us. It was always a joy for me to eat with Will and Jessie.

Afterward, I eagerly joined Jessie in the living room where we talked and talked, while my uncle worked at his desk in another room. Sometimes he walked in when I was in tears and roared: **"What is it now? Another one of those bums from the candy store?"** As he shouted, I felt crushed. He didn't even know what I was talking about, or why I was crying. Worst of all, he didn't want to know. That troubled me all the more. As I got up to leave, I whined, "I'm not coming up here anymore!"

That's when Jessie became the mediator. She stepped in and spoke in a low, calm voice: "Billy, it's okay, she'll be all right. Getting upset is not going to help any. Please, Billy, try to understand, have some patience…"

Will left the room, mumbling something under his breath. Jessie heaved a sigh and nodded her head. "Your uncle has no patience; it's terrible." She paused and then softly said, "Dear, he's very worried about you. He gets upset and he can't contain himself." But I was too upset to hear her.

There were times when I ran out of their home into the street, sobbing bitterly. My uncle's words cut like a knife and I couldn't get hold of myself. I wandered the streets in a fog until I was able to pull myself together; then I found my way home.

These bitter fights left me in a state of despair for days at a time. I would tell myself: *I'll never speak to him again.* But I couldn't hold on to my anger for long. My uncle had become too important in my life, and so had Jessie. I looked up to both of them. Soon, I overlooked my upset and went back to them, as if nothing had happened.

Despite our continuous miscommunications and disagreements, I still had a silent longing for my uncle's love and approval. *If only he could be gentler with me and accept me for myself.* And then, I was pleasantly surprised. In rare moments, Will dropped his austere manner and interacted with me in a very calm, caring way. I reveled in those moments. I felt that I was about to have a close relationship with him when suddenly I saw a frown on his face. I must have aroused his irritability with something I said— something trivial to me but significant for him. He was obviously annoyed with me and once again, there was dissension and ill feelings between us. I felt disheartened. I gave some thought to this, and I concluded that my uncle wasn't able to sustain a tranquil, tender relationship with me; I sensed that he had to keep himself at a distance—why, I didn't know. But how I appreciated those moments when he could be gentle and thoughtful. I was so sorry it couldn't last.

One day I saw a mutual affection between him and Jessie. He went over to her and kissed her gently on the forehead, and with a loving grin, called her "Golden Flower." She looked like a teenage girl as she flashed her glowing smile and laughed. These two people loved each other, and it made my heart feel good to see this. Even the way they spoke to each other—in a kind, thoughtful way—told me there was a genuine caring between them. It was something I enjoyed being a part of.

But sometimes, when I discussed my problems with both of them, I was shocked to see them in a war of words and it was all about me. I listened to their differences of opinion, which were vast, and I couldn't help but feel horrible because I had caused dissension in a household that was otherwise peaceful and calm. When Will became angry with me for disrupting his peace and quiet with my ongoing problems, he lashed out: "We have a life of our own to live!" That cold, unfeeling tone once again! I felt shredded. I couldn't speak. I couldn't think. I couldn't hear anything. I felt in the way. Again, I told myself: *I'll have to stop seeing them.* But it never got that far. I valued them too much, and the wisdom that only they could give me.

My mother continued to be resentful because I was seeing the two people she hated the most. She asked me about my visits, and I told her that Jessie was asking for her. "Jessie wants to know if you'd like to come over."

"Me go up to my brother's house? I don't want any part of him or his wife. It's bad enough you go up there. Leave me alone!"

I retorted, "Jessie is very worried about me. She sees how lost I am; she knows how much I'm suffering. Jessie cares about me very much." I was trying to convey a message: *See how Jessie cares for me? Why can't you care for me like that? Why can't you love me?* She was not in the least moved, and we didn't talk about it again.

I had become so attached to Jessie that whenever I found something pressing or disturbing, I wrote it down for her. Whether she was on vacation or only a few blocks away, it didn't make any difference; I had to let her know what was going on inside of me. I was despondent when I wrote these notes to her:

I love my mother—I don't know if she really realizes it, but I do. I wish she could be happy and on her feet like before I was born. This alone would make me a happier girl.

I miss my father so much and I often wish I could just experience some of these pleasures that little children experience with their fathers. It must be wonderful! It must be wonderful to feel secure with your father and not have to cling to your mother. To be able to kiss your father, walk hand in hand with him—that's all I have ever really wanted. And now it's all too late. Now I realize all that I never really wanted to know. It is all very painful and lonely to understand. My father once told me, a little while before he died, that someday I would understand a lot of everything that I never knew then. And he was right. I see what he meant...

As I expressed my feelings on paper, I found some emotional relief from the tensions I was carrying around.

Out of the blue, my uncle said, "You have the best of both worlds! You have your mother's intelligence and your father's temperament. If it were the other way around, you'd be in a lot of hot water!" From the way I felt, I couldn't see how things could be any worse.

When I was leaving their home one day, my uncle walked me to the door and said: "I want you to know you're the only person who can come here at any time without calling or making an appointment." I felt confused. I would think about my uncle and the things he said. I wondered: *Does he really care about me, or is he just putting up with me because of some moral responsibility?*

One day I found the nerve to ask, "Will, why do you yell and scream at me for the least thing?"

I was quite surprised to hear his response. "I have patience with others who are not as intelligent as you, but for someone with your intelligence, who is walking on her head instead of on her feet, I lose all patience!"

41

Getting Around New York

On one of my visits to Uncle Will, he said: "We want to take you to a well-known restaurant in Manhattan. It's called Toffenetti's. We think you'll enjoy it."

At the age of nineteen, I had never even entered a restaurant. I was filled with anxiety and dread at the very thought of it. But I had an opportunity staring me in the face, and I would not let it pass by. I went home and told my mother. As usual, she was not very happy to hear that I was going places with Will and Jessie. But I wasn't listening to her dictates like I had before. If I wanted to do something that she disapproved of, I would just go ahead and do it. I had become quite a rebellious young lady.

Part of me wanted to try new things, while another part wanted to maintain the status quo and be left alone. Each new experience put me on edge. I knew I would have to eventually eat in a restaurant. How much longer could I hold out? So somehow I found some courage and took another step outside my door.

Toffenetti's: What a place! It was huge, exquisite, and totally packed! I stood there looking around in amazement. *My goodness, there are so many people here!* I felt vulnerable and very much out of place. I wanted to leave immediately, but how could I tell that to

Will and Jessie? They had been so eager to take me to this classy restaurant. Before long, someone showed us to a table, and we were seated. I knew I was stuck; I would have to stay.

Soon, a young man came over to our table and handed out something called a menu. He stood there waiting for us to order our meal. I looked at this menu and I was confused. *What's an entree? What's a combination dinner? What do they mean by "a la carte"?* I was glad that Will and Jessie solved my dilemma and ordered for me. The young man quickly jotted it all down on a pad, and then he was gone.

When the food came, I had the most dreadful feeling. *Am I doing this right? Am I eating with the right silverware?* I felt a million eyes upon me saying, "You don't know how to eat in a restaurant!" *How embarrassing. Could people look inside of me and know that this was my first time?* What a terrible thought! But then again, I told myself: It can't be as bad as all that. I already had some experience eating at Will and Jessie's. They had shown me which spoons to use for soup and which to use for dessert. At home it didn't matter if I ate with a fork, a spoon, or my fingers—I could even eat right out of a pot. I didn't need to have fine manners; I didn't need to pretend for anyone. But here, I had to know.

So, I sat quietly and chewed my food slowly. I tried not to show any discomfort. I muddled through the meal as best I could, not knowing what I was eating and caring even less. We didn't say much during the meal. I watched Will and Jessie and observed their manners at the table, and then I did the same. That felt pretty safe. As we were about to leave, Will looked pleased and said, "Now you've made a start. We have taken you to one of the finest restaurants in New York!"

I smiled and said, "Thank you." I never let him know how I really felt.

Shortly after that venture, I joined Jessie in Jahn's, a well-known ice cream parlor in the Bronx. With a big, happy smile on her face, she said: "You told me you never had a Coke—well, you're going to have one right now." Soon, I was staring at a dark liquid fizzling in a glass. With a spirit of adventure, I decided to try it. *My goodness, what a terrible taste!* I wanted to spit it out, but I was ashamed. There was Jessie, sitting next to me, having an ice cream soda, looking like the cat that swallowed the canary. I managed to get a few drops down and paused. Then I had some more. By the time I reached the bottom of the glass, I had barely begun to tolerate it. On my last sip, I was startled; I heard a weird, gurgling whistle that echoed loudly in my glass. I could have sworn that everyone in the place had heard it. I had no idea that sipping soda through a straw from an almost empty glass could make such a loud sound. If my face hadn't flushed red, I would have been as white as a sheet. I took a peek around the room. No eyes had turned in my direction—not even Jessie's. She appeared to be enjoying her drink. A few seconds later, Jessie was smiling, and with a twinkle in her eye, she said, "So how did you like your first Coke, dear?" I didn't have the heart to tell her, so I muttered, "It was okay…"

Will and Jessie kept talking about the places they wanted to take me to, and I felt my heart leaping in my chest. I wanted to tell them how afraid I was, but each time, I had a need to meet the challenge. I had to somehow learn about life outside my four walls. Soon, they were telling me about the Statue of Liberty. Jessie gushed, "It's enthralling. You have to see it!"

So, on a warm summer day, we took the subway downtown to Battery Park. There we sat, waiting for a ferry to arrive. I had never seen a large body of water before, and there, in front of me, were waves rippling in the bay. It was fascinating, but I couldn't really appreciate it; anxiety was blurring my view. Every so often I would glance at Will and Jessie. They appeared comfortable and relaxed talking to each other, as they gazed out at the water. I tried to act nonchalant. I couldn't let them know how frightened I was of this new experience. I wasn't about to spoil their day.

Finally, the ferry arrived, and we got on. I blocked out everything around me. When we got off on Liberty Island, I looked up and who should be standing there before me but Miss Liberty! She was tall and awesome with that torch in her hand. Will started to laugh. He pointed up to the Statue and said, "We're going all the way up there. And we're going up in an elevator!"

I froze. *What is an elevator?* I soon found out. There I was, squeezed into a box that closed like a cage. Suddenly, it began to move. It seemed so strange—being trapped within the four walls of something that was moving; and moving we were! The elevator was going higher and higher. How I wanted to get out! I looked around; no one seemed alarmed but me. *What will happen if the elevator gets stuck? Or if it suddenly plunges downward and crashes into God knows what?* I was holding my breath until the elevator stopped and the door slid open. There I was, out in the open, with my feet on solid ground once again. I was so thankful for that. We had traveled some ninety feet and had arrived at the top of the pedestal of Miss Liberty.

"You are now looking out at New York Harbor," said my uncle. He pointed to places in the distance, but what I saw had no meaning for me. Both he and Jessie seemed to be enjoying themselves as they conversed with each other. I tried to conceal my anxiety as best I could.

I recall one happy moment in the afternoon, and that was when Jessie softly murmured, "We've been here for some time now. I guess we'd better go."

But my happiness didn't last long. It was back to the elevator, and then another ferry ride. Good grief! I had forgotten about that.

It felt good to be back in Battery Park. I now delighted in the aroma that was wafting on the breeze, as we sat on a bench and watched the boats gliding by. I felt tired in the moment, but I had a good feeling because I ventured out into the unknown and nothing terrible had happened. There was nothing to be afraid of.

A few weeks later, Jessie said to me, "Dear, we'd like to take you to the Empire State Building. It's the tallest building in the world, and we want you to see it."

Even though I had a fear of heights, I wanted the experience, no matter how dreadful I perceived it to be. I had no idea of what I was getting myself into. Soon I was in an elevator with Will and Jessie when they announced that we would be going up to the 86th floor, and then, to the 102nd floor. It was the same fear as before: *Let me out of here!* But I never said it; I was too ashamed. So, I stood there, scared, as the elevator began its journey upward. Suddenly, the people around me became invisible. I kept staring at the floor numbers, but I didn't see a thing. And then the door opened. I rushed out of there like a bat out of hell. My uncle was smiling as he happily declared: "We are now on the 86th floor of the tallest building in the world!" I felt a hot sweat go through me as he spoke.

We were now entering the Observation Deck, and I heard my uncle say: "You can see all five boroughs from here." I wondered what was so important about that. My first impulse was to look down, but I pulled back. Temptation prevailed and I took a quick glance. My goodness, people had become nothing more than dots on the street below. *How amazing! What a sight to behold!*

Will and Jessie were now talking to me about the surrounding view and I tried to appear interested, masking the fog I was in. But I couldn't partake in it. I only heard Jessie saying, "Let's go up to the 102nd floor; there's more to see up there!"

My God, will I ever get through this? I knew there was no way to back out; I had come with Will and Jessie, and I would have to leave with them. Whatever they were going to do, I'd have to do, too!

When we arrived on the 102nd floor, I felt that same urge to look down below. This time, it looked somewhat different; it seemed that the dots had multiplied! I had a queasy feeling in my stomach; I quickly turned away. Soon, Will and Jessie were talking to each other, pointing out places in the distance. Names and more names of places I had never heard of, and then I heard nothing. I just wanted to go home.

Soon the sun faded and darkness stretched over the city. I felt mystery and intrigue as I looked out over a luminous world of sparkling lights set against a black background and I thought: *How beautiful it is here at night!* For a moment, I forgot where I was, and then I heard Jessie say, "It's getting late. Why don't we stop off at the Automat and have a bite?"

I could feel my stomach rumbling, and I welcomed Jessie's suggestion. As we made that seemingly long journey down in the elevator, I kept telling myself: *You're not alone. You're with Will and Jessie. Jessie is happy. She's smiling; and Will seems relaxed. It's not so bad!* I nervously held on to that thought, even as the elevator door opened and we stepped out.

We were now heading over to eat in a Horn and Hardart Automat. This was a huge, self-service restaurant that had small glass windows set in a wall, through which you could see all kinds of food. You would put some coins into a slot; the door would open and out would come the food of your choice. How fascinating that was. And the food tasted so good. What I especially liked was the atmosphere. There were no waiters and waitresses pressuring you for orders. It was nice, quiet, and informal; there were plenty of tables and chairs, and you could sit and talk for as long as you wanted to—and we did just that.

"There are so many more things to see, dear. We'll be showing you more wonderful sights in the city…" I heard the enthusiasm in Jessie's voice when she said that, and I wondered what else they had in store for me, but in the moment, I wasn't eager to find out.

The next time I ventured out with Will and Jessie, we returned to Battery Park. I recall marveling at the great big Staten Island ferries in the distance. A short time later, we were on one of them. I crawled on to the ferry like a tortoise, while Will and Jessie moved along steadily with the crowd. I was hoping to take a seat on a lower deck, when Jessie called out, "Come on, we're going upstairs. Follow us!"

I nervously watched her climb the stairs to the upper deck as the ferry began to move. She was very casual and relaxed. As she glanced back, she gave me a great big smile. Will seemed at ease, too, as he followed her. I kept lagging behind, when the ferry started to pick up speed. I was trying my darndest to keep up with them. With a fear that I might lose my balance and fall, I held on to a rail for dear life.

I found my way up to the deck where Will and Jessie were waiting for me. We found seats together and occasionally, they got up and walked around. I observed my uncle and aunt, talking, smiling, and every so often, we exchanged small conversation. Jessie commented, "How refreshing it is to breathe in the nice cool air." She verbalized what I was feeling. The breeze carried a scent that I found delightful. As I began to relax a little, I slowly got up from my seat and walked a few feet over to the rail. Much to my astonishment, I found myself basking in the beauty of the summer

day. It all felt so good. I wondered: *What is there to be afraid of?*
As I looked out over the water, I said to myself: *It's okay. It's okay.*
And it was okay.

42

My Father's Family

I used to hear about my father's family as I was growing up. My mother would talk about them with contempt. I wondered who they were, and what they were like. Were they really as bad as she made them out to be?

My first introduction to my father's family was when I was twelve years old, and met my father's brother, Marvin. My first recollection of Marvin was seeing him on a warm summer day in Spring Valley when he was with Grandma and Hedda huddling together, whispering about something that apparently was not for my ears. I sensed something awful had happened, but just what, I didn't know. The look of intense sadness on their faces told a story of its own. As I looked at them, I was overcome with dread. Suddenly, I didn't want to know what happened; I was there but not really there, as I withdrew into myself. I guess I was trying to protect myself from some painful reality. Soon, Marvin was driving us back to the city. I didn't speak to him, nor did he speak to me. When we got out of his car, we remained total strangers. Sometime later, I learned Marvin had come out to Spring Valley to deliver the terrible news: my father had just died.

Sometime later, when I was in my early teens, Marvin came to visit. He was eager to talk about his brother: "You never knew George? What a shame!" As he spoke, I felt terrible. With tears in my eyes, I had a wish to be back in time with my father. His stories were touching, and Marvin seemed so sincere, so caring. He sounded like a really nice guy.

Later, Grandma was in our home and I told her that Marvin had recently visited us. She asked, "Did he talk about your uncle Irving? Poor Irving, he's a sick boy—they had to put him away in an institution. I can see him as if it were only yesterday. He's tall and thin, and he looks a little like Abraham Lincoln." I didn't know what to say. I didn't know anything about Irving, and I wasn't really interested. I was too preoccupied with my own little world.

Shortly afterwards, Marvin came over with a frail-looking young man. Marvin smiled and said, "Lenore, this is your uncle Irving. He's been asking to meet you."

What a surprise! I was meeting Uncle Irving after all these years. Yes, he was tall and thin, but I didn't see any resemblance to Abraham Lincoln.

Marvin volunteered, "I'm taking Irving out on a supervised visit, so we can't stay too long; I have to bring him back before sundown." Irving appeared happy to meet me and immediately extended his hand to me. I noticed that his hand was shaking continuously, and he could hardly speak as he stammered, "Hel-lo Lee-nore." There was so much sadness in his eyes and yet he was trying to smile. I wished there were something I could do to alleviate his suffering. I felt helpless as his eyes met mine.

I watched Marvin relate to his brother, and I was deeply touched. He explained things to Irving in a low, protective tone, almost like a parent speaking to a child. It was heartwarming. My mother sat quietly in her chair. She showed no emotion and appeared oblivious to everything around her throughout the visit. They stayed for a short time and then they were gone.

Marvin came back a few times with Irving. I stopped focusing on Irving's disabilities, as I perceived the person within. I thought he was a sweet guy—a very gentle soul. I was feeling pretty much the same about Marvin. He was outgoing. He had a great sense of humor and enjoyed telling a joke. They both appeared to be good people, but what did I really know about people? I just knew how I felt when I was with them.

I would hear my mother say, "I'm sorry for Irving, but the rest of that crowd could go to hell. They're all no damn good!" My mother was on the warpath and I wasn't about to participate.

I now had a strong desire to meet my aunts Bea and Rose. If I were to pass them on the street, I would not have known them. I ran over to a store in the neighborhood and thumbed through a number of phone directories. I found a phone listing for Bea, and I raced home to make the call. (We now had a phone in the house.) A hot sweat passed through me as I dialed her number. Soon, I heard a woman's voice at the other end. I asked anxiously, "Is this Bea?"

A soft, sweet voice replied, "Yes, this is Bea."

I found the courage to say, "Hi, I'm your niece. I'm George's daughter, Lenore."

Bea seemed startled as she said, "You're George's daughter?"

I was very uncomfortable as we started to talk. The phone was shaking in my hand. I guess my mother's badmouthing of Bea over the years had a profound effect upon me. And soon, I heard her say, "Why don't you come out to see me? I live in Brooklyn...."

Me go to Brooklyn? Besides anything else, I wasn't ready to travel out there, so I said, "I'll call you back and let you know when I can make it. Right now, I'd like to get in touch with Aunt Rose. Could you give me her phone number?"

Bea replied, "She doesn't have a phone. She lives in the Bronx. I'll give you her address."

I quickly jotted it down and I thought: *Maybe she lives right near me. What a surprise it will be for her; and what a wonderful moment it will be for me!*

As I said goodbye to Bea, I had mixed feelings about meeting her. I wondered if, and when, that would occur. Meanwhile, my primary concern was seeing Rose.

I had a lot of anxiety when I went over to my mother and said: "I'm going to visit Aunt Rose, and then, I'm going out to see Aunt Bea."

She looked as though she were about to fall on the floor. "What? You're going to see those bitches? They're a bunch of good-for-nothings! They don't think of anyone but themselves. All they know is to eat. They're like a bunch of pigs! And what a stupid lot they are! I have no use for that crowd. They're no damn good!"

I had a simple reply to her outburst: "I want to see them because they're my aunts. I have a right to meet them."

Hedda grumbled, "You're in for more trouble. You don't learn. You don't learn…"

Maybe I didn't learn, but I knew I wasn't going to learn by sitting in the house with my mother.

On a hot, humid day in August, I boarded a bus in the Bronx and nervously asked the driver to call out Spofford Avenue. Rather reluctantly, he said he would — but what if he didn't? As I sat there anxiously looking at unknown signs and streets, the bus crawled through areas I had never seen. I had no idea of where I was or where I was going. It seemed like an endless ride when suddenly the driver shouted out my stop. *Thank God he didn't forget!* I jumped out of my seat and flew off the bus.

My heart was beating fast as I approached one person after another, asking for street directions. I finally found the building that Rose lived in. How relieved I was when I saw her name in the building directory. However, as I put my finger on the bell, I was struck by an alarming thought: *What if I came all this way and she wasn't home?* Suddenly the buzzer echoed back. I became more nervous as other thoughts came rushing in. *What is Rose like? What if she doesn't like me? What if she doesn't want me dropping in on her like this? What if she turns out to be a nasty person?*

I swallowed down my anxiety, entered the old, narrow walk-up, and slowly climbed the long, dimly lit stairway. Some of the bulbs were out on some landings, and I had an eerie feeling that the building was deserted. My imagination was running wild, and I had all kinds of scary thoughts. My heart was pounding, but I forced myself to keep climbing the stairs. Soon, I heard a voice from somewhere: "Who is it? Who is it?"

Thank God, there is some sign of life in this building!

I heard some footsteps on the stairs and yelled back: "I'm George's daughter, Lenore."

Suddenly I saw a short, slightly plump lady at the top of the stairs. I repeated, "I'm Lenore, George's daughter."

With a wide-eyed stare and open mouth, she cried out: "Well, for heaven's sake!"

I ran up to meet my aunt Rose at the top of the landing, and with a look of joy on her face, she reached out and grabbed me. "George's daughter! I can't believe it!"

We embraced, and then together, we climbed the rest of the way to her apartment on the top floor. As she opened her door, I heard her mutter: "My brother's daughter! "

I stood there, staring at her. My aunt Rose wasn't at all what I pictured her to be. I was told that she had small ugly marks all over her face from the chicken pox. I didn't see any such thing. She looked youthful, with short reddish-brown hair framing her sweet, round face. Her dark brown eyes sparkled when she spoke. She was lively and vibrant. Here before me stood this lovely, warm lady inviting me into her life!

"Can I get you something to eat or drink?"

I replied, "All I want is your company."

She soon went into the kitchen and came out with a tray full of fruit. Then she sat down beside me. "How is your mother, dear? It's been years since I've seen her. When I knew her, she was a beautiful young woman."

I detoured quickly from that topic, and went on to ask, "Have you seen Marvin lately?"

She laughed and said, "We're not a very close family. I rarely see my brother or Bea."

I confided, "I've never met Bea. What is she like?"

Rose frowned. "Bea is only interested in herself and her family. My sister likes the rich. We don't talk that often. When we do talk, it's usually me calling her on a phone in the candy store, and it's brief. That's about it!

"Honey, let me show you around the house." Rose's apartment was a cozy, immaculate little place. What immediately caught my eye was a large, framed picture of a handsome young man. He looked a lot like my father. Rose proudly said, "You have a cousin, Barry."

And she went on to tell me that Barry was her only child, married, and living on Long Island. "You know, I'm a grandma. I have nine grandchildren, and I become a grandmother every other year. My son's married to a Catholic girl, and they practice Catholicism." *What did she mean by "practice Catholicism"?* I didn't want to appear ignorant, so I didn't ask.

I soon heard a key in the lock. Rose's husband was home. Soon, a short, thin, grey-haired man was standing before me, smiling. Rose couldn't wait to tell him: "Eddie, you'll never guess who is here. It's Lenore, George's daughter!"

A shocked expression appeared on his face. He laughed heartily and said, "After all these years!"

As soon as he sat down, he started to talk and didn't stop. He was telling me all kinds of stories about people he met and places he had been to; and he was constantly chuckling as he spoke. My mind kept wandering. I heard my grandma's voice saying: "Eddie never worked a day in his life. He could never find a job. It's either too hot or too cold, or there aren't any jobs. It's always something."

At some point Rose interrupted: "I work as a waitress in the East 70's. It's a very busy place. I'm back and forth on my feet all day. My feet hurt, but what good is complaining? What can you do? You have to make money to live. That's life!"

I was observing Eddie as Rose spoke. Sometimes he would laugh and refer to Rose as "Mom." I wondered how he could call her "Mom" when I was told he was twenty years her senior and looked it. But Rose didn't bat an eyelash.

Soon Rose went into the kitchen and started to prepare dinner. There was an aroma from the kitchen that took my breath away. Home cooking! I was thrilled when she said: "You're going to have dinner with us!"

Sometime later, the dining table was filled with platters of meat and gravy mixed with vegetables and potatoes. It was a delicious meal. I couldn't help but say, "You're one terrific cook, Rose."

She heartily replied, "Well, don't forget, I work in a restaurant!"

We spoke about little tidbits at the dinner table. We shared some smiles and a few laughs, as we lingered over our food. It was a carefree, relaxing atmosphere, and I was feeling comfortable. At the end of the meal, Rose brought out a lavish dessert and coffee. I was full, but I was still eating. I don't know when I enjoyed a meal more. And soon, we dragged ourselves back to the living room. And we talked.

Rose looked sad as she confided, "I didn't see my brother for twelve years, and in the last two years before he died, he came to see me three times."

I asked her why things were like that, and she angrily replied, "Because, dear, your mother didn't like us. She poisoned his mind against us."

She was speaking against my mother, and I didn't particularly like it. I ignored it, as I opened my heart to her about something that weighed heavily on my mind: "I miss my father very much. I never stopped crying about him through the years."

Rose frowned, then said: "On his last visit, George said to me: 'My daughter doesn't love me. Did you ever hear such a thing? She doesn't love her own father!' "

Rose stopped, as if to reflect for a moment, and said: "What a shame. Your father died, never knowing how much you loved him."

She said this as casually as one might open a faucet and pour water into a glass, but those words cut into me like a knife. I was startled that my father would say something like that. I didn't feel loved by him either.

"It's a tragedy. But at the time, things couldn't be helped...."

Rose continued to speak, but I couldn't hear what she was saying. "My daughter doesn't love me..." It was whirling around in my head. I wanted to cry.

I came back to the present as Rose was saying, "Your father would be very proud of you if he could see you." She added, "I'm proud of you, too."

But she didn't even know me. Was she being kind?

We sat and talked for a while, and then it was time for me to leave. As I walked towards the door, Rose went to a drawer, pulled out an envelope and whispered, "Here, dear, some pictures of your father."

And then she slipped a couple of dollars into my hand. I was shocked. How could I take money from my hard-working aunt? I told her I couldn't accept it. Her voice must have risen an octave as she said: "Come on, it's nothing! I won't hear it. It's just a little carfare!"

I felt embarrassed as I put the two dollars into my bag. It didn't feel right. The amount she gave me was not huge, but I knew that money didn't come easily to her. I didn't want to take even one penny from her. But she was one gracious lady. She opened her door to me. She fed me and made me feel at home. And then she gave me money. I was moved by her generosity and loving spirit.

Going home on the bus, I kept thinking about things Rose said—especially about my father. I remembered Jessie telling me something similar: "Your father loved you. All he ever wanted from you was your love." It was very disturbing.

A few days later, I went to the park. I was lying on the grass, basking in the sunlight of a beautiful summer day when I saw a man and a little girl sitting on the grass nearby. He was hugging and kissing the little girl. Suddenly I wanted to be a small child again and have my father hug and kiss me. I tried to ignore them, but I couldn't. As tears rolled down my cheeks, I got up and left. On a slip of paper, I wrote down what I felt:

"I see many such scenes and now I know what I have missed and what I have always cried for. It hasn't been for a sweetheart — it's just been for my father."

I started to see Rose more often, and we spoke a lot about George. "I loved my brother very much and because you are George's daughter, I feel that love for you, too." I was touched.

Rose went over to her jewelry box. "I have a lot of things for you, honey. I hope you like them."

My eyes opened wide and my jaw dropped. She gave me a 14K gold Benrus watch, a choker, a beaded bracelet, and a heap of fine necklaces. I was never a lover of jewelry, whether it was real or costume, but I wanted every piece that Rose offered me. I could feel a token of affection tied to each one. Each time I saw Rose, I came away with a little something of hers that was given to me with love.

Like Jessie, Rose had a "common sense approach" to life. I was quite impressed by the things she said. I would go over to Rose's house with a yearning to find my life; I had to learn more about living in the real world. I was especially curious about family life. "Rose, what does it feel like to be a part of a family?"

She answered, "We are not all fortunate to be part of a family. Look at me. My family separated when I was very young; that couldn't be helped because of the war. We were never close; everyone went their own way. But I got married. I made my own family. There are many, many people who come from bad homes and have nothing—and they find a way."

"Suppose I don't find anyone who wants to marry me, then what?"

Rose smiled warmly and chuckled, "Well, do you think it was easy for me? I didn't have boys interested in me when I was young, and I didn't go to school dances. I didn't think I was ever going to meet anyone when I finally met Eddie. I wasn't attractive, and no one paid any attention to me. But you see if it's in the cards—if it's fate—it will happen. When you go to bed at night, say a prayer to meet someone nice and kind, who will be good to you. Believe that it will happen and it will happen."

When I told her I was not brought up to be religious, Rose laughed and said, "Neither was I. It's something you learn to feel in your heart. You don't have to go to synagogue to pray. You pray in your heart for what you want. You ask God for help, and to give you what you need to make you happy and content."

I came away with hope that things could become better. Rose had all kinds of answers for coping with life, and there was a certain amount of love that trickled through. Perhaps the wisdom she acquired had something to do with the loss of her child. I had heard that Rose's firstborn was very sickly; she was bedridden and couldn't walk. She died when she was only five. Both Rose and Eddie were heartbroken. Rose rarely spoke about this, but when she did, I could see pain in her eyes. It seemed her encounter with the hardships of life enriched her capacity to feel and to understand.

"So often you hear that people who have money are happy. It's not true. You can have lots of money and be miserable. You have to do what makes you happy. That's the secret of life."

I asked her: "Are you doing what makes you happy?"

Rose replied, "Well, I don't have a job that makes me happy. I don't have the education. But I have learned to do things that make me feel pretty good. I go dancing. Eddie doesn't like it, but I do. I love it!" Her eyes were glowing as she spoke. "I take myself out to Yorkville. I have a few drinks, and I enjoy myself. And you, too, can find something that will have meaning for you — something you can enjoy!"

I told Rose how much I wanted to have friends — people who would accept me for myself. "Rose, what shall I do? Please help me, tell me what you do to have friends."

"Not everyone will be your friend. So often I trust people and when I turn my back, they say things that aren't true. My boss will flatter me to my face and when my back is turned, she will say nasty things about me. That's how the world is. I'm very naïve. I trust too easily and I get hurt. That's why I'm telling you, dear, have faith in yourself, and look to yourself more, look to others less."

She was giving me sound advice, but I found it very hard to take in. Sometimes I would tell her, "But Rose, I can't do what you say. I don't know what to do. Everything in my life is so upside-down."

"It takes time, but you will do the right things. It doesn't happen overnight."

I said, "But Rose, you don't understand. It's the way I grew up. My mother and the things she did. Everything was so weird, so unreal. It's hard to put into words."

With a frown Rose replied, "Your mother was a very sick woman, dear. There's nothing that can be done about the past. The only thing we can work with is the present."

I thought it was wisely said, and I added, "I hope you're right."

There were times when she became excited and raised her voice. I couldn't understand why she would fly off the handle so easily, and for trivial things at best. Was it me? Did I do something to upset her? I became flustered, but I wouldn't say a word when she was in one of those moods. Things would blow over in seconds, once her tension was released, and she was back to her old self. We would resume our talks as if nothing had happened.

I kept asking about Aunt Bea. "What is she like? I've heard so much about her…"

Rose would snap, "Go out to Brooklyn and see her! I've told you before she's not interested in anyone but her own family. She's a social climber, and she likes people with money. That's all I'm going to say."

I soon spoke to Bea again, and once more she invited me to come out to Brooklyn. I told her I would be visiting her real soon.

Now where in the world is Brooklyn? As I thought about my forthcoming trip, I began to panic. It seemed that Brooklyn was on the other side of the world. *How will I ever make it out there?* There I was, a girl in my late teens, worried about going out to new places, taking wrong turns, and ending up God knows where. Goodness gracious, I was acting like a little child and I didn't like it. I felt infantile and ashamed. However, there may have been some validity to this since my sense of direction was never developed and it was easy for me to lose my way. It was a problem all right, but I couldn't give in to it for then I would be sitting in the house and not doing anything with my life.

But why was I feeling so much pressure to go out to Brooklyn and meet Bea? From the things I heard about her, she wasn't a very nice person. Nevertheless, that didn't seem to matter to me. I wasn't going to let my anxieties rule me. This was another challenge I had to meet and I wasn't about to avoid it.

It was a long, daunting trip on the subway. I finally found my way to Bea's apartment on Ocean Avenue. When she opened the door, I saw a short lady with dark hair and a friendly smile. Like Rose, Aunt Bea looked young and attractive. But while Rose had made a big fuss over me when she met me, Bea was more reserved.

She invited me inside and, as I looked around, I felt that I was in the lap of luxury. This apartment looked like something I had seen in my movie magazines when I was growing up. There was this beautiful huge beige sectional sofa that spiraled around the living room. The carpeting was thick, and I loved the feel of this plush beige carpeting underneath my feet. I was captivated by what I saw as I said to Bea: "You have a beautiful home."

Bea held her little dog in her arms as she sat down on the sofa. I was standing there, gaping at the beauty of my surroundings when Bea said: "Would you like to join us?" And I sat down. So, there I was, experiencing a different way of living. It didn't seem real. *What am I doing in a place like this?*

In no time Bea was talking continuously about her three children and their accomplishments. She was very proud of her daughter, Lisa, the concert pianist. She also boasted about her two sons: the dentist and the schoolteacher. She had so much to say about them but showed no interest in me whatsoever. I just sat there and listened. I felt invisible and annoyed.

At some point she took me into one of her bedrooms and opened a chest drawer. "Your cousin, Lisa, crocheted this sweater." It was a beautiful blend of gold thread running through beige wool. I stood there, holding it in my hands, admiring it. "You can have it," Bea said, with a big smile on her face. "You can consider it a gift from Lisa."

I was choked up with emotion. I thought this was a lovely gesture and I was impressed by her giving nature. But then a thought hit me: *She's giving away Lisa's sweater. How would Lisa feel if she came home and found it gone? Would this be upsetting to her?* I know I would have been devastated. But I didn't mention this to Bea. I took the sweater and said thank you.

Bea soon said, "Let's go out and take a walk. I'd like to show you around Brooklyn." It sounded like a good idea, so I went out with her. As we strolled along, I didn't think the streets of Brooklyn looked that much different from the streets of the Bronx. When it started to turn dark, we went back to Bea's apartment. Soon Bea made a tempting offer that I couldn't refuse: "Why don't you stay overnight? It's late and it's a big trip back to the Bronx."

I was elated. I loved the thought of staying in her luxurious apartment, but at the same time I was a little uneasy. I wasn't used to sleeping away from home, but I couldn't pass up this opportunity. I called Hedda to let her know that I wasn't coming home. She was upset and scolded me, but it was what I expected.

I worked up the courage to speak to Bea about something that was on my mind: "What's wrong with Uncle Irving? Why is he in an institution?"

Bea sadly replied, "Irving has problems. It's difficult for him to function in the world like, let's say, you and me. He's been in a state institution since he was a little boy. He needs the special care that the institution offers. Marvin takes him out regularly on supervised visits. And that reminds me; Marvin is coming over tomorrow morning with Irving. He's going to Staten Island first to pick him up, and then they're coming over here. We'll all be going out on a picnic after that. We'll have a great day!"

My timidity was aroused. *A picnic? I've never been on a picnic. The last thing I want is a picnic.*

I couldn't sleep that night.

When Marvin and Irving arrived in the morning, I was in a state of frenzy. I didn't feel safe, but I didn't want them to know how unsafe I felt. I tried to hide my feelings as best I could. The unknown had a way of paralyzing me with fear and anxiety, and now I was entering the unknown again.

Marvin drove us over to a huge picnic area with tables, benches, and trees. Bea and Marvin sprawled out a huge tablecloth and placed upon it platters of pork tenderloin, potato salad, lettuce, tomatoes, peppers, fruits, and rolls. I had not tasted many of the foods that were on the table and suddenly, I was eager to experience what it all tasted like. I forgot to be nervous as I sat down to eat with my father's family and indulged myself with all the delicious food that was there before me.

Afterwards, Bea and Marvin became involved in conversation while Irving sat there, staring off into space. He looked rather lost in a world of his own. I felt an achiness inside. Bea and Marvin were so busy engaging in talk and more talk they didn't once look my way to see me sitting there, sad, and silent. I didn't know what to say so I didn't say anything. I was afraid of making a fool of myself. I felt lost and lonely with people who were my father's family and yet, total strangers to me. Oh, how I wished I hadn't come. Over and over I said to myself: *This is just awful. What am I doing here?*

I was in downcast spirits for the rest of the time we were together. It seemed like a great big cloud was hovering over me. I tried not to reveal how bad I was feeling as I sat there, immobilized. I was relieved when Marvin said: "Time to get going!" We said our goodbyes, and Marvin dropped me off at a nearby subway station.

Now I was confronted with the reality of trying to get home on my own. There were some train and bus connections to make, and I felt shaky as I held the travel directions in my hand. I don't know how I made it, but I found the inner strength to move through my fears and get home safely.

Later, I thought to myself how silly it was to be so frightened. It was only the thoughts in my mind that made things appear so unsafe. Things were not as bad as I built them up to be. I guess the unknown can be very scary. But I still was very depressed and didn't know how to shake it.

I soon went back to Rose and told her about my visit. And I added, "At times, Bea can be a bit standoffish. She's very wrapped up in her family, like you said."

Rose smiled but did not comment.

Nevertheless, I felt an urgency to see Bea again. Because she was very close with my father, I thought she could tell me things about him I didn't know. So, I went out to Brooklyn to see her again. Bea started off by saying, "I loved your father very much. Did you know that we used to go out dancing together? We loved to dance. We even won dance contests! We spent a lot of time together. When he married your mother, I didn't see him anymore."

That was news to me. I was shocked to hear that. I always thought my father was running around to meet women at dances. I never knew that he and his sister were champion dancers! *Wow!*

"You know, your mother killed him. My poor brother, he was always working and saving money. When he died, your mother became wealthy. She's still living off that money all these years after his death."

I heard the hatred in her voice, and that stirred up intense anger in me. On some level, I agreed that my mother was responsible for George's death. I wanted to tell Bea that, but somehow, I couldn't find the words. As I sat there listening to her rant, I felt sick to my stomach. I was twisting inside with hurt and anguish. I couldn't formulate a thought. I sat through it all until I couldn't any longer. When I had enough, I said: "I think it's time for me to go." Then I got up and left.

When I got home that night, I was filled with pent-up hostility. I told Hedda, "You caused my father's death. The way you hollered and screamed at him drove him out. When he was ill, you wouldn't give him any of the money he earned, so that he could get treatment. I think you're despicable!"

Hedda's cheeks reddened and she lashed out: "I knew this would happen. Going over to that clan has put all these crazy ideas in your head." Then she walked out of the room. I sat there in gloom and pain for I don't know how long. I was brooding about things that could not be undone.

I soon visited Rose and told her, "Bea was telling me how my mother killed George. I was wiped out by her rage."

Rose quickly responded, "She never should have said that, but that's the way she is. She says whatever's on her mind, and she doesn't care who she hurts."

"Bea also told me something that astonished me: She said she and George would go out dancing when they were young. What a surprise."

"Oh yes, they loved dancing," Rose replied. "It was a big thing for both of them. It runs in the family. We all love music and dancing."

"Well, Rose, when all is said and done, I have to agree with you. Bea's only out for herself and her family. I don't think I'll be going back there again…"

Rose laughed and said, "I'm glad you found out for yourself. She doesn't give a hoot about you or me. I guess we all have to experience things for ourselves."

I felt fortunate to have Rose in my life—someone I could turn to for sound advice, plenty of support, and a certain amount of love and warmth.

I still couldn't get Bea's voice out of my head. A few days later, I was walking around in the street feeling rather low, when I was overtaken by a very disturbing thought: *Bea dumped on me all the things she wanted to tell my mother. She talked to me as if I was Hedda. She can't see me for myself because I'm Hedda's daughter. All she can see is Hedda.* I was driving myself crazy thinking about Bea and the things she told me. I had to stop dwelling on this.

Meanwhile, I was spending more time with Rose. She was kind to me, and I knew that she liked me. She only tried to make things better; she did not dwell on the traumas of the past, and I was thankful for that.

It was summertime, and Rose was talking to me about going to the beach. I wondered what it was like, but I was in no hurry to find out. I admitted to her: "I'm already nineteen and I've never been to a beach!"

Rose looked at me with furrowed eyebrows and a rather odd expression. "Well, let's go! You'll come here early in the morning, I'll pack a few sandwiches, and we'll take some fruit. The bus on the corner will take us right over."

The thought of it made me sorry I spoke. I bit my lip. "I don't know how to swim. And I'm scared of the water. I don't even have a bathing suit…"

When Rose heard that, she almost hit the ceiling. "So, you can't swim, you don't have to swim. I can't swim either! But that doesn't mean you can't go in and get your feet wet! Get yourself a bathing suit! You and I—we're going to the beach!"

I had an awful feeling in my stomach. I knew she wasn't kidding. I dreaded the thought of going, but her spirit to live and do things drew me in. On the spur of the moment, I said, "Yes, I'll go with you."

Early one morning we got on a bus heading for Orchard Beach. I said to myself: *It's a mistake. I shouldn't be doing this.* My fear of the unknown was surfacing again, and I was very anxious. But I wasn't going to give in to my fears, especially when I was with my aunt Rose.

When we got to the beach, we walked on the grass for a short distance until we approached the boardwalk. Nearby, I saw something tan covering the ground. *So that's what sand looks like! It doesn't look very appealing to me.*

Beyond the sand, I saw a huge body of water. Something about it appeared beckoning, and frightening, at the same time. I looked at Rose. She was smiling as she said, "It's so lovely here, so peaceful, so cool. Look at the water. It's beautiful! I'm going in."

Then and there, Rose started to slip out of her street clothes, which covered her bathing suit. I was sort of in a daze as I watched her throw her outer clothes into a tote bag. She was now glowing. "I'm going to stand in the water. Come with me. You'll love it."

I was suddenly feeling very unsafe. *What am I doing here with all this sand and water?* I didn't know how to tell my aunt how frightened I was, as I withdrew more into myself. Within moments, Rose ran off the boardwalk and dashed out into the sand, cheerfully calling back, "I'm going to get myself wet. Come on in and join me." And she ran ahead — straight towards the water!

I looked around and didn't see a person in sight. Somehow, I couldn't find my voice to call out to her. I was frozen in fear. I stared at my aunt disappearing in the distance, but I didn't really see her. I was just standing there. *Oh, my God, she's leaving me here all by myself!*

A feeling of dread passed through me. I pulled off my pants in a panic and threw them into my bag. I used to wonder what it was like to wear a bathing suit, and now, I was on the beach in this beautiful black bathing suit, my first ever, and it seemed very trivial to me. I had to get down to the water as quickly as my legs could carry me. Nothing else seemed to matter.

But there was a problem: In front of me was a huge expanse of this tan powder. I thought I would be able to run through it, but it was slowing me down. *How strange this feels under my feet!* But I couldn't pay any mind to it. I kept focusing on trudging my way towards my aunt Rose.

I kept seeing a hazy vision of Rose calling to me. Soon I was close enough to see her. She was standing in the water, smiling from ear to ear. She yelled out to me: "It's wonderful in here. I love it. Come on in!"

My heart pounded as I stepped closer.

"What is there to be afraid of?" she happily screamed out. "It's just a little water."

I finally surrendered, my feet barely touching the shore's edge when Rose, laughing like a girl of sixteen, splashed water all over me. "Hey, it isn't so bad. It's lots of fun!"

I had to admit: *It's not as bad as I thought.*

Although I shared many more experiences with Rose, what stands out in my mind now is that first meal I had in her home. There were smiles, a few laughs, and informal, relaxed chatter around the dinner table. It seemed to be what family life is all about. And I became a part of it that night.

43

Finding and Losing A Friend

I was walking down a street in my neighborhood not very far from home. I saw a tall young man a few feet away, coming towards me. He said hello, as if he knew me, but from where, I had no idea. From a quick glance he somehow looked familiar. But I had to turn away. Something about him made me feel very uncomfortable. My heart started to race as I turned around and moved in the opposite direction. I just felt, *I must get away as quickly as possible!*

About a week later I saw him again. I was standing in front of my building, when he came over to me and said, "Hi. I'm Tony. What's your name?"

I was plainly annoyed. I was minding my own business, and from out of nowhere, this stranger was intruding upon my privacy. In no uncertain terms I told him, "I don't want to go for a walk, I don't want to have a little talk, I don't want to do anything; I just want to be left alone!"

But Tony was persistent; he kept talking. It was all casual talk. I soon found myself engaged in conversation.

I noticed he was tall—at least six feet or more, with a slight hook in his nose. He looked down a lot when he spoke, and I observed his drooping eyelids. He was exceedingly unattractive, but there was something nice and simple about him. He seemed interested in speaking to me—and I did not perceive any sexual overtones. I found this appealing. Suddenly I wanted to hear what he had to say. So, we spoke some more. Yet there still was something about him that made me uncomfortable.

I went upstairs and thought about Tony. *Of course, I know him! He's one of the guys at the corner candy store—the guys who talk about me and make nasty remarks when I pass by.* I was not very happy about that. In the days that followed, I kept seeing Tony around the neighborhood and we'd stop to talk. He soon admitted to me, "I used to hang out at the candy store, but I gave that up. Now I stay by myself." I decided not to make this an issue, so I let it go.

It appeared that Tony and I had something in common: we both were loners, with a need to talk. Our lonely, divided selves seemed to unite and form a whole when we got together. Tony was paying a lot of attention to me; sometimes, too much—but I enjoyed it. He always remained a gentleman, and I must confess that it was wonderful to be treated with respect. I suppose that's why I, in turn, treated him with so much respect.

All through the years, the movie magazines and love songs nurtured an image of false romance and sexy allure that had sunk deep into my mind and caused me to see life in a rather unreal way. Tony was not my idea of a Don Juan. He did not represent romantic love, or even a facsimile of it. He had no charm, no finesse, and no allure. Tony was dull and drab and did not appear especially intelligent. But I could relax with him. He made me feel that I could be myself. I would confide in him when we took walks in the neighborhood. That meant a lot to me. But there were times when I felt angry with myself. *Why can't I do better?*

I was seeing Tony regularly for several months. Then I did not see him at all. *Where is he? Why haven't I seen him around?* I decided to inquire about him at the private house around the corner where he lived. His landlady came to the door and looked at me peculiarly. What was I doing bothering her when I should have known better! She came right out and said, "Tony is dead."

I stood there in shock. The landlady barked, "Didn't you know that Tony had epilepsy? He's had it all the time he's been living here. Many attacks. Some of them bad too."

"You mean he died from epilepsy? Nothing could be done to save him. What about medication? Do you know if he was taking anything?"

In a matter-of-fact tone, she responded, "The last attack was bad; they couldn't control it. They did what they could."

It seemed incredible. Tony never told me he was ill. I uttered, "I'm at a loss for words . . ."

She added, "His wife and children were too."

Wife and children? He said nothing to me about being married. And then she corrected herself. "I should say ex-wife and children."

We had spent quite some time together, yet Tony was unable to talk about his personal life. I was amazed and hurt. I had told him so much about myself. *Why couldn't he talk to me?*

Soon after, I was standing in front of my building, feeling sad about Tony, when I saw a young man, short and slim with tousled black hair and long sideburns, walking toward me. I had constantly admired him when I saw him in the street; he looked just like the movie actor, Marlon Brando. The very handsome Billy Braunson was about to approach me. *What could he possibly want with me?*

"I'm a friend of Tony's. I've seen you around with Tony. His death hit me like a thunderbolt—I'm still shaking. I can't believe he's gone."

Billy talked about his grief and sadly said, "Tony's in the funeral parlor near Fordham Road. I'm going there tonight. Good Lord, it doesn't seem real!"

His voice dropped low and his words were slurred; his eyes were red.

I hesitated for a moment, and then worked up the nerve to say, "Would it be possible for me to go along?"

Spontaneously, Billy responded, "I'll meet you in front of my door at eight o'clock. You know where I live, don't you? I live next block in that boarding house on the corner."

Of course, I knew where Billy lived; Billy Braunson was notoriously known in the neighborhood. He was often referred to as

"Bayonet Billy" because he was said to have a bayonet in his possession. At the time that he approached me, he and his brother had just been involved in a street brawl. Billy had pulled out a knife, and the police soon appeared on the scene. As a crowd gathered, the police were separating the two boys. The next time I saw the Braunson brothers, Billy's wrist was bandaged, and his brother's arm was in a sling. But this was nothing new; the Braunson boys were known to have street fights that brought out the police, but somehow it did not really bother me that Billy was known for violent outbursts and for carrying around sharp instruments. With my silly-girl heart, I suppose I was too impressed with Billy's striking good looks to care.

That night in the funeral parlor was one I shall never forget. The room was deserted, except for Billy and me. I felt very uncomfortable as I came near the casket in which Tony lay. It was hard to believe that Tony was gone. It seemed like only yesterday when he and I were standing at the door, talking about a lot of things that made sense—and no sense. Now, here I was, at a funeral parlor, with Tony's body in a casket.

Numbness crept over me, shielding me from the pain I didn't want to feel. I stood to the side, as Billy walked over to the casket. He got down on his knees and started to sob: "There never was anyone like you, Tony. You are my only friend. I love you, Tony. You are my mother, my father, my brother, and my life. I have nobody, Tony. Why did you leave me?"

I felt helpless as I watched Billy writhing in anguish. Billy was now sobbing uncontrollably. I was feeling sick, as I stood there.

We soon stepped out into the warm night air and began our long walk back. We trudged through the streets crossing one, then another, and it seemed like forever. Not a word was spoken. I was lost in my gloom, and Billy seemed very lost. Finally, we arrived at Billy's boarding house. I was surprised to hear him say, "Why don't you come on up for a while? We'll keep each other company."

At first, I felt, *It might be a mistake—me going to a man's apartment, and so late at night? But Billy is so miserable; and I'm so distraught. What could be wrong with it?*

As soon as I entered his room, I thought, *Oh, my God, it's nothing more than a cupboard!* It was so small one could barely walk in it without bumping into the chest of drawers, or the bed. I knew I had made a mistake. It was obvious to me that I didn't belong there. I wanted to leave, but didn't know how to say that to Billy without promoting hard feelings between us.

So, I stood there, kind of dumbfounded, not knowing what to say or do. Billy turned on the radio, twisting the dial from station to station until he found some slow, dreamy music. In the small space that surrounded his bed, Billy took me in his arms and began to dance with me. Then he started to kiss me passionately. Before I knew it, he threw me down on the bed. He was on top of me in seconds, as he continued to kiss me.

I cried out, "**No, Billy, please, no!**"

He did not stop. Then I let out a loud scream. Spontaneously, he raised his hand to cover my mouth and then quickly pulled himself off me. "You know, I should get out my bayonet and kill you for that! Screaming like that in my room! You'll have the whole neighborhood over here. The police will be banging on the door!"

His look of anger held me captive; I couldn't move. He then darted over to the window, opened it from the bottom and stuck his head out. Then he turned back to me and hissed, "Fortunate for you, no one's out there!"

I knew I had to get out of there and as quickly as my legs could carry me. There was only one way to do it, and that was to level with him—to be as honest as I possibly could at the right moment.

I was still sitting on the bed while Billy stood at the window, scratching his head, and looking at me as if I were crazy. "Why did you come up here if you didn't want to do anything?"

My eyes were now wet with tears, and I had trouble forcing the words out, but this was the time to tell him. "I just wanted to be with you after seeing Tony at the funeral parlor. I didn't want to have any sex. You wouldn't stop, and I was scared. So, I screamed. I'm sorry, Billy."

A few seconds later, Billy said, "Go ahead, leave! Get out! It's okay with me."

I flew down that long, narrow flight of stairs, out of the building and into the street. Then I ran all the way home.

44

Nobody Cared

The more I was out in the world experiencing how difficult it was for me to fit in, the more I was in touch with my anger and rage. I decided to visit my uncle Will and Aunt Jessie and talk to them about it. I began to express my angry feelings about the way I grew up when Will started to pontificate, "Your mother bears the personality and temperament of her father's family. It's a kind of insanity! They all have the illness from way back when. They are unbelievably stubborn, possessed of will power without the wisdom that should accompany it. They drive people out of their minds and kill those they come into contact with!"

It was very unnerving to hear this again. Many times he told me, matter-of-factly, that my mother (his sister) had stubbornness and an inability to listen to reason. Now, he was going a step further. "It's insanity. It's an insanity that runs in the family! Each and every one of them has the same characteristics." (It was rather amazing to hear him speak so nonchalantly about this, for he was one of these family members. Obviously, he did not include himself as part of this lunatic tribe.)

It felt like another lecture, and I didn't feel like listening; I was too lost in my own distress to care about the details behind my mother's bizarre behavior. But I listened just the same.

"I could tell you stories about every one of them and the people they've destroyed. There's a commonality shared by the entire family: they all have a need to create their own reality. In other words, their perception of reality is different, distorted by their own views of how the world should be. Reality, then, is a derivative of their truth, their stubbornness, their insanity . . ."

He kept dwelling on the word "insanity", and it was driving me crazy. Perhaps the family did carry a gene in their bloodline that determined this type of behavior. But so what if they did? Did it matter? Was this proclamation of "insanity" supposed to account for, ameliorate, or mitigate my suffering—the suffering that was thrust upon me by my mother's family line? Hearing that they were insane did not resolve my problems, nor lessen my pain. In no way was this good enough to compensate for the agony of my childhood, or the abnormal life I had with my mother. And if my mother and her paternal family were all "insane," then why was I living with my mother in the first place?

"I've been angry at your mother all these years for the damage she did to you. Your grandparents were responsible too. They are not your friends!"

I looked at Will in anguish. How could he say that? Grandma knocked on our door when no one else would set foot into our home. Just seeing Grandma was a source of inspiration for me. How could I renounce my loyalty to her, just because my uncle was telling me, "She is not your friend"?

"I wanted to get psychiatric treatment for your mother. But I couldn't get any support from your grandparents or your father. Your grandparents were violently opposed to getting outside help for her. Your grandfather said, 'She's the mother, she knows what's best for her child!' And your grandmother cried, 'She'll snap out of it! Leave her alone!' Together, they were a team I could not fight."

My uncle spoke in an authoritative tone of conviction. And why wouldn't he? He sounded like the skilled lawyer he was, as he made this informal presentation. However, the more I listened to him present his case, the more agitated I became.

And he went on. "Your father George was a nice guy. I knew him well over twenty years. But he was weak, very weak. He didn't know what to do, or how to fight people who were stronger than he. So, he took his coat and ran.

"I will never forgive my parents for what they've done to you. Do you know what your grandmother did at a time when your mother was in desperate need of treatment? She went to a fortune teller!"

Will paused, sadly shook his head, and commented, "Incredible!"

I finally found the courage to voice my disdain. I was nervous and a bit shaky, but I was suddenly speaking up. "Where were you all those years? Why didn't you come up to see me?"

Will then reiterated what I had heard so many times: "No one was allowed in your home. Your mother wouldn't open the door."

Sure, it was easy for people to talk. It was easy for Will, and my father's family, to say, "No one was welcome in your home." But how many times had anyone tried?

"We didn't have people ringing our bell or knocking on the door. What would have been the worst that might have happened if someone did come? My mother would not have opened the door. But there were times when she did open the door. Grandma came, although she was not wanted."

"Generally, people don't go to places where they're not welcome."

"You're saying that you stayed away because Hedda didn't want any visitors?"

My anger intensified and my pain was speaking. "People are so afraid of becoming involved. Didn't anyone care about the life of a little innocent child wasting away? Didn't anyone care whether I lived or died? How was I to survive, locked away in the house with a mother who was 'insane'? Why didn't you take me away from her? I was only four years old when she was put away in Bellevue. Why did you allow me to go back to her?"

My uncle responded in a cold monotone, "Nothing could be done without the support of your father and your grandparents."

"What happens when a family is unwilling to come to the rescue of a child?"

"No judge would have removed you from your home. There were no bruises on your body; there was no physical neglect; there was food in the refrigerator. Your grandmother and grandfather, and even your father, would not testify against your mother. And if you came before a judge, and he asked you if you wanted to leave your mother, what would you say? No, of course. So, what was there to do? Then, when you were older, you certainly would not have left your mother; you know that yourself."

There was a lot of truth in what Will said, but I could not accept his legal analysis. "Are you aware of all the things that happened after my mother came home from Bellevue? Do you know how I've been living all these years? My mother was, and still is, very disturbed. And yes, I was abused emotionally and physically. I did have black and blue bruises on my body from her physical attacks. She used her fists on me. She would shake and pummel me . . ."

Jessie looked astonished. She frowned and interrupted, "Dear, we never knew that you were pummeled . . ." I wondered what would have been different if they had known.

As I spoke, I was violating the sacred bond I had with my mother. But it was time to come out of hiding. "I could never speak about it; I could never say anything bad about my mother. Even now, I'm struggling with it, but it's time for the truth to come out."

Jessie listened with a look of concern. Will was silent.

"I now have curvature of the spine. My teeth and my eyes are also affected. It's all because of her neglect! Her terrible neglect! She never got me that brace for my back, and Grandma tells me my curve is getting worse. She let my teeth go until they had to be pulled. I was studying under a 40-watt bulb, and she didn't give a damn about my eyes. Are you saying that this is not serious?"

In his judicial manner, Will repeated, "Nothing could have been done any differently. Generally speaking, a child usually stays with its mother. Only in severe cases is a child removed from the home. There must be severe neglect or proof of physical molestation that determines this. If a child has food in its mouth and a roof over its head—which was the case with you—the child is not likely to be removed from its home."

I thought to myself, *How could my uncle know how I was living with my mother? What did he or anyone else know about what was actually going on in our home? Grandma came and went. The tutors came, spent a short time going over my schoolwork with me, and then they were gone. And that was the extent of our visitors. No one was around long enough to see what really went on behind closed doors.*

"Yes," I admitted, "I did have food in my mouth and a roof over my head but that is not the whole story. I don't think you're hearing me. My mother was living in another world. She was not in reality. I told you I was abused mentally and physically. How much abuse is warranted before something is done? I would think that anything which is injurious to a child's health might be considered cause for alarm."

Will didn't show any real emotion about what I was saying. He was rather cool as he reiterated, "It was an unfortunate situation, but I could not fight this family."

I found his response to my revelations of a brutal childhood very unsettling. He was beginning to sound like a broken phonograph record. It seemed as if he was justifying his own inaction, while blaming others in the family for their weak, unsupportive behavior.

It was tearing me up inside to listen to my uncle talk about my life as some kind of cut and dry legal case. It was my life, and I could no longer hold back my emotional pain. I said, "I don't care what the laws are. A crazy parent should not be allowed to keep a child! Hedda was crazy. She was doing crazy things. The worst of everything was her physical and emotional abuse of me. It didn't stop. Her neglect was something else; the fact that she wouldn't get a brace for my back speaks for itself. I was always sick and home from school. Don't you think Hedda had something to do with that? And why weren't people allowed in the house? I saw my grandparents and my father only briefly, and even then, I wasn't allowed to talk to them. I think that's cruelty beyond cruelty. I lived in isolation in Hedda's asylum, more like a prisoner than anything else. It's incredible to believe that I was never permitted to have a friend and at nineteen, I still don't know what it's like to have a friend. Do you know that the only friends I had growing up were my radio and my rocking chair?

"There's more. Do you know what it's like to see your mother standing at the sink, scrubbing her hands with water so hot that blood comes oozing out? Do you know what it's like to watch your mother airing out books in the refrigerator to kill germs while dust, and dirt were accumulating all over the house? Can you imagine what it's like not to take a bath or shower? Grandma said we have to take baths because we're all animals and if we don't bathe, we start to smell. I worried about that, but Hedda didn't think it was important. She never spoke about washing up unless the doctor was coming. When I looked in the mirror, I saw strands of long stringy hair. I wanted to look nice and pretty. I looked anything but pretty in those hideous checkered jumpers. I hated the way they made me look: fat and dumpy. How ugly they were! But Hedda didn't care. As long as I didn't bother her, I could have walked around in a barrel! But what does it matter? Nobody cared about me. I was an invisible child."

A hush fell over the house. Nobody said anything. But once I got started, I couldn't stop.

"I am not convinced that, at the age of four, 'nothing could be done' to salvage me from this life. I should never have been sent back to my mother when she came out of Bellevue. That was the worst mistake of all: returning a child to a mother who was just put into a psychiatric institution!"

I wondered where I found the courage and the words to release all the anger I was carrying around for so long. When I was through, my uncle looked crestfallen. "Lenore, you have an attitude, and you are not about to listen to reason or facts."

Is that all he could say? I thought, *Why should he care? It's not his life. People just sit back and let things happen. There are no angels. There are no innocent bystanders. Everyone in a family bears responsibility for what happens to a child. Everyone is to blame!*

I had shared some very painful stories with my uncle, and I wondered, *Did he hear me at all?* He seemed too preoccupied with the facts he placed before me to take in anything new.

He went on to tell me, "I have a friend, Frank Shay. He's a psychologist I've known over the years. He knows about your situation. Do you know what he told me at the time? He said, 'Your niece should be taken away from her mother and immediately placed in an orphanage. I wouldn't wait another day.' I asked him, 'Do you think it's better for a child to be in an orphanage than with her own mother?' He didn't answer because there is only one answer. A child belongs with its mother!" My uncle had a sour look on his face as he spoke.

I was infuriated. "I agree with Mr. Shay. In an orphanage, I would have had friends. I would have seen people. I would have been out in the world. And I would not have the problems I have today."

"Nonsense!" Will responded. "You don't know what you're talking about . . ."

Will continued to speak, but I wasn't listening. A strange feeling came over me. Maybe Will didn't want to see it; maybe he didn't want to recognize that his sister had something more severe than "a case of stubbornness, a kind of insanity that runs in the family. Maybe it was something more."

My thoughts drifted, and suddenly, a vision of Grandma came before me. Her face was covered with that horrific look of misery as she spoke to a visitor about her four-year-old grandchild: "She's such a bad child. My daughter is in the hospital because of her. Oy, what I've lived to see . . ." Grandma was blaming me for my mother's mental illness! Maybe deep down, Grandma didn't really like me; maybe she wasn't my friend. She stopped by for a few minutes, on her way to Grandpa's store, and then disappeared. She left me sitting in the house with my mother. Maybe things would have been different if Grandma truly cared.

And what did my father do? He ran off and went out dancing. There was no father!

My uncle Will was the educated member of the family; he had insight, know-how, and several academic degrees. His wife, Jessie, was a school secretary, who boasted of helping children with their problems. How could they allow this to happen? Why did Will and Jessie allow me to grow up in an environment that was so emotionally crippling?

They all walked away. It was as if their hearts were made of stone, and their hands were tied behind their backs. Why did my family fail me?

I was angry with everyone. I was angry with myself. I hated what I was: helpless, weak, and hardly able to do anything for myself. I was devoured by fear and anxiety. I wondered if there was anything I could do to help myself.

I soon heard Jessie speaking to me in her soft, calm voice: "Dear, you don't know how many nights Will has lost sleep over you. Your uncle loves you very much, and he's been very worried about you through the years. You have no idea just how much he's worried about you . . ."

As Jessie voiced my uncle's concern, something about the whole thing made my stomach turn. Okay, he was losing nights of sleep over me, but I was losing my life! What do people really know about a life that is wasting away, and the spirit within that longs to live?

I had tears in my eyes when I left their home. Walking in the street, I just couldn't get it out of my mind: *Nobody cares!*

That night I had another bitter fight with my mother. "You're responsible for all my problems. You never cared about me. You never loved me. I was with Will and Jessie today, and I told them I'm not able to function in the world because of you and all the damage you've done to me."

She answered, "I know you hate me. You have your grandmother to blame. If it weren't for her, you wouldn't be the way you are."

I was astonished to hear her say this. Where was she coming from? She was disclaiming all responsibility for her behavior. I guess I should have known better. I ran out of the room crying.

I sat in my room and sulked for a while. I was lost in my own world. The words of Mr. Shay kept spinning around in my head. Maybe an orphanage would have been the way out of my nightmare.

Maybe when I was a small child, it would have been a refuge for me, but then again, maybe not.

My thoughts strayed to other possibilities. Grandma might have been able to take me in, but she wasn't that well. My father? Hell, no! I could hear him saying, "I have to make a living . . ." Will and Jessie were the most qualified to take care of a child, but they didn't want children.

So, I guess there was no one; however, as I reflected upon my childhood, I perceived, *There has to be something better, and different, than what I experienced with my mother. For children who are abused and don't have a home, there has to be some place of refuge that they can go to. They need to have some sense of safety* . . . I truly believed that, and I wouldn't be deterred from my beliefs.

The next time I saw Will I said, "You know, I should write a book and call it *Nobody Cared*."

He nodded and casually said, "You could do that . . ."

I replied, "You're agreeing with me then, that nobody cared about me—not even you."

He paused for a long reflective moment, then looked me straight in the eye and said, "Yes, that is correct."

I was crushed.

When I left my uncle that day, I really started to think about my life. I remembered that Jessie had suggested psychotherapy to me. I started to think seriously about it. I knew I would have to do something about my anger and my emotional pain. I was determined to make something of my life.

It may have been true that nobody cared—but I cared

PART TWO

BECOMING VISIBLE

45

Therapy

"Help me. Please help me. Why don't you help me?"

I was lying on the floor, sobbing bitterly at the feet of my therapist. He just sat there, stoically observing me. I felt like something less than human.

I had a vision that I would sit down with a therapist, talk about my problems, and the therapist would help me overcome my emotional pain. But it was nothing like that.

I was almost twenty years old. My uncle and aunt agreed to pay a nominal fee that enabled me to go twice a week to a therapist in training at a psychotherapy center in Manhattan. I was excited, so I immediately told my mother the good news: "Will and Jessie are sending me for therapy!"

Hedda gave me a strange look and said, "You're going to see one of those nutty doctors? Sounds like more of my brother's mixing in. Now you'll have one of those head doctors talking against me, just like my brother and his wife."

I said, "That's not true. I need help and I'm going to get it."

"I saw that crazy psychiatrist who walked around with his hands shaking. What did he know? He told me to stop washing my hands. That's all he said. And that's what they put me away for. It's crap! And now you're going to one of those nuts! Well, go! I'm tired of all that nonsense. You're not going to listen to me, and I'm not going to waste my breath."

There she was, trying again to put a damper on something that had meaning for me. But I didn't react to her gloom. I knew what I wanted, and this time, it was real. It was happening. I just hoped that my therapist would be able to help and understand me.

My therapist, Stuart Martino, was a short, good-looking young man with large brown eyes and dark, curly hair. The receptionist told me: "He's cute as a button. All the girls are crazy about him!" When I met him, I knew exactly what she was talking about. He had a sweetness and tender quality, but there was also a shyness that gave him a boyish appeal. Then I noticed a huge gold band on his finger, and I was disheartened. *He's married!* I told myself I would not let that bother me; I was there to get help for my problems.

I was going around saying to myself: *There's no me…There's no me…* I didn't know what I meant by it, yet I said it to myself all the time. I even had it written all over my little journal. It was one of the many things I wanted to talk about in therapy. I started to make categories of my problems. I wondered where I would begin. My book was a jumble of hurt and pain that needed immediate attention. But there was something else I had to deal with: What was I going to do with my life? I wanted to find a way to live in the world, but so far, I wasn't doing very well. Would I ever be able to become a part of the outside world? I suddenly was spending an awful lot of time fretting about my future. As I focused on the things that frightened me most, I wrote in my journal:

Never could function without mother — and still can't. Scared that I can't support myself. Need of money to live. How will I manage? What will happen to me?

I'm afraid to spend $7 on shoes. I don't want to spend the money for I'm always afraid of being down to the last dollar. Drives me crazy. Mother is using up every red cent we have in the bank. Maybe we should go on relief and hold on to that money?

I obsessed about having a job so that I could have money for food, rent, clothes, and carfare. But I felt immobilized. I worried that after such an abnormal childhood, how would I be able to do anything with my life? I was a bundle of nerves.

Mr. Martino just sat there, listened, and took notes. Sometimes he might interject a few words like: "How do you feel about that?" But mostly, he remained silent. My frustration grew.

I continued to talk about the things that appeared earth shattering to me. I spoke about my mother and what a hell it was living with her. She said things that made me feel I had no right to live. I thought at least my grandma cared about me, and then one day she upset me terribly when she said: "If your mother gets sick, see who'll take care of you. You'll have no one!" It was the very same thing my mother would tell me when I was growing up. It scared me and tore me to pieces to hear Grandma talk like that to me.

Mr. Martino sat there taking notes and remaining silent. When I told him, "I want to have love and happiness in my life, I don't know what to do," he didn't blink an eye.

"Why don't you talk to me? Why don't you say something?"

There was a slight smile on his face and more silence. Once again I felt like a nonentity. I was talking and he was writing. Was he really there with me? My therapy sessions went on like that for several weeks when I said, "I think I want to get a different therapist."

Mr. Martino looked concerned. He asked, "What's wrong, Lenore? Don't you think I understand?"

I melted. He was so sweet and his smile was so warm. There was nothing I could say. I wasn't aware that Mr. Martino had been trained in the Freudian method to just sit, listen, and say nothing for long periods of time. I was even more confused because, although I was disappointed with him as a therapist, I found I was falling in love with Stuart Martino, the man.

I kept watching him take notes. Sometimes I said, "What are you writing?"

He would smile and evade the question. One time he replied, "I'm writing down what you're telling me."

I wondered why he had to do that. Still another time, he offered his pad to me. "Here, Lenore, you can look at it."

Something about that did not feel right. I couldn't find words to say how I felt or why I was feeling so upset. "I don't want to see it." That's all I could say. I didn't mention it again, but as he kept taking notes, I continued to feel uncomfortable.

I would visit Will and Jessie and tell Jessie about my sessions. I cried, "He doesn't talk to me. He just sits there and takes notes. It's driving me crazy. I want another therapist."

Jessie, with concern in her eyes, responded, "I met Mr. Martino. He is a very sensitive man. Give him some time, dear. He's trying to help you."

That was the last thing I wanted to hear. One day Will came into the room and overheard me describing my therapy to Jessie. Will broke out laughing. "You know, Jessie, when Lenore leaves, this poor guy Martino must go into the next room, lie down on a couch and talk to his analyst."

How could my uncle say something as heartless as that? I didn't find it funny at all. I was hurt but I covered my true feelings. I thought Jessie might come to my rescue, but she just sat there and looked on.

And I continued to see Mr. Martino.

I kept staring at the ring on his left hand. What was his wife like? She had to be beautiful to be the wife of Stuart Martino. Having been mesmerized by the glamorous world of show business since I was a small child, it seemed that one had to be beautiful, and in show business, to have anything or to amount to anything. The thought consumed me: *Mrs. Martino must be an exquisite woman; undoubtedly, she's an actress or a singer. She has the career I yearn for, and the love I want so badly—the love of Stuart Martino.*

One day I went in and told him, "I hate your wife. The thought of her tears me to pieces!"

He sat there staring at me for a while, then asked: "Why do you hate my wife, Lenore?"

I didn't know how to answer that; I only knew that I hated her. I spent my session that day agonizing about her. I was in severe emotional pain. When I went home, I obsessed about her some more.

The next time I saw him, I continued to lament about "that gorgeous woman." It felt strange because I didn't even know what she looked like. Yet I cried and cried, "Oh, why can't I be like your wife?"

Session after session, Martino listened, as I expressed my despair. My therapy had become exceedingly painful. One day I found the courage to say, "I'm not coming here anymore."

His soft, gentle response was, "Why do you want to do that, Lenore?"

Who was I kidding? I didn't have the emotional strength to leave. Good Lord, what kind of a hold did this man have over me? I began to dread seeing Martino. Then I had a great idea—I would skip an appointment and not call him. It would be my way of making a protest for the way he was treating me. I was exhilarated as I thought about it; I went out and bought myself a pretty pink and white lace dress to celebrate my joy. As therapy time approached, I must say I was a little anxious, but I felt I was doing what I had to do.

When I next saw Martino, he looked annoyed. "Lenore, what happened? You've missed a session and you didn't call."

I stood there, feeling rather pleased with myself—but not for long. Martino firmly said, "I'm going to charge you for that session."

I hated wasting money, even if it was not my own, and couldn't bear the thought of paying for a session I hadn't received. I tried to invent a good excuse, but all I could say was, "I just couldn't make it."

Martino reiterated: "Well, I'm going to charge you."

Suddenly, I became nervous. He wasn't kidding!

"I can make up the time. I won't do it again. But please don't charge me. It's not fair to charge for a session I didn't have."

Martino retorted, "It was your therapy time and you were not here. You have to pay for your session. It's the Center's policy that sessions missed without twenty-four-hour notification be subjected to immediate payment."

I was seething as he spoke, but I knew he was right. The following week I begrudgingly gave him the money I owed him. I felt resentment as Martino held it in his hand and smilingly said: "Thank you." But I had learned a lesson. I would never allow anything like that to happen again.

I continued to see Martino and constantly begged him for answers to my problems, as if he were a magician who could pull the answers out of a hat. "Why am I so moody?" "When will I feel different?" "When will I function normally, like anybody else?" "Why can't I like myself?" When I asked any of these questions, he usually tossed the ball back in my court and said: "What do you think?"

One time, however, he was more precise. He said, "How many years did it take for you to get like this? Do you think I have a magical solution to solve your problems overnight? This all takes time."

Well, enough was enough. One day I took a few pillows from the couch and flung them at him. As the pillows came hurtling toward him, he held his hand across his face and ducked. His face turned a little red, but he did not lose his cool. He went on observing, and taking notes, as if nothing had happened. He was immovable! I was seething with rage, and trying to get a reaction from him, but whatever I did made absolutely no difference. Then I had an idea. Why didn't I think of it sooner? I blushingly said to myself: *I'll make him notice me!*

I came in one day and started to undress. Martino's face reddened, as he sheepishly said, "Lenore, you can't do that in this office. We don't do things like that around here!"

By that time I had undressed down to my bra and panties. I didn't intend to go any further, but he looked a little unsettled. I sat down on the couch and he remained in his chair. He was still smiling and blushing as much as when I had begun disrobing. I wondered what he was thinking and feeling as I sat there, acutely embarrassed and perplexed by what I had just done. I went through the session that day in my underwear, as a smiling, though concerned, Mr. Martino cautiously watched my every move. I thought to myself: *What's the use? He can't be budged.* Soon, I put on my clothes and left.

As Martino continued to observe me and take notes, I was feeling more worthless than ever. I wanted to be close to him; I wanted him to touch me, to hold me, to make up for all those years when no one came near me. I was yearning for Martino's love, but I could feel him looking at me as though I were just some object to study and write about.

Another idea came to me. I would ask him to sit on the couch with me, so that I could be near him. Then I could place my head on his lap. Reluctantly, he agreed to sit on the couch, but did not sit very close to me, nor did he consent for me to put my head on his lap. I went home emotionally bruised. If I couldn't rest my head on his lap and have him near me, I felt that I couldn't go on.

When I saw him the following week, I sat down and cried and cried. "You don't care about me. I have no purpose in being alive."

Martino explained, "I am here to help you with your problems. We need to talk about them. We cannot act them out."

I responded, "You don't understand. When I was growing up, nobody showed me any love. I wasn't allowed to be touched, hugged, or kissed by anyone. My mother didn't want anyone to show affection to me. And now, I'm starved for love. To feel love… to feel affection… I'm desperate!"

The following week when I saw Mr. Martino again, he said, "I've been thinking about it. It's okay for you to sit on the couch with me and put your head on my lap."

I felt as if he was doing me a favor and I said, "You're just trying to be nice—you don't really care about me. I don't want to sit on the couch with you anymore."

Again, I spent the session crying. I told him how hurt I was from his initial rejection. I couldn't stop sobbing about it. I felt so bad, I didn't think I would ever recover. I felt just as invisible as when I was growing up. *There's no me… There's no me…*

Mr. Martino listened and remained silent.

I began to lose my appetite; I was having trouble sleeping. I had to do something about it. At my next session I said, "Is it still okay to sit on the couch and put my head on your lap?"

He smiled and said, "Sure, Lenore."

He got up from his chair and went over to the couch. Then I sat down on the couch beside him and tried to rest my head on his lap, as he sat there, rather stiffly, probably feeling as uncomfortable as I. I jumped up. "It's no good! If you had just let me do it when I wanted to, my whole life would have changed. But you rejected me. You're just like the others! You're just as rotten!"

Once I said this, it was over. I could no longer strive for his love. And I no longer was in love with Stuart Martino.

When I left his office, I felt lower than low. I cried: *Why can't I be loved?* I started to feel, now more than ever, that I would never be loved by anyone. How terribly sad and hurt I was.

Soon I was in a session when my sadness turned into anger. Then I burst into tears and started to tremble. Mr. Martino softly said, "You are a very frightened girl." I needed to hear that just then; I was becoming more aware of just how frightened I was. Mr. Martino made a good point. And he had spoken to me. It felt so good to hear him say something… anything…

I struggled with my therapy until Mr. Martino left the institute and went into private practice. I was then assigned to another male therapist whose approach was very different: he talked! And I talked with him. I felt I was being heard, and that gave me a feeling of being alive and seen as a person. In this training institute, I found myself with a new therapist every so often, but I never again experienced the intense acting-out behavior that I had with Mr. Martino.

As I continued in therapy, I learned about an intriguing phenomenon called "transference." I became aware that feelings from childhood are transferred from patient to therapist. Had I transferred my pent-up feelings from childhood to Mr. Martino?

As I began to reflect upon my experience with Mr. Martino, I could see him in another light. It's true that his silence-and-listening technique was not the best approach for someone like me who needed interaction with her therapist, but there is another side to this. Mr. Martino gave me the opportunity, and the freedom, to express feelings that were locked away inside of me for so long. He provided a safe place for me to be whatever I needed to be. I could lie down on the floor and bang my head against the couch if I so desired. I was allowed to cry my heart out and say whatever I felt in the moment without fear or recrimination. He had the sensitivity to accept me the way I was, regardless of how difficult it might have been for him. He could have shown me the door many times, but he didn't. It felt like a disaster at the time, but I began to see it as something I needed to experience.

I was becoming more aware of how empty I felt inside. I felt I had nothing to live for. Possibly Love might give my life the new meaning I was seeking. But the same old question surfaced: How was I going to find it? Maybe I could sustain myself in therapy. What else was there?

46

Maury and Me

I was twenty years old and eager to work. I was scanning the employment columns, but the more I searched, the more discouraged I became. I didn't have any of the skills required to get a job that was halfway decent. I worried whether there would ever be any job available for me. And I kept looking.

I became anxious when I thought about going out on job interviews. What would it be like? The isolated existence I lived as a child was a major deterrent to my functioning in the outside world. With no real social skills, I had trouble interacting with people. Anxiety constantly reared its debilitating head, and I felt unable to cope with the simplest things that ordinary people would not give a second thought to. So how would I manage on a job?

Regardless of these obstacles, I still had a strong need to be out there in the world, working like everyone else. I was determined to find something I could do. My spirits were dropping lower and lower as I went through all those ads, but I persevered. If I looked long enough, something just might turn up.

I finally came upon an ad for a part-time job in a Bronx lamp factory. Not knowing what I was getting myself into, I went for the interview and got the job. I wound up standing on my feet for hours on end, on an assembly line, dusting lamps—one after another—all sizes, all shapes. My back was hurting, and my feet were sore, as I dusted each lamp that came down the conveyor belt. Under my breath I muttered: "If I never see another lamp, it will be too soon!"

After a few weeks, I left. I was trying to feel better about myself by getting a job and earning some money, but working in a lamp factory didn't seem to be the answer. I was finally out in the world, but I felt awful inside. I walked around in a fog.

I was on my way home one day, forlorn and confused, when I heard a voice call out, "Heavy traffic!"

I looked up, startled. There before me stood a young man wheeling a hand truck stacked with cartons. I had to quickly move out of the way, for he was about to plow into me. What was going on here? To top it off, he was chuckling! For a moment I was annoyed, then I broke out laughing, too. There was something contagious about his laughter, and I couldn't help but think: *He's so cute!* And I went on my way.

I started to think about that young man when I got upstairs. He had an irresistible smile and such a contagious laugh. He looked a little like Cornel Wilde, the movie actor. Later that week, I noticed him coming out of the grocery store on the street where I lived. This was the same store where my mother bought our groceries; she would give in orders and have deliveries sent to our door. I learned that Mr. Owens was no longer there and that this young man was the new owner.

While I rarely did food shopping, I started to buy Tropicana Orange Juice in his store. I never knew that a quart of juice could get used up so fast. Soon I introduced myself to the handsome owner. He told me his name was Maury. I stared at his jet-black hair and dark brown eyes that sparkled as he spoke. There was only one thing on my mind: *How can I get him interested in me?*

I found a tight-fitting, lime green dress in my closet that I thought might grab his attention. I rolled my hair into a bun and applied bright red lipstick to my lips. As I stepped into my high heel shoes, I was eager to go downstairs and flirt with him.

As I picked up a container of orange juice and placed it on the counter, I noticed something was wrong. Maury didn't waste any time telling me: "I'm a divorced man. I don't want any serious involvements. When I go out, I go out to have a good time."

That felt like a slap in the face. Was I that obvious? As I turned to a side, I noticed a tall young man standing in a corner, snickering. What an embarrassing moment for me. I didn't know what to say. Flustered, I paid for my juice and quickly edged out the door. How was Maury able to see through me like that? I told myself: *I'm never going back there!* But I kept thinking about him. I soon found myself buying more Tropicana, and we continued to talk as if nothing had happened.

One day Maury told me that he played the clarinet and loved music, especially jazz. It was my opportunity to say: "I love music, too. I have a lot of records. I think you'd like them. Why don't you come up to my house? I live just a few doors down." I gave him my address, and Maury smiled that charming, infectious smile. "If I have a little time, I'll stop by tonight."

I told my mother about Maury from the grocery store. I said he might be visiting me. I was surprised that she didn't have any objection. That night, at nine o'clock, the doorbell rang and there was Maury. I noticed a gleam in my mother's eyes when I introduced him. When he came into our living room, I felt my cheeks redden. Our apartment looked poverty-stricken and I felt ashamed. As Maury looked around, I wondered what he was thinking, but he didn't say anything. I was relieved. Soon he asked to see my record collection, which he thumbed through very quickly. He pulled out a record and asked: "Mind if I put this on?"

He then went over to my rinky-dink phonograph and soon I heard Dean Martin singing a charming little ditty, "Aw C'mon." Maury asked me to dance. I was on the spot. My face flushed as I said, "I don't know how to."

He laughingly replied, "I'll show you—there's nothing to it. Just follow me."

I was tense and nervous as I followed him around the floor. I wondered: *Is this what dancing is all about?* Then, as I looked at the man in my arms, I said to myself: *My, he's handsome!* I became more nervous. *He's much too good-looking for me.*

I glanced at my mother sitting nearby. She was actually smiling. She was watching us dance and she had that broad cat grin, which she reserved for someone or something she really liked—a rarity in itself.

When the record ended, Maury went back to my record collection and thumbed through it again. I said, "You'd be surprised if you knew how many songs I know by heart." He seemed amused as he continued to search for a record he liked, and when he found one, we went on dancing. The music was enjoyable, although I could barely focus on anything—not even Maury.

Soon, it was time to sit down and talk. The big question was: *What am I going to say?* A photograph album came to mind. It contained pictures of me from the time I was a baby to the present. I said, "Maury, would you like to look at my pictures?"

Before he could respond, I had the album in my hand.

"I never saw pictures like these in my life! This is you as a baby? You could have been a child model! Look at those expressions! Incredible!"

The look on his face astonished me. I was speechless; I didn't know how to accept the compliment. I sat there intrigued, as Maury turned each page and continued to rave…

All in all, the evening seemed to be going pretty well, but I couldn't relax. *Am I making a good impression on Maury? Can he see through me and know how nervous I am? Will he want to see me again?*

At ten o'clock, Maury got up. "Time to go! Tomorrow is another workday." He smiled at me with a mesmerizing smile as he walked toward the door, and I melted. *What is a gorgeous guy like Maury doing with a nobody like me?* I was relieved that the evening was over. I could give up the pretense that all was well when I felt so frazzled inside.

On a warm summer evening, I had my first real date. Maury met me in front of my building and cheerfully asked, "Why don't we go out for a drive?" I was reticent about this. I did not feel safe. Even though I knew Maury from his store, I didn't know if I could trust him. Something inside of me told me to go with him anyway.

When he stopped his car, I said, "Where are we?" He replied, "We're by the Tappan Zee Bridge." *Now where is that?* I was afraid to ask. I was nervously wondering: *What's going to happen next?* Much to my surprise, Maury took out a flute and started to play. When he put it down, he took me in his arms and kissed me. I became very uncomfortable. I perceived that this was a prelude to sex, and I panicked. *This doesn't feel right. I got to get him to stop!*

I soon found myself back in my mother's apartment, unhappy and distressed as ever. *Sex! Sex! Sex! Is that all they think about! Why is it always about sex?* I worried that Maury wouldn't speak to me anymore because I didn't give him what I knew he wanted.

How relieved I was when, in a few days, I saw Maury again and he was still speaking to me! I was walking down the street on a lovely spring day when Maury spotted me and came over with a warm smile asking: "Would you happen to know the words to the song, 'It Might As Well Be Spring'?"

"Not only do I know the words, but it's one of my favorites."

"Could you write it out for me?"

I immediately answered: "I'll have it for you in no time."

With a big smile on his face, he went back to his store as I headed a few doors down to my building.

"It Might As Well Be Spring" is a romantic song reeking of restlessness, melancholia—and a fantasy of love. It's a beautiful song that awakens a sort of moodiness in me every time I hear it. What made Maury select this song? I wondered about it as I ran up the stairs in my building.

My spirits were high as I sat down at the kitchen table and started to write. The lyrics came whirling into my head and I quickly jotted them down. Then I ran back downstairs to Maury's store. I approached Maury with a vibrant smile and said, "Here it is Maury, 'It Might As Well Be Spring.'"

He stood there, flabbergasted. "Wow! That was fast!"

"I told you that you'd be shocked by all the songs I know by heart."

His eyes widened as he browsed over the lyrics. He exclaimed: "I'm amazed." I could feel his joy. It was contagious.

I soon said: "I have this wonderful record by Otto Cesana. It's a beautiful instrumental with a lot of strings. It's called 'Devotion.' You have to hear it…"

Maury showed an immediate interest. "Come on over to my apartment; it's just around the corner. I'll play the record for you on my hi-fi. The sound is so powerful, you get the feeling of being in a great big auditorium. Every instrument is amplified. I promise you it will sound much different on my phonograph than the one you have in your mother's apartment. And you know what? I have a favorite that I want you to hear. It's called 'Tamboo,' and I think you're going to like it."

It all sounded good, but I felt uncomfortable about going to Maury's apartment. It felt like a prelude to something I wanted to stay away from. I said, "I'll come over, but not right now. Someday soon, very soon…"

I started to hang out in Maury's store. I had a strong need to be with him, even though he was busy most of the time. I soon met Maury's mother, Emma, who came in a few days a week to help out. She was a short lady with glasses and a pleasant, cheerful smile. She would wait on customers and stand at the cash register until she became tired. Then she would sit down for a few minutes and be right back at the job. I wanted to make friends with her, but she seemed unapproachable. Still, I didn't let that keep me from stopping by and saying hello to Maury.

One day when I was visiting Maury in his store, he joyfully confided: "My mother is the greatest. They don't come any better. She comes in a few days a week and she does a great job."

I said, "I rarely hear you and your mom speak to each other in English. I was wondering what that's all about."

"We're Spanish Jews–otherwise known as Sephardic Jews. My mother, father, my three sisters and myself, we all speak Spanish." He went on to tell me his parents came here from a tiny island off the coast of Turkey. He was all smiles, as he shared stories with me about this most colorful group of people. I was shocked when he told me his parents were cousins. I heard somewhere that cousins usually don't marry because it might be detrimental to the wellbeing of their offspring. When I mentioned this to Maury, he shrugged it off and didn't seem very concerned. I didn't go any further.

Maury shared myriad stories with me about his early youth. I was taken aback when he said: "My father has a terrible temper. When I was about three or so, he'd come looking for me with a shoe in his hand. I had to hide under the bed."

"It must have been frightening to see your father so angry."

"I was scared, but what could I do?"

"How is life with your sisters?"

Maury's response was not very flattering: "They're all very spoiled—especially the schoolteacher. She thinks her shit doesn't smell. I see them mostly at holiday get-togethers, and I'm okay with that."

From what he told me, I was not eager to meet his father or his sisters, but I was happy Maury could talk so openly to me. I sensed he was a genuine person and that he was speaking from the heart. I liked that. He soon told me his age. It was hard to believe that he was ten years older than me; he looked like a kid out of school.

When I saw Maury again, he revealed to me, "I've been married before and I have a little girl. My wife walked out on me, and it was a terrible shock. But it's just as well. I couldn't live with her. She had a lot of problems…"

It sounded like he was still enmeshed in his marriage, but I wasn't about to probe. I sensed that he would eventually tell me whatever he wanted me to know. Soon, I told him dribs and drabs about myself. I wondered if my abnormal background would be a turn-off, but he appeared interested and accepting. I felt so glad that he wasn't looking down on me or walking away.

Maury started to visit me regularly. My mother frequently left the room when he came over, so we could be alone. Soon Maury said, "You have to come over and see my apartment. It's gorgeous. You'll love it. It's just a couple of blocks from here."

I began to think about it: *Maybe I'll go over to Maury's. It's not as if he's a stranger to me; we're friends, and I feel safe with him…* Yet I felt anxious and uncomfortable when I thought about it. But maybe I was just being silly. I finally decided to stop fretting about it. I told myself I would put aside my fears and trepidation as

I nervously headed over to Maury's apartment. I had the Cesana record with me and I thought about how nice it would be to hear it on Maury's hi-fi—whatever that was. Still, something felt strange about this, and I just didn't know what it was.

Maury had a big, radiant smile on his face when I arrived. "Let me show you around." The apartment was small, but it was something to see. As I entered the living room, I saw two small beautiful red Castro convertible couches on a light beige carpet. On the opposite side of the room were heavy greenish-gold drapes covering the windows from the ceiling to the floor with a dark green valance overhead. Behind the drapes were multi-colored lights, adding a glow to the romantic atmosphere. I marveled at the way he decorated it. I looked around, entranced by what I saw.

Maury soon asked, "Did you bring that record with you?"

"Yes, I have Cesana's "Ecstasy" with me, and my favorite, "Devotion" is on it. It's wonderful. Wait till you hear it."

I handed the record to him and he placed it on his turntable. He had not exaggerated; it sounded as though there was an orchestra in his living room. Every note was vibrant and crystal clear. I never knew anything could sound so beautiful, so enthralling. I was listening to a record called, "Ecstasy," and that's exactly how I felt. The sounds of the instruments felt like a gentle ocean breeze sweeping over me.

I was in another world when Maury came over and sat down on the couch beside me. He put his arms around me and kissed me. "I want to make love to you."

Suddenly, my heart sank. I no longer heard the music. "I don't want to have sex. I never had sex before, I'm a virgin."

He laughingly replied, "You got to be kidding! You never had sex? What are you saving it for—the worms? Let's do it. You'll love it!"

No, I wasn't saving it for the worms. I was looking for love—but what Maury was offering me was sex! I guess, on a subconscious level, I surmised something like this might happen if I were to visit Maury. And then I became aware—and I felt sick to my stomach. Sex! It was all about sex! Sex! Sex! Sex! I didn't know what sex was, and I had no desire to learn. Sex was an enigma to me. It frightened me. My fear of pregnancy dominated my thinking. But on another level, I had a hope in my heart of giving myself to someone who could love me and make me happy—someone with whom I could share a mutual bond of love. I would wait until I found that love. Within that context, I thought of sex as sacred in marriage. I couldn't find it in my heart to turn against my heartfelt beliefs by engaging in casual sex.

But Maury was persistent. He had the look of love in his eyes and his smile was so captivating, it was hard to resist. After much coaxing, I finally said yes.

If he did not believe I was a virgin, he soon found out. One towel after another was covered with blood. What was happening to me? I now was crying and filled with fear. Maury stood there, perplexed. "Do you want me to take you to the hospital?"

He kept handing me towels while I continued to wipe away the blood. Finally, the bleeding stopped. I was still in shock when Maury took me back to my mother's apartment.

The following day I saw my doctor. "That's normal—some women bleed more, some less, when the hymen is broken. It's nothing to worry about." He gave me the go-ahead to have sexual relations, adding, "Just go slowly."

With no real interest in sex, I tried to forestall it as long as I could, but it was uppermost on Maury's mind. Weeks passed before I finally agreed to try again. It happened one night in my mother's apartment. It was the first time I had sexual intercourse, and I was taken aback. *Is that all there is?*

Maury was now visiting me every night after work. He stayed late, and often fell asleep in my arms. He soon stopped living in his apartment and began to stay with me at my mother's. He left a beautiful, immaculate apartment to be with me, and when I thought about it, I found it hard to believe. He never spoke about how dismal and depressing it was in my mother's apartment, and so very different from what he was used to. But as gorgeous and romantic as his place was, I had no interest in living there. I guess I still had strong ties to my mother, and it didn't feel safe to break away and leave her. I was just glad that Maury didn't complain. He accepted things the way they were.

As I eventually began to feel closer to Maury, I could enjoy making love with him. He was tender and gentle, and I lost many of the bugaboos I had about sex. It felt strange though, knowing that my mother was in the next room. She acted as though she didn't know what was going on, and that lessened a lot of the embarrassment I was experiencing.

Strange as it may seem, things were going very well with my mother. Maury had become a part of our household, and the three of us were now sharing smiles, laughs and casual talk. It felt good to see such a radical change in my mother. She looked so happy when Maury was around. She really surprised me, but I was also aware that handsome young men beguiled her, and Maury was exceedingly handsome. I still couldn't get over how much she had mellowed. My goodness, my mother was an entirely different person! Sometimes I wondered whether my mother was living vicariously through me and then I quickly put the thought out of my mind.

I was different, too, and so was my relationship with Maury. Our bonding intensified and our relationship turned into a full-blown romance. Maury was calling me "honey" and I melted. He was hugging me, kissing me, and making love to me with a lot of passion. I could be lying in bed beside him, speaking about things that were on my mind when he would gently move my hair to the side away from my face. As he gazed into my eyes, he made me feel cared about and loved. What a wonderful feeling that was. As I stared at his long, black eyelashes and radiant smile, I could feel the magnetism of his charm. Out of the blue, Maury proclaimed: "I never met anyone like you. I think I'm going to marry you. I never said that to anyone—except Molly."

I was thrilled. Maury could love me enough to want to marry me! It felt so real and true. I was feeling pretty special and so very happy that Maury could show so much love to me, so much adoration. My years of lovelessness seemed to be a memory of the past, as I opened myself to Maury's love and warmth. I was afraid to say how happy I was for fear that the spell would be broken. I was enjoying the moments I spent in ecstasy just thinking about Maury.

I felt like a new me. With a happy heart I put on my radio. I was not listening to the radio that much after I started breaking away from my mother and going out of the house. By the time I met Maury, I found the music on the radio quite different from the music I knew in my childhood. Most of it didn't appeal to me, but there was one song I liked very much. It was all over the radio dial—you couldn't escape it. When I heard *Volare* I was filled with joy. I was walking on air. It was a sprightly, charming little melody that brought out my feelings of love for life—and my feelings of love for Maury.

I was feeling stronger emotionally as I held on to the hope that I would be marrying Maury in the very near future. I rejoiced in the thought that I no longer would be living out of wedlock. I never liked the idea of living together without marriage, but I went along with it because I was so elated that Maury wanted to be with me. And now, things were changing for the better—or so I thought.

It wasn't long before my joy began to fade. Maury began to speak to me about his ex-wife. "Molly was tall. Molly was beautiful. Molly knew how to dress. Molly loved sex..." And he continued on and on.

I was stunned. Why was he telling me all this? Did he want me to be like Molly? Couldn't he see I was hurting? Why was he trying to make me upset and jealous?

"I'm only teasing you, honey."

But was he? What kind of game was he playing?

He would watch me and laugh. It seemed as though he was looking for some kind of reaction from me, but I didn't know how to respond. I was thoroughly confused. Maury was displaying love for me—enough to say he wanted to marry me—and yet he was speaking to me with passion about his ex-wife. I sat there silently, staring at him, allowing him to rant about Molly and her charms. I felt like crying. He must have sensed this from the look on my face for I would hear him say, "You poor thing," as he held me tightly in his arms. That only made me feel worse.

I felt sick to my stomach, as he laughingly pulled me closer to him and sighed, "Molly, you've come back to me." He had a warm, glowing smile, as he caressed me, but I was holding in my pain and agonizing about it. His cruelty cut like a knife. He stuck the knife in and twisted it with words that stung. And he didn't stop. I wondered: *Why is he being so mean to me?*

As much as I hated to hear about Molly, I was compelled to listen. I was eager to hear what he had to say. What was it about me that was not as good as Molly? What could I learn about her that would make me more like her? Perhaps if I were to become like Molly, then Maury might adore me the way he seemed to adore her.

He continued to taunt me with things about Molly, and it was driving me crazy. She had become my competition. My goodness, what was I going to do?

47

Friends

In the midst of Maury's antics, he enthusiastically said to me: "I have friends I want you to meet. Some of them go all the way back to elementary school. They're really great. You're going to like them." The frightened little girl within me cried: *Oh no! Maybe they won't like me. Maybe they'll think I'm strange. Then what?* Although I was working hard at fighting my fears, I still didn't feel safe around people. Yet another part of me wanted desperately to socialize with Maury and his friends. How could I throw away an opportunity like this?

I soon found I had nothing to worry about. Most of Maury's friends were regular, ordinary people, unpretentious and nice. Their friendliness and warmth allowed me to drop my guard a little and peek out of my shell. How wonderful it was to watch Maury interact with them. It was so natural for him to laugh and crack jokes, but what amazed me the most was how relaxed he was. He carried the conversational ball, and I came along for the ride. A lot of the time I forgot to be self-conscious as I lost myself in Maury's happy-go-lucky manner.

People getting together, sharing some smiles, a few laughs, and enjoying each other's company: I wondered if this is what life is all about. I continued to ponder that thought as I nervously encountered the challenges of everyday living.

Once in a while, when I was in Maury's apartment, I heard a knock on the door. It was his friend, Joe, a cab driver who lived in his building. He was a big, friendly guy who loved to schmooze about his problems and everyone else's. When Maury complained about tiredness, Joe said: "I have just the right pill for you!"

Maury asked: "How do I know it will work?"

Joe's response was, "I take it all the time, and it works wonders for me."

That was all Maury had to hear. "Give me one."

I was appalled that Maury was about to take someone else's medication and I tried to stop him. "Just because it's good for Joe doesn't mean it's good for you."

Maury paid no attention; he put the pill into his mouth and swallowed it with a smile. I sat there frowning, all upset about this act of stupidity.

One day Joe came in and said something that startled me: "We're going to the insane asylum, yes, we're all going!" I laughed at this and he said it once again: "You think I'm kidding? We're all going! Just you wait and see…." I thought that was an odd thing to say. What made him say something like that?

Maury and I were sitting in his car one evening when he became animated and excitedly told me: "I have two people I want you to meet. They're very special. They don't come any better. They're married and they have a little girl. I used to work in the used clothing business with Jay. He's very smart, he teaches himself whatever he wants to know. That's how he became a baby photographer. And Amy's an artist—she's a wonderful girl. You're going to like her. We're going over there right now."

My heart beat rapidly when Maury's foot hit the gas pedal. I couldn't tell Maury how frightened I was of meeting people, so I sat there with bottled-up emotions, dreading what was about to take place.

It was a short ride and soon we were at their door. When Maury introduced me to Jay, I was shocked. I immediately recognized him as the man who stood in the corner of Maury's store, snickering, when Maury said he didn't want any serious involvements. I didn't like him then, but my gut feeling was to be cordial and not mention a word about that incident. And neither did Jay.

Jay appeared to be in his 30's, well over six feet tall, with dark hair and hazel eyes. His deep resonant voice made me think he would make an excellent radio announcer.

Soon I met Amy. I liked her right away. She was a quiet, soft-spoken, serious young woman with long black hair and dark brown eyes. A sad expression covered her face, as she sat at a table in her living room, painting colors on baby photos. But as busy as she was, she made time to talk with me. I got the impression that she was a very sensitive, caring person and I felt comfortable in her presence. However, I couldn't help wondering how much more attractive she could be if she were to take better care of herself and lose a few pounds. But she appeared too preoccupied with her work to let it bother her.

Their daughter, Lucy, soon came in to say hello. She was a beautiful little child, about six or seven years old, with long black hair and big brown eyes. As she threw her arms around Maury with so much warmth and affection, I thought: *What a wonderful little girl with so much love to give!*

On the way home, I said, "Maury, I do like Amy very much. She's really nice. I think I can have a friend in her." Maury replied, "I knew you would like her. By the way, I should tell you that Jay has an opinion about most everything and says whatever's on his mind." I wondered why he was suddenly telling me this, but I wasn't about to ask any questions. We didn't discuss it further.

One night, when we were visiting Jay and Amy, there was a gathering of friends in their home. Everything seemed to be going well until Jay began to ridicule some poor soul in the room. How did this come about? I was not paying much attention to what was going on, but there he was, shredding this poor guy with sharp, cruel words that made my skin crawl. I was ashamed to be in the same room with Jay. Maury was sitting beside me, but he didn't seem to mind. I was hoping Jay would stop, but he kept jabbering away and soon I didn't hear anything; I tuned him out and became oblivious to everything around me. I sat there, afraid to move or make a sound. I was experiencing a childhood moment of trauma. At some point I whispered to Maury, "Let's get out of here."

Outside, Maury said, "Jay can be very nice, but he can also be very vindictive." I didn't like Jay, but I didn't say anything to Maury about it. Jay frightened me and I didn't want to see him again. I thought he was despicable. I kept thinking about man's inhumanity to man, and I thought about what I had just witnessed. I didn't want to be around an explosive scene like this. I found it very disturbing.

But we did go back. This time Jay was boasting about how he could "rip into people." I was aghast. Why would he want to do that? From the way he was gloating, I had a feeling that he took pleasure in being obnoxious. *Would he be picking on me too?* I was terribly afraid that he might attack me with nasty words and I wouldn't be able to handle it. I all the more wanted to stay as far away from him as possible. I wondered how Maury tolerated Jay's hostility.

However, my need to have Amy as a friend became greater than my fear of her husband. I started to visit Amy on my own. I became very nervous when Jay was around but most of the time he wasn't there, and I was grateful for that.

So Amy and I got together and shared our thoughts and feelings as she sat at her table and colored photos. I told her about my problems—anything from the way I grew up to the joy and pain in my relationship with Maury. Amy reminisced about the early years of her marriage and how happy she was with Jay. As she spoke, I felt she wasn't being honest with herself and that made me uncomfortable. There were many times I saw her with Jay and he reprimanded her for the least thing. I recall when we were in Maury's store and Amy reached for a muffin on the counter. Jay growled, "Put that down!" My goodness, his voice had the sound of thunder in a storm. Amy just stood there with hurt written all over her face as she dropped the cake on the counter. I felt awful. I wondered how she could allow him to control her like that. At other times, he ignored her altogether. How was she able to dwell upon the happiness of her marriage in the past when her marriage in the present reeked of so much havoc and pain? Poor Amy. She seemed so unhappy and yet so contented within her unhappiness.

It was on my mind and I was troubled by it. Amy was in an abusive relationship and she was accepting it as the most natural, normal thing in the world. As much as I liked Amy, I found I was losing respect for her. But I continued to visit her.

During one of our visits, I was shocked to see another aspect of Jay. Jay was sitting comfortably in his living room amongst a group of friends and he was speaking about a multitude of topics with confidence and ease. I was astonished that Jay was so well versed in the ways of the world. I marveled at his presentation. I thought it was absolutely brilliant. I could see Maury was fascinated, too, by the expression on his face as Jay spoke. Jay now seemed to be an altogether different person. I wondered how he could be so sweet, so bright, and charming one moment, and then so nasty and mean the next.

Maury and I were invited one night to another small social gathering in their home. Alcohol was being served, and I really didn't like the stuff, but everyone was drinking, so I had a little, too. Soon I became giddy and said funny things. Before long, Jay was smiling and whispering to Maury: "She's so cute when she's drunk!" Truth of the matter: I was just a little high, but it looked as though I had consumed too much. Soon Jay was laughing out loud and Maury was all smiles. People in the room also seemed to be having a good time as they kept their eyes peeled upon me. In a way, I liked the attention I was getting, so I didn't have the heart to spoil it and say I wasn't drunk; I just played along with it.

When I saw Jay again, he was very sweet and mild-mannered. Surprisingly, after that night, his attitude towards me changed and he appeared to genuinely like me. I was not that nervous around him anymore, and it was a relief. What made for this change was a mystery, and it baffled me. I found it amazing that Jay could be so cruel towards others and yet so very nice to me.

Maury and I were now spending quite some time with Amy and Jay. It was a jubilant moment for me when Lucy came running out to greet us with a joyous smile and some great big hugs. As she spoke, I was amazed at how well Lucy could express her thoughts and feelings in words. She seemed so much older than her age. I enjoyed our get-togethers, and I began to feel as if I were a part of one happy little family.

Maury soon asked my mother if she would like to join us on our visits to Jay and Amy, and with some skillful coaxing, he got her to say yes. She came with us many times, and although she didn't have much to say, she was smiling and we could see she was glad to get away from her shut-in existence.

I was in Maury's store on a beautiful sunny day when a young man came in carrying an umbrella, looking rather somber. Maury ran over to him, and they started to talk. It wasn't long before Maury introduced me to Nat. I liked him right away. I sensed something really nice about him. He had the funniest Cheshire cat grin when he laughed. I found it contagious and I would start to laugh, too. Soon, all three of us were laughing. This was the beginning of a special friendship that Maury, Nat, and I shared when the three of us got together.

Maury also introduced me to other friends who I later considered my friends as well. It felt good to have each and every one of them in my life. The heartfelt joy of these friendly get-togethers lingered with me but deep down, I longed for the quiet moments when I could be alone with Maury. I wanted to feel his charm and warmth—and the love that only he could give me.

48

Molly Madness

Out of the clear blue, Maury would speak to me about his ex-wife. If it wasn't about Molly, the Marvelous, it would be about Molly, the Malevolent. I was shocked to learn that there was actually a dark side to her: "Molly was a pathological liar. She told me all kinds of things; I never knew what to believe. I'll never forget the night I came home and found the house bare. Molly was gone. She took her clothes, our baby daughter, and everything else—and went back to her parents. I didn't know what hit me!"

I found the voice to ask, "You mean she just picked herself up with a baby and walked out like that?"

"I slapped her a few times and her mouth was bleeding. Sometimes my temper gets the best of me."

I looked at him in disbelief. I was appalled. It troubled me that Maury was capable of raising his hand to a woman.

Maury continued to talk about Molly. I perceived he was still very connected to her. Sometimes it sounded as though he never left her emotionally, especially when he put his arms around me and glowingly said: "Ah, Molly, you've come back to me!"

I felt a stinging pain. *What kind of cruelty is this?* I finally worked up the courage to say, "What's all this about Molly? Don't you care for me at all?"

Maury's response was a laugh. "You poor thing…" Then he took me around and hugged me. But I didn't want to be hugged. My spirits were dropping lower and lower, and I found myself in a whirlpool of despair. No matter how much I tried, I knew I would not be able to compete with the memory of his ex-wife. I kept telling myself: *I'm not like Molly. I'm nothing. There's no me… there's no me….*

I began to go for more therapy, but it was nothing more than a Band-Aid on a gaping wound. I desperately thought about ending my relationship with Maury, but then he would flash his charming smile and say: "Honey, you know I don't want anyone but you!" My pain dissolved as he spoke and I was mesmerized all over again, but it was only momentary. Maury continued to praise the charms of Molly, and I became more despondent. *Molly… Molly… Molly… Won't he ever stop?*

Maury and I were now having arguments about anything and everything. Maury usually went back to his apartment until we were able to straighten out our differences. Then we would get back together until the next eruption.

After I discontinued with Mr. Martino, I stayed on at the Center and was assigned to other therapists in training. One therapist, a verbose young psychiatrist, said to me: "I don't understand your case. I have your records here, and it looks like you've been seeing many therapists. I don't think the others understand you like Mr. Martino. I suggest you go back to him. He seems to have the best understanding of you." *What? Go back to Martino?* I was amazed to hear him say that, if not a little annoyed, but he had a point; I was speaking my heart out to therapists who appeared puzzled and confused. Although I had traveled a rocky road with Martino, it seemed to be worse without him. So, I finally made the phone call. I told Mr. Martino I wanted to resume therapy with him. He was gracious and readily accepted me back. And soon, I began my weekly sessions.

But it was not enough. Between my sessions with Mr. Martino, I was desperate to open up and talk my heart out to someone who could understand me when I was in my very dark moods. So, I began to run over to the Emergency Room of a local hospital with the hope that a doctor on call would be able to help me out of my despair. More and more, I found myself sitting in the hospital in the middle of the night. Sometimes I had a long wait, which made me even more on edge, but it didn't matter, as long as I could get out of my system the things that were troubling me. It seemed like the only way I could alleviate the mounting tension I felt inside.

It was comforting to know that there were trained individuals who could see me on the spur of the moment and pull me out of my doldrums with their soothing manner, words of comfort, and an insight or two. I was seeing young interns who I thought were full-fledged psychiatrists. Although I was disappointed at first, it didn't really matter as long as I had a compassionate mental health professional who would hear me and help me deal with my pain. Soon, I felt some relief. Then I would calm down, leave the hospital, and find my way home. And the cycle would start over again.

I hated those journeys to the hospital. *How can I stop this turmoil? What can I do to pull myself out of this state of emotional upheaval?* Then I had an idea. Maybe if I made myself more attractive, I could be more like Molly; and then Maury would really love me and stop telling me stories about how wonderful she was.

I always wanted to have black hair like Elizabeth Taylor, and I just knew it would look good on me, especially with my fair skin. When I told Maury about dying my hair black, he didn't like the idea at all. "If you want to dye your hair, make it titian. Titian would look good on you—but not black. It's too harsh."

One of Maury's friends, Cora, had become extremely chummy with me. With a great big smile she said: "I think you would look fabulous with black hair! I'll be only too happy to do it for you. Just let me know when."

I didn't really want to dye my hair, but I felt it was the thing to do. So, one night I went over to Cora's apartment. I felt pretty shaky as I said, "Okay, let's do it." I must have been in trauma, for I blocked out everything around me. When it was over, I heard Cora's voice: "Wait till Maury sees how pretty you look." Cora was beaming as she handed a mirror to me. I was overcome with delight. I thought I looked just like a movie star. I excitedly called Maury on the phone and told him the good news: "I now have black hair! Wait till you see how good it looks on me. Can you pick me up at Cora's?"

His response startled me: "I told you not to do that."

I said, "But it's really nice, Maury—you have to see it. When are you coming over?"

"I just got home. I'm tired, and I'm not going out again. I don't love you **that** much!"

Oh, my God, he doesn't love me!

I felt myself shaking. I couldn't let Cora see me like that; I had to make an excuse and leave. There was only one place where I could go when I felt so dejected and lost. It was late at night when I arrived at the hospital. Soon I started sobbing my heart out to the intern on call. "Not even Maury can love me… Maury can't love me… But he can love Molly!" I added, "I can't go on… I can't go on…"

I was immediately referred to a psychiatrist, Dr. Brewer, a short, red-haired man, who had a worried look on his face. He sat there, scrutinizing me. "Are you suicidal?" he asked.

I didn't answer; I cried and cried some more. He was now asking me myriad questions and taking down a bunch of notes. We were talking and talking, and I felt I was getting a hold of myself and calming down. I guess I needed to feel cared about, and my talk with Dr. Brewer helped me not to feel so alone and lost. After a while, my bad feelings dissipated. I said, "I think I can leave now."

But Dr. Brewer had a strange look in his eyes that troubled me. I was used to journeying over to the hospital when I was very upset, but this turned out to be one journey too many. "You're not going anywhere!" he firmly said. "I'm concerned about you, and I feel it would be best to keep you here in the hospital."

Oh no! They're going to lock me up! What am I going to do? I felt fear soar through me, as my heart began to pound. *What is going to happen to me?*

I was soon interviewed by another psychiatrist, who asked me: "Why are you here?" It felt awful to say: "I was dying my hair to make myself more attractive for my boyfriend, Maury, but he rejected me. He loves his ex-wife, and I don't know what to do." The doctor wrote down some notes, as I sat there staring at him, and then he was gone.

I must have panicked something terrible, for everything around me had once again become a blur. I looked around and found myself on a ward. There were strange faces wherever I turned. Some had weird expressions. *My, they look creepy! Am I safe here? Will they harm me? My God, I don't feel safe. I want to go home.*

I was worried sick. *Maybe I won't be able to get out!* My mind was racing with all kinds of thoughts. Soon I asked for permission to make a phone call. I was anxious to speak to Maury. I wanted to let him know I was in the hospital. Maury was surprised and asked, "What are you doing there?"

I said: "I want to work out some problems while my therapist is away." He accepted that and asked no further questions. That disappointed me because he didn't seem too concerned. Yet when I heard his voice, I wanted to run out of there and straight into his arms. Only now, I was stuck on a mental ward. *What have I gotten myself into?*

I remained agitated and upset. I asked to see a psychiatrist and soon I was seeing one after another. I had the hope that someone there could help me with the gnawing ache I felt inside. This ache was not new to me, but it was profoundly aggravated by Maury's stories about his ex-wife. I wondered: *Can't anyone hear me and take this terrible pain away?*

I guess I was wishing for magic. Most of the young doctors seemed utterly astonished when I told them about my childhood. Some looked mystified. One was asking questions, trying to understand, as his glasses dropped from his nose. I perceived that it was hard for them to comprehend how a child could live locked up in a house with a crazy mother for her whole childhood, survive, and be able to tell the story. None of them seemed to understand.

One psychiatrist came over to me and asked, "Are you in therapy?"

I said, "Yes I am but my therapist, Mr. Martino, is away on vacation. He'll be back in two weeks."

That seemed to interest him. He repeated, "He'll be back in two weeks?"

In my mind I panicked: *I have to wait two weeks before I could speak to Martino again! Will he be able to get me out of here when he gets back?* I was on pins and needles, fearful but hopeful at the same time.

Every day, like clockwork, there came a time for medication. If there was one thing I did not want, it was Thorazine. As soon as it was handed to me, I put it into my mouth, walked into the Ladies' Room, spit it out and threw it into the garbage. I didn't think a pill could help me with the problems I had.

I was missing Maury something terrible. Every day, I was in the phone booth making calls to him. He kept asking me, "When are you coming home?" I wished I knew the answer to that. Then he made a joke: "You'd better be careful; they just might take the key and throw it away!" I didn't find that very funny, but I laughed; I was enjoying Maury's sense of humor, even though I thought it was a little crude.

Maury didn't come to see me; neither did my uncle Will. I certainly never expected Hedda to visit me in a hospital. And so, there were no visitors. I felt alone and anguished as I drifted around the ward.

For the most part it was quiet, and there was no real violence or disturbances—except for two teenage girls, Joan, and Gail. They were scaring the patients with their antics, as they came running up and down the corridor laughing, screaming, and making noises. I was very nervous when I saw them coming my way; I knew they were up to no good. *What are they going to do next? What kind of havoc are they about to create?* I managed to stay out of their way. How I wanted to go home—especially during times like these.

Soon I saw two elderly ladies sitting in their chairs, lost in what appeared to be a world of their own. I got a surprise that I would never have expected when I learned that one had been employed as a schoolteacher, and the other, a social worker. How did they end up like this? Something like this awakened me out of my trance.

This showed me there is no one beyond the realm of mental illness; we are all vulnerable, no matter what your walk of life is. We are all one.

I went to one of the dances that were given regularly for the patients on the ward. They looked so depressed, so forlorn, as they managed to creep along with the music that was playing on the phonograph. I looked in and walked out.

I found a happy moment in the Ladies' Room when I peeked at myself in the mirror; I couldn't help but admire the way I looked with my jet-black hair. *Not so bad at that!* Despite the mess I got myself into, I was still glad that I had dyed my hair. I stood there for a few moments, deep in thought, when I turned to a side and saw an attractive young woman who was applying her make-up like an artist. As I watched her, I said what I was feeling: "You have such beautiful eyes!"

She casually replied, "There's nothing to it. I'll teach you how to make your eyes look just like mine." She took out an eyebrow pencil and showed me how to apply it on my lids and under. As I looked in the mirror, I thought this was incredible. I was filled with joy as I said: "I'm indebted to you for making me look so pretty."

She replied: "I have an extra pencil and I'm going to give it to you." She smiled and then walked away. How truly wonderful it was to have this little eye pencil in my hand! From there on I began to apply it regularly to my eyes. I became aware of the dramatic, sensual look it gave me. I thought: *How pleasantly surprised Maury would be if he saw the way I looked now!*

As I wandered around the ward, I saw a tall young woman looking my way. She smiled and said, "This place is something, isn't it?" And the conversation began. Toma was so friendly and outgoing. I wondered what her problem was. She soon revealed she was hit over the head early one morning when she was on her way to work. The details of her story were not clear to me, but it sounded as though she had been through hell. I liked her. I think it was her openness and down to earth quality that appealed to me.

Toma took me over to a table in the Day Room where her friend was sitting. "I want you to meet Tessie." Tessie was a pretty young woman with a warm, charming smile. She told me she had a little girl and missed her very much. I learned she was hospitalized because she was scrubbing the floors of her apartment over and over again in the middle of the night. I listened to her speak and soon felt comfortable enough to share some of my problems with her.

She enthusiastically said, "When we get out of here, I'd like to get together with you." I thought it was a great idea. Like Toma, she was expecting to be discharged at any time.

Another young woman soon entered our group. Ann was from the south and had suffered a nervous breakdown while pursuing a singing career in New York. The four of us gathered around a small table in the Day Room, and there, we could talk, share our problems, and be supportive of each other. It didn't feel like a mental ward when these ladies were around. I found their warmth and compassion essential to my recovery from Molly madness. I don't know what I would have done without them.

My hankering to go home remained as strong as ever. It was just about two weeks when Mr. Martino returned from vacation. I got him on the phone and said, "Thank God you're back! I'm trapped in a psych ward of a local hospital. Help!" I went on to tell him what happened when he was away. He immediately contacted the admitting psychiatrist, Dr. Brewer, and they spoke. They agreed I should not be in the hospital. Dr. Brewer soon paid me a visit. "I made a mistake committing you. You don't belong here. I spoke with your therapist, Mr. Martino, and we both feel your big problem is that you were locked up in your childhood and being here is more of the same."

My goodness, how my world brightened when Dr. Brewer said: "You can go home." I didn't think I would ever be able to get out of there, but now Dr. Brewer was telling me that I could leave. *Hallelujah!* I was crying tears of joy.

I always thought psychiatrists were the ultimate, that they didn't make any mistakes. But now I was learning that they were not infallible. This psychiatrist made a mistake and even admitted it. I found it amazing.

The first thing I did when I got home was rush over to Maury's store. He was loading a carton of eggs into his station wagon. I stood in back of him for a few minutes and when he turned around, I said, "Hi, Maury."

He seemed ecstatic to see me. This was the first time Maury saw me with my black hair and makeup on my eyes. He blinked several times and said, "Hey, you look great! You look different. You look fantastic! Who showed you how to put on that eye make-up?" And we started to talk. It was as if I had never been away.

He laughed as he said, "Don't you go checking into hospitals anymore! They might just keep you there and throw away the key!" I knew he was kidding, but why did he have to harp on that?

It was a frightening experience, but I learned a lesson I will never forget—and that is if you go into a hospital or mental health facility, you have to be very careful about what you say to a doctor, nurse or an attendant in charge. It is very dangerous to say "I can't go on, I can't go on" if you are experiencing emotional despondency. A feeling of fleeting despondency could be mistaken for actual suicidal tendencies. and if this is the case, it is grounds for immediate committal. And I was mistakenly committed. I became frazzled as I worried, *Will I ever get out of here?* When I was finally released, I told myself: *Under no circumstances will I ever allow myself to get into such a frenzy that I wind up on a mental ward of a hospital.*

And I stopped running over to the hospital in the middle of the night.

49
Into the World of Work

I kept thinking about the lesson I learned: I vowed I would never allow myself to become so upset that I would wind up in a mental hospital again. Nothing is that important. If Maury teased me about Molly, I would let it slide or leave the room. But I would not succumb to it.

Maury himself appeared somewhat different. He was low in spirits and seemed to have things on his mind that were taking up his time and energy. He was in a downcast mood when he came to me and said: "I need help in the store. There's more work than I can handle, and my mother isn't always available. You said you wanted to work. Why don't you come in on the days when my mother's not there?"

Me working at a cash register? I shuddered at the thought of it. I knew I wasn't good at making change and I had no desire to face that challenge. But that wasn't my only reason. I knew Maury was difficult to work for; I would see him having fights with his mother in between customers. I was not about to partake in that scene. He continued to pressure me and I flatly refused. I said, "Maury, I am not a good cashier." And I would not yield.

Soon, the unthinkable occurred: my mother agreed to work in Maury's store. What a shock that was. After all those years locked away from the outside world. I didn't think anything would ever move her to leave the house, but she went downstairs to work for Maury on the days his mother didn't come. She had no complaints about waiting on customers or ringing up the cash register. She did have a problem with Maury: "He's screaming all the time! I'm getting sick from it. So much aggravation…" Still, she managed to stay on for several months until she came down with the shingles, and then she quit. It amazed me that she never made a big to-do about it. Despite the hard times she experienced with Maury, she remained on good terms with him as if nothing had happened.

And Maury continued to work hard. In the morning, he was usually behind the counter or in the back room candling eggs to look for impurities. In the late afternoon, he would load up his station wagon with cartons of eggs and then go out on his route, making deliveries to his many customers. He came home late and tired. I was surprised to hear him say, "I'm having trouble paying my bills. They keep piling up on me…" I wondered why he was having financial difficulties when he was working so hard.

Maury soon told me that he had palpitations of the heart. "When I was little, about 3 or 4, I had a strep infection with a very high temperature. There was no penicillin in those days, so it couldn't be treated, and I wound up with rheumatic fever. I have a heart murmur, and sometimes I may get skipped beats—what they call palpitations. That's about it. It can be annoying at times."

He spoke about it in a matter-of-fact way, and it sounded like a harmless condition, however, in the days that followed, Maury complained about his health. "I'm not getting enough rest, and I have this low blood pressure…" There were mornings when it was hard for him to get out of bed to open his store. There were times when he didn't feel well enough to go to work, but he persisted, and I was concerned.

A red flag went up in my mind. Maury was pushing himself too hard. I saw him lifting heavy cartons, and I thought it was a strain on his heart. I said, "Maury, you're bright. You speak well; you're attractive. I watch you load big, heavy cartons into your station wagon and it bothers me. You might be hurting yourself. Don't you think you could do better?"

He had a quick reply: "I don't have any skills. This is how I make my living. The egg route does it—the store doesn't. I need both."

I had an awful feeling. How could he sell himself short like that? I continued to talk to him about finding other work. But he just wouldn't hear me.

Grandpa was now in his 70's, and very ill with hardening of the arteries. He was still going to work, staggering on and off buses, in hot and cold weather. Then one night, as he was about to lock up, he fell down in front of his store. No one knew what happened to him, but I knew he died the way he wanted to—by his store. I had not been very close to him, but he was my grandpa, and I felt a sense of loss. I turned to Maury for comfort and support, and he was there for me.

I continued to feel restless and eager to be out in the world doing some kind of work. While Maury was asking me to help out in his store, my uncle Will was telling me that he wanted to send me to business school. The truth of the matter: I was not interested in either.

Soon Maury said, "I have an old rinky-dink typewriter—maybe you could make some use of it." He took me to the back of his store and hidden in a corner was a Royal manual. "Why don't you try it out?"

I pecked at a few keys and they felt stiff. I didn't think I would ever be able to use it, but Maury had a different viewpoint. "Look, it's an old machine. I don't use it, but it's a start for you. If you decide to go to business school, you can practice on it. Why don't I just bring it upstairs?"

I liked the thought of having it in the house, just in case. Once the typewriter was in my mother's apartment, I started to play around with it. I could make words, even whole sentences. I was amused by what I could do. Maybe I could type fast instead of pecking at the keys. The challenge became appealing to me.

I went over to my uncle and said, "As you know, I don't like the idea of office work, but at least I'll be doing something more than cleaning lamps. If you still want to send me to business school, I'm willing to give it a try—but only typing, no shorthand!" (I didn't think I would ever be able to read back my shorthand notes.)

After attending classes for almost a year, I was amazed that I could actually touch-type fifty words a minute. It fascinated me that I didn't have to look at the keys—all I had to do was type.

I felt indebted to my uncle for making this possible. Soon I went into Maury' store and threw my arms around him. "I never could have done it without your typewriter. Thank you, Maury. Thank you so much."

Maury had a joyful smile as he said, "I knew you could do it."

I was now ready for a job in the business world. The school I attended sent me out on an interview and I got the job. It was like nothing I ever imagined. I was now working as a typist with a hospital collection agency and did nothing but type cards and form letters all day long. I was nothing more than an automaton spitting out mail. As I looked around, I observed my female co-workers. They were talking to people on the phone, reminding them about unpaid bills while I was slaving over a typewriter seven hours a day. Their work seemed so interesting compared to my work, which was so draining, so very boring. A feeling of nothingness came over me.

The workplace itself was extremely intimidating. Things had to get done in a certain rigid manner. People had to look, dress, and act in a formal business-like fashion. Work had to be performed without flaws. Everything had to be perfect. Would they fire me if I made a mistake? It seemed that as long as I did a fairly good job, I could feel safe. When I made a typographical error, the supervisor was there to admonish me, and my anxiety soared to new heights. I tried hard to appear confident, but I felt like a frightened little child with an authoritarian figure hovering over me. I wondered how long I would be able to stay in such a setting.

I didn't like the business world and I went moaning to Maury, my uncle Will, my therapist, and whoever else would listen to me. But the problem was mine. I had chosen something that wasn't right for me and I had to find a way to deal with it. However, griping about it served a useful purpose; I was able to release some of my built-up tensions and that gave me the emotional strength to go on.

Despite all the pressure I was under, I was still very eager to have a rapport with my co-workers. I secretly yearned for the acceptance, approval, and even the love of my peers, but somehow I couldn't make a connection. That made me feel pretty bad, but it didn't stop me from studying them: how they dressed and wore their hair, how they walked and talked, how they interacted with each other. How were they able to do everything so well? I had a hard time just getting by. I was trying to make sense of things around me and to learn how to become more like the people I admired. That was a job in itself.

When I felt rejected, my need to belong intensified. When someone in the office walked past me and ignored my overtures of friendship, I felt a hurt that was as strong as physical pain. I wondered what I had to do to be accepted into their world.

I soon got the impression that the business world was artificial. People didn't seem real or caring, and it was very disappointing. Perhaps I was looking for something more—like the family I never had. But what could I really expect? I wasn't there to seek out a family; I was there to work. I understood this on an intellectual level, but on an emotional level I couldn't feel it.

I was despondent and wanted to quit, but I desperately needed to prove to myself that I could function in the outside world. As I tried to play the game, I struggled with feelings of inferiority and incompetency. I thought the work experience would bring me out of myself and make me feel better; instead, I was feeling more worthless than ever.

I felt fortunate to have Maury in my life. Throughout my tension-filled days, I fantasized about coming home to him in the evening and being in his warm embrace. I found solace in thinking about the tender moments I would share with him.

It was high anxiety for me when, one day, I came to work and was told I had to relieve the receptionist on her lunch hour and that I would have to learn the monitor switchboard. *Oh, no!* I was sure I would be disconnecting people right and left, as I sat at the board, pushing buttons up and down. Soon I had a pleasant surprise: the switchboard was simple and not that busy. I was talking to people, putting calls through, and I kind of enjoyed it. But when several calls came in at one time, I became flustered and didn't do so well. It was like a simple game that suddenly became more difficult. I had to remain calm and make all the right moves at the right time, but I wasn't all that calm. It was a challenge. Somehow I managed, and I was glad to have something to break up the monotony of all that typing.

I soon found someone in my office to talk to; she was another typist who also stayed by herself. A short, stocky young woman in her 20's, she had stories to tell about her troubled relationship with her boyfriend. I was hearing the same things over and over, but I was so glad to have someone to talk to, I really didn't care what she spoke about—as long as she talked to me.

It came to a point where I couldn't stand typing one more card. I stayed at this job for over a year and that was enough. It was time to leave. I had acquired some office experience and I was now ready for something more to my liking, although I wasn't sure just what that would be. I was in high spirits when I started perusing the want ads, but soon, I became discouraged. I went out on interviews, but the jobs I wanted did not want me, and the ones I didn't want were offered to me. Maury encouraged me to "keep looking," and alerted me to the ways of the business world: "Don't let them tell you that they'll call you. If they want to hire you, they'll let you know then and there. Before you leave, ask them if you have the job."

I thought this was a sound piece of advice; I did just that. I found more work, but nothing that I was happy with. I rationalized that there were some good things about being in the business world. I was now out of the house for some ten hours a day and away from my mother. I was experiencing life through my own eyes—not hers. This allowed me to separate myself even more from her. I was learning about something called self-reliance. It was not easy to stand on my own two feet and do things on my own. As I fell down, I got up. As I learned to do one thing, I found I could do another and yet another....

Best of all, I was rewarded for my typing skills with a salary. I was actually earning money! I could squirrel it away in the bank, and see the dollars growing in my account. This was a source of security for me. As I thought about it, I was proud of myself—if only in the moment.

50

Putting My Fears Aside

Working at the hospital collection agency was my first experience in the business world and I was overly sensitive to my environment. Everything was so new to me, and I had to be on my toes at all times. It was especially difficult since I was encountering a way of life so very different from the isolation I knew with my mother.

While I was caught up in the stress and anxiety of the workplace, I found some aspects that were actually appealing to me. I never expected to see a quaint little kitchen in the middle of a business office, but there it was. A smile came to my face when I saw a pot of coffee on the stove. I enjoyed inhaling its fresh aroma as I watched my co-workers scurrying back and forth to grab another cup. The environment was cozy and comfortable. I could have my lunch there if I so desired. It had a nice, homey quality about it that I enjoyed.

When one of the workers had a birthday, there usually would be a big cake waiting for her. On my birthday, as I anxiously approached the kitchen, one of my co-workers, Jane, came over to me and said: "There's a cake waiting for you on the table. And you didn't think we liked you!"

I was overcome with emotion. "A cake for me? What a wonderful surprise!"

My goodness, I never dreamed they would have a cake for me. For the most part, I didn't think my co-workers liked me. But there I was, facing the reality that told me just the opposite—they did like me!

While I was impressed by this positive gesture, Jane's comment triggered myriad feelings in me—especially feelings of not being safe or comfortable around people. I had trouble connecting; I didn't know how to make casual conversation. Maybe not having gone through the socialization process had something to do with it. I didn't know how to put my feelings into words, and in a way, I was afraid to. My feelings about people were muddled and mixed. I wanted so very much to be liked but, for the most part, it seemed that this was not about to happen.

I was going for therapy to understand myself better and to have a better self-image. I thought I was making progress. Apparently not. I was perplexed, as I told my therapist how uncomfortable I was in everyday situations. His response was simply: "There is no growth in life without discomfort." I figured if that were the case, I must really be growing and changing. But I didn't feel it.

Truth of the matter, I felt pretty bad about myself. When I looked in the mirror, I felt even worse. I saw a nose that was much too bulbous for my face. I was able to ignore it when I was younger, but now that I was out in the working world, I was more self-conscious than ever. I felt people were looking down on me because of it. I was feeling, all the more: *No one will ever like me!* And I was obsessing about it. I soon realized: *Something has to be done!*

However, I had anxiety just thinking about plastic surgery. The thought of it sent shivers through me. I was a girl with hardly any education or knowledge of the world. In many ways I was quite infantile—and I had plenty of fear. I asked myself: *How will I be able to go through something so drastic? By going under the knife will I be taking my life into my hands?*

When I got a hold of myself, I made up my mind to find out all I could about the procedure and the doctors who might be performing it. Soon I was asking others for their opinions. I started with my mother. She just stared at me with a vacant stare and did not respond—which is what I expected. Grandma, who would call me "shaina meidala" (a Yiddish name for "pretty girl") said, loud and clear: "Leave well enough alone! You don't need it." When I asked Maury, he casually replied, "If you want to, you could do it, but it isn't necessary. You're pretty the way you are." Will and Jessie were very opposed to the idea; they knew someone who was seriously injured when the surgeon cut into a nerve. "We really don't think you should do this." But I couldn't hear what they were saying. I was too intent upon one thing—making myself look more attractive so that I could fit in better with my peers.

Then I found out my cousin, Lisa, had plastic surgery. I saw pictures of her before and after, and what a difference there was. The hook in her nose was gone and she looked radiantly beautiful. This gave me the impetus to make an appointment to meet with her surgeon.

Dr. Maxwell Maltz, a world renowned cosmetic surgeon, was middle-aged, gray-haired, and a little on the gruff side. He asked several questions, one of which was: "Did you ever have an accident, such as falling off a bike?" I told him: "I've never been on a bike." And we talked. Soon he said: "I think plastic surgery will make a big difference in your life." At the time I left his office I felt somewhat safer and reassured.

I still was distraught and worried about going through with the procedure. After all, it was still surgery and something could go wrong. At times, I was petrified with fear just thinking about it. But there was a spark of faith in me that told me everything would be okay, and I so wanted to believe that.

I eagerly worked at squirreling away five hundred dollars for the surgery with Dr. Maltz, and soon I was ready. Again, my co-workers came through in a warm, caring way that surprised me; they sent me off with a beautiful pink nylon bed jacket. I was happily taken aback that they would do something so wonderful for me.

I wasn't feeling well when I arrived at the doctor's office. I weakly uttered: "I think I have a cold in my system. I have to go home and get some rest. I'll come back when I feel better." Dr. Maltz wasn't happy to hear that. He looked at me in a peculiar way and barked, "If you leave now, you won't be coming back. If you're going to do it, do it now or forget about the whole damn thing!" I cringed. The doctor had spoken!

I was a nervous wreck when I entered the operating room. Soon, the surgery began. I was awake during the entire procedure and I heard the doctor talking to his assistants. At one point, they were discussing the excessive blood flow. In a panic I attempted to sit up. I squirmed: "I have to get out of here!" In a loud tone Dr. Maltz fired back: "Now, you shut up and lay there!" Oh boy, I was stuck, and I knew it: *What have I gotten myself into this time?*

I don't know how I got through it—but somehow, I did. It was over and I could breathe easier. Over-all, the surgery went well. I had black and blue eyes for a short time, which is to be expected, but there was no real pain. When it was time to remove the bandages, the doctor handed me a mirror. I couldn't believe my eyes; my nose was beautifully formed, shortened and tilted upward. Is this really me? When Grandma saw me, she was beaming with joy as she said, "He gave you an Irish pug!" Maury was filled with pride when he said, "I'm taking you over to my parents to show you off." Will and Jessie also expressed their approval and delight, despite their initial protests. Back at the office, my co-workers agreed, "You look fantastic!" As for myself, I was thankful I found the courage to go through with this on my own. I was thrilled that it turned out the way it did. I was so worried but my fear was overridden by an overwhelming need to make myself look the very best I could.

During this time, I left my office woes on the back burner, and soon I was back at the grind. I was grateful for the gift I gave myself. When I looked in the mirror, I felt really good—something quite new for me.

51

One Thing After Another

While I struggled to sustain myself in the work force, things were going better in my personal life. I was experiencing precious moments with Maury. But I wanted more of Maury's time, love, and attention—much more than he could give. I guess I needed to make up for all those years of a lonely, loveless existence; I just couldn't get enough. I went to my therapist with all my complaints and he said: "You want love, but you don't know how to receive it." I thought about that. Maybe I didn't know how to accept the love that was given to me. But knowing that did not help any. My uncle Will, frustrated and annoyed, spoke out: "If you keep on like that, you're going to lose him!"

Maybe he was right, but I didn't want to hear it. When I saw Maury again, I calmed down and stopped my lamenting—until the next time.

Maury came in one night and told me that, out of the blue, he received a phone call from Molly. "She's remarried, and she has another child. She's calling me about Francine. My daughter is asking to see me, so I'm going over there. I'm going to spend some time with her."

My heart started to pound. *What is this all about? Why is Molly calling him now when he hasn't seen his daughter in years?* Something about this seemed strange and it troubled me.

Maury began to visit his nine-year-old daughter on weekends. I was feeling jealous and neglected. Then one night he came in, low in spirit, and said, "Molly wants me back after all these years! She wants to leave her husband. I told her I didn't think it would work." He paused and said, "I have some thinking to do."

I worried myself sick. I could only think about one thing: *Is he going to leave me?*

In the weeks that followed, Maury walked around like a man carrying a load of bricks on his back. Then the cloud lifted, and he came in looking relieved. With a great big smile, Maury made the announcement: "I just saw Molly. I told her she has a husband and another child, she's made a new life for herself—and I have a new life, too."

I took a deep breath. Thank God for that! It felt like he had finally resolved his issues with Molly and closed the door on his past. I had hopes that he would not mention her name again and that he would now give himself fully to me.

Maury was now paying more attention to me than ever before. When I visited him at his store, he put aside whatever he was occupied with at the time. I basked in those delightful moments we shared. A few hugs and kisses, and some loving smiles, brightened my day.

I still wasn't comfortable with Maury's mother. Whenever I came into the store, Emma was usually there, waiting on customers or working at the cash register. She looked worn and tired, as she went from one chore to another. Maury would tell me what a wonderful woman she was, but I didn't get that feeling. Maybe that's because she and I hadn't hit it off. She seemed distant and I didn't know how to approach her. I felt she didn't like me, or perhaps it was my insecurity speaking. For a while, I tried to avoid her as much as possible.

Then, as we started to speak to each other, I was surprised at how sweet and caring she was. Emma now greeted me with a smile and a great big "Hello, honey," and it appeared that we were getting to like each other. But soon, there was a problem: when I came into the store, Maury would go rushing over to her and say, "Mama, Lenore's a nice girl. She's not like Molly. Go over and give her a big hug!"

I had the strangest feeling when he said that. Emma would look at me and I would look at her, then we would break out laughing. At Maury's command, we would share a quick embrace. I could see she was just as embarrassed as I. Sometimes he would push us together to kiss. That felt even worse; it was a forced thing, an awkward moment for both of us. As a result, we never really got to know each other. I once again felt uncomfortable in her presence, and I could sense she felt the same way.

Maury soon said, "I'm going to visit my parents and I want you to come with me." I was reluctant to go but I went anyway. I met Maury's father, Noah, a gruff, heavy man who had a severe case of diabetes. He sat in his recliner munching on cookies and other snacks. I was only there for several minutes when I witnessed the strained interaction between him and Emma, and I found it disturbing. Noah criticized his wife in a rude, loud tone, talking over her, and disregarding what she had to say. She either ignored him or laughed it off. It was an unpleasant scene, and I wondered how she could be so complacent. She seemed to be swallowing her feelings to avoid conflict, but I was swallowing mine as well. I was appalled at the way Noah treated Emma, but I didn't think it was my place to say anything.

One day, we were sitting in their living room and Maury said, "Lenore does an imitation of Marilyn Monroe. It's fantastic! Sing that song for my parents—you know the one I mean…." Maury had that jubilant smile on his face, and he was coaxing me with all his charm. Soon, self-conscious me forgot to be self-conscious, and I was sitting and singing "I Wanna Be Loved By You."

Emma had a grin on her face and seemed to be amused. Maury just sat there, smiling. He looked like the cat that swallowed the canary. What really astonished me was the reaction of Maury's father. He was sprawled out on his recliner, laughing so hard that his belly couldn't stop shaking. I thought he looked so funny. What was going on with Noah? I was only singing, no gyrations or anything like that. But he sure seemed to be having one hell of a time.

After we left, I felt ashamed. Where had I ever found the guts to sing in front of Maury's parents? Later, when we were alone, Maury said, "I've been meaning to ask you where did you ever learn to sing like that? You must have seen a lot of Marilyn's films."

"I never saw any of them. I heard that song on the radio many times and I just sing it the way I feel it. It's natural for me." I'll never forget the expression on Maury's face as he stared at me. I began to think about seeing a Monroe flick, but I wasn't that interested. I continued to sing that song when I was alone with Maury, for I knew he got a big kick out of it—and so did I.

Maury was now taking me around to meet his extended family. Most of his relatives were kind, friendly people who opened their doors and hearts to me. Maury's grandmother was especially fond of me, and I liked her, too. A plump little lady with a warm, friendly smile, she radiated love and joy whenever she saw me. She would rush over to me, put her arms around me, and give me a great big kiss. I felt genuinely cared about in that moment. One day when we were walking in the street, Maury was beaming. "My grandmother said I should marry you. She knows good people and she likes you very much." My heart was dancing with delight. She said what I wanted to hear. I only hoped that Maury was feeling the same way.

While I liked Maury's relatives, I had no desire to participate in family gatherings. However, when the holidays rolled around, I went to these social functions only because I knew Maury wanted me to be there with him. I couldn't tell him that these socials made me extremely uncomfortable and brought out in me feelings of anxiety and shame. I would find myself tightening up inside and withdrawing into a corner. It seemed strange that I could feel more alone in a group of people than if I were by myself. On the outside I tried to be friendly, but inside, I was squirming. I would have liked to disappear from the scene and find some comfort in seclusion, but it didn't feel right to pick myself up and leave.

As another family get-together approached, Maury asked me to meet him at his grandmother's. I was working at the time and recall rushing over for the beginning of the festivities. I rang the bell and found the door open. I walked in and will never forget the fantastic surprise that awaited me. Maury and his relatives were standing together in a row and as soon as they saw me, they began to sing the song, "Let Me Call You Sweetheart." I knew the lyrics and was touched as they sang:

"Let me call you sweetheart, I'm in love with you.
Let me hear you whisper that you love me too.
Keep the love-light glowing in your eyes so true.
Let me call you sweetheart, I'm in love with you."

It was a beautiful moment for me. I didn't know how to accept this display of love. I was overcome with emotion, and at a complete loss for words. *Is it really me they're lavishing with all this attention and affection? What can I say or do to express my appreciation?* I just hoped they wouldn't notice how flustered I was. I never experienced anything quite like this.

"I have something for you, honey." Maury came into my mother's apartment one day with a radiant smile on his face. He reached into his pocket and pulled out a tiny box. "Look, honey, a cultured pearl ring! It's a friendship ring. I hope you like it."

My heart dropped. *What's a "friendship" ring and why is he giving it to me?* I thought he wanted to marry me. I tried to hide my disappointment as he continued. "Honey, you're looking at two genuine cultured pearls and little diamonds on both sides. Look how beautiful they are; they're so small and dainty…." It felt like he was trying to sell me this ring.

Maury's joy continued to accelerate, while I felt like crying. *My goodness, a friendship ring?* I didn't know what to say. I swallowed my sadness, slipped the ring on my finger and barely uttered, "It's lovely."

"I have to get back to the store now." Maury gave me a peck on the cheek and whispered: "I'll see you later." And he was gone.

I began to brood. When I saw him again, I found the voice to say, "I thought you wanted to marry me…"

Maury took one look at me and said, "Honey, you can consider this an engagement ring." *Really? Is he just saying this to appease me?* I would have been more than happy if he had come in with a cheap engagement ring from Woolworth's and said, "Let's get married." But he didn't do that. I had an ache inside and I couldn't find the words to tell him.

Nevertheless, I went over to see Amy to show her my ring and Jay was there. I said, "Maury just gave me this. He said it's an engagement ring, but it doesn't look like one." I wasn't overly zealous, and I might have appeared a little down.

Jay looked at me and blasted off: "You know, Maury's running around with women. You think he was like that years ago? No way! He's only been running around since Molly left him. He was crazy about that girl. She broke his heart. He was the quietest fellow you would ever want to know. He was so shy he couldn't talk to a girl. I had to push him to go out on a date. It's hard to believe, but it's true."

I was flabbergasted. Jay had regressed to his brutally blunt, belligerent self. My heart was pounding as I looked at him in disbelief. "Why are you telling me this? I know Maury loves me. I can't believe he's running around with women." Jay shrugged it off with a sneer. Amy continued to color, seemingly oblivious to everything around her. The sound of silence filled the air, and I was hurting. I soon got up and left.

I was pretty shook up on my way home. I couldn't put the things Jay told me out of my mind. I told myself, *Jay is just being nasty. But what if the things he said are true?*

In the days that followed I walked around with a hurt I couldn't talk about. Was it possible that Maury was betraying me? I didn't want to know the truth.

I avoided going over to Amy for a while. I soon received a phone call from her: "I have bad news. Jay and I have split up. He's seeing someone. She's a close friend of mine and you know her too." Amy paused for a moment and said, "It's Mindy."

Mindy? How could that be? "Are you telling me that Jay is having an affair with Abe's wife? (Abe was Jay's boss, whom Jay worked with on weekend wedding jobs.) I was shocked to hear of Jay's entanglement. Mindy was an older woman with grey hair and a little fat across the middle. I thought she looked quite a bit older than Jay, in fact, old enough to be his mother. It staggered my imagination that the two of them would be romantically involved. And I wondered about Abe; how did he fit into this? I recalled that in recent times, when I came over to visit Amy and Jay, Mindy and Abe would usually be there. So, what was this all about?

I was amazed at how calm and collected Amy was as she spoke about Jay and his affair. She went on to tell me: "Jay has disappeared, but I think I know where he is." She didn't reveal much more, but I knew she was hurting, and I empathized with her. In my heart I felt she was better off without Jay. I couldn't tell her that, but I did say, "I'll speak to Maury and see if he's heard from Jay."

When I spoke to Maury, he looked baffled. "I don't know where Jay is. I didn't even know he left." It remained a mystery: *Where is Jay?* There were many questions, but no real answers.

Maury and I were visiting Amy frequently during this time when Amy sadly revealed, "Jay is staying with Mindy and Abe. It's a complicated story and I'd rather not go into it now." We didn't discuss it any further. When I saw Amy on my own, she continued to speak about her happy times with Jay and I found this very disconcerting. I wondered why she was so blind to reality. But who was I to talk? I had on my own blinders.

Another family gathering was about to take place and I wanted to look my very best, so I decided to wear my long blue floral dress that usually made me feel pretty and confident. I still felt uneasy, but as usual, I forced myself to go.

I soon met Maury's sister, Evie. I remembered what Maury said about her: "Evie's the baby of the family. She's immature and very spoiled." Evie was a petite little redhead, who wore her clothing short and so tight, she wiggled as she walked. I couldn't help but stare at her gyrations. As I watched her moving around and talking with the other guests, I perceived a funny feeling in the pit of my stomach. I didn't like her.

I was meeting a lot of people and most of that evening became a blur in my mind, but at one point I saw Maury looking troubled. I went over to him and asked, "What's wrong? You look all upset."

He was quick to reply. "My sister Evie said your hair is too long, and your dress is so long it makes you look matronly. She said, 'Couldn't you do better?' "

My heart sank as Maury spoke. I just stood there, staring at him. Did he have to repeat to me something as cruel as that? Suddenly I agreed with Evie: My dress is wrong. My hair is wrong. Everything about me is awful. As much as I try, I can't make myself attractive. I was hurting and then my hurt turned into anger. "She doesn't like me. Well, she doesn't have to. I don't like her either! I don't want to ever see her again." Maury didn't respond. He looked like he had just eaten a radish. It turned out to be a gloomy evening for both of us.

I eventually met up with Maury's two other sisters, Miriam, and Regina. Miriam, a housewife with two children, was warm, down-to-earth and a really nice person. She could laugh easily and be spontaneous with her thoughts and feelings. She joyfully asked Maury and me to "come on over" and visit with her and her family. But Regina was something else. Maury spoke with a passion: "Regina is a snob. Just because she's a teacher, she thinks she knows it all, so she thumbs her nose at people." When I met Regina, I found she was quite aloof. I thought to myself: *Maury's right. I'm going to stay away from her.*

Back in my mother's apartment, Maury had a happy smile as he announced: "I'm going to teach you about foods—all kinds of foods. Instead of always eating the same things, you're going to have variety in your life!" And he wasn't kidding. Maury loved to cook, and he was good at it. He started to bring all kinds of foods into my mother's home, including non-kosher meat. Hedda used only kosher meat, but it didn't seem to bother her; she permitted Maury to do whatever he pleased in the kitchen. And I watched Maury whip up one delicious platter after another, including bacon and eggs. That was one of my favorites. Maury laughed and said, "Don't ever tell my mother I make bacon. She'd have a fit. My mother keeps a kosher kitchen."

Hedda smiled. She appeared fascinated. Although Hedda didn't eat the foods that Maury made, she was having a great time watching him at the stove.

Maury was showing me a new way of life and I was surprised that Hedda had no aversion to it. She didn't seem to care one way or another. She remained, for the most part, passive and uninvolved. I was glad she was over her emotional outbursts and I wondered: *What made for this big change in her? Was Maury responsible for this?* I noticed she had become very fond of Maury. She appeared happy and laughed like a young girl when he was around.

Eventually, Maury said, "I'm going to teach you how to cook." Hedda sat back and didn't say a word. I soon found myself making an egg omelet and French toast, but I wasn't very motivated. It worried me when Maury said, "I want you to cook like my mother. My mother makes delicious rice dishes with spicy yellow sauce. I'll take you over there and she'll teach you." Then he would become busy and forget about it. I would say to myself: *Thank God for that!*

Truth of the matter, I wasn't ready for an apron and a kettle. It didn't feel very glamorous to stand behind a stove. I wanted to get out of the house and make something of my life. I didn't want to get trapped in the house in a life of drudgery.

About this time, Maury began to take me out to local restaurants. I was eating simple, ordinary food, but I enjoyed it like I never knew I could. It was great to be out of my mother's house and in the atmosphere of a nice cozy restaurant. I wondered why I had ever been so afraid of this.

But Maury wasn't too happy about eating out. He continued to rave about his mother's cooking. Soon he stopped taking me out. One night I found the courage to ask, "Why don't you take me out to eat like you used to?"

"I don't take you out because you don't deserve it!"

I saw red. He spoke with a calm voice, but I could see he was seething inside. And so was I. "You're not taking me out because I don't stand in the kitchen and cook for you like your mother?"

Maury smiled and said, "You got it!"

We continued to have petty arguments that turned into big fights. We separated for days at a time. Then we missed each other and made up. Maury continued to force the issue: "When are you going to cook like my mother?" It was the same old story. It was a problem we couldn't resolve. Maury concluded, "There's always TV dinners."

But I knew Maury wasn't happy with TV dinners, and I recognized his persistent nature. He didn't quit easily when he had something pressing on his mind. "Hey, I got an idea. Let's go over to my mother. We'll have a delicious meal and she'll give you her recipe for making rice. You'll see how easy it is."

I figured it couldn't hurt if I just went over there, and I knew it would make Maury happy. This time I was in for a big surprise. Maury's sister, Evie, was there and she didn't want to come out of her room to say hello. Maury and his mother went to see what was wrong, while I sat alone in the living room. I soon heard loud screaming: "**Maury, Maury, stop it! Your sister's mouth is bleeding. Stop it!**" Maury's mother sounded frantic. Soon Maury came running out. "I had to sock her. She was talking about you. She said you never went to school, you never went to parties, you never had a boyfriend, and she went on. Let's get out of here!"

I was stunned. Somehow Evie found out about the way I grew up and Maury had defended me in the only way he knew. The truth was out and she was looking down on me while I was looking down on myself.

I couldn't get this incident out of my mind. Evie knew things about me that I didn't want her to know. I was not like everybody else. I wondered how much Maury's family knew about the way I grew up. I felt more shame than usual. Somehow, I had to fight these feelings and get on with my life.

I soon realized there were bigger problems than how I looked in Evie's eyes or what the family thought of me. Maury complained: "The laundry is really piling up. We'd better go over to my apartment and use my washing machine." *Oh, no! How I hate that machine.* Several times I tried to assist Maury with the wash, but I only made things worse. Sudsy, soapy water came gushing out of the machine, spilling all over the kitchen floor. Maury's temper blazed. "This is no good. How many times have I told you how to use the machine? How come you don't learn?"

I countered: "But that machine is not working properly, you said that yourself."

Later, he said: "Maybe the answer is that laundromat on the corner."

So, I began to use the laundromat but, for the most part, I became the washing machine. I soon found myself doing his long underwear by hand. One night his friend, Nat, was visiting Maury in my mother's apartment, and it came out that I was washing Maury's long johns in the bathtub. Nat cracked up laughing. "You're making this poor girl do your underwear? How could you?" I pretty much felt the same way, but I couldn't say no, especially when Maury complained about being tired all the time. I continued for a while until Maury said he was going back to the washing machine in his apartment.

"I guess I'll have to keep you as a pet." Maury said that many times with a chuckle and a broad grin. I thought it was cute at first, but then I sensed a tone of annoyance in his voice. I knew he wanted me to learn how to cook and clean and become domesticated like his mother, but I just wasn't doing it.

"I guess I'll just have to be your pet."

52

Up, Down and Around

Despite our many ups and downs, Maury was taking me around. When he went to visit a friend or relative, I was there. When he went out to a restaurant, I was with him. Wherever he went, I was usually at his side. But it was not that easy or enjoyable because most everything was new and challenging. The little child inside of me was very scared, and I didn't feel safe enough to reveal how very unsafe I felt. There I was, on a journey into the unknown that aroused feelings of anguish and dread. How was I to cope with this new foreign world that was opening up to me?

I kept on moving towards the things I was afraid of, as I continued to travel around with Maury. If I were to reveal my fears and anxieties to him, I thought it would only make things worse, for then he would be watching my every move and I didn't want that. Mostly, I was ashamed. But when Maury asked me to go somewhere with him and do something that was unfamiliar to me, I couldn't refuse; I had to go. His overpowering personality, combined with love and warmth, enabled me to face new challenges. However, fleeting it was, I could feel some sense of safety with him in the moment, and this gave me the impetus to do more. Maury loved to live and enjoy life, and it came through in just about everything he did. His emotional strength and love of life were rubbing off on me.

Maury was now taking me out on the town with him. He especially enjoyed Manhattan and the many things it had to offer. He would find a space to park his huge white station wagon and soon we became a part of the busy throng of Times Square.

This was entirely different from anything I had ever seen. As I walked down Broadway, I saw a fairyland of theaters and glittering lights. *So, this is the Great White Way I heard so much about!* I could understand why my father wanted me to see it, and now, I was in the heart of it. It was a magnificent spectacle, very colorful and unique. No doubt, it was an exciting tourist attraction, but as for myself, it didn't take my breath away.

On 42nd Street I saw a dazzling display of movie theaters, one after another. *My goodness, how does one select a film?* As we gazed up at the marquees, we looked at each other and asked: What are we going to see? It was overwhelming but most of the time we found something we both liked. At other times, we just walked around, grabbed a bite, and went home.

Once in a while, we took in a Broadway show. It was fascinating to see real live people moving around on a stage, emoting before my eyes. I especially enjoyed the musicals. I found the melodies of one musical, "Subways Are For Sleeping," so enchanting they kept twirling around in my head for days afterwards.

Soon Maury was teaching me about alcoholic drinks called "ladies' cordials." I didn't like the taste of alcohol, but when we went out to a nightspot, I usually ordered an alcoholic concoction to please Maury. I thought Brandy Alexander was the best from all the alcoholic beverages I tasted. I didn't tell Maury how much more I preferred chocolate milk.

I soon got my first taste of nightlife. Maury started taking me around to several small nightclubs in Manhattan. If we got there early, we would sit down at a table and have a drink. Then a band would appear on the platform and play a medley of jazz music. The music was a bit too loud for my taste and I couldn't stand the smell of smoke that permeated the room. I found the whole scene unappetizing, but I never mentioned anything to Maury about this for I sensed it was important to him that I have these experiences.

"Now I'm going to take you to some great jazz spots in Manhattan." Maury was in high spirits when he introduced me to the Metropole. I tried to get used to the jazz Maury loved, but I couldn't bring myself to tell him that this wasn't my kind of music. The melodies were so distorted, I couldn't recognize the original tune.

I continued to have new experiences. While it was exciting, it was also fatiguing at the same time. I was only too glad to have quiet time with Maury. When he was in a musical mood, he took me over to his apartment and played the music he loved so much on his clarinet. Sometimes he put a favorite record on his phonograph and danced to it. I loved to watch him dance. He put his heart and soul into every beat. He often tried to teach me. Then he would say, "You don't follow the rhythm!" I had heard that one before and it bothered me.

Nevertheless, Maury took me to a fantastic ballroom in Manhattan called Roseland. It was a wonderland of music, dance, and romance. One melody was flowing into another and myriad lights were changing colors before our eyes. I was dazzled, as Maury held me in his arms and danced with me.

My experience was very different at Coney Island. I went with Maury and his friends to see the amusement park. When we got there, I knew it was a mistake. As I looked up and saw the rides spinning around into the sky, I couldn't believe my eyes. One ride was turning upside down, and it looked especially scary. And it made me wonder: *Are they out of their minds?* I stood there watching in awe. I didn't know how anyone would ever attempt something like that, but there were long lines of people waiting to get on.

In his inimitable way, Maury began coaxing me to go on the rides with him and wouldn't stop until I said yes. There I was, spinning upside-down on a ride that I thought would never end. I was frightened out of my mind. But it didn't stop there; terrified as I was, I went on other rides with Maury. Soon I found myself holding on to a bar for dear life. I was shaking on the outside while churning on the inside. It was devastating. Afterwards, I told myself: *Never again! Never again!*

One Saturday night, I was with Maury in his apartment. We were having a pleasant time when the doorbell rang. I was surprised to see Maury's friend, Matt, a guy who spent his spare time making sexual conquests, standing there with a pretty blond on his arm. They both were smiling jubilantly as Maury turned to me and said, "We have to get out of here; I loaned them the apartment for the night."

"What? You loaned them the apartment? How could you do that? You never told me...."

I was furious, as we left the building. "You're a good guy, Maury. You're doing great favors for your friends, but what about you and me? We have to leave your apartment so that Matt can bring his girlfriend over to do whatever. That's horrendous!"

Maury had a guilty look on his face, and he mumbled: "It won't happen again." We walked around the street for some time without saying a word. I didn't know what to do with my hurt and anger.

A few weeks later, Maury said he was taking me to see a new movie, "The Apartment." As we were watching it, Maury leaned over to make a comment on the Jack Lemmon character: "That guy reminds me of myself, loaning out his apartment. He's a good-natured schnook!" I couldn't agree more. I sensed an irritation in his voice and I wondered if Maury was going to give up being Mr. Good Guy.

Out of the blue, Maury started gesturing to me with his fingers. "This is sign language used by the deaf and I'm going to teach it to you." Why he wanted me to know it, I had no idea and I didn't ask. I attempted to learn it, but I wasn't doing very well. My heart wasn't in it. Eventually, he stopped, and I sighed a sigh of relief. I felt annoyed with myself. *Why can't I stand up for myself? Why am I allowing Maury to take me over like that?*

It seemed that Maury was trying to make a new person out of me. One of the things he wanted to do was to make me more aware of myself. He kept pointing out whatever he thought I needed to change. "Don't stare!" I was taken aback when he said that. "You have a wide-eyed stare. You got to do something about it." Then he opened his eyes wide and said, "This is what you look like." My goodness, did I look that weird? "I'll show you how to fix that easy enough." Maury lowered his eyes. "Now, you do it."

It wasn't so easy to do. I was used to that wide-eyed stare. I guess it began when I was a little girl and my mother was yelling and screaming at me. I would sit at attention, widen my eyes and stare at her. Over time it became a habit. I realized that I had to work at changing this behavior. I soon discovered how hard it was to lose that which had become so much a part of me.

When I least expected, Maury zeroed in on the way I wore my hair. I was used to wearing my hair long and straight or tied in a ponytail. He thought I could look better, so he introduced me to a beautician-friend and asked, "What can you suggest for Lenore?" She mentioned various hairstyles, including bangs, but Maury didn't like any one of them and neither did I. Soon, it was not an issue. I had my hair cut short in a pixie style, and when I looked in the mirror, I saw for myself how much better I looked.

On a Sunday afternoon, Maury said, "Let's drop over to see my mother and show her your haircut. She'll be happy to see the new you." I was all for it. However, when I saw Evie there, my heart skipped a beat. I thought I was in for more trouble, and I wanted to leave immediately, but I was in for a surprise. Evie came over to me and with a smile, she exuded a joy that made her nose wrinkle and eyes sparkle. "Oh, you cut your hair! You look so cute in short hair! Don't ever let it get long."

My goodness, she likes me now because of the way I look! From that moment on, the tension between Evie and me lifted and we could talk to each other with respect. Maury's mother soon chimed in, "You look great with that haircut, honey."

I was amazed: They all liked me better because I looked better. Maybe the way you appear on the surface is the way people will judge and treat you. *Wow!*

Maury took an intense interest in the way I dressed. "Your clothes are too matronly. They're too long." My spirits dropped. There was a time when I wore clothes that were too tight and sexy; now, my clothes were "too long and matronly." I was confused; I didn't know how to dress.

I came into the kitchen one morning wearing an outfit of brown and black. Maury was sitting there, having his breakfast when he saw me and went bonkers. "Those colors clash! They look atrocious! You can't go out like that! Take it off!" He was so excited; I didn't know what hit me. I became flustered and clammed up. What did I know about clashing colors?

It was frustration and more frustration. *Oh dear, what am I going to do?* Maury was now giving me advice about the kind of clothes I needed to wear to make me look "sharp." As we were walking down the street or riding in his car, Maury suddenly became animated. "Look at that girl over there. She's a sharp dresser. I want you to dress like that!" I stared at the girl. *Oh, my goodness, how can I ever dress like that?* I wasn't comfortable wearing the latest fashions; it didn't feel like me. As I thought about it, I felt really bad: *Why can't I be like that girl?*

I was overwrought with resentment; Maury kept telling me about things that needed to be "fixed" or made over, and most of the time, I felt I couldn't comply. I wanted to tell him to stop, but it was important for me to hear his opinions. I knew he had splendid taste and great ideas, and I wanted to improve in any way I could. So, it went on, and so did my frustration.

There was a time, however, when I said no on the spot. I liked to wear shoes with a medium high heel. It made me look a little taller than my 5'2" frame, and I liked that. But I must admit I wasn't very comfortable wearing them. Maury was cognizant of this. "I don't like the way you walk in those shoes, and besides, they're not good for your back. The American Girl shoe has a small heel and it would be ideal for you. Here, I'll give you money for the shoes."

Maury reached into his pocket, and I stopped him. "I don't like the American Girl shoe. It looks like something an old lady would wear." It amazed me that Maury pressured me to dress in the height of fashion, and yet he was urging me to wear something that wasn't very fashionable. But I didn't talk about it. I foolishly stuck with what I was wearing, even if it meant sore feet and a slight limp.

Soon, Maury had me on the trail of a new adventure: "Let's go up to Bear Mountain." I dreaded the thought of going up to the mountains, but there was something inside of me that was compelling me to experience it. *If I don't do this now, I'm going to miss out; I may regret it later.* Maury was begging me to go, and I couldn't put him off any longer. So I went. And how astonished I was to find myself in a rowboat on a lake with Maury at the oars. *Wow! Me in a rowboat! How did he ever get me to do that?* My heart was in my mouth as one thought ran through my mind: *How do I get out of here?* But I couldn't just get up and walk out of a rowboat. I managed to keep my panic down so that Maury wouldn't see me in such disarray. I believe my trust in Maury helped to tide me over this rough time on the water.

When I was on my own, life became more complicated for me. I had to face daily obstacles and I didn't have the necessary experience and knowledge to guide me. I still had to deal with the pain of my past and the way I grew up. Feelings from my childhood were spilling over and imprisoning me in the present. When I had all that I could handle, I went over to a chair in my mother's apartment and sat down; I couldn't move, nor could I put into words what I was feeling. I was lost. Maury would come over to me and take me in his arms. "Everything's okay, honey. Nothing's changed. It's okay…" I would hold Maury tight and cling to him. I so wanted to believe him.

I soon thought Maury was acting strange. He sat down with me at the kitchen table and playfully grabbed my hand; then he pushed my fingers back. It felt like a game at first, but soon he pressed harder and my fingers began to hurt. *Why is he doing this? And why is he laughing?* Somehow, I wasn't able to ask. As much as I wanted to cry "**Ouch!**" something inside me wouldn't allow it. I hated what he was doing, as I sat there, expressionless, holding in my pain. I was able to catch my breath when he stopped.

He continued to play this game with me. Soon, he was pressing my fingers more forcefully. Then Maury asked, with a quizzical look on his face: "Why can't you say 'Ouch'?" I stared at him, somewhat bewildered. It seemed as if Maury was giving me permission to say what was going on inside of me. In a loud, clear tone I hollered: "**OUCH!**" And he stopped. Just like that! It was a moment I will never forget. It was a breakthrough for me; I could actually express my pain. From then on, I would allow myself to voice "OUCH" when I had to, without any hesitancy. And Maury stopped bending my fingers.

I reflected back on this scene many times. I was so afraid to reveal my pain, Maury had to communicate to me that it was all right to say I was hurting. I had learned, at an early age, to squelch my feelings and suffer in silence. I was used to hiding my feelings from my mother. I could not show her my fear, anger or hurt, for she might get upset and go berserk. So, I went numb.

One evening in my mother's apartment, Maury was in bed when he heard me sobbing. I was having a terrible fight with my mother. In his long underwear, he stormed into the living room, ran for the belt from his pants and flung it at my mother. **"You don't love her!"** he shouted. **"You never loved her! That's why she has all these problems! I ought to beat you to a pulp!"**

My mother ran from him, and he ran after her. I started to cry, **"Please Maury, don't hit her!"** I don't know how many times I screamed, as I managed to get between them. He finally backed off, and I was relieved. It felt good to have Maury stand up for me, but who knows what would have happened if I hadn't stepped in between them.

Maury had a ferocious temper, and it frightened me. He could become enraged over something miniscule. I recall the time I was drying a pot with the paper towels that came from his store. He flew into a rage and screamed at the top of his lungs: **"Hey, look at all those paper towels you're wasting! That costs money!"**

I stopped what I was doing. I looked at him as if I had never seen him before. My mind went blank, and I just stood there. A few minutes later, when I came out of my trance, I saw my mother standing a few feet away from me. I stared at her, as she held her finger to her mouth making a "shush" sound. Was this my mother, who made my life a living hell as I was growing up, signaling for peace? I was utterly astonished.

Nevertheless, I was becoming closer to Maury, even though I was walking on eggs around him. I was very worried about stirring his wrath. I was in dread of causing a violent reaction, and it happened one day when I was in his apartment. We had a silly disagreement and Maury became enraged. He yelled at me, then grabbed a lamp off the table and swung it at me. I ducked and he soon came at me and slapped me hard across my face. With eyes blazing, he said, **"You little runt! How dare you tell me what to do!"**

I ran out into the street, shaking. Tears rolled down my cheeks, as I wandered around in a stupor. I finally wound up at my uncle's. When Will opened the door, he looked appalled to see me standing there, my face all red and puffed up. "What happened to you?"

I told him: "Maury was angry at me and he slapped me across the face." Will told me "Sit down in the living room." He ran into the kitchen and came back with an ice pack. I applied it immediately, and it took away some of the sting. Will then ran into the bedroom. I heard him angrily talking to himself, "I'm going to get him on the phone and tell him a thing or two!" But he couldn't get through. "Damn! It's busy! He must have taken the damn phone off the hook!" And he continued to dial Maury's number.

I was sitting in the living room, dazed, and hurting, with an ice pack on my face, when my aunt Jessie came in. I immediately told her what happened. She looked distressed and left the room. A few minutes later, I saw her putting on her coat. She nonchalantly said, "I'm going out now. I need a few items from the supermarket."

I stared at her in disbelief. "You're going to leave me like this — my face all red and swollen — and go out?"

Jessie retorted in a loud angry voice: **"I am not your mother!"**

I was shocked. What a thing to say at a time like that! It was another slap in the face—only this one was verbal. *Is this my aunt Jessie talking, my beloved aunt Jessie who I've grown to value so much? Is this the precious lady I've trusted with all of my secrets and painful feelings?*

As if her comment was not hurtful enough, she soon mumbled: "I should have gotten a divorce years ago. I never should have stayed in this crazy family!"

I didn't know this woman who stood before me.

Just then, my uncle came into the room. "What's going on? You're going out, Jessie? Look at Lenore. You're going to leave her like that?" He looked horrified. They soon quarreled, as I sat there watching them say unpleasant things to each other. Then Jessie left the house in a huff.

My world was turning upside down once again. Not only had Maury slapped me, but my aunt Jessie had lashed out at me with words that really stung. My uncle sat down on the couch beside me. There was a look of gloom written all over his face. "Lenore, you'd be a damn fool if you went back to him!"

His comments only made me feel worse. I said, "I have to leave." I had to get away and be by myself. My uncle looked worried as he walked me to the door. I had seen another side of Jessie. I also saw another side of Will.

I swore I was through with Maury. He had raised his hand to me. But I found myself missing him something terrible. I guess I was a glutton for punishment; I couldn't wait to see him again. But I didn't want to pick up the phone to call him and he was not contacting me.

I had a habit of standing at the window and watching for his station wagon. Sometimes I saw him loading it for his egg route; once or twice, I saw him parking late at night. And then I didn't see him at all. I became anxious; I wondered where he was and what he was doing.

I was very distressed when I went over to Amy and asked, "Where's Maury? Is he going out? Is he seeing someone?" Amy just sat there with a smirk on her face, as she continued to color her baby photos. I stared at her, and my heart was pounding. "Aren't you going to tell me what's going on?" She didn't respond. Did she know something she wasn't about to divulge? I suddenly felt an ache inside that made me want to cry. I couldn't find the words to tell her how awful I felt, as I stood there, watching her color her photos. Why couldn't she level with me? I thought she was my friend…

I reached out to a few of Maury's friends, but no one seemed to know his whereabouts, or perhaps they didn't want to become involved. When I turned to Cora, she said, "He loves you, Lenore, I know he does. You don't have any cause to worry." (I didn't know that Cora had been intimate with Maury and they maintained a cozy rapport, even as we spoke.)

Out of the blue, Maury returned with a sparkle in his eyes and a great big happy smile. He didn't waste any time asking: "When are we getting married, honey?" I sat there, stupefied, not knowing what to say. "Do you know when I fell in love with you, honey? When I saw your baby pictures. Anyone who can pose like that has to be pretty special!" The look on his face was sincere as his eyes gazed into mine. My spirits soared. A few caring words were enough to obliterate my pain.

Then he said: "You know, honey, I'm tired of living at your mother's. We spend too much time there. Let's go over to my place. I have things to do and besides, I want to be alone with you."

I had mixed feelings about this, but in a way, I thought it might be a good idea. From the time I arrived at his apartment until the time I left, his phone kept ringing. Each time I answered it, I heard a woman's voice. I looked at Maury with a hurt expression and asked: "Who are all these women?"

He laughed. "They're just old friends." I wanted to believe him, but just how "old" were they?

One day I was in his apartment and saw him writing on the back of a note pad. I asked, "What are you doing?"

He didn't answer, so I went over and playfully pulled it out of his hand. He chuckled, "I'm making up a list of all the women I've slept with. So far, I have thirty-four. And you're one of them!"

I couldn't believe my ears. "A list of women you slept with? Thirty-four women? You slept with thirty-four women? How can you say you love me?"

I sat down. I was bewildered. Maury broke out laughing once again, then got up from his chair and came over to sit down next to me. Endearingly, he put his arm around me. "Are you for real? You know I love you!"

There was a certain cruelty in his charm that now made those words meaningless. I got up from my chair, sad and confused, and went back to my mother's. I rationalized that he must have known those women long before he met me. It was a soothing thought, and it took away some of my hurt. But I still had an uncomfortable feeling whenever I ruminated about it.

On a warm, sunny afternoon, we were casually strolling down a street in our neighborhood. Maury looked pensive, and I asked him what he was thinking about. "I don't know why I love you. What do you do for me? What's so special about you?"

Ouch! What a terrible thing to say! It seemed just awful to have to explain to Maury why he should love me, but I made an effort. "I'm honest. I'm a caring person...." Suddenly it seemed so very wrong. Maury was reinforcing what I felt all my life: *No one will ever love me because I'm not good enough to be loved.* I didn't see him for days after that.

When I first met Maury, he told me, "I don't want any serious involvements." I thought about that a lot, but never brought it up; I was afraid to. I began to wonder if Maury was picking fights with me so that he could have the freedom to be on his own and see other women. Was I interrupting the life he wanted to have?

Soon Maury was at my door and we were together once again.

I was in Maury's store one day when he began to complain about heart palpitations. They became so severe, he asked me to go with him to a hospital emergency room. I became very frightened. *Will he be okay?*

The doctor on call examined him and gave him a pill. He said, "This should help," and then asked Maury, "What kind of work do you do?"

Maury said, "I own a grocery store."

I added, "Maury also has an egg route and makes deliveries to customers. He lifts heavy cartons of eggs, and spends long hours in the store."

The doctor admonished him. "You shouldn't be doing that. You're working too hard. You should think about changing your job. And you have to rest more. You have a heart murmur."

Maury quickly responded, "I had rheumatic fever when I was very young...."

Before he could finish, the doctor said, "That explains your condition. They didn't have penicillin back then."

He handed Maury a prescription and said, "Go home, take it easy, and you'll be all right."

But Maury didn't listen; he continued to schlep heavy cartons and remain active in his store. He was working as hard as ever and he kept having abnormal heartbeats. We were making regular trips to the Emergency Room, and Maury would see various doctors, only to disregard their words of caution. I would plead, "Maury, you can find other work. You can do better; I know you're capable. You're only killing yourself!" Maury continued to turn a deaf ear, as I continued to harp on this. Every time I watched him lift a carton, I thought to myself: *He's committing suicide and there's nothing I can do about it!*

There was a time Maury was so exasperated with me, he gave a loud holler: **"Mind your own business!"** There I was, worrying myself sick about him, and there he was, responding with anger and defiance. It was time to separate once again.

One evening Amy and her daughter were visiting me in my mother's apartment when the doorbell rang. It was Maury. I hadn't seen him for several weeks, and all of a sudden, I heard him speaking to my mother: "I have to see Lenore — I need to see her right away!" He sounded very excited, and I wondered what this was all about. I hurried to the door, and Maury anxiously said: "I have to talk to you."

I said, "I have company. Amy's here." As I looked at the eagerness on his face I said, "Okay. I'll be right down." For the life of me, I couldn't imagine what would drive him into such frenzy. I excused myself, ran down the stairs, and met Maury in front of my building.

"I miss you. I've been thinking about you. I just came from my sister's wedding and I want to marry you as soon as possible!"

Maury looked tense and worried. Why would he suddenly make such a demand? It felt very strange. "I'll have to think about it," I said. "I can't discuss it right now. I have to get back upstairs."

Maury didn't seem to be listening. He pressured, "When will you let me know?"

I thought this was absurd. We weren't even on speaking terms. I didn't think of asking him, in the moment, *Why the urgency?* Instead, I said, "I'll get back to you." I returned to my mother's apartment, agitated, and confused.

The next time I saw Maury, we spoke about marriage. He was more like his usual, carefree self as he smilingly said, "What do you have to lose? If it doesn't work out, we'll get a divorce. It's as simple as that!"

Somehow, in the moment, it made sense.

After all those fights and separations, this did not feel like the love I dreamed about in my childhood. But I couldn't resist the idea of joining with Maury in the union of marriage. My gut feeling told me: *Don't do it!* But my heart had a mind of its own.

As my wedding day approached, I was flooded with myriad thoughts about wedding ceremonies. From the time I was a small child and became aware of traditional weddings, they had no appeal for me. I had no desire to be married in a white wedding gown with a multitude of people gathered around in what appeared to be a very superficial setting. From as far back as I can remember, I always felt that marriage is a sacred union where two souls are joined together in a pledge of love before God. It is a warm, tender, intimate moment to be shared between two people. Why would I want a crowd witnessing it as if it were some kind of spectator sport?

On a day in May, I wore a simple pink and white lace dress, and along with my mother and a few friends, I went with Maury to a justice of the peace. There, I became Maury's wife after a tumultuous three-year relationship.

So, there I was, at twenty-three, a married woman. I was finally leaving my mother and moving in with Maury. Was I doing the right thing? Only time would tell…

53

Married Life

It was the evening of our wedding. Maury and I were having dinner in our apartment and I noticed he was staring at me in a peculiar way. Soon, he had a big smile on his face. "You know, honey, you chew your food just like Molly."

What a nauseating thought! I felt so sick to my stomach, I wanted to get up and walk out then and there, but I didn't; it was our special day. I was fuming, but I didn't show it. *What kind of cruelty is this? How can he speak to me about his ex-wife on the day we are married? It's abominable!*

I found the voice to say: "Don't tell me you're starting that Molly business again."

Maury laughed. "I'm only kidding, honey. I like the way you chew your food."

I didn't feel like eating anymore. He was playing his game again, but this time I didn't show how really annoyed I was. I continued to have my meal as if nothing had happened, and Maury stopped talking about his ex-wife. I thought to myself: *Why can't this guy let me love him?*

Whether Maury's behavior became outlandish or not, I tried to cope as best I could. We both had our respective problems, and sometimes they would intertwine, but we managed to get through them. We had some good times and some very difficult times. I was still glad I made the move. I was glad to be away from my mother. I was surprised by how nicely I was adjusting to the transition from my mother's apartment to Maury's. I didn't have any negative feelings about leaving her. In fact, it felt good to be on my own in a lovely, small apartment that was neat and clean, with a charm of its own. I enjoyed looking at the décor, as I walked around admiring Maury's excellent taste. However, I kept bumping into a great big empty birdcage in our little hallway. It looked so lonely, so deserted, standing there all by itself, I wondered what could be done about it. I asked Maury, "Do you think you would like to get a bird?"

Maury staunchly replied, "No, I don't want any more birds."

I soon began to think about what I could do to make the cage into something unusual and pretty. Suddenly a thought came to me. I ran down the street to the local Woolworth's and purchased a bunch of artificial flowers and greens. Then I rushed home and began to decorate the cage. When I finished, I was delighted with the way it looked. When Maury came home, he looked at it and smiled. "I see we have a flower garden in a birdcage. I like it. It's a novel idea." I reveled in the beauty of my little "flower garden" as I walked around the apartment.

All in all, things were going pretty well. Then, one evening, I was about to put a potato in the oven. I opened the oven door and with a match in my hand, I attempted to light the gas, but it did not ignite. So, I tried once more. I stuck my head into the oven to get a better view, and I have no recollection of what followed because it happened so fast. The next thing I knew, parts of my hair were singed, and I was on my way to the hospital.

At the hospital, I panicked as I was checked for burns. Fortunately, I escaped a catastrophe. I was warned, "Do not light the stove a second time when gas has escaped. First, close the jet and wait a few minutes to make sure the gas has dissipated. Then go ahead and light it again."

I was shaky for a while after that and I had a temporary dread of lighting the oven. Maury came home one night, upset. "Who were you talking to? There's a rumor going around that after marrying me you stuck your head into the oven to commit suicide."

"That's incredible! I did tell a few people about the incident, but who would make up such a weird story? Only a mean-spirited person would do something like that."

Maury looked annoyed and said, "I think I know who it is."

He was about to say more when I stopped him. "Maury, I don't want to know. I think the whole thing is ridiculous. I want to put it out of my mind." We didn't discuss it any further.

I felt a lot of stress during this time. I was frequently getting sick, very similar to the days of my childhood. After seeing a doctor, I wound up taking penicillin and cough syrup. Maury said, "I'm sending my mother over to take care of you."

I wasn't sure that was a good idea, especially since his mother and I were not bosom buddies and could not establish a real rapport. Nevertheless, she came over and served me hot tea in bed. She broke out laughing: "You're just like a little baby—you're always getting a sore throat or a cold." I couldn't dispute it. It seemed that the more stress I was under, the more prone I was to coming down with a respiratory infection.

I continued to go for therapy. I talked and talked about whatever was on my mind, but the sessions didn't seem to be going anywhere. Nevertheless, therapy had become an important part of my life. If Maury was home when I got back from a session, he would laugh and say, "Hi, honey. Did you get your shot in the arm?"

I didn't think it was funny. In fact, I found it annoying, as I tried to convey to him what therapy meant to me. I struggled to come up with the right words and I wound up saying: "I'm trying to find myself." But something about that didn't feel right. And I wondered: *Why am I going?*

One day, a thought hit me that made me laugh out loud; Maury was comparing my therapy to a drug, and in some way, he may have been right. I had become very dependent on seeing my therapist as if, by some kind of magic, he could take away everything that was wrong and make it right. Sometimes I came away feeling more positive and self-assured in the moment, and at other times my spirits were low. In any event, the effects of therapy were short-lived and soon I was craving another "shot in the arm."

Maury had a fantastic ability to laugh and make light of things that seemed earth shattering to me. I think this playful quality was a part of his charm that drew people to him. He could even make my mother laugh, and that's saying a lot.

But then, there was this not-so-carefree side. I recall how upset Maury was when he saw me walking around the house wearing pantyhose that had runs. He let out a scream: **"Hey, take that off! I don't want you wearing that. It's ripped!"** I became flustered and immediately pulled off the torn stockings, fearing he was going to pull them off himself.

"I don't want my wife going around like that. You're not a poor girl.'

Maury's outburst overwhelmed me and I didn't know how to respond. My heart was leaping in my chest as I felt a hot sweat pass through me. It didn't bother me to wear torn pantyhose, so why was Maury having a fit over it?

Maury continued, "I want you to have nice things. I will buy you clothes—nice, expensive clothes—whatever you want when I make some money. You'll be able to hold your head high when you leave the house…"

I was very uncomfortable when Maury talked about this. I didn't feel that I should have "nice, expensive clothes." I winced at the thought of it and I didn't know why. And it troubled me. Why would I not want "nice, expensive clothes?"

About this time, Maury was agitated about still something else. "…And I don't want us living like your uncle and aunt. He sits at his desk and she sits at hers—that's no way to live." This came out of the blue and I was startled. I had no idea that Maury had an aversion to the way my uncle and aunt lived. Although they both worked and were busy most of the time, they appeared to be very close when they were together. I admired the lifestyle of Will and Jessie and I wanted to copy their way of life.

"…And I don't want any wife of mine working." I found this very disturbing. I had no idea that Maury felt that way. I wanted to work. It had become very important for me to be productive in some way. Sometimes I felt I needed it to survive. To placate Maury and avoid an argument, I simply said, "I'll stop working, but not right now."

Soon, Maury went around the house gleefully singing: "I can't give you anything but love—and a baby…" I didn't think it was funny. I nervously said, "I don't want a baby, Maury. We agreed to that. You know how I feel." He laughed it off, but I was very uneasy. Although we weren't sexually active, I worried that he might try to impregnate me to keep me at home. The thought of it sent me into a tizzy.

I felt a need to get away from it all, but what could I do that would take my mind off my problems and make me feel better? I thought about seeing Amy again. She and Lucy had moved to Yonkers, near the baby photography studio where Amy was now working. I hadn't seen them in quite a while. I suddenly had an urge to visit them and see how they were doing.

And I was pleasantly surprised. Amy was smiling and in great spirits. There was a glow about her that I hadn't seen before. I said, "Amy, you look beautiful. You lost weight. You fixed your teeth. You look utterly fantastic. I'm so happy for you. What has caused this amazing transformation?"

She joyfully went on to tell me about her steamy sexual encounter and then she added: "I had wounded feelings after Jay left me and I guess I needed to prove to myself that men could still find me attractive."

I didn't think she could resolve her problems by using her sexuality that way; it sounded like a superficial outlet for healing her wounded pride. But who was I to tell Amy how to live?

Lucy soon joined us, and how delightful it was to see her again. She was somewhat older, quite a bit taller, but sweet as ever. For a while, the three of us sat around and chatted, and then I asked Amy if Lucy could come over and spend time with Maury and me. With a smile, Amy gave her approval as Lucy's eyes lit up with joy. These were happy moments for me as I observed that both Amy and Lucy appeared to be on a better, more positive path. I came away feeling good about my visit with them.

In the weeks to come, Lucy became a frequent visitor in our home. I loved having her over and Maury seemed to be enjoying her visits as well. Then one day Maury said to me, "I want more time alone with my wife." I was somewhat taken aback, but I respected his wishes. I cut back on seeing Lucy, but when I was with her, I treasured the moments we spent together. Lucy was still only a child, but I was amazed that she was able to step out of her child self and become adult-like with a depth of understanding and insights far beyond her years. Her beauty of spirit and ability to care never ceased to fascinate me. I considered her a precious gem in my life.

My time with Lucy, however, was short-lived and Maury remained busy at his egg route and in the store. I wasn't working, and I walked around my neighborhood feeling lonely and more useless than usual. I wondered what could give my life some meaning. I scanned the classified section of the New York Times and came upon a position to work part-time for a prominent Manhattan psychiatrist in the East 60's. I applied for the job, never thinking I would get it, but I still went for the interview. I met Dr. Russell, an elderly gentleman with a ruddy complexion and graying hair. I liked him right away, and I guess he liked me, too, for he hired me on the spot. My job was to greet clients and maintain office records. The salary was meager, but that didn't bother me. The setting seemed ideal.

There was no pressure on me to perform. I sat at my desk with not much to do. When Dr. Russell was free, he came out and chatted with me. He proudly told me he had treated many show business people over the years and was counseling a well-known radio personality at the time. I was very impressed. To think that a psychiatrist, who worked with top-notch celebrities, wanted to hire me, and spend time talking with me!

As the weeks passed, I noticed that Dr. Russell was giving 2 to 4 hour sessions to some clients and I wondered about that. I finally found the nerve to ask him why he was giving some clients such long sessions. He revealed a disaster occurred when he stuck to the traditional fifty-minute hour: a patient left his office, went out into the street, and committed suicide. I was stunned. I could see why he wouldn't want to stop a session just because "Time is up!"

Dr. Russell soon began talking to me about personal things in his life. I was amazed that he could be so open and outspoken with me, a complete stranger, but I was thrilled about it. He trusted me, and that made me feel really good inside.

If Maury was upset about me working for the doctor, he never mentioned it. He continued to work long hours at his store and egg route. He came home tired, but usually in good spirits. The happy moments I shared with Maury were precious to me. When he was nice, he was the very best. But when he became the Maury who was enraged over myriad nothings, I was torn up inside and didn't know how to handle my fluctuating feelings. The climate of our relationship was continuously changing from the sublime to the ridiculous. It was like being on an emotional roller coaster; I never knew when it would be heading for the sky or plummeting towards the ground. I guess this was nothing new; it's just that I had developed more awareness about the way we were living, and I wanted something better.

At times, I had thoughts about leaving Maury but then I felt the most horrible sensation in the pit of my stomach. As unhappy as I was, I felt it would be worse without him. I was emotionally tied to him as I had been to my mother.

When I came home from work one evening, I found a note on the kitchen table: "Thanks for the sandwich. I want you to know I'm very happy since I'm married to you." I was surprised that Maury felt that way; I thought he was unhappy, too.

I soon found out that Maury was about to do something that I would never expect from him or anyone else. A few days before my twenty-fifth birthday my mother said to me: "I thought you should know that Maury is planning a surprise party for you."

What is a surprise party?

Hedda explained it to me, and then I really froze. *Oh, my goodness, I'll be walking into a dark room, and suddenly, the lights will go on. Everyone will be singing Happy Birthday, and I'll be standing there, the center of attention. What am I going to do?* The thought of it sent shivers through me. I had to find a way to stop it.

On the night of my birthday I intentionally came home earlier than usual. I put on the lights in the hallway, and as I was about to enter the living room, Maury screamed: "The lights! The lights! Turn off the lights!" But it was too late.

I watched Maury storm out of the living room and make a mad dash into the bedroom, slamming the door behind him. I wanted to follow him in, but something told me it would be a mistake. Suddenly, I felt awful. I had no idea Maury would become so upset. I had spoiled his surprise. He tried to create a perfect moment for me, and I ruined it. I was only thinking about myself. But then again, I was very uncomfortable with people and parties; I might even say I was terrified. Deep down, I had a gnawing feeling that nobody liked me and this alone put me on edge. These were my little secrets that I would not divulge to anyone.

So, there I was, lingering in the hallway of our apartment. I didn't know what to do. My heart was pounding in my chest as I slowly entered the living room. There was a great big cake awaiting me, and a room full of people. I was flustered, but I didn't want my guests to see just how flustered I was, so I smiled and put on a happy face as I greeted them.

Soon I excused myself. *What's happening with Maury?* I walked towards the bedroom as Maury's mother was coming out. She looked very upset. "Maury's crying. He's sitting on the floor and stamping his feet. And he's crying." Suddenly, I was feeling Maury's hurt as if it were mine. I wanted to fix it and make it go away, but I didn't know how. I stood there, dumbfounded.

Maury's mother went back into the bedroom, and my mother followed her in. After a few minutes, Maury came out. I went over to him and said: "A surprise party for me! I never had a party in my life. How wonderful that you would do this for me. I want to thank you so much." I threw my arms around his neck and kissed him. Slowly, a smile came to his face. I could feel his distress melting away and so was mine. Together, we joined our guests.

I looked around the living room and marveled at it. There were decorations all over the place. Huge multi-colored letters were dangling from wall to wall that said:

HAPPY BIRTHDAY LENORE

On a large table that extended from one wall to another was an overflow of food. It was set up like a buffet and included corned beef, pastrami, and coleslaw, amongst other delicacies. A variety of breads were spread out all over the table, as well as soft drinks and liquor. It was a breathtaking sight to behold. I had never seen anything like that, and it was all for me on my birthday!

I was in the spotlight and I didn't know how to handle all the attention that was being lavished upon me. At first, I felt knotted up inside, but then there were moments when I found myself eating it all up. How very exciting it was! I recall how I would clam up at Maury's family gatherings, but this was not just any social event— it was my party, and it was very special to me. I was the guest of honor, and I had to play the role as best I could. Much to my surprise, once I got into it, I found I could steal some happy moments that came my way.

Grandma came over to me with a bewildered look on her face. "I never saw anything like this. It's like a wedding." I had never been to a wedding, so I didn't know what she was talking about. But I didn't want to know; there was so much going on around me, right then and there. People were talking, laughing, and running back and forth filling up their platters with food. My goodness, they were stuffing themselves as if there was no tomorrow!

Maury's friend, Nat, came in with two girls, one on each arm. Grandma whispered to me: "Look at the way the three of them are eating. There's pastrami and coleslaw hanging out of their mouths!" I was too overwhelmed in the moment to notice any of this. The sound of sweet, soothing music filled the air as I danced with Maury, and then with Lucy. These were some of the most enjoyable moments of my evening.

Later, as the guests were about to leave, one of Maury's friends, Jacob, a tax lawyer, who had been drinking a little too much, started to sway as he sang to his wife, "I had a hat when I came in, I'll have a hat when I go out…" I thought it was so funny, for the hat was perfectly perched on his head. As he was dancing towards the door, a conga line was forming, and the guests were following him out. That was something to see.

When all the guests were gone and we were cleaning up the mess together, I was thinking about the event that had just occurred. I was touched. Maury gave me my very first party; he did something very special for me. He created an atmosphere of music, laughter and casual talk that was warm and loving. And I was with people who came to acknowledge me on my birthday. I wasn't used to having anything like that in my life; I couldn't believe it was real and happening to me. I don't think I was able to truly appreciate it as much as I would have liked to, because it was so very different from anything I had ever experienced. But I will say it was a marvelous evening that I will never forget.

A few weeks later, I was sick in bed with another virus, when the doorbell rang. I heard Maury speaking to someone in the hall. "Lenore's home?" With a broad smile, Jay walked into the bedroom and sat down on the edge of the bed. "I thought you were working. I never expected you'd be home. What a pleasant surprise!"

I was also surprised. There was something different about Jay. Not only was he thinner and more relaxed, but his voice had a gentler tone. That hard edge was gone, and he was smiling. *What happened to Jay?*

Maury soon joined us, and an exuberant Jay said, "It's really great to see both of you. I know it's been a long time. Things didn't work out between Mindy and me. It's pretty much over with Amy, too." I detected a tone of sadness in his voice, but also an unusual calm. Soon, he revealed the reason for his visit. "I need a place to stay, and I wonder if you could put me up for say … three weeks?"

"Of course, it's all right. You can stay for as long as you want." Maury said without hesitation. But I wasn't sure I wanted a visitor. Nevertheless, I chimed in, "We'd love to have you."

Many a time I was alone with Jay and we got to talk. For the first time, I felt really comfortable in his presence. He showed an interest in what I had to say, and I found it easy to express my feelings to him. We could talk about anything, and even when we didn't talk, I could feel camaraderie. Jay had his heartaches and I had mine. It takes one lost soul to recognize another.

At the end of three weeks, Jay made an announcement: "It's time for me to go. I appreciate all you've both done for me." And, just like that, he was gone. He didn't tell Maury or me what his plans were. Maury said, "I have a hunch he's going home to his wife and daughter." I was already missing him, and the brief friendship we shared. How I hated to see him go.

Maury was now looking very tired. He had put on a few pounds and he appeared to be aging. His spirits were low and I could see that he wasn't well. He continued to complain about his heart skipping beats, and he was taking naps whenever he could.

Maury made an appointment to see a cardiologist. I felt it was long overdue. I looked forward to going with him, but when the time came, I was once again sick in bed with yet another virus. I was upset and angry with myself: *Why did this have to happen now?*

When Maury returned from the doctor, he had a very casual attitude. "Nothing new—same old, same old." He didn't want to talk about his condition, so I decided not to probe. But I was worried. *What did the doctor say?*

Maury soon was back at work. As I saw him loading heavy cartons into his station wagon, I once again said to myself: *He's killing himself! If only there was something I could say or do to make him stop this insanity.* But whom was I kidding? It was pretty clear that Maury had to do things his own way.

More and more, Maury was sitting on the floor in front of the TV screen. Sometimes he was slumped over, and sometimes he was leaning against his recliner. I sensed something was very wrong. One day I approached him: "Maury, how come you're sitting on the floor? What about your new recliner?"

I was jostled by his response: "I can breathe better this way, I'm more comfortable in this position." He did not say more and again, I did not probe; I knew he didn't like to talk about his health. But each time I saw him bent over like that, I felt a pang in my heart.

Maury soon complained, "I don't know how I'm going to pay off my debts. I can't work like I used to. The money's not coming in, and the creditors are at my door. I don't know what to do…"

"Why don't you try to sell baby photos like Jay taught you? I think you would do very well. You have the personality for it."

"I've been thinking about it for some time now," Maury replied. "I can't go on like this. I have to give up my business."

Finally! I was thrilled. The part of me that still cared for Maury was revived in that moment. I now had new hope—hope that we would be able to make a fresh start.

Maury soon found work as a salesman with the baby photography studio. He was going into people's homes with pictures of their babies and he was making great sales. He looked handsome in a suit, and he was glowing with enthusiasm as he said, "Why didn't I do this sooner?"

"I've been telling you that all along."

Maury soon asked me to send out appointment cards to his customers. I thought that was a great idea. One night, however, he came home irate: "I went to see my customers, but they weren't home. How come you didn't send out the cards I gave you?"

I was taken aback. "What are you talking about? You never gave me any cards."

He then reached into his jacket and his face turned red. "Well, what do you know? They're right here in my pocket."

When Maury started fights with me, and he was at fault, he made up for it by buying me something to wear. I recall two items I especially liked: a pair of plaid velveteen slacks and a long white cardigan sweater. My goodness, I could have had a brand new wardrobe based upon Maury's outbursts!

More and more, I began to see Maury in a different light. So many things he once said that seemed so "cute" to me were now very annoying. In many ways, he appeared childish and immature, and his magnificent charm was becoming stale. Thoughts kept running through my mind: *If only he were a deep thinker like his friend, Jay; if only he were an intellect like my uncle Will.* But he wasn't.

I soon found myself picking on Maury for the most miniscule things. I believe this was my way of retaliating for his callousness and neglect of my feelings. Afterwards, I became irritated with myself because I wasn't dealing directly in the moment with my feelings of anger and hurt. And it continued like this.

Maury came home one evening with a wooden carving board that had an inscription on it: "When I did well, I heard it never. When I did ill, I heard it ever." That bothered me, maybe because it was true.

I went over to my uncle Will with complaints about Maury. With a look of disgust on his face, he bluntly lashed out: "You're gutless! You're just like your father. If you can't live with Maury, then pick yourself up and get the hell out of there. Shit or get off the pot!" I wanted to cry. Instead I sat there silently in awe of him. So, what was I going to do?

I had a fantasy. I dreamed about being held and kissed by a warm, wonderful, sensitive man. There would be a genuine understanding between my beloved and me, with never a harsh word spoken. We would have a unique harmony in a union of love. My marriage to Maury was nothing like that, and I was deeply disappointed.

I allowed myself to feel how very unhappy I was with Maury, and that I had been pulling away from him for some time. I became aware that I no longer was in love with him; I wasn't even sure that I liked him. I began to give more thought to leaving, and when I found enough inner strength, I cried: "I'm sorry, Maury, I made an awful mistake. I never should have married you!" And I ran out the door. I went back to my mother, frustrated, and anguished, after approximately two and a half years of marriage.

54

Afterwards

I was back at my mother's, thinking about how Maury glibly said: "If it doesn't work out, we'll get a divorce." When Maury asked me to marry him, I felt it was something I had to do. Now I was kicking myself for not trusting my intuition that told me, "Don't do it!"

Maury was constantly calling me at my mother's, but I wasn't about to speak to him. I knew he would be coaxing me to come home and I didn't want to deal with it. My immediate goal was to avoid a confrontation. Eventually I did meet up with him and we talked. The only thing that came out of our meeting was the understanding that I needed some time for myself to think things over. Maury did not take favorably to this, but he didn't argue the point. We parted on amiable terms.

Early one morning I received a phone call from Maury. "I have some music I want you to hear; it has a fantastic sound, and you're going to love it. Come on over!" I wasn't keen on this, but he sounded so excited I became curious. When I got there, he put the record on and exclaimed: "Listen to the rhythm, the beat, the sound—it's fantastic! It's going to be a best seller." Maury was right; I loved the sound of the bossa nova, Desifinado, as performed by Stan Getz. It did become a big hit. Thereafter, whenever I heard it, I couldn't help but think about the first time I listened to Desifinado with Maury. How ecstatic he was, and how jubilant I felt to hear music like that.

In the weeks that followed, I saw Maury several times at our apartment. Each time, I noticed a young man sleeping on the couch. I thought it peculiar, and I asked Maury: "Who is that guy? Every time I come over, I see him sleeping on the couch."

Maury laughed. "He's a friend of mine. He's just tired. Don't worry, he's a good guy."

It wasn't long before I got another phone call from Maury. This time he was very upset. "There was a robbery in the apartment. Many things are missing: your Ampro tape recorder, the pearl ring…." And he went on.

"What? My Ampro? My uncle, my grandmother, even Hedda, all chipped in to buy me that great big tape recorder for my birthday. It cost over $200. And my ring…"

Maury continued to talk about the robbery, but I didn't hear a thing he said. I was becoming more and more agitated as he spoke.

"This is terrible. I'm coming right over!"

I rushed out into the street. Tears were running down my cheeks, and I was barely able to see where I was going. When I saw Maury, I hollered at him. "I'm not surprised at all. I was very suspicious of your friend lying on the couch, sleeping, every time I came over. Your friend seemed very strange to me. I even mentioned that to you, but you pooh-poohed it. He was eyeing up the place, waiting for an opportunity to rob you."

Maury sadly agreed. "I guess I should have known better."

"Yes, you should have, but now it's too late."

I went back to my mother's feeling ripped up inside. Maury was soon calling me again, "I miss you very much and want you to come home. Let's meet and talk about getting back together…" I didn't think it was a good idea, but finally, I gave in, more to appease him than anything else. We met in a Howard Johnson's on Fordham Road, and it was almost as if we spoke two different languages. He had grown a mustache, and I thought he looked terrible. I told him that, as he reached for a cigarette. Suddenly, he seemed like someone I didn't know. It was a meeting that was over before it began. I wished I had listened to my instincts that told me: *Don't go!*

I was miserable. Being in the house with my mother only made me feel worse. The sound of her voice stirred up anger in me and I couldn't handle it. It was like being back in my childhood with her.

I was so glad I had a job to go to. Even if things were slow, I always found something to do. At times Dr. Russell paced back and forth between rooms with a troubled look on his face and his hands clasped behind his back. And I would hear him say, "I forgot again! Oh, my God! I hope I'm not losing my mind!" I was shocked to hear a psychiatrist talking like that. He didn't seem to be aware of my presence, and that I was overhearing everything he said.

One day Dr. Russell nervously said, "They're in my house! I can't go home tonight."

"What?"

"I don't go home when my in-laws are there."

I was astonished. An educated, professional man like that, afraid to go home because his in-laws were visiting? He added: "I'm going to have to sleep here again on the couch."

I didn't know what to say. How do you respond to a psychiatrist about his problems when he's supposed to be the one with all the answers? I wondered what he would have advised a client if the client came to him with the same problem.

As I observed Dr. Russell, I realized that a professional could be as fragile and burdened down with troubles as anyone else. I usually put professional people (especially psychiatrists) on a pedestal and looked up to them as if they were holy. How wrong I was! But I was learning. Soon it became clear to me that while it may be easy to be objective with someone else's problems, it can be oh so difficult if the problems are your own—even if you are a psychiatrist.

As the doctor kept on sharing bits and pieces of his life with me, I found it intriguing that a prominent man, like Dr. Russell, could turn to a person like myself, with no formal education or degree, and trust me with so many of his intimate problems. I couldn't get over it; he was confiding in me as if I were his best friend. I came out of his office feeling a sense of wonderment and awe.

I frequently had an urge to talk to Dr. Russell about the things that were troubling me, but I managed not to reveal any of my own problems. I didn't feel right using my boss for psychological consultations.

I soon had a big surprise. Nat came to pay me a visit. There he was at the door, in his usual long dark overcoat, hat on head, umbrella in hand, and a solemn, worried expression on his face. With concern, he said to my mother: "I was thinking of Lenore and wanted to see how she's doing."

It was wonderful to see Nat. He was the big brother I wanted but never had. He was so nice and sweet, with a great big loving heart. He usually was very serious, so when he broke out into a huge cat grin, I burst into laughter, too. I never ceased to be amazed at the things he would say, especially when he felt strongly about something; he just had to get it off his chest. His friends knew him as "an amateur social worker" because he was constantly reaching out to help others—including me.

"Lenore, I want to take you out to a singles' dance. I think you'll like it, and you'll meet plenty of people." A confirmed bachelor in his thirties, Nat enjoyed the social scene and he wanted me to experience it as well. I thought it might be a good idea, so I joined him one night. He soon got lost in the crowd, and I was left on my own. I didn't like it at all. There were so many young women standing around, waiting for someone to come over and ask them to dance. I thought the whole scene was pathetic, and there I was, a part of it. No one came over to me and I felt old feelings of rejection and loneliness. For the rest of the evening, I moved around demoralized. I couldn't wait for Nat to take me home.

Later, I told Nat that I was very uncomfortable at the dance. Nat persisted: "You're over-reacting. You have to get out more. You just might meet someone who could appreciate you, unlike your husband."

Although I knew Nat had my best interests at heart, I was dubious about going out with him to more singles' events. Each time I had the same revulsion. The whole singles' scene made me sick to my stomach. When Nat asked me to go once again, I declined. "It's just not my cup of tea."

Soon, we were sitting and talking when Nat, looking especially intense, said: "I was just thinking. You should consider going to college. This office work is not for you…"

College? Oh No! "Nat, it's a great thought, but I don't think I can do that."

I could see Nat was disappointed, but he did not give up. "I'm going to make another suggestion to you. Have you ever thought about law? I think you have the ability to be a great lawyer."

"You got to be kidding!"

Later, Nat was back with still another idea: "I think you should find a man who can take care of you. Get a divorce from Maury and go down to the Waldorf Astoria. Sit in the lobby and see if you can meet someone who has a lot of money. You're a frail girl, and you need someone to look after you, someone with money."

I thought that was the most ridiculous thing I ever heard. "Me, at the Waldorf, looking for someone with money? No way!" I laughed it off and said, "I don't think so."

Nat countered, "You're making a big mistake."

Nat was not a stupid guy, but in his attempt to be helpful, he frequently said things that didn't make any sense to me. But I knew he meant well. Because I knew he was so genuine and caring, I regarded him as a very special person in my life. Nat and I continued to be best of friends, enjoying each other's company whenever we got together.

I was moping around the house one night, feeling sorry for myself, when I received a phone call. I was surprised and excited to hear Jay's voice. He was feeling gloomy and wanted to say hello. We resumed our friendship at a time when we both needed to lift our spirits off the ground. Jay would tell me, "You're my tranquilizer," and I would respond, "I feel pretty much the same about you." I was so much more alive and relaxed when Jay was in my world.

About this time, I was walking down the street near my home, when I bumped into Maury's friend, Joe, the cabdriver. He had the most exuberant look on his face, and I sensed he had some exciting news to tell me. Sure enough, he couldn't wait to blurt out: "Maury has a girlfriend. He's going out and having one hell of a time!" I was not shocked to hear this; in fact, I expected it. I was now motivated to ask Maury for a divorce. I rushed to the phone and called him; I said I wanted to see him right away. He told me to come on over, and within minutes I was there.

Maury seemed happy to see me, but I can't say I felt the same. We had barely begun to talk when Maury joyfully boasted: "I just paid off my bills, honey. Aren't you happy? No more creditors! No more money problems!" I was startled; I knew he had no money. I asked him how he was able to do that, and he laughed, "You know the money you put into our joint account? I took out five hundred dollars and used it for my debts!"

I was infuriated because he didn't tell me; he just went ahead and did it. But I tried to conceal my feelings. I wasn't there to talk about money or to argue with him.

"When are you coming home? I miss you, honey." He made a facial expression as if he were about to cry. "Look at my tears, honey; they're all for you."

I felt his insincerity and I was flooded with anger. "Those are crocodile tears! You're not fooling me. You've been running around with women ever since I've known you. I happen to know you're seeing a woman right now. How can you have the nerve to ask me to come back?"

Maury broke out into his usual laughter. "You're catching on to me, honey."

As I stared at him, he looked like a laughing devil. I picked myself up and ran for the door. I was out of there as fast as my legs could carry me. I never told him what I came over for.

A few weeks later, I decided to pay Maury a surprise visit. I vowed that nothing would stop me this time from speaking about divorce. I turned my key in the lock and walked into the living room. Maury was slumped over on the floor, in front of his TV set. He looked pale and drawn, and in a weak voice, he murmured: "I'm sick. I can hardly breathe, and it's hard to walk."

I became very upset. "What are you doing about it?"
"Nothing."

"You have to see a doctor, Maury. You can't go on like this. My boss is not only a psychiatrist, but he's also a medical doctor. I think you should see him the first thing in the morning. I'll go with you." Reluctantly, Maury agreed. When I went back to my mother's that night, I couldn't stop thinking about him. He looked very ill, and I knew he needed immediate medical care. I was thankful I came in when I did. I worried that he would not go with me to see Dr. Russell as he promised.

In the morning, there was a knock on my mother's door, and it was Maury. He still appeared very ill, but he managed to make it over. He came in and looked around the apartment as if he had never seen it before, and sadly said, "I don't know how I could have ever lived here. I must have loved you very much."

I was touched. There was sincerity in his voice, and I suddenly forgot all the bad things I said about him. I wished I were back in time with him. I missed the warm moments we shared together, even the crazy fights we had. And now, we were two strangers on our way to a doctor's office.

As soon as Dr. Russell examined Maury, he said: "You're on the verge of congestive heart failure! You need to go to a hospital right away. Don't wait!"

Heart failure? I panicked. Then my mind went blank and I stood there in a fog. I soon heard Dr. Russell repeat, "Get him to a hospital. There is no time to lose!" His words echoed in my head, and soon we were in a cab, zooming towards the one hospital we were familiar with: Jacobi Hospital in the Bronx.

At the hospital, the attending doctor said, "He's going into congestive heart failure. It's good you came in when you did!" Then Maury was taken away, and I was left standing there. I was filled with anxiety and fear. I wondered if I would ever see him again.

I tuned out everything around me as I nervously sat in the waiting room. Suddenly, it seemed as if we had never parted. The only place I wanted to be was with Maury.

And I continued to wait. I was still pretty much in a fog when I saw Maury again. I heard him say, "They took two quarts of liquid out of my lungs." Maury continued to speak, but I couldn't take it in.

When I returned the following day, I heard some more alarming news from Maury, "They took some more tests. They want to remove a valve in my heart. They say it's calcified, and they want to put in a plastic one."

Maury became very quiet as he stared out the window. I was in turmoil, as I sat by his bedside and realized the implications of open-heart surgery. This was a big risk. I knew he was frightened, but I didn't know what I could say that would be comforting or reassuring to him. I sat there watching him staring out the window, with a blank expression on his face. My feelings of helplessness only made me ache more. Soon I heard Maury say: "They don't want to do surgery right now. They say I'm not ready for it. They want me to lose a few pounds. I'll be here for a while before they do anything."

I was glad to hear the surgery was postponed. I would have more time with him, and I could find out more about the procedure. When I found out the name of his surgeon, I made an appointment to see him.

Dr. Roland told me, "There's damage to Maury's aortic valve from childhood rheumatic fever. The valve will have to be replaced as soon as possible. Your husband has a serious heart condition and the only option we can offer him is surgery. Otherwise, there is no hope."

"What are Maury's chances for survival?"

The doctor replied confidently, "I give your husband an eighty percent chance if he goes through with it." That was somewhat encouraging, but the thought of this surgery still petrified me. At home I couldn't stop worrying about how dangerous this was. But the doctor was telling me, "There's no other way." And I wanted to trust him.

I visited Maury every day. I smiled to hide my fears as I walked down the long hospital corridor to his room. I was trying hard to be strong; I had to be courageous for Maury.

How astounded I was when I came in one day and saw Maury sitting in bed, eating his mother's food. He was supposed to be on a diet, but there he was, munching away at fatty Spanish cooking.

It was not the kind of food that you would give to a heart patient. Exasperated, I asked, "How did you get that?"

Maury laughed and said, "My mother came up the back staircase and brought it in when no one was around. I can't eat this hospital food."

I got upset and reprimanded him. "You're on a restricted diet. That food you're eating is fried and greasy. Why are you eating it? It's no good for you!"

Maury responded as if it were a big joke. "Are you kidding me? This food is great! It couldn't be better."

I went away shaking my head. *He's impossible!*

I came in one day and saw Maury lying in bed, silent, deep in thought. I asked him, "What are you thinking about?"

He looked into my eyes and with a serious expression on his face, he said, "I'm thinking about the ten thousand dollar life insurance policy I recently cancelled."

I was stunned. "A ten thousand dollar policy! What are you talking about?"

"When you left me, I canceled the policy."

I sat there, not knowing what to say.

A short time later, I saw Maury looking very somber. I knew he was worried about the operation and I asked, "Do you want to speak to a psychiatrist in the hospital? It can help to reassure you that things will be okay."

Maury said: "I don't want that. I'm okay and I don't need to speak to anyone." I didn't think he was okay, but who was I to tell him his feelings?

On one of my visits, I came in earlier than usual. I was walking down the corridor, when I saw a young woman coming out of Maury's room. She was rushing towards the staircase as if she had a train to catch. I felt a thump in my chest. She was very attractive in her coiffed pageboy hairstyle and a dark navy suit. I recalled the words of Maury's neighbor, Joe: "Maury has a girlfriend...." I thought to myself: *This must be her.*

This was a jolting experience for me. I tried not to think about it, as I stood in the corridor for a few minutes. Then I pulled myself together and went into Maury's room. I didn't mention a word to him, and we had a very pleasant afternoon together.

One evening, I came home from the hospital so tense and distraught; I rushed to the phone to call Maury. I had to hear his voice. We had a long conversation and Maury said, "I loved you so much. You'll never find a guy who'll love you the way I have."

I wanted to cry. I asked him if he would ever be able to love me again. He thoughtfully replied, "I don't know…"

That wasn't the answer I hoped for. I suddenly had a feeling of loss. Genuine loss. Maybe it wasn't all his fault; I played a role in it, too. I thought about my life with Maury and I was aching inside. He had his problems, but I had my own. I was not perfect and I could not blame him for all the things that went wrong. I found myself caring for Maury much more than I ever imagined I could.

My need to help Maury through this crisis became uppermost in my mind. I firmly declared: "When you come out of the hospital, Maury, I will take care of you. I will do whatever it takes to get you back on your feet."

But that never came to pass. Maury had surgery, and within approximately twenty-four hours, he was dead. He was only thirty-four years old.

I was devoured by guilt. I had left him, not knowing he was so very ill. He needed me and I wasn't there for him. Dear Lord, what had I done?

55

What Really Happened?

I was walking around in a daze. I could barely get on the subway and go into Manhattan. I arrived at Dr. Russell's office hoping to do my work, but when I got there, I found I was unable to do the simplest things. It was an effort to file away a few papers. I felt more like a patient than a part-time office worker. There was nothing I wanted to do but cry.

Dr. Russell noticed I was upset and commented. "Grief in the mourning process is normal, but I sense something deeper, and I'd like to help you with it."

As we talked, Dr. Russell asked me a question that was quite profound: "Have you ever lost anyone close to you?"

I said, "I was twelve years old when my father died. My mother never told me. She buried him, and I found out some time later."

Dr. Russell grimaced. He appeared deep in thought. "You were not allowed to express mourning for your father. Your mother didn't allow you to go through the grieving process. Most probably, the grief you didn't express then is coming out now. If issues are not resolved from the past, they come alive and haunt you in the present."

I found this hard to grasp emotionally. As Dr. Russell continued to talk, I found my mind wandering to Maury and his operation.

"Maury should never have had that surgery," I said. "The surgeon talked me into believing that he would survive. He said the aortic valve had to be replaced and then Maury would be just fine. I so badly wanted to believe it. And look what happened."

"I don't think your husband died of open-heart surgery. I think he lost his will to live."

What made Dr. Russell say something like that? Why was he telling me something so disturbing when I already was in so much pain? I couldn't bear the thought of it. "Can you please explain that to me?" I asked.

"I just have a hunch."

That's all he said, but it got me thinking. The surgeon had told me: "Your husband has an eighty percent chance of survival…." If that were the case, then what went wrong? It must have been something medical, I thought. Maury would never give up on life. He loved to live. But Dr. Russell didn't believe that. He stuck by his premise and I fought the notion. I reminded Dr. Russell that Maury had been ill for some time.

"Maybe so. But with your permission, I would like to speak to the doctor who performed the surgery."

I suddenly felt frightened. Suppose he was right? I didn't think I could deal with it.

The next day, when I came to work, Dr. Russell approached me and said, "Yep, I spoke to the doctor and he agrees. He said Maury was on the operating table for seven hours, and everything went well. He lived for some twenty-four hours after. There was no problem. He, too, feels that Maury, for some reason, didn't want to go on living."

I pointed out, "Maury couldn't breathe after the operation. They made an incision to open his trachea, and that didn't help."

Dr. Russell didn't waver. "The first twenty-four hours are the most difficult, but he got beyond that. Both his doctor, and myself, are thinking along the same lines…"

I was shaking. If this were true, then maybe I had somehow caused his demise. I always felt responsible when things went wrong.

Dr. Russell and I had a talk. Then he said, "There's only one way to find out."

I didn't want to hear it. The sound of it revolted me. But I had to find out the truth.

I went to the hospital the next day and spoke to one of the doctors in charge. I asked, "Is an autopsy necessary if you don't know what really happened to someone?"

He told me, "If you really want to know, an autopsy must be done. It is the only way we'll ever find out just what went wrong. If we understand this, then we might have the knowledge to save the lives of others."

The thought of an autopsy was very upsetting, but it seemed that in order to truly know, I would have to sign that paper and give the necessary permission.

I spoke to Maury's mother because I knew this would be very upsetting to her as well. "It's against Jewish law," she adamantly said. Then I told her what the doctor told me: "Somebody's life could be saved if they find out exactly what happened to Maury." She was still against it, but she finally agreed.

The autopsy report came back, and it did not reveal anything of a physical nature. Dr. Russell said, "That's what I thought."

It was hard to believe. I started to ponder what had happened when I went to see Maury right after his operation. He was lying in bed with his eyes wide open, and he held his hand to his head as if deep in thought. He looked as though he wanted to say something, but he wasn't able to form words; he could only make sounds. That troubled me, and I approached a doctor on call. "Why can't he speak?"

The doctor was rather abrupt and didn't seem to know. I was going to speak with Maury's doctor in the morning, but he never made it through the night.

It preyed on my mind. It was a terrible tragedy. But I couldn't think of a reason why Maury would give up on life. The more I thought about it, the more confusing it was in my mind. He seemed to be motivated to go through with the surgery and "have a new life."

In the days that followed, I was wracked with guilt. There were questions, and more questions, with no answers, and a lot of tears. But it was out of my hands. There was nothing I could do about it.

I would sit in a chair and feel my heart racing. When I was worried enough, I went to a doctor, who assured me, "There's nothing wrong with you." I didn't know if I could believe that. I left the doctor's office in a daze and walked in front of a car. "Hey, lady, do you want to get killed?"

I nervously went from one thing to another. I didn't know myself anymore; I was a completely different person, walking around in a trance. And the fast heartbeat continued. I soon went to other doctors, who confirmed it was just a matter of nerves.

I eventually complained to Dr. Russell and he said: "I think you're identifying with your husband." It was hard for me to comprehend. How is that possible?

I soon forced myself to focus on things outside of myself. I stopped worrying about a condition I didn't have, and I found my palpitations becoming less and less. I continued to drag myself through the day, doing the best I could—and that wasn't very good. Dr. Russell held firm to his conviction about Maury's death, and I still didn't know what to believe. It hurt whichever way I looked at it.

In my grief, I began to think about Maury and the five years I spent with him. I was just beginning to experience the outside world when Maury came into my life. I was on the brink of destruction. He helped break through my feelings of despondency and oriented me to a new way of living, as he took me around and exposed me to various aspects of being in the world. Because of his genuine concern, I was empowered to move forward and meet the challenges that lie before me. Through it all, Maury was nurturing me with love and affection, and I was thriving on it.

Although Maury displayed outlandish behavior at times, I couldn't think about the bad; I could only dwell upon the good. He was a very special person in my life. He was my first boyfriend and my first real love. It is very possible that, if it wasn't for Maury, I might have remained in the house with my mother for the rest of my life.

Maury meant more to me than I realized—and now, he was gone…

56

Living with a Married Man

I was waking up in the middle of the night in a sweat. *This has to be a bad dream; it can't be real. I can't believe that Maury's gone.*

I knew Maury wasn't well and I was regretting that I hadn't given more thought to his health issues. But I was too busy drowning in my own personal hell. I could barely take care of myself. Now, it was too late. I had failed Maury and there was nothing I could do about it.

I was cleaning out Maury's apartment when I came upon a pile of papers. I found something that was very disturbing to me. It was a pawn ticket. I couldn't believe my eyes. Maury had pawned his beloved black and gold clarinet for thirty dollars! How dearly he cherished that clarinet. Was he that desperate for money?

In grief, I decided to call my aunt Rose who now had a phone. I told her the bad news and she appeared shocked. "I'm so sorry, honey. I don't know what to say…" She said she would contact Bea and let her know. When I got off the phone I was just as despondent as before.

Several days later, Rose called me back and she sounded upset. "I spoke to Bea and told her about Maury. She said, 'I'm not interested in Lenore. I don't care about her problems. I have my own family to worry about'." I was devastated. My father's sister, Bea, who claimed to love her brother so much, had no compassion or regard for his daughter. It made me sick to my stomach. I told myself that I would have nothing more to do with her. And was it really necessary for Rose to regurgitate her sister's unkind remarks?

I was in too much turmoil to be alone; I wanted to be with someone I could relate to. I suddenly thought of Maury's mother. I was soon knocking on her door. As she welcomed me into her home, tears were rolling down her face. "My son loved you," she cried. "He would say, 'Lenore's an orphan, be good to her, Mama.' He gave me money to buy you gifts. He gave me $85 for your charm bracelet…"

I had no idea that Maury was behind that beautiful gold charm bracelet that I cherished so much. What a loving gesture! He was having money problems, and yet he was giving his mother money to buy me gifts. I was deeply moved.

But what astonished me even more was to learn that Maury was telling people, "Lenore's an orphan." Yes, I felt like an orphan, but I never spoke about it to anyone and no one ever mentioned anything like that to me. How intuitive of Maury. He could feel what I couldn't put into words, and he cared enough to tell others, like his mother, "Be good to Lenore." If only he had been able to tell me that he knew I was an orphan, it would have made a world of difference to me. In knowing that he understood, I would have felt closer to him, and our relationship might have been very different. If only I had known…

But I couldn't go back in time. It seemed that I would never feel anything but remorse and guilt, as I dwelled upon the many mistakes I made. When I left Maury's mother that day, I knew I would go back many more times. I felt closer to the memory of Maury when I was with her.

I rarely saw any of Maury's friends during the months I was separated from him—including Jay. He visited me a few times, and then he stopped coming around. I wondered what that was all about, but I decided not to pursue it.

Jay came back into my life soon after Maury's death. He began to see me regularly at my mother's. Sometimes we would go for a drive or we might go somewhere in the neighborhood to have a bite. We usually wound up talking about Maury, how he lived, and the tragedy of his death. Sometimes we both broke down and cried together. With tears in his eyes, Jay said: "I loved Maury."

Soon, Jay shared with me stories about a childhood that was filled with agony and abuse. As the son of an alcoholic father, he witnessed his father having affairs with women and beating up his mother during bouts of drunkenness. "My father liked my sister, but he was jealous of me. I must have been about ten when he punched me in the nose and it made me bleed. I told him, 'If you ever put your hands on me again, I'll beat the hell out of you! And if I can't do it with my hands, I'll do it with a chair or whatever I can get my hands on!' I was a big kid for my age, so he wasn't about to start up with me."

Jay and his family lived in chaos until his father disappeared one night, never to be seen again. Jay knew a life of rejection and I empathized with him. It was very easy for us to understand each other; we were speaking the language of pathos. He seemed to know me so well. He amazed me with intuitive insights, which were remarkably on target. More and more, I wanted to be with Jay—and only Jay.

I was not thinking very clearly when I went over to see Amy. I thought their marriage was over, so I confided in her about my feelings for Jay. She looked as though she had seen a ghost. I realized I had made a terrible mistake, but it was too late to retract my words. Amy sounded frantic as she spoke. "He just recently came home. Do me a favor, Lenore, please stay away from him."

Suddenly I was very upset, too. I couldn't make the promise she wanted to hear. I was torn between my feelings for Jay and my friendship with her. We tried to calmly discuss the situation, but our emotions got in the way. Soon, what I was saying didn't seem to make any sense, and I couldn't hear what she was saying to me. As I got up and walked towards the door, I knew that my friendship with Amy was a thing of the past.

I went home distraught. *How could have I done something so stupid?* But then again, how was I to know that Amy still had feelings for Jay? They had been apart for several years while Jay was living with Mindy. During that time, Amy was seeing other men. Her eyes were sparkling and she had the happiest glow on her face as she told me about the intimacies of her new life. It sounded to me as if she had moved on. But apparently, she had not.

Jay made it clear to me: "There's nothing between Amy and me. I'm staying with her so I can be with my daughter." Then he emphasized: "It's over between me and Amy." But there was something about this that troubled me, and I pondered: *Why was I feeling that I was wrecking their marriage when it had already fallen apart?* I was in conflict. I knew I should not have gotten involved with a married man, but I also knew that Jay was not just any ordinary man; he was my confidante and friend, he could understand me like no one else, and that was especially attractive to me.

I was torn up inside. I was haunted by Amy's anguished face, and I could hear her heartfelt pleas. I had a need to go off by myself when I felt so down. There was one place I wanted to be, but I had to travel to get there. How fortunate for me that the subway had become my friend; it took me to wherever I wanted to go. I would just hop on a train and in no time, I would be in Battery Park at the lower tip of Manhattan. There, I would find a bench by the water and soon I would gaze at the ripples, the ebb and flow of the waves, and the ships moving slowly in the distance. People were passing by, but I didn't see them; I was at one with the universe. This was my place of peace and calm. This was my sanctuary.

This time, however, I was wracked with guilt. Then I remembered one of the last times I saw Amy. She looked radiant and was bubbling over with joy as she told me about her latest sexual encounter. I blushed as I listened. Amy was no angel. So why was I feeling like a villain?

I went home and patiently waited to hear from Jay. Then, late at night, he phoned to tell me he was on his way over. It was wonderful to hear his warm, sensuous voice. I couldn't wait to see him. And before I knew it, he was knocking on my mother's door. "Where would you like to go?" I could only think of one place.

It was after midnight when we arrived at Battery Park. It was especially lovely on a warm summer night, and very romantic. Soon we were on a great big ferry, gliding over the water in the dark of night, heading towards Staten Island. I amazed myself; I forgot to be afraid. Standing there at the rail of the ferry, looking out at a darkened world that glowed with lights across the water, I thought: What a beautiful sight this is. Soon Jay came over to me, took me in his arms and gently kissed me. I felt that my life was beginning again.

Jay continued to visit me late at night. My mother laughingly referred to this as "the midnight rides of Paul Revere." I thought it was silly and paid no mind to it. And we continued to go down to Battery Park.

It wasn't long before Jay didn't go home at all. My mother didn't voice any complaints about it, just as she hadn't shown any objections to Maury living in her apartment with me. Sometimes I thought she was rather pleased. She liked Jay and got along with him very well. They conversed about simple things, and when we wanted to be alone, she understood. She tiptoed out of the room and made herself scarce. I found it hard to believe that this woman, my mother, who was so fierce when I was growing up, had become nothing more than a pussycat. How astounding it was. No longer was she the screaming, abusive monster who scared me out of my wits. I wondered if the men in my life had anything to do with it. Sometimes I felt Hedda was living her life through me. But it didn't matter; I was grateful for the positive change in her.

One day I approached Jay and asked: "Does Amy know you're here with me?"

Jay looked at me as if I were crazy. "Who cares? I'm not going back there anyhow!" He seemed pretty adamant about this, so I didn't ask any further questions.

Jay and I continued to share a nice, cozy existence until reality reared its ugly head: I was living with a married man. How I abhorred the thought. I knew, at an early age, that such a relationship could never work for me. It would never make me feel truly loved, and it was not the kind of life that I could respect. But I rationalized that Jay was a very special person with whom I shared a very special bond. I thought we truly loved each other, so I eventually found the nerve to ask the big question: "Are you planning to get a divorce?"

He stoically answered my question with a question: "What will I do with my daughter?" I was startled. I didn't know what to say. I was staring at him, and he was staring back at me. He had successfully deflected my question by asking me something I didn't know how to answer. Jay had been away from home for several years and during that time Lucy was living with her mother. Why was he asking me this now? I concluded that he was avoiding the topic of divorce because he didn't want to marry me. Ouch! I walked around with tears in my eyes.

In the midst of my turmoil, my resentment for Hedda was coming out in moments when I least expected. I wanted to move out and away from her once and for all. I thought about moving into Maury's apartment that I had been holding on to for quite some time. I wasn't very comfortable with the thought of living there, but I didn't want to give it up either. Eventually, I decided to move there with Jay although I continued to have many reservations.

My uncle Will was very disturbed about my involvement with Jay. He chastised me: "He's a married man! Tell him you will have nothing to do with him until he gets a divorce!"

No doubt, my uncle was right. I told myself that I would stop seeing Jay, and if he really missed me, he'd know what to do. But it never got that far. Jay began to call me "baby." How I loved to hear him say that. The way he said it made me feel cared about and cherished; I wanted to reach for the stars. When his vibrant personality overshadowed my fears, I felt a sense of safety; and when he was able to wrap his loving warmth around me, I felt that nothing could harm me and the world was good.

I began to get lost in Jay's thoughts, opinions, and ideas. He would say things like: "Baby, the reason you feel like that is because…." Or he might say: "Your thinking is wrong, and I can prove it; I know what you're feeling, but you don't!" I was mesmerized. I thought Jay was a genius at defining emotions. His ability to tap into my inner world was especially appealing since I was desperately trying to find an identity and make sense of the world around me. It never ceased to amaze me that not only could Jay read me like a book, but he could also tap into the thoughts and feelings of others with astute clarity.

While I continued to be fascinated by Jay's intelligence, I began to feel a downside. It became exceedingly difficult for me to have a thought of my own; Jay would reject just about everything I said as he tried to show me a better and different way of looking at things. At times, I was completely overwhelmed. He flooded me with so many thoughts and insights, it became exceedingly difficult for me to take it all in. His need to make me understand his views became overbearing and filled me with frustration. I was becoming more tense and irritable, but I couldn't ask him to stop because I had a profound interest in what he was telling me. Maybe I could learn to do better if I kept an open mind and listened to what he said.

In therapy, I was seeking answers to a multitude of problems, which I would present to my therapist. "What do you think?" was the question that came back to me. Most of the time I didn't know, and my therapist gave me very little feedback. Then I turned to Jay. He had answers within minutes! It was mind-boggling. *Why am I going for therapy when Jay understands me better than my therapist?* Or so I thought.

I was becoming more and more dependent upon Jay's opinions. He seemed to know so much and I knew so little. Then I thought about Amy. She looked up to Jay as though he were a deity, and yet I had seen him belittle and ridicule her. He became irate and raised his voice when he disapproved of something she said or did. She never fought back and I looked upon her behavior with disdain. I wondered how she ever allowed Jay to have so much power over her. It was ironic that I soon found myself in a similar situation; I was also intimidated and swallowing my feelings. My sense of worth, so little to begin with, was sliding into the sewer even more. Why did I think Jay would treat me any differently than he treated his wife?

I was confused. I revered Jay, but I was seeing so many aspects of him that I didn't like. I began to face the reality that Jay's cool exterior was only a facade, and underneath was a sleeping rage. I became nervous when he was angry. I sensed a volcanic explosion could occur at any time. I was choosing my words carefully, so as not to set an eruption into motion. It was so similar to the way I lived with my mother.

Jay was an altogether different person when he was working with children on his photography route. On several occasions I went out with him and watched him in action. I marveled at the delightful expressions he got out of those babies. His love of children was apparent and came through in his photos.

Because Jay was such a good photographer, I suggested he open his own studio. But he wasn't very happy to hear this. His response was: "I don't want the headache and responsibility that comes with having a business of my own."

I could readily understand that, for Jay had a propensity to relax, enjoy life, and watch the passing parade. In his spare time, he read just about everything he could get his hands on, going through newspapers and magazines as if there were no tomorrow. Although I felt neglected, I admired his thirst for knowledge. I wondered how he could get so wrapped up in reading something like The Scientific American; I didn't have any interest in opening a book. Nor was I really interested in television. Jay loved to watch football games and science fiction shows. I often wondered: *What does Mission Impossible have that I don't have?*

When things were quiet and appeared to be going well, shades of the not-so-nice Jay would reappear. This was the Jay who was hurtfully blunt, who would ridicule people in his home and make them feel terrible; only now it was me he was needling and making fun of. When I said something that he considered dumb or silly, he had a weird, mocking expression on his face and then he either burst into laughter or made a derogatory comment that had a sting to it. *Ouch! How can he be so cruel?*

I didn't like Jay in those moments. Jay knew I grew up in isolation and lacked an education. So why was he ridiculing me about things I didn't know? Was he playing some kind of game with me? I wondered if it made him feel better to belittle me while he made himself superior.

When Jay mocked me with a nasty remark, I silently agreed with him. I was very ashamed that I hadn't gone to school like everyone else, and it seemed that everyone knew more than I. I felt that discomfort wherever I went, and I wanted to fix it, but I didn't feel I could do anything about it.

One day we were having a dispute over some triviality when Jay came over to me and said, "Baby, you know what your problem is? You don't have a sense of humor!"

When he said that, I became infuriated. "Really? I happen to have a terrific sense of humor. I just don't find it funny when the 'joke' is on me."

"Baby, you happen to be very bright. You're just too sensitive. Lighten up. I told you many times that you're a very bright girl, but you're ignorant and there's a big difference between ignorance and stupidity. You are certainly not stupid; you're just not knowledgeable. You don't know about the world and how people live...."

Even though I could see the validity in what he said, what was I going to do about it? Maybe if I could somehow make myself "knowledgeable," then I could feel better about myself and lose that feeling of shame I carried around with me. Then maybe Jay would treat me differently. But where would I begin? It seemed like an impossible task. When I turned on the radio, I heard talk about what was going on in the world, but I couldn't make any sense out of what I heard. I heard words and more words that had no meaning to me. I liked the thought of becoming knowledgeable, but I didn't know how to approach it.

I was interested in other things—things I couldn't talk about— like marriage, because I was afraid of hearing the horrific **"No!"** that my mother inflicted upon me throughout my childhood. But Jay wasn't my mother. When I felt enough frustration, I found the courage to say: "I need to talk to you, but I'm afraid."

"If you don't ask for what you want, baby, how am I to know? I'm not a mind reader."

I just sat there silently and stared at him. I found it difficult to articulate my feelings in words. Could I trust him not to hurt me?

When I finally found my voice, I asked, "What do you think about getting married?"

Suddenly, a blank expression covered his face. Jay appeared disinterested, if not completely detached. I found it disheartening; it was pretty clear that the topic of marriage was taboo.

But I quickly forgot my distress when Jay came over to me, put his arm around me, gave me a kiss, and called me "baby." How easily I would forget my hurt when I was shown a little love. Grandma did not spare my feelings when she said, "You're such a foolish child. They can spit in your face, then all they have to do is say, 'I love you' (singing those words), and you go back for more!" I felt a sting as she spoke. How could I deny the truth?

I was on another emotional seesaw. When I was on an upswing, everything looked so good; it was hard to imagine that things would ever change. But when I was down, I was so morbidly miserable, I didn't think I would ever get out of the muck. I found myself with mixed feelings about Jay; I was loving and hating him at the same time. Through it all, the good and the bad, I wondered: *Why do I want to marry someone who isn't interested in marrying me? Do I really want to marry Jay?* I became depressed; The whole thing seemed wrong, so very wrong.

But I couldn't give in to the distress of the situation I found myself in. I reached out to my radio to find some soft, soothing music that could give me a sense of peace and calm. What a jolt it was to realize that the music I loved so much was no longer on the radio. I guess I was so wrapped up in my emotional woes, I wasn't aware that times had changed. This was the mid-60s. The age of the crooner and the songstress was over. Lyrics were becoming more muffled and unclear. Music didn't sound like music anymore, just a lot of noise. It was the age of rock 'n roll. The whole scene was very unappetizing to me. No dignity. No substance. No nothing. Not my cup of tea.

So, what was there that I could turn to? Although there were problems with Jay, there were also positive aspects to our relationship. Among those were the things we liked to do together. For one, there was a certain joy we experienced taking rides away from the hustle and bustle of the city. So often we stopped off at places to eat. We both enjoyed going out to simple, cozy, inexpensive restaurants with good food. We frequently took a drive up to Yonkers and wound up having a bite in a place called IHOP (the International House of Pancakes). It was a treat for me to be with Jay and relax with him over a pancake platter in this odd-looking, quaint little house with a slanted roof.

While we were in the restaurant, I was taken aback by Jay's behavior towards the waitresses who were serving us. With a sexy, teasing smile, Jay would flirt as he engaged them in trivial conversation. He ignored me as if I wasn't there and this annoyed me no end. *How can he be so disrespectful of my feelings?* I was biting my tongue, as I boiled up inside. I wanted to get up and walk out, but I didn't want to create a scene. So, I sat there, fuming, as I watched him with that gleam in his eyes.

Jay presented an enigma to me. It seemed that the longer I knew him, the less I was able to understand him. He certainly was very close-mouthed when it came to anything personal. He would continuously pontificate about the external world, while he kept a tight lid on his own inner world. Why was he so guarded? Why was he flirting with waitresses in restaurants? It troubled me, but I couldn't find it in me to confront him.

We were in a restaurant when I felt a need to speak to Jay about his income. He never spoke about it and I was curious. "Did you have a good week, Jay? How are sales going these days?" I saw a look of discomfort on his face. "Why so secretive, Jay? I don't want money from you. You know me better than that." He deflected my query with some meaningless chatter that made me feel small and insignificant. Suddenly, I was back in my childhood, feeling lost and lonely.

As I thought about what would give my life some meaning, I continued to wander around department stores in awe of the beautiful garments that surrounded me. I was now schlepping Jay along with me because I valued his opinion so highly. To get a better view of me in an outfit, Jay would squint his eyes and if he liked the way I looked in it, he would say, "I'm getting this for you." I was happy with whatever he bought for me. But as usual, most of the clothing hung in my closet, unworn.

Jay, on the other hand, didn't care about clothes or appearance. He was putting on weight but because he was so tall, it wasn't that noticeable. He was content to wear a loose shirt and baggy pants in and out of the house. However, when he went to work, he was always neatly dressed, and when he had to shoot a wedding, he would put on a nice dark suit. I enjoyed seeing him look so elegant.

But I didn't enjoy seeing Jay lighting up one cigarette after another and drinking all that coffee. What was so appealing about cigarettes and coffee? I sampled a cigarette, took a few puffs, and started to cough. I couldn't stand the taste it left in my mouth. As for coffee, I could only tolerate it if there was plenty of milk to cover up the bitter taste. I didn't find anything in either that would make me want more. I wondered how he could consume these with such a passion.

I could see that Jay was distressed and unhappy. He was walking around the house with a cigarette dangling from his lips and his eyes were sad. He had a long face and I felt as though I was looking at my mother. There was a time when she, too, walked around with a cigarette in her mouth, looking tense and forlorn. I felt responsible for her sadness and now, as I stared at Jay, I was experiencing the same feeling. I kept wondering: *What's going on in his head? Why does he look so troubled and worn?* I finally asked, "Are you angry at me, Jay? Have I done something to upset you?" He didn't respond and I was perplexed. Had he even heard me?

Jay wore many faces and each one presented a challenge for me. However, there was one side of Jay that really astonished me— the one that could be so genuinely caring and emotionally involved. He had a compelling way of encouraging me to do things I didn't have any interest in. Once or twice, he said, "You know, my 11-year-old daughter knows more about the solar system than you do." I felt shame. I knew I had to do better.

Jay finally got me to open a book, and that was a feat in itself. After so many years, I soon found myself reading again, and I don't know how he did it; I must admit I had a lot of resistance. Perhaps it was the way he spoke to me about the world we live in that aroused my curiosity.

Although my resistance remained strong, I found I was slowly learning, and Jay was teaching me. With my very limited background, it was difficult for me to grasp the things he was telling me, and I struggled with concepts. He explained each thing to me as if he were talking to a child. At times I thought he had the patience of a saint. His persistent eagerness and faith in my ability to learn motivated me to do more all the time. I began to wonder: *What would I ever do without Jay?*

"Be honest, baby. Say what you mean. Say what you feel." But I found that so hard to do. I lacked the courage to speak my mind and I sensed a reprimand was just a heartbeat away. But Jay persisted: "Be true to your feelings, don't be afraid to speak the truth." He chastised me when he perceived I was covering up what I was feeling, and I fought him every inch of the way. Despite my protests, I was learning to become more honest with others and myself, and Jay was showing me how.

Dental issues were still something else I didn't want to deal with. I avoided dentists the same way my mother had, but with severe consequences. "Your gums are all red and swollen. I'm getting you over to a dentist right away. You'll need special treatments for that." Jay appeared tense and upset as he schlepped me into his car and drove over to a dentist in Yonkers. The dentist concurred that I needed special treatments for gum disease. This was the start of ongoing dental work for me.

There was a time I was very ill with aches, pains, and high fever. I felt Jay's anxiety as he hovered over me with pots of chicken soup and other foods that he brought to me in bed. He took care of me like a baby. He never told me, until afterwards, that I had the dangerous strain of the Hong Kong flu. I realized how very caring and concerned he could be in difficult times. There was goodness about Jay that I could not dismiss.

One day Jay came in with a big smile. "I have a surprise for you, baby. We're going to the Catskills this weekend. Take a few nice outfits with you and we'll go." I thought it was short notice, but I wasn't about to ask any questions. It was going to be a new experience, but Jay would be with me. So, I put aside my apprehension, packed up a few things, and I was ready to leave.

I had never been to an exclusive Catskills hotel before, but as soon as we got there, something about the whole scene didn't feel right to me. There was something artificial and unreal about it, just what it was, I didn't know. I did know I didn't belong there. I wanted to leave right away, but I couldn't bring myself to tell Jay how out of place I felt.

When we went into the dining room that night, I was frozen in fear. As I looked around, I observed how the people interacted with each other, exuding an air of superiority and standoffishness. The women were elaborately dressed in long gowns, some beaded and spangled, with lots of jewelry. Their make-up was way overdone. I thought the heavy black eyeliner and mascara made them look like a bunch of ghouls. They looked just ghastly to me. *Didn't they have mirrors? Couldn't they see how utterly grotesque they looked?* I would not have liked to bump into any one of them on a Halloween night.

As Jay and I sat at the dining table, waiting for our meals to be served, I found myself unable to speak or move. Everything around me became a blur, and it remained pretty much like that for the rest of the evening. As we left the dining area, I recall asking Jay: "When are we going home?"

"Baby, we just got here, and we're all paid up for the weekend."

Oh, no! How awful! This is a waking nightmare!

I spent the rest of my time there immersed in trauma, unable to articulate to Jay what was going on inside of me. I was amazed at how completely oblivious he was to the change in my mood. Couldn't he tell by the way I was acting that there was something very wrong?

The best part of my experience in the Catskills was when Jay said: "It's time to leave." *What a relief!*

How good it felt to be home. The neighborhood restaurants, so simple and plain, appealed to me all the more. I could feel comfortable and safe in a place that was not elaborate or pretentious.

One night we were having a bite in a coffee shop when Jay smiled and said: "Amy is seeing someone, and I think it's serious. She met him at work, and it seems like they're more than friends. I met the guy. He seems very nice. I like him."

"I'm very glad to hear that. I hope Amy will be happy."

Jay replied, "I hope so, too." And we left it at that.

I had a nagging need to call my uncle. I hadn't spoken to Will for some time since our disputes about my involvement with a married man. I felt a sweat soar through me, and my heart beat a little faster as I dialed his number, but soon I was pleasantly surprised. We were able to speak to each other as if our heated controversies never existed.

"I've made a lot of progress, Will. I couldn't open a book but now I'm reading…" And I went on to tell him about my other accomplishments with Jay, but Will seemed to be disinterested. That put a damper on my spirits. I was sorry I called. I didn't think I would be speaking to him again any time soon.

However, a few days later, I was surprised to receive a phone call from Will. "Jessie and I would like you to come over and visit with us. You can bring Jay." *Wow!* I was thrilled to hear him say that. Jay and I soon joined Will and Jessie in their living room, and this was the beginning of a nice, friendly rapport that the four of us shared.

I was very proud of Jay. I considered Will to be the epitome of knowledge and Jay was able to converse with him on just about any topic. They especially liked to discuss politics and world events. Sometimes Jessie joined in. I didn't have anything much to contribute, so I just sat there silently and listened to them talk. I wondered if they knew I was in the room. I was just glad that we all were together like a family.

There was a time when the four of us were in a restaurant, and Will and Jay were having an intense conversation. Jay stepped away from the table to make a phone call and a woman sitting nearby, who overheard the conversation, was so impressed by Jay, she leaned over and whispered to me: "Is that man a doctor?"

Yes, Jay had a way with words, but how he could overdo it. When I went out with him and his colleague-friends and their wives, (all very nice, down-to-earth people), Jay was pumped up and ready to fire away with the latest information he had acquired from magazines and newspapers. I thought he sounded like an intellectual automaton. I sat on the edge of my seat and cringed, as Jay rambled on and on. I found it boring and monotonous. I wondered if others felt the same way. I sensed they, too, were a part of his captive audience. I just didn't have the heart to tell him.

Out of the blue, Jay gave me a half smile and proclaimed: "You know, I don't like you, baby—I love you." I was astonished. What in the world did he mean by that?

Then, one evening we were sitting in the living room, watching some silly program on television, when Jay looked into my eyes with the sincerest expression on his face and soulfully said, "I want to grow old with you." I perceived it was said with love and that he meant it. I thought to myself: *He wants to grow old with me—but he doesn't want to marry me.* Suddenly, I was very sad. I felt myself pulling away from him.

Maybe I expected too much. When I complained about Jay, my uncle would usually remind me: "You have a roof over your head and food in your mouth. What are you complaining about?" But I sensed there was much more to life than food and rent—just what, I didn't know.

The things I once found so appealing about Jay were not that attractive anymore. I was getting tired of him being a Mister-Know-It-All. It was getting on my nerves. It came to a point where I wanted to feel my way through things by myself, instead of being told what I'm feeling, how I'm feeling, or what I needed to feel.

But I still was very attached to Jay emotionally. In my heart there still was a lingering desire to marry him. But what did I really know about marriage? The marriage between Hedda and George was a plain disaster. My marriage to Maury was a fiasco. Yet I fervently held on to the belief that marriage represented the ultimate pledge of love between two people. Perhaps those love songs on the radio had a stronger effect upon me than I cared to admit.

One day, I sat down with Jay to discuss marriage. Jay looked at me with a questioning stare and said, "You know, baby, I told you about this some time ago, maybe you weren't listening or maybe you didn't hear me. Marriage is a great institution for having children. People should get married for the sake of procreation. I don't see any point in getting married unless you want to have a baby. If you want to have a baby, I'll marry you."

I felt wiped out. I somehow managed to say: "I do want to share the sacred bond of marriage with you, but I don't want to have a baby. I thought you were aware of that. I can't even think of having a helpless human life in my hands. I can feel myself in a panic just thinking about it."

I was torn when I realized there was no point in arguing this further. There was nothing I could do but let it go.

Much to my dismay, Grandma soon approached me, sounding quite distressed. She was telling me the same thing she had told my mother so many years ago: "You need someone to take care of you in your old age." She was now working on me diligently, as she had on my mother, to have a baby. She made some very good points, and I began to ruminate about what she said. Soon, I went back to Grandma and firmly stated: "You know it may be good to have a child for one's old age, but not everyone can, or should, have a child. I am not going to have a baby, so please, let's **not** talk about it anymore."

She made a face and said, "I think you're making a big mistake." But something seemed to click this time and she didn't bring it up again.

Soon Jay made a startling announcement: "Amy is coming over to discuss divorce."

What a shock! I dreamed of marrying Jay so many times, but it was only a dream. In reality, I began to wonder: *Do I still want to marry him?* I didn't know. My feelings were swaying to and fro like a pendulum.

Soon, Amy was sitting opposite me in my living room. My once close friend, with whom I had shared my most intimate thoughts and feelings, was now here to talk divorce so that I could marry her husband. It didn't feel real.

Amy had the same sad expression on her face, and she spoke in the same cool stoic tone that I recalled from years ago. It seemed like only yesterday when she and I would get together and talk for hours in her living room. Now we were strangers on this strange, stormy journey.

Our conversation was very strained, but that was to be expected. As I heard the cold indifference in Amy's voice, a chill soared through me. I wanted to speak, but I couldn't find words that would make any sense. I was sizzling in my own personal hell when Jay came in and sat down in a corner of the room. I looked to him, desperate for some sort of input, but he didn't say a thing. How could he be so detached? In my dismay I asked, "Don't you have anything to say?" He shrugged his shoulders and casually remarked, "You know me. I'm just an observer." *Oh no, he's playing his games again! Typical Jay!*

Amy continued to speak in a slow monotone. "...I had done some detective work on my own. I didn't want to believe it, but I had a sneaking suspicion that Jay was living with you. I came over to your building one night and I saw his car parked in front of your door. I wanted to put my hands around your neck and strangle you—but I thought twice."

The icicles in her voice gave me the eeriest feeling. I wondered how she could speak about something so emotional and yet not show a trace of emotion. I squirmed in my seat. I wanted to say something, but I realized there was nothing I could say or do to alleviate the pain I had caused her. I sadly acknowledged: "It must have been a terrible shock. I can see why you were so angry."

"Yes, it was a shock. But that's in the past. And besides, I have someone in my life now." She turned to Jay and matter-of-factly said: "If you want a divorce, there won't be a problem."

I sat there with my feelings in a jumble. Soon, Jay and Amy started to talk about divorce. I didn't want to hear what they were saying. I tuned out, as thoughts entered my mind and drifted away. Soon there was the sound of silence. I felt a sense of despair as Amy got up and walked out the door.

The rest of the evening became a time to reflect, as I sat alone with my thoughts and feelings: *Poor Amy. She looks as sad as ever. And poor Lucy growing up without her father. It's all because of me and my foolish need for love. I've been selfish, very selfish, and I know I've caused them pain and grief. Damn!*

"You can't attain happiness at someone else's expense." Where had I heard that? I couldn't recall, but I could see the truth in it now.

57

Muddling Through

Jay didn't follow through on the divorce, but I didn't think he would. Our living arrangement had been established and I continued to abhor the life I had chosen for myself. I kept thinking about leaving, but where would I go? I was feeling as alone as ever. I kept fantasizing about meeting someone who could truly love me and make me happy.

I felt fortunate to have the support of Jay's mother and sister. I really liked them, and I sensed they genuinely liked me, too. Every so often, mostly on holidays, Jay and I got together with them, and we shared some laughs and casual talk. I liked the way they made me feel—as if I was part of the family.

Jay's sister, Jackie, was a cheerful, outgoing person. She was married, with three children, and she also drove a bus. Despite her busy schedule, she let me know: "My home is always open to you and Jay." I was moved by her graciousness.

One day I called her and told her I was applying for a learner's permit. Jackie immediately said, "Come on out and I'll teach you to drive. There's nothing to it. It's all country out here and there are plenty of parking lots we can use." So, Jay and I went out to Suffolk County.

Jackie, with her patience and sense of humor, did a marvelous job at coaching nervous me behind the wheel. She would say to me, "You're doing great. You're a quick learner. You'll be driving in no time." And I was learning. It was a marvelous feeling. This gave me the impetus to do even better.

Jay's mother was a lovely little lady with grey hair and big green piercing eyes. We all called her "Mama." She had a love of life that showed up in just about everything she attempted to do. She must have been in her 80's when I first met her. She was so sprightly, so full of life and laughter; I just loved to be around her. I recall the time she was in our home and there was music on the radio that moved her. Mama sprang out of her chair, came over to me, took me in her arms and waltzed me around the floor. *Was I hit by a hurricane?* My goodness, Mama was strong! I broke out laughing and said, "Mama, you're too much. I can't keep up with you." She laughed her hearty laugh and whirled me around some more. Yes, Mama was a wonderful lady. I always let her know how much I enjoyed her.

Then there were times when Mama came running over to me with a very serious, strange expression on her face. I was rather bewildered as she placed her fingers on my forehead and pulled out a couple of hairs. I cried, "Mama, what are you doing? That hurts!"

Very stoically she would say: "I don't want you to have gray hairs. No gray hairs for you!" That was a real "Ouch" moment for me. But I felt a tinge of love with that "Ouch."

Both Mama and Jackie expressed concern about the way I was living with Jay. I was sitting and talking to Jackie in her car when she became angry and said: "How come my brother doesn't get a divorce and marry you?" I felt humiliated. My cheeks flushed and I didn't have an answer, but I gave some silly excuse to counter my embarrassment. And then I felt worse as Jackie continued to express her anger. Sometime later, Mama gently asked me, "Why don't you and my boy get married?" I wanted to know that, too.

I was jostled out of my complacency; the truth was back to haunt me: if Jay really loved me, he would have married me a long time ago. My resentment was stirred up again, but it only lasted so long, and then it was gone—until the next time. Other people who knew I was living with a married man approached me with the same question. I didn't have a good answer, so I would casually slough it off. But it was getting me down. As I ruminated about my life with Jay, it felt so wrong. This was not the kind of life I wanted, and I felt ashamed. *If only I could run away and hide.* But I knew I couldn't, and I was hurting inside.

I hadn't taken much interest in the decline of our neighborhood until I heard about the numerous muggings and burglaries that were now commonplace. I nervously spoke to Jay about it: "Our neighborhood has become crime-ridden. It's not safe to live here anymore. We have to move!"

It wasn't long before we went to the real estate broker who found an apartment for Will and Jessie in the Pelham Parkway section of the Bronx. In no time we were living just a few blocks away from them. I hoped that things would be different between Jay and me in this new locale, but whom was I kidding? The location was different, but we were the same.

Pelham Parkway was a quiet, countrified area with tree-lined streets and many private homes. It wasn't like the noisy streets of the old neighborhood, and I liked that. Jay and I were now living on the first floor of a private house and adjusting nicely to our new environment. A shopping area and a subway station were only a few blocks away. It seemed like we had made a good choice.

It troubled me that my mother was still living in the old neighborhood. My uncle also had concern about her. Somehow, we both convinced her that she had to move. Before too long, she was living nearby in a basement apartment of a private house. We were happy to learn that she liked the landlady and her daughter and had good things to say about them.

The beauty of the Parkway brought out the artist in me. Every so often I walked over to an area thick with trees and greens. I opened my folding chair, sat down, and reached into my bag. Out came my pen and sketchpad, and I began to make swirling lines. I drew and drew some more. I wondered why anyone would ever want to turn to anything as damaging as drugs and alcohol when something as spirit lifting as the movement of a pen on paper could produce a natural, incredible high. At least, that's the effect it had upon me. I made one line after another, and I saw branches forming; and then leaves coming out of the branches, and soon, I had a tree. The flow of the lines seemed to have a rhythm of their own. What a jubilant feeling it was to capture the beauty of my surroundings on paper! I was grateful for moments like these when my spirits were soaring, and I was so full of life.

One day I had a big surprise. Jay came in and his daughter Lucy was with him. Some time had passed since I last saw her. Lucy was now in her early teens and quite an attractive young lady. I didn't know what to say to her and she was very cool towards me. That was understandable. I remembered the warmth and loving feelings we had once shared, and I felt bad. But what did I expect? I certainly had made a mess of things. I had been very possessive of Jay, and I didn't want to share him with anyone, including his own daughter. It was a terrible mistake that I could not undo.

Like myself, Lucy had grown up without a father in the home. How hurt I was when I learned that my father was seeing other women. And now, I was no better than the women I resented. How hurt Lucy must have been when she learned I was living with her father. I was looking at myself in a mirror, and the mirror was Lucy. I felt shame and guilt as I looked into her eyes.

Despite the discomfort I felt in Lucy's presence, I was hopeful that Jay and I would be able to get together with her and make up for lost time. Soon Jay was bringing Lucy over regularly. One day he came in and told me, "Lucy's pregnant." *Oh no! How awful. Lucy's going to have a baby? She's only a baby herself!* It bothered me; it didn't make any sense. Lucy was too smart to get herself pregnant. Yet, there she was, about to have a baby. I wondered what that was all about.

We tried as much as possible to be supportive. It was during this time that Lucy and I renewed our friendship. She was pleasant and cheerful, and I felt like a kid when I was with her. At one point we were so close, Jay would call out to me, "Your sister's here," when he brought her over.

Underneath her carefree, easy-going manner, I sensed Lucy was hurting, as she vacillated between giving her baby up for adoption and keeping it. I encouraged her to do what she felt was best for herself and the baby. And we had long talks. One afternoon Lucy shocked me when she came in with a short haircut. "Lucy, you cut off your beautiful long black hair…" She responded with an emotional outburst towards her father that came out of the blue—and there were many more after that. Lucy's true feelings were now spiraling out of control. She came over a few more times and then she disappeared from our lives.

Lucy soon gave birth to a baby girl. She decided to keep the baby, and I was not surprised. I later learned she was living with her baby, the baby's father and his family. I wondered how she was, and how things were going for her.

I soon was back in a state of depression when I said, "I'm very unhappy, Jay. I can't go on like this. We have to do something about the way we're living. I've been over this many times with you."

I don't know what I expected, but I just had to get it out of my system. "Relax, baby! Don't get all upset." There was a blank expression on his face as he sat there and read his newspaper.

But I was upset. I was struggling with my anxieties and depression, and a relationship that wasn't working. I couldn't accept things the way they were. I tolerated as much as I could. I didn't feel strong enough emotionally to make a change. I felt trapped.

I walked around with tears in my eyes, dreaming about finding someone who could really love me, if that were at all possible. After all those years, I still felt loveless and alone. Love… Love… Love… Would I ever find that love?

On one of my walks in the neighborhood, I came upon a little boutique just a few blocks from where we lived. I went wild with delight over the latest styles I saw in Venus' Closet, and it was all so reasonably priced. So, there I was, once again escaping from my inner turmoil and indulging myself in my favorite pastime. It was just a momentary fix that was so good while it lasted, but when it wore off, I felt as bad as before, maybe even worse.

Jay took a look at me and said, "Let's go out for a drive, baby. You'll feel better." I dragged myself out of the house, but I was too depressed to even care where I was going. Sometimes we wound up at Friendly's in Yonkers and I would delight in my favorite, a hot fudge sundae. There was something I loved about the taste of chocolate; it seemed to alleviate my yearning for something I couldn't describe. But, of course, it was just another temporary fix.

There were times when we got away from the Bronx and did a little traveling. We went to Pennsylvania and rode around the Amish country. We viewed the White House in Washington, D.C. We did some sightseeing in Cape Cod and enjoyed the beautiful scenery in Canada. All of these places were delightful to see—but it felt so good to get back.

I had some wonderful moments with Jay and some very trying times. But I couldn't get away from the truth: I was living with a married man.

58

"Work is Your Salvation!"

I was in my 30's and every so often my uncle looked upset with me and he would say, "Lenore, you need a raison d'etre. That is to say, you need a purpose in life." He didn't like the way I was living, and I agreed with him.

An aching sadness continued to dwell inside of me and wouldn't go away. And how forlorn I was because I was feeling so unloved and misunderstood. I felt like a small child in a dangerous, hostile world. Yet my need to do something meaningful remained strong. What would give my life some meaning, some happiness, some joy?

My uncle was now telling me, "Work is your salvation." I began to think about it. Maybe he was right. But maybe that was a deception in itself. I once thought that a job would give me some sense of worth and fulfillment. I secretly was hoping for a job that would give me a "raison d'etre," but the jobs I found only made me feel more insignificant and bad about myself. But I wasn't about to give up.

Again, I began to search the employment section of the New York Times and contact various employment agencies. I went out on interviews and presented myself as a person eager to work—

someone who would work very hard if given the opportunity. I was greatly disappointed. With the skills I had, I couldn't find anything that was halfway decent. I was once again rejecting the jobs that required the same old straight typing. I was also rejecting anything that had to do with figures. I wouldn't dare attempt anything like that.

I had an opportunity to learn a plug switchboard and it sounded exciting—so I took the job. I didn't think it would be so hard to do, but the cords had a way of becoming entangled, and I couldn't determine quickly enough which plug went into what socket. Meanwhile, more calls were coming in. I became flustered. *What am I going to do? If I keep on like this, they're going to fire me!* Then the board became really busy, and I was losing calls right and left. I was asked to leave. I was only there for a few days.

I went home in tears. I became sick with despair. I wondered: *Why can't I do anything right?* My self-esteem was very low, and I was becoming even more insecure. *Will I ever find more work?*

In desperation, I took a job as a waitress in a busy restaurant in Manhattan. I said I had experience, but they found out soon enough. When the lunch hour was over, so was my job.

I soon found jobs doing general office work that consisted of typing, filing, and handling a push button phone. The many new things I had to learn confused me, so I nervously went to my bosses and co-workers with questions and more questions, as if my life depended on it. "Is this the way you want it?" "Am I doing it right?" I don't know how they put up with me; I felt like I was driving them crazy.

Along the way, I met some very nice, patient people and some who were not so nice. If I felt anger or annoyance directed at me, I became very distraught: *Oh, they don't like me!* It was so easy for me to identify with criticisms and condescending remarks because that's what my life was all about as I was growing up. Underneath it all, I felt that my peers knew everything, and I knew nothing. An awareness that I wasn't like other people continuously came up to taunt me.

So, I was working again and earning a salary, but it wasn't filling the empty void inside of me. Still, it felt great to have money in my pocket, although I had no real desire to spend it. I liked to stash it away in the bank and see the dollars grow. So, I continued to be frugal, trying to save a dollar whenever possible. On my lunch hour, I just about starved myself so that I could save a few pennies. I wound up in a Chock Full O' Nuts, where I would indulge myself with a small cheese and walnut sandwich. I usually came away hungry.

I soon got a job with a carpeting firm as a general office assistant. I worked with a cranky middle-aged bookkeeper in a two-female office. She walked around with a chip on her shoulder and was especially nasty to me. If I said, "There you are," (handing some work to her), she barked back, "No, there you are!" in a tone of contempt. Her caustic remarks bothered me and made the environment a very unpleasant place for me to work in. The more she slapped me down emotionally, the more I felt a need to make conversation and connect with her. I was looking for some way to fix this problem, but I was only making it worse for myself. It was the same feeling I experienced with my mother when I tried to communicate with her. Frustrated and depressed, I left that job after nine months. I went home and cried to Jay, as he sat there, smoking a cigarette.

I soon heard about taking dictation from tapes. This appealed to me; it was an opportunity for me to use my good spelling and grammatical skills—and it paid more. I eagerly registered for a mini-course with the Dictaphone Company. I learned to use a machine that played tapes called dictabelts. With earphones on my head and a pedal for foot control, I passed the course in a few weeks and received a Certificate of Proficiency. I was walking on air.

I tried out for several positions using my new skills. I was told, "You don't have the experience." I wondered how I was going to get the experience if no one was willing to take a chance on me. I continued to trudge the city streets answering ads from various newspapers. I was feeling down and worn out when I came in off the street and applied to an adoption agency. I was astonished; there was an opening! I was immediately assigned to transcribe tapes in a Dictaphone pool. *What will this be like? Will I be able to do the work? What will my co-workers be like?*

It turned out that my co-workers were five middle-aged ladies, easy-going and eager to be of help. If I had a problem with a tape, I could easily turn to any one of them. I liked my new work environment. I also felt good about the young social work students who were supplying the dictabelts we had to transcribe. They provided myriad case studies about their clients. I was learning the ins and outs of the adoption/foster care process, and how heavily screened people are when they request a child. I found it all very fascinating.

But transcribing the dictabelts was no easy task. I was now listening to voices on tapes that were not very clear. The sound was often muffled, and I had to play the tapes several times to make sense of what was being said. When I was really stuck, I called over one of my co-workers. If she had a problem in deciphering it, I wound up calling on the student who made the tape. That took time. I was also losing valuable time trying to regulate the speed; words were coming at me too fast or too slow. I found it very frustrating and a drain on my energy. I came home at night exhausted and just about plopped into bed.

As more tapes kept coming, there was more pressure to get the work done as quickly as possible. I felt as though I was drowning in tapes. Most of the ladies in the Dictaphone pool also felt that there was too much coming too quickly. Sometimes we took a breather to gripe amongst ourselves. At times we shared personal tidbits and had a laugh or two. There was a nice, warm rapport amongst us, and this gave me some sense of belonging. There was a sense of camaraderie that was quite different from anything I experienced before on a job.

But while I was enjoying this special comfort, I was becoming more disenchanted with the Dictaphone. At the end of the day, I dragged myself out of the office. My energy was spent. I couldn't wait to go home, get into bed, and cry. I had graduated from the role of a copy typist to that of Dictaphone typist, and it didn't feel much different. I was still nothing more than a typing machine. But I found this could divert my mind and give me a sense of having some control over my life.

One day I was sitting at the Dictaphone machine when I looked down and saw my left ankle puffed up like a balloon. *Oh, my goodness, what happened to my ankle?* I was scared out of my wits. I immediately called my neighborhood doctor and he told me to come right over. I then told the office manager I had to leave and rushed over to the doctor's office. I was sweating and the worst thoughts entered my mind, as the doctor examined my leg. He asked a multitude of questions and then he casually said, "I don't think it's anything to worry about." But he couldn't tell me what was wrong.

I went with Jay to an internist in a well-known hospital in Manhattan who said, "It looks like an edema—a fluid build-up. My wife has the same thing—one ankle swollen, no pain. No one knows what it comes from." He seemed unconcerned, but I still had a need to know.

Jay was now accompanying me from one doctor to another. One of them said: "It looks like occupational hazard. Are you sitting for long periods of time in one position?"

The answer to that question was yes. I then told him: "I'm continuously moving my right foot up and down to control the pedal of the machine, but I am not using my left foot."

He still couldn't give me a medical explanation for what was causing the swelling, nor did he make any suggestions. I was in the dark about what to do next, and I was worried. The swelling was not going down.

Jay soon found an internist in Queens who had a reputation for making an accurate diagnosis, and in no time, we were visiting this doctor. I studied the expression on his face as he examined my leg. He didn't look as alarmed as I felt. He said: "Looks like there's a problem with the venous return."

It sounded scary. I anxiously asked, "Is it serious?"

"No, not really. This is called venous insufficiency. That means there's not enough blood being returned to the heart…." He went into a technical description. I heard words and more words, but I couldn't take in what he was saying. I just knew that he was putting the medical pieces of the puzzle together. He spoke in a matter-of-fact tone and didn't appear concerned. That gave me a sense of relief.

"I'm working at a job where I sit a lot. Do you think that has something to do with my condition?"

"Yes, it does!" he responded. "Get up and walk around. Do not sit in one place for any length of time. Right now, I want you to go home and elevate your leg in an upright position, so that your leg is above the heart. Get an Ace bandage and wear it on your leg during the day until the swelling goes down."

I went out and bought myself a bandage, and for months I wore it wrapped around my ankle, going all the way up to my knee. When I was in bed, I elevated my leg in an upright position. In the office, it remained on my mind to get up, move around, and not to stay glued to the transcribing machine. Eventually, much of the swelling went down.

It was dawning upon me that a steady diet of Dictaphone was not good for me. It was time to look for another job. I began to check the employment ads once again. I was using a pay phone in the adoption agency lobby, but I wasn't on guard. Someone from my office must have overheard my conversation and reported me to Management. I was called in and dismissed on the spot.

What a shock! *Who could have done that?* I thought all my co-workers were my friends—apparently not. It was very upsetting, but a part of me felt good about it. I wanted to get away from all those tedious tapes. I had been with the adoption agency for two years and now I was free.

I didn't stay idle very long. I was eager to explore new possibilities and I soon found an opening in an export firm. There was one problem: my fear of self-service elevators. The job was on the fifteenth floor and the elevator went right into the office. What was I to do? I didn't mind going in with other people, but I hated to be in the elevator by myself. My need to have this job, however, was greater than my fear. So, scared as I was, I went into the elevator and I pressed the button that said 15. My heart was throbbing wildly in my chest, as I stood by myself in this moving closet. Finally, the doors opened. *I made it!* I was on the fifteenth floor. And I had a job!

I was now going up and down in the elevator every day. I continued to be nervous and I may have been holding my breath, but I got through it each time without incident. This was a big accomplishment for me and soon much of my fear was gone.

My new boss, Mr. Sternberg, was an elderly gentleman who believed in handwritten notes and loaded me down with them. I was sitting at my desk, trying to decipher his chicken scratches, when suddenly I heard one of the other bosses calling his secretary. He had a strong German accent and couldn't say her name, Gracie. Instead, he said, "Crazy, Crazy, please come in, I have dictation for you." It sounded so funny; I sat there and chuckled to myself. This was one distraction I needed and welcomed.

Unfortunately, there was also some Dictaphone on this job, but I remembered my physical condition. I got up, walked around the office, and made sure that I didn't sit for hours in one spot.

Here, too, there was so much to get done and it all took time. There were deadlines to meet and I worried: *How will I ever get all this finished?* Mr. Sternberg walked up and down and said: "Is it ready yet?"

I was once again complaining to Jay: "I can't stand the pressure any longer. What am I going to do?"

Jay surprised me one night. He came in with a bunch of phonograph records and a book called: "How To Learn Shorthand At Home." *Me learn shorthand? Never!* I dreaded the thought of stenography. It was another language, and I didn't think I could ever learn it. Nevertheless, I thumbed through the steno book and was overwhelmed by what I saw. *This is utterly fantastic—circles and lines that make up words. How will I ever make sense of these symbols? How will I read them back? But then again, stenography might just open doors for me in the business world...*

I was in anguish when I asked my mother for help. She had worked as a secretary in her youth and was familiar with Gregg shorthand. I plunged into the steno book with her assistance. I worked at building my speed by playing the shorthand records and testing myself. Every spare moment was spent studying. With a lot of perseverance, some tears, and plenty of hard work, I achieved my goal in less than four months. I was doing ninety-three words a minute! I was thrilled. I was grateful to my mother and Jay for making this possible.

When I felt ready, I told Mr. Sternberg I could now take shorthand and asked him to dictate his mail to me. He seemed reluctant at first, but then agreed. I was a little nervous, but there I was, sitting opposite my boss, making lines and circles—and I could read it all back. I was very happy with this accomplishment. I was now a stenographer! In a few days, however, he stopped; he went back to the Dictaphone and his handwritten notes. What happened? He never told me, and I didn't ask.

Disheartened, I walked a few doors down the street on my lunch hour and answered an ad for a secretary with stenographic skills. I was immediately accepted. My heart was leaping with joy.

I was now working in another export firm. My new boss, a tall, lean, Harvard graduate, whom I shall refer to as Mike, was a tense, arrogant young man who could be quite overbearing at times. I didn't have a moment to myself. I was now taking shorthand for long stretches of time, and strange as it may seem, it wasn't as bad as I thought. It no longer presented a threat to me. In fact, I was getting to like it. However, I didn't like being a robot, carrying out the orders of my master to the point of fatigue. But somehow, I was managing…

I was sitting at my desk knee deep in pages of stenographic notes, when I looked up and saw Mr. Von Linn coming my way. He was one of the other bosses in the firm. A small, kind, elderly gentleman with white hair, a big thick mustache, and a twinkle in his eye, he could be very serious, but he also liked to clown around. Most often, as he passed my desk, he would give me an impish grin or a wink. Sometimes we would share a few friendly words.

On this particular day I felt a need to talk to him about my workload. I complained, "I have so much to do…." He pointed his finger at me and with an angry look on his face, he raised his voice and gave a command: "Don't talk about it! Do it!" In the moment I was taken aback. *Is this the Mr. Von Linn who's always so nice to me?*

"Yep," I responded. "I'm doing it, I'm doing it." For a long moment we stared at each other and then he broke into a great big laugh—and I laughed, too. He then walked away with that impish grin on his face. It turned out to be a fun-filled moment for both of us.

How I wished my own boss had a sense of humor. I would describe Mike as a slave driver and a grouch. I recall the time I was taking dictation for over an hour when I had to go to the Ladies' Room. When I returned, Mike was standing at the door of his office, with his hands on his hips, biting his lip as he looked down at his watch. "You know, you were gone for seven minutes! What took you so long?" I was aghast. From that time on, I tried to be prepared whenever I thought he might be calling me in for dictation. But I wasn't always able to predict when that would be.

I was so frustrated when I sat down and talked to Jay about my various episodes with my boss, Mike. He said, "These are good experiences, baby. You don't know it, but your boss is teaching you a lot." A lot of what? I didn't have the guts to ask him, it sounded utterly ridiculous to me.

For the most part, life in the workplace was rough and even painful at times. But I persevered. It was still better than cleaning lamps. Many a time my uncle saw me unhappy and brooding. He would reiterate what he told me so many times: "Work is your salvation!"

I wondered about that.

59

My Visits with Hedda

The relationship between my mother and me was quite complicated. I was in my 30's and I told myself I would have to stop seeing her. I found when I visited, my emotions were getting the better of me and I was becoming very upset. Although she had become calmer and more civilized—no longer the tyrannical mother I knew in childhood—I could not undo the emotional damage she had inflicted upon me in my youth.

When I came out of my mother's house, I was lost. Sad, lonely, and confused, I felt an ache inside wherever I went. I felt rejected and different from everyone on the planet. As I carried around my pain, I was brimming with anger at my mother for cutting me off from contact with the outside world, isolating me to live within the confines of her needs and wants. I had become nothing more than my mother's possession, her captive. Because I was not allowed to be a child, I wound up swallowing my feelings while resentment festered inside of me.

Most debilitating: I didn't have social skills. I didn't know how to fit into this strange, difficult world I found myself in—a world that never stopped being alien to me. I was overwhelmed and distraught as I tried to find my way around. How was I to function?

I struggled with the thought of it. And then I struggled with the reality of it. And the struggle didn't stop.

I walked around in a whirlpool of anxiety. While I was besieged by hostile feelings for my mother, I wasn't able to break away from her. When I visited her, I was overcome with a need to express painful pent-up, unresolved feelings from yesteryear. That's when my feelings came bursting forth. It might have been better to stay away, for I became consumed with rage as I lamented about the way I grew up. "You've ruined my life! You've caused me insurmountable pain and suffering. I grew up with no family, no friends, no love, no nothing. And it's all because of you!"

It became even more upsetting when she just sat there and didn't say a word.

I came over one day more distraught than usual. As I entered her apartment, she said with a long face: "You haven't been here lately. I guess you're too busy. You don't have time for me?"

"You know what? Maybe I don't like coming over here. You've always made me feel bad about myself. You always told me I'm rotten, I'm no good, you never had anything good to say about me. And now I feel really bad about myself. Not even therapy helps! I hope you're happy."

"I did the best I could," was her usual response said with no feeling in her voice, no expression on her face. She remained devoid of emotion or remorse while I smoldered within.

Sometimes she became incensed and soon it was a battle of words. She complained: "I'm getting sick from all this aggravation. My blood pressure—you're going to give me a stroke!"

That really scared me, but I wasn't able to help myself once I got into my pain. Many times, I went over with the intent of holding my tongue and having a nice, pleasant visit, but my hostility was just below the surface. Sometimes it got so out of hand, I would run for the door, hurry home, and then sit there and worry: *Will she be all right?*

I spoke to my uncle Will about my tumultuous visits with Hedda. He listened but did not say much. Then one day he looked amused and laughed. "A friend of mine, who knows about the way you grew up, remarked, 'It's a wonder Lenore hasn't gotten a gun and shot her mother by now. It wouldn't be surprising if she did'."

I was startled to hear this. Yes, I was very angry but why hadn't any of those murderous thoughts entered my mind? And if they did, I would have dismissed them just as quickly.

One of my therapists said, "You were 'identifying with the aggressor' as you were growing up. A person will agree with an aggressor when she perceives danger or feels threatened and is trying to feel safe. Then it becomes a matter of survival. Another aspect of this is when a parent—the aggressor—dislikes, neglects, and treats a child badly. The child will then do whatever is necessary to receive the love and approval the child wants so badly. The child will then follow the dictates of the aggressor. In both cases, you were coping with your mother's brutality. You might say you were 'holding the hand of the aggressor'."

This insight gave me an understanding as to why I needed to feel closer to my mother and cling to her the meaner she was to me. I wondered if there wasn't a part of the little girl in me that still craved her mother's love. Maybe it was something I didn't want to see.

In spite of the turmoil I experienced in my visits, I was still unable to stay away. I put my heart and soul into trying to get her to understand my pain and frustration. She had one response: "What would you do if you didn't have me to blame?"

While a rageful side of me continued to feel contempt for my mother, there was another side that could feel compassion for her— a side that was actually concerned about her. It troubled me when I came into her basement apartment and felt the coldness and smelled the stench of mold in the air. I hated to see my mother living like that. I thought it was very unhealthy and depressing. I spoke to her about it, but she said it didn't bother her.

When I saw a sick, morose look on her face, I had a strong desire, emanating from childhood, to change it into a smile. I became distressed to see my mother sitting there as if the world had collapsed upon her. I wanted to help her so badly, but it seemed that an invisible wall existed between us. Hedda remained in a state of despair and so did I.

On one of my visits I noticed something different about her. It was summer and she was wearing a white short-sleeved blouse and black skirt that gave her a youthful, neat appearance. She seemed rather relaxed as we sat down on folding chairs in her living room and talked. I soon noticed tears in her eyes. "I've been listening to a religious program about the word of God…" I perceived that she had found some meaning and comfort in the belief of a higher power and I strongly encouraged her to stay with that program.

A short time later, she raved about the actor, Andy Griffith. Her eyes lit up and there was a smile on her face when she asked, "Have you ever seen his show?" No, I hadn't, I rarely watched TV, but that wasn't important; she had found a source of pleasure that was able to take her out of her troubled world and make her smile. I realized the importance of this, as I thought about my own lonely existence in my youth.

While Hedda had mellowed over time, she was still very detached and enmeshed in her own world. There were times when I wanted to put my arms around her, but she pulled away. She still wasn't amenable to touch, let alone a hug or kiss. I felt like a leper in her presence. I could never find the words to tell her how awful it felt to be pushed away by your own mother.

Then one morning Hedda called me and excitedly said, "Please get me a record by Englebert Humperdinck."

Who? I had heard that name before, but what in the world was this all about? She went on to tell me, "He's a singer and he recorded a song about love…" She gave me the name of the song, and then burst into tears. "It's a beautiful song. I never heard anything like it. It's all about love. I want you to promise me you'll get that record for me. I don't know what love is…I always wanted to know what love is about,"

Tears welled up in my eyes as I heard my mother telling me something I sensed all along that I couldn't admit to myself. Then, that day, she revealed it to me herself. Now, my suspicions were confirmed. My mother was incapable of love.

It was a strange, crazy relationship. My mother often said, "I know you hate me." Yes, a part of me did, but there was still this other part that cared. Ambivalence is the only way I can describe it. Regardless of all the wrong she did, she was still my mother.

60

Gale Force

Jay and I were taking a walk in Manhattan when we came upon a feline pet shop, and my eyes opened wide. I've always loved cats, and here before me was this lovely little shop that seemed to cater exclusively to cats. I just had to go inside and see for myself.

It was fascinating. I saw breeds of cats that I had never seen before. How beautiful and exotic they were. We walked around, admiring the kittens in their cages. I was most impressed by the ones that had a dark mask with cream-colored coats and sable brown markings. There was a look of alertness about them that intrigued me. I was drawn to one in particular. What a magnificent looking creature! I thought. Soon, a tall, attractive redhead came over. "They're all pedigreed. The one you're looking at is a Siamese. His parents were champions in cat shows. He's an exquisite little fellow, isn't he?"

Yes, I had to agree; I never saw anything quite like him. I kept staring at the kitten, and he was staring right back at me. He soon was performing for me on his scratching post.

Jay said, "Do you want him?"

It's hard enough for me to take care of myself, what am I going to do with a cat? I thought it was very noble of Jay to ask me, but I couldn't give him an answer in the moment. A couple of nights later, we went back; I wanted to see that kitten again. I stood there admiring it, and Jay asked the same question. Again, I had no answer. But Jay did. He took eighty-five dollars out of his wallet and handed it to the redhead. She introduced herself as Mrs. Gale and said, "You can call us any time if you have a problem."

I was startled. Just like that, I became the mother of a Siamese kitten!

The owner, a short, pudgy man, soon came over and said, "My name is Myron Gale. If you have any questions, day or night, feel free to call me or my wife." We thanked him and left with the kitten.

Jay called the cat Charley Brown and said: "I think it will be a good experience for you to have this cat. Maybe you'll want to have a baby…"

While I was sure I didn't want a baby, I now was overjoyed with having a cat in the house. I loved to look at it and watch it do its cute little maneuvers. I adored little Charley. I had a burning desire to take him in my arms and hold him, however, his claws looked very sharp, and I was extremely uncomfortable. I watched Jay caress him and I marveled at it; he showed no fear or hesitation. *Why can't I be like that?*

Within a few days, we noticed a problem; Charley wasn't eating. We both were worried, so Jay brought him back to the Gales. When he returned, he told me, "They're taking care of him. They're going to find out what's wrong." I had a very uneasy feeling about this, but I hoped everything would be okay.

A few weeks later, Jay came home with another Siamese kitten. "They sent Charley back to the breeder, and they're nursing him back to health." I was disappointed by this news. It troubled me that Charley was not coming back. Something did not seem right, but I let it go. Holding the new kitten in his arms, Jay smiled and said: "The Gales told me this is a really sweet cat—robust and healthy."

Soon, I saw for myself. Our new kitten was a little daredevil. He looked so cute scooting up and down the apartment, and then looking at me as if he had done something wrong. There were times when he hid for hours and I went crazy looking all over the house for him. Then, all of a sudden, he appeared and wailed like a baby.

Those loud, demanding tones caused me concern. *What is he trying to tell me?*

In the pet shop we were told, "Every cat has its own personality. The Siamese are known to wail. It's normal. Nothing to worry about." But when he let out a wail, I couldn't help but worry.

I was now grasping the reality that we had a new family member whom we had to take care of and be responsible for. I was on the phone constantly with Mr. and Mrs. Gale, who assured me that I was not bothering them with all my questions. "That's what we're here for. We want to be of help." I thought of that with every phone call I made.

Eventually, we decided to call our new kitten, Hanky. As I became more comfortable with Hanky, I was able to touch him. When my love overcame my fear, I was able to pick him up and hold him in my arms. I felt like I was holding a bundle of love.

Hanky was a little clown, performing all kinds of tricks for our attention. As he kept getting into everything, I was becoming a nervous wreck. He was scratching the furniture. He was chewing on the cork of his scratching post. He was overeating and throwing up. He once swallowed a string that was tied around a cake box. It finally came out the other end, but those hours of watching and waiting made me frantic. I didn't know how to deal with a rambunctious little kitten. What was I going to do? Call Mr. Gale, of course.

Mr. Gale, (who liked to be called "Gale"), was a brilliant man with a dynamic personality. He was about 5'3" tall and over two hundred pounds. He wore his hair flat, parted in the center, and he would stride around the store in a short white lab coat. He was blatantly outspoken to the point of callousness, and he was terribly opinionated. He often referred to himself as an "intellectual sadist." On another level, he exuded an exceptional sense of humor and a gift of gab. He took pride in being a radio and television personality. I found him interesting and amusing. But I was also in awe of him.

Gale's wife, Tammie Carlson, walked around the store in a short, white medical jacket over a pair of black pants. He referred to her as "T.C." She smoked a small, slim cigar and flashed a smile that she could turn on and off like a faucet. She and Gale worked together as a team.

I came in one day to speak about Hanky. I was quite surprised when Gale flippantly said, "I'm looking for a secretary-assistant. Would you be interested?"

I had mixed feelings. I loved the idea of working in a place with cats, but I wondered if I would be able to work for Gale. He seemed like more than I could handle. He casually smiled, "Take your time, and let me know."

It was another challenge for me. I felt I needed to take this job. Why? I didn't know. But I soon found myself calling Gale and accepting his offer.

Right off the bat, Gale yelped, "One thing I don't like is the way you dress. You dress like Old Mother Hubbard! Those long, ugly Mother Hubbard skirts — I don't need that around here. I want to look at something pretty… something sexy…."

He sneered as he spoke. And I was afraid to open my mouth. He was right; my clothes were rather long and old-fashioned. A few days later Gale stormed into the store with a package in his hand. He just about threw it at me as he snarled, "Here, take this and put it on right away!"

I opened the bag and saw two short cotton dresses; one was orange with white polka dots, the other was a dark blue floral design. I was startled. "Put them on! And I mean **NOW!**"

He spoke in a loud, stern voice, and I became flustered. I hurried into the back room and changed; and then I looked in the mirror. *My goodness, they both look great on me!* I was thrilled to have them. When I modeled them for Gale, he snapped, "That's much better. Now you're presentable. I don't want to see you in any of those Old Mother Hubbard clothes!"

From then on, I pranced around the store in my new dresses. I liked the way they made me feel. And Gale liked the way I looked; I could see him eyeing me up and down with a great big cat grin on his face. The dress bottoms were approximately one inch above the knee, and I began to think that shorter would be better. I went out and bought myself some real short miniskirts. And that was the start of my miniskirt craze.

Jay was now encouraging me to wear my miniskirts way up on the thigh: "If you got it, baby, flaunt it!" I was doing just that. And Gale continued to beam with joy.

"Jay also likes me in short skirts."

Gale made a face and became annoyed. "Jay is a pseudo-intellectual. His opinions don't count." What a thing to say! But I was not about to argue with him. I thought Gale was a knowledgeable man and somehow, what he had to say was important to me.

Gale's wife, Tammie, seemed very guarded as she puffed on her slim cigars and took care of the customers. Gale held her up as a role model, "Watch T.C. and imitate her. She has style and class."

Funny he should say that; I could hear him shouting at her across the store, and I would see her clamming up. That didn't make me very comfortable. Why was he screaming at her? And would he be screaming at me next? Gale could be very overbearing at times. I was becoming more and more nervous in his presence.

Sure enough, the same thing happened with me. Gale would have what I call "yelling fits." When he was in one of his moods, he would explode over anything and everything. He roared like a lion, showing he was the top cat. He had to be heard—only I didn't want to hear him. I was trembling inside, but I wouldn't let him know. Soon it was over; it was back to the old Gale who could be so jovial and witty. I found it confusing. I never knew how to behave in his presence; I was always afraid that he'd have an outburst and be all over me with his rage.

One day Gale came in exuding a lot of joy. "You have to start wearing mink. T.C. has several of them, and she loves them. I get them at auctions, and I can get one for you, too. I want you to experience the luxury that comes with mink. There's nothing like it. Wait till you wear one...."

I winced at the thought of it, but I didn't say anything; I knew it would create dissension if I told him how I felt, so I listened to him talk. I wondered: *Why is this so important to him?* And he continued to boast about the magnificence of mink.

A few days later, Gale came into the office with a mink coat over his arm. "You'll feel like a million dollars when you put this on!" His eyeballs were rolling around, and his smile spread from ear to ear.

I told him: "I don't especially like fur coats, and I wouldn't feel comfortable wearing one."

But that made no difference. He was now badgering me: "Put on the mink!"

I finally appeased him; I put it on and went out to lunch. I'll never forget how terribly self-conscious I was, as I walked down Lexington Avenue. It just wasn't me; I couldn't wait to get it off. In a pout Gale said, "You just don't know what the good life is!" Maybe so, but I never saw that mink again, and I was happy about that.

He also had something to say about the hat I wore. "You look like an old lady in that hat! Take it off!"

It was a very cold winter day. I was about to go out on my lunch hour, and I couldn't find my hat. I was looking all over for it and I became frustrated. I was glad I had a sandwich with me. I decided to stay in and watch the cats in their cages. One cat had a beautiful deep brown coat. I admired its fur. It was curled up in a ball, with its rear end facing the outside of the cage; its face was not visible.

When Gale and his wife came in, they were all smiles, and then they burst out laughing. Gale said, "See that cat over there—the exotic brown cat—really something, isn't it? Well, I thought you'd like to know—that's your hat!" I was flabbergasted. *So that's where my hat had disappeared!*

Things like that made me laugh. But some things made me shudder—such as the time Gale had to check on a kitten delivery. Gale put on his helmet and turned to Tammie: "I'm heading down to 16th Street and I want her to come with me. I'm taking her on the scooter."

Me on a scooter? No way! Tammie chuckled and said, "Go ahead, go with Gale. You'll have a lot of fun!"

I stood there, trembling in my shoes. "No, I'm not going anywhere."

Gale barked, "Hey, dearie, you're going on that scooter with me if I have to carry you out there and put you on it myself!"

How am I going to get out of this one?

Gale got his way—as usual. It was night, and I was too scared to think about how scared I was, as I sat on the back of Gale's motor scooter. My arms could barely fit around his bulging waist, and there I was, holding on to Gale for dear life. We were zooming through traffic, and I felt my hair flying in the breeze as we flew through the night; other than that, I blocked out everything else. I was frozen in fear. How sorry I was that I ever got on that scooter. Pretty soon we reached our destination and Gale growled, "Wait here! I'll be right back!"

My heart was beating fast as I stood there, waiting for Gale. In a few minutes he returned, looking tense. "No cat deliveries tonight. Get on the scooter! We're going back."

I swore to myself: *I'll never do this again.*

As we entered the store, Gale wanted to know if I had a good time. To keep the peace I timidly said, "It was okay." If only he knew…

I couldn't wait to get home that night. How could have I let him talk me into going on a scooter with him? The next time he asked me to go on the scooter, I said, "Nope. Once is enough!" And I was so very thankful that he did not pressure me to take any more rides with him.

Gale came running in one day and said, "I'm taking you out to lunch, get ready!" *What's this all about? What does Gale have in store for me now?* Soon enough Gale was driving me over to a restaurant, taking me by the hand and forcefully telling me: "Now you're going to have duck!" I found myself in a panic. *Who ever said I wanted to eat duck?* I felt forced to comply because Gale had made the decision. I was so traumatized I didn't even know what I was eating, and later, I felt annoyed with myself because I couldn't say no.

Soon, a new problem arose: *How am I going to deal with Gale's amorous onslaughts?* "Give me a little kiss," he would say, and then he would pucker his lips. I ignored his flirtations as much as I could, as I tried to divert his attention with my humor. Sometimes that worked, but there were times when he became persistent. He would get out of his chair and chase me around the office. I thought he looked ridiculous. I wound up ducking under my desk and hiding there; I was talking fast and playfully swaying his attention to something else. Soon he stopped and I crawled out. I liked to believe it was all in the name of fun, but sometimes I wasn't so sure about that. We often wound up laughing together when these silly moments were over. But I will admit that I was very uncomfortable at the time.

He kept inviting me to the many wild parties he held in his penthouse apartment. Each time I said: "No, I'm not going." He would make a silly face and laughingly reply, "You don't know what you're missing!" He didn't give up trying, and I didn't stop saying "no."

"I want you to learn a new word every day, and I want you to tell me what it is." I looked at Gale; I didn't think I heard right. *Goodness gracious! What is this all about?* Gale burst out laughing as he said, "Then go over to T.C. and use the word in a sentence. See if she knows what it means…" I thought to myself: *This sounds wacky. How am I going to do this?"* And I sat there, gaping at him. "Sacrosanct: that's the first word we'll use. I bet she'll never know what it means."

I looked up the word in a dictionary, then went over to T.C. and used it in a sentence. She looked at me startled and said: "What are you talking about?"

I told her, "Don't worry about it. Gale is just having a little fun." I watched Gale, several feet away, rolling over in laughter. I thought: *My Goodness! What is so funny?*

Gale kept playing around with words, but that's as far as it went; he talked about it, but nothing came of it. I was tickled that I didn't have to get involved in any more of that tomfoolery.

Soon, he was telling me about hairstyles and what would be ideal for me. I was becoming upset because I didn't think I could follow anymore of his dictates. He continued: "Get rid of those nylon stockings and buy dark brown pantyhose; they're sexy and they'll look great on your legs." The next day he asked me to come into his office. "I've been thinking about it: cut your hair short, very short, and get yourself a pair of glasses with large, round frames, like Jackie Kennedy's. Wear your miniskirts with long socks that go all the way up on the knee, and (rolling his eyes) you'll look great!"

My goodness, how am I going to wear those oversized glasses? I'm not tall, and they'll look horrible on my face! And I don't want to cut my hair or walk around in those silly knee-high socks. That's not me! What am I going to tell him? He'll go crazy!"

It didn't pay for me to worry about this one; he forgot soon enough. Usually, when Gale got a new idea, the old one would get wiped out quickly enough. But that was not always the case. He was coming up with numerous ideas, so I didn't know which ones would stick. He was shaking me up emotionally as he continued to flood me with new thoughts and ideas. I couldn't say yes and I was afraid to say no. Some of them seemed rather bizarre. I never knew what Gale would present to me next. I became scared when I heard him say, "I have a great idea…" *Oh, no!*

I began to feel as if I were Gale's experiment. Whenever he cracked the whip, I had to obey. I became frazzled, trying to carry out his demands. I kept thinking of leaving, but for the life of me, I just wasn't able to walk away. I complained to Jay and I was taken aback by his response: "I think it's a good experience for you, baby." I wondered: *What's so good about it?*

I came into Gale's office one day, prepared to take dictation. Out of the blue, Gale yelled: **"Get out of New York! It's better to be a big fish in a small pond than to be a small fish in a big pond!"** His face reddened and his eyes bulged. He was in a rage.

I sat there and stared at him. I was dumbfounded as he went on to tell me why New York wasn't good for me. *Who was he to tell me what to do?* When I left the room, I was in tears. His words were overwhelming, and I resented him no end. He was shaking up my world and making me more confused than I already was.

Frustrated, I spoke to a close friend who scolded me: "The man's a nut! What are you staying there for? Get out of there!" I agreed with him. I just didn't know how to do it. Why was I there? I didn't know…

Suddenly, I would see Gale dancing and prancing around his store. My goodness, he looked so funny. I wondered: *Who is this man? What is he all about?* I couldn't figure him out for the life of me.

I came into the shop one day and Gale was beaming with joy. "I am now the pilot of a Cessna airplane and I want you to see it. My artist-friend did a great job of painting cats all over it. You've never seen anything like it!" His eyebrows rolled up and down as he said, "You have to see it. You'll just love it!"

That old feeling of anxiety was bubbling up within me, and I didn't know how to respond.

"Tomorrow afternoon, you and me are going to Teterboro Airport!"

There was something about this that sent a shiver through me. I cautiously asked: "Can I bring Jay along?

He replied, "Sure. Bring Jay. I'm bringing T.C."

That sounded reassuring; I wouldn't be alone with Gale and coerced into something I didn't want to do, like flying in an airplane. I felt compelled to go. Why? I didn't know. I told Gale, "Jay and I will meet you tomorrow at the airport."

Gale was in an upbeat mood at Teterboro. He ignored Jay and T.C. as he pointed to his plane. "Just look at those cats! Did you ever see anything like that?" I gaped at the artwork—cats in every position, covering the entire plane. It was very unusual, to say the least.

Jay and T.C. were standing nearby as Gale said: "Let's all go inside and see how nice it feels."

All of a sudden, I had a queasy feeling in my stomach. I sensed what was ahead, but somehow, I didn't want to stop it. Once we were inside, Gale unfastened the chains that anchored the plane. He came in, touched some controls, and slowly, the plane began to rise above the ground. We were taking off! We were flying!

In some strange way I welcomed this experience. I didn't know why, but again, it felt like something I had to do. Soon Tammie put a tablet in her mouth and offered me one. "It keeps you from getting dizzy." I shook my head no; I was too petrified to speak.

We were gliding on an even keel, slowly and smoothly in the air, when I faintly heard Gale remark something to Jay about "a change in the weather."

Jay replied, "It's cloudier than when we started out."

Gale didn't respond, and we continued to glide in the air for another few minutes. Soon Gale circled around the airport and suddenly brought the plane down. I wondered: *What was that all about?* But I didn't dare ask. I felt much better with my feet on the ground. I could breathe a sigh of relief.

As we left the plane, Gale made the announcement that he would be right back. I wondered where he was going in such a hurry. I lingered at the airport with Jay and T.C., and it wasn't too long before Gale returned with a trophy in his hand. It was a miniature airplane mounted on a long gold colored pedestal, with the words "FIRST FLIGHT" in huge letters on the marble base. Gale was beaming. "I bought this for you. I'm proud of you. You did very well."

He gave me a kiss on the cheek and said, "It got cloudy up there and for a few minutes, I lost my way, but I didn't say anything. I knew you'd be screaming, and I didn't want to hear it."

Oh my God, was it as bad as all that?

Jay and Tammie exchanged a smile, while I stood there, holding the trophy, and admiring it. It was a beautiful piece of work. It felt heavy in my hand. I couldn't believe that Gale would buy something so exquisite for me just because I flew in an airplane with him. I felt an inner glow as I held the trophy close to my heart.

I must say that working for Gale was more than just moving through weird experiences. In my role of secretary-assistant, I worked hard. I would hear Gale call me: "Hey, Slave, I have more work for you. Come on in." There, on his desk, would be a pile of mail waiting for me.

Sometimes I sat at my desk, overwhelmed. He was giving me a lot of dictation. I had a habit of saying to myself, "Oh, my God…"

I don't know how Gale heard me, but he would come waltzing in, and in a peculiar voice he would say: "Did you call?" He had such a funny expression on his face, I laughed out loud and laughed some more. I couldn't contain myself.

But then I got back to work. Gale's correspondence consisted of letters going out to breeders, cat lovers, and radio/television hosts who invited Gale to be a guest. There was also a curious public that wanted to know about his work with felines. He answered just about every piece of mail he received. I felt a sense of accomplishment when I finished my typing and sent the mail out. Then I would hear my master's voice: "Here, Slave, I have more for you!"

I didn't complain about the work, for I found it interesting. But I didn't think I would ever get used to the word, "Slave." After a while, however, I thought of it as a term of endearment.

As I was going through the files, I learned the truth about my little Charley Brown. He was "put away." My heart dropped. My suspicions were now confirmed. I went home despondent. I spoke to Jay and he said: "I didn't want to upset you, baby—and neither did the Gales."

The Gales just shrugged it off. "It happens all the time."

I was sad about this for a while. I was also distressed that I had to read about it in a file. Eventually, I came to terms with Charley's death.

I continued to work for Gale for a few more months. I tolerated his screaming fits and his changing moods. I shared his happy moments. I listened to his keen perceptions. I gave him my shoulder to cry on when the cats were dying from a bad batch of vaccines.

I still didn't know why I was there. I could say I was learning about life, but it was a huge price to pay. I lived in constant fear. It was wearing me down. I was drowning in stress, and I soon became ill with bronchial asthma. I couldn't stop coughing and spitting up green phlegm. Gale said, "I'm tired of seeing you choking. Get out of here and go home!"

I was out sick for a couple of weeks. "Hey, dearie, we can't afford to run a business like this!" Gale barked. **"Either you're here or don't bother to come back!"** I heard the fury in his voice, as he hung up on me.

I finally had a way out. This was the opportunity I was looking for. I was breaking my ties to Gale. I was upset and yet relieved. I did not go back.

Sometime later, I had occasion to see Gale again. He was laughing so hard; I wondered what in the world was so funny. Then he told me: "I sure pushed you around. When you had enough, I knew you would leave me, and that's exactly what happened. I got you to stand up for yourself!"

I was shocked. I couldn't find words. He looked like the cat that swallowed the canary. But as I thought about it, I realized Gale was a powerful force in my development. He once said: "I want you to have new experiences." And he made sure of that. He forced me to do things I never would have done, and I survived. I grew emotionally in the process.

Before I left that day, Gale made a prediction: "When I'm fifty-five, I will be dead."

How can he say something like that?

One day I received a phone call from his wife. "I thought you would want to know: Gale just died."

He was fifty-five years old.

61

Finding My Way

I was having one sore throat after another and bronchial infections, like when I was a child. But it didn't keep me in the house. When I felt sick enough, I went to a doctor. This time, however, the doctor did not focus on my respiratory condition. Instead, he showed concern about my back. "What's happening with your scoliosis? You have quite a pronounced curve. Does it bother you?"

I hadn't thought about it because I didn't have pain. But he made it sound urgent when he said: "Get a work-up at New York Hospital, and don't wait!" I became very anxious, and immediately called the hospital for an appointment. When I arrived there, a number of x-rays were taken. I worried: *What will the x-rays reveal?* I was in a state of panic.

When I returned to get the results, I was seen by the chief orthopedist who pointed to the curve on the x-ray and said: "You have severe scoliosis—what we call an S-shaped curve…" As I sat there listening to him speak about my condition, I became too nervous to hear what he was saying. He soon called in several doctors, who huddled together to study the x-rays and inspect my curve. They talked amongst themselves using medical terms I didn't understand. One of them said, "I do not recommend surgery—not with that curve!"

The others agreed. One doctor asked: "How is your breathing? Do you have shortness of breath?" I didn't know how to answer his question. Sometimes I felt discomfort—a sort of tightness across my midriff; I didn't know what that was, but I didn't connect it with scoliosis. I replied, "I never gave any real thought to it."

The doctor continued: "This condition can be very debilitating, and it can worsen as you grow older. Do you get tired easily? Do you feel fatigued when you are active?" My answers were definitely yes.

"Do not lift anything over five pounds. Don't do any housework. Don't even sweep a floor! And be very careful about the way you bend." I wondered: *What would happen if I did any one of those things?* I couldn't find words to ask any questions, and I was too afraid to hear the answers.

Soon, another doctor asked, "Why wasn't this curve corrected in childhood? Scoliosis can easily be treated with a brace or surgery when a child is very young."

The question hit a nerve and I wanted to cry. Instead, I sadly replied, "My mother was very ill."

The doctor's response was: "That's really too bad. There's nothing we can do for you now."

I left the hospital in a state of frenzy. I was being pummeled by a multitude of feelings. Fear and anxiety were the strongest. *How debilitating would this condition become?* The doctors said it would worsen as I grew older. I paced the streets as I thought about it. They made scoliosis sound like a treacherous disease. Yes, I was feeling a lot of fatigue and I did have breathing problems. *Oh, my God! Could this all be coming from scoliosis?*

I was in deep despair. As I thought about what the doctors said, I was overwhelmed with anger towards my mother. My scoliosis could have been prevented, but she didn't care. Dr. Gross told her: "She will have to wear a brace to correct this...." My mother disregarded what he said. How I begged her for that brace! Tears came to my eyes as I heard her "No!" ringing in my ears. How could she have denied me medical treatment to straighten my back? Was she that disturbed or just plain evil?

I thought of the top-notch Madison Avenue back specialist that Will and Jessie brought me to several years before. He told me: "There's nothing to be concerned about. You have an innocuous curve." Could he have been wrong? Were the doctors in New York Hospital correct? I was thoroughly confused.

I had to find a way to deal with my emotional turmoil. I had to keep busy. I had to keep going. So, what was I going to do?

After my nerve-wracking experience with Gale, I decided not to tie myself down to permanent employment. I didn't want to be a "slave" any longer to the commands and dictates of a boss. I wanted to work, and it seemed that temporary office work would be ideal. I thought of the many ways in which it would be good for me: I wouldn't have to follow the same monotonous procedure every day. I would have freedom to come and go as I pleased. I could travel all over the city and meet a lot of people. I could see what different work environments were like. I might even find a job I liked if that were possible.

So, I went out to explore the world of temporary work. On one of my interviews with a temp agency, a rep told me, "We need someone who can take shorthand—about eighty words a minute—and read back her notes with accuracy. We have a problem finding that." I suddenly felt a surge of confidence because I knew I had good skills. I took a shorthand/typing test and was immediately hired by that agency. I also registered with several other agencies. As soon as someone was ill or unavailable for work, I received a phone call. Sometimes I didn't know what kind of firm I would be assigned to, or where in the city I would be working until the last minute. But it didn't matter; I eagerly looked forward to each new assignment. I soon chose one agency over the others because it provided me with steady employment.

It was an incredible story: I lived the life of a hermit with my mother. I went in one door of a school building and out the other. I couldn't find my way around the corner. My contact with the outside world came from a radio. My transportation skills were almost zero. And there I was, traveling all over the city into some of the most luxurious, high-class buildings on Madison and Fifth Avenues. How amazing it was—me taking shorthand from bigwig corporate executives! What was even more amazing is that I took it all in stride. I didn't think there was anything unusual or wonderful about my being able to accomplish all this with a background like mine. If I thought about it, I most probably would never have attempted it. I knew, however, that I could type and take shorthand. I also had an intuitive grasp of grammar. With a striving for excellence, I was able to use these skills to my advantage. But still, I couldn't find any real meaning in anything I did. No matter how much I tried, I couldn't find a way to feel good about myself. But that didn't stop me from trying to do better with each new assignment.

Because I felt very uncomfortable with anything new, I had the queasiest feeling about going into a strange setting—but I dealt with it, as a flood of anxiety engulfed me. I never knew what to expect when I opened the door of an office for the first time. *What will this be like?* My nervousness gradually lessened as I became more accustomed to my new environment. I tried to conceal my insecurity as best I could.

I suppose what was even more devastating was to walk into an unknown setting and see all those faces gaping at me. My goodness, you would think I came from outer space! Soon, I was introduced as "The Temp." Something about the whole scene made my stomach churn. I wondered: *Are they going to accept me? Will I be able to work here?*

The assignments kept coming in and things were moving along nicely, despite the tension I felt inside of me. I continued to be concerned about maintaining my calm; although I'm sure at some point my nervousness was apparent. However, I could not allow that to interfere with my assignments. I was most intent upon doing my very best on each job. Every one of my assignments was very important to me—so important that I rarely turned one down. If I were unable to go out on an assignment, I would fret as if the world were coming to an end. I was constantly on the go, scurrying from one place to another.

Some assignments lasted a day or two, a week, and possibly a month or more. Sometimes it wasn't clear just how long an assignment would run. I was exploring new territory all the time, and it presented a huge challenge for me. There was usually something to contend with on each job, and I became more anxious as I struggled with situations that arose every day. I worried about the reactions of the executives when I made mistakes. I became nervous: *Is the boss satisfied with my work? Is he going to ask me to leave?*

While I was gaining emotional strength dealing with the complexities of office life, I still had to struggle with my overwhelming fear of riding up and down in a closed box. It continued like this, as I went from building to building into strange new elevators. To add to this, my assignments were usually on high floors. But I developed a strategy for dealing with this problem: I waited for others to go in, and then I joined them. Not being alone made me feel a little safer, but I still found myself fighting to control my panic as my heart raced wildly in my chest. I could breathe easier when the doors finally opened, and I made it to my floor.

If there was no one around to join me in an elevator, I was in trouble. I felt ashamed as I spoke to building attendants and told them my problem. Many times I received the response: "There are others who feel the same as you. We see them all the time." One attendant told me: "There's a man in the building, an accountant, who walks up to the twenty-fifth floor. He will not use the elevator!" I was so relieved to know that there were others like me. And I dealt with the problem each time it came up.

The best time of my workday was the lunch hour when I could get away from the office and its rigidities. The elevators were usually packed, and I struggled to push my way into a cluster of people that were squeezed together like sardines in a can. When I arrived on the main floor, I ran out into the street like a bat out of hell. How invigorating it felt to sniff in a breath of fresh air.

I scurried around, looking for an inexpensive place in which to eat, and usually wound up at a Chock Full o' Nuts. Wherever I worked in the city, there were plenty of them around, so I didn't have to go far. They were usually packed during the lunch hour, and

I waited a while to get a seat. As I grabbed a quick cheese and walnut sandwich, I looked down at my watch and it was just about time to get back to work.

Traveling around the city usually presented a problem for me because I didn't know my way around, and I would have to ask for directions. It may have been annoying to the people I bothered, but what could I do? I had to get to my job.

I worked in some beautiful, modern offices and in others that were not very attractive. It didn't make a difference to me, for I was there to work, not to admire my environment. But some of these places were breathtakingly gorgeous, and so often my feet would sink into thick, plush carpeting. One office was so modern, I bumped into a glass door; my myopic eyesight didn't allow me to see the glass in front of me. I was not hurt; I was just shaken in the moment. Thereafter, I was very much on guard when I came into an ultra-modern office. I preferred the old fashioned offices that were not so elegant in style, but more practical for me to get around.

I was soon receiving assignments to work as an executive secretary in some of the most prestigious firms in the city. I was in awe; I was taking dictation from presidents and vice-presidents of corporations. I didn't think I could measure up to the standards of working for men of that caliber. I scared myself with negative thoughts about messing up in some way and getting fired, but it didn't happen. I usually had no trouble reading my stenographic notes or doing other office work that came up. A few of my bosses complimented me on my skills. I was pleasantly surprised to receive this praise and I was able to feel good in the moment.

As I went around the city, from one place to another, I had a hope that maybe I would come upon a job that would make me happy and fulfilled. But it was just wishful thinking. There were no right or wrong jobs—just jobs. I didn't come upon any job that I would have wanted to make permanent.

It amazed me that I usually didn't give a thought to the people I was replacing. I knew many of them were out ill, and while I grew up with a certain amount of fear about germs and contamination, I wasn't worried about any of this when I was on an assignment. One time, however, I was told that I was replacing a young woman who was out ill with the very contagious mononucleosis. That scared me. I uncomfortably approached one of the office workers and asked, "Has anyone in the office come down with this illness?" I was assured that there was nothing to worry about, but for a while I still felt considerable concern about this. I can't recall any other time when I was so upset about contracting an illness on an assignment. For the most part, I was very wrapped up in the tasks that were presented to me.

As a temp, I was always under stress to perform exceedingly well. I perceived that I was under continuous scrutiny from my superiors. That applied to the clothes I wore as well. My agency advisor would call me up and tell me: "Dress really sharp for this one. I'm sending you to a posh office on Madison Avenue." I received many such assignments, and each time I became a little shaky because I knew I wasn't a "sharp" dresser; I wore what was comfortable and what I was used to, which was something simple like a blouse or sweater and skirt. I usually didn't give much thought to my appearance, as long as I was dressed nice and neat when I left the house. Soon, I added a jacket to my attire.

I continued to wonder how others perceived me in the workplace. I worried that the people around me would see through me. I couldn't have them see the real me—the me who was so very unsure of herself. What would they think? They might not want me around; they might even ask me to leave. So often, I wore a smile on my face to cover the doubt and confusion I felt inside. I had to hide my fears and anxieties under the mask I wore—my protective mask—the smile that said I was okay, and everything was all right in my world.

When I looked around, I saw my co-workers, confident and poised, holding down permanent jobs, while I came in as a measly fill-in. When I compared myself with any one of them, I felt small and insignificant. A sense of worthlessness was making me feel I didn't deserve any better. All I could do was feel those bad feelings until they went away.

I guess I had a lot of guts. I came out of isolation to leap into a world of business that I knew nothing about and found even more difficult to understand. I was functioning on a drive to succeed. I continued to work diligently at whatever was offered to me, treating each job as if it were my very own. Many of my bosses recognized this, and when they had a build-up of work, they called the agency and asked for me. I felt joy in being appreciated.

In my travels from office to office, I had a secret wish to make a connection with a coworker. In a rare instance or two it might happen, but it was short-lived. I wasn't in a place long enough to establish any real rapport. I did admire the friendships I observed; I wondered how people could become so close.

Slowly, I began to discover that temp work wasn't very good for my frail ego. Temp workers were not well respected. They had a bad reputation for not showing up for work, coming in late, or leaving an assignment in the middle. The permanent staff made remarks about temps being "unreliable and incompetent." I didn't fall into this category, but I sensed they had the same misgivings about me, and I was very sensitive about that.

Many a time I overheard my co-workers referring to me as: "only the temp." How I hated to hear that—but it was true. I was an outsider coming into a place where people knew each other, worked together, and belonged. I could never get used to being on the outside looking in; it made me feel so sad, so despondent, so unlike everybody else, and so very alone. Yet I had chosen work where I would be just that: an outsider. I tried to adjust as best I could, clinging to a hope that I would be liked and accepted for myself. But it wasn't happening, and it was wearing me down. I was as invisible as ever.

At the end of the workday, a feeling of emptiness hovered over me. I went home and cried to Jay: "They say I'm 'only a temp.' I'm not seen as a person, and it kills me. I don't know what to do."

Jay listened and lit a cigarette. Then I heard his usual response: "You're upset, baby. I'll take you out to eat and you'll feel better." I loved going out to eat, but it didn't help me find a solution to this problem.

I complained to my therapist about my temp jobs, as well as my unhappy life with Jay. But it was just talk. I couldn't stop doing temp work anymore than I could leave Jay. Therapy helped me calm down considerably while I was there, but when I left, I reverted back to my same old self. My uncle remarked: "You relieve yourself by talking, but there is no change." He made a good point, and I was saddened by the truth.

Nevertheless, I continued to believe in therapy where I could talk to someone who would hear me, offer me support, and provide occasional insights, but I avoided getting in touch with what was already there. I was so busy fretting about what was going on outside of me I didn't bother to ask: What's going on inside?

I was overlooking my physical problems for some time, so I began to go out for long, brisk walks. I was told that exercise is essential for dealing with scoliosis. One day I overdid it and my lower back began to ache so badly, I didn't think I would be able to make it home. I was a couple of blocks from where my mother lived, so I painfully limped over and rang her bell. When she opened the door, I was in panic as I uttered, "I have terrible back pain. I have to lie down right away!"

Once inside, I looked for a place to lie down. I noticed a bench loaded down from one end to the other with cans of food and paper products. I stood there staring at it, while my mother, a few feet away, looked at me with a blank expression on her face. I could see she wasn't about to make space for me. I cried, "What about your bed?"

I now had a frantic need to get off my feet, but from the weird expression on my mother's face, I perceived it wasn't about to happen. "You mean you're not going to let me lie down on your bed?"

She slowly responded, "Maybe yes, maybe no."

I will never forget how those words tore me apart. I looked at her in disbelief and asked, "Is it germs?"

She did not reply.

I can't believe it! My mother isn't going to give me a place to lie down when I feel so sick, I'm about to fall on my face.

I was devastated. I guess I should have known better. Hurt and angry, I hobbled out into the street. I couldn't help thinking: *What a bitch!*

Bent over and sobbing, I staggered a couple of long blocks until I reached the parkway. There, I found a bench. I sat down and cried some more. How could she be so mean?

I stayed away from my mother for some time after that. It was just as well. When I did see her, we continued to have words as I blamed her for my emotional pain and physical health problems. As usual, I was desperate to hear her acknowledge my pain or at least show some remorse for her wrongdoings. I believe my burden would have been a little easier to bear if she had once said, "I'm sorry." Instead, she stared at me, seemingly oblivious to what I was talking about. It happened time after time, but I didn't give up. In my heart was a secret hope that my mother would change; maybe she would lose her indifference and show some caring for me. How silly I was to think I could go to a well for water when the well was dry.

When I went to see my uncle, it wasn't any better. I still looked up to him as if he were a deity, but I couldn't relate to him either. I would tell him about my emotional pain, but he'd look at me as if I were speaking another language. He seemed to have no use for the language of feelings. I wanted to scream out my frustration, but I knew it wouldn't help any. And I no longer was that close to Jessie. After I saw them, I usually felt more alone than ever.

My therapist at the time made a statement that haunted me: "From what you've told me, your best bet is to move far away from your family—3,000 miles, at least! Have no contact with them! They're poison for you." I sensed he was right, but emotionally, I wasn't strong enough to sever ties and leave.

One morning the phone rang, and it was Hedda. "Can you come over? I have something I want to talk to you about."

I was surprised to hear from her. We hadn't spoken to each other in some time. I grabbed my coat and went right over.

When I arrived, she looked worried. She told me somberly, "I'm having problems. The money your father left us is running out."

I was taken aback. "You still have that money after all these years? I don't know what to say. Maybe you can apply for welfare."

There was anger in her voice. "Don't tell me about welfare. I don't want any part of that."

"Then what do you want to do?"

She did not respond. It was then that I reminded her about working in Maury's store. "You made a tremendous leap when you left the house. I think it was a huge accomplishment, close to a miracle. You came out of isolation and you were amongst people. You were waiting on customers and taking care of the store when Maury was out on his route. Truly remarkable."

I suggested temporary work to her. She was reluctant at first, but she soon bought a typewriter and brushed up on her typing. Then she applied to a Manpower agency for temp work in the Bronx. She was given part-time assignments as a typist in her local area. She dressed neatly, spoke well, and looked decent. She left her apartment early in the morning with a sandwich in her bag and came home in a fairly good mood, with interesting tidbits about her day at work. I couldn't believe this was my mother, working and functioning in the outside world!

She was especially happy about one of her assignments. She was working in a firm that specialized in handbags and small pocketbooks. She happily gave me several small items she received from this firm, and I was delighted. I still have a beautiful small red hand purse. I could feel the joy she was exuding from having this experience. I thought this was a tremendous undertaking for her. I was surprised and fascinated to see her doing so well.

As for myself, I continued to scurry around the city from one temp assignment to another. There were times I felt so alone and distraught amongst people in the workplace, I had to take a few moments to run into the Ladies' Room so that I could steady myself and go on. I was feeling like an orphan in the storm of life.

I was becoming more and more alienated from the temp work environment I chose for myself, and I ruminated about finding other work. But again, it was the same old story: what else could I do? I was stuck; I didn't have any other skills, but I did have an overwhelming need to be active and accomplishing in the outside world. And I was fulfilling that need.

During an intense bout of melancholia, I received a phone call from the temp agency. "Lenore, I have an assignment for you in a well-known jean company on the sixty-fifth floor of the Empire State Building…" I didn't know what to say. I was flabbergasted. *Me going into an elevator all the way up to the sixty-fifth floor? Never! Not with my fear of elevators and heights!* "I'll call you back in a few minutes and let you know if I can make it." I agonized about it, then I called back and accepted the job. I guess my fascination with clothing was greater than my fear of elevators.

I managed to be in the lobby of the Empire State Building well before 9 in the morning. It was the height of the rush hour and there I was, with all my anxieties, waiting for an elevator. Fortunate for me there were plenty of people going to higher floors, so there wasn't any chance of my being alone in an elevator. I squeezed into a crowded elevator and before I knew it, I was on the sixty-fifth floor.

Soon I was inside the wonderful world of fashion. My heart was leaping with joy as I looked around and saw shirts and jeans hanging all over the walls. It was very exciting. I found it breathtaking. I wanted everything in sight.

I was now at a typewriter, mindlessly typing away like an automaton. There were several young, hard-working executives who constantly kept my nose to the grindstone. They liked my work and made kind remarks about my skills. I liked the feeling of being liked, so I worked harder, but there was always more to do. I soon asked if I could work overtime. "I don't want money for this; I would like to have merchandise instead." They wholeheartedly agreed and said, "You can have whatever you want." I was elated.

I went through racks of shirts and jeans, and I made piles of items that appealed to me. I told my bosses what I was taking, as I stashed them away in shopping bags. I then made several cumbersome trips on the subway to get it all home. How happy I was when I tried on these fashionable styles. They all fit like a glove! I was walking on a cloud.

For several weeks I continued to work into the evening in this house of fashion. I dealt with my fear of going down in the elevator by leaving when the evening staff left. I would not allow myself to be defeated by an elevator.

Afterwards, I reflected upon the good moments I had with this company. I was so glad I didn't run away from this challenge. Even though I had to fight the overwhelming anxiety of going up and down to the sixty-fifth floor of the Empire State Building, it turned out to be a wonderful experience for me. In fact, I would say it was one of my finest assignments. The things I dreaded the most were actually opportunities for my growth.

I traveled around some more, and soon met up with a fascinating boss. Brad was a sweet young man, very friendly and outgoing. I liked him the moment I saw him. He asked me, "How come you're doing temp work?"

I said, "Truthfully, I can't stand being tied down to a job; I really don't like office work."

That opened a door to communication. I was surprised when he said, "You might consider an acting career."

I replied, "Me doing acting? I don't think so."

He responded in a tone of enthusiasm. "You show a lot of emotion when you speak. Your eyes are very expressive. I could see you with an acting career."

I was taken aback by the interest he was showing me. We soon were having long, enjoyable conversations on a multitude of topics, and neither one of us really wanted to do any work. I felt guilty about that and wondered why he called an agency for a secretary when there didn't seem to be anything for me to do. It was like that for the several days I was scheduled to "work" for him. All we did was talk.

Brad soon pointed to a stack of papers on his desk. "See all those papers? I don't worry about them; they'll sit there and collect. When I'm ready, I'll go through them. By that time, most of those papers will be ready for the garbage!" His cavalier attitude surprised me. I wished I could deal that way with my own stuff, which was accumulating but not "ready for the garbage."

He soon shared with me his love for music. As he expressed joy and delight in his operatic singing lessons, I was intrigued. I felt like I knew Brad all my life. What a funny feeling to have about someone I just met!

As I turned around, I noticed his assistant standing nearby. She was a young woman with an odd expression on her face as she watched us talking. I sensed something was bothering her, and I confided in Brad: "I think she's jealous of me."

Brad's eyes widened. "How did you know that?" He smiled and said, "You are very perceptive!"

His response surprised me. I replied, "It's only an observation."

Unfortunately, the week went by quickly, but the pleasant memories remained. The time I spent with Brad was precious to me. I was thrilled that an executive like Brad would spend so much time talking with me, setting aside any work that had to be done. I never experienced anything like that. Brad was warm and sensitive, and he made me feel worthy of his attention as he confided aspects of his life to me. His interest in me filled my heart with joy and made me feel special. I will always value those moments I shared with this very dear person. I considered this a rare occurrence in my life.

Soon, I had an altogether different experience. I was given an assignment at a swanky hotel in the East 50's. I remember climbing the plush staircases in the Hotel Drake. I thought to myself, "What an exquisite place this is!" I was working there at the time my grandmother became ill. I could hardly keep my mind on what I was doing; I was so worried about her.

Grandma was suffering with a heart condition, angina, and it was getting worse. She was now in a nursing home in Brooklyn. As I visited her, tears ran down my face. *Will she be all right?*

On one of my visits, I spoke to her doctor who bluntly told me, "Your grandmother had a heart attack. When she has a second one, she will die." *My goodness, how can he speak so bluntly?* He spoke with no feeling or compassion in his voice, and he had a bland expression on his face. He continued to talk, but I didn't hear anything he said. I left the nursing home in shock.

In the days that followed, I tried to busy myself as much as possible, but my anxiety was getting in the way. I couldn't keep my mind off Grandma. Jay met me after work, and we went over to visit her. Grandma looked pale and didn't speak much. When she did, she complained of chest pain. It was making me ache to see her so ill.

I felt it was time to let my mother know about Grandma's condition. I was hoping that Hedda would visit Grandma before it was too late. Hedda was adamant. "I'm not going out there. There's nothing I can do for her."

I was appalled at her response. I felt like my heart had been ripped from my chest.

"Jay will take you by car…."

But she coldly said "No." Her mother was dying, and she had no desire to see her one last time. I thought my mother had changed—that she had possibly become human. I was very disappointed to see shades of the old Hedda reappearing.

Within a few days I received a phone call from my uncle Will. He told me the bad news. Grandma was eighty-six years old. I loved her. I wanted her to live forever. Grandma was a very significant person in my world, and now she was gone. I was demolished.

I turned down all temp assignments. I was frightened when I thought about going out of the house and just as upset when I stayed in. My spells of panic were overwhelming. Just about everything was putting me on edge. Sounds and noises became very disturbing. The least thing jostled my nerves. Even eating in a restaurant, which I normally loved to do, was now a challenge. I was another person, someone I did not know. It felt like a piece of me died with Grandma.

I tried to disguise my illness however I could. I dared not tell anyone, not even Jay, lest I give in to it and lose the little of myself that I had. I was surprised that neither Jay, nor my uncle, noticed a difference in my behavior.

I fought my fears and nervously went out of the house one morning. I walked over to a local pharmacy and inquired about psychological help in the neighborhood. I was told about a therapist, Dr. Hans, who was only a few blocks away. I made an appointment to see him that same day.

Dr. Hans, a plump little man with a hearty disposition, prescribed medication as soon as he saw me. I filled the prescription, then went back to him and nervously said, "I don't know if I can take this. I don't like drugs."

He laughed and told me there was nothing to be worried about. "Cut the pills into quarters and take one-quarter with a meal. Then we'll slowly increase the dose, and you'll be better in no time."

I began seeing him every week, and when he asked about the medication, I told him I was taking it. But each time I attempted to take one-quarter of a pill, my hands shook, and a gripping fear overpowered me. I couldn't trust the pills, but I wanted to trust Dr. Hans.

I was now relying on Dr. Hans for my survival, and he could be mighty tough. When he became annoyed, he got up from his chair, came over to me, and tapped my knuckles lightly with a ruler. "No, my girl, that's not how you do things. Why do you think like that? I don't like that!"

I was disconnecting from reality and he was trying to pull me back. As he probed my feelings and challenged my thinking, I was connecting with him. His persistence, wit, and a certain amount of toughness, were empowering me to get a hold of myself. In several months, Dr. Hans brought me out of my black hole and back into reality.

One day, with a laugh, he said, "You don't have to take those pills anymore. One-quarter of a pill could never be useful anyway."

I smiled and said: "I never took them—not even one-quarter!"

An amazed expression covered his face.

Just before Dr. Han's untimely death, he introduced me to his physician-wife. Dr. Anna was soon to become my medical doctor, and one of the most important people in my life.

As I recovered from my grandmother's death, my hunger to find meaning in my life grew more intense and I began thinking even more about my future. As I became more aware of how precious life is, and that it's over too soon, I realized how very important it is to do things that we love to do—things that will make us happy and fulfilled—while we can, the sooner, the better.

62
Going to College

My uncle Will was encouraging me to go to college and I told him, "I can't do that. It's ridiculous! How can I go to college when I barely went to elementary school?" The thought of college sent a hot sweat through me and made me cringe.

Will persisted, as he stressed the importance of a college education. "It opens doors to you. Good-paying jobs become available. A whole new world is there for you to explore…" It sounded intriguing and soon I began to think it might be possible. Perhaps I could try….

I found out about a test given for people like myself who needed a high school diploma to get into college. Courses for the High School Equivalency (HSE) exam were given in various schools throughout the city. I found a school in my neighborhood and registered for a preparatory course. I bought a slew of HSE books that reviewed the course material and contained multiple questions and answers. I was full of hope and enthusiasm when I began, but when I became aware of the subjects on the Exam, I was aghast. *My goodness, there's an awful lot to absorb! How will I ever be able to learn so much at one time? This is like years of school wrapped up into one huge exam!*

I studied a lot on my own, but it was overwhelming; I wasn't familiar with any of the subjects in the books. I turned to my uncle Will to lend a helping hand. I went over some of the study guides with him, but even with his help, I knew it was up to me to ultimately do the work myself. For almost two years, I kept my nose to the grindstone as I attended classes and continued to study on my own.

At some point, it was time to stop preparing and take the test. And what a shock it was! The test was nothing like the material in my courses or in the study guides. It was exceedingly difficult. I was struggling to answer questions on an exam that lasted for approximately ten hours over two days. I recall meeting with my uncle at the end of the exam and sobbing, "I failed—I know I failed!"

"You don't know that," he thoughtfully replied. "It may seem that way, but it's very possible you passed."

I couldn't hear those words. I was too despondent.

In the weeks that followed, I silently mourned the education that I would never have. There was a gnawing pain inside of me that said I had not given the answers that would have opened the door to a new life for me. How I dreaded the time when I would open my mailbox and find the letter that would confirm my suspicion. Soon I had to face my fear. My heart raced as I held the envelope in my hand. I started to tremble as I opened it. What a happy moment it was for me to learn I had passed! *Hurrah!*

I wasted no time. I applied to a local community college and was accepted for the fall semester. My uncle Will, an experienced Social Studies teacher, gave me some practical advice. "Take just one non-credit course, and we'll see how it goes. Western Civilization would be a good start. I'll help you with it. If you do well, you may want to go further and take credit courses towards a degree." I enrolled in the course.

So, there I was, in my 30's, going to school! I arrived at the community college in awe and wonderment. I was both scared and excited at the same time. I saw a big spread of land with trees and buildings scattered all about. Students were scurrying to and fro, with overloaded packs on their back. But I wasn't really interested in my surroundings. I was too flooded with anxieties about this new adventure.

There was one huge problem: I had no background in history. I looked over the course textbook and I panicked. Not to sound flippant, it all seemed like Greek to me. *What have I gotten myself into now? This course is a big mistake. Maybe college is a big mistake, too.*

As I struggled to digest the material, I kept turning to my uncle for help. He went over aspects of the course with me. I still found it hard to comprehend. He advised me, "Keep reading your shorthand notes over and over. The more you work at it, the more you'll learn." I diligently continued to study, but I didn't feel that any of the material was registering.

The final exam turned out to be a 3-part essay. I didn't recognize the question and I became flustered. I looked it over and over and then, as I gained my bearings, I found myself writing. Still, I thought for sure that I had flunked. I was astonished when I found I passed the course. I was even more shocked that I had an A!

I soon forgot about my agony with this history course and I started to plan for the next semester. This time I would matriculate, and I chose a subject I was more familiar with: psychology.

In my second semester I stepped out of my trance a little. I opened my eyes and looked around. The students were talking, laughing, and kidding around. I couldn't help but envy them. It all looked so simple, but apparently, there was an art to socializing. I wondered: *How are they able to do this? What's their secret?* It preyed on my mind and remained a mystery to me. But then again, what did I really know about socializing? I rationalized that I wasn't there to socialize, but to study and make something of my life.

I once was sitting in the Students' Lounge when a student smiled my way. I began to talk to her. I mentioned some tidbits about the courses, and I welcomed the verbal exchange we shared. Afterwards, I was smiling as I thought about how very much I delighted in the contact.

In the classroom, I experienced the same feelings I had as a child. Although my peers had the courage to speak up and express their thoughts, I was petrified. There were numerous times when I had an answer on the tip of my tongue, but I was too timid to take the risk. I listened to others, frustrated, as I said to myself: *That's what I wanted to say!*

Learning was no easy task for me. As much as I tried, I didn't feel like I was absorbing the material. Teachers were giving new assignments all the time. I could barely finish writing one paper before the next one was due. As a slow reader, I was feeling the mounting tension of reading one book, then another and another. In a state of anxiety, I wondered how I would ever get through all the work that was confronting me.

What a nightmare it was for me when a test was scheduled. I was in a frenzy as I studied. I was drinking one cup of coffee after another to keep stimulated and alert. When the test came, I had the most horrible feeling in the pit of my stomach. I just knew I would fail. My uncle emphasized: "The material at first may not look familiar to you, but as you read it over, you will recognize what you have learned." But that didn't ease my anxiety.

When the teachers returned a test, I held my breath. Each time seemed like the first time as I imagined the worst. I just couldn't believe that I got an A! It was mine. What a thrill it was. In fact, it was exhilarating. How I needed to give myself a sense of worth. But the joy didn't last long, and the moment of glory wore off too quickly. Soon, I was back at the grind.

I dealt with my feelings of inadequacy by working harder and longer hours. This was my opportunity to prove to myself and to the world that I could accomplish and be smart. School was all that mattered. I became miserable, and even guilty, if I wasn't plugging away at my studies. At times, when I was so overwhelmed by stress, I felt an urge to give it all up. I cried to myself: *What do I need this for?* As I put my books down, I felt my tension release. When I felt better, I went back to studying some more.

I felt fortunate to be able to take shorthand notes in class. I often went up after class with all sorts of questions about things I didn't understand. I felt I was making a nuisance of myself, and I was ashamed, but my teachers were kind and accepting. They were only too glad to give me more insight into the coursework I needed help with, and this gave me the impetus to work harder.

"I can't learn Spanish—it's impossible. I'm going to drop out!" I was in a state of panic when I went to talk to Professor Alvarez, an academic advisor at the school. A tall, soft-spoken man with a short graying beard, he wore glasses that gave him a scholarly look and an air of distinction. He softly responded, "Please calm down. Many people have trouble with a new language. You are not alone. Don't tell yourself that you're unable to do it. We have tutors in the school who will be glad to help you. But whatever you do, please do not give up."

I sat down in a chair opposite him and told him my story. He appeared sympathetic. Then I told him: "This is the first real school I ever attended. I've heard of cultural shock, but I think I would call this educational shock. Maybe I don't belong here. Learning this language is a nightmare. I don't think I can do it much longer. "

He sounded genuinely sincere as he reassured me "I know you can do the work." The warmth in his voice was comforting. As I looked into his eyes, I saw a man who was kind and caring. The storm inside of me was subsiding. He told me: "If you keep trying you will succeed." When he walked me to the door he gently said, "If you need me, I am here for you. Please don't hesitate to stop by. And don't forget to contact a tutor."

The next day I found a tutor and began to work long, tedious hours. I still had my doubts, but I learned just enough Spanish to pass the course. I was very grateful to Professor Alvarez for his encouragement and support. But there was constantly some project or course work that was overwhelming to me, and I found myself running over to his office with the same cry: "As much as I study, it's hopeless. I just can't do it!"

He was quick to reply: "You're too hard on yourself. You need to relax more. You are doing well. Just hang in there." I needed to hear that; I would leave his office a little less frazzled. As many times as he said, "You can do it!" it always felt like the first time. And it didn't stop; the least thing jostled me. It didn't take much for me to feel like I was falling apart.

I was having trouble with another required course; this time it was mathematics. For the life of me, I just couldn't make any sense of it. Jay was now working very hard to teach me, but I just wasn't grasping it. I said, "I can't feel it."

Jay became upset and said, "What is there to feel? They're just numbers!" But numbers didn't have much meaning to me. As I tried to understand algebra, I wondered what those signs and symbols were all about. It seemed that the more I worked at it, the less I comprehended. I kept trying, but I wasn't doing well on the math tests. My anxiety was percolating. *How am I going to pass this course?*

I soon found a tutor in the Math Lab and began to work long hours with him. He was a young man who smoked a pipe, laughed a lot, and had a contagious sense of humor. I found that relaxing at times; it was something I needed to keep me together. I studied some more at home. When I saw the actual test, I recognized material that I was fairly familiar with, and that calmed me down considerably. But I still thought I had failed. I was on edge for days until I found out that I just barely passed the test and the course as well. I made it! Thank goodness for that.

But I still didn't understand math.

It became very clear to me that one needs to have some elementary or high school background before tackling something as intensely challenging as college. I felt this strongly, as I continued to struggle with one course after another.

My art classes gave me some sense of satisfaction. When I was painting and drawing, I felt connected to the universe. I had a feeling of calm. One day my instructor came over and said, "You catch the essence of a person and an object like the lens of a camera. Have you considered art as a career?" I was moved by her compliment. But as much as I loved art, I never thought of it as anything more than a hobby that gave me a lot of pleasure.

When it came time to choose a major, I gave this a lot of thought. Psychology seemed to be a logical choice. I was always curious about people and why they behave as they do. There are commonalities we all share, and yet we all are so different. I thought the things I learned about myself in therapy might make it easier for me to understand and be helpful to others.

One time I struck up a conversation with a fellow student who, like myself, was waiting to see a teacher. I had never seen this girl before, and suddenly, she was telling me the story of her life. It amazed me that she could talk so openly and trust me, a complete stranger, with her innermost thoughts and feelings. I made some suggestions that put a smile on her face and a great big "thank you" on her lips.

I had similar encounters that gave me an opportunity to experience closeness with my peers. As I interacted and empathized with a person in distress, I forgot about my lack of social skills and became completely natural with my responses. I was stepping out of myself. I was using myself for a worthy purpose. It was a rewarding feeling to help others help themselves. It felt right to choose psychology as my major.

As a psychology major, I was required to take a Communications course. An elderly Irish professor, gentle and spirited, gave us numerous verbal exercises to perform in class. One time he gave us an unusual assignment. He asked that we choose from a variety of controversial issues and write an essay on the opposite of what we believed in. My goodness, this sounded complicated and it evoked considerable anxiety in me. What was I going to write about?

I finally chose the topic of abortion. I had never been an advocate of abortion, but I believed abortion is indicated in certain cases—like when a woman is raped, or in pre-existing conditions that present a threat to the life of the mother or unborn child. To get more information for my assignment, I hurried over to the school library and did research. Soon, I was ready to present my material in class. I entitled my paper: "Abortion is Murder."

On the day of the presentations, I recall how flustered I was, sitting in my chair in the first row as I began to read aloud. It was only a page long and I tried to emphasize my points with a certain amount of emotion. I wondered if the class, or the professor, could sense my discomfort. When I finished, I had a great big surprise; the professor got out of his chair, rushed over to me and with a spurt of intense emotion, kissed me on my cheek. "That was wonderful!" There were tears in his eyes and a warm, radiant smile on his face.

I felt honored as my face reddened, and an exhilarated excitement soared through me. This was a moment of joy—a moment I will never forget.

I felt fortunate to have taken that course, for I had another wonderful experience: I met a lovely, soft-spoken young woman in the class. Doreen was tall with long blond hair and deep blue eyes. When it came her turn to introduce herself to the class, she simply said: "I know I need to take this course for my major, but I'm terrified to speak in front of a class. In fact, to be perfectly honest, I dread it."

She was very open with her feelings and I admired that. Later, I went over to her and confided: "I feel the same as you. I'm also afraid to talk in front of a group. You took the words right out of my mouth!"

And that was the start of our friendship.

I had known Doreen for a short time when she made an astute observation. "Lenore, I think you're frightened of your feelings. You don't have to be. It's okay to say what you feel."

Was I that obvious? Or was she that perceptive?

Doreen had problems of her own, but she didn't allow them to get in her way. She had a sad smile on her face when she spoke to me about her alcoholic father: "I see him on the street but we don't speak. I wave hello, and he passes me by…" Tears were in my eyes as Doreen continued to speak. My, she was courageous! She had a quiet strength that I admired. I didn't think I could ever be that stoic, but I welcomed anything I could learn from her.

I knew I had a lot of work to do on myself in order to improve emotionally. How was I going to deal with the problems of others when I had so many of my own? However, when I heard about a fieldwork course that was opening up for psych majors I immediately applied.

I soon was accepted and informed that I would be working with geriatric patients in a Bronx psychiatric hospital. It was not exactly what I had hoped for, but I couldn't refuse. This was an opportunity staring me in the face.

I was told that the hospital was located in a secluded grassland area, but I didn't know just how "secluded" it was. I asked the bus driver to call out my stop, and I was bewildered when I got off the bus. I found myself in a wide-open field. My goodness, I was in the middle of nowhere! I didn't know which way to go, so I waited there and before long, some people straggled by. They pointed to several tall buildings in the distance.

I crossed the huge grassland, and there before me were the hospital buildings. My, they looked creepy! I stood there, staring at them. There was something dark and morose about this huge complex that catered to all types of mental disorders. Suddenly, I got cold feet and wanted to turn around, but how could I do that? I had already made a commitment to be at the hospital. Besides, I didn't know where I was, or how to find my way out. A feeling of anxiety crept over me as I checked the numbers on the buildings surrounding me. There were so many. It seemed as though I was walking in circles when I finally found the right one. I became knotted up inside as I stood at the entrance; I didn't want to go inside. I had the eeriest feeling as I entered the building.

I approached the receptionist at the front desk and asked to see the psychologist, Grace Franklin. Soon a young woman appeared before me. She had a tender, warm smile, and the most sensitive eyes. She introduced herself and told me she was going to be my supervisor. As we began to talk, I heard a tone of sincerity in her voice that impressed me. Within fifteen minutes I wanted to accept this placement. The tension that enveloped me earlier had begun to subside and I could breathe easier.

Grace proceeded to show me around the ward. I saw some very distressing sights and I was overwhelmed. I began to retreat into myself. In a trance-like state I faintly heard Grace's voice: "Let's go to my office and I'll tell you about your assignment." I tried to maintain my focus as I followed her down the corridor.

"I'm giving you two patients. One of them is depressed and manipulative, and the other is extremely difficult—she's a catatonic schizophrenic. You have the option of reading the charts first, seeing what other therapists have already written, and then writing down your observations as you see the patients; or making your own first-hand assessments as you see the patients, and then reading what is in the charts. Whichever you choose, you will give your reports to me. If you have any questions, please don't hesitate to come to me. I am here to help you."

So, what was I going to do? I didn't give this a second thought; I knew right away.

I began to meet with my patients. One of them, Rosie, a small dark-haired lady in her 60's, would stand in one spot, immobilized, with her arm outstretched. As I talked to her, she was totally unresponsive; she kept staring straight ahead. I wondered what was going on inside of her: Can she see me? Can she hear me? Something terrible must have happened to her! I went to Grace and said: "I'm feeling kind of helpless with Rosie. What can I do to be of help to her?"

Grace's reply was, "There's nothing you can do. This is called a catatonic state. Just meet with her and observe her behavior and we'll talk about it." As I watched Rosie, I remained hopeful that one day she would snap out of her trance and speak.

My other patient, Greta, was an elderly, frail little lady who sat in a wheelchair. How she hated to talk! I felt like I was pulling words out of her mouth but when she needed something, like cigarettes, she became overly friendly. How grumpy and caustic she could be if she didn't get her way. I noted the drastic change in her, and I shared my frustration with Grace. She said, "It's very good that you picked up on that. Just continue what you're doing. You're on the right track."

And what was I doing? I was coming around to see them. I was spending time with them. I was observing, trying to understand their behavior, and I was providing support when I could. But I wondered if I could be doing better.

I went to Grace with my concerns. We had long discussions about the geriatric population. I soon felt comfortable enough to share some aspects of my early life with her. As I spoke, I noticed tears in Grace's eyes. I could feel her empathy and compassion. I was touched by her genuine caring. I felt I had a friend in Grace.

When I wasn't seeing my clients, I made it my business to involve myself on the ward. I walked around saying hello to the patients. Most of them looked lost; some appeared frightened. I kept coming back. I was speaking to anyone who wanted to speak to me. It brightened my day if I could make someone smile just a little.

Another student, also assigned to this ward, said: "How can you take this? This is so depressing; I just want to get out of here." I agreed with her; this was a very difficult placement. But I was learning to cope with situations that I might have otherwise run away from.

Grace soon called me into her office. "Have you been reading the files?"

I replied, "No, I decided not to."

Grace looked astonished. "It's incredible. The things you have here. It's almost identical to what our professionals have in the files. I am amazed!"

I found the voice to say, "If I read the files, I would be influenced and then the work would not be mine."

Grace looked at me for a long moment. "Your insights are keen. You are doing very well."

My spirits soared. How I valued her comments. I was on top of the world. At the end of the semester, Grace handed me an Evaluation sheet. It said:

"The quality of Lenore's work is excellent. She has shown much insight and genuine interest, for example, when one of the patients was trying to fend off closeness, Lenore wanted to learn about the manipulation and how to handle it. She was aware of her own feelings in response to the patient—which is a most valuable indication of her aptitude. Her productions are superior and her motivation is strong."

I was astonished by her evaluation. Tears filled my eyes and I could barely speak. "I never expected anything like this. Thank you so much, Grace, I never could have done it without your help."

This turned out to be a valuable experience for me. One of the things that made it so special was the very meaningful rapport I shared with Grace.

Community college turned out to be an exceedingly difficult experience for me. In that I had not attended school formally, I questioned my ability to function within a college setting. I wasn't doing very well, and I didn't think I would be able to make it through—but I was mistaken. My instructors had excellent teaching skills and an ability to reach out to students who needed special attention, like myself. They were kind and considerate, and the atmosphere was warm and nurturing. I am also grateful to my academic counselors for their patience and encouragement in helping me to move ahead when I wanted to give up. These were wonderful human beings who motivated me in my struggle to attain an education. And in the process, I was learning.

Going to college. Persevering. Hanging in there. I was getting stronger emotionally by attempting things I was afraid to do. Most astonishing of all: I rarely became ill. This was a miracle. I thought back to my childhood and how I was constantly becoming ill with respiratory infections that were so severe, I was unable to go out of the house and attend school. But now, I couldn't afford to get sick—there was so much to do and my need to succeed was very strong. Acquiring a college education had become the most important thing in my life.

63
Making Changes

It was harder than I thought. What was I thinking? With no real education, how could I possibly expect to get through college? It was a crazy thought, an impossible goal, and I found that out soon enough. I was struggling, sweating, and bursting into tears when the challenge became too difficult for me to handle. I was disheartened. I was beginning to see my striving for an education as another one of my disastrous mistakes.

But when I was doing really well, I was overcome with feelings of how wonderful it is to be able to go to college and acquire an education that I never thought I would have. These were the times when I knew I would not give up; I would continue to persevere.

Jay was immersing himself in my studies as if they were his own. He worked diligently at trying to teach me advanced mathematical concepts. He critiqued my English essays and taught me more about writing than my own English teacher. Whenever he could, he provided meaningful comments. I was amazed at his academic skills, and the patience he had with me. I thought he was simply marvelous. I don't think I would have been able to pass myriad courses if it weren't for him.

But he was still treating me like a child, telling me what I was thinking and feeling. My therapist commented, "He takes over so much, and he gets so powerful, you can't exist. He wipes you out." That was pretty much how I felt.

Jay had plenty of his own problems and yet he was constantly analyzing mine and everyone else's. There came a time when I said: "You never cease to amaze me. While you have solutions to everyone else's problems, you're not able to solve your own."

"I'm like an ostrich burying its head in the sand."

"I couldn't agree with you more," I replied.

We continued to have our disagreements, as I traveled down the road of pain and pleasure with Jay.

One night Jay's mother called and joyfully said, "It was such a lovely wedding. Lucy looked so pretty. Too bad you weren't there...."

I was shocked. "What? Lucy got married? I didn't know that."

Her voice dropped. "You mean my boy didn't tell you?"

I sat there, staring at the receiver in my hand. In a daze I heard Mama say, "I'm so happy for her. The poor kid! After all she's been through. Her child needs a father..."

I was dumbfounded. I couldn't hear anything else. I felt an ache inside; it was more pain and disappointment. I was living with a man whose daughter got married and he didn't even tell me! It was mind-boggling; I was living with a stranger. Jay was not the Supreme Being I had built him up to be in my mind.

I approached Jay: "How come you didn't tell me Lucy got married?"

He meekly said: "Amy was there, and I didn't think it would be a good thing to have you both there together."

I was boiling up inside. I felt awful. I told him: "I'm very hurt. You could have at least said something. I didn't have to find out from Mama."

"Sorry baby, I did what I thought was best."

But it was not best for me. This did not feel like love. I felt more alone than ever.

I knew what I had to do; I just didn't know how to do it.

It was St. Patrick's Day. Spring was quickly approaching. There was a chill in the air, but the chill I felt inside was even greater. I put on two sweaters, a scarf, and my heavy winter coat, and headed for school as usual. When I got there, I learned that my late-afternoon English class had been canceled. Disappointed, with time on my hands, I decided to go to the college library.

I was eagerly rummaging through psychology books and I couldn't find what I was looking for. Standing nearby was a young man with long, dark brown hair tied in a ponytail. He was wearing a multicolored striped shirt that caught my eye because the buttons were bulging out. He was also engrossed in browsing through the shelves. I turned to him and asked: "Is this the right section for books on bioenergetics?"

He replied: "I'm not sure, but I will try to help you."

Soon we started to talk. He said, "My name is Jon. I'm trying to get a degree in accounting, but I'm not really interested in the courses. Eventually, I want to go to Israel and live on a kibbutz…"

I thought he was a bit talkative, but I liked his friendly, engaging manner. We continued to talk for a short time and then, when it got dark, I said: "I have to leave."

I was surprised when Jon asked: "Can I have your phone number?"

I felt uneasy and told him: "I'm sorry. I can't give it to you right now."

Jon cheerfully responded, "Well, I'll give you my number. If you ever feel like calling, please don't hesitate."

I walked away thinking: *This is a nice young man, but I'll probably never see him again.* I thought about him some more on the bus going home. He didn't look like someone who had just stepped out of a Hollywood movie magazine. I didn't like the way he looked with that ponytail hanging down on his neck. In general, I was not a fan of ponytails on men. But there was something nice about him—something really nice. It seemed like he might be a good friend. He had said that he was twenty-two, while I was in my late thirties, and I wondered: *What would we have in common?*

At home, things had become pretty cool between Jay and me. My nose was constantly in the books, and I was also studying hard in the Math Lab. I was under extreme pressure and more irritable than usual. I hardly spoke to Jay and when we talked, we usually wound up in an argument.

We had a bad fight one evening and things got out of hand. Jay raised his cup and smiled as he spilled cold coffee all over my hair. I stalked out of the room, terribly upset. I thought to myself: *I've got to get away from him. I just have to get away. I can't live with him any longer!*

I had a need to talk to someone. It was right before Passover, and I thought of the young man I met in the library. I made a phone call to Jon, and he seemed pleasantly surprised to hear from me. As we talked, Jon asked: "What are you doing for the holiday?

"I'm not going anywhere."

I was rather surprised to hear his response: "My parents are having a Seder. Why don't you come over here? It's not good to be alone on Passover."

I thought he was very kind to invite me, but I didn't know how to respond. Again, I felt very uneasy about venturing into any new experience, but something within told me to go. On the spur of the moment, I surprised myself and said yes.

On the night of the Seder, I was getting ready to leave the house, when Jay walked in. "Where are you going?" He had that blank expression on his face that made me want to shake him and scream.

I defiantly snapped, "Out! I'm going to a Seder." I rushed past him and headed towards the door. On the bus to Jon's home in Co-op City, I felt a gnawing discomfort inside of me. I worried: *Am I doing the right thing?*

I arrived at Jon's parents' home just as the Seder was about to begin. Jon's aunt, Iris, a stout, soft spoken lady, welcomed me into their home. Jon then introduced me to his mother, Edna, a short, plump, dark haired lady, and his father, Oscar, an attractive man with deep piercing blue eyes.

As I joined them at the Seder table, my tension mounted. It was more stressful than I thought. There I was, with people I didn't know, observing a holiday I knew very little about. I had mustered up the courage to come to this gathering, making myself amenable to whatever was about to take place, and I was scared. But as I observed what they were doing, I did the same. Things began to look less frightening as I became absorbed in the ceremony. We recited passages from the Seder book, the Hagadah. We ate matzoh and horseradish with glasses of wine. We had a holiday meal. We even sang a few songs. As the evening went on, I let my guard down a little and interacted with Jon and his family.

When it got late, Jon's mother made an announcement: "I'm calling the cab company. We're sending Lenore home in a cab." It was a kind gesture, and I came away feeling that these were fine people.

In the cab going home, I thought to myself: *Maybe President Roosevelt was right; there is nothing to fear but fear itself.* I wondered how long I would be able to hold on to that thought.

Several days after the Seder, Jon and I met in a coffee shop in Manhattan. Even though Jon hardly knew me, he surprised me when he opened up about some very personal matters in his life. He began by telling me about his mother. "Edna's afraid to go outdoors alone; she has agoraphobia. She also has a dread of being in the house by herself. That's why my aunt is there. When my father comes home from work, he eats his dinner and goes to his room…"

As Jon spoke, I could perceive strong similarities between his family and mine. His mother had severe psychological problems, like my mother, and his father was in the role of a non-person, like my father. I felt a kinship with Jon.

Jon continued. "I'm afraid to talk to my sister. When she's not ignoring me, she's criticizing whatever I do. She is super-cold. I can't speak to her or anyone else in my family."

I listened but remained silent for the most part; I didn't know what to say. I felt a need to "fix" his problems. Then I realized how ridiculous my thinking was. There was nothing I could do to take away his pain. I said, "I'm so sorry you're having such a hard time."

Jon replied, "It's not all that bad. I do have things in my life that are positive. I do really well in math. I finished in the 99th percentile in the country when I took my math SATs. When I graduated from the Bronx High School of Science, I received a Regents scholarship and I was all set to go to Syracuse—in fact, I was about to put my acceptance letter into the mailbox—when my mother and aunt came running down the street and stopped me. 'You can't go! We don't want you to go! You can go to a school here in the city. You can even stay at a dorm, but we don't want you leaving New York!' Reluctantly, I agreed to their demand."

I thought: *What a terrible thing they did. They stopped him from pursuing his goal! How painful that must have been for him.*

"So, I went to NYU instead, but I didn't do well. I became very depressed when my friend, Judy, said she didn't want to see me anymore. I really cared for her, but she wasn't that involved with me. It was a one sided relationship. Afterwards, I couldn't concentrate on my class work, so I dropped out and got a job as a shipping clerk. I was very depressed for a while, until I enrolled at the community college. I'm not really interested in the accounting courses I'm taking. I'm not sure what I want to do."

I was listening to him, but I didn't know how to respond. I wondered if I would be scaring him away if he knew how I lived with my mother. How could I tell him that I didn't go to school like everybody else? What would he think of me?

In the days that followed, in between classes, I spent a lot of time with Jon. I enjoyed his company, and I was very careful not to talk too much about myself.

Back at home, Jay inquired: "What's going on? What are you doing these days?"

I simply said, "I have some friends in school. My new friend, Jon, is a very nice fellow…"

Again, Jay looked at me with that blank expression on his face. I wondered if he had even heard me. I kept thinking: *What kind of life is this? This is no good.*

Sometimes it's hard to tell when one is changing because it's a slow process that occurs over a period of time. I wasn't aware that I was changing, as I kept going through my metamorphosis. I still was very unhappy with myself and the way things were. I very much wanted to make things better and find my life. Would I ever find someone who could love me—someone who truly cared?

I was glad to have met Jon. He seemed to be a sensitive young man who was very sweet and thoughtful. There was a tenderness about him that I found appealing. He also was interested in me and what I had to say.

It was very different with Jay. At times I felt like a nuisance to him. Sometimes I wondered if he even liked me. So often I spoke to him and he didn't reply, he was so wrapped up in reading a newspaper or magazine. I felt neglected. I didn't feel worthy of his attention.

As I became closer to Jon, I soon realized that what I had with him was more than a friendship. There were times when we were walking down a street and Jon suddenly stopped, took me in his arms and kissed me. I was filled with joy, so happy and alive in the moment.

I usually was very slow to take action, but several weeks after I met Jon, I went over to my uncle and said: "I want to leave Jay. Can I stay with you and Jessie for a little while?"

I was surprised that Will didn't ask any questions. He simply said, "I don't think it's a good idea—but you can stay here for a short time." I sighed a sigh of relief as I thanked Will and hurried out the door.

When I got home, I wrote a note to Jay telling him I was leaving. I told myself I would have nothing more to do with him. I took a few pieces of clothing and then I found the inner strength to pick myself up, walk out the door, and head over to my uncle.

Jay began to phone me: "I can't eat. I can't sleep. I miss you terribly."

I was shocked. When I lived with Jay, I felt, for the most part, that he disregarded my feelings, but now that I was away from him, he was falling apart. I was feeling his grief and didn't know how to cope with it.

While I was spending more time with Jon on campus, I continued to see Jay. He was calling me, and I sensed an urgency in his voice that made me want to meet with him. I was distressed to see him so pale and gaunt and in so much pain. Jay had tears in his eyes and my heart melted. He was suffering and it was all because of me. I knew I couldn't go back in time and suddenly, I feared going forward. What was I to do?

I had to admit to myself that a part of me still cared for Jay and I felt a sense of loyalty to him. When he called me, I ran out to meet with him. We usually wound up in a neighborhood restaurant and had a bite. Then we sat around and talked about living together and where we went wrong. I felt confused and distraught in our meetings, but I felt that by listening to Jay, I was helping him with his pain. In some ways, I was also helping myself, for I was hurting as well.

During one of our meetings, Jay proclaimed: "I'm going to get a divorce. I want to marry you. You can have my money. I'll give you whatever I have in the bank." I never expected that. Through the years Jay was most secretive about everything—especially his earnings. I was startled by this sudden turn-about. But there was nothing that I wanted from him.

Another time Jay told me: "I was never unfaithful to you in all the time we were together." I heard the sincerity in his voice, and I was taken aback; I didn't know how to respond.

I was spinning around on an emotional merry-go-round that didn't stop. I found myself worn and frazzled, caught between two people I genuinely cared for, who seemed to care for me. I worried: *What am I going to do? If I stop seeing Jay, something terrible might happen to him. If I open my heart to Jon and reveal my involvement with somebody else, will he still want to see me?*

I finally told Jon about my relationship with Jay. He looked upset as he said, "I understand. I trust you will make the right decision." My heart was lighter when I heard that, but I was still worried and confused.

We had known each other only two months when, out of the blue, Jon said, "Do you want to get married?" I couldn't think of anything I wanted more, but I was too distressed to give him an answer. Then, one night after classes, we met in a deserted college classroom and we talked. I said, "Let's get married right away."

To my surprise, Jon replied, "I'm not sure, I have a problem with intimacy. I've never been this close with anyone before." He then broke down and cried. "I don't want to have a marriage like my mother and father. I don't want to be like them. They don't even talk to each other. I don't want to hurt you. Maybe I'm not right for you."

With just a few words, my world crumbled. "We don't have to be like Edna and Oscar," I murmured. "We could make a different life…." My heart was talking, but I could see Jon wasn't hearing me. He was very upset and so was I. Soon, nothing seemed to make any sense. We both were in despair when we left the campus that night.

I went home and thought about what Jon said. Maybe he was right. Maybe he wouldn't be good for me. I needed someone with insight, so I thought of my friend, Doreen. I called her on the phone and said, "Doreen, you've been honest with me in the past. I'm seeing a young man. I would like you to meet him and have your opinion,"

Doreen said, "Sure, I'd love to."

After she met Jon, she called me and exclaimed, "Oh, Lenore, he's so nice—he'll never hurt you."

That's all I had to hear. But I was still troubled about that night in the classroom and Jon's fear of emotional closeness. I wanted to stay positive about my relationship with Jon, so I decided not to dwell on it.

One evening, Jon and I went into Manhattan to see the film, *Murder on the Orient Express.* As the movie was about to begin, I turned around and who should be standing several feet away but Jay! I was shocked. *What is he doing here?*

Soon he was signaling to me. When I did not respond, he moved in closer and demanded: **"I want you to leave—and now!"** He was speaking in a loud voice and creating a scene, so we passively got up and walked out. We followed him into his car to wherever he was taking us, which turned out to be a nearby restaurant.

The three of us sat down at a table and a waiter came over. Jay and I ordered coffee, and Jon said he wanted scrambled eggs and home fries. When the waiter left, we began to talk. I said, "Jay, I've lived with you for so many unhappy years. I think we should let bygones be bygones. I'm with Jon now, and I want to stay with him."

Jay turned to Jon and asked, "What are your feelings for Lenore?"

"I want whatever will make Lenore happy."

Jay looked distraught as he sipped his coffee. Pain was written all over his face. I was hurting, too, as we lingered over words, but the talk was going nowhere. Meanwhile, Jon hardly said anything as he munched on his meal. I wondered how he could be so detached. Jay suddenly picked himself up, paid the tab and walked out. I found the whole scene very disturbing.

The next time I saw Jay, he said: "This guy, Jon, is very selfish. He's not right for you. Besides, he's too young. You deserve much better. If you're going to leave me, then you should leave me for someone who cares about you. This guy doesn't care for you!"

I was enraged. *Who the hell is he to say something like that to me? I wouldn't be looking for love elsewhere if I felt he truly cared about me.*

I said, "Jay, you need to see a therapist. Your behavior in the movie theater was atrocious. I could say more, but I really don't want to. I think you're out of control and badly in need of help."

Jay gave me a half smile and assured me, "I'll look into it."

As I walked away, it dawned upon me that I never asked him how he found us in the movie theater. Then I realized that my uncle was the only person who could have told him, and that upset me. Why would he tell Jay where I was going with Jon?

Jay began to visit my uncle when I wasn't around. They became very close. I was stunned to hear my uncle say: "Jay's complaining that you dumped him for a younger man." Did Jay really believe that? Or maybe he didn't want to look at the ugly truth: I didn't leave him for a younger man; I left him for a single man. When Jay got through telling my uncle about his sorrows, I was in the role of the ogre, while Jay was in the role of the betrayed martyr. Ouch!

It seemed so ridiculous as I thought about it. For years I spoke to Jay about marriage, but he disregarded my feelings entirely. Now he wanted to marry me because I left him for somebody else?

My therapist said, "Let's look at the relationship that existed between you and Jay. When you were with him, he was controlling.

He made you feel bad about yourself. He took care of you in a way that made you dependent upon him and unable to separate yourself from him. It sounds like a repeat of your life with your mother."

Yes! Why hadn't I seen this? I actually had my mother in Jay. So, when I left Jay, it was like leaving my mother all over again! Thinking about it made my head spin. *Will I always be getting into relationships with people who are like my mother?*

Soon, my uncle admonished me. "You're making a big mistake leaving Jay. He really cares for you. This fellow Jon is too young. He is not for you!"

How does he know that? He never even met Jon. I kept asking Will to meet him, but he refused. "Under no circumstances! I am not interested."

I overheard Jessie comment to Will: "She's acting like a teenage girl. It's only a passing phase. She'll get over it."

It was pointless to try and make them understand; I would only be running out into the street in tears and I didn't want that. I spoke to them when I needed to, the rest of the time I tried to avoid them.

Graduation from college was only a few months away and I began to worry: *How am I going to graduate when I hardly have any time to study?* When I opened my books, I could barely concentrate, but I kept on going to class.

During all this turmoil, I received a letter from the college. It was an invitation to attend a ceremony to become a member of the honor society, Phi Theta Kappa. It was for students who held a 3.5 grade point average or better, in a 2-year college. It sounded wonderful! This was an opportunity to feel good about myself and to be rewarded for my hard work in maintaining an "A" average. I had to be a part of this memorable event. I had to go.

I told Will and Jessie about the ceremony and they were overjoyed. My uncle Will was a member of Phi Beta Kappa, a 4-year honor society, and he would talk about it with pride. They told me they would be there and asked if it was all right to bring Jay. I said he certainly could come. "You've all worked hard to make this possible."

I went to the ceremony dressed in a simple white cotton shirt and a long black skirt. I didn't know what to expect, and the thought of what was ahead paralyzed me with fear. I was so glad to see Will and Jessie there—and even Jay; I needed all the support I could get. When my name was called, my heart started to race, as I found my way to the platform. In front of me, numerous candles were spread out over a long table. I felt nervous and out of place, being the center of attention. My hand was shaking like a leaf as I lit the candle that inducted me into the honor society. The lighting only took a few moments, and it was over. I heaved a sigh of relief as I hurried away from the table. Only when I was back in my seat did I feel the exhilaration of the moment that had just gone by.

"Congratulations!" beamed Jessie. "That was a beautiful ceremony. All your studying paid off!" I gave Jessie a big hug and then embraced my uncle Will, who was usually rigid and uptight when it came to displaying affection. While we were commemorating this joyous event, Jay was taking pictures of me, one after another. Usually, he didn't want to take even one picture. He claimed, "I can't take pictures of people I'm close to. I can't be objective." I was astonished by his sudden change of behavior.

Afterwards, I realized that despite my anxiety, this was an event I would not have missed for the world. Even though I couldn't enjoy it as I would have liked to, this was something quite unique in that I was able to acknowledge to myself that I could excel by working hard and not giving up during times of extreme adversity.

I was disappointed that Jon did not come.

Soon it was back to the classroom and into the reality of my everyday existence. School still had meaning for me, but not like before. I didn't have the patience or desire to sit down and study for tests. I stopped obsessing about attaining an "A" in my classes. More than anything else, I wanted to be with Jon. In the evening he frequently met me in front of the private house where I stayed with Will and Jessie. We would sit on the stairs and hold each other. Sometimes I would cry in Jon's arms, as I reflected upon the bind I found myself in.

In the heat of an argument with my uncle I asserted, "I'm tired of going to school. It's too much pressure. I want to give it up. I want to marry Jon."

My uncle gave me a dirty look and then he barked: "You can do whatever you want. I don't care if you drop dead!"

I was devastated. I felt myself burning up with hurt and rage as I ran from the room. Then I broke down and cried and swore I was through with my uncle forever. I wanted to move out then and there, but where would I go? I had never been on my own and I was frightened at the thought of it. I went to Jon and told him I needed to leave my uncle's home. I asked him: "How do you feel about living together?"

He appeared nervous. "I'm not sure if that's a good idea. I never lived with anyone before."

This was a moment for me to stop and think about how unhappy I was living in an out-of-wedlock situation. But there I was, willing to repeat a scenario that had given me so much pain and grief. My goodness! Why couldn't I learn?

Jon and I began looking for a furnished room. We moved into one place, then another and still another until we settled into a tiny room near the college.

Jon continued to share childhood experiences with me. I was touched that he trusted me enough to allow me into his world and that he was not afraid to share his innermost feelings with me. Jon's sensitivity was one of the things that drew me to him. He was especially sensitive about his father. "When my father's home, it's as if he's not there. My mother treats him like a dog. I can only speak to him on a superficial level. We usually talk about how some local sports team is doing. We never get any deeper…"

I felt helpless as I listened to Jon speak. It seemed that I was just sitting there, listening to his turmoil without saying anything useful. What could I say to be of help? Maybe just listening to him was what he needed in that moment.

One day I found the courage to say: "Jon, I need to tell you about the hell I lived through in my life." He listened with concern and looked sad as I spoke. We both had experienced an awful lot of emotional turmoil in our families, and we were finding our way through it together. We were bonding on a deeper level.

Jay was now joining Will and Jessie every Sunday morning for breakfast. It seemed ironic: my uncle and aunt, who had once chastised me for living with a married man, were now treating Jay like family while I had become the outsider. How outlandish! I was infuriated when I thought about it. *How could this be happening?*

Soon Jon came in with startling news: "My sister is getting married, and her room will be available. My mother asked if we would like to live in Co-op City."

I wasn't very eager; Jon had told me so many unappealing things about his family, but it might be better than living in a furnished room. A week later I had a new home—again. The apartment, painted in delightful beige and green earth colors, was beautiful and homey. I experienced a warm, cozy feeling just being there. Things were going well: I was enjoying delicious meals, I had a lovely room to sleep in, I found people who seemed to like me, and I was with Jon.

I soon found a friend in Jon's Aunt Iris. I could talk very easily to her and she seemed to be interested in me. She impressed me as a sweet lady with a heart of gold. When I was sick in bed with the flu, she brought large bowls of chicken soup to me and said, "I made this especially for you. You'll eat this, and you'll feel much better!" She showed me the kind of concern and involvement that a loving mother would show her child. I enjoyed that and ate it up as much as the good food she put before me.

But I didn't like Edna. Jon's mother was very much like my mother in so many ways. Her rage was usually right below the surface. She would drop into a tirade for the least thing. I found it scary seeing her standing opposite me, staring at me with an angry expression on her face. Her arms were stiff at her sides, her fists clenched, her eyes bulging, and her cheeks all puffed up. She looked as though she was ready to explode. Although she never became physically violent, that angry look on her face gave me the creepiest feeling. What in the world made her get so worked up?

In one of her episodes, Edna was pacing up and down as she lamented: "I'm a failure! I'm a failure! Look at what I married! I never should have married Oscar! There are so many millionaires I could have married. (She mentioned names I never heard before.) I knew so many fellows who became rich! And I had to marry Oscar.

Life is rotten. It stinks!" She spoke in a loud, harsh voice. I thought this was especially cruel since her husband was in the next room.

More and more, I found her talk incredible. Where was she coming from? Was this woman in reality? I didn't think so. It sounded like psychotic talk to me. She was so much like Hedda, who also ranted and raved, non-stop. And like my mother, when Edna got into one of her emotional tantrums, she was oblivious to everything around her for God knows how long. I wondered how Edna could ramble on like that, and not care whether anyone was listening or even there. I told Jon, "When Edna comes on like a bulldozer, she runs over anyone who gets in her way."

I finally asked Iris, "Do you know why Edna is so disturbed?"

Iris replied, "Since our parents died, she's been like that. We've been to psychiatrists and they prescribed medication for her, but she doesn't take it." There was an agonized look on her face. I perceived her pain and didn't say anything more.

Edna rarely went out of the house. She claimed to be agoraphobic and openly stated: "I can't go out if Iris isn't with me. We don't go far anyway."

I thought Iris had the patience of a saint. She did the cooking, cleaning, and shopping. She stayed home and nurtured Edna as if she were her very own child. Iris never complained. Once in a while she expressed a desire to go to a movie. I recall the time we spoke about going to a museum together and Iris looked so happy as we made plans. When Edna heard about it, she loudly roared: **"No! You're not going anywhere! You can't go! You can't leave me alone!"**

Iris looked distraught as she retreated to her room. As I empathized with her, I felt angry. It seemed so unfair that Iris was being denied the simple pleasure of going to a museum.

Soon, Iris confided, "I was married for only nine months when I had to leave my husband. My sister was suicidal—she needed me." I was anguished. This lovely lady was sacrificing her life and her happiness to take care of her demanding sister, who did not show any gratitude or appreciation for all Iris was doing for her. I didn't know what to do with the anger that was building inside of me. I felt Iris was more like Edna's slave than her sister, catering to all of Edna's whims and wants. I was amazed that Iris could remain so gracious and loving under those circumstances, but she was steadily putting on weight. I surmised she was eating to soothe her frustration. Poor Iris: she was caught in a trap.

Jon was rarely at home to witness the unpleasant scenes that occurred. He was usually overextended, doing myriad things like going to classes, meeting up with friends and involving himself in activities I had no interest in. Sometimes I thought I was spending more time with Iris than with Jon, and that bothered me. I felt ignored by Jon and I was brooding a lot.

There were times, however, when I would meet Jon after class. If it were sunny and pleasant, we would lie down on the campus grass, hold each other, and kiss, and talk about whatever was on our minds. I felt so young, so carefree, so much in tune with the universe, nothing else mattered to me. These were rare moments that I cherished.

One day, in Jon's parents' apartment, I got a call and Jay was on the phone. I was amazed when he said: "I'm in front of your building. Come down now, I want to see you."

"What? You're in front of this building?" I was flabbergasted. Without thinking, I reached for my scarf and coat and flew down the stairs.

I was distressed when I saw Jay. I looked at him in disbelief. I asked, "How did you get my phone number and how did you know where to find me?"

He somberly answered: "Let's go across the street to the coffee shop and talk."

We were soon sitting opposite each other. With tears in his eyes, Jay said: "I'm ashamed to tell you this, Lenore—I never did this before—but I opened your handbag and I got Jon's address and phone number from your address book."

I was aghast. "What? You opened my bag? Where was I when that happened?"

I was too devastated to hear his response. *How did he get into my bag and invade my privacy?* I wanted to tell him how angry I was, but I couldn't find the words. I became the docile little girl I was trying so hard to get away from. How I hated the fear and weakness that wouldn't allow me to stand up for myself and say what was on my mind.

In the days that followed I received more phone calls from Jay. "Lenore, I'm downstairs." And off I went. One night I met him in the coffee shop, and I noticed the most jubilant smile on his face. Jay lit a cigarette and sipped his coffee. "I saw your mother this morning. I did her shopping and dropped it off in her hallway."

I asked, "Is she still stacking up on all that stuff?"

Jay said, "Oh, yes. I go over there every week and whatever she wants, I get for her. She has so much canned food and paper products, I don't know where to put it."

I replied, "I haven't seen her for some time. I stopped going over there. It's too much aggravation for me."

"I'm sorry to hear that," Jay responded. "You should look in on her. I think she misses you."

"She misses the fights we have when we see each other. Well, I've had enough of that."

Jay replied, "I think you're wrong, but I can't tell you what to do."

We spent a few more minutes together and then we both had to leave. Afterwards, I thought about Jay. I was astonished that Jay was still shopping for my mother after our break-up. How many men would do that? And he wasn't griping about it either; he appeared very happy to do it. Again, I felt that soft spot in my heart for him. I couldn't stop thinking about his goodness. How could I tell him goodbye?

Jon saw me coming in one night after a meeting with Jay. He looked upset and said, "It's been some time now and you're still running out to see Jay. When are you going to stop seeing him?"

I wanted to know the same thing, as I found myself spinning in different directions. I couldn't walk away and abandon Jay in a state of emotional turmoil, nor could I stand to see the pained expression on Jon's face. It all was tearing me apart. I was succumbing to nervous exhaustion when I said to Jon: "This is a terrible problem and I'm struggling to find an answer. I'm worried about Jay and I can't stop seeing him now. I'm asking you to please wait a little longer." Though Jon did not respond verbally, I could see he was hurting. An aching sensation continued to gnaw away at me as I told myself I had to find some way to resolve this dilemma—and soon.

A few days later I was in Jay's car when I found myself saying to him: "We have to stop seeing each other. This is not good for you, and it's not good for me."

When the light turned red, I opened the door and rushed out. I was halfway down the street when I heard screeching brakes in the distance. My heart was palpitating as I started to run towards the accident scene. I anxiously stopped someone on the street and asked, "Do you know what happened?

I was told: "Oh, it's nothing. Some kind of crash, no one was hurt."

I was shaking as I headed towards a bus stop. In the distance, I saw a police car with red lights flashing as it raced in the direction of the accident scene. I wanted to turn back, but my body wouldn't permit it. My energy was depleted, and I felt as if I were about to fall on my face. When I got home, I collapsed into bed.

The following morning, I called Jay. He told me: "I was taken to the hospital and I stayed overnight. I wasn't really hurt. They just wanted to make sure I was all right."

My dreadful fear that Jay might wind up harming himself had now become a reality. I couldn't allow that to happen again. I felt even more compelled to watch over him as best I could.

I was living two lives. I felt like I was in one of those soap operas I would listen to when I was a little girl. But this was real. I was confused: *How can I possibly love two men at the same time?*

I went to my therapist with tears in my eyes and said, "It's crazy! I should stay away from all men. They're no good for me and I'm no good for them. I keep thinking I should walk away from both and start over…"

"That might not be a bad idea. It would give you some time to be on your own and think about what you want to do with your life." His response made me even sadder; I knew I couldn't do it. So, what was I going to do?

As the days passed, Edna was getting on my nerves more and more. Her atrocious behavior was making me tense and nervous, but how could I say anything when I was a guest in her home? When

Edna got into one of her spells, I wanted to be as far away from her as possible. But I was also concerned about her, simply because she was Jon's mother and Iris' sister. Jon would speak to me about his mother with hurt in his voice, and Iris showed her relentless devotion by the way she took care of her. I wondered: *Could I be of help in any way?*

When Edna was in a calm mood, I went into her room, sat down by her bed, and tried to talk to her. "Your family loves you, Edna, and they're very concerned about you…" But she didn't seem to be listening; the look on her face told me she was somewhere else. I kept trying—but to no avail.

Jon's father, Oscar, said very little. When he came in from work, he smiled hello, and soon shut himself away in his room. He remained unapproachable, which made me want to know him more. Sometimes he had an outburst of anger and then he crawled back into his shell. I was careful to speak to him only when he made the first move.

It was a chaotic household, but I was grateful that Jon's family allowed me to stay in their home. They were strangers who had taken me in at a very difficult time in my life. And, strange as it may seem, I felt a sense of belonging.

The days were long and hectic. There were myriad things to do. Then the phone rang, and it was Jay: "I want to see you…" I stopped whatever I was doing and ran out of the house. It was madness. During one of our get-togethers, Jay let me know: "I'm going for therapy." I thought this was an excellent move, even though his therapist turned out to be the same one I was seeing. I wasn't happy about that, but as long as he was going for psychological help, I could breathe a little easier. Soon he was not calling me that often, and I was seeing less of him. I thought this was healthy for both of us.

Many a night I was sitting alone in the living room feeling down and dejected. I wondered what I could do to take my mind off things. It was then that I thought about my old hobby, drawing: *Why not try sketching some things in the apartment?* I grabbed a sheet of pad paper and a pen and set my sights upon anything that looked appealing enough to draw. How wonderful it was to feel my tension dissipate, as I once again felt the swirling lines under my pen. I even drew Jon when he was sound asleep on the couch.

I still had my schoolwork to deal with. I continued to have very little interest in my courses. There were too many diversions cropping up from day to day that didn't allow me to focus on any one thing. I might say I was in a constant state of flux. As things around me were changing, I seemed to be changing, too. And yet so much of me remained the same.

Finally, in my late 30's, I graduated with an Associate's degree in Psychology. It was my first official graduation from any school. My perseverance paid off with honors and a 3.9 grade point average. But I wasn't that happy with any of my accomplishments. Once it was over, it did not have any real meaning for me. I felt a need to strive harder and accomplish more. I had to get ready for my next round of sweat and tears: senior college.

About this time, Jon and I were strolling down a street in Co-op City when we bumped into Jon's friend, Gary. He was beaming and eager to make the happy announcement: "I'm getting married and I want you both to come to my wedding. And Jon, I want you to be my best man."

Jon's eyes lit up. "Great! I'd love to do it. When?"

Gary looked amused. "Hey, how come you guys aren't married? You two are soul mates, if ever there were!"

Jon evaded the question, but my emotions were stirred. It was the same old story, and it was all about love: *Why can't I be loved enough to be married? Ouch!* I wanted to disappear, but I couldn't move, I couldn't think. I had to shut down.

I came back to the moment when I heard Gary say, "Why don't we make a double wedding? You guys can get married with us…" As Gary spoke with vibrant enthusiasm, I looked at Jon. The blank expression on his face said a lot to me. I found the inner strength to say, "We're not getting married now."

"Well, whatever you decide to do, I'm looking forward to seeing you both at our wedding."

This was not the first time that one of Jon's friends said to us: "How come you're not married? You guys are real soul mates!" Jon did not respond, and I was very hurt. I could feel so much love between us, and yet, Jon did not want to make a commitment. Soon, I would be going to someone else's wedding. How I hated the thought of it.

At the wedding, I was so distraught, I ran out into the street. Tears were flowing down my face as I found myself walking along a congested highway. I had no idea where I was going and I cared less. I just barely escaped being hit by oncoming traffic as I moved along in a daze for I don't know how long. Suddenly, I came to my senses and realized it was worse to be out walking nowhere than to be somewhere safe. I quickly turned around and headed back.

As I came in, the wedding was ending. Jon rushed over to me and said, "I was so worried—I've been looking all over for you. Where have you been?"

I didn't tell him then how upset I was, but I think he knew. It was time for me to face the painful reality I didn't want to see: Jon did not want to get married. This was enough to make me pull back and look at things as they really were. It was then that I lost my urgency to be bonded in marriage.

A week later, Jon and I were sitting on the bed in our little room. I was telling him about my pain at Gary's wedding. Jon's response was, "Well, let's get married now. We don't have to wait—when do you want to get married?"

Is he appeasing me by asking me to do this now? I said: "I don't think your heart is in it. You don't really want to marry me and that wedding only dredged up more pain for me."

Little did we know that Edna had been eavesdropping outside the door. She suddenly flew in like a hurricane and yelled at Jon: **"You can't do that! The time isn't right. You're not working. You can't support a wife! I won't have it! Lenore can live here for as long as she wants, but you can't get married!"**

I was outraged as Edna exploded into one of her tirades. It wasn't long before Iris, hearing her sister screaming, came running in, looking astounded. "What's going on?" She instantly sided with Edna, and soon they both were yelling and screaming on top of their lungs that we were not to get married. They were going berserk!

I was horrified. I had befriended Edna and I adored Iris. How could they turn on me like that? How could they dictate to us what we could and could not do? My heart was leaping in my chest, and Jon just stood there, looking perplexed. My world was collapsing before my eyes. This did not seem real. I had lived with Jon's family for four months and they treated me like a princess. I had grown attached to them. Now they were telling me we couldn't marry because Jon didn't have a job? Were they just being nice to me because they saw me as a stabilizing agent for Jon? Did they feel I wasn't good enough for him? Maybe it was all a sham. Maybe they were just using me. I didn't want to find out. I said, "I'm leaving!"

Jon immediately said, "And I'm going with you."

Sometime later in the day, there was a knock on the door. It was Edna and Iris. "Please don't go. We want you to stay. We'll make a wedding for you if you will stay…" I was flabbergasted. *Are they kidding? I don't want any part of it. All I want to do is get out as quickly as possible.* I came away feeling as if I had been stabbed in the back.

Jon immediately found a cozy little studio apartment on the other side of the Bronx, off the Grand Concourse. More changes and more moving around. I remembered a time when I could barely move myself out of the house. How amazing it was; I counted six moves within one year!

There were also changes in my school life. I enrolled in a nearby senior college and I chose an independent work-study program. I now had two majors, psychology and art, plus regular courses. I was very busy. I found the independent study program more intense than I thought.

When I was flooded with schoolwork, intermingled with personal stressors, I went to talk to the school psychologist, Dr Ronald. He was a sweet, warm man, with white hair and a delightful personality. I found him blatantly honest and down to earth. He once said to me, "My door is always open to you." It was a relief knowing I could turn to him at any time without feeling like a nuisance. I took him up on his offer and went to see him regularly. His keen understanding, straightforward approach, and marvelous sense of humor helped me in coping with situations as they came up.

Over a year had passed since my break-up with Jay. When I saw him again, he looked better and seemed to be more in control of his emotions. He, too, had made many changes in his life. He moved out of the private house where we had lived together and into an apartment building. He was making new friends and doing new things. He didn't seem so despondent anymore, and I didn't have that pressing need to carry around his problems as if they were my own. I could now let go of my guilt about leaving him and feel some sense of inner calm, knowing he was safe and doing well in his life.

It wasn't long before the silence was broken between my uncle and me. We made our peace and I was speaking with him regularly. He phoned me one night and spoke in a somber tone: "Jay came here from a therapy session in tears and told us, 'Lenore was right. I was living out some crazy fantasy from my childhood when I was living with her. I never saw her the way I should have'." I felt there was something very wrong with the way Jay was treating me. I thought it was something I said or did that made Jay so cold and distant. Now, Will was confirming my belief that Jay didn't really see me; I was invisible to him. We didn't discuss it any further.

A few weeks later, Will phoned me again: "Jay is getting a divorce." A buried anger was aroused in me. He was finally getting a divorce. After all those years!

Undoubtedly, my leaving Jay turned out to be a good thing—a blessing in disguise—for it snapped him out of his complacency and made him real.

Meanwhile, things were not going well between Jon and me. We continued to have one disagreement after another. It didn't take much for Jon to become rebellious or defiant over some miniscule thing. He complained that I was treating him like a child, and I was stunned. I didn't know how to respond when he flailed about in rage. He reminded me of an angry little boy who didn't get his way, and I didn't hesitate to tell him. I sensed that he was relating to me as if I were his mother and it troubled me. *Why can't he see me for myself?*

I hardly knew Jon, yet I bonded with him without thinking twice. I was only too eager to live within my fantasy of love. I knew

Jon had personal problems, but I also knew that underneath, he could be a very kind and caring person. So, I accepted him with his emotional baggage, the same as he accepted me with mine. And I realized that if we were going to stay together, we had a lot of work to do.

There were times when I longed for something I could not get from a human being: unconditional love. I thought about my Siamese cat. I craved the comfort and companionship that only Hanky could give me. I could see him cuddling up in my arms and gazing into my eyes with his adoring look. I got Jay on the phone and said: "Please give my Hanky back to me."

"Nothing doing!" was Jay's response.

I knew when Jay said no, there was usually nothing that could move him. But I kept bugging him. He finally said, "I'll get you another cat, but Hanky stays with me!"

I soon became the owner of an adorable "Golden Siamese" kitten. She had the rich sable-brown markings of the Siamese and the dark brown coat of the Burmese. I named her Joy. Like Hanky, she had a loud Siamese wail. Her needs and wants had to be catered to immediately; otherwise, she would scream until she got her way. I wasn't too happy about that. But then, she looked into my eyes and expressed her gratitude with a great big purr. Or she just might lick my face, opening and closing her eyes as if in a swoon. I grew to love Joy very much, but my longing for Hanky, the cat I left behind, didn't go away.

We weren't living that long in the studio apartment when we decided that we needed more space. We soon found a larger apartment right around the corner. We were moving again and making another adjustment to living in a new place.

Jon soon graduated with an Associate's degree in Accounting, and then moved on to a senior college in Manhattan, where he switched his major to computer science. We both continued to work diligently on our college courses. Things had become so hectic for us, we were passing each other like two ships in the night.

Although I was immersed in my studies, I started to think about getting a doctorate in psychology. The thought was very exciting, and I was feeling good about it until I realized a course in statistics is required for psychology majors. It was a disturbing thought, for I dreaded anything that dealt with mathematics. I wanted to get the statistics course out of the way as quickly as possible, so I decided to take the course over the summer. This turned out to be a huge mistake because months of coursework were crammed into only a few weeks, which meant I would hardly have enough time to digest the material.

When I saw what I got myself into, I panicked. *I can't do this work! I just can't do it!* But I knew that I would have to try. Jon, a math whiz, volunteered to work with me. We often worked around the clock, but I still couldn't understand the material. I just couldn't absorb what Jon was trying to teach me.

The statistics teacher was a lovely young woman, kind and understanding. With a tone of caring in her voice, she said, "On the day of your final you can use a hand calculator for the test, and this should be helpful to those of you who have a dread of statistics." I attempted to get ready by working with Jon on this little device at home, while he helped me with the basic concepts. When it came time to take the actual test, the material looked vaguely familiar to me, but I didn't have any real understanding of what I was doing. I was shocked when I found out that I passed the course. I didn't think I could ever do it again.

I became aware that statistics would be a major stumbling block in pursuing a doctorate in psychology. The realization that I wouldn't be able to work in my chosen field left me distraught and on edge. I thought about applying for a Psy D degree that is not so heavily focused on statistics, and I wanted to discuss this with a person knowledgeable in the education field. I thought of my uncle Will.

However, when I met with him, I got sidetracked and discussed something that was weighing heavily on my mind for some time: "Will, I want you to meet Jon. He's really nice, and I know you'll like him. I need you to meet him. Please, Will, please…" It was an awkward moment for me, but how surprised I was when he agreed. Soon it happened, and what a fantastic time it turned out to be. I was ecstatic with joy. Their rapport was so natural it seemed as though Will and Jon had known each other all their lives.

Unfortunately, I didn't get around to discussing the topic of a Psy D degree with my uncle.

From time to time, Jon would say, "Let's get married. Now that I want to get married, you don't. When are we going to get married?" Jon was asking me once again, and once again I went within and couldn't find an answer. I thought back to the time when I first met Jon; I would have married him in a heartbeat, but he wasn't ready. Sometimes, it seemed that he would never be ready. I was very hurt and disillusioned by this, but I didn't talk about it; I held it inside and pretended the problem didn't exist. And we went on living together. Jon was involved in his own little world and I was involved in mine.

Love. Romance. Marriage. I often asked myself: *What is it all about?* I gave it quite some thought, but it still remained an enigma to me. However, the concept of marriage remained the epitome of love for me—but its luster had worn thin. I had grown to be cautious, like a child who puts her finger into the fire and gets burned. I was learning to care more about myself, and my own feelings. In the process, I began to realize that maybe my expectations were unrealistic. Maybe they were all based on a myth of love and romance. Maybe I didn't need to be married to be loved…

I soon received my Bachelor's degree in psychology and art, and I was in an exhilarated mood. The world looked good to me, and Jon once again mentioned the thing that was uppermost on his mind: "We've been living together for over three years now. Marry me. I'll make you happy."

I could see the caring expression on his face, and he sounded so sincere. I began to give it some thought. Soon Jon urged: "Our friends are moving to Oregon, and I want to have them at our wedding before they go. I know a rabbi who will do it right away. All we have to do is call him. Let's do it!"

Something within told me that this was the right time. We hurried down to the Municipal Building in Manhattan to get a marriage license. Then Jon called the rabbi who said the ceremony could be performed the next night in his home. I contacted my uncle and a few close friends, and they said they would be able to come. How nervous I was. *I'm really getting married!*

The following night Jon and I were at the rabbi's house in Brooklyn. Our guests met us there. In a daze, I heard Jon tell me: "Members of the rabbi's family and friends will be joining us so we can have a minyan."

"A minyan, what is a minyan?"

Jon replied, "At least ten adult males are needed to be present. It's tradition." I heard words, but I was barely able to take it in; I was too excited. Foremost on my mind was my need to change into my wedding dress. Jessie was with me, and we scurried around until we found a room. I recall how nervous I was, as I slipped into my simple long off-white cotton peasant dress. We then hurried back to the living room, where Jon and the rabbi were waiting for me under a canopy. Jon looked very handsome and somber in his white ceremonial robe, while I was very shaky. Soon I heard the rabbi say: "I am ready to conduct the ceremony."

Somehow, I forgot to be self-conscious as I became involved in the proceedings, but my anxiety persisted. I remember being told by the rabbi, "Circle around Jon seven times." But I lost count. I whispered to Jessie, who was standing nearby, "How many times was that?"

She smiled: "Just one more time."

And there I was, a married woman!

Afterward, the rabbi joyfully sang and played the guitar as we danced and frolicked around his living room. My uncle Will became our photographer that night. I just couldn't believe this was happening—it all seemed so unreal.

We later found a kosher restaurant near the rabbi's house, where we had a reception meal. And then it was over. Our guests went their separate ways, and we went home. I wondered why we couldn't do this sooner. I rationalized that neither one of us was really ready to make the big leap.

We didn't take any time off to celebrate our marriage. Jon was back at school and I was restless, hankering to be working again. This time I was hoping to find a job in the mental health field, but it was harder than I thought. A Bachelor's degree was not enough.

I was very disappointed and soon found myself at the door of a temp agency. I was offered a long-term assignment in a one-girl office working as an "administrative assistant" for an industrial psychologist. It sounded interesting but I wondered: *What is an "administrative assistant"?* The sound of it made me uncomfortable as I wondered if I was eligible for the job. Nevertheless, I decided to take the risk.

So, what was this assignment all about? Nothing new. It was the same old monotonous office work that, in the past, made me feel so insignificant and like a robot. I now had a Bachelor's degree but I was back where I started from at the same old secretarial grind, taking care of the mail, manning the phone, and typing up notes from dictation. Ouch! And I wondered: *Is "administrative assistant" just a glorified term for secretary?*

Here, however, I didn't mind office work as much as before. The atmosphere in this office didn't feel like the usual tense Manhattan setting. My new boss, Harvey, was not a typical slave driver. He was a gentle, sensitive man who had a way of making a person feel special. I thought that was a magnificent trait. I didn't feel like an office worker in his presence. He related to me as if I were a close friend or family member, as he shared tidbits about his wife and children with me. Harvey made me feel that we were on an equal footing and what could be better than that?

One thing I admired so much about Harvey was his laid-back, nonchalant manner. He was not driven by ego needs. We would speak to each other in a simple, unpretentious way and share many laughs together.

Soon, however, I learned that Harvey was not as easy-going as he appeared. When he spoke to me about his confidential files, there was a look of worry on his face. Harvey was out of the office for long periods of time and he was fearful that his confidential files might fall into the wrong hands. He came to me and said, "Lenore, I'm entrusting you with the keys to my file cabinet. You are the only one now, besides myself, who has this access, and I know you will take good care of these files while I'm away."

I felt ten feet tall. But I also felt the great responsibility he bestowed upon me, and I didn't take it lightly.

There were times when I felt a need to discuss personal problems with Harvey, but I never confused him with a therapist. As much as I wanted his input, I held back. I wasn't comfortable mixing my personal life with my work life, even though I had a great rapport with him.

During this time, Jon received his Bachelor's degree in Computer Science. He soon was running all over the city trying to find employment and came away discouraged when he couldn't find anything. When I saw Jon depressed, my spirits dropped low. Harvey would softly reassure me: "Don't worry, Lenore. Jon will find a job."

And Harvey was right. Jon did find work and I was astonished at the amazing transformation in him. Whereas he once had no real goals, interests, or purpose in life, he suddenly became a responsible young man totally committed to, and engrossed in, doing well at his job.

Sometime later, when I spoke to Jon's mother again, I was surprised to hear her say: "If it weren't for you, Jon would never have been able to accomplish all he's done. We tried, but we failed." I would like to think that I was responsible for Jon's success, but I know better. I was only the catalyst; Jon did the work himself.

My marriage with Jon is still a work in progress. We have experienced a lot of good times as well as many hardships. A genuine caring for each other and many shared interests pull us over the rough spots, as Jon works on his self-improvement and I work on mine. We have come a long way together since we first met in the college library.

64

Graduate School

I continued working for Harvey and I was having a fine rapport with him. But I was still restless. Every now and then my thoughts would stray to getting a doctorate in psychology, but Harvey soon made a suggestion that gave me something to think about. "Social Work requires only two years to get a graduate degree and you wouldn't have to deal with statistics. There are many aspects of social work you can pursue—including counseling."

It sounded like a great idea. I began to apply to social work schools in Manhattan. I was excited when two top schools accepted me for interviews. I was debating in my mind which one I wanted to attend. I soon turned to my uncle Will, now a retired teacher, and he immediately told me which one to go to. "This one is more prestigious and will look better on your resume." I thought: *Who would know better than my uncle?* However, I wasn't so sure that this "prestigious" school was the best choice for me. I heard some negative things about it, but my uncle was swaying me to go there.

As Fate would have it, both schools scheduled interviews for me on the same day. Unfortunately, at that time there was a transit strike in the city that made it exceedingly difficult to get around. I was frantic with anxiety. *How will I be able to make both interviews? I have to make a choice, which one is it going to be?*

The word "prestigious" stuck out in my mind, so I decided to go over to the school that my uncle recommended. As it turned out, the "prestigious" school was only a few blocks away from where I was working in the Union Square area, while the other school was all the way over by Columbus Circle; I would have to take a cab through dense midtown traffic to get there, and that would take more time away from my job. As I scurried over to the "prestigious school," I wondered if I was making the right decision.

Soon, the Fieldwork Director, Mr. Charman, a short, arrogant young man was interviewing me in his office. He started off by asking me a slew of questions. At one point he said: "I detect an accent. Where do you come from?"

When I meekly said, "The Bronx," he gave me a funny look. Then he remarked, "It figures."

Suddenly, I felt like I had put my neck into a noose. And he went on. "I see here on your application that you also went to college in the Bronx. The way you talk indicates that as well. And you use the word 'like' too much. You'll have to do something about that too."

He was taking apart whatever I said. I was now afraid to open my mouth. I still tried to sound confident, but I felt awkward each time I defended myself. I wondered if he could sense it. At one point he said in a harsh tone: "This school is all about feelings and you're too much in your head. There's a good possibility you won't be accepted here."

With my uncle's words fresh in my mind, I replied, "I know this is an excellent school; it has a wonderful reputation, and I would very much like to be a part of it." As I spoke, I couldn't help feeling: *He doesn't like me.*

At the end of that brow beating he coldly said, "I want you to meet with my assistant, Mr. Gold. He will be contacting you in the next two weeks." Thank God the interrogation was over. Saying goodbye to Mr. Charmin was the best part of the interview.

I came away feeling dejected: I'm not good enough to go to that school. They'll never accept me. I rushed back to Harvey and tearfully told him about my interview. I was taken aback by his casual attitude. "Don't worry, Lenore. If they don't accept you there, you can go back to Fordham. I went to that school myself and I had a great time. It was a lot of fun!" I began to feel even more despondent. Was I turned off by the words: "it was a lot of fun"? I was used to a lot of struggle. Strangely, I now felt more intent upon being accepted by this "prestigious" school that had already caused me distress.

Two weeks later, I met the man who would decide my fate. Mr. Gold was easy-going and not at all like Mr. Charman. But he also had a lot of questions to ask. I wondered: *Am I saying the right things?* I tried to hide my nervousness as I sat there, answering questions for over two hours. I was becoming exhausted. *How much longer is this going to take?*

How relieved I was when the interview came to an end. Mr. Gold casually said: "I'll be getting back to you to let you know our decision." I felt very pessimistic when I left his office.

Soon I received a letter in the mail. How excited I was when I found out I was accepted. *Bravo!* Yet a part of me felt uneasy. How gratifying it was working for Harvey for almost two and a half years. True, I was "a permanent temporary," but my boss liked me, and I was comfortable in my environment. I was safe. Somehow, this new school did not feel safe to me.

I went back to Harvey and told him the good news. He smiled and said, "I'm so glad that you were accepted into the school of your choice."

With joy in my voice, I said, "Harvey, I want you to know what a great experience it's been working with you. I've had so many wonderful moments here, I can't put it into words."

Harvey warmly replied: "It's been a pleasure working with you, too."

Before I left, Harvey asked me to join him in the Executive Dining Room. This was a huge, elaborate place where all the bigwigs met to eat and shmooze. With reluctance I had lunch with Harvey, and felt very much out of place, but I still thought he was very kind to allow me to have this experience with him.

Soon, a new chapter of my life was beginning…

I arrived on my first day at Graduate School not knowing what to expect. In the casework classroom, the instructor, Ms. Rosen, a short, serious-looking, middle-aged woman, informed the students of their fieldwork placements. I was assigned to a state psychiatric hospital. "This is a very difficult assignment for a first-year student. You will be working with psychotic patients. It is a demanding setting, and you can decline this placement, but I will say that while it is very challenging, it is a true learning experience."

I was startled. I had filled out a form requesting a placement in an outpatient mental health clinic. I felt a knot in my stomach telling me there was something wrong; that accepting this placement might be a terrible mistake. However, when I learned it was the same psychiatric hospital where I had worked before, my spirits lifted. *That was a positive experience, so why not go back?* But this time I would not be working with a geriatric population. I would be on a locked ward with deeply disturbed psychotic patients. I wasn't really sure how I felt about this. Nevertheless, I decided to accept the placement.

Ms. Rosen went on to tell us: "In this class we will be studying casework theory and reviewing what is going on in the field. A student is expected to be at her field placement three days a week. The other two days of the week will be spent in class. Every time a student sees a client, a process report needs to be written up about the interaction between the student and the client. This is to be handed in to the fieldwork supervisor for review. Select cases are to be presented in class."

I was somewhat overwhelmed as I listened to Ms. Rosen speak about the many facets of schoolwork that were required in the curriculum. Besides the necessary classes and fieldwork, I didn't realize how much heavy reading and paperwork all this would entail.

When I went over to the psychiatric hospital, I met my fieldwork supervisor, Pauline. She was a tall, thin, masculine-looking woman, who immediately let me know: "This is a training ward, and there is a problem getting patients for all the students who are coming in. Right now, there's a shortage. Patients will be assigned shortly. In the meantime, observe the patients on the ward."

I was very disappointed. Ms. Rosen didn't mention anything to me about a patient shortage, but I followed Pauline's advice and moved around the ward. Soon I felt like I was in another world. Screaming, shouting, people walking around like zombies—there were all kinds of nerve-racking sights to behold. I was repulsed. I saw patients who were unresponsive and staring off into space; they looked as though they were on heavy medication. Still other patients were in a state of agitation, extremely restless and excitable. A few were flailing about, out of control. They looked really scary. A creepy feeling came over me. When Ms. Rosen said it would be a difficult assignment, she didn't exaggerate!

A thought kept racing through my mind: *There's still time. I can change my mind. Maybe I should go back and ask for another placement....* But I was too intent upon getting started to pay attention to my inner voice.

Days were passing and I still had no patients. My frustration was growing. I kept thinking to myself: *What am I doing here? When will I begin my training? This feels awful.* I went to Pauline and complained. "My classmates have two or three clients, and they're discussing their cases in class. When do you think I'll be getting a client?"

She asserted: "Second year students, who have first choice, are also griping. You'll get patients, but in the meantime, I suggest you continue to observe the patients on the ward."

My God, is she kidding? What is there to observe? It didn't make any sense to me, but she was my supervisor and who was I to challenge her? I was boiling up inside as I aimlessly wandered around the ward. As I stood there watching people suffering in severe emotional pain, a feeling of helplessness crept over me. I couldn't help feeling morbidly useless. I thought to myself: *This seems like such a waste of time. How can this be "a true learning experience" without clients to work with? I have to go back and get myself another placement.* But somehow, I didn't pursue it.

I started to speak with Pam, the occupational therapist on the ward. She was a tall, dark-haired young woman who appeared to be very involved with her work and her patients. I found her easy to talk to, and I could easily be myself with her. One day I said to her, "Let's get out of here and find some place to talk." She had a big smile on her face as she quickly replied, "Yes, I think that's a great idea. Let's go."

So, we found a small restaurant in the area and we sat and talked over some tea. Tears came rolling down my cheeks. "I can't stand it any longer. I'm going to leave my placement. I don't have one patient. What am I going to do?"

"Don't let it get you down," Pam replied. "I just know that everything will turn out fine. It may be a little slow, but you will get your patients…" How very much I wanted to believe that. And we talked some more. When we were about to leave, I felt guilty that most of the time we spent together was focused on how upset I was in my placement. However, that didn't stop our friendship from developing and I was very happy about that.

I began to look forward to staff meetings. There, staff members, including the interns, talked about relevant issues. I didn't have anything to contribute, but I was listening and trying to absorb whatever I could. I thought this might be useful when the time came for me to work with patients.

As part of the staff, I carried around a giant key to lock and unlock the heavy metal doors when I went in and out of the ward. As I placed the key in the lock, I had the most eerie feeling. I could perceive danger lurking beyond the door; the key was symbolic of that danger. Patients could become violent at any time. In a staff meeting, one of the nurses spoke about a pregnant nurse who was attacked and beaten up by a patient in an elevator. That made my heart jump. How did that happen? No one knew, but it was not a rare occurrence. When I walked down a lonely corridor and saw unsavory characters a few feet behind me, I became nervous and moved faster.

You could feel chaos in the air. As patients became more violent, screaming and acting out, they were given psychotropic medications to calm them down. Drugs so commonly used to treat mental disorders could also induce tremors, and many patients were walking around the ward shaking as a result. I thought it was terrible that medication, which is used to benefit patients, could also produce such horrific side effects.

As I observed the caregivers on the ward, it seemed that they had a mighty tough job to perform. I wondered how much this environment affected them. In one of the staff meetings, I heard about a ward psychiatrist who didn't come in for several days. One of the staff members interjected: "He hanged himself! Didn't you know that?" There was silence in the room. Then suddenly someone volunteered: "I'm not surprised—it's happened here before. Other psychiatrists have also committed suicide…"

I was shocked: *What? Psychiatrists committing suicide? What would make them do such a drastic thing?* I thought it strange that a person in the helping profession, like a psychiatrist, could not help himself, and that he would wind up taking his own life. Maybe this extremely stressful environment had something to do with it. I all the more realized that this is, indeed, a very difficult workplace to endure; for some, it might even be deadly.

I began to wonder if I could be useful in this placement. You had to have a strong stomach to work on this ward. I realized this was not the kind of setting I would want to work in for any length of time. Some of the sights I observed were really gruesome. A nervous twinge soared through me as I watched a patient being put into a straitjacket and hauled away.

But I was quite familiar with mental illness. My mother was not only out-of-control, but she was also out of reality. Her behavior was unpredictable, and anything could happen at any time. I guess, based upon my experience with my mother, I felt that I could deal with this psychotic setting. Maybe I had to prove something to myself, I don't know. But I felt it was something I had to do; I would not retreat and walk away.

While I was very distressed by these experiences, my greatest distress occurred in the classroom. I was amongst a group of young women who came from upper-class families and had attended prominent schools such as Vassar and Barnard. They presented themselves as gutsy, opinionated, and overly confident. I admired them and very much wanted to connect with them, but when I tried to make overtures of friendship, they were exceedingly aloof and ignored me as if I wasn't there. If any one of them spoke to me, it seemed as if they were doing me a favor. I'm sure they sized me up as not being one of them. Nevertheless, I ached to belong and be a part of their group, and it greatly disturbed me that they were not allowing me to connect with them.

But whom was I kidding? I was not like them. I watched them interact with each other with such an air of indifference and superficiality it made my skin crawl. I was intimidated by their arrogance and standoffishness. I wondered how they could possibly work with people who are troubled and disturbed when they exuded such a lack of warmth and caring. As I perceived their coldness and callousness, it appeared as if I was in a room full of Heddas and that felt just awful.

So often, I would sit in the classroom, immobilized. I felt trapped. I didn't want to be there, but I was there. However bad I felt, I still managed to attend classes regularly.

I picked up the courage one day to voice an opinion in class. My cheeks were burning and I could feel myself choking on my words. A student came over to me afterwards and spoke in a loud harsh tone that sent a sting through me: "I thought you were going to have a heart attack!"

I was jostled by her words. I couldn't think of a thing to say, and we stood there looking at each other. Soon she was gone, and I was feeling like a first class jerk. *Damn! Why did I have to do something stupid like talking up in class?* After that, I tried to keep as low a profile as possible.

But the problem persisted: when there was a go-around, the students were expected to volunteer some personal aspect of their lives that might have significance in casework. I felt much too vulnerable for something like that. *How am I going to make myself inconspicuous, so that I wouldn't have to speak about myself?* It was another heart-pounding episode for me in the classroom.

It was the same old story. Sitting in the classroom, I felt lost and alone. I wanted to reach out to a fellow student and talk about my problems at the school, but as I looked around, I didn't see a friendly face in sight. There didn't seem to be anyone who would listen to me and support me in my distress. I felt like I was treading on foreign soil.

I decided to stop off at the synagogue in my neighborhood to see Rabbi Schwartz. I would turn to him from time to time when I had a pressing problem. I was in tears as I stumbled into his office. "Rabbi, it's awful! The students are so arrogant and nasty, and I'm not getting any clients. I'm ashamed to show my face in the classroom…"

The rabbi's response was: "Calm yourself and sit down. You're not looking at this very clearly. You're getting yourself all upset. You're in school for a purpose, and you're letting all kinds of things pull you down. You tend to focus on miniscule things while overlooking the bigger picture. I know you, and when your sensitivities get in the way, you over-react to just about anything and everything. Things become overwhelming and then you lose sight of the things that matter most. As I've already said, you are in school for a purpose. You are not in school to form a friendship club or have people like you. You're only shortchanging yourself. Keep your eye on the donut, and not on the hole! Remember that when you're down in the dumps."

"Rabbi, I know you're right—I just hope I'll be able to follow through."

Soon, Pauline came over to me and said: "I have a patient for you. Her name is Kristin. She has a bipolar disorder which manifests cycles of mania and depression. Kristin says crazy things happen to her when she comes to New York. Kristin has a habit of not taking her medication. Lithium is essential for Manic-Depression. Meet with her and see what you can do."

I was ecstatic. Kristin was my first client in graduate school and I was very eager to work with her. She was a highly intelligent young woman who poured her heart out to me about her multifaceted experiences in the big city. "Life in a small town is not for me, but here in New York, there's so much to do…" I perceived Kristin was having a hard time keeping up with the fast, stressful pace of city life. I pointed out to her that it can be particularly overwhelming when you have a manic-depressive condition and you're not taking your medication to control it. She vowed: "I will be taking my Lithium from now on." And we talked and talked...

At the time of her discharge, she adamantly said, "I'm going home and I'm not coming back to New York. I'm just a country girl who doesn't do very well in a big metropolis."

I think you're making a wise decision," was my response.

Several weeks later, my supervisor let me know that she heard from Kristin. "She said she's taking her meds and seeing a therapist. She's doing much better, and she says she owes it all to you." It was a wonderful feeling to know I was a part of helping her sort out pieces of her life that were in drastic disarray.

I amazed myself; I had my own problems that I was struggling with, but I still was able to function in this tumultuous psychiatric setting. I marveled that I was an altogether different person when I was working with a client. I felt alive and energized knowing I was needed and fulfilling my passion to be of help to others. Even though I had feelings of anxiety, I didn't allow any of it to spill over into my work environment. I was finally beginning to feel competent.

Soon, it was back to square one. Again, there was no one to work with, and my spirits plummeted. Once again, I moved around the ward, trying to make contact with patients who were lost in their own reality. Again, time was flying, and I was heartsore. I didn't have one client! I once again complained to Pauline. She said, "You look very upset…" Yes, I was very upset. I wanted to walk out then and there, but something within told me to wait.

Within approximately two weeks, Pauline came over with a young dark-haired woman who had the saddest expression on her face. I could see she was hurting and in emotional pain. Pauline introduced me to Cathy and said: "Set up an appointment when you two can meet."

So, I now had a new patient. Unfortunately, it was the end of the day and I was getting ready to leave. I sensed Cathy had a need to unburden herself, so I assured her: "We'll meet tomorrow at 2 p.m. and we'll have lots of time to talk. Will that be okay with you?" She nodded her head yes, and we parted.

On my way down the corridor, I passed the Nurses' Station and noticed it was vacant. It was between shifts and I didn't see anyone in sight. An eerie feeling passed through me; I was alone on the floor. That always made me tense. Then suddenly I heard a sound. When I turned around, I saw Cathy. I was surprised to see her. She meekly whispered, "Do you have a few minutes for me?"

Spontaneously I said, "Sure, Cathy, we can talk for a few minutes." Without thinking I went with her into a secluded office and closed the door behind me. Suddenly, Cathy became hysterical and started to scream, **"Help me! Help me! You gotta help me!"**

Her screams became louder and louder. She came towards me and lowered herself to the floor. Kneeling at my feet, she started to pull on my skirt. I was frightened out of my wits. *Is she dangerous? Will she attack me? What am I going to do*? I hadn't looked at her chart and I didn't know anything about her. My preference was to meet with the client first and read the chart afterwards so as not to be biased in my observations. But what a mistake that was in a setting like this.

Somehow, I found the voice to firmly say, "I would like to help you, Cathy, but I'm going to need you to sit down and talk to me. That's the only way I can be of help to you." I repeated this several times, as my heart beat like a drum. Cathy slowly removed her hands from my skirt and pulled herself up. I was able to breathe a little easier. She then sat down on a chair, talking, and sobbing at the same time. I could barely hear her; all I heard were muffled sounds.

What am I going to do now? I knew intuitively that I had to remain calm, but firm. "I will be coming to see you tomorrow afternoon, Cathy, and we can talk about all the things that are bothering you. We'll have lots of time to talk, and that is a promise."

I was amazed that Cathy stopped crying almost immediately. My own inner tension had been building, but I was not giving in to it. I continued to speak to Cathy in a firm, reassuring way, as I maintained an outer calm. When I took her back to the ward, I was rather shaky, but I covered it with a smile. I approached a nurse who was just coming on the evening shift. "Cathy's been kind of upset.

Could you please keep an eye on her?" The nurse agreed to watch Cathy, and I felt I could leave.

I was still shaky as I found my way downstairs. I waited in the lobby for my bus to come. For the most part, I was oblivious to my surroundings, but I do recall how wonderful it felt to see the bus pull up in front of the building. I couldn't wait to get home and lie down.

That evening I kept thinking: *Nothing in any textbook could have prepared me for the experience I had with Cathy!* I wondered if I would be able to work with her. I didn't think I could handle her case, but I knew she was counting on me. I worried that I might have to break my promise to her.

I decided to meet with Cathy as scheduled. However, I checked her chart first and it stated: "paranoid schizophrenic with delusions." In my initial session with Cathy, she cried: "My family is trying to poison me…" And from there on in, that is all she spoke about.

I discussed Cathy's case with my supervisor and asked how I could be of help to her. Pauline's response was: "This is psychosis and there is nothing you can do but be there for her. Talk to her; listen to her. be present for her. That's the only help you can give her now."

As I continued to meet with Cathy, I tried to have some dialogue with her, but it was useless. There didn't seem to be anything I could say or do that would make a difference. It was pulling me down. I felt helpless and frustrated. What was I doing there?

I thought back to my mother's mental illness. It was different from Cathy's, but it was psychosis, nonetheless. My mother was also living in her own world. I was not a stranger to psychosis, yet now, I didn't know how to handle this aspect and it felt as though I was experiencing psychotic behavior for the first time.

I was now aware that this placement was one great big mistake. Why had I, a first year student, accepted a second year placement? The instructor strongly asserted that this would be a very difficult assignment, especially for a first year student, and I had the option of saying no. Instead, I put my head into the noose and accepted it without thinking it through. At the time it sounded like an awesome challenge, and I wanted to have the experience. But I wasn't ready for the trauma it presented to me.

Suddenly, Cathy stopped talking to me altogether. I was perplexed and didn't know what to make of it. Pauline said, "You weren't here for a couple of weeks during the winter break, and she's angry. She feels you abandoned her."

I was startled. I didn't think I held that kind of significance in her world. I kept trying to establish some sort of rapport with her, but she kept clamming up. I had a feeling that she was through talking to me.

I continued to bring my concerns to Pauline who, in her cold, austere manner, told me: "Don't worry about it, you're doing fine. Continue to meet with Cathy, that's all you can do." I reluctantly said, "I'll keep trying."

And try I did, but to no avail. Cathy remained mute. By now I was feeling superfluous. *This is awful. She has no intentions of talking to me! What the hell am I doing here?*

The second year students on the training ward now had two or three clients. My fellow classmates were discussing their cases in class and I felt ashamed and angry; I didn't have one case to present.

In supervision, I bitterly complained to Pauline: "My only patient is not talking to me. I need patients to work with so I can have a true learning experience. This placement is not working out for me. I want to leave."

Pauline replied: "I know how you feel. We'll have someone for you real soon, but you'll have to be patient…"

Be patient? Be patient for what? This is abhorrent! My school term is slipping away. I had taken out a loan for thousands of dollars for an education I wasn't getting. I was becoming angrier and more upset with every passing day. I said to myself: *Am I supposed to sit in a corner and not do anything about this?*

It was time for me to take action. I made an appointment with the dean of the school, Dr. Stiller. A tall man with a graying beard and pensive eyes, he listened intently to what I had to say. As I told him about the situation at my placement, I also spoke a little about myself. He commented: "You've certainly experienced a lot of grief in your life and you seem to understand what human suffering is all about. Stay a little while longer at your field placement. I know they're trying to get clients for you as we speak."

This was not the answer I had hoped for. Suddenly, my spirits dropped. *What a disappointment!* The dean seemed like such a nice man, but he, too, was telling me to be patient and wait. *But how much longer could I wait?* I wanted to cry as I walked out of his office. I felt like I was being given the run-around and I didn't like it.

When I went back to my placement the next day, Pauline's face was like stone. "I heard you met with your dean. What did he say?"

I avoided her question; I couldn't look at her. I was fuming with anger.

"Come into my office," she said. "I want to speak to you." Her voice was like ice. "I don't like your attitude," she adamantly declared. "You said you wanted to leave—well, now you're leaving!"

Suddenly, I felt sick to my stomach. I now had a change of heart; I wanted to stay and work it out. My goodness, what had I done? The shame I felt, I could not put into words.

I was getting ready to leave the placement when Cathy came running up to me. "You're leaving because of me. Please don't go. I'm sorry I was mean to you. I want to make it up to you. I'm begging you—please stay."

Cathy was speaking! I was amazed that she suddenly found her voice. I was aching inside as I told her I wasn't leaving because of her, but there was no way I could convince her. I couldn't tell her it was my supervisor's decision—not mine.

More than half of the term was over, and I was in a state of panic as I rushed back to the school to speak to Mr. Charman. I tried to be composed as I told him about my unhappy experience at the state hospital. I then asked: "Is it at all possible that you might have an opening for me in an outpatient mental health clinic? That was my original choice on the Placement form I filled out."

"The slots are all filled," he barked. "You'll be lucky if we're able to find anything at all!"

I could feel him looking down on me in his condescending manner. I was now at his mercy. His face reddened and his eyes were blazing with anger. "You just might be finished in this school!"

Oh, my goodness! What had I done now?

My heart was racing as I sat there, staring at him, while my world was collapsing around me. He continued to reprimand me for losing the placement and I couldn't find the words to respond. I couldn't understand how this was all happening to me simply because I was asking to receive clients and have a true learning experience.

As I got up to leave, I suddenly found the words to stand up for myself: "By the way I worked at that very same psychiatric hospital in a college program, and I never had a problem like this. I received clients, I had an excellent evaluation—in fact, there's a copy of my evaluation and other assessments of my work in your file."

He looked astonished as I walked out the door.

I soon received a phone call from Mr. Charman. "I have a placement for you at a skilled nursing home facility in the Bronx. Now, don't get yourself kicked out!"

Ouch!

My goal was to succeed, but this new placement was extremely depressing. It made me very sad to see people strapped to wheelchairs or lying in bed, unable to feed or clothe themselves. Some were stooped over and drooling. Many were staring off into space or spending most of their time sleeping. There were those who had such morbid expressions on their faces; they looked as though they had lost all interest in life. It was hard to take it all in and not be stirred by these sights. At some point, I shut down. I wondered if I would be able to work with this population, but I was going to make every effort.

I recall overhearing a social worker talking to a colleague. "Thank God for this lunch break—it's so damn depressing in here!" It sounded strange to hear a staff member speaking like that, but then again I realized he's only human.

My new field supervisor, Sarah, was a very plain lady, slightly overweight, with graying hair and a friendly disposition. She appeared soft on the surface, but as I got to know her, I found out how very strong and firm she could be.

Sarah introduced me to my first client, a disoriented gentleman who mistook me for his sweetheart. When I came around to see him, he would nervously say: "We need to be careful—they may tell my wife about you." I was very sad because there was nothing I could say that would dissuade him from his belief. I went to Sarah and asked: "Can you please take me off this case? This patient cannot relate to a female. He is confused about his relationship with me. He thinks I'm his girlfriend, and that his wife will find out. He has a problem with mistaken identity. He needs to work with a male therapist."

It was obvious to me; nevertheless, Sarah pooh-poohed it. She asserted, "I want you to work with this client for a while longer and we'll think about what to do if things don't change." I couldn't understand her thinking, but there I was, paying visits to a client who became very upset each time he saw me. A few weeks passed and this case was assigned to a male therapist.

Sarah soon gave me another client: a sweet, frail little white-haired man, who could barely stay with a thought for more than a few minutes. His thinking was very jumbled, and I could barely understand what he was struggling to say. I felt morose; I couldn't make contact with him either. *What am I to do? This placement is just as bad as the last. I don't have a single patient to work with.*

I was distraught when I went to see Sarah. I said, "I'm having a hard time communicating with my patients."

She looked at me with a sorrowful expression on her face. "These patients are all very ill. This is a skilled nursing facility. These are the only clients we have for you."

My heart dropped. I understood what she was telling me. This was another terrible situation. I didn't know what to do.

My casework instructor, Ms. Rosen, was soon informed about my problem. She immediately agreed to have a conference with Sarah, with me present, at the nursing facility.

On my way over to the meeting I stopped off at a luncheonette. I had change in my hand and I wanted to make a phone call, but I didn't know whom to call. I asked myself: *How can things be so bad?* The pain inside was tearing me up and I thought about my education coming to an end. I sat down at a table and cried. *Are they going to kick me out of this placement, too?*

I arrived at the meeting. Sarah and Ms. Rosen were waiting for me. They immediately began to discuss my future at the nursing home and in graduate school. Was there to be any future? My fate was in their hands. My heart was in my mouth as I listened to them talk about me as if I weren't there. For a while, it looked like a hopeless situation. Then I heard Sarah say, "We could let her go, but her work is so good. Her process reports are excellent!"

There I was, on pins and needles, as they were about to make a decision: would I stay or would I go? Regardless, there weren't any clients available with whom I could have a reasonable working relationship. I thought it was mind-boggling; whichever way I looked at it, it was a no-win situation. Still, I remained anxious as they continued to deliberate.

Finally, Ms. Rosen said to me: "You will have to manage to do the best you can, under the circumstances. You can stay on, but if you find it too difficult, then you are certainly free to leave." I knew what my answer would be.

The meeting was over. I felt weak in my knees as I pulled myself out of my chair and headed for the door. With anxiety and tears, I struggled to get through the rest of the semester in the nursing home. I catered to Sarah, kept my mouth shut, made no more complaints, and behaved like a good little girl. *Ouch!*

One afternoon, towards the end of the semester, I went to the graduate school cafeteria and was feeling bluer than blue when I saw a classmate sitting all by herself. Betty, an older woman with short brown hair and a friendly smile, openly shared her thoughts and feelings in the classroom. She was one of the few who came across as witty and introspective. This felt like a good opportunity to speak with her. I found the nerve to go over to her table. She smiled when she saw me, and I asked her if I could join her. She was pleasant enough, and I couldn't wait to tell her what was on my mind: "This is a hard school. It's been very difficult for me to endure."

"You're not alone," she amicably replied. "It's very difficult for many of the students."

Her smile was warm and reassuring, so I went further. "The girls in this school are so arrogant. They come from backgrounds of wealth; they consider themselves the elite. Their lives are so perfect. It seems to me that they look down upon anyone who is not like them."

Betty appeared interested in what I was saying, so I trustingly went a step further; I told her the story of my life. Bit by bit the tale unraveled, as I bared my soul to her. A strange expression covered her face. She exclaimed: "This is a horror tale!"

She continued to listen and remained silent. I got lost in details, and the time was flying. After a couple of hours, we got up to leave. Out in the street, Betty said: "You spoke about the girls who come from elite backgrounds. You know, I have similarities to them. I live in Connecticut. I have a husband and two children. My husband is a lawyer. He makes a very good living, and we have a house. I can put myself into the same classification as those girls."

I was floored. Whatever made me think she was any different? Suddenly I wanted to disappear; I was so embarrassed. By knocking those elite, arrogant women, I was knocking Betty as well. Even worse, I made the mistake of telling a very personal story to a total stranger. She said goodbye with icicles in her voice. I walked away in a fog.

I saw Betty several times after that. She didn't speak to me. She didn't even look at me. Why was she snubbing me? Was it because I shared with her the pathos of my life? I found it very disturbing. I was extremely anxious to find out what the problem was. I was in the classroom one day when I saw Betty get up from her seat and walk out. I figured she was heading for the Ladies' Room. I waited a few minutes and then I followed her in. She was washing her hands when I went over to her and said, "Hi, Betty. You pass me by and you don't say hello. You seem to be upset. I hope I didn't overwhelm you with my stories."

She had a grim expression on her face, as she looked me straight in the eye. "Yes, you did." She took a deep breath and went on. "In fact, I am quite overwhelmed with all you told me."

Before I could say anything, she turned towards the door and walked out. I stood there feeling awful. She was dismissing me because of my problems. I thought to myself: *This is a person who wants to be a social worker?*

That was the last time we spoke. I reflected upon this incident. I had poured out my heart to Betty, and I expected to find a sympathetic ear, but instead, she turned her back to me. I had a habit of opening myself up to strangers and talking too much, then getting the most unexpected reactions. I would need to be much more careful in the future.

I will never forget my first year in graduate school. It was Hell—but I survived.

65

The Nightmare Continues

I hated the thought of going back to graduate school. My first year was a disaster and it left me with a dread of going through more of the same in my second year. Getting my degree was still very important to me. I felt at a loss; I didn't know what to do. I finally decided to take time off and explore my options.

I found a job as a stenographer in a Manhattan insurance company. I was unhappy as ever doing what I considered to be mindless work, but I was relieved to get away from the intense pressure I experienced in graduate school. Tears were welling up in my eyes, however, when I realized that I was postponing a degree that would enable me to do something really meaningful with my life. In the weeks and months that followed, I remained ambivalent about returning to school.

I thought that group therapy might give me a new perspective. I soon became aware of an informal self-help group where people get together to speak about whatever is on their minds. It sounded good to me, so I decided to give it a try.

This group provided an altogether different experience for me. There were 8 to 10 members from all walks of life. We met on a Sunday afternoon in alternate homes and shared commonalities, as we confided openly and freely. These people were lovely and warm, and genuinely supported each other with helpful suggestions and sincere interest.

As I discussed my problems at graduate school, some members chimed in: "Don't let them push you around. Stand up for yourself! Go back there and get your degree!"

This was sound advice. I knew I had to be strong and try again. The school had now moved to upper Manhattan, which meant I had to take two local buses to get there. It was quite a long, cumbersome trip but I made it my business to be there, rain or shine.

Again, I asked to be placed in an outpatient mental health setting, but this time, at the beginning of my second year, I was sent to another nursing facility in the Bronx. I met with an interviewer who spoke about the setting and said: "This is an end-of-life placement. Do you think you could work in a place like this?"

I looked him in the eye and sadly said, "No. I cannot accept this placement."

When I left, I felt morose. I walked around for a while and then called Mr. Charman. I told him I wouldn't be able to work in that setting, and then cautiously asked for another placement. He didn't seem hostile or annoyed, and I was relieved. He immediately assigned me to work with children, ages eight to twelve, in a Jewish elementary school a few blocks from my home.

But what did I know about children? Not having mingled as I was growing up, I didn't have the slightest idea of what they were like or how I would work with them. But there was only one way to find out, and that was to meet the challenge.

I felt apprehensive at first, and then I met my fieldwork supervisor. Mr. Shapiro, a community organizer, appeared charming and pleasant, and I was hopeful that I would have a positive experience with him at the school.

As I interacted with the children, I found that some were outgoing and friendly, while others were quiet and guarded. They all shared one commonality: they had trouble talking about what was bothering them. The usual response to any question I asked was: "I don't know." This left me frustrated and in a quandary. I persevered and responded with patience, warmth, and genuine concern. Much to my surprise, I found many of the children slowly crawling out of their shells and speaking to me.

One day I saw a little girl sitting on a staircase, crying. I went over to her and asked her, "Why are you crying?" Cindy turned out to be the eight-year-old daughter of a teacher in the school. As we talked, she told me she was crying a lot since the birth of her baby sister. "My mother is paying a lot of attention to my sister, and she doesn't pay any attention to me. She says I'm acting like a baby." She continued to cry, as we spoke some more. I told her: "I'll look into it and I'll see what I can do."

I met with her mother, Myrna, and together, we explored the possibilities for Cindy's disturbance. Myrna confided: "You may be right. I think she's jealous of the baby. She probably needs more attention and affection."

The next time I saw Cindy, she was smiling. I asked: "How are things going?"

She replied: "Better!"

I was becoming more comfortable interacting with the children. I recognized their need to be loved and cared for and their desire to belong. But I was still tense and worried; I was trying to understand the children and their feelings, and I wasn't sure if I was saying or doing the right thing.

I went to Mr. Shapiro with a lot of questions. When I asked him: "How am I doing?" his usual response was: "Relax! You're doing fine." But I knew there was so much to learn, and I was frustrated because I felt I wasn't learning fast enough.

As I got to know Mr. Shapiro, I found he was a very bright, overly confident young man, who wore many faces. He could be kind and sweet, but he could also display a nasty temper. At times, I thought of him as a little dictator. What he said was law and he was not to be challenged.

One day Mr. Shapiro assigned me to work with a seven-year-old girl. Rivka, a pretty child with dark hair and green eyes, was a troubled little girl who came to school with her hair disheveled and her clothing soiled. When I first met her, I was taken aback by how very well she articulated her thoughts and how self-assured she appeared for her age. When I read her file, I thought it was horrific that her mother was bringing men into the home, having sexual encounters with them, and that Rivka was being exposed to this. It seemed incredible that she was able to handle herself so adult-like within the turmoil of her chaotic world.

I met with Rivka every week and we spoke briefly in a vacant classroom. Rivka was not open to speaking about her mother, but she was able to state her needs clearly and precisely: "Please take me out of there. Please take me away from my mother."

Her pleas went straight to my heart. I immediately went to Mr. Shapiro and told him: "Rivka is very upset. She's begging me to take her out of her home. What could be done about this?"

I was shocked to hear his response. "She's a manipulator and a liar. Don't let her manipulate you. I know about her problems, and we're doing what we can. I'm in touch with Children's Services, and it takes time. They're looking into her case. Tell her that when you see her."

He was speaking in a very forceful tone, and I was biting my tongue. I wondered: *How can he, a mental health professional, speak like that about a troubled little child? And why does he have such an intense dislike of Rivka?* It bothered me that he wasn't showing any compassion for this child and what she was going through. But foremost on my mind was one thing: *What can I do to get Rivka out of her sordid environment?*

Each time I met with Rivka, as with any of my other clients, I wrote the necessary process report about our interaction. I handed over these reports to Mr. Shapiro. In supervision, he went over my notes and made suggestions. I would ask: "Do you have any news about taking Rivka out of her home?"

His usual response was: "Stop worrying about her! She's a bitch! She's taking advantage of you. She knows how to reach you, all right!"

I looked at him in disbelief. It was terrible talk, and I was very troubled. *How am I going to deal with Mr. Shapiro and his hostility toward Rivka?* I wasn't very good at confronting authority figures and this presented a problem for me. I was holding back the anger he aroused in me until I found the guts to say: "You're talking about a little girl who needs help. She's in a lot of trouble. How can you say those awful things?"

He responded with a snicker, "Because she's a little bitch and that's all there is to it! I told you that before and I'll say it again because you need to hear it!" I couldn't help but feel disdain for him.

Rivka was on my mind day and night. Her pleas touched me deeply, and I walked around in dismay: *How can I ask Mr. Shapiro to have some mercy for this little girl? Is there anything more he can be doing to get her out of her home or were his hostile emotions getting in the way? And is there anything more I could do to be of help?*

I was afraid to step over Mr. Shapiro's authority. He made it very clear that he didn't want me to intervene. He emphatically told me: "I'm in touch with Children's Services. Your role is to see the kid and counsel her, and that's all. We'll take it from there."

I was appalled. He wasn't allowing me to take any action on Rivka's behalf. What was I going to do? After giving it some thought, I reached for the phone. My heart beat faster as I called Children's Services. I introduced myself and asked about Rivka's case. I was told, "We don't have enough evidence to remove her from her home." I was repulsed. *How can they allow a child to live like that?*

I went back to Mr. Shapiro and told him what I had done. His response surprised me. He was not angry; he was actually gloating! "I told you things are not as easy as you think. No physical abuse. No truancy on her record. There's food in the refrigerator, and a roof over her head. She stays in her home." It was the very same argument my uncle gave me for my own case! It was mind-boggling.

In my next visit to Rivka, I said: "Mr. Shapiro told me to let you know we are doing everything we can for you." And I was ashamed; I couldn't tell her that Mr. Shapiro and Children's Services informed me that under the circumstances "nothing can be done."

Rivka's cries were an echo of my own childhood. I could never forget the fantasy I had about someone taking me away from my mother, and the ache I felt inside because there was no one to rescue me. I could see myself in Rivka. However, there was one big difference: Rivka could voice her pain and plea for help. I suffered in silence.

"Get it into your head there's only so much a social worker can do and no more. Learn that now. There's nothing you can do for that kid." I could feel the sting of his words and the contempt in his voice. But it did not alter my thinking: Rivka was in harm's way, and something needed to be done.

Mr. Shapiro and I continued to have our differences about this case and others as well. He would raise his voice: **"Your way is the wrong way! I know what I'm doing!"** I would often leave his office in tears. One time he screamed so loudly, people gathered in the hallway and were staring at me as I came out. I tried to hold my head up as I walked past them, but inside, I was squirming with shame.

I felt alone in a storm with the wind and rain pounding on my face. It was one crisis after another, as I went back and forth between the classroom and my placement. I was barely able to eat or sleep. I didn't think I could persevere any longer. I felt defeated and ready to give up. I went to Mr. Shapiro and told him: "I can't stand this aggravation. I'm leaving!"

All of a sudden, his attitude changed. "Calm down. Let's work out our differences. I want you to stay!" He pleaded with me, but I was too angry, too hurt, to hear anything he had to say. I wound up running out of his office in a huff. I was pretty sure I wasn't going back.

A thought occurred to me: *Maybe I can transfer out. Maybe if I went over to the other school that accepted me and told them my story, they might allow me to come into their program.*

I made an appointment to go over there. I was a little early for my appointment, so I found a place where I could sit and wait. My anxiety was running rampant. I felt a need to talk, so I was very glad when a young woman sat down next to me. I opened up to her and told her all about my experiences at my school. "I have so many problems in my school. I never should have gone there. Mr.

Charman, the program director, never liked me from the start. He criticized just about everything I said."

"Did you say Mr. Charman? He's the Social Work Director of your program? He was here the other week. He gave a lecture, and he was on fire! He's full of hostility. I feel sorry for anyone who has to deal with him."

I agreed. "It's been one problem after another. It's a terrible school. I want to get out of there in the worst way. That's why I'm here."

"I love it here. This is a wonderful school. I think you'll like it, too."

I was amazed at how warm and friendly this young woman was. In all the time I was in my social work program I didn't have the rapport with any of the students there that I was having with a student I just met. So, there I was, enjoying a friendly exchange the first time I stepped into this building. I felt joy. It was a wonderful experience for me, and my hopes mounted as I thought about becoming a part of this program. I recognized this school as an altogether different environment from the one I was in. There was a welcoming feeling in the air. Even the walls were painted in light, bright, cheerful colors. I liked the feeling I got from just being there. I wanted all the more to transfer over.

We were so involved in our conversation, I hated to get up and leave, but it was time for my appointment. I could feel my heart leaping in my chest as I explained my situation to the school advisor. Then I heard what I didn't want to hear: "Stay where you are and work it out. It's only a 2-year program."

But what did I expect? I surmised the answer before I got there. But I was still disappointed and upset. And then, as I was about to leave the building, I ran into a student I knew from the senior college I attended. What a surprise! Sophie, a tall, attractive young woman, was sparkling with joy as she said, "I've been so happy here. This experience has been really wonderful. I'm about to graduate and I'm opening a private practice when I leave here. I've already set it up."

Wow! That was a mouthful! I was happy for Sophie, but as we talked, I couldn't help but feel envious. She had made a wise choice while I was struggling to survive in the school I had chosen.

I was in tears when I approached Jon and said: "I can't stand it there any longer. I'm going to drop out." He was vehemently opposed to this. He said: "You have to do your best to hang in there. If you leave now, you may never go back." This made a lot of sense to me, but I wasn't convinced.

Almost everyone I spoke to told me not to leave. Dr. Anna, who was not only an excellent doctor, but also a dear friend and a precious person in my life, had my welfare at heart. I would go over to her with my many problems and she spent long periods of time listening to me and advising me. She was adamant when she said, "You can't quit now. It's very important you follow through and get that degree!" In the moment I agreed with her, but with each passing day, I found it was becoming more difficult for me to even think of staying in the program. I was desperate to find a solution to this problem.

I immediately thought about seeing a South American psychiatrist, who I knew from a psychotherapy center in Manhattan. Dr. Charles had dark brown eyes, thick black hair falling over his forehead into saucer bangs, and a flamboyant personality. He could be a character at times, but he had a wonderful way with words. He was outlandishly blunt and honest with me. There were so many things I liked about him, especially the way he could make light of an issue that I considered critical and show me another way to look at it. He was gifted with astute viewpoints and creative ideas that made me think, think, and think some more. He certainly could break through my trances and allow me to see what was really there. I knew Dr. Charles was the therapist I wanted to see.

My hand was shaking as I nervously dialed his number, and I soon heard his voice. I gave him my name and anxiously told him I needed to see him right away. He was somewhat reluctant, but after some cajoling, he agreed to meet with me in his office in mid-Manhattan.

It was a jolt to my nervous system when he opened his door and I saw the horrific look on his face. With a tone of exasperation in his voice he said: "I **hate** working with patients—but I'll work with you because I like you."

What a startling welcome that was.

The first thing Dr. Charles said to me in our therapy session was: "Don't come to me when you're in crisis! I repeat, don't come to me in crisis!" His tone was harsh, and his words pierced me like a jab from a needle. I thought that was an obnoxious thing to say and I didn't know how to respond.

This was the side of Dr. Charles that I didn't like. I knew from past therapy sessions that he could be gruff—even nasty at times. In an instant, he could become temperamental, irritable, and impatient. I never knew how to deal with his outbursts. I would sit there smoldering in frustration when he became overly aggressive with his admonitions. When I cried, he called me "Camille." Who was Camille? I didn't know, but when I saw him sneering, I didn't want to find out. I dared not ask.

But I had to disregard all that because I desperately wanted his help. He taught me things about myself that really helped me, and I was grateful for that. And now I needed his wisdom to keep me on track and in school.

As Dr. Charles sat there, looking at me as if I were a freak of nature, he was shaking his head from side to side. I could feel tension in the room. There was silence and he soon softened his approach as he thoughtfully said: "I understand you're having a rough time, but we have to look at this intelligently. You have a golden opportunity to get a professional degree and make a new life for yourself. Why would you screw it up and sabotage your chances of succeeding?"

We did a lot of talking about this, and within two weeks, I went back to Mr. Shapiro, and rather sheepishly told him: "I want to stay on."

He had a great big smile on his face as he said, "Welcome back!"

Soon, one of the teachers at the elementary school became my friend and ally. Jeanine was a sweet, warm, outgoing young woman who had been working in the school for many years and was aware of Mr. Shapiro's shenanigans. She advised: "Don't give in to his abuse. When he becomes a pain in the butt, come on over, and we'll talk about it. Then we'll see what to do." It felt wonderful to hear her say that. With Jeanine's support behind me, I came away more confident in my ability to cope with Mr. Shapiro.

Despite my troubles in the placement, I was attending casework class regularly. My second year casework instructor, Ms. Stern, was an attractive young woman with an easy, soft-spoken manner and a friendly way of communicating with the students. As for the students, they were the same as ever: snobbish and enmeshed in their cliques. They ignored me and I didn't dare approach them. But when I made a twelve-page presentation about Rivka, pandemonium broke out. My classmates and Ms. Stern were jumping all over me with questions and different points of view about the case. The over-all theme was: How could a child be permitted to live in such an unhealthy environment? What was being done to get her out of her home? And most of all, what was I doing about it?

I explained that my field supervisor and I were in touch with Children's Services and had been advised that nothing could be done under the present circumstances. As long as there's food in the refrigerator, a roof over her head, no physical abuse or truancy, she stays in her home. But the agitation of the class continued to escalate. I strongly agreed that Rivka should have been taken out of that environment a long time ago, but my classmates weren't able to accept that there wasn't an immediate solution.

As they vented, I was choking up with shame and anger because of my inability to do anything that would help Rivka out of her plight. I painfully reflected upon the disagreements I had with Mr. Shapiro about the way the case was being handled. (I never mentioned Mr. Shapiro's terrible attitude toward Rivka because I didn't want to cause any further havoc in my placement or at the school.)

When I next saw Ms. Stern in class, she looked troubled and worn. "I couldn't sleep that night after your presentation. I'm coming over to your placement tomorrow to meet with you and your supervisor. I want to discuss Rivka's case further." I didn't see anything wrong with that; in fact, I thought it was a great idea. I was hoping that a conversation amongst the three of us might result in something positive.

When Ms. Stern arrived at the children's school, she immediately expressed her concern to my supervisor. "I am very worried about Rivka. What is being done to get her out of that house?"

Mr. Shapiro was strong and confident as he declared, "I know the tough times she's having, but it's not so easy to take a child away from its mother. There's a lot involved." He detailed the rules for removing a child from its premises and went on. "I'm working with Children's Services, and I can assure you that we're doing everything we can to get Rivka out of there."

As I sat there and listened to him speak, I thought he was doing a marvelous job. I couldn't get over how well he was performing in front of Ms. Stern. I said to myself: *My goodness! He's showing all that concern for a child he can't stand!*

When he stopped speaking, I told Ms. Stern about my experiences with Rivka. "My hands are tied. I want to help her, but there's only so much I can do…" I continued to talk about my interactions with Rivka, while Ms. Stern expressed her concern. In many instances I persisted in explaining how and why I handled Rivka's case the way I did. She soon asked to see some of my other process reports. As she thumbed through them, she commented, "You're not asking enough questions. You can get a much clearer understanding of your clients if you do." As she continued to read, she made another comment that jostled me: "You're giving too much advice. This is not about lecturing—it's about asking why."

I was dumbfounded. I explained, "When I ask questions, the children clam up on me. It's not easy to get them to open up and talk about what's bothering them. As for lecturing, no one has ever told me that I lecture…" And we talked some more. Mr. Shapiro soon joined in, and everything seemed to be going well. All in all, I thought Ms. Stern left on a pleasant note.

Later, I thought to myself: *Funny, I gave every one of my process reports to Mr. Shapiro and he never once mentioned anything about asking questions or lecturing.*

I gave more thought to the things Ms. Stern said. I did have a problem asking questions. However, as a counselor, I knew I was required to ask questions as part of my job, and I would have to do better. But this thing about lecturing—that was news to me. Was I lecturing without being aware of it? I told myself that I would need to be much more aware of these things in the future.

Next time I came to class, Ms. Stern asked me to meet her in her office afterwards. There, she said, "I'm putting you on probation."

A cold sweat went through me and my heart started to palpitate. I looked at her in disbelief. "Why are you doing this?"

She casually replied, "Because of your defensiveness."

I was stunned.

She went on: "When I saw you at the placement, you were justifying your actions. You were being defensive."

What? She's putting me on probation because I defended the way I was handling my cases? That's incredible!

I stood there befuddled as she continued to speak. "I want a copy of all your process reports with Rivka. I want to read each and every one of them, then I'll give them back to you with my comments."

I came out of her office in a tailspin. *Am I not supposed to say anything? Am I supposed to just sit there, listen to her, and acquiesce to whatever she has to say?* Suddenly, I felt I had no more freedom to express myself than when I was a little girl in my mother's asylum. How appalling!

I now felt the pressure of being under the intense scrutiny of Ms. Stern, in addition to coping with the loud pompous mouth of Mr. Shapiro. I was squirming inside. It seemed like much more than I could handle, but I surmised if I wanted to graduate, I would have to somehow comply with their demands.

I went back to Mr. Shapiro, angry and wounded. "Ms. Stern said I was being defensive, so she put me on probation."

He had a great big knowing smile on his face as he replied, "I told you to speak less and listen more!"

His response made me even angrier, but he had a point. "You know something? You're right!" (No defensiveness there.)

When I had my next supervisory session with Mr. Shapiro, I came right out and said: "I have a problem. I have a tendency to over-identify with clients, young and old. I hear horrible stories and I want to make everything come out right, but I know I can't tell clients what to do or how to feel. There are times when I feel really helpless."

"In this field, you cannot solve or 'fix' anyone's problems. Each person is responsible for his or her own life. And be aware, when a client is ready, the client will make the necessary changes. It doesn't come from you!" I could feel the truth in what he said. It was something to think about.

I began to listen to the children more intently, and I was asking more questions. I was very careful not to give any advice. I started to work diligently on my process reports, reading and re-reading them. I became obsessed with the thought that I might be writing up notes that would be in conflict with Ms. Stern's requirements. I was overwrought with doubt and anxiety. *Is my work adequate? Oh, my goodness, maybe I'm doing this wrong! Then what?*

And the pressure continued. Each time I handed in my process reports, one after another, I asked Ms. Stern, "How am I doing? Is there any improvement in my work?" But she wouldn't give me any feedback. I couldn't understand it. *Why isn't she telling me about my mistakes, so that I can correct them? Why isn't she saying something...anything...?*

As I stopped by her office with more reports, I asked the same question again: "Have you read any of them?" Each time she gave me a different response: "I'm still reading them..." "Oh, I forgot, I left them on my desk as I was walking out the door..." "I'll get back to you next week..."

I didn't know what to make of this. I wanted to believe her, but I didn't know how I could. I was beginning to feel silly asking her the same thing over and over, but I was desperate to get her feedback. One day I was in her office when I felt rage welling up inside of me. Somehow, I couldn't say anything, as she just sat there, giving me another one of her lame excuses. Her voice was cold and lacked emotion. It made me cringe. As her eyes met mine, she was staring at me, as if she were analyzing me. Soon I was staring back at her. It felt awful. Why couldn't I put her on the spot and ask, "Why aren't you giving me the feedback you promised me?"

I remembered something Dr. Charles told me: "Don't be afraid to speak up. Be spontaneous!" Those words stuck with me. He had spoken with such heartfelt sincerity. But I was in anguish because I just couldn't do it. I wondered if I would ever have it in me to "be spontaneous."

Once again, I left Ms. Stern's office in defeat. I thought about making a complaint against her, but I didn't want to make any more waves in the school than I already had.

So, I went home and sulked: *That Ms. Stern is such a bitch! Why is she so damn evasive? Is she playing some kind of mind game with me? Her guarded responses make me want to scream. How am I going to pass this course if she isn't reading my reports and giving me feedback? What the hell is going on? This is torture!*

And I worried myself sick.

I was aching to get away from it all. I needed some sort of diversion, an outlet for my tensions. And soon it happened. I was on a recess break from school and I made a phone call to Jay. I was shaky as I said, "I need Hanky. It would mean the world to me if you could consider giving my cat back to me."

I thought it was a miracle when Jay said, "Yes, you can have Hanky." But there was a catch. "My daughter found this grey tabby and she gave him to me. Hanky is very attached to his companion, Precious. If you want Hanky, you'll have to take Precious, too."

Was he kidding? "I'd be only too happy to have both." I soon had three bundles of love: Joy purred when I spoke to her; Hanky came to me and curled up on my lap, and Precious performed his amusing feats—anything from rolling on his back to jumping high on top of our great big hutch in one great leap. It was wonderful to watch. I thought it was incredible how they could restore my sanity when I felt my world crumbling around me.

Vacation time was brief. Before I knew it, it was time to get back to the chaotic social work program. How I hated the thought of going back. I worried: *How am I going to get through more of this?* I took a peek in the mirror and said to myself, "You look lousy!" I was gaunt and pale and I had to make myself look better. I cut my hair short and put on plenty of make-up when I left the house. I thought if I looked better, I might feel different—at least on the surface. It was a helpful camouflage. I kept telling myself that I had gotten through tough times before, and I would do it again.

I continued to work with Dr. Charles. I was sitting in his office one day, talking with him as usual, when he had a most pensive look on his face. "I'm going to tell you something that may shock you, but I think you should know. I have worked in hospitals for years as a consultant, and I have counseled many, many students, and social workers. I have never met a social worker that liked her supervisor. I will tell you now, if you ever get a job where you find you're having trouble with your supervisor, grab your hat and run! Don't hang around!"

My jaw dropped. I was flabbergasted. I knew so well what he was talking about. My experiences with social work supervisors, past and present, were extremely negative, and I was very unhappy about this. But I pointed out to him that I couldn't just grab my hat and run at this time. I had to deal with it. So, I continued to talk to Dr. Charles, and he gave me support to stay on.

Mr. Shapiro soon called me into his office. With a glowing smile on his face, he said, "I'm going to teach you to do art therapy with the kids. You can intersperse it with your counseling, and it will give us more insight into what's going on in their heads."

Me doing art therapy with the kids? Oh, no!

"It's very simple," he went on. "You'll ask the kids to draw a picture of their parents and themselves, and then you'll ask them to talk about the picture. You'll come back to me and I'll show you what it all means. For example, if a kid draws his mother and father as very large and puts himself in the middle as very small, you'll know that the kid feels unimportant. This is just one aspect of art therapy. It's symbolic of many things. There are hidden messages in each drawing. I'll help you with whatever you need to know." As I began to understand bits and pieces, I thought art therapy was a great therapeutic tool for uncovering many aspects of the unconscious. I tried to use it whenever I could.

The children were now coming over and asking: "Can we talk?" I often stayed overtime, talking with them about whatever was on their minds. Teachers were approaching me with questions about the children's behavior. I was receiving phone calls from parents who were expressing their concerns and I made myself available to meet with them. I thought things were coming along nicely, although I wasn't really sure; I was working mostly on instinct and perception. I recall running over to Mr. Shapiro and asking him my usual question: "How do you think I'm doing?"

His response was: "Relax!" Then he started to laugh out loud.

"What's so funny?"

"You! You have nothing to worry about!"

But I did have something to worry about—something real big: Probation. It never left my mind. There was a good possibility that I might not graduate.

I continued to nervously write up process reports about every child I worked with. I remained exceedingly careful about what I said. I also kept my own copies of each report I handed in. Mr. Shapiro looked over these reports and appeared satisfied. When I completed the Rivka reports, I immediately handed over one of my copies to Ms. Stern. At one point, I counted twenty-two that I had submitted to her. Still, there was no feedback. *How can she collect all those reports and not make any comments?* She might have said: "You're doing fine" or "Your work needs improvement." But I got nothing. This became more nerve-wracking than anything I could put into words. I tried to maintain my facade as I struggled to keep a lid on my anxiety.

While waiting in the classroom one day for the class to begin, several young women were sitting together and chatting. "Did you hear that forty percent of second year students are on probation?" *Yikes!* I couldn't believe my ears. Then I heard the names of some of the brightest students in my class. Apparently, it was not an unusual occurrence to be on probation in the second year. I was aghast. As I mulled this over in my mind, I found it all very disturbing.

Soon I was back in Mr. Shapiro's office. He was in an exceptionally cheerful mood. "I have good news for you, I just received word that Rivka's mother left her alone in the apartment for several days with hardly any food in the house. As a result, Children's Services was able to remove Rivka from her home. I thought you'd be happy to hear that." I was relieved. I had a prayer in my heart that Rivka would receive the care and attention she so desperately deserved.

I continued to scurry back and forth between the two schools, while paperwork from both the field and the classroom were piling up. I was overwhelmed. I found myself fizzling out when I looked at the reading lists that were pages long. *How am I going to get all this done?* I was rushing from one project to another and there was no time to think about any one thing, I just had to do it. How emotionally draining it all was, and how very quickly I was losing the little energy I had. I never experienced anything quite like this before. As much as I tried to get everything done, I soon realized it was impossible; there was always more.

I recall standing in the school corridor one day when I overheard a conversation between two students. One was saying, "I don't know how I'll ever be able to finish this work…." The other replied, "I think they want us to suffer, so we'll know what our clients go through. Do you really think I do all that reading? I got news for you—I don't read half of it. They have to be crazy to think we can do all that work!" I knew then that I wasn't the only one who felt so overwhelmed with schoolwork. I admired that student for being so open and honest. From then on, I tried not to push myself so hard with my assignments.

In the classroom, I noticed that Ms. Stern avoided eye contact with me. I saw her walk out into the corridor on a break and light a cigarette. I was standing near the door of the classroom when she returned and walked right past me. Her body language seemed to say, "Don't bother me, stay away!"

I knew something was radically wrong. There I was, working diligently to perfect my counseling skills, while my casework instructor was actively ignoring me. *What the hell is she up to?* I sensed I was in trouble, and I traced it back to my first placement. They weren't giving me patients and I complained vehemently. I was finally asked to leave the placement. Then it was one thing after another. I found myself fighting to stay in the school and receive an education.

The present problem seemed more severe than squabbling over a bunch of client reports. Could it be that I was not wanted in the school because I was seen as a nuisance, a troublemaker, and a pain in the butt? Were they trying to get rid of me? I sensed Mr. Charman didn't like me from the start. And why would Ms. Stern put me on probation for stating my views? She said I was "being defensive." She mentioned it that one time in her office and didn't discuss it any further. There was no attempt made to help me understand the problem and how I could remedy it. I sensed there was something very wrong, and I didn't know what to do.

I had a strong need to speak with Dean Stiller. I worried, however, that I might be opening a Pandora's box and making things worse for myself—if that were at all possible. My instincts were telling me to keep my mouth closed, put blinders on and work feverishly to finish the rest of the school year. By now, I was barely hanging on by a thread—but I was persisting.

In agony, I went to speak with my uncle Will. A brilliant man with several academic and law degrees, he knew how to make people sit up and take notice. I told him about my ordeal at the school, and he stoically said, "I'll take care of it." He then sent a nine-page letter to the dean, spelling out my problems in detail. "When your dean receives my letter, you will see changes taking place!"

I still worried: *What can come out of this? Did I do something wrong again?* It wasn't long before Mr. Shapiro called me into his office. "Your casework supervisor was called on the carpet by the dean…"

Suddenly, my mind went blank. He was speaking in a loud tone. I was listening, but I didn't hear a thing. When he finished, he was sitting there and looking at me intensely. I could see he was waiting for me to respond. We were now staring at each other. How very embarrassing it was.

I soon found words. "I'm shocked to hear that. I don't know what to say."

He smiled and casually said, "Well, if you want to discuss this further, you know where to find me."

I was only too glad that he wasn't pressuring me for a response. I assumed that the dean had received my uncle's letter, but I wasn't about to discuss it with Mr. Shapiro.

I felt a bit calmer, if only on the surface. I wondered what was going on behind the scenes, but I was too afraid to ask. I did notice a change in Mr. Shapiro's attitude. He was now treating me more like a peer than an incoming novice. One day he told me about a case and said something that astounded me: "How would you handle this case? I want your professional opinion."

"You want my opinion?"

"I need your expertise," he said sheepishly. And he started to smirk. "You know, your ideas are pretty solid!" I was very surprised to hear that. I didn't expect any such praise from Mr. Shapiro.

Just as my days were coming to a close at the elementary school, the principal, Rabbi Ginsberg, came over to me and said, "You've developed quite a rapport with the children here. The kids are telling their mothers about you, and the mothers come here asking for you. They want you and only you to work with their children. And now you have to leave. What a shame!" He grabbed my hand and said, "Well, keep up the good work!" It was a compliment that touched my heart and made me feel that I wasn't wasting my time. As I thought about it, I was so glad that my anxieties hadn't interfered with the quality of my work. It felt like things were looking up.

It was the final day of the casework class. When I came into the classroom, Ms. Stern looked at me in a peculiar way. I went over to my seat, sat down as usual, and soon I heard her say: "I have good news. All of you have passed the necessary requirements for the Social Work program. Congratulations!" She went on to read the names of the candidates. Was my name on that list? I held my breath and felt my face flush. Goodness gracious, how relieved I was when my name was called!

I felt like a prisoner who was released from a jail sentence. I could feel Ms. Stern's eyes upon me as I got up, left my seat, and walked towards the door. I held my head high and didn't look back.

How liberated I felt in that moment! I said to myself, *Thank God I'm rid of that wretched Ms. Stern — and this awful school as well!*

Mr. Shapiro soon called me in. "The cat's out of the bag! While you were waiting to receive feedback from Ms. Stern, she was sending all your process reports up to a special committee."

I was stunned. "Why? What made her do that?"

Mr. Shapiro shrugged his shoulders and said, "I don't know. It was something about reviewing your work."

Although I perceived something strange was going on, I still was in shock. I guess I didn't want to believe it. It seemed so incredible to me. "How did you find out about this?" I gently asked him.

"Does it matter?" he glibly replied.

I sat there in awe. "So that's what she was doing! I knew there was something radically wrong. Call it a hunch. She didn't go over one process report with me, and I sensed she was avoiding me."

Mr. Shapiro echoed, "You know, social workers are known for their hunches, and it sounds like you were right on target with that one."

Maybe so, but that didn't make me feel any better. I was in denial. I didn't want to see what was going on before my eyes. It seemed that my casework teacher wasn't going over my process reports with me because she wanted me to fail. I avoided the awful truth. I was very good at it. Avoiding reality was nothing new to me. I grew up dodging the things I didn't want to see or feel. My ex-boss, Gale, would tell me, "You have a bag over your head. Get that damn bag off!" But I didn't want to hear it. Reality was much too painful for me.

I didn't discuss anything further with Mr. Shapiro, but I did reach out to my uncle Will. "The letter you sent the dean was really effective. My field instructor told me that the dean called in Ms. Stern and had a talk with her. I found out that all my work was going up to a committee for 'review.' That's why she wasn't working with me on my cases. Isn't that something? I think she was planning to fail me."

Will had an angry look on his face. "No doubt, she was holding back your work to stop you from graduating. That's pretty apparent."

"I was wondering how I was going to graduate with no input from my casework instructor. If it hadn't been for you, my chances for graduating would have been pretty slim."

"There shouldn't be people like Ms. Stern in the education field!"

I wholeheartedly agreed.

Ms. Stern had a lot in common with my mother. I never thought there would ever be another human being on the face of this earth with Hedda's deviousness, but I was wrong. I never thought that a teacher, who is supposed to be there to help and guide her students, could do just the opposite and cause someone the anguish and distress that she caused me.

I felt fortunate to have the dean of the social work program, Dr. Stiller, as my one true friend who stayed by me through thick and thin. He was an unusually understanding person with whom I developed a close rapport. The dean knew my story, and he was aware of my work with clients. He was my mentor when I wrote my Master's thesis about my life in graduate school. It was quite a detailed study about the mistakes I made, the things I learned, and how I was able to grow. Soon after, I met the dean in an elevator and nervously asked, "What did you think about the paper I submitted to you?"

The very serious dean broke out into a broad smile and replied, "It was excellent, Lenore—just excellent!"

Tears welled up in my eyes as I said, "I'm so glad you liked it."

When he awarded the MSW degree to me at my graduation ceremony, the dean embraced me, kissed me on the cheek and whispered, "I knew you could do it. If anyone can make it, you can!"

Those loving actions and kind words touched my heart. The only other person he kissed at the ceremony was his daughter.

On my school evaluation, it was said: *"Lenore was able to utilize her unusual sensitivity and her creativity with very good results.... Lenore was an insightful, thoughtful and intelligent student. Her deep commitment to the profession and to her further development, together with her compassion and diligence, will make her an asset to any agency."*

I received my Master's in Social Work in my mid-40's but as I held the piece of paper in my hand that spelled out success, it had no real meaning for me. I wondered if it was worth all the pain I had to endure to attain it. In my heart I felt like a failure. All that I had to go through left me feeling trampled on, stepped over and discarded like a piece of waste. I lost what little respect I had for myself.

When I started the social work program I was eager to obtain professional credentials that hopefully would lead to a rewarding career and personal satisfaction. I was even thinking about opening a private practice. I came to the school with hope in my heart and I came away downtrodden and disheartened.

Graduate school was over, but my nightmare continued. New heartaches were just beginning for me. My experience at the school had a debilitating effect upon me. My spirit was shattered, and I lost interest in life. I sat at home or took walks in my neighborhood in a state of despair. I was demolished in my sadness. I was now a stranger to myself.

I hadn't experienced anything as gruesome as this in any of my endeavors. I usually bounced back after a defeat or hurtful experience and I continued where I left off. I now needed to pull back, look at my life, and piece things together again before I could go on to anything else.

I gave a lot of thought to the mistakes I made. As I began to sort out my feelings, I realized the school I had chosen was wrong for me from the start. My uncle impressed upon me, "This is the school you should go to, it's a good school and it has a lot of prestige. It will look good on your resume." How could I not trust an educator like my uncle? I now realized how very wrong he was, and how very wrong I was for not pursuing any other alternatives at the very beginning.

I guess I should have known better. In my very first encounter with Mr. Charmin, the Field Director, I was made to feel I didn't belong there, but I disregarded my intuition. Soon, I was in the school and one problem followed another. I moved around in tears, from class to class, and to my field placements as well, under extreme duress, as I struggled to get my Master's degree.

A feeling of rejection hovered over me. I was in a state of frenzy when I hurried to see a psychiatrist with a plea for him to help me stay in the school. Talk only helped so much. When I left Dr. Charles' office, I found I couldn't turn off the anguish I was feeling inside.

One of my worst heartaches in the school was my encounter with deception and connivery. I found it hard to believe that such dishonesty could exist in an educational institution—but it did. I was deprived of the training and feedback that I so justly deserved and paid dearly for. The treatment I received in this institution was absolutely abominable. My life at graduate school was a living hell.

This experience was especially painful since I was programmed as a child to be silent and not have any thoughts or feelings of my own. Here in this academic environment, I unhappily found myself in a similar situation. I hated being in the role of a docile little girl who is not allowed to express her thoughts and feelings less she be reprimanded. I thought those days were long gone and over. But this social work program only reinforced the negative belief system I was trying so hard to break away from.

Yes, it was a terrible struggle to get through social work school. I was in extreme mental anguish, but I didn't feel safe enough to approach any school official about my problems, including Dean Stiller. I couldn't talk about how upset I was not to receive clients and to be paying for an education I wasn't getting. It was safer to disregard what was going on inside of me, as I tried to avoid any further conflict at the school. So, I suppressed my feelings and suffered consequences that were severe. I needed to recover.

It is said that time heals all wounds, and it was taking some time to heal mine. But I was healing. I was also becoming stronger emotionally, as it became clear to me that I had to get hold of myself and start over.

66

Working with a Client

It's back to the present as I continue working with one of my first clients, Nancy. She has been in a state of turmoil since she broke up with her boyfriend, Danny, who is a batterer. I fear that at any time she might return to her life of abuse, and I am very careful about the way I speak to her. She is very sensitive and depressed. I am concerned that she might be suicidal, and that anything I say to her might be misinterpreted and set her off.

I speak to my supervisor. She tells me: "Watch her carefully, and we'll take it one step at a time."

Several weeks have passed and Nancy's behavior continues to fluctuate. Nancy has an appointment to meet with me, but she's more than a little late. Soon, there's a buzz on the intercom, and the receptionist lets me know: "Nancy is in the waiting room." I exhale a sigh of relief.

Nancy looks worn. "I apologize for being late. It takes longer to get here since I moved out of my neighborhood. I'm staying with a friend in Brooklyn now, so I can avoid bumping into Danny." She cries: "I keep thinking about him. What did I do to make this happen?"

I reinforce what I had said so many times: "You are not to blame. Women who have been abused usually think it's their fault. It is not your fault, Nancy. No one deserves to be battered emotionally or physically. It's a crime to assault anyone. Your boyfriend could go to jail for his behavior."

Nancy looks bewildered. I ask: "What keeps you attached to him?"

"I don't really know. He can be sweet and warm. Then something gets into him and suddenly he's a changed person."

That sounds familiar. I ask, "What causes him to change?"

"Anything can do it." Nancy continues to tell me how jealous he is and how he over-reacts. "We'll have these fights and he'll yell at me over things that don't make any sense. When he's in one of his moods, he starts using his fists, and I can't make him stop. That's when I tell myself I have to break away from him—no matter what!"

The thought of it sounds great, but I have a hunch that Nancy will not be able to do it. I know what it's like to be attached to someone who has a ferocious temper. I see traces of myself in Nancy's plight for I, too, have suffered from physical and emotional abuse.

When I see Nancy again, she tells me: "I'm able to eat a little more, but I'm having trouble sleeping. My friend tells me I'm brooding too much. She says I should forget Danny—that I should go out and meet other men. There's plenty of fish in the sea. "

"How do you feel about that? Do you think you're ready to go out on dates?"

Nancy's eyes look downward as she replies, "I don't think so. But I'm always listening to what people tell me."

That's something else I have in common with Nancy, although I've grown somewhat beyond that now. I tell Nancy, "You have the option to choose what you want. You can always say no. From what you've told me, you have a need to please people. It sounds as if you depend upon others to make decisions for you."

"I've always been that way. I don't know any other way to be…"

In our sessions, Nancy is learning there is another way.

As Nancy continues to obsess about Danny, I detect anger in her voice and that is a good sign. But it's brief. I know Nancy needs to express her anger and I wonder how that will come about.

I am frustrated. I want to scream: "Don't take that abuse! Why are you with someone who hurts you like that?" But I can't tell her that; she's my patient. Instead, I empathize with her. "I understand how helpless you must feel. Have you ever experienced anything like this before?"

"Yes. My mother was married to a man who was very abusive…"

I am aware that Nancy is responding to an old pattern of behavior. I would like to make a connection between the abuse of Nancy's childhood and her present abuse, but my intuition tells me this is not the right time. I am concerned that this is a missed opportunity.

I soon hear Nancy saying, "I miss Danny. I'm aching inside. Do you think I'll ever get rid of this ache?"

I know all too well what that kind of pain feels like, and I'm not sure how to respond. This is a crushing pain that comes from severe emotional trauma. I feel I need to reassure her: "It's normal for you to have this pain—you're in the grieving process. In order to heal, it's important for you to feel your feelings and not avoid them, no matter how painful they are." Nancy has a wide-eyed stare … and we talk.

I think about how important it is to express our emotions at the time we're feeling them, and how awkward it is to actually say what it is we are feeling in the moment. If only we had the courage! I recall how I would constantly suppress my feelings. Then I became aware that these feelings do not go away. If you ignore or hold down your emotions, they will appear in some other way. Not good. Freud said: "Depression is anger turned inward," and it is apparent that Nancy is holding in her anger. I am hopeful that she will eventually be able to get in touch with her anger.

One day Nancy comes in, distraught. "He's calling me at my job. He wants to see me, but I don't want to see him. He says he loves me and can't live without me. What am I going to do?"

I don't like the sound of this, and I want to tell her to disregard his calls, but I know it must be her decision. I respond, "You sound as if you're afraid he's going to take you over. You know, you are not his captive. This man has caused you tremendous grief and pain. Do you really want to go back to him?"

"Danny said he would be different if I give him another chance. He said he's changed, and he needs me in his life."

In my studies about domestic violence, I learned that batterers don't change, and inevitably, revert to their old pattern of abuse. I know Danny is on his best behavior, and I am hoping that he won't persuade Nancy to go back to him. I wonder how to best approach this very delicate issue. Then Nancy gives me an inroad.

"I keep thinking: How can Danny treat me like this if he loved me? He's always telling me he's going to change—but he never does."

I validate Nancy's point: "So Danny is constantly promising to be different—but does he really change? What I'm hearing is that he makes promises and more promises, but he doesn't keep any."

"I guess that's true," Nancy agrees, then adds: "But I always have a hope that things will be different…"

What I like here is that Nancy is beginning to question the things that Danny tells her. She is becoming less vulnerable to his charm and more aware of her own feelings.

Nancy soon comes in very anxious. "Danny is still calling me at the office. He wants to meet me in a restaurant. He says he wants to speak to me—that it's very important." And we talk about it.

Nancy is struggling with her emotions, as they keep pulling her in different directions. I am aware that Nancy will have to look deep within to find the answers that are right for her. It must be her own realizations. I cannot fix it for her, and I am frustrated. I find it hard to be patient, but I am doing the best I can.

When I next meet with Nancy, she tells me: "Danny was in front of my office building. I saw him when I left work yesterday, but he didn't see me. He was sitting in his car, and I ran by. It must be terrible to be a fugitive."

I never thought like that, but I suppose Nancy has a point. I feel she is acting strong in the face of temptation. I compliment her on how well she is handling herself. But Nancy is still very confused and worried about being manipulated by Danny. Batterers are especially known for their magnificent manipulations.

Nancy comes in one day, smiling. She is eager to tell me, "I have a surprise for you. I went back to my apartment. I couldn't stand living with my friend any longer—she was always telling me what to do, as if she were my mother. It's good to be back in my own place and stand on my own two feet."

But I'm concerned about this. I am linking this sudden move to her anticipation of meeting up with Danny. I know he is living in the same neighborhood, and I wonder if, on an unconscious level, she is hoping to bunk into him. The thought of it repulses me, but I feel, over-all, that Nancy is showing emotional strength.

When I see her again, she is more nervous than usual. "I saw Danny the other night. He was in a restaurant in my neighborhood. I have a feeling that any day now we're going to meet. What will I say? How will I handle it?"

"It sounds to me like you're frightened of your feelings—especially your anger."

Nancy starts to cry. "I'm scared to death. There's a lot I'd like to say, but I wouldn't know where to start. I hate him for the pain he's caused me, yet a part of me misses him and still cares for him. How mixed up can you get?"

"Let's go back to the reality of your situation. Of course, you're upset. You're out working and he's bringing other women into your apartment and having sex with them. It sounds like you're very angry."

Nancy's face reddens. "Yes, I am very angry. I'm boiling over with anger!"

"If you can feel your anger and understand where it's coming from, this might help you to find relief from your pain."

The next time I see Nancy, I hear intense fear in her voice. "I have a message on my answering machine. Danny wants to see me. He tells me how much he misses me and how much he loves me. But if that's true, why was he running around with other women?"

I am glad that Nancy is finally seeing through Danny's words of deception. But I am also worried. What will happen when she finally meets up with him?

In our next session, Nancy appears very disturbed as she tells me: "I met him at my job. He was waiting in front of the building for me—and this time, I talked to him!"

I'm not surprised, but I am concerned.

She continues: "I'm very upset. I told myself that I was going to keep away from him, but I backed down on my promise to myself. If I keep on making these mistakes, how will I be able to have a decent life?"

I don't have an answer to this very pertinent question. I am reminded of a saying: "Two steps forward and one step backward."

My supervisor tells me, "Things have to take their course—as long as her life is not in danger. If that were the case, we would have to take immediate action. But don't worry about it. Right now, you're right at the place where the client is—and that's what really counts."

I'm feeling more helpless. I don't feel good about her seeing the batterer.

The next time I see Nancy, something about her appears different. She tells me, "I just saw Danny and I let him have it! I told him all the things that are on my mind. I told him he's no good for me. I said he never loved me—if he had, he wouldn't be beating me up and making love with other women. Words came out of my mouth and I couldn't stop…"

This is great news. Nancy is finding her voice. She is vibrant. Nancy is not only feeling her anger, but also openly expressing it to the object of her rage. I think this is a big step in progress for her. She is finding the inner strength to verbalize what she has been holding in for far too long. And I am delighted.

When I asked her how it felt to tell him off, she simply replied, "Great! He still asked me to come back to him. I told him, 'You'll have to show me how different you are.' He said he would prove it to me, but now I'm sorry I said that; I don't think I can go back to him."

Again, I feel she's doing very well, and I share that with her. She's making emotional strides, and she seems to be better able to deal with the challenge that Danny presents to her. However, Danny has a very volatile personality, and I am concerned about Nancy's ability to handle him.

When I see her again, Nancy looks dejected but anxious to talk. "I'm seeing Danny after work—and I'm very upset about it. He drives me home and we talk. I still have a need to see him. Is it possible that I still love him?"

How familiar those words are to me. I listen to other abused women who say the very same thing. It seems that when the battering phase is over and things return to normal, there is a tendency for the abused woman to overlook her recent agony and resume the relationship—until it happens all over again. I've had similar experiences and I understand how awful it feels to be in a situation like that.

I feel it's time to explore Nancy's pattern of abuse. "Tell me, Nancy, about your years growing up. What were they like?"

Nancy begins to talk about her childhood. "My stepfather was very mean to both my mother and me. He hit me a lot and he hit her too—especially when his temper got the better of him. When he was drinking, he could be really rough."

"I'm sorry to hear that. It seems like you've had quite some abuse in your childhood. Do you see a connection between the abuse in your early life and what is occurring in the present?"

Nancy reflects upon the question. Then very slowly, she says: "That abuse... Oh, my God! My stepfather... Danny... they both abused me! I never thought of that."

As we start to put the pieces together, it becomes apparent: Nancy has lived with so much abuse in her life, it has become a part of her. She gravitates towards it. As I help Nancy to look at the pattern of her life, it all begins to make sense. Love and abuse are apparently connected for her. Danny perpetuates what she has been used to all her life. As she becomes cognizant of this, she adamantly states: "This is no good! I'm not going to allow myself to be abused anymore!"

In my heart I am applauding her. I am hopeful that she will be able to sustain and utilize this insight as she continues to have contact with the batterer.

Nancy is now getting more sleep and she's eating better, but in some ways she seems to be more anxious. She reports: "I had dinner with Danny after work and it was a very pleasant experience. I made another date to see him. I just hope I'm not being drawn back in."

I hope so, too. Once again, I'm afraid that Nancy is heading in the wrong direction and I don't know how to help her with this. I'm constantly discussing her case with my supervisor, who tells me, "You're doing very well." I'm not so sure about that, but with some apprehension, I keep following my intuition.

Once or twice, Nancy reports that she saw Danny on the verge of an outburst. "I picked myself up and walked away. I don't need that. I've had enough of that!"

Nancy is vacillating constantly, but that is to be expected. Although Nancy continues to struggle with her emotions, she is finding her way. Her depression has lifted, and her anger is being released. Nancy is working hard at turning things around and making things better for herself, and I'm praising her for this.

Like a mantra, I keep repeating: "You deserve better! You don't deserve to be emotionally or physically abused!"

This seems to be making some impact upon Nancy, for she comes in one day and says: "I saw Danny and I told him I'm in therapy. I said I'm learning about myself and abuse, and I'm not going to be abused anymore—I deserve better! And now that I'm aware of this abuse trap, I'm not going to fall into it again!"

Was this Nancy speaking?—the withdrawn, depressed young woman who could barely voice an opinion? I thought this was incredible. I am especially proud of Nancy because she is becoming bolder as she asserts herself.

Several months have gone by, and our short-term therapy is coming to an end. A smiling Nancy sits down opposite me and exudes pride as she speaks: "Things are looking up for me. Although I'm still spending time with Danny, I'm doing so much better on my own. I care about myself. I want to have a happy life, and I'm doing everything I can to make that possible." I have a feeling that Nancy is on the path of making it happen.

As we are saying goodbye, I compliment Nancy on making great strides in a very short time. She throws her arms around me and kisses me, as she says: "I never could have done it if it wasn't for you. You're so genuine, so caring—and you have wonderful insights. You've helped me more than any therapist I've worked with in the past. Is it possible I could continue to see you?"

I respond that because of agency policy, it isn't possible. I point out how very important it is for her to continue her emotional growth with the help of ongoing therapy, and that she realizes batterers usually don't change; eventually, they return to their abusive behavior. "The emphasis is on you—nobody else!"

Nancy warmly says, "I just can't thank you enough." I am moved by her gratitude.

I thought back to the time when Nancy first came for counseling. It appeared that she was suicidal. I watched her move through this horrendous period—and away from it. Through it all, she displayed a sense of strength and determination. I am grateful to have accompanied this courageous young woman on her journey. I, too, have grown in the process.

As I worked with Nancy, I could see similarities between her and myself. We both grew up in households of emotional and physical abuse. As an adult, Nancy continued the unhappy pattern of her childhood, and so did I. As she tried to free herself from the pain of her past, she found herself pulled back into it, very common for victims of abuse.

In our sessions, Nancy was struggling to find a better way. With a strong desire to overcome obstacles on her path, Nancy persevered. As she became aware and empowered, she was able to gain control over her life. I was amazed, and truly delighted, to have witnessed her rapid progress and emotional growth.

Working in the field of psychotherapy is demanding, but it can also be quite rewarding. I feel fortunate that over the years I've developed an intuition that has been especially helpful to me in my work with clients. I am grateful to be able to help people with their problems, as I have been helped with mine. I consider every client special and unique. Each person needs to feel safe in an environment where thoughts and feelings can be explored and freely expressed. Clients must know they will not be judged or criticized for being who they are. I remember how I would turn to a therapist in my darkest moments and how much it meant to me to know that I was not alone in my distress. In my work with clients, I have found the therapist and client travel a special journey together. It is a journey of soul-searching … discovery … and enlightenment.

67

Realizations

I was in therapy for many years when I found a young, sensitive female therapist who said to me: "I think you're ready to calm yourself long enough and feel safe enough to face the deep-seated wounds of your childhood." In the weeks that followed, Dr. Suzanne and I had intense discussions about my mother and me, and what it was like living with her.

"From what you've told me, it sounds like your mother wanted you all to herself and was worried about losing you. It seems that she wanted to keep you near her so that you wouldn't leave her. You were like a part of her; you and she were one. You formed a unit together and she didn't want anything to threaten that. She couldn't tolerate you becoming close to anyone else because that would have jeopardized her connection to you."

Dr. Suzanne was tapping into the dark, chaotic world I lived in so many years ago. I was intrigued by her interpretation. "You're saying my mother kept me isolated in the house because she was afraid of losing me?"

"The unconscious mind works in strange ways. I think her mind manufactured a germ phobia. Her germ phobia made you frightened of becoming ill and scared you enough to fend off contact with people. It also made you as frightened of the world as she was. She wanted to keep you clinging to her. But being with your mother didn't feel safe and being without her felt even less safe because she made the world seem so terribly threatening and dangerous. Going to school was unsafe. Going outside your home was unsafe. Even going near your father was unsafe. Your mother didn't want your father to have contact with you, so she used her germ phobia to keep him away from you. Don't forget this is all on an unconscious level. Your father didn't know how to handle it—so he acquiesced."

"It wasn't only my father she kept me away from—she kept me locked away from the world!"

"A truly terrible way to live."

"I was in constant dread."

"There was no one to rescue you, and I don't know if you would have left your mother even if there were someone to take you away from her. You needed your mother to feel safe. When you were a very young child and she was pulled away from you, your whole world collapsed. There was no one else that you felt connected to, except her. Your sense of yourself crumbled because you felt you couldn't exist without her—a cause for trauma in itself. Your entire sense of survival was based on being with your mother. And then she was gone. That caused you to feel even more unsafe."

"I can feel what you're saying is valid and real. I didn't have a sense of myself as a separate entity, and I would constantly say to myself, 'There's no me. There's no me.' There was no me. There was only her."

"Your mother was obsessed with keeping you all to herself."

"She was always ranting about how bad people are and instilling a fear in me that made me cling to her. I was rarely out of her sight—except when I went to the bathroom, and even then, she was there. It seemed that she was hanging on to me for dear life."

"While she needed you to cling to her and to fear being separate from her, she was isolating you and neglecting your needs."

"I wasn't supposed to have any needs. I was afraid to say anything, but I couldn't always be quiet. At times I became cranky and spoke back. That's when she would tell me: 'You're bad. You're making me sick. You're a rotten little bitch—you'll be the death of me yet.' Because she was my mother and I was only a little child, I believed I was killing her."

Dr. Suzanne responded: "You became the container of all the bad feelings she had about herself. None of this was about you. It was all about your mother and her crazy internal world."

"I told you about the lady psychiatrist at Bellevue, who wanted to know why this woman hated her child so much. I feel the psychiatrist was right in saying my mother hated me. I could feel her hatred."

Dr Suzanne paused briefly and said: "Let me sum it up. She created you and experienced you as a part of her, so whatever she was feeling about herself, she was feeling about you as well. No separation between the two. In other words, I think she put her hateful feelings about herself into you and then you felt hatred for yourself."

Yes, my mother was full of hatred and she was projecting it on to me. I now had a better understanding of why I had such a terrible self-image.

"When my mother was taken to Bellevue, I thought I had done something very bad to her and that I would never see her again. I felt my life was over. From my uncle's file I learned that she was on the brink of taking her life and mine. Her hospital record indicated 'undiagnosed psychosis'. "

"I understand that this was an especially upsetting time for you. In her psychotic state, she might have wanted to kill herself—and you, too. Don't forget she couldn't separate herself from you. You were like an appendage of your mother."

"That makes sense. When she came out of the asylum, she appeared to be different. But she was not really different. The things she said and did seemed wacky to me, but what did I know then? I was just a child, and I didn't know that my mother was mentally ill—or just how ill she was."

As a door opened into my past, the enigma of my mother's illness began to unravel. I could now allow myself to "feel" the reality of growing up in my mother's home.

The words of Dr. Suzanne stayed with me: "Your mother did not want you to have a life of your own because she needed you to be with her. It's important that you realize it was about her and her psychosis—not about who you were. Your mother's psychosis dominated your experience of the world."

I felt a chill go through me, then a shift of consciousness. For all those many years my mother was brainwashing me with her twisted thinking. Somehow, the things she told me, which caused me to have unrelenting shame and guilt about myself, no longer had the same hold over me. I was grateful for this understanding. It was as if a load had been lifted from my heart. But this was not enough to free me from the emotional pain I carried around with me.

This was the beginning of a new chapter in my life. As I continued to work with Dr. Suzanne, I began to seek out other sources of insight and enlightenment. I went to psychological lectures and listened to inspirational programs on the radio. I was in a state of flux. Sometimes I felt so different I didn't recognize myself, and yet so much of me remained the same. I persevered with an intense desire to find my true self.

I began to attend spiritual lectures, and I was drawn to a spiritual teacher who came to New York to speak about self-realization and the silent mind. I was captivated by the sincerity, love, and truth in his voice. He smiled a lot and heartily laughed out loud as he spoke about the frenzied way in which people live. He asked, "Who are you? What do you want?" He kept on repeating those questions. Then he declared: "This is a slave planet. We are all motivated by fears and desires. Everyone is in a trance. Parents pass on the slavery that was passed on from their parents. Parents teach you who you are—a bad baby, a good baby. It takes months of hypnotic suggestion just for you to identify with your name. It's the origin of the false self. It's all part of the ego trance. **It's time to wake up!** You don't need to search; you won't find it outside of yourself. Who you are is already there."

His words, said with such conviction, pierced my heart; I was fascinated. His message was: **"Stop! Enough!** The way to stop is to sit in silence. Silence is your true nature. Silence is freedom. Stay in the moment in silence. Emotions cover your true heart. It's the heart that is real, that experiences itself through feelings...."

He emphasized that negative emotions be experienced in order to be free of them. "Drop all the way through your feelings. Under each layer, there is still something deeper; feel it fully, in your own silence, and don't run away from what you feel. If you bear it, you will find hurt, and under that, terror, and under that, despair. Underneath it all is emptiness … true peace … intelligence … and limitless love."

I realized that I, too, was in the hypnotic trance he spoke about, and that my continuous seeking and striving didn't allow me to find any happiness or inner peace. It was time to stop. It was time to fall into the depth of what was already there.

A therapist once said to me: "Cry! You have an awful lot to cry about!" As bad as I felt then, I just couldn't—but I knew he was right. There were endless layers of tears bottled up within me that, like an onion, had to be peeled away. I was now willing to "drop through" those many layers of unresolved feelings, wherever they would take me. As I sat in silence, I allowed myself to feel my grief, as I had never done before. I got in touch with my anger and I began to feel the pain of my existence. I surrendered to it, no matter how unbearable it felt, and gradually, I plummeted into deep sorrow. I cried and cried some more. Each time I came through it a little stronger emotionally. I then experienced a sense of joy and peace that was very new to me. I began to feel good about myself from just being alive and living in the moment. I found I could enjoy the simplest things, like taking a walk, smelling a rose, or looking at a beautiful blue sky. And while I have always loved music, it now touches my soul in a way it never has before.

68

My Theory

"How could your mother be protecting you and beating you up at the same time?" Dr. Suzanne asked me that question and I had no answer. I started to think about it.

I kept wondering what happened to my mother. What made her drift out of reality and become so violently out of control? From what I read in my uncle's file, she was an excellent student in school. After she graduated from high school, she got a job as a secretary. When her mother became ill with a back injury, she stayed home and attended to her. She was used to sitting in the house with her mother, going out shopping for food and leading a very simple, uncomplicated life. It was only after she gave birth in her 30's that she developed symptoms of psychosis.

But what is psychosis? One definition depicts psychosis as a mental derangement characterized by a loss of contact with reality, but there is no definitive answer as to what causes a person to create his or her own reality. However, if one has a predisposition to psychosis and stress becomes unmanageable, psychosis can result. So, what made Hedda's life so unbearable?

The unconscious is a complex mechanism. Stored away in it are memories and events from the past that cause us to behave the way we do in the present. There may be numerous reasons for Hedda's bizarre behavior, but the one thing that stands out in my mind is what she herself told me: "I never wanted to have children. It was your dear grandmother's idea. She said it's important to have a child for my old age. It took ten years, but she finally talked me into it!" Ten years? I flinched at the thought of it.

Apparently, Grandma, with her persistent, powerful, and persuasive skills, succeeded in convincing Hedda that having a child was crucial. So, Hedda becomes a mother and finds herself stuck with a colicky, screaming baby she didn't want, couldn't love, and was unable to handle. She finds herself facing the reality of an actual life in her hands. She is robbed of her freedom as she discovers a child is not a doll. It is human and has a lot of needs and wants. She discovers that taking care of a child is a huge full-time responsibility as she obsessively watches her child to make sure she is safe and protected. She develops a germ phobia and makes rules for warding off germs: no touching, no kissing, and no contact with people. She keeps washing her hands and anything that the child handles that might contain germs. Her fears permeate just about every aspect of her child's existence, as her child remains isolated in the house with her.

Hedda now has an emotional noose around her neck. There is stress compounded with more stress that looms larger and appears unsolvable. Beset by fear and depression, mixed with rage and resentment, she is finally overcome by madness.

But this is only the tip of the iceberg. She winds up briefly in two psychiatric facilities and doesn't stay in either long enough to receive any kind of meaningful treatment. When she comes out, there is no after-care surveillance of her condition. She continues to live in an unreal world, driven by the overwhelming dictates of her illness. This includes airing out books in the refrigerator and scrubbing her hands with soap and hot water as blood comes oozing out of open sores. Through her fits, frenzies and foibles, Hedda remains trapped in a web of turmoil that she, herself, unwittingly created.

So there I was, with a mother who is supposed to be protecting me from the hazards of Life, as she pummels me physically and abuses me verbally. What was this all about?

I asked a therapist-friend for his professional opinion. Over a period of time, Bob had endeared himself to me as an intuitive person with a lot of empathy and knowledge. He knew my story. He bluntly said: "You know, your mother wanted to kill you!"

At first, I was shaken at the thought of it, but it actually made sense. Why hadn't I thought of that myself? But how could I think like that? She was protecting me!

Bob went on: "Your mother had thoughts and urges of wanting to kill you and this is what the psychiatrist at Bellevue Hospital was concerned about. Sometimes your mother was the Monster personality and acted on this urge. More often, she just had feelings and thoughts to kill you. When someone has feelings like these, they have feelings of shame and want to hide these thoughts and feelings from others and from themselves. One way is to unconsciously place these feelings on to something else. So your mother took her murderous feelings and placed them on to germs. This resulted in her germ-phobia, where she could supposedly protect you from germs and protect herself from the shame about her murderous feelings as well.

"She was seething with feelings of wanting to harm you and she even used the germ-phobia to cause further harm to you. She did not allow you to speak to people and did not allow anyone to speak to you. She kept you from school and from having friends. She did not care about your back and eyes. Sometimes she was out and out mean and nasty with you. At times her madness was more extreme but her madness was always with her, even when she appeared more stable."

I interrupted. "Wouldn't you say that washing one's hands continuously is a way of washing away guilt?"

Bob agreed. "Yes, that is true. People do wash their hands excessively because they have disturbing impulses and want to rid themselves of their guilt, as they try to wash the guilt away. Your mother had murderous feelings and wanted to dispose of them by washing them away. This was the side of her that wanted to kill and it was oozing out."

As I thought about the way I grew up with a fear of the "imminent doom," it's very likely I sensed my mother's murderous feelings all along. I was in Harm's Way and didn't know it. But I could feel it. How disturbing it was. I am grateful to Bob for showing me a new slant to my mother's bizarre behavior. Yes, I sensed the validity in what he was saying. I could feel my mother's resentment and hatred for me, but I never thought it extended into murderous feelings. Yet, I am not surprised. It is said, "The truth will set you free," and the truth becomes clearer to me as I continue to try to piece together the parts of my life that I struggle to understand.

Out of the blue I had a thought that boggled my mind. Hedda was very opposed to having a child. Then, after many years, she succumbed to Grandma's pressure and had a baby. She convinced Hedda that having a child was crucial for her in her later years. It seems that this was the origin of Hedda's obsession with keeping me alive to take care of her in her old age. It might sound surreal—but it feels real enough to me. And this became my theory.

When I met with Bob again, I told him my theory. I asked him: "Does this make any sense to you?" Bob simply said, "You're saying your mother's murderous feelings were overcome by her overwhelming need to preserve you for old age. Yes, I like your theory. I think it makes sense. And, by the way, the premise of your theory just might have saved your life."

In my early teens I began to break away from my mother, and her efforts to maintain control over me eventually failed. When it became obvious that I was no longer amenable to taking care of her in her old age, her psychotic symptoms dissipated and she became docile.

Dr. Suzanne put it so well when she said: "The unconscious mind works in strange ways." As I thought more about my theory, I feel confident that I am on the right path. But it's a theory, only a theory—my theory.

69

In Denial

I was making an entry in my journal when a light bulb went on in my head: Where was my family when I was growing up, when I needed them! What happened to them? I realized in that moment: my mother was not solely to blame. She was seriously ill—but they were not!

I started to think about my early years. I am back in time. I am a young child, very sad and frightened, and I am all alone with my mother. She is acting kind of strange, and I am crying. She is crying, too.

My father soon signs a statement: **"…My wife and the baby have not been getting along very well lately. On one or two occasions, she threatened to take her own life and that of the baby's. I do not believe that either she or the baby are safe… The family doctor has advised us to send her to Bellevue for observation…"**

It was the beginning of a realization that could no longer be avoided: Hedda was mentally ill. Not only was she an imminent threat to herself, but to her child as well. Dragged out of the house screaming, she was pushed into an ambulance and whisked away to

Bellevue. Hospitalized for a brief time, she was then released upon her father's demand.

My mother returned from hospitalization as tyrannical as ever. Her rules were enforced without question. And there I was, a little child, not allowed to be held, touched, or kissed. Nor was I allowed to speak to anyone, lest I stir my mother's wrath. Behind the scenes, Hedda continued to raise her fists to me in fits of frenzy and violence.

My father, my uncle, and grandparents were aware of some of Hedda's outrageous behavior, and the abnormal way I was growing up—yet they did nothing about it. I must say I am astonished as to why they were not stirred into some kind of action. Couldn't they see that my mother was not in touch with reality? Grandpa, in particular, was adamant in proclaiming: "There's nothing wrong with Hedda. Lenore's a bad child!" And Grandma, more or less, agreed.

I sadly think about the many times Grandma came into our home loaded down with shopping bags of groceries, hardly able to catch her breath, and the first words out of her mouth were: "Did she go back to school?" She was speaking in a loud, excited tone, making me feel my life depended on whether or not I was in school.

It was daunting. There I was, a helpless, frightened little girl, isolated and abused, living in neglect and filth. I was suffering with debilitating bouts of viruses and bronchial asthma that took my breath away. But Grandma didn't seem to be aware of any of this. Couldn't she see that I was much too ill, much too traumatized to even go out of the house? Couldn't she perceive how difficult it is for an abused, neglected child like myself to function in the outside world?

Things continued in pretty much the same way, with Hedda intermittently in and out of control, while I sat there, grateful for the times I wasn't choking on a cough and so glad I had my radio to listen to and comfort me.

It was abhorrent the way my family deadened their hearts and feelings to what was going on right before their very eyes. They lost sight of what was most important—and that was the safety of a child. They denied there was a child in danger.

So, what happens to a child caught up in such an abnormal life? And how was Hedda, who had such a severe mental illness, allowed to go on without some kind of intervention?

Of course, my mother was the main culprit in this horror tale, but my family were culprits as well. They knew she was ill—but they detached themselves from the situation. I believe it is a serious offense to turn your back and walk away from a child who is sick and traumatized, for you are robbing that child of its birthright to grow naturally, develop emotionally, and to function in the world with a sense of identity, dignity, and well-being. I consider everyone in my family complicit and accessories to the crime because they turned away from their moral responsibility of protecting a child in danger. To this very day, I cannot understand how these people, my family, could have been so blind to the suffering of a child.

There was no one in my family who wanted to recognize that Hedda had a serious psychosis. Being cognizant of a problem necessitates doing something about it, but apparently, they didn't know what to do—or perhaps they didn't want to know. I believe it was less burdensome for them to withdraw into a state of denial.

I began to think that my family was living in denial, but could I really be that objective to make such a statement? I needed feedback and thought of my social worker friend, Bob K, who read my manuscript and knew me well. I decided to contact him: "I've been mulling this over in my mind and I need to have your expertise about my invisible childhood. It seems that my family was oblivious to the way I was growing up, and as I think about it now, I believe my family was in denial. You know my story. What do you think? Do you agree?"

Bob replied, "I read over that section on your early years and yes, I would say your family was in denial and I'll tell you why. They knew your mother was diagnosed to be mentally ill but did not use that fact in their calculations on how big the problem was and what to do about it. They did not move to protect you. The State also failed to protect you. Child welfare should have been contacted and a worker assigned to monitor your mother and your care. Your uncle was not in denial about the problem initially, and he did take action to help you. But he did not take action to protect you from your mother when she came home after her hospitalization and make sure you had proper care. He was in denial when he stated that he could not do anything further for you, although he saw a need for action. He could have gone to the courts. He could have contacted Child Welfare. Your father also could have stood up and fought for you. He had the power to take you out of there. It sounds like he was a wimp."

I interjected, "Yes, he was a wimp. But my uncle was not much better. I was shocked when he looked me in the eye and said: 'I didn't take any action because my parents were against it and I couldn't fight them.' So, he leaves me alone with his sister, who was just hospitalized for an undiagnosed psychosis. I agree there should have been some kind of follow-up when my mother came home from the hospital. With no professional supervision, we were left to fend for ourselves. What a disaster that was!"

"Your mother was mentally ill and that is her excuse as to why she should not be held accountable for punishment, but she was still committing immoral behavior. She is still responsible in that she did do the crimes, and she continued to commit her criminal atrocities unimpeded while your grandmother kept your uncle Will abreast of what was going on in your household.

"Your uncle was abetting the crime. It is a tragedy that such an educated man didn't do what a family member is morally responsible to do and make sure you were protected and brought up properly."

"Thank you, Bob. You raise some very important points. My family had to be in denial to allow a little child to live in such an isolated, dangerous environment, and now you've confirmed it. Yes, my family was in denial. And you know what? I'm angry!"

"You have a right to be."

70
Bits and Pieces

I had occasion to meet with my supervisor, Pauline, who dismissed me from my psychiatric placement in graduate school. I let her know that I now had my Master's and was working with victims of abuse. She nodded her head in approval and said, "I was a novice. It was my first job. It was a mistake to let you go. I didn't know any better at the time…"

I couldn't find words. I was blown away.

At about the same time, I was attending a professional conference and I saw the name of my first therapist on the program. But now it wasn't Mr. Martino, there was "Dr." before his name. I didn't recognize him at first; his hair was graying, and he looked much older. But there he was, to my utter disbelief, Stuart Martino standing at the podium, about to give a lecture.

After the lecture, I excitedly approached him and said, "Dr. Martino, do you remember me?" He stared at me and appeared puzzled. I introduced myself and reminded him that I was a patient of his many years ago. I proudly said, "I now have a professional degree and I'm working as a therapist."

He looked shocked. "Lenore! It's incredible!" He became silent for a moment and soon we talked. He confided, "Your case was the most difficult one I ever had. I didn't have a clue as to what was going on!"

What a revelation! I was stunned. I told him, "I'm still in therapy, and my uncle is quite distressed about it. He says that thirty years is much too long."

Dr. Martino appeared amused and replied: "With your background, it's amazing you didn't end up in a mental institution."

I proudly replied, "I made a choice."

"Well, you certainly made a wise choice. You have come a long way." Dr. Martino smiled, and we continued to have a warm, wonderful conversation. It was hard to believe that I was so contemptuous of this man at the time I was in therapy with him. But I was so very different back then. I was going through transference.

As we parted I asked, "How shall I address you?"

Very casually he replied, "Just call me Stuart."

I was thrilled; Dr. Martino had recognized me as a colleague.

I was in therapy with Dr. Suzanne and I grew to admire her very much. She was very natural and unpretentious. She wore little makeup and dressed very simply. One day I said to her: "I love the way you dress. You always look so nice and neat in a shirt or sweater and a pair of pants. I have so many things in my closet that I hate to wear. Some are so fancy, I don't even know why I bought them."

Dr. Suzanne looked at me in astonishment and responded: "Maybe you're buying those clothes for the person you'd like to be."

Wow! What a great insight that was. When I became aware of this, my obsessive shopping came to a halt.

Many years after Maury's death, I was speaking with his close friend, Jacob. He opened up to me as he spoke about the last time he saw Maury. "He paid me a visit after he saw a cardiologist. He said he was very ill. The doctor told him he had only six months to live if he didn't have heart surgery. Maury said he was thinking about going for the surgery, but he had a feeling he might not come through it."

I was shocked that Maury never said anything about this to me. I couldn't find words to express the anguish I felt when I heard this.

I was in my 30's, speaking to my uncle Will on the phone: "I went to the optometrist and he said my eyesight is getting worse. I must get stronger eyeglasses. It was no joke studying all those years under a 40-watt bulb! Hedda wouldn't allow my father to get me a lamp." Suddenly, my uncle flew into a rage and screamed into the receiver: "If that were my child, and my wife said I couldn't put a lamp on the table, I'd throw her out the window!"

I was sitting in a restaurant with Jay, waiting for the food we ordered, when I looked out the window and was amazed by what I saw. There was Rosie, my patient at Bronx Psychiatric, who suffered from catatonic schizophrenia. Standing in a catatonic stupor, with arm outstretched, I wondered whether she would ever be able to come out of it. Well, there she was, arm straight, walking with a woman, as well as anyone else. It seemed like a miracle.

My uncle Irving spent a great part of his life in the Willowbrook State Hospital. Diagnosed with a condition that is now referred to as "intellectual disability," Irving was living under brutal conditions, but he remained stoic and never complained. On supervised visits with his brother Marvin, he went to see a chiropractor for ongoing treatments. Marvin also brought Irving over to visit with me. The look of sadness in Irving's eyes awakened a feeling of helplessness in me. I wondered if there was anything I could do for him.

Fate intervened when we learned that Maury's friend, Ira, opened a small legal practice in Harlem and was looking for a part-time messenger. He met Irving and hired him on the spot. I thought it was wonderful that Ira was willing to take a chance on Irving and overlook his disabilities. When Irving began to work, he was released from the institution to his brother's care.

Irving worked hard and was determined to succeed. He became remarkably astute at getting around the city, as he traveled from one place to another with bold confidence. He soon found small living quarters in New Rochelle and he continued to thrive under the care of his chiropractor. Gradually, his arm straightened out, the shaking of his hand stopped, and his stammering lessened. It was something to behold.

I was delighted to accompany Irving on long walks and talks. In Irving I found a beautiful person with a golden spirit and a passionate desire to live and learn. I was so proud of Irving as I watched him make numerous strides in a relatively short time.

What brought about the healing of Irving's debilitating illness? Irving attributed it to Dr. Jacobs and the chiropractic treatments he received.

Thank you, Dr. Jacobs. You did a great job!

PART THREE

MY LIFE IN REVIEW

My Life In Review

In this review, I explore the many aspects of my life that I consider most important to me in my struggle for personal development and personal growth. This encompasses a multitude of experiences that I've encountered on my on my unusual journey through life.

My life has been an amazing adventure of turmoil and triumph. As I look back, I am astonished at the way I lived my life with my psychotic mother, trembling in fear of her rage and physical attacks upon me. I was growing up isolated from the world. And I survived.

As I reflect upon my life, I am most grateful that I had a radio. It saved my life. It helped me live through torturous times and became the family and friends I never had. My radio programs enabled me to separate myself from my mother for the time I was able to listen to them and gave me access to a range of emotions I couldn't experience with her. I heard happy songs that took away the bleakness of my existence. There were sad songs that made me cry, and I heard songs that gave me hope. The popular singers, and their music, awakened in me a spiritual awareness of something wonderful in the world. Through these musical encounters, I experienced a glow inside that made me feel alive. I had a feeling that this might be what "love" is all about.

Then there were dramas and mystery shows that sparked my imagination and led me down a path of excitement and intrigue. The comedy programs brought a smile to my face; they could actually make me laugh! I felt close to my radio friends; it was a connection to life outside my four walls. I would never have been able to appreciate the love and beauty of the world if it were not for my radio.

Although I lived in fear of Hedda, I wanted to believe in her because she was my mother. She conveyed the message to me, verbally and non-verbally, that the world was a dangerous place and people were "no damn good." From what she said, it seemed that the outside world was far more threatening than being in the house with her. But I didn't know how very disturbed my mother was. I was only a child.

I remember how I used to wait for Grandma's knock on the door, interrupting my isolated existence. I believed she was coming up to see me. How disappointed I was when I found out her visits were mostly about dropping off food for my mother and me. It was only minutes before there was a war of words between her and Hedda, and I would hear my mother telling her "stay away a few days." My heart began to pound. Suppose Grandma didn't come back?

My father came home after work, gulped down a meal of sour cream and potatoes, and was gone before I knew it. I wondered why he was such a stranger to me. Within a fantasy, I adored my father. But that's all it was—a fantasy. In real life, there was no father.

And there I was, growing up with a kind of yearning I did not understand. The love and affection, so essential to a child's growth and development, were denied to me. Hedda had rules that I was not to be touched or shown any love or affection. The words, "I love you," were never said to me. The only time I heard those words was on the radio. It was strange and disturbing that my father and grandparents were not allowed near me and I was not allowed near them. When you are not to be touched, held or kissed, you begin to feel like a pariah, a scourge that no one would ever want to go near. And that's exactly how I felt. Was I that repugnant?

However, there were times when my mother did touch me— mostly when she punched me with her fists. I lived in terror of her beatings—especially when she turned into that horrible monster that pummeled me mercilessly. I had the dreadful feeling that something awful was about to happen to me, and I cringed in fear. If I escaped her fists, she beat me emotionally with her words. As I sat on my rocking chair, staring off into space, I found myself disassociating from the pain she inflicted upon me. I couldn't think; I couldn't speak; I was unable to move. I was in trauma. When I recovered, I turned to the radio for comfort.

There were so many sides to my mother's personality. A new Hedda was constantly emerging before my eyes. I never knew which one she was going to present to me; I was constantly on guard.

In my early teens, I struggled to separate myself from my mother. It seemed too threatening to set foot outside my door, but I found the courage to persist. When I came out of the house, I was a frightened child who didn't know what to expect. She had me locked up like an animal for my whole life, and now I was going to find out what it was like to be out in the world.

But it didn't feel so good out there. I felt fear as I stood in front of my building. I saw people moving about in what seemed to be some kind of blur. The outside world seemed cold and unfriendly— or maybe that's the way I perceived it after all those years, a captive of my mother. What a strange feeling it was. Suddenly, there I was, alone on the streets of the city, with just my mother's brainwashing to guide me. I felt lost, as a host of feelings moved in to overwhelm me.

But this did not stop me from pursuing something I was yearning for most of my life. My heart palpitated as I thought about it. I soon began to roam the streets in search of the love I heard about in the songs and soaps on the radio. The thought of having this love became uppermost in my mind. I didn't even know what it was—this magnificent thing called love—but I was going to find it.

I dressed to get attention and to attract a wonderful man into my life. I started out in eager anticipation, but I frequently found myself in panic and turmoil, as I meandered around the streets of the Bronx trying to find that love. I sensed anything could happen at any time, but in some way it was exciting, it was a challenge. I was living off many different feelings that were pulling me in different directions. I felt all mixed up inside because I didn't know much about anything; I surely didn't know how to take care of myself, nor did I stop to think I might be in harm's way. I had no time for that, as I floundered about in my hapless existence.

I was having unsavory experiences with men, but I wanted to be loved so badly, I couldn't stop myself from pursuing these atrocious contacts. I was obsessed, I was hurting, and I was getting into trouble. When I think about that Sunday morning in the park, I realize how lucky I was to have come out alive. I didn't know enough to know I was taking my life in my hands. I cringe when I think about that experience. My disturbing encounters with men only fostered my belief that no one would ever love me. Through it all, I strongly held on to the hope that someday, somehow, my true love would appear and I persevered with that thought in mind. But what I was searching for was nowhere to be found.

So, at last, I was in the outside world. My heart was in my mouth and my legs felt kind of wobbly under me, as I moved from one distressing incident to another. Not only was I seeking this most precious thing that people write songs about, but I was also reaching out to strangers to make a friendly connection. I don't know what I expected; maybe I just wanted to hear a friendly "hello." Instead, I found people distancing themselves from me, as if I were some strange creature from outer space. I felt left out of life.

When I was a child, I recall my doctor stressing the importance of mixing with children my own age. I wondered what all the fuss was about. For a long time, my schoolwork mattered more than anything else. How wrong I was! It is crucial for children to have social contact to learn how to interact with each other and the world. As I began to mingle, I realized what I had missed. What did I know about social contact? What is appropriate behavior? How do you interact with others? What do you say?

I wanted to crawl back into my cave, but I couldn't do that; I had to keep going. And I kept feeling sad, awkward and frightened as rejection stared me in the face. I had a thought that plagued me: *Why would anyone want to know me when my own mother pushed me away?* But I wouldn't let that defeat me. I had to learn how to function in the outside world and to find the love I was looking for. I would do whatever I could to make this possible.

------♠♠♠------

I was shocked. Suddenly, as I was walking down the street in my neighborhood, I bumped into my mother's brother and his wife. My heart began to beat wildly. *What am I going to do?* From the time I was a little girl, my mother had poisoned my mind against them, and I grew to fear them. And there they were before me and, somehow, I couldn't walk away. I stopped to speak with them, and they invited me to come to their home. This was the start of a very complex relationship with my uncle Will and my aunt Jessie that touched just about every aspect of my life.

I desperately needed help in coping with the outside world. Will and Jessie had suggestions for how I might be able to fit in and become a part of it. Although I tried to meet their standards, my inner child was crying out to be noticed and cared about for just being me. I knew they were trying to be helpful, but I had a lot of resistance to change. At times I became despondent because I couldn't be what they wanted me to be.

I kept turning to men for the kind of "love" I encountered in my radio fantasy world. I wanted so very much to fill the void in my heart. But real life is not radio life and I kept looking for something I couldn't find.

Will came to me one day with a provocative insight: "There's something you do that turns men on. I don't know what that is. It may be a certain look…" That look he saw was a longing for love. In all likelihood, men intuited my loneliness and longing as a call for sex. It was anything but!

And I was getting myself into more trouble. I recall the night I went up to Bayonet Billy's room, and he was about to rape me when I screamed. The next day I went over to Will and Jessie to cry about the incident. My uncle scolded: "You went up to a man's apartment at midnight. What did you expect him to do? Sing you a lullaby?" I suddenly felt myself sinking into shame. Yes, it was an incredibly stupid thing to do; I had put my life at risk again. I had to stop doing crazy things like that!

And my search for love continued…

Will and Jessie suggested I see a therapist to help me with my problems. When I started therapy, I seemed to be reliving all kinds of feelings I experienced in my childhood, many of which I projected onto my therapist. I knew nothing about "transference" at the time. So many times, I left his office in confusion and tears.

———⁂———

I was fortunate to meet my first real love in a very strange, unusual way. I was walking down the street in my neighborhood, minding my own business, when a young man wheeling a hand-truck almost knocked me over. Maury was all smiles, but I was plainly annoyed. And that's how it all began.

Maury was sweet, handsome, and extremely charming. He had a unique sense of humor that could make me laugh when I wanted to cry. When he appeared on the scene, I was lost, lonely and heading towards self-destruction. But Maury's interest, although sexual at first, turned into something more profound, and soon I could feel he genuinely liked me. He was showering me with hugs and kisses, and I was ecstatic. Suddenly, there was new meaning in my life. I felt I had found love.

Maury was making me aware of life outside my four walls, and I was gravitating towards it. He was taking me around, opening doors for me, exposing me to the myriad things I had never experienced or even knew existed. Combined with his magnetic personality and love of life, I was finding the emotional strength to pull myself out of the painful existence I was living with my mother and become a part of Maury's world. This presented a huge challenge to me. I was consumed with anxiety when I forced myself to go out of the house. Yet I was finding courage and motivation to enter life experiences that were totally alien to me. I was frightened—too frightened to reveal just how frightened I was. Through the many things we were doing together, Maury exuded joy and laughter that I found uplifting and contagious, and I was better able to cope with my fears of the unknown.

I have memories of Maury that touch me to this day. How surprised I was when I learned that Maury had been telling family members: "Be nice to Lenore, she's an orphan." I was amazed that Maury could comprehend that although I had a family, in reality there was no one. My heart was beating with delight when I found out that Maury was able to recognize this. How very well he could understand, how very well. But I didn't know this at the time, and I had deep regrets later on.

Another wonderful moment was the birthday party he planned for me. It was the first birthday party I ever had—and it was exquisite. I never expected anything like that, and I was too overwhelmed to appreciate it. But Maury made it happen.

On the other side of the coin, while I found pleasure and joy with Maury, I also experienced a lot of heartache. Maury, like my mother, was easily excitable and displayed a ferocious temper. He also had a belief system that was hurting him—and me as well. Even though he had a serious heart condition, he was obsessively concerned about making a living. Doctors warned him against working at a job where he had to shlep heavy cartons, but he believed he couldn't do anything else. I worried about him as I watched him load and unload his station wagon. With an ache inside, I cried out: "Maury, Maury, you're killing yourself!" He turned around and hollered back: "Mind your own business!" How very sad it was. How tragic. Maury was only 34 years old when he died.

After Maury's death, I became closer with his best friend. Jay was a very unusual person with remarkable qualities. His brilliance and insights never ceased to astonish me. He encouraged me to develop my intellectual abilities and live up to my fullest potential. So often he would say, "Lenore, you're a very bright girl; it's just that you don't believe it." His belief in me motivated him to work diligently to help me through college. Like Maury, he was teaching me things that children in elementary school knew. There was no end to his patience. He even entrusted me to drive his car, with a Learner's Permit and my myopic eyesight, from the Cross-County Shopping Center in Yonkers back to our neighborhood in the Bronx. I cried: "I can't do this!" But I did! He had more faith in me than I had in myself.

He was a good friend, a very good friend. But I wanted something more. I couldn't live without love in my life. As our friendship deepened, I wanted to believe there was a genuine love between us. However, the fact that Jay was a married man cast a shadow over my hope of having any real happiness with him. He had told me his marriage was over, but if that were the case, why would he be holding on to something that was supposedly defunct?

It was a big mistake. Living with a married man is not a good or wholesome way of life. At least, that's the way I felt, as the little self-worth I had kept slipping further out of my grasp and into the toilet. This wasn't the kind of life I was looking for, or the love I had been dreaming of. Yet, there were some aspects of my relationship with Jay that were healthy and nourishing. For this, I am most grateful.

⚬⚬⚬

In my early 20's, I had hope of going out into the world and making something of myself. I can't say exactly where I got the spirit from, but there was a burning spark in me that made me want to move ahead and not sit in the house like my mother.

There were problems, however, that got in the way and I wasn't coping too well—but I was trying. For one, I had no real life experience to guide me in a world where knowledge and skills seemed to reign supreme. And my childhood trauma was ever-present. I ruminated about the terrible emotional pain that dwelled inside of me, and I wondered what would take it away. I was quite despondent. What was going to happen to me? I was overcome with anxiety and mental anguish.

But I found a resilience in me and I was bouncing back. When I was able to pull myself out of my morbid moods, my inner child could once again feel hope and a goodness in the world. How very much I wanted to feel better about myself. I wanted to have meaning in my life, some purpose, a sense of accomplishment. But where would that come from?

Perhaps I could find fulfillment by performing well on a job. Maybe it would be an office job—the type of work my uncle praised. He often said work would give my life some purpose. But was there anyone out there who would be willing to take a chance on me? I didn't think so. I worried myself sick. I didn't think I would ever find a job.

How wrong I was! My uncle sent me to business school to learn a trade. There, I learned touch-typing. Later, I studied shorthand at home. I went from dusting lamps in a factory to working as a typist, then as a stenographer/secretary in some of the most prestigious offices in the city. I was working for presidents and vice-presidents, but what astounded me even more was that I had built up a reputation for excellence. Some of the bigwigs of the firms I worked for were specifically asking for me when they needed a skilled stenographer. I couldn't believe the success I was achieving. Although I was never happy or content with office work, I was gaining some much needed self-esteem.

However, I didn't like office work, but I didn't know what else I could do. I anxiously wondered when I would begin my life and I obsessed about it. I didn't realize I was already in the process; I just wasn't ready to accept the strides I was making. I felt I was nowhere, and that alone gave me a feeling of despair.

How well I remember the time I began going to work. Taking the subway to and from Manhattan during the rush hour can become somewhat of a trauma for someone like me. It was so very different from the isolated life I lived with my mother. I found it overwhelming standing on a subway platform, watching crowds of people waiting for a train. When a train pulled into the station, there would be a mad scramble, as people were fighting their way off the train, while others were pushing and shoving their way in. As I stood there observing, I thought: How ludicrous it is to try to squeeze into a train that is already packed to the gills! This is crazy! Trains were pulling into the station every few minutes and some of them were not that crowded. I couldn't understand such a mad dash for a train when the next one was just a few minutes away. But there they were, like a herd of wild animals, gravitating towards what looked to me like a mad stampede. As for myself, I waited a few minutes, and usually, everything worked out just fine.

But I was not out of the woods yet. Many a time, I would board a relatively empty train and it would fill up so much there would be hardly enough space to breathe. When I got to my destination, I said to myself: *Thank God—not for another few hours!*

As I moved around the busy Manhattan metropolis, a fear of rejection lingered in a corner of my mind, but that didn't stop me from pursuing a connection with someone I might meet in an office, on a train, a bus, a park bench, or on the street. So strong was my need for love and acceptance, I wanted to bond with people instantaneously. "It takes time to build a friendship, it doesn't happen overnight." Where had I heard that? I could not recall, but it didn't have much meaning for me. I must say I was severely disappointed when I realized it does take time to form a friendship. And I kept my eyes open for opportunities to connect.

On my path, I kept meeting people who were self-absorbed, angry, and controlling (so similar to my mother). I didn't like to experience that negative energy. I also encountered people who were very anxious and full of fear. It sort of shook me up, for I was seeing things in them that I didn't like in myself. In other words, it was like seeing a reflection of myself in a looking glass.

After many of these encounters I was feeling worse about myself. What was I doing wrong? I was feeling more alone with people than when I was by myself. I couldn't find warmth or caring anywhere. I continued to long for some kind of recognition of my existence but, for the most part, people didn't seem to see me, nor did they acknowledge me as one of them. While it was getting me down, I had a spark of Pollyanna that told me things would somehow get better.

So there I was, drifting at sea. Sometimes I felt like I was about to drown. I wondered: *Why am I unable to connect with others? How do people perceive me? Do they sense something strange about me? Am I that different from other people? And what am I going to do about this?*

I was like a little girl, frightened and vulnerable, as I reached out to acquaintances and asked for their opinion of me. I desperately needed to know how others perceived me so that I might become aware of my inadequacies and possibly make changes. As I waited for feedback, I felt anxiety swelling in me. But I couldn't hide from this, I had to know the truth. Maybe then I would feel better about myself. Maybe people would begin to accept me, too.

But I was finding it more difficult than I thought. People were giving me all kinds of advice, but could I really hear what they were saying? And was I able to learn? I found it exceedingly difficult to hear unkind comments, anything from the way I talked to the way I dressed. My heart would sink and I felt shame. I still gravitated towards hearing all the bad stuff about myself, probably because it mirrored the way I felt deep down. I was making myself miserable, but I couldn't stop. Sometimes I thought I was a masochist. Why was I so open to hurt and pain? Maybe because it was all I knew.

Distraught as I was, I moved forward and came upon people who I perceived did not like me. I felt shattered. I had the queasiest feeling in my stomach over every little thing. If someone looked at me the wrong way, I wanted to cry. My extreme sensitivity was getting me down. I carried around a bundle of hurt, anger and resentment that I didn't want anyone to see.

My sense of humor was something I called upon in my darkest moments. Sometimes I was able to laugh at myself when I wanted to cry, and then I was able to move forward. But that didn't happen too often.

I was observing my peers wherever I went. I tried to pattern myself after women I admired on a job, who exuded self-confidence and appeared to be comfortable in their own skin. It was all so appealing and yet so disturbing. I was angry at myself because I was nothing like the people I admired. That didn't mean I couldn't study them and learn how to become more like them.

I stared at women on the streets, in restaurants and other public places. I marveled at how they could make themselves so stunning. They knew how to wear their hair, apply make-up, and carry themselves. They dressed in style and knew what to wear. What could I do to make myself look more like them?

Wherever I went, I was very attuned to the way people spoke to each other. I became immersed in a tone of voice, a facial expression, a mannerism, and a way of being in the world. Some people articulated their thoughts and opinions with so much clarity. I had a problem with that. Would I ever be able to speak like them?

It was becoming apparent to me that I couldn't be like these people any more than they could be like me; people's life experiences were so very different from mine. As I walked along the streets of Manhattan, I was engulfed in a sort of nothingness, a feeling of nonexistence. I didn't think I would ever come out of it or feel any different. But I was able to get hold of myself as I continued to fight the dark, depressing feelings that hovered over me. I forced myself to be at my job every morning, rain or shine, no matter how bad I felt.

And I continued to watch the passing parade…

As I kept observing people on my path, I was especially drawn to a contagious laugh and a happy demeanor. I found myself picking up expressive gestures and laughing a similar laugh. Like a sponge, I was sopping up bits and pieces of others' personalities. When I became aware of this, I was delighted. I was growing and changing, and I didn't even know it. It's amazing how things get into the unconscious and pop up when you least expect.

So, there I was, experiencing some uplifting moments in my travels. But I wasn't very happy for long. As I wandered along the hustle-bustle of Manhattan streets, I suddenly became very sad. I saw people who exuded profound joy and radiance, and that made me feel everyone else had a wonderful life while I was just trying to survive. My habit of comparing myself with others was driving me crazy.

I got a grasp on this when I talked about it with one of my therapists. She said, "You didn't grow up like other people, so you can't compare yourself to them. There is always someone prettier, smarter, someone who has more money and wealth, and so on—but those people have their own heartaches and headaches…" I tried to hold on to that concept, especially when I was overcome with feelings of envy and jealousy.

Just as I was complaining about my poor self-image to my therapist, my aunt Jessie approached me and said: "There's such a change in you, dear. You don't know what you looked like when you came out of the house. You're so different now, it's incredible—just incredible!" And she sat there, staring at me. I was astounded. Did I really look that bad? Since I was constantly in flux, I couldn't remember what I was like when I started out. But although I couldn't perceive my progress, my aunt Jessie had. It started me thinking. Maybe I had come a long way, but still, no matter what I did, I couldn't lose the sadness that accompanied me from childhood.

I thought about taking drugs for my emotional pain, but I never felt comfortable doing so. I had to cope with my angst as best I could. Talking it out in therapy was one helpful, temporary way of finding relief. But, for the most part, I had to endure the pain for the time it lasted—until the next time.

While I was struggling to overcome the negative programming of my early years, my resistance to change remained as strong as ever. When I found a nice comfort zone, I just wanted to hide there and avoid the pain that comes with change. In that we are creatures of habit, we tend to revert to what we know and are comfortable with.

I continued to dread the unknown and the many challenges it brought to me, but I couldn't afford to stand still. I would have to work harder at fighting my fear of new experiences by forcing myself to do the things I feared. I had to muster up every bit of inner strength to face the unknown and the things I was afraid of—which was just about everything. For me, confronting the unknown was threatening, even dangerous.

But not taking a risk can even be worse. I had missed so much of my early life. How could I deprive myself of new life experiences? How could I afford to miss more? If I were to deny myself new things that came my way, I would be depriving myself the way my mother had, and I couldn't afford to do that.

But first, I would have to master even the smallest tasks before I could go on to larger ones. And there was plenty to do. I was flooded with the multitude of things I hadn't experienced when I was growing up. I was continuously pushing myself to learn the things that little children learn, while dealing with the things I had to do in the present as an adult.

There were times when I became so overwhelmed, I wanted to quit. But I just couldn't give up. My inner need to find myself, to find my identity, and a new, better way of living in the world was propelling me forward. I continued with a pressing need to have a real sense of achievement; maybe then I would have a feeling of self-worth.

As I continued to meet people, I was perplexed. I just couldn't figure out how to become one of them. I was trying my darndest to make friends, but I was more alone than ever. I was craving caring and closeness, but all I was getting was coldness and indifference. I was seeing a smile and hearing a cheerful hello, but it was just a greeting, nothing very substantial. My goodness, I was going crazy! I was sinking into the pits of despair. I wondered: *What makes people so mean?*

Nevertheless, I continued to hunger for social contact to fill the void in me. When I was fortunate to find someone with whom I could feel some sense of safety and comfort, I opened up and talked my heart out. And what would I talk about? Mostly the topic I knew best: my horrific childhood. I suppose it was a plea for sympathy and the attention I never got when I was growing up, but it was also a way of reaching out for intimacy and bonding with another human being. I must say it felt great to be heard, but I didn't find any real satisfaction. Most of the time I talked too much and scared people away. And soon I was alone again.

❦

My emotional development was long and slow. The world around me continued to be a very strange, frightening place. Many times I felt like a small child alone in this great big metropolis. But I fought my fears as I kept traveling around, observing people, places, and things. On a subconscious level, I was making mental notes, selecting what I felt was important and filtering out what was not. I was making discoveries about what seemed to work for me and what didn't.

Because there was so much I didn't know about living and functioning in the outside world, I could never be sure about any one thing. Simple everyday problems were cropping up all over and without the necessary knowledge and experience to guide me, I was lost. So, when I was stuck in a difficult situation and needed immediate answers, what was I going to do?

In desperation, I turned to acquaintances I met along the way, with the hope they could lend a helping hand. A surge of shame soared through me as I worked up the nerve to approach people I hardly knew with my problems. Sometimes I thought I was a nuisance, but I needed all the help I could get. Many responded to me with kindness and concern, but some were callous and abrupt. They made me feel they knew it all and I knew nothing. But I continued to ask questions.

I felt a need to please those I was receiving advice from, even though I didn't always agree with them. It seemed if I were to do what they suggested, I might have a friend. So, like a chameleon, I was changing my emotional colors to blend in with those I wanted to impress. But I wasn't feeling good about it. I went around saying: *There's no me… There's no me…* There was no me. So, who was I really? Just an extension of a lost little girl crying within for the love and approval she never had?

I trace my need to please and appease others back to my early childhood when I learned to appease my mother by attending to her feelings and shifting moods, rather than what was going on inside of me. But the more I discounted my own feelings and needs to take care of hers, the more invisible I became to myself. Nevertheless, I had to be very careful not to say or do the wrong thing so as not to upset my mother and stir her wrath. My life was less dangerous if I listened to her, agreed with her, and was able to entertain her. If I was lucky, I might even get a smile out of her.

As I struggled with myriad issues of everyday living, I thought of someone who might be able to help me navigate my world. My former boss, Gale, had spoken about his wife, Tammy (T.C), with deep regard. "She's brilliant. Watch her and learn from her. She's a great role model and a real mentor."

I was in Tammy's Manhattan penthouse apartment, having a pleasant conversation, when out of the blue she announced, "I know a great alcoholic beverage you can order when you go out—Scotch on the rocks with a twist of lemon! Now repeat that after me: Scotch on the rocks with a twist of lemon." I didn't tell Tammy that I couldn't stand alcohol because I was afraid that it might create dissension between us and she wouldn't like me. A sort of helplessness came over me and I felt powerless to voice my feelings: "Enough already!" So, I kept repeating this phrase for I don't know how long until I got it exactly the way she wanted me to say it.

I had many such encounters. So what was this all about? Undoubtedly, these people were trying to change me, they were trying to make me over. I became angry and resentful when I thought about it. I just wanted to self-improve, to learn from others, but they were trying to mold me into something I was not, something they thought I should be.

Because I was in the process of becoming my own person, I had yet to form my own true identity, and I was vulnerable to their manipulations. I guess they sensed my vulnerability and were reacting to it.

I worried about the validity of things that people told me. Were the things they said really true? With a strong need to follow my own gut instincts, many times I ignored what others told me and proceeded to do what I felt was right. My uncle Will expressed his annoyance as he barked: "You ask a lot of questions and then you do whatever you damn please!" That had a ring of truth to it. He refused to see that I had to ask questions, and even more questions, because there was still so much I didn't know about living in the world. Eventually, I concluded that there is nothing wrong with turning to others for feedback—as long as I, in the final analysis, do what I feel is right and don't give my power away.

As I started to take more risks, I found that many of my decisions led to mistakes that made me cringe, and I had to deal with the consequences of my actions. I began to realize that making mistakes is a part of living, learning, and growing. In retrospect, each of the experiences that I found so unpleasant and upsetting at the time, were actually a stepping-stone in my emotional development. These were lessons that helped me form my own identity and become my own person.

⸻ ❧ ⸻

Therapy became my safe haven in the Jungle of Life. I don't think I could have survived without it. The understanding and acceptance given to me by my therapists was invaluable to me. No judgment, no reprimands, just a listening ear, some keen insights, and a lot of support. I might compare this to a child in turmoil whose parent provides the comfort that says, "I'm here for you."

Initially, I used therapy as an outlet to talk about things that were troubling me in the moment. I intellectualized a lot of what I was feeling without going deeper into what was actually going on inside of me. It was much too threatening to go deep into that dark place and struggle to untangle the emotional cobwebs of my life.

But many times I did go deeper and speak about the way I grew up. As I talked about my mother, each of my therapists concurred she was paranoid schizophrenic. They found it hard to believe that she was not on any kind of medication for her condition. So often I heard the question: "Wasn't there anyone to take you out of there?" There was a look of astonishment on their faces when I said: "There was no one."

One caring psychologist shared her heartfelt feelings with me: "I am angry. No, I'm more than angry, I'm infuriated! You grew up in a torture chamber and there was no one to get you out of there. It's outrageous!" She declared her disdain for my family. I was touched by her empathy and compassion for me.

Another therapist praised me for my ability to overcome adversity, adding: "I don't know how you found the courage to persist, but I think you're doing a marvelous job!" Although it was encouraging to hear her say this, I didn't feel very heroic; I just wanted to be free of my emotional pain and find my life.

Feelings presented a great big mystery to me. Because, as a child I wasn't allowed to express my feelings, I worried: Is there a right or wrong way to feel? It seemed so confusing. A therapist clarified this for me when she said, "There is no right or wrong way, there is no good or bad. Feelings are what they are; they come and go. It's okay to feel whatever you are feeling in the moment."

It seemed like a cloud lifted when I heard that. I began to realize that when I feel my feelings, it is not a test where there is a right or wrong answer and there is a grade. I soon allowed myself to feel my feelings without chastising myself. As I began to accept my true feelings, I was better able to understand my true self.

I also became aware that negative emotions can stress the immune system and then illness can occur. I wondered how much of this contributed to my childhood infections. It seemed I was healthier longer and didn't become ill that often when I was able to talk about my feelings in therapy. How amazing the mind-body connection is.

I continued to go for therapy twice a week, although it didn't seem to be enough. I was distraught, I was confused, and I was in trauma. I was depending upon therapy to keep me together. I didn't know any other way to deal with my turmoil. Sometimes I felt so bad I didn't think I could face another day. In my sessions, I was rambling on and on, saying the same things over and over. It was talk, talk, and more talk. My therapists allowed me to vent and express my anxieties without restriction. I was able to feel a sense of freedom I had never known. On the other hand, I felt I wasn't making any real progress and wound up in deep distress because of this.

So there I was, barraged by the same fears, anxieties and shame that brought me into therapy. I was talking about the things that made me hurt, but nothing seemed to change. I felt I was moving at a snail's pace, but it didn't seem like I could do any better. And I kept going for my sessions. I released some of my built-up tensions while I was there and felt relief for a short time, but soon I was feeling bad all over again.

My frustrated uncle Will spoke to me about therapy: "It's like opening and closing a valve for you. You let off steam and then you're right back to where you started. Where is the progress? I don't see it!"

I didn't see it either.

"So, Will. how come I can't do better in therapy? Why can't I make any progress?"

Will looked me in the eye and said, "Your thoughts are in your head. When your thoughts reach your feelings then things will begin to change." I was startled to hear him say that, for he usually didn't give much credence to feelings. Afterwards I thought about it: *It sounds right, but how am I going to get there?*

I began to think about leaving therapy. Then I realized it wasn't very practical. I needed someone with whom I could be completely free, open, and honest—someone with whom I could easily speak, who would listen, be objective and then exchange thoughts and opinions with me. The process was stimulating, and that contact helped me to hang in there when I was at my lowest. Therapy was a door that opened into a place where I could feel safe. Outside that door, I did not feel I had the luxury of saying what was on my mind and in my heart without feeling I was being scrutinized and judged.

But it seemed like I wasn't getting anywhere with my problems and that continued to trouble me. Wasn't there anyone out there who could actually relieve me of my emotional pain? Where was this Miracle Worker who would wave a magic wand and take away all my hurt and despair?

Maybe I was expecting too much. I rationalized that therapy was serving many purposes. It was easing the anxiety that made me feel so helpless and vulnerable. It was sustaining me and keeping me intact when I felt like I was falling apart. It also helped me to have a better understanding of myself in the world. And I was gathering bits and pieces of insight from every therapist I worked with.

I might say I was taking baby steps until I could take larger ones. Mr. Martino, my first therapist, once said to me: "How long did it take you to get like that?"

Eventually, it became clear to me that I was the only one who could go within and give myself the answers I needed. A therapist could assist me on my journey to find out who I am and what I'm all about. A therapist could help me find the truth of my heart. But a therapist could not solve my problems for me. Only I could do that.

Although my therapists were accepting me, I still wasn't accepting myself. I wondered if I would ever be able to truly like myself. I was working hard to overcome, but the negativity of my past would not go away. My mother's contempt for me was deeply embedded in my unconscious and continued to fester there. I could not eradicate her voice in my head saying: ***I'm the only one who will ever care for you***. The hatred in her voice mocked the meaning of her words.

I can still hear my mother screaming her infamous war chant, **"She doesn't need that!"** I was a little girl when I was indoctrinated with that belief. Programmed by my mother's voice in my head, it impacted just about everything in my life with a feeling there wasn't anything I should need or want.

After many years of continuing a pattern of self-deprivation, pain, and impoverishment, I became aware that I didn't have to live like that. In breaking through the pattern of "she doesn't need that," I began to replace it with "she does need that!" A door was opening for me into a world where I could be free to make choices and not cringe about it.

I was struggling; I was driven; I had to succeed—but at what? I really didn't know. I just knew I had to keep going. I kept wondering: What's it all about? It seemed that the more I learned, the less I knew, and the more I remained the same. I still couldn't make any sense of the world around me. It felt like a mystery—one great big mystery that I wanted to unravel and understand.

Anxiety and Fear, my constant companions, were with me to alert and protect me at all times. Hot and cold sweats and a pounding heart made me aware that danger might be lurking anywhere around me, and I was constantly on guard. So much of the time I was walking around in trauma and didn't even know it. But it was nothing new; I was raised on trauma—the trauma of Hedda.

I continued to feel nervous and threatened as I exposed myself to more new surroundings and different experiences. I remember how frightened I was going out of the house and doing new things. I didn't feel safe. It was a difficult transition going from the insulated shelter of my home environment into the fast moving raucous of the outside world. Many a time I felt as if I were stepping off a cliff as I traveled from one new adventure to another. How I dreaded it, but somehow, I felt it was something I had to do. In the process, I was slowly opening myself to an awareness of what was going on inside and outside of me.

And I continued along my path. In many instances, I was so frightened tears would fill my eyes. But when it was over, a smile came to my face. Somehow, I had gotten through it—whatever it was! The worst was over and I could feel relieved. A lot of the time what I feared was not so bad at all; it was just bad because things were so new to me. There was really nothing to worry about. Then, I could really laugh at myself for being such a silly goose.

When I was overstressed and run-down, I became ill with a debilitating respiratory infection. Then there was a nagging tightness across my solar plexus that gave me cause for concern. I went to many doctors, who had mixed reactions: "It could be coming from stress—or it could be your scoliosis…"

And I continued to plod along.

I was in my thirties and attempting to do more with my life, even if it scared the dickens out of me. That included going to college. How would I ever be able to go to college when I barely attended elementary school? Could I dare attempt it? It presented a humongous challenge for me. My fear of failure was heightened in the school environment, but Jay was there to support me and help out with courses that were over my head. He encouraged me when I had no faith in myself. He was telling me, "You can do it!" when I said, "No, I can't!" And I was able to make it through college.

But our relationship wasn't working. There is no real happiness with a man who is married to someone else. He told me his marriage was over, but apparently it wasn't. I found myself suffering the consequences of my selfish, thoughtless behavior, as I experienced the piercing shame and guilt of living with a married man.

While I didn't find the love I was looking for, I still had a hope in my heart to find someone who could love me and whom I could love. Then we could join our hearts in the holy bond of matrimony. I began to wonder if this love existed.

It was St. Patrick's Day, and my English class was canceled. I had time on my hands, so I went over to the campus library. As fate would have it, I met a young man there. Jon was sweet, mellow, and a student at the college. In the weeks that followed, I was enjoying long walks and talks with him. Because we were alike in so many ways, I found myself becoming close with him.

During this time, I found the courage to pick myself up and leave Jay. We were living together for eleven years and I finally admitted to myself that we should have parted a long time ago. But it wasn't as simple as all that. Both Jay and I were in deep grief as we mourned the loss of our relationship.

What a tumultuous time this was for me. I wasn't interested in much of anything, including my college courses. I struggled to complete my Associate's degree, which I did—surprisingly, with honors. I soon made the decision to register in a four-year college. Once there, I forced myself to do the very best I could. When I fell down, I picked myself up and went on. Somehow, I found the stamina to continue. When I was stuck with an assignment that I was having a problem with, I gave a holler to my uncle Will or Jon. So often, I found myself scurrying over to the school psychologist for guidance and support. I was quite surprised when I made the Dean's List.

And I graduated! I now had a BA degree in psychology and art. I was astonished, but grateful, that I made it through as I did. I acknowledged to myself how amazing and utterly ludicrous it is to think one can attend college with almost no formal education. But somehow, with hard work and perseverance, I did it!

Soon after I finished college, I was in an exuberant mood, and Jon spoke to me about marriage. It was a big leap for both of us, but it felt like the right thing to do. Jon and I were like two kids when we first met. Together, we've been able to overcome a lot of the negativity we both grew up with. The problems we had to face have helped us become stronger emotionally, as we weathered them together. We continue to work at our relationship as we deal with the myriad issues of everyday living.

As I continued to work on myself in therapy, my passion to give of myself increased. I went on to graduate school in social work with the hope of learning how to help people who were struggling with emotional pain. I often wondered how I was able to work with clients in all kinds of anxiety-ridden situations without my own anxieties getting in the way. I felt a sense of fulfillment when I could touch someone with a word, a thought, or a helpful insight.

While I could maintain my objectivity with clients, when it came to my own problems, I was still very much in the dark as I fumbled to find the switch to turn the light on. There was still so much of my own emotional pain that I had to cope with. In graduate school I was feeling my fragile nature all the more. I fought my way through and came out with a professional degree, but I was beaten down by all the hardships I had to endure in the program. I felt robbed of my inspiration to be of help to others, as well as myself.

I walked around in a funk. I no longer had the drive or persistence to do anything that held meaning for me. My spirit was broken and I had to heal.

When I was able to start over, my old companions, Fear and Anxiety, were still accompanying me on my journey and keeping me on my toes. As I worked with my clients, I was still concerned: *How am I handling this? What can I say or do that would be of more help to my clients?* I would speak to my supervisors about my many concerns and the feedback I received was encouraging. They liked my work and let me know I was doing a good job. But I could never feel that secure. As I obsessed about the quality of my work, I was receiving compliments from my clients. I was doing better than I thought.

One day I was going over process notes with one of my supervisors when she said to me: "You are much too hard on yourself. You have to learn to be gentler with yourself—you need to treat yourself better." I agreed with her, but how was I going to do this?

With some trepidation, I revealed to several of my supervisors the struggles I had to overcome and the fact that I was in therapy myself. Much to my surprise, they were not taken aback by anything I said. One of them replied: "I think it's necessary to be in therapy so that you can better deal with your own feelings as you work with your clients." I knew what she was talking about. I, too, felt that my own therapy enabled me to be more present and clearer with my clients.

The time came for me to open my eyes and face the reality of my traumatic childhood. Dr. Suzanne was there to assist me. As we pulled the lid off the enigma of my mother's strange behavior, I could now see things in a different light. It wasn't my fault; I didn't make my mother ill—it was the other way around: my mother made me ill! Not only did I understand this intellectually, but now I could feel it emotionally.

Without realizing it, I was carrying around bits and pieces of my mother's negative belief system. Her distorted reality became a part of me and appeared when I least expected. A feeling of being "bad"—the bad child I was made out to be—never left me, and I was treating myself the way my mother treated me. In other words, I was not very kind to myself. The shame and guilt that haunted me throughout my childhood could spring up at any time. As a child, if I just opened my mouth to speak, I was made to feel that I was committing a crime and I felt the agony of shame. As for guilt, it was not much different; if something went wrong, I felt responsible and blamed myself for making a mess of things. Dr. Suzanne commented: "More of your mother's brainwashing." I couldn't deny it; my mother was an expert at it.

I worked with Dr. Suzanne for many years and I felt grateful to have benefited from her astute intuition and genuine concern. However, I was still drowning in my own emotional hell, even after so many years of therapy with her. Intermittently, I searched for various other ways to deal with my trauma, but they were not resonating that well with me. Eventually, I continued with talk therapy, with an emphasis on breathing techniques and being in the moment.

⸻ ❧ ⸻

As I traveled around to different lectures in the city, I came across a spiritual advisor who said: "In order to stop feeling every little thing in a negative way, you will have to continually observe yourself and change your thoughts and feelings. You will have to develop a new perception of yourself. Come from a more positive perspective and you will have a different experience. You can then act with calm, rather than with hurt, anger, and all the negative feelings that are associated with being a victim."

While this all sounded appealing, I found it easier said than done, as I floundered about in a whirlpool of doubt… confusion… and hope.

—⁂—

Sunday meetings of my self-help group had become an integral part of my life. One of the members said something to me that had a profound impact: "Why don't you think about people the way you think about food? I know you are very particular about what you eat—you like organic vegetarian food and you wouldn't eat anything that you knew wasn't good for you—so why would you want toxic people in your life?"

—⁂—

For some time, I was relentlessly trying to get people to like me, or even love me. I was still a little girl at heart. I longed for a friendly smile, a loving gesture, a kind word, that would make me feel good and alive. But instead, I was getting hurt. I had become a magnet for attracting unwholesome, negative people into my life. In these encounters I was experiencing distress that left me depressed and emotionally drained. I talked about it in therapy, but to no avail. I didn't realize I was attracting men and women into my life that displayed the same negative characteristics of my mother and father. Despite the myriad insights and depth of understanding I had acquired along the way, I continued to repeat the same unconscious, destructive behavior.

I became aware of the concept, "Repetition Compulsion," while reading about the great psychoanalyst, Sigmund Freud. He observed that people would repeat, over and over, patterns of painful behavior that originate in childhood. Psychotherapist Harville Hendrix expanded on Freud's views when he proposed that people are attracted to and develop the strongest chemistry with those who trigger their deepest issues and wounds from childhood. Underneath this is an unconscious desire to play out and resolve the unfinished business of their early lives by attempting to create a new, different, happy outcome in the present.

I was shocked and appalled when I realized I was enmeshed in Repetition Compulsion. I was attracted to men like my father, who were not emotionally available to me—and yet I pursued them. The results were chaotic. Similarly, my female friends were angry, controlling, and very much like my mother. I was constantly falling prey to Hedda substitutes and their hostilities. I hated the way that made me feel. I was actually making the same ludicrous mistakes and repeating the same behavior over and over with an unconscious hope that I could create a new, positive outcome. But it just wasn't working, and I was unhappy as ever.

It finally struck me how much of my life was based upon the disastrous relationship I had with my mother and the non-relationship I had with my father. I told myself I would have to stop this madness and put an end to the painful relationships I was getting myself into. I had grown to abhor the thought of any more toxic people in my life and the suffering that goes with it. In my pain, I told myself that I do not need the love and approval of others, I can actually give this to myself.

I don't think there is any easy way to resolve Repetition Compulsion. As I began to understand more, I became mindful of how Repetition Compulsion was occupying a huge part of my life. In my experience, I have found that self-awareness is key to turning this around and sending it out the door. If I sense Repetition Compulsion creeping up on me, I will nip it in the bud and re-direct my energy to something that is constructive. Repetition Compulsion is no longer welcome in my life.

I began to realize that underneath it all, I had been searching for the good mommy and the loving daddy. Unconsciously, I was seeking out people who I thought could rescue me with the love I never had as a child. But I could not find the special love and caring I had not received from my parents. There was an unresolved emptiness and an unidentifiable longing that lingered within.

As I grew stronger emotionally, I began to go within and re-parent my inner child, giving myself the unconditional love I was seeking for so long. I decided I was worthy of it, and I deserved it. When I learned to re-parent myself, I could say to myself: *Okay, my mother didn't love me, my father didn't love me—but that doesn't mean I can't love myself!*

I came to the realization that in order to have a good, healthy relationship with another person you first need to have a good, healthy relationship with yourself.

Yes, it is a wonderful thing to find the right person, someone with whom you can share your life and work together to create harmony and joy. I still hold a special reverence in my heart for the realm of love and marriage. To me, marriage still represents a validation of being truly cared about and loved. However, I have come to realize, over the years, that you don't need a ring and a piece of paper to be happy and loved. Signing a contract does not give you assurance that you will find happiness and fulfillment with your partner. I have found that one has to work at a marriage or a partnership like anything else.

My striving for perfection entered into just about every aspect of my life. I believe it all began when I was a little girl seeking my father's approval. While I tried hard to please him, there wasn't anything I could do that would bring a smile to his face. As he became more critical of me, I began to obsess about doing things better and better. My drive for perfection had begun.

For much of my life, my world was centered on striving for perfection. I had to do exceptionally well in order to prove to myself, and to others, that I was smart, worthy, and as good as anyone else. For example, if I performed well on a school test, my reward would be an "A" grade and a temporary burst of good feelings that came from it. My spirits were lifted and there was new meaning in my life. How desperate I was to lose those bad feelings I carried around, if only for that moment.

While I was continually striving for perfection, I was making mistakes all the time. I was anything but perfect. After beating myself up for one agonizing mishap or another, I began to realize that making mistakes is normal and a part of life. Moreover, I could learn from my mistakes and grow in the process.

As I began to feel better about myself, I became aware that I do not need to be perfect to like myself or to have others like me. I realized I have never been perfect or even close to it. Part of being human is making mistakes and I've made so many. Some of my mistakes were quite serious and have troubled me deeply over the years and still do. I sincerely regret the pain I may have caused others, as well as myself.

While I no longer strive for perfection, I continue to feel a need to do my best in the things I attempt to do—and I'm okay with that.

As my self-image improved, I became stronger emotionally and I began to appreciate myself. As I got in touch with my own thoughts and feelings, I found the opinions of others no longer had a commanding control over me. My world did not crumble if someone didn't like me or said something unkind. I began to understand that people unconsciously project and/or transfer their own thoughts and feelings on to those they encounter or are close with. I realize that in most instances, people are coming from, and reacting to, their own life experiences as they interact with others. I no longer blame myself for the behavior of others.

It had always troubled me that I was not like everybody else. I have finally come to the conclusion that I do not have to be like anybody else. I am fine just the way I am. What is more, I do not want to be like anybody else. As I learn to accept myself for who I am, I no longer am troubled about "being different" or "belonging." As I change my thoughts and beliefs, I am able to make authentic changes in my life. At last, I am more real and visible to myself.

When I was writing An Invisible Child, I turned to a friend for feedback. This is what she said: "It makes me so angry. Your father left you with your mother and went out dancing. Your mother was mentally ill—but he wasn't. Shame on him!"

Her reaction startled me. It was something I needed to hear, and I guess I was ready to hear it. I was suddenly jostled out of my complacency into a reality I didn't want to face. Through the years I silently pined for my father's love and the relationship I never had with him. But now I could see this man was a father in name only—a biological father. He never fought for me when I needed him. He abandoned his sickly daughter to a lion in a cage while he went out to find happiness and a new life for himself. The truth hurt—but it was the truth. When I could feel this emotionally, I could close the door to another painful chapter in my life.

There was a time when I felt a profound disdain for every member of my family. These were people who turned their backs when they saw a child suffering in abuse and neglect and walked away. They paid no mind to what was going on around them, as long as their lives remained intact. It was clear to me that members of my family were plainly despicable. I remember a psychiatrist telling me: "Stay as far away from your family as you can. They're poison for you!" How right he was!

I soon found that my intense dislike for my family was giving me more grief and pain than I could handle. In order to save myself, I had to back off and let go of my anger and disdain and replace it with something of a spiritual nature.

It took years and years of hard work, but so much of the anger and resentment I harbored against my mother was eventually washed away with the sweat and tears I experienced in therapy and on my own.

My mother spent the last years of her life in a nursing home. Despite the way she treated me in my youth, I felt a need to see her. When I saw her sitting in a wheelchair in the corridor of the Home, she looked so lost and lonely. A big smile brightened her face and her eyes lit up when she saw me. In that moment, I felt at peace with her.

On one visit I was startled to see my mother sobbing profusely: "I'm sorry for what I've done to you…" And she went on sobbing. I didn't know what I was feeling, and I didn't know what to say. As I sat there, observing this woman, my mother, she appeared as much an enigma as ever. I didn't know her—but she was still my mother.

⸺⠒⠒⠒⠒⠒⸺

For the most part, I try not to think about my mother and the past. However, there are times when I can't help myself, and I think about my mother with anger and rage. These are the times when I experience recurring tightness in my solar plexus and difficulty in breathing. One orthopedic doctor referred to this as "a spasm caused by the curvature of your spine." Several doctors pointed out that this condition might have been prevented with the proper treatment in childhood.

At about the time I was ten, Grandma was talking about my "crooked back." I didn't like to hear it, but what could I do? I was only a little girl, and troubled by this. As a few more years passed, my curve could be readily observed. How well I remember the doctor saying to my mother: "She has a curvature of the spine and she needs a brace to correct it. If it's left alone, this condition, known as scoliosis, will only get worse…" I was jostled by those words. What did he mean by that? It sounded urgent, and I felt a gnawing pain inside from wanting the brace so badly. I knew my mother would never get it for me because she didn't believe I needed anything—including a brace for my back. In my mind I cringed when I thought of those horrible, debilitating words that my mother abided by: **"She doesn't need that!"**

So, there was no brace. Nothing changed—except my curve that was steadily progressing. And Grandma was worried. Grandma came in and showed concern about my posture. "You're not sitting up straight. You're hunching over again." I didn't know what I was feeling as Grandma thrust her shoulders back and showed me what good posture looks like. Hedda came running in, screaming, **"She doesn't need to know that! She knows enough—too much!"** She and Grandma got into one of their verbal battles and soon Grandma ran to the door. Was there some sort of inherent evil in my mother that made her so mercilessly cruel?

I was emotionally torn to pieces when I realized that my scoliosis might have been averted with something as simple as a brace. As I grew into adulthood, I became aware that neglecting a child's health is one of the cruelest things a parent can do. I consider the neglect of my scoliosis one of the worst crimes, if not the most atrocious crime, committed by my mother.

⸺∞⸺

I soon became aware of the treacherous ways in which scoliosis works. I saw a top neurologist at Mount Sinai Hospital in Manhattan who explained: "There are three components involved in your scoliotic condition: the upper chest, the stomach below, and the diaphragm in between. The diaphragm is between two cavities: the abdomen and the chest. Because of your crooked back, the abdomen and the chest cavity compress the diaphragm, and that causes a problem in breathing. It's a corkscrew effect—a kind of twisting— and it's characteristic of scoliosis.

"Pace yourself. Take five-minute breaks. Sitting up straight or standing for long periods of time will have a tightening effect. It can feel like someone is sitting on your chest. If you have trouble with breathing, sit down and catch your breath. When you have tightness across the diaphragm, lean back in a chair or lie down. That causes a stretch to occur, and there no longer is pressure on the diaphragm. That stretch will help with the corkscrew effect. Shortness of breath will indicate when to take breaks." From the doctor's astute clarification, I had new, useful information to guide me.

Other practitioners have suggested stretching as well as breathing exercises. One orthopedist said: "Walk! Walk! Walk until you drop!" And yet other doctors tell me that periods of rest are indicated for the fatigue that accompanies scoliosis. I try to use a little of each.

However, I don't usually ruminate about resting or relaxing when there is something I want to do. For example, I recall the time I was shopping in a large clothing store and became immersed in buying a few winter scarves for myself. I completely forgot about my condition. I was standing for some time when I felt tightness across my diaphragm and shortness of breath. As it worsened, I thought I might collapse. I looked around for a place to sit, but there wasn't any. What was I going to do? I limped over to the cash register, reached into my bag, and tossed a few dollars at the cashier. I then found my way to the door. Lucky for me, there was a subway station on the corner. I staggered down the stairs onto a platform and sat down on a bench until I felt able to get into a train and go home.

Each time I have an episode like the one I just mentioned, I come away with a heightened awareness of how devastating scoliosis can be, and that I have to be vigilant when I am outside busily engaged in a project for any length of time.

I was having a pleasant chat with Will when he casually asked: "Do you think you can ever forgive your mother?"

Forgive my mother? I was taken aback. Suddenly, a subdued anger surfaced. It felt as though rockets were blasting off into space.

"Even if I were to forgive my mother for all her outrageous behavior, I couldn't forgive her for my back, my teeth and my eyes. I feel sick when I think of it. Let me refresh your memory.

#1: She wouldn't get me a brace to stop the curvature of my spine—and look what happened!

#2: What about my eyesight? I was a child studying under a 40-watt ceiling bulb, straining to see, and she refused to put a lamp on the table. It makes me want to scream!

#3: At the age of fifteen, she took me around the corner to a butcher-dentist and he pulled out two of my front teeth just like that!

I was devastated. Other dentists have told me a simple capping would have been sufficient. I've had problems with that dental work like you would never believe.

Let's not forget all the physical and emotional abuse I had to endure. Now, I ask you, Will, could you forgive her?"

My uncle didn't say a word. I don't remember ever seeing him speechless like that. He just sat there, staring at me. I could feel the pain of my past welling up inside of me, as if it were only yesterday. The things my mother did to me: cruel… cruel… so brutally cruel!

I was flabbergasted when I found out my uncle Will wanted to write a book about me. I was sitting with a friend in a restaurant having a bowl of soup, when I felt a need to tell her about my uncle's project. She said, "I would be very angry if I were you."

I guess I was, I just didn't want to acknowledge it to myself. It was just too painful. When I overcame the initial shock, I wondered why my uncle wasn't trying to rescue me from his sister's insane asylum instead of obsessively collecting information about me for the purpose of writing a book. I felt the anguish of being more like a lab experiment than a human being. As I gave more thought to it, I was even more appalled. Did my uncle have the belief that I would remain under my mother's thumb for the rest of my life, locked away in the house, forever her appendage?

My uncle stopped collecting information about me when I started to visit him at age nineteen. As I began to write the book myself, I decided to give my time and energy to this difficult task and put aside my negative feelings about my uncle's questionable book writing ambitions.

My uncle Will wore many faces and my feelings towards him fluctuated with the way he reacted to me. There were moments when I revered him because of his intelligence, and at other times,

I couldn't stand his guts. He tried his darndest to drum things into my head to give me a proper perspective about the world when I wasn't ready or willing to listen. He felt he knew what was "best" for me and if I didn't listen to him, he might act like a two year old having a temper tantrum. At times he could be outlandishly cruel. We would fight like cats and dogs over the most miniscule things. I often wondered how he could be so cold and remote, but then I realized he came from the same dysfunctional family as my mother. However, despite all our disagreements, I grew to admire and respect him for the learned man he was. My uncle Will is deceased, and I can now understand that his heart was in helping me to learn the ways of the world and how to live in it. I would not have been able to overcome all that I have without his help and support.

As I got a handle on the life I lived with my mother, the delusional belief system that she instilled in me began to collapse. I became aware that I do not need to suffer and make myself feel bad to be a part of the world. I began to feel more compassion for myself and the hardships I experienced in my life. The love I've desired so much from others I am now able to give to myself unconditionally. As I write about this, tears of joy fill my eyes, for I have found a self—my true self—that I can turn to and value.

A person who has lived a life such as mine cannot escape unscathed. As residues from the past emerge, I strive not to dwell on the negativity of my past but instead, I find myself compassionately curious when old feelings arise. I allow room within myself in order to recognize and feel my feelings. I often find I can then let these feelings go. It requires attention, perseverance, and emotional space for both anger and tears. Moment by moment, I am becoming a new Lenore.

As I continue to evolve, my focus is on living in the here and now. I understand that Love is the strongest force in the universe. I think it is our purpose for being here. I believe the caring and kindness we give to others comes back to us in countless ways.

Love is the healer and it can help us to surmount the hurdles that Life sends our way.

Basically, I am a student of Life. For me, there is no end to self-exploration and there is always room for self-improvement. I strive to do better all the time. My life is built around being the best I can be. From my understanding of spiritual teachings and life experiences, I recognize that we all have obstacles on our paths that cause distress and grief. All kinds of problems come our way that seem insurmountable. We struggle to overcome and in so doing, we are subjected to more discomfort and pain. Ultimately, we can change and grow—if we want to enough—and if we are open to the positive opportunities that emerge on our paths.

I have suffered the consequences of a disastrous childhood. My life has been a succession of challenges, failures, and disappointments, from which I have changed my attitudes and beliefs. In rising above my suffering, I have become a more caring, compassionate human being. Perhaps if it were not for the obstacles I encountered and overcame, I would not have developed into the person I am today.

Writing this book has given me the opportunity to be blatantly honest with myself. It has made me examine things that I might otherwise have pushed aside to avoid the pain of my past. In trying to be open, honest, and objective, I have endeavored to face my fears, faulty thinking, and the myriad mistakes I made on the path of emotional growth. I must say, however, that it is not easy to capture the past in words of the present. Reliving a memory is very different from experiencing a thought or feeling in the moment. And, of course, telling this story is not the same as having lived it.

I have had to work on this book for many years and redo it many times until I was able to find the right words and feelings to describe what it was like to be me, struggling to overcome my traumatic childhood, and trying to find a life that is livable with meaning in the here and now. In so many ways it has been a therapeutic process for me.

My message to you is:
If I could do it, then you can do it, too!